DATE DUE

09	21	08	

Demco No. 62-0549

A Companion to Victorian Poetry

Blackwell Companions to Literature and Culture

This series offers comprehensive, newly written surveys of key periods and movements and certain major authors, in English literary culture and history. Extensive volumes provide new perspectives and positions on contexts and on canonical and post-canonical texts, orientating the beginning student in new fields of study and providing the experienced undergraduate and new graduate with current and new directions, as pioneered and developed by leading scholars in the field.

A COMPANION TO

VICTORIAN POETRY

EDITED BY **RICHARD CRONIN,**
ALISON CHAPMAN AND
ANTONY H. HARRISON

Blackwell
Publishing

© 2002 by Blackwell Publishers Ltd
a Blackwell Publishing company

350 Main Street, Malden, MA 02148-5018, USA
108 Cowley Road, Oxford OX4 1JF, UK
550 Swanston Street, Carlton, Victoria 3053, Australia
Kurfürstendamm 57, 10707 Berlin, Germany

First published 2002 by Blackwell Publishers Ltd

Library of Congress Cataloging-in-Publication Data has been applied for.

ISBN 0-631-22207-3 (hardback)

A catalogue record for this title is available from the British Library.

Set in 10½/12½ pt Garamond 3
by SNP Best-set Typesetter Ltd., Hong Kong
Printed and bound in the United Kingdom
by TJ International Ltd., Padstow, Cornwall.

For further information on
Blackwell Publishing, visit our website:
http://www.blackwellpublishing.com

Contents

Editors' Preface

In England, the period from about 1830 until World War I is normally distinguished by historians as 'Victorian' in honour of the longest-reigning monarch in British history, who dominated the era as a kind of cultural icon. These years witnessed an extraordinary flowering of literary culture, comparable in many respects to what occurred under England's other long-lived and remarkably influential female monarch, Queen Elizabeth I. Despite the virtual absence of significant drama produced for the stage during most of the Victorian era, every other genre flourished. (Much great dramatic literature did in fact emerge, but not in the form of stage plays.) The productivity of poets, novelists and writers of self-consciously artistic prose non-fiction remains, from the vantage of the early twenty-first century, breathtaking.

The work of the poets, on whom this volume focuses, retains its ability to enchant, amaze and inspire. Victorian poetry, as a vast and extraordinarily complex body of productions, employs every established verse form in the language and exploits every established poetic subgenre, while refining upon some, such as the dramatic monologue, the verse drama and the pastoral elegy, in ways previously unimagined. Produced by authors of both sexes in every social class from all districts in the British Isles (and indeed the colonies), it engages a remarkable variety of cultural discourses – political, religious, social, economic and scientific – in both direct and nuanced ways that still strike readers as highly original, and also aesthetically and ideologically powerful. Coming to critical terms with this diverse body of materials is a project that in itself raises many critical and theoretical issues, issues that the editors of this *Companion* have attempted to address openly in both the content of its chapters and its organizing principles.

Readers of this volume will immediately notice its differences from some of the other Blackwell *Companions*, as well from other works that attempt in some way to present a critical or historical introduction to Victorian poetry. Instead of collecting essays that treat significant Victorian poets or poems individually, we have brought together specially commissioned chapters that reflect both the multifariousness of Victorian poetry and the variety of critical approaches to it – many of them richly informed by recent developments in textual and cultural theory. Thus, rather than presenting a single chapter on *Idylls of the King*, we provide readers with a number of chapters in which Tennyson's great epic is discussed, along with other significant Victorian poems, in terms of genre (Tucker), marketing (Erickson) and reception (Shattock), but also within a variety of cultural contexts, such as Victorian medievalism (Harrison), Victorian concerns with nationhood and empire (Linley), and Victorian attitudes to gender (Saville) and sexuality (Maynard). A detailed topical index allows readers to trace such connections. This volume is thus designed, at one level, to demonstrate the ways in which a given poet or poem can be seen to emerge from a number of cultural matrices and participate in a variety of cultural discourses. At another, it seeks to explore the relationships – generic, stylistic, thematic – between work by different poets, and in doing so resuscitate a considerable body of poetry of the period that has fallen into neglect.

In her introduction on Victorian poetics, Carol T. Christ offers a commanding overview of the whole period. The remaining contributions are organized in three parts: 'Varieties and Forms', 'Production, Distribution and Reception' and 'Victorian Poetry and Victorian Culture'. Part one surveys the generic range of Victorian poetry and the variety of its schools and styles. In part two the focus shifts from the form and content of Victorian poetry to the means of its production. Chapters deal with issues ranging from the new print technologies and the economics of the production of poetry to the structure of the marketplace, and to the influence of anthologies, lending libraries, illustration and reviewing on the reception of Victorian poets and their work. Part three attempts to position Victorian verse in what the editors see as crucial cultural contexts and to explore the interactions between the poetry and dominant cultural discourses.

This book offers itself as a companion to a body of work most of which had almost disappeared from view in the mid-twentieth century, and much of which has still to attract the attention that it deserves. In the 1960s Victorian poetry had been all but reduced to the work of three poets: Alfred Tennyson, Robert Browning and Matthew Arnold. Gerald Manley Hopkins and Thomas Hardy remained, but by virtue of being enrolled as moderns before their time. The work of Victorian women poets had been effectively erased. Much has changed since then, and this *Companion* reflects that. But it seeks to do still more: to lay out an agenda for the study of Victorian poetry in coming years. It suggests, for example, that the work of women poets no longer needs special defence. It is treated here not in one chapter but in every chapter. This *Companion* maps areas that invite future research, in chapters such as Florence Boos's on Victorian working-class poetry, and it recalls to attention poems that remain unread, as in Herbert F. Tucker's chapter on the Victorian epic. In place of the tastefully minimalist shop window that the New Critics of the last century displayed to their readers, this *Companion to Victorian Poetry* offers a window that is richly and chaotically cluttered. But there is an appropriateness in that: Victorian shops after all had windows of precisely that kind.

Notes on Contributors

Florence Boos, a professor of English at the University of Iowa, has published book-length studies of the poetry of Dante Gabriel Rossetti and William Morris, and edited Morris's *Socialist Diary* and *Earthly Paradise*, as well as a more recent special issue of *Victorian Poetry* devoted to nineteenth-century working-class poetry. She is currently at work on a book on working-class women poets of Victorian Scotland.

Matthew Campbell is Senior Lecturer in English Literature at the University of Sheffield. He is the author of *Rhythm and Will in Victorian Poetry* (1999) and co-editor of *Beyond the Pleasure Dome: Writing and Addiction from the Romantics* (1994) and *Memory and Memorials, 1798–1914: Literary and Cultural Perspectives* (2000). He is currently working on Irish poetry in the Union, 1801–1921, and editing *The Cambridge Companion to Contemporary Irish Poetry*. He is editor of the *Tennyson Research Bulletin*.

Alison Chapman is a lecturer in English Literature at the University of Glasgow. She is the author of *The Afterlife of Christina Rossetti* (2000). She is editing a collection of essays on Victorian women poets for the series *Essays and Studies* (2003) and, with Jane Stabler, co-editing *Unfolding the South: Nineteenth-Century British Women Writers and Artists in Italy* (2002) and a special issue of *Forum* (2003) on Anglo-American expatriate communities in Italy.

Carol T. Christ is Professor of English at the University of California at Berkeley and until recently was Vice-Chancellor and Provost of that university. Her books include *The Finer Optic: The Aesthetic of Particularity in Victorian Poetry* (1975), *Victorian and Modern Poetics* (1984) and *Victorian Literature and the Victorian Visual Imagination* (1995), and she has edited *The Mill on the Floss*.

Richard Cronin is Professor of English Literature at the University of Glasgow. His books include *Shelley's Poetic Thoughts* (1981), *Colour and Experience in Nineteenth-Century Poetry* (1988), *Imagining India* (1989), *1798: The Year of the Lyrical Ballads* (1998), *The Politics of Romantic Poetry: In Search of the Pure Commonwealth* (2000) and *Romantic Victorians* (2002).

Lee Erickson, Professor of English at Marshall University, is the author of *Robert Browning: His Poetry and His Audiences* (1984) and *The Economy of Literary Form: English Literature and the Industrialization of Publishing, 1800–1850* (1996).

Dino Felluga is an assistant professor at Purdue University, West Lafayette, where he teaches nineteenth-century British poetry as well as theory and cultural studies. Articles of his have appeared in *SEL: Studies in English Literature, Criticism, European Romantic Review* and *ARIEL*. He is currently completing his first book, entitled *The Perversity of Poetry: The Market, Romantic Ideology, and the Masculine Poet*.

Pauline Fletcher is a professor of English at Bucknell University and general editor of the *Bucknell Review*. Her publications include the monograph *Gardens and Grim Ravines: The Language of Landscape in Victorian Poetry* (1983) and, edited together with John Murray, *Wordsworth in Context* (1992), as well as numerous essays on Victorian poetry.

J.-A. George is a graduate of Vassar College and King's College, London. She has taught in the Irish Republic and currently lectures at the University of Dundee, where she also runs the Mediaeval Drama Group. She has published on Old and Middle English language and literature, sixteenth-century drama, the Pre-Raphaelites and translation theory.

Antony H. Harrison is Professor of English at North Carolina State University. He has edited *The Letters of Christina Rossetti* (4 vols), *Gender and Discourse in Victorian Literature and Art* and *The Culture of Christina Rossetti*. His authored books include *Victorian Poets and the Politics of Culture: Discourse and Ideology* (1998), *Victorian Poets and Romantic Poems: Intertextuality and Ideology* (1990), *Christina Rossetti in Context* (1988) and *Swinburne's Medievalism: A Study in Victorian Love Poetry* (1988). He has held fellowships from the National Endowment for the Humanities, the National Humanities Center and the American Council of Learned Societies. He is currently writing *Matters of Taste: Victorian Poetry and Desire*.

Natalie M. Houston is an assistant professor at the University of Houston. She has published articles on Victorian women writers, nineteenth-century sonnet anthologies and the poetry of the Crimean War. She is currently completing a book on the cultural history of the Victorian sonnet.

Richard Jenkyns is a Fellow of Lady Margaret Hall and Professor of the Classical Tradition at the University of Oxford. His books include *The Victorians and Ancient Greece* (1980), *Three Classical Poets* (1982), *Classical Epic: Homer and Virgil* (1991), *The Legacy of Rome* (1992), *Dignity and Decadence: Victorian Art and the Classical Inheritance* (1992) and *Virgil's Experience* (1998).

Lorraine Janzen Kooistra, Associate Professor of English at Nipissing University in North Bay, Canada, has published numerous articles on visual/verbal relations and

Victorian poetry. She is co-editor, along with Mary Arseneau and Antony H. Harrison, of *The Culture of Christina Rossetti: Female Poetics and Victorian Contexts* (1999) and author of *The Artist as Critic: Bitextuality in Fin-de-Siècle Illustrated Books* (1995) and *Christina Rossetti and Illustration: A Publishing History* (2002).

Margaret Linley is an assistant professor of English and member of the Print Culture 1700–1900 Specialized MA at SFU. She has published on literary annuals, Tennyson, Christina Rossetti, Felicia Hemans and Letitia Landon. She is currently working on a book on Victorian poetry, the British nation and imperialism.

Catherine Maxwell is Senior Lecturer in English in the School of English and Drama at Queen Mary, University of London. She is the editor of the Everyman edition *Algernon Charles Swinburne* (1997) and *The Female Sublime from Milton to Swinburne: Bearing Blindness* (2001). She has published essays and articles on Christina and D. G. Rossetti, Browning, George Eliot, Shelley, Ruskin, Swinburne and Vernon Lee, and is currently writing the volume on Swinburne for the series *Writers and their Work*.

John Maynard is Professor of English at New York University, where he served as Chair from 1983 to 1989. He has published *Charlotte Brontë and Sexuality* (1983) and *Victorian Discourses on Sexuality and Religion* (1993) as well as two studies of Robert Browning. He is co-editor of *Victorian Literature and Culture*. He is currently working on a project on reader theory.

Roderick McGillis is a professor of English at the University of Calgary. He is the author of *The Nimble Reader* (1996), *A Little Princess: Gender and Empire* (1996) and *Children's Literature and the Fin de Siècle* (2001). He has recently published his first novel. His current work deals with the construction of masculinity in popular culture.

Seamus Perry is Reader in English Literature at the University of Glasgow and author of *Coleridge and the Uses of Division* (1999), editor of *Coleridge: Interviews and Recollections* (2000), and co-editor, with Nicola Trott, of *1800: The New Lyrical Ballads* (2001). He is an editor of the journal *Essays in Criticism*.

Linda H. Peterson is Professor of English at Yale University. She has recently published *Traditions of Victorian Women's Autobiography: The Poetics and Politics of Life Writing* (1999), as well as articles on Tennyson, Letitia Landon, Barrett Browning, Christina Rossetti, Margaret Oliphant and Mary Cholmondeley.

Stephen Prickett is Regius Professor of English Language and Literature at the University of Glasgow. His books include *Coleridge and Wordsworth: The Poetry of Growth* (1970), *Romanticism and Religion: The Tradition of Coleridge and Wordsworth in the Victorian Church* (1976), *Victorian Fantasy* (1982), *Words and the Word: Language, Poetics and Biblical Interpretation* (1986) and *Origins of Narrative: The Romantic Appropriation of the Bible* (1996).

Alan Rauch, Associate Professor of Literature, Communication, and Culture at the Georgia Institute of Technology, researches the cultural studies of science in the nineteenth century. He is the author of *Useful Knowledge: The Victorians, Morality, and the March of Intellect* (2001). His current projects include *Private Reading: Public Knowledge*, which focuses on nineteenth-century private subscription libraries and their role in the dissemination of knowledge, as well as a reprint of William Paley's *Natural Theology*. Rauch has also edited Jane Loudon's 1827 novel *The Mummy! A Tale of the Twenty-Second Century* (1994) and, with George Levine, *One Culture: Essays in Science and Literature* (1987).

David Riede is Professor of English at Ohio State University. He is the author of *Swinburne: A Study of Romantic Mythmaking* (1978), *Dante Gabriel Rossetti and the Limits of Victorian Vision* (1983), *Matthew Arnold and the Betrayal of Language* (1988), *Oracles and Hierophants: Constructions of Romantic Authority* (1992) and *Dante Gabriel Rossetti Revisited* (1992).

Matthew Rowlinson teaches English at the University of Western Ontario. He is the author of *Tennyson's Fixations: Psychoanalysis and the Topics of the Early Poetry* (1994) and numerous articles on Victorian Literature. His current research links literary allegory and the history of money forms in nineteenth-century Britain.

Julia F. Saville is Associate Professor of English at the University of Illinois at Urbana-Champaign, specializing in Victorian poetry and the relation between nineteenth-century poetics and the visual arts. She is the author of *A Queer Chivalry: The Homoerotic Asceticism of Gerard Manley Hopkins* (2000) and various essays. Currently she is working on a book provisionally entitled *Bathing Boys: An Aesthetics of the Male Nude in Victorian Literature and Culture*.

Adrienne Scullion teaches in the Department of Theatre, Film and Television Studies at the University of Glasgow. Her publications on Scottish cultural issues include articles in the journals *Comparative Drama*, *New Theatre Quarterly* and *Theatre Research International*, and essays in the collections *Group Identities on French and British Television* (2001), *The Cambridge Companion to Modern British Women Playwrights* (2000) and *A History of Scottish Women's Writing* (1997). She also works on early women playwrights and is the editor of *Female Playwrights of the Nineteenth Century* (1996).

Joanne Shattock is Professor of Victorian Literature and Director of the Victorian Studies Centre, University of Leicester. She is editor of *The Cambridge Bibliography of English Literature*, third edition, vol. 4, 1800–1900 (1999), and has recently published *Women and Literature 1800–1900* (2001). She co-edits a monograph series, *The Nineteenth Century*, for Ashgate.

W. David Shaw is Professor of English at the University of Toronto. Amongst his books are *The Dialectical Temper: The Rhetorical Art of Robert Browning* (1968), *Tennyson's Style* (1976), *The Lucid Veil: Poetic Truth in the Victorian Age* (1987), *Victorians and Mystery: Crises of Representation* (1990), *Elegy and Paradox: Testing the Conventions* (1994) and *Origins of the Monologue: The Hidden God* (1999).

E. Warwick Slinn is Associate Professor of English at Massey University, New Zealand. He has studied in Canada and England and has been a Fulbright Scholar at the University of Virginia and Duke University. He has written essays on literary theory as well as poetry and is the author of *Browning and the Fictions of Identity* (1982) and *The Discourse of Self in Victorian Poetry* (1991). He is currently completing a book on Victorian poetry as cultural critique.

Chris Snodgrass has published numerous articles on figures such as Carlyle, Swinburne, Wilde, Dowson, Symons and Beardsley, among others. He is the author of *Aubrey Beardsley, Dandy of the Grotesque* (1995) and is currently writing a second book on Beardsley and *fin-de-siècle* sexuality.

Herbert F. Tucker has published *Browning's Beginnings: The Art of Disclosure* (1980) and *Tennyson and the Doom of Romanticism* (1988), edited the Blackwell *Companion to Victorian Literature and Culture* (1999), and co-edited with Dorothy Mermin a teaching anthology of poetry and prose, *Victorian Literature 1830–1900* (2002). Recent articles discuss the epic poetry of Barrett Browning, Tennyson, Browning, Swinburne and Morris; recent auguries portend completion of *The Proof of Epic in Britain 1790–1910*. At the University of Virginia he serves as associate editor of *New Literary History* and series editor in Victorian Literature and Culture for the University Press.

J. R. Watson is Emeritus Professor of English Literature at the University of Durham. His books include *Picturesque Landscape and English Romantic Poetry* (1970), *Browning's Men and Women and Other Poems: A Casebook* (1974), *Everyman's Book of Victorian Verse* (1982), *Wordsworth's Vital Soul: The Sacred and Profane in Wordsworth's Poetry* (1982), *English Poetry of the Romantic Period, 1789–1830* (1985), *The Poetry of Gerard Manley Hopkins: A Critical Study* (1987) and *The English Hymn: A Critical and Historical Study* (1997).

Chronology

Date	Poetry volumes	Other literary and artistic events	Contexts
1827	John Keble, *Christian Year* Robert Pollok, *The Course of Time* Alfred Tennyson, *Poems by Two Brothers* John Clare, *The Shepherd's Calendar* L. E. L., *The Golden Violet*		First Reform Bill introduced to Parliament and rejected by House of Lords Riots in Bristol, Derby and Nottingham
1828	Felicia Hemans, *The Records of Woman*	First publication of *The Keepsake*, instituting vogue for annuals	Thomas Arnold appointed headmaster, Rugby
1829	L. E. L., *The Venetian Bracelet* Ebenezer Elliott, *The Village Patriarch*		Catholic Emancipation Metropolitan Police Act
1830	Tennyson, *Poems, Chiefly Lyrical* Hemans, *Songs of the Affections*		Charles Lyell, *Principles of Geology* Railways begin George III dies; William IV becomes king
1831	Elliott, *Corn Law Rhymes*	Arthur Hallam, 'On Some of the Characteristics of Modern Poetry'	Discovery of chloroform Discovery of electromagnetic current First cholera epidemic
1832	Tennyson, *Poems* (dated 1833)	*Penny Magazine*	First Reform Bill Harriet Martineau, *Illustrations of Political Economy* (1832–4) Babbage's Difference Engine No. 1 constructed
1833	Elizabeth Barret, *Prometheus Bound* Robert Browning, *Pauline*	Start of Oxford Movement and the *Tracts for the Times* (1833–41) Thomas Carlyle, *Sartor Resartus* John Stuart Mill, 'What is Poetry' and 'Two Kinds of Poetry'	Abolition of slavery in British Empire

Date	Poetry volumes	Other literary and artistic events	Contexts
1834	Henry Taylor, *Philip van Artevelde* Benjamin Disraeli, *The Revolutionary Epick* Hallam, *Remains*		William Henry Fox Talbot produces photographs Death of Samuel Taylor Coleridge Poor Law Amendment Act ('New Poor Law')
1835	Browning, *Paracelsus* Clare, *The Rural Muse* William Wordsworth, *Yarrow Revisited and Other Poems* Eliza Cook, *Lays of a Wild Harp* L. E. L., *The Vow of the Peacock*	David Friedrich Strauss, *Leben Jesu* (*Life of Jesus*)	John Elliotson, *Human Physiology*
1836	Joanna Baillie, *Dramas*	Charles Dickens, *Pickwick Papers*, begins Augustus Pugin, *Contrasts*	
1837	Browning, *Strafford*	Carlyle, *The French Revolution* Dickens, *Oliver Twist*, begins	Accession of Queen Victoria
1838	Barrett, *The Seraphim and Other Poems* Cook, *Melaia, and Other Poems*	Dickens, *Nicholas Nickleby*, begins	Stereoscopy invented People's Charter published (May) Anti-Corn Law League (1838–46)
1839	Philip Bailey, *Festus* L. E. L., *The Zenana and Other Poems*	Mary Shelley's edition of Percy Bysshe Shelley's *Poetical Works* Carlyle, *Chartism*	Chartist riots Daguerreotyping process announced in France
1840	Browning, *Sordello* Richard Barham, *Ingoldsby Legends* Caroline Norton, *The Dream and Other Poems*		Penny post introduced by Rowland Hill Stereotyping begins Victoria marries Albert C. H. Townshend, *Facts in Mesmerism*
1841	Browning, *Pippa Passes*	*Punch* begins publication Carlyle, *Heroes and Hero Worship*	

Date	Poetry volumes	Other literary and artistic events	Contexts
1842	Browning, *Dramatic Lyrics* Tennyson, *Poems* Thomas Macaulay, *Lays of Ancient Rome* John Westland Marston, *Gerald*	Mudie's Circulating Library established J. M. W. Turner, *Steamboat in a Snowstorm* First issue of *Illustrated London News*	Chartist riots Copyright Bill Income Tax introduced
1843	R. H. Horne, *Orion*	Macaulay, *Critical and Historical Essays* Carlyle, *Past and Present* Wordsworth poet laureate Turner, *Approach to Venice* John Ruskin, *Modern Painters*, begins Dickens, *Martin Chuzzlewit*, begins Dickens, *A Christmas Carol*	
1844	Barrett, *Poems* Coventry Patmore, *Poems* William Barnes, *Poems of Rural Life in the Dorset Dialect* (1844–62)	Horne, *A New Spirit of the Age* Chambers, *Vestiges of Natural Creation* Talbot, *The Pencil of Nature* (1844–6)	Friedrich Engels, *On the Condition of the Working Class in England* Factory Act
1845	Browning, *Dramatic Romances and Lyrics* Thomas Cooper, *The Purgatory of Suicides*	Disraeli, *Sybil*	Irish Famine (1845–51) John Henry Newman converts to Catholicism
1846	*Poems by Currer, Ellis and Acton Bell* Edward Lear, *A Book of Nonsense*	Marriage of Elizabeth Barrett and Robert Browning George Eliot, translation of Strauss's *Life of Jesus* Dickens, *Pictures from Italy*	Repeal of the Corn Laws
1847	Tennyson, *The Princess* Christina Rossetti, *Verses*	Emily Brontë, *Wuthering Heights* Charlotte Brontë, *Jane Eyre* William Thackeray, *Vanity Fair*	Ten Hours Factory Act

Date	Poetry volumes	Other literary and artistic events	Contexts
1848	Arthur Hugh Clough, *The Bothie of Toper-na-fuosich* Dora Greenwell, *Poems*	Pre-Raphaelite Brotherhood founded Dante Gabriel Rossetti, *The Girlhood of Mary Virgin* (1848–9) Monckton Milnes, *Life, Letters and Literary Remains of John Keats* Macaulay, *History of England*, vols i and ii Dickens, *Dombey and Son* Elizabeth Gaskell, *Mary Barton*	Karl Marx and Engels, *Communist Manifesto* Democratic revolutions in Europe
1849	Matthew Arnold, *The Strayed Reveller* Clough, *Ambarvalia* (with Thomas Burbidge) Edward Bulwer-Lytton, *King Arthur*	D. G. Rossetti, *Ecce Ancilla Domini* *Eliza Cook's Journal* (1849–54)	
1850	Wordsworth, *Prelude* Tennyson, *In Memoriam* Barrett Browning, *Poems*	Wordsworth dies; Tennyson poet laureate Development of wood engraving Launch of the *Germ* (Pre-Raphaelite magazine) John Everett Millais, *Christ in the House of his Parents* Dickens, *David Copperfield* *Household Words* launched	Restoration of Catholic hierarchy in UK
1851	Barret Browning, *Casa Guidi Windows* Browning, *Christmas-Eve and Easter-Day* Baillie, *Dramatic and Poetical Works* George Meredith, *Poems*	Millais, *Ophelia* Gaskell, *Cranford* begins Ruskin, *Stones of Venice*	Great Exhibition Singer's sewing machine patented Henry Mayhew, *London Labour and the London Poor* (1851–2)

Date	Poetry volumes	Other literary and artistic events	Contexts
1852	Arnold, *Empedocles on Etna and Other Poems*	William Holman Hunt, *On English Coasts*	Herbert Spencer coins the term 'evolution'
1853	Alexander Smith, *A Life Drama* Arnold, *Poems: A New Edition* Patmore, *Tamerton Church-Tower and Other Poems*	Dickens, *Bleak House*, begins Holman Hunt, *The Awakening Conscience*	
1854	Patmore, *Angel in the House* (1854–62) Sydney Dobell, *Balder* W. E. Aytoun, *Firmilian* Arnold, *Poems*, second edition	Dickens, *Hard Times* Gaskell, *North and South*, begins	Crimean War (1854–6) John Maurice founds Working Men's College in London
1855	Browning, *Men and Women* Tennyson, *Maud, and Other Poems* Arnold, *Poems*, second series	Dickens, *Little Dorritt*, begins Macaulay, *History of England*, vols iii and iv	Spencer, *The Principles of Psychology*
1856	Barret Browning, *Aurora Leigh* (dated 1857)	Henry Irving's debut on London stage William Morris and Edward Burne-Jones, *Oxford and Cambridge Magazine* Lewis Carroll takes up photography	
1857	Edward Moxon publishes illustrated edition of Tennyson's *Poems* Alexander Smith, *City Poems* Arnold, *Poems*, third series Charles-Pierre Baudelaire, *Les Fleurs du Mal*	Pre-Raphaelites, Oxford Union frescoes Gaskell, *Life of Charlotte Brontë* Anthony Trollope, *Barchester Towers* Gustave Flaubert, *Madame Bovary*	Indian Mutiny Matrimonial Causes Act
1858	Adelaide Anne Procter, *Legends and Lyrics* Morris, *The Defence of Guenevere* Clough, *Amours de Voyage* Arnold, *Merope*	George Macdonald, *Phantastes*	Lionel Rothschild becomes first professing Jewish MP

Date	Poetry volumes	Other literary and artistic events	Contexts
1859	Tennyson, *Idylls of the King* (completed 1885) Barnes, *Hwomely Rhymes* Edward FitzGerald, *Rubáiyát of Omar Khayyám*	Mill, *On Liberty* Dickens, *A Tale of Two Cities* Wilkie Collins, *Woman in White*, begins Eliot, *Adam Bede* Samuel Smiles, *Self-Help*	Charles Darwin, *Origin of Species* Charles Blondin crosses Niagara Falls on a tightrope
1860	Barrett Browning, *Poems Before Congress* Augusta Webster, *Blanche Lisle and Other Poems*	Rise of giftbooks *Essays and Reviews* First issue of *Cornhill Magazine* Dickens, *Great Expectations*, begins Eliot, *The Mill on the Floss*	
1861	D. G. Rossetti, *The Early Italian Poets* Smith, *Edwin of Deira* Greenwell, *Poems* Francis Palgrave, *Golden Treasury of Songs and Lyrics*	*Hymns Ancient and Modern* Barrett Browning dies in Florence Eliot, *Silas Marner*	Prince Albert dies American Civil War (1861–5) United Kingdom of Italy proclaimed
1862	Barrett Browning, *Last Poems* Meredith, *Modern Love* Christina Rossetti, *Goblin Market and Other Poems* Alfred Austin, *The Human Tragedy*	Formation of Morris & Co Death of Elizabeth Siddal	Richard Gatling invents his gun
1863	Janet Hamilton, *Poems and Essays* Jean Ingelow, *Poems*, first series	Alexander Gilchrist, *Life of William Blake* Julia Margaret Cameron takes up photography	John Colenso deposed as bishop of Natal T. H. Huxley, *Man's Place in Nature*
1864	Tennyson, *Enoch Arden* Browning, *Dramatis Personae* William Allingham, *Bloomfield in Ireland*	Newman, *Apologia Pro Vita Sua* Dickens, *Our Mutual Friend*, begins Gaskell, *Wives and Daughters*	Louis Pasteur invents pasteurization

Date	Poetry volumes	Other literary and artistic events	Contexts
1865	Algernon Swinburne, *Atalanta in Calydon* Newman, *Dream of Gerontius*	Carroll, *Alice in Wonderland* Arnold, *Essays in Criticism* Leo Tolstoy, *War and Peace* Ruskin, *Sesame and Lilies*	Formation of the Kensington Society for Women's Suffrage
1866	Swinburne, *Poems and Ballads*, first series Christina Rossetti, *The Prince's Progress and Other Poems* Webster, *Dramatic Studies* Robert Buchanan, *London Poem*		Riots in Ireland Dr Barnardo opens his first home
1867	Mathilde Blind, *Poems* Webster, *A Woman Sold and Other Poems* Jean Ingelow, *A Story of Doom* Arthur O'Shaughnessy, *Epic of Women* Ellen Johnston, *Autobiography, Poems and Songs* Arnold, *New Poems* Morris, *Life and Death of Jason* Greenwell, *Poems*	Carlyle, 'Shooting Niagara: And After?'	Marx, *Das Kapital*, vol. 1 Second Reform Bill
1868	Browning, *The Ring and the Book* (1868–9) Eliot, *The Spanish Gypsy* Hamilton, *Poems and Ballads* Barnes, *Poems of Rural Life* Morris, *Earthly Paradise* (1868–70)	D. G. Rossetti, *Beata Beatrix* Keble, *On the Mysticism Attributed to the Early Fathers of the Church* (*Tract 89*) Collins, *The Moonstone*	Suez Canal opens First Trades Union Congress
1869	Tennyson, *Idylls*, second series Carroll, *Phantasmagoria, and Other Poems*	Arnold, *Culture and Anarchy* Mill, *On the Subjection of Women*	Francis Galton, *Hereditary Genius*

Date	Poetry volumes	Other literary and artistic events	Contexts
1870	D. G. Rossetti, *Poems* Webster, *Portraits*	Austin, *The Poetry of the Period* Dickens dies Christina Rossetti, *Commonplace and Other Stories*	Married Women's Property Act Franco-Prussian War (1870–1) Education Act Elementary Education Act Darwin, *Descent of Man* Religious tests abolished at Oxford and Cambridge
1871	Tennyson, *Idylls*, third series Browning, *Balaustion's Adventure and Prince Hohenstiel-Schwangau* Swinburne, *Songs Before Sunrise*	Carroll, *Through the Looking Glass* Buchanan, 'The Fleshly School of Poetry'	
1872	Samuel Ferguson, *Congal* Tennyson, *Idylls*, fourth series Browning, *Fifine at the Fair* Christina Rossetti, *Sing-Song*	Eliot, *Middlemarch* Friedrich Nietzsche, *The Birth of Tragedy*	
1873	Browning, *Red-Cotton Night-Cap Country*	Walter Pater, *The Renaissance* Mill, *Autobiography*	Invention of the Remington typewriter
1874	Ingelow, *Poems*, second series James Thomson, 'City of Dreadful Night'	First Impressionist exhibition Thomas Hardy, *Far from the Madding Crowd* Christina Rossetti, *Annus Domini* and *Speaking Likenesses* Tolstoy, *Anna Karenina*	
1875	Browning, *The Inn-Album* Alice Meynell, *Preludes* Christina Rossetti, *Goblin Market, The Prince's Progress, and Other Poems*		
1876	Carroll, *The Hunting of the Snark* Morris, *Sigurd the Volsung* Browning, *Pacchiarotto* Swinburne, *Erechtheus*	Eliot, *Daniel Deronda* Henrik Ibsen, *A Doll's House*	Victoria proclaimed empress of India Alexander Graham Bell invents telephone
1877	Patmore, *The Unknown Eros and Other Odes* Buchanan, *Balder the Beautiful*		Russo-Turkish War Thomas Edison invents phonograph

Date	Poetry volumes	Other literary and artistic events	Contexts
1878	Swinburne, *Poems and Ballads*, second series	Webster, *A Housewife's Opinions*	London University degrees for women
	Browning, *La Saisiaz and the Two Poets of Croisic*		Zulu War (1878–9)
1879	Browning, *Dramatic Idylls*, first series	James Whistler versus Ruskin	
	Webster, *Disguises*	Hardy, *The Return of the Native*	
		Christina Rossetti, *Seek and Find*	
1880	Browning, *Dramatic Idylls*, second series		National Eisteddfod Association established
	Tennyson, *Ballads and Other Poems*		
	Swinburne, *Studies in Song, Songs of the Springtide, and the Heptalogia, or the Seven Against Sense*		
1881	Amy Levy, *Xantippe and Other Poems*	Christina Rossetti, *Called to be Saints*	Married Women's Property Act
	Christina Rossetti, *A Pageant and Other Poems*		Irish Land Act
	D. G. Rossetti, *Ballads and Sonnets* and *Poems, a New Edition*		
	Webster, *A Book of Rhyme*		
	Oscar Wilde, *Poems*		
1882	Swinburne, *Tristram of Lyonesse and Other Poems*	Walter Hamilton, *The Aesthetic Movement in England*	
		D. G. Rossetti dies	
1883	Meredith, *Poems and Lyrics*	Pater, *Appreciations*	
	Browning, *Jocoseria*	Christina Rossetti, *Letter and Spirit*	
1884	Levy, *A Minor Poet and Other Verse*	*Oxford English Dictionary*	Third Reform Bill
	Tennyson, *Becket* (performed 1893)		Fabian Society founded
	Browning, *Ferishtah's Fancies*		Voting Act
			'Crofters' War'

Date	Poetry volumes	Other literary and artistic events	Contexts
			Married Women's Property Act (granting status as independent agents)
1885	Tennyson, *Idylls*, fifth series Tennyson, *Tiresias and Other Poems* Ingelow, *Poems*, third series	Christina Rossetti, *Time Flies*	Marx, *Das Kapital*, vol. 2 Age of sexual consent raised to 16
1886	Tennyson, *Locksley Hall, Sixty Years After* Rudyard Kipling, *Departmental Ditties* Edith Nesbit, *Lays and Legends*, first series Morris, *Pilgrims of Hope* W. B. Yeats, *Mosada: A Dramatic Poem* Stephenson, *Underwoods*	William Sharp, *Sonnets of this Century* Robert Louis Stevenson, *Strange Case of Dr Jekyll and Mr Hyde* Hardy, *The Mayor of Casterbridge*	
1887	Browning, *Parlayings* Meredith, *Ballads and Poems of the Tragic Life*	Arthur Conan Doyle, *A Study in Scarlet*	Victoria's Golden Jubilee
1888	Nesbit, *Leaves of Life* A. Mary F. Robinson, *Songs, Ballads and A Garden Play* Blind, *The Ascent of Man* Meredith, *A Reading of Earth*	H. Rider Haggard, *She*	Heinrich Hertz produces radio waves
1889	Tennyson, *Demeter and Other Poems* Browning, *Asolando* Swinburne, *Poems and Ballads*, third series Michael Field, *Long Ago* Yeats, *The Wanderings of Oisin*	Browning dies	'The Red Flag' written

Date	Poetry volumes	Other literary and artistic events	Contexts
	Levy, *A London Plane-Tree and Other Poems* A. Symons, *Days and Nights*		
1890	Morris, *Chants for Socialists* and *Poems by the Way* Kipling, *Barrack-Room Ballads* (1890, 1892)	Tennyson dies	
1891	Francis Thompson, *The Hound of Heaven*	A. H. Miles, *Poets and Poetry of the Century*, 10 vols (1891–7) Wilde, *The Picture of Dorian Gray* Hardy, *Tess of the D'Urbervilles*	
1892	Tennyson, *Death of Oenone and Other Poems* Nesbit, *Lays and Legends*, second series W. E. Henley, *Song of the Sword and Other Verses* Field, *Sight and Song* Wilde, *Poems* Meredith, *Poems* Symons, *Silhouettes*	Christina Rossetti, *The Face of the Deep*	
1893	Field, *Underneath the Bough* Blind, *Songs and Sonnets* Christina Rossetti, *Verses* Henley, *London Voluntaries and Other Verses*		Sigmund Freud and Josef Breuer, *Studies on Hysteria* (1893–5) Independent Labour Party established Second Irish Home Rule Bill defeated
1894	A. Mary F. Robinson, *Retrospect and Other Poems* Swinburne, *Astrophel and Stella and Other Poems* Symons, *London Nights*	*Yellow Book* (1894–7) George du Maurier, *Trilby* Kipling, *Jungle Book* Death of Christina Rossetti	

Date	Poetry volumes	Other literary and artistic events	Contexts
1895	Webster, *Mother and Daughter* Nesbit, *A Pomander of Verse* Yeats, *Poems* Wilde, *The Sphinx* Lionel Johnson, *Poems*	Max Nordau, *Degeneration* Hardy, *Jude the Obscure*	Marx, *Das Kapital*, vol. 3 Lumière brothers develop cinematography Trials of Wilde
1896	Mary E. Coleridge, *Fancy's Following* A. E. Housman, *A Shropshire Lad* Ernest Dowson, *Verses* Swinburne, *The Tale of Balen*	First issue of *The Savoy* Morris, *Kelmscott Chaucer*	
1897	Mary E. Coleridge, *Fancy's Guerdon* Lionel Johnson, *Ireland, with Other Poems* Symons, *Amoris Victima*	Christina Rossetti, *Maude* Bram Stoker, *Dracula*	Henry Havelock Ellis, *Studies in the Psychology of Sex*
1898	Nesbit, *Songs of Love and Empire* Hardy, *Wessex Poems and Other Verses* Wilde, *The Ballad of Reading Gaol*		Marie Curie discovers radium
1899	Dowson, *Decorations* Yeats, *The Wind Among the Reeds* Symons, *Images of Good and Evil*	Symons, *The Symbolist Movement in Literature*	
1900			Freud, *The Interpretation of Dreams* Max Planck propounds quantum theory
1901	Hardy, *Poems of Past and Present* Yeats, *Poems*		Victoria dies; Edward VII accedes Freud, *The Psychopathology of Dreams* Guglielmo Marconi transmits wireless messages

Introduction: Victorian Poetics
Carol T. Christ

In developing a characterization of Victorian poetics, it is important to recognize that literary periods are historical hypotheses that depend not only upon assumptions about historical change but also upon historical accident. The organization of literary history into historical periods is a fairly recent phenomenon. It develops from the historicism that dominated nineteenth-century thought, a historicism that was motivated by a distinct sense of modernity. John Stuart Mill begins his essay 'The Spirit of the Age' by observing the relationship between modernity and historicism:

> The 'spirit of the age' is in some measure a novel expression. I do not believe that it is to be met with in any work exceeding fifty years in antiquity. The idea of comparing one's own age with former ages, or with our notion of those which are yet to come, had occurred to philosophers; but never before was itself the dominant idea of any age.
>
> It is an idea essentially belonging to an age of change. Before men begin to think much and long on the peculiarities of their own times, they must have begun to think that those times are, or are destined to be, distinguished in a very remarkable manner from the times which preceded them. (1963–90: XXII, 228)

We have come to rely so heavily on the interpretative categories of Romantic, Victorian and Modern that we forget that these categories were constructed as a way of defining historical progress towards the modern, from a modern perspective. The poets that we call the Romantics did not think of themselves as Romantics, any more than the Victorians thought of themselves as Victorians. Poets writing in the 1830s and 1840s conceived their work in the context of the major writers of the two previous generations – Wordsworth and Coleridge, and Byron, Shelley and Keats. The characterization 'Victorian' depends in part on the accident of the beginning, length and end of Victoria's reign and takes polemical force from the efforts of early twentieth-century writers to define themselves, in Mill's words, as 'distinguished in a very remarkable manner from the times which preceded them'. In seeking to characterize Victorian poetics, it is important not to assume distinct breaks with the writers that we call the Romantics or with those we call the Moderns. The history of poetics in the nineteenth and twentieth centuries is a continuous development that has sometimes been obscured by modernist polemics and by the structure of academic specialization.

The poetry that we have come to call Victorian develops in the context of Romanticism. The birth dates of writers whom we identify as Victorian are not many years distant from those of the second generation of Romantics. None the less, these earlier poets defined what poetry was for the young Tennyson and Browning. When Browning first read Shelley, at the age of fourteen or fifteen, Shelley quickly became his God; in his early autobiographical poem, *Pauline*, Browning writes that Shelley's poetry seemed 'a key to a new world' (l. 415). When Tennyson, at fourteen, heard that Byron had died, he felt the world had come to an end, melodramatically carving in stone 'BYRON IS DEAD'. Later, when Tennyson was at Cambridge, his close friend Arthur Hallam placed his poetry in the school of Keats and Shelley. Although Victorian poetics came to distance itself from Romantic poetics, the first generation of Victorian poets initially saw themselves as writing in a Romantic tradition. Had the second generation of the Romantics not died so young, we would not have so sharp a sense of division between these groups of writers. Wordsworth, after all, was still writing poetry in the 1830s and 1840s, and served as poet laureate until his death in 1850, when he was succeeded by Tennyson.

Even in early Victorian poetry, however, we can see assumptions that would generate a distinct poetic project. Both Tennyson and Browning develop a poetic mode, distinct from each other but with important points of contact, that embodies a poetics from which most subsequent poetry of the century derives.

Tennyson's friend Hallam reviewed Tennyson's first independent book of poetry, *Poems, Chiefly Lyrical*, in a remarkable and influential essay that defines the principles of Tennyson's early poetics. Hallam indicates the boldness of his critical ambition in the title of his review, 'On Some of the Characteristics of Modern Poetry'. He begins by differentiating the poetry of Shelley and Keats from that of Wordsworth. Wordsworth too frequently writes a poetry of reflection, whose aim is to convince rather than enrapture. Hallam contrasts this with what he calls the poetry of sensation. He describes poets of sensation in the following way:

> Susceptible of the slightest impulse from external nature, their fine organs trembled into emotion at colors, sounds, and movements, unperceived or unregarded by duller temperaments . . . So vivid was the delight attending the simple exertions of eye and ear, that it became mingled more and more with their trains of active thought, and tended to absorb their whole being into the energy of sense. Other poets *seek* for images to illustrate their conceptions; these men had no need to seek; they lived in a world of images; for the most important and extensive portion of their life consisted in those emotions which are immediately conversant with the sensation. (1943: 186)

Hallam argues that such poetry is not descriptive; it is 'picturesque'. It consists of a combination of sense impressions through which the poet experiences and evokes a poetic emotion. Hallam grounds this poetry in the physical laws of association. Although the poet's impressions are necessarily subjective, they can be re-experienced by any individual willing to exert the effort of repeating the process of their combination.

Hallam's description of the poetry of sensation resembles what John Ruskin would later criticize in *Modern Painters* as the pathetic fallacy, the attribution of human emotion to our impressions of external things. Ruskin distinguishes between 'the ordinary, proper, and true appearances of things to us' and 'the extraordinary or false appearances, when we are under the influence of emotion' (V, 204). Indulging in the latter is a sign of weakness in the poet. Ruskin feels that both Keats and Tennyson display this weakness. He thus faults the very state that Hallam claims for the highest species of poetry – emotion so powerfully felt that it imbues all impressions of sense.

For Hallam such poetry is self-sufficient; its only motive and standard is beauty. He claims that the delicate sense of fitness from which the poetry of sensation springs 'acquires a celerity and weight of decision hardly inferior to the correspondent judgments of conscience'. It is weakened by 'every indulgence of heterogeneous aspirations, however pure they may be, however lofty, however suitable to human nature' (1943: 187) . This, according to Hallam, was Wordsworth's weakness; he too often indulged such heterogeneous aspirations, motivating philosophical reflection rather than sensation.

Tennyson's early poetry uses sense impressions in the way in which Hallam describes. He constructs a scene through a combination of images that convey a subjective experience. Here, for example, is the first stanza of 'Mariana':

> With blackest moss the flower-plots
>   Were thickly crusted, one and all;
> The rusted nails fell from the knots
>   That held the pear to the gable-wall.
> The broken sheds look'd sad and strange:
>   Unlifted was the clinking latch;
> Weeded and worn the ancient thatch
>   Upon the lonely moated grange.

In his review of Tennyson's early poetry, John Stuart Mill praises Tennyson for the power of creating scenery 'in keeping with some state of human feeling; so fitted to it as to be the embodied symbol of it, and to summon up the state of feeling itself'. Hallam praises Tennyson in similar terms: he is distinguished by his power 'of embodying himself in ideal characters, or rather moods of character, with such extreme accuracy of adjustment, that the circumstances of the narration seem to have a natural correspondence with the predominant feeling, and, as it were, to be evolved from it by assimilative force' (1943: 191–2). In 'Mariana', for example, Tennyson conveys Mariana's desolation through the landscape that surrounds her – the moss-encrusted flower plots, the falling rusty nails, the broken sheds. This is a poetry whose focus is subjectivity, not as a universal category – the 'I' of the Romantic poet – but as a particular mood or character. It uses a language of sense impressions, predominantly visual impressions of landscape, to convey these moods. Any philosophical statement is motivated by character or mood.

The poetry of sensation that Hallam describes does not place great emphasis on the cognitive capacity of language. Indeed, Hallam describes a role for pure sound in poetry, apart from meaning. He claims that there are poems in which sound conveys meaning where words would not:

> There are innumerable shades of fine emotion in the human heart, especially when the senses are keen and vigilant, which are too subtle and too rapid to admit of corresponding phrases. The understanding takes no definite note of them; how then can they leave signatures in language? Yet they exist; in plenitude of being and beauty they exist; and in music they find a medium through which they pass from heart to heart. The tone becomes the sign of the feeling; and they reciprocally suggest each other. (1943: 194–5)

Hallam here articulates the principle that gains increasing prominence as the century advances, that poetry aspires to the condition of music. He provides a theoretical basis for the characteristic of Victorian poetry many have remarked upon – its pursuit of what seems like pure sound, as in these lines from Tennyson's 'The Ballad of Oriana':

> My heart is wasted with my woe,
>   Oriana.
> There is no rest for me below,
>   Oriana.
> When the long dun wolds are ribbed with snow,
> And loud the Norland whirlwinds blow,
>   Oriana,
> Alone I wander to and fro,
>   Oriana.
>
>   (ll. 1–9)

Like the use of sensation that Hallam describes, the use of sound contributes to a poetry that produces its effects through evocation of mood.

In one of the most prescient parts of his essay, Hallam observes that the poetry of sensation that he describes results from what T. S. Eliot would later call a dissociation of sensibility. Hallam felt that the different elements of the poetic temperament – sensitive, reflective and passionately emotional – had originally been intermingled but now had become divided from each other. This division, Hallam argues, has given rise to the melancholy that characterizes the spirit of modern poetry, the return of the mind upon itself, and the habit of seeking relief in eccentricities rather than in community of interest. Modern poets thereby necessarily become alienated from their audience. The sense of the modern that Hallam describes is a burden that troubles all of Victorian poetics. By the end of the century writers of the Aesthetic movement and the Decadence were to embrace the alienation and eccentricity that Hallam laments; critics who locate themselves more conservatively, as we shall see, construct a poetics whose explicit goal is to escape this sense of the modern.

The poetics that Hallam defines in his review of Tennyson's early poems resembles John Stuart Mill's early conception of poetry. In 'Thoughts on Poetry and its Varieties', Mill, like Hallam, distinguishes the poetry of Wordsworth from the poetry of Shelley. In

Wordsworth, Mill argues, poetry is almost always 'the mere setting of a thought' (1963–90: I, 358). The highest species of poetry represents feeling rather than thought. Its object is to act on the emotions by exhibiting a state or states of sensibility. For Mill as for Hallam sensibility pervades the nervous system and operates through the senses; it follows physical laws of association. A dominant feeling generates a combination of images and thoughts. Thought is always subordinate to feeling, the medium of its expression. Likewise description has no place in poetry; objects like thoughts must be represented through the medium of feeling. It follows from this conception of poetry that it is of the nature of soliloquy – in Mill's words, 'feeling confessing itself to itself' (1963–90: I, 348).

After Mill wrote these two essays, he reviewed Tennyson's first two volumes of poetry: *Poems, Chiefly Lyrical*, which Hallam had reviewed, and the 1832 *Poems* (published 1833). Although Mill praises much of what Hallam had praised in Tennyson's early work, his review shows him modifying the concept of the poetry of sensibility that his earlier essays had held up as an ideal. Now Mill argues that poets must apply the faculty of cultivated reason to their nervous susceptibility and to their sensitivity to the laws of association. He warns Tennyson that he must continue to develop this faculty and finds evidence in poems like 'The Palace of Art', with its criticism of aesthetic isolation, that he has begun to do so. Tennyson's development as a poet shows his sensitivity to the conflict that Mill's early essays on poetry reveal. Tennyson feels a tension between an imaginative allegiance to the poetry of sensation and a troubled aspiration to a higher level of generalization that would enable him to address a society from which the poet has been alienated. Before I address the way in which the poetics of mid-century considers this dilemma, I will describe the poetics of Browning's early poetry, for it explores a different and in some ways more radical way of representing subjectivity than Tennyson's.

No review of Browning's early poetry gives it the synoptic overview that Hallam provides for Tennyson, and Browning's own descriptions of his poetic project are fragmentary. After his first long confessional poem, *Pauline*, which reflects the powerful presence and influence of Shelley, Browning turned to dramatic forms. In 1842 he published the volume *Dramatic Lyrics* with the following advertisement: 'Such poems as the majority in this volume might also come properly enough, I suppose, under the head of "Dramatic Pieces"; being, though often Lyric in expression, always Dramatic in principle, and so many utterances of so many imaginary persons, not mine.' Two things are significant in this definition: the combination of lyric and dramatic utterance and the conception of an imaginary speaker, separate from the poet. Through his development of a dramatic principle for lyrical utterance in the form that came to be called the dramatic monologue, he can at once represent and question the nature of subjectivity – how the self creates a world and constructs the character of others to support its views. Through the speakers he creates, Browning explores the power and failure of language in representing the self and the way in which history constrains what his characters can see. His speakers range from madmen like Porphyria's lover or Johannes Agricola, who parody the Romantic sublime, to historical characters like Cleon or Karshish, who allow us to explore the limitations that one's place in history imposes on consciousness, to imaginary figures like Childe Roland, whose perceptions of the world we have a much smaller basis for judging. The form allows a wide range in its application of irony, permitting the poet to create grotesque characters whose distortions we delight in discovering (like the speaker of 'My Last Duchess') and characters whose blindness is shown to be our own.

The dramatic monologue is the single most important formal development in Victorian poetry. It ultimately shapes modernist assumptions about poetic personae. In 'The Obscurity of the Poet', the modern poet and critic Randall Jarrell identifies both the innovation and the debt: 'The dramatic monologue, which once had depended for its effect upon being a departure from the norm of poetry, now became in one form or another the norm' (1953: 13). The form is so important an achievement in the history of modern poetics because it enables the poet to move beyond the dilemmas that Romantic assumptions about poetic subjectivity had seemed increasingly to pose. Modern poetry as Hallam defined it represented the individual sensibility, a sensibility that had become alienated from society. Browning makes this a dramatic situation; he frees the poet from the burden of alienated subjectivity by attributing it to a specific character and thereby extends poetry's representational range. Tennyson also moves increasingly towards a poetry of dramatic mask, as he provides mythological identities for his lyric speakers. Using sensation to depict mood and character, his poetry is closer to the dramatized subjectivity of Browning's monologues than the contrast between their poetics would seem to suggest. Both approach, though from different directions, what in *Retreat into the Mind* Ekbert Faas has called 'a new psychological poetry' (1988: 5). Each transforms the universal subjectivity of Romanticism, in which the 'I' of the poet claims to represent each of us, to a dramatic representation of individual psychology that treats any such claim with irony.

The implications of such a poetics were not ones that all writers and critics were prepared to embrace. In the preface he wrote for his 1853 *Poems*, in which he removes his own poem *Empedocles on Etna* from the collection, Arnold proposes a poetics that specifically counters what he feels are the inadequate poetics of the modern age. He identifies the modern with 'the dialogue of the mind with itself' (1965: 591). It too easily leads to poems that represent a state of continuous mental distress, 'unrelieved by incident, hope, or resistance; in which there is everything to be endured, nothing to be done' (1965: 592). Although Arnold is describing his own *Empedocles on Etna*, he could have as easily been describing any of a number of Tennyson's early lyrics, such as 'Mariana' or 'The Lotos-Eaters', or one of Browning's dramatic monologues. Arnold defines the aim of such a poetics as 'a true allegory of the state of one's own mind in a representative history' (1965: 598–9). This is not an adequate description of the poetics of even his own *Empedocles*, much less Tennyson or Browning, because it ignores the irony that the dramatic character of the poems gives to lyric utterance. Nevertheless, Arnold's characterization is significant. It reflects his effort to distance himself from a subjectivist epistemology that he associates with Romanticism.

As an alternative to the poetics that he criticizes, Arnold advocates a poetry which focuses on the representation of excellent human actions. Such actions 'most powerfully appeal to the great primary human affections: to those elementary feelings which subsist permanently in the race, and which are independent of time' (1965: 593–4). Such an art escapes the predicament of the modern: the alienation of artists from his society, their

confinement to subjectivity as the material of art, and their location in a mundane con-
temporaneity. Arnold advocates a style appropriate to poetry as he conceived it: the grand
style, in which beauty or elaborateness of expression does not offer itself as an independent pleasure, distracting the reader from the action. Elsewhere he criticizes the styles of
Keats, Tennyson and Browning for too fervent an embrace of 'the world's multitudinousness' (Arnold 1932: 97). Arnold associates a poetics of subjectivity with the kind of
elaboration in style that for both Tennyson and Browning represented the movements of
consciousness.

Arnold's poetics is a reactionary one in that it does not result in a poetry, even in his
own work, that successfully reflects it, as his turn to criticism suggests. It is most valuable in the insight it gives us through what it rejects. Furthermore, it demonstrates the
pressure in Victorian poetry to address more ambitious subjects than either the poetry of
sensibility or the dramatic lyric seemed to allow. Poetry at the mid-century is a fascinating set of experiments in using the poetics of sensibility and the dramatic monologue in
long forms with considerable ambition of social statement. The question of the appropriate subjects for such poems, as Arnold's preface indicates, absorbed all poets writing
in those decades.

Arnold believed that the Classics offered the noblest and most significant personages
and actions from which to take the material of poetry. He is critical of the 'domestic epic'
dealing with the details of modern life. In her verse novel, *Aurora Leigh*, Elizabeth Barrett
Browning articulates the opposite view. Her heroine, the poet, Aurora Leigh, claims that
poets' sole work:

> is to represent the age,
> Their age, not Charlemagne's, – this live, throbbing age
> That brawls, cheats, maddens, calculates, aspires,
> And spends more passion, more heroic heat,
> Betwixt the mirrors of its drawing-rooms,
> Than Roland with his knights at Roncesvalles.
>   (V, 202–7)

Aurora then calls upon poets to 'catch / Upon the burning lava of a song / The full-veined,
heaving, double-breasted Age' (V, 214–16). This passage reflects not only Barrett Browning's epic ambition but her belief that such an ambition must be realized in a contemporary narrative with the sweep and fullness of detail of the novel.

Both Arnold and Barrett Browning paint a vivid picture of the poetry they feel takes
upon itself the wrong subject. Arnold abjures poems 'representing modern personages in
contact with the problems of modern life, moral, intellectual, and social' (1965: 594);
Barrett Browning mocks the poet who does not understand that 'King Arthur's self / Was
commonplace to Lady Guenever' and Camelot as flat to minstrels 'as Fleet Street to our
poets' (V, 210–13). It seems that both Arnold and Barrett Browning could be describing
Tennyson. This paradox indicates the complexity of Tennyson's engagement with the issue
of poetry's appropriate subject. He writes poems in which he uses classical models for
contemporary materials, as in his 'English idylls'. He also writes dramatic monologues on

subjects from Greek myth, like 'Ulysses' and 'Tithonus'. Robert Browning displays a similarly complex engagement with the idea of poetic subject. He creates both contemporary and historical characters but always with the kind of detail that makes them novelistic. Although Arnold and Barrett Browning seem to articulate a stark choice in poetics, the practice of Victorian poetry is more eclectic. The most characteristic Victorian poetic projects combine aspirations from the two. Victorian poets rifle history and legend for characters and stories that ground and give resonance to thickly detailed representations of sensibility; they also seek in classical forms a way of elevating domestic realism.

The question of the appropriate subject for poetry is closely linked to the issue of the long poem. Tennyson's and Browning's early poetics find their appropriate realization in short poems. In mid-century both Tennyson and Browning write ambitious long poems which none the less remain grounded in their early poetics. After writing dramatic monologues of increasing length and complexity, Browning conceives *The Ring and the Book*, a daring experiment in which ten monologues offer different perspectives on an obscure seventeenth-century Roman murder trial. Tennyson's long poems reflect a more eclectic set of experiments. He termed *The Princess* a 'medley'; it combines a modern frame with a vaguely medieval story concerning the modern issue of woman's education, and a long narrative with lyric interludes. *In Memoriam* is a long poem, in T. S. Eliot's words, 'made by putting together lyrics' (1964: 291). Tennyson calls *Maud* a monodrama in which 'different phases of passion in one person take the place of different characters'. *The Idylls of the King* is the most conventional of Tennyson's long poems, a set of twelve narrative romances, each of which focuses upon a character who offers a perspective upon the Arthurian ideal. As diverse as these poems are, however, each places a poetry of sensibility in a larger framework that is not articulated in a unifying and authoritative manner by the poet himself but is implied by the juxtaposition of parts. As in *The Ring and the Book*, the form operates by a dramatic principle, in which lyric elements are placed in a larger context that invites ironic reading. Neither Tennyson nor Browning abandons the dialogue of the mind with itself which Arnold feels is so inadequate a basis for poetry, yet both aspire to the weight of moral and social statement that Arnold believes is the poet's responsibility by juxtaposing lyric panels.

We can begin to understand how so large a poetic ambition can rest on so fragile a foundation by exploring the relationship between subjectivist and objectivist accounts of perception in Victorian aesthetics. Both Tennyson's and Browning's poetics seem grounded, as I have shown, in an understanding of perception that stresses the subjective organization of vision. Yet Victorian aesthetics contains a number of powerful objectivist accounts of perception that emphasize transparent vision of the object. In 'The Hero as Poet', Carlyle defines the ideal poet's sensibility not as 'a *twisted*, poor, convex–concave mirror, reflecting all objects with its own convexities and concavities' but 'a perfectly *level* mirror'. He urges the poet, first of all, to see: 'The word that will describe the thing follows of itself from such clear intense sight of the thing' (1896–1901: V, 104). In 'The Function of Criticism at the Present Time', Arnold repeatedly describes the ideal in all branches of knowledge, including poetry, 'to see the object as in itself it really is' (1960–77: III, 258). Ruskin's *Modern Painters* contains volumes of advice about depicting the truth of rocks, the truth of clouds, the truth of water, the truth of space, the truth of trees. His strictures against the pathetic fallacy stem from a conviction that the poet's responsibility is to provide a true account of the appearances of things. It is tempting to argue that Victorian poetics contains competing, mutually exclusive accounts of perception, one objectively and one subjectively based, but such an argument would obscure the way in which objectivist and subjectivist accounts of perception in Victorian poetics tend to approach each other. Hallam grounds his poetry of sensation in universal laws of association; Ruskin's account of the truth of natural phenomena in *Modern Painters* provides a defence of Turner's impressionism. Both objective and subjective accounts of perception in Victorian poetics anchor themselves in the visual. The prominence of visual detail in Victorian poetry reflects this uniform emphasis on the visual in what are competing accounts of perception. A number of Victorian writers share the view that either perspectivism or impressionism could accommodate both a uniquely subjective point of view and an objective model of perception. This commitment to perspectivism as mediating between subjective accounts of perception and the aspiration to see the object whole sheds light on the form of the Victorian long poem. The long poem juxtaposes a set of perspectives in order to imply a whole. Because the vision of the whole is implicit, not explicit, such a form lends itself to ironic readings in which no single vision emerges.

Victorian theories of poetic style amplify this effect. Victorian poetic style is often baroque; it is thickly detailed, it delights in alternative formulations; it is ornate and elaborate. In *The Stones of Venice* John Ruskin provides a suggestive formulation for this idea of style in his concept of the Gothic. Although Ruskin is describing Gothic architecture, his insistence that the term 'Gothic' applies not to a set of architectural features, but rather to a set of mental tendencies of the artists, allows critics to use the term more broadly. The key elements of the Gothic for Ruskin are savageness, or rudeness; changefulness, or variety; naturalism, or love of natural objects; grotesqueness; rigidity, or energy giving tension to movement; and redundance, or love of accumulation and ornament. Ruskin did not intend to provide a description of contemporary poetic style. Moreover, Victorian poetry is so diverse and eclectic that it is difficult to make a single characterization of its style. Nevertheless, Ruskin's definition of the Gothic reflects the way in which critics and writers valued a style embracing elaboration, accumulation, luxuriance of energy, profusion of natural objects, variety. However different, Tennyson's and Browning's poetry shares a superfluity of detail and expressive formulation. In a review published in 1864 of Tennyson's *Enoch Arden and Other Poems* and Browning's *Dramatis Personae*, entitled 'Wordsworth, Tennyson, and Browning; or Pure, Ornate, and Grotesque Art in English Poetry', Walter Bagehot criticized both poets for an excessive elaboration in their style. Bagehot's ideal, which resembles Arnold's, he calls 'pure literature', literature that describes the type in its simplicity, that is, 'with the exact amount of accessory circumstance which is necessary to bring it before the mind in finished perfection and no more than that amount' (1898: II, 341). Bagehot opposes pure art to ornate art, whose exemplar is Tennyson. The ornate style attempts to surround the type 'with the greatest number of circumstances which it will bear' (II, 351), working not by choice and selection but by accumulation and aggregation. The grotesque, exemplified by Browning, abandons the type altogether to take as its subject the mind in difficulties, abnormal specimens, struggling with obstacles, encumbered with incongruities. In his definitions Bagehot connects subject matter to style. He understands that choice of subject matter for Tennyson and for Browning carries with it a commitment to a certain style. What is at stake for Bagehot, as it was for Arnold, is the power of generalization. The commitment that Tennyson and Browning both have in their distinct ways to representing a singular subjectivity commits them to principles of elaboration in style that Arnold saw as domination by the world's multitudinousness. Bagehot's criticism at mid-century shows that the linguistic elaboration of Victorian poetry was recognized as an important question in poetics, linked to ideas of poetic subject.

At mid-century, then, both Tennyson and Browning had evolved a distinct poetics from their Romantic roots: representation of a singular subjectivity in a dramatic context that allows ironic distance and implication; use of visual detail to mediate between subjective and objective ideas of perception; experiments with perspectivism to generate large poetic forms with ambition of social and philosophical statement; and an embrace of elaboration in style. Conservative critics like Arnold and Bagehot understood the radical implications of this poetry and proposed in reaction a conservative poetics. For Arnold the stakes were very high. He believed that poetry could replace religion and philosophy. It could interpret life for us, console us, sustain us. He placed upon it a responsibility for truth and high seriousness that neither Tennyson's nor Browning's poetics accommodated in the way that Arnold imagined. It is ironic that the elevation to which Arnold raises aesthetic experience, his insistence upon its separation from the world of practice, contributes ultimately to aestheticism, a view that would have been abhorrent to Arnold.

The Victorian debate about the proper role and value of aesthetic experience takes on even greater complexity in relationship to gender. The emphasis, in one strand of Victorian aesthetics, on sensibility as the most important element of the poetical character led to an identification of poetry as feminine. Tennyson, for example, most frequently represents the imagination as female, as in 'The Lady of Shalott' or 'The Palace of Art'. By the 1860s the effeminization of literature had become a topic of critical debate. Alfred Austin, who was to succeed Tennyson as poet laureate, writes that in contemporary literature, 'we have, as novelists and poets, only women, or men with womanly deficiencies, steeped in the feminine temper of the times' (1869: 96). He is particularly critical of what he sees as a feminine mode of verse, characterized by lyrical fluency, erotic ardour and circumlocution. Tennyson receives particularly harsh criticism; the muse of Mr Tennyson, Austin asserts, is 'a feminine muse'.

As Austin's criticism suggests, the increasing presence of women poets and novelists in the literary marketplace in part motivates the debate about the gender of literary sensibility. Wordsworth's predecessor as poet laureate, Robert Southey, instructed the young Charlotte Brontë that literature 'cannot be the business of a woman's life, and it ought not to be'. Hundreds of women proved him wrong. The growing prominence of women writers led to a discussion of the nature of women's writing, with many critics arguing that men and women writers had distinct poetic modes. In *Female Writers* (1842), for example, Mary Ann Stodart argues that the epic belongs to man, the lyric to woman. Contemporary feminist criticism has paradoxically reinscribed the Victorian separation of men's and women's writing. Women writers, it is argued, share experiences and circumstances so distinct from those of men that they write a poetry with a unique tradition and set of characteristics. Critical work building on this assumption has brought attention to unjustly neglected women writers and provided powerful insight into the representation of gender in their poetry and into the effect of gender on poetic stance and persona. However, it has also contributed to a blindness with regard to the role of women poets in Victorian poetics. Barrett Browning, for example, did not think of herself as a poet isolated from the contemporary poetry of men; she wrote an epic in *Aurora Leigh* about the development of a woman poet that is very much engaged in contemporary aesthetic debates. Christina Rossetti, similarly, is very much part of the Pre-Raphaelite movement. Separating women poets from their context limits our understanding of their work and of Victorian poetics, of which they are part.

Most writing on Victorian poetics sees a sharp distinction between poetry in the first and second half of the period. Although Tennyson and Browning continue to write through the 1880s, poets of the later part of the century see them as members of an earlier generation from whose example they have departed. Yet the continuity is greater than the poets acknowledge. Just as Tennyson and Browning evolved their poetics from elements in Romanticism, the poets of the 1850s to 1880s develop aspects of the poetics of Tennyson and Browning.

The Pre-Raphaelite Brotherhood was the first group of artists to articulate what they saw as a new aesthetic. The term 'Pre-Raphaelite' is a difficult one to define in the history of Victorian poetics. It initially described a movement in painting, the principles upon which Dante Gabriel Rossetti, John Everett Millais and William Holman Hunt based their revolt in the late 1840s against the academic art of their day. They insisted that they wanted to return to the purity of art before Raphael. Their painting combines microscopic fidelity to detail, abundant use of symbolic objects, medieval and religious subject matter, a white ground that produces luminous colour, and a sharply outlined depiction of the human figure. The group fell apart to reconstitute itself almost a decade later with Rossetti, William Morris and Edward Burne-Jones. This second phase of Pre-Raphaelite painting was quite different from the first. Closely aligned to the Aesthetic movement, later Pre-Raphaelite painting is characterized by richly patterned canvases picturing heavily stylized erotic subjects to which are attached symbolic meaning.

The extension of the term 'Pre-Raphaelite' to poetry seems at first glance an accident of personal association. Two of the painters of the Pre-Raphaelite movement were poets – D. G. Rossetti and Morris – and other poets, including Swinburne and Christina Rossetti, were linked to it by personal relationship. Nevertheless, these poets were seen as a group by their contemporaries and successors, and the term 'Pre-Raphaelite' is useful in describing their work and its contribution to Victorian poetics.

The Pre-Raphaelites were initially known for their fidelity to detail. The early poetry of D. G. Rossetti and Morris uses minute particulars in a way analogous to early Pre-Raphaelite painting. Tiny sensual details convey the emotion that is the centre of the poem. Here, for example, is a stanza from Rossetti's 'The Woodspurge', about a man in a moment of grief:

> My eyes, wide open, had the run
> Of some ten weeds to fix upon;
> Among those few, out of the sun,
> The woodspurge flowered, three cups in one.
>
>   (ll. 9–12)

Rossetti introduces the possible allusion to the Trinity only to insist that the flower of the woodspurge is merely a sensuous impression given significant context by his grief:

> From perfect grief there need not be
> Wisdom or even memory:
> One thing then learnt remains to me, –
> The woodspurge has a cup of three.
>
>   (ll. 13–16)

Like Rossetti, Morris is interested in the connection between sensation and emotion. In *The Defence of Guenevere and Other Poems*, he combines a use of sound and visual detail derived from Tennyson with the dramatic techniques of Browning to depict characters in the midst of passionate conflicts that they barely understand. Morris brings together the vertiginous epistemology of a poem like 'Childe Roland to the Dark Tower Came' with the Tennysonian lyric.

What separates the Pre-Raphaelite project from Tennyson and Browning is an interest in the relationship of the sensual to the symbolic. In D. G. Rossetti's poetry this interest takes two forms. He portrays mythological female figures with a fullness and intensity of sensuous detail that make symbolic conventions concrete. His Blessed Damozel leans on the gold bar of heaven until she makes it warm. Rossetti also uses a language of shadowy personification and abstraction to depict erotic experience that cannot be articulated. Here, for example, are some lines of the Willowwood sonnet sequence, about the pain of love's loss:

> And I was made aware of a dumb throng
>   That stood aloof, one form by every tree,
>   All mournful forms, for each was I or she,
> The shades of those our days that had no tongue.
>
> They looked on us, and knew us and were known;
>   While fast together, alive from the abyss,
>   Clung the soul-wrung implacable close kiss;
> And pity of self through all made broken moan.
>
>   (II, 5–12)

These lines achieve their eerie effect not only by embodying past selves in the dumb throng that surround the speaker but in representing in disembodied form the kiss and pity of self. Rossetti experiments with a disjunctive, dissociative poetry as a way of exploring emotion that frustrates articulation.

Swinburne was the most radical of the Pre-Raphaelite circle in his exploration of the way in which a language emptied of concrete references can convey powerful emotion. As T. S. Eliot understood, Swinburne writes a poetry in which 'the object has ceased to exist' (1964: 285). He creates poetic emotion from a language so abstract, set so free from referents by its accumulation of metaphor, so dominated by its patterns of sound that his poetry tests a certain limit in poetics. Here is an example from his 'Hymn to Proserpine':

> Far out with the foam of the present that sweeps to the surf of the past:
> Where beyond the extreme sea-wall, and between the remote sea-gates,
> Waste water washes, and tall ships founder, and deep death waits:
> Where, mighty with deepening tides, clad about with the seas as with wings,
> And impelled of invisible tides, and fulfilled of unspeakable things,
> White-eyed and poisonous-finned, shark-toothed and serpentine-curled,
> Rolls, under the whitening wind of the future, the wave of the world.
>
> (ll. 48–54)

The transformation of natural objects to figures of speech (foam of the present, surf of the past), the use of adjectives that refuse sensual definition (invisible, unspeakable) and the use of metaphors that offer conflicting images (shark-toothed and serpentine-curled) all create a welter of words that evoke emotion without mimetic or cognitive referents. It seems paradoxical to treat poetry this abstract as part of the same poetic movement that valued minute sensuous particulars, but there is a conjunction between them. The Pre-Raphaelites share an interest in the relationship of the sensuous, the emotive and the symbolic. Swinburne portrays sensuous experience to which he gives mythic dimension by obscuring particular context. D. G. Rossetti explores the nexus and the disjunction between the particular and the symbolic in erotic experience. Morris writes intensely realized dramatic lyrics of which he obscures the context.

Contemporary critics saw the unity of the Pre-Raphaelite movement not in its poetic experimentation but in its scandalous subject matter. In a vitriolic review of *Poems and Ballads*, John Morley condemns Swinburne for depicting 'the unnamed lusts of sated wantons, as if they were the crown and character and their enjoyment the great glory of human life' (1866: 145). In a review of D. G. Rossetti's *Poems*, Robert Buchanan gave the label 'the fleshly school of poetry' to the work of Rossetti, Swinburne and Morris. He calls the school 'sub-Tennysonian'; it derives from the sensualism of 'Vivien' and *Maud*. Buchanan's definition is instructive because it shows that more is at stake than simply erotic subject matter, although that no doubt would be enough to earn his ire. 'The fleshly gentlemen', he writes, 'have bound themselves by solemn league and covenant to extol fleshliness as the distinct and supreme end of poetic and pictorial art; to aver that poetic expression is greater than poetic thought, and by inference that the body is greater than the soul and sound superior to sense' (1871: 335). Despite the prurience and hyperbole of his attack, Buchanan understands that Pre-Raphaelite subject matter is linked to a set of assumptions about poetry. He formulates a crude version of Arnold's criticism of Browning, Tennyson and Keats: that poetic expression offers itself as an independent pleasure.

In a response to Morley's attack on his poetry, Swinburne defends the poetry he writes as a kind of lyrical monodrama, not dissimilar to *Maud*, in which each passion represents a new stage and scene, whether the sadomasochistic love of 'Dolores' or the longing for oblivion of 'The Garden of Proserpine'. His defence resembles Browning's assertion of the dramatic character of his work. Swinburne writes, 'With regard to any opinion implied or expressed throughout my book, I desire that one thing should be remembered: the book is dramatic, many-faced, multifarious; and no utterance of enjoyment or despair, belief or unbelief, can properly be assumed as the assertion of the author's personal feeling or faith' (1925–7: XVI, 354). Despite his kinship to Browning and Tennyson, however, Swinburne presents his phases of passion with much less irony. Browning and Tennyson developed dramatic forms to distance the lyric voice; Swinburne uses them to embrace lyric energy.

The poetry of the Pre-Raphaelites shows a far greater engagement with lyric forms than that of Tennyson or Browning. The most powerful lyric poet among the Pre-Raphaelites is Christina Rossetti, but, like Morris, D. G. Rossetti and Swinburne, she is interested in obscuring the context from which the lyric voice speaks. She uses an abstract vocabulary in which physical objects are often figures of speech and emotions approach but do not quite reach personification. Her great subject is negativity; she defines the lyric voice through where it is not and what it has not. Here is a characteristic stanza from the poem 'Three Stages':

> I looked for that which is not, nor can be,
> And hope deferred made my heart sick in truth;
> But years must pass before a hope of youth
>   Is resigned utterly.
>
> (ll. 1–4)

The idiom that Christina Rossetti develops allows her to represent the constraints on women's emotional lives with particular power. She often places herself in the position of woman as men regard her and explores the constrictions of that position. She also uses the idiom of negativity that she creates to write powerful religious poetry. Christina Rossetti develops her style in a Pre-Raphaelite context, which she turns to a set of subjects that subvert conceptions of gender and passion characteristic of her brother's work.

The poetry of Gerard Manley Hopkins also reflects the increased presence of lyric forms in the poetry of the 1870s and 1880s. Like Tennyson and Browning and like the Pre-Raphaelites, he is concerned with the relationship between the sensual and the symbolic, with how to mediate between psychological experience he sees as uniquely particular and an objective world he wants to make generally accessible. Like them he explores the consequences of this epistemological dilemma for the shape of the poem – its form, its language, its rhythm. Language for Hopkins, as for Swinburne, is a medium with its own texture and identity that creates poetry's unique experience.

Hopkins believes that the identity of every individual thing in the universe – natural object, person – consists in its inscape, the unique characteristics that define its particular being. To comprehend the inscape of an object, one must perceive it with a thrust of energy that Hopkins calls instress. Instress is a dynamic act; Hopkins defines it with verbs like 'greet', 'meet', 'catch'. Hopkins crafts the shape of his poems to dramatize the act of instress. The poems themselves constitute inscape in two senses: they realize the inscape of the object that the poet seeks to capture, and they create their own inscape as they themselves become unique objects in the universe. Hopkins avoids the dilemma of solipsism and non-communicability that would seem implicit in this poetics by understanding identities as unique intersections of characteristics. Metaphor thus becomes critical to his poetics, as it is to Swinburne's, for it is by the piling up of metaphor that Hopkins portrays both the effort of instress and the unique mapping of inscape, as in the opening lines of the sonnet, 'The Starlight Night':

> Look at the stars! look, look up at the skies!
> O look at all the fire-folk sitting in the air!
> The bright boroughs, the circle-citadels there!
> Down in dim-woods the diamond delves! the elves'-eyes!
> The grey lawns cold where gold, where quickgold lies!

The set of metaphors that Hopkins generates in this sonnet for the starlight night represents the instress of inscape much as Swinburne's amassing of metaphor evokes the passion that is the subject of his poems. However, there is a critical difference. Swinburne amasses metaphors to obscure the referentiality of language. Hopkins believes in an organic relationship between words and things in which the way that words acquire multiple meanings through metaphor allows one to grasp not only the unique characteristics of an object but its place within the web of the universe. A passage from an early diary gives a sense of how Hopkins understands language to work. A horn, he states:

may be regarded as a projection, a climax, a badge of strength, . . . a tapering body, a spiral, a wavy object, a bow, a vessel to hold withal or to drink from, a smooth hard material . . . , something sprouting up, something to thrust or push with, a sign of honour or pride, an instrument of music, etc. From the shape, *kernel* and *granum, grain, corn*. (Hopkins 1959: 4)

Ultimately Hopkins's poetics derives from the identity of Christ with the Word. The name of a thing is an essentialist connection for Hopkins, as it is not for most of his contemporaries. We can instress the web of sensual particulars that constitutes the universe through the web of language, with its metaphorical principles embedded in the origins of words and the spread of their meanings.

In his play with language, the poet must not fall into the ease of convention. Like Swinburne, Hopkins feels that the writing of the highest kind of poetry requires a mood of intense passion. In a letter to his friend A. W. M. Baillie, in which he confesses that he has begun 'to *doubt* Tennyson', Hopkins differentiates the language of inspiration from what he calls 'Parnassian'. Hopkins argues that the poetry of inspiration can only be written in 'a mood of great, abnormal in fact, mental acuteness, either energetic or receptive, according as the thoughts which arise in it seem generated by a stress and action of the brain, or to strike into it unasked' (Hopkins 1956: 215). Parnassian does not require this mood; it is the grand style adopted as a conventional mannerism. Like Bagehot, in his definition of the ornate style in poetry, Hopkins illustrates it with *Enoch Arden*. The language of inspiration for Hopkins requires a deformation of conventional syntax. It resembles Ruskin's idea of the Gothic. Hopkins intensifies the sense of syntactic deformation under the pressure of inspiration by a unique system of poetic rhythm he calls sprung rhythm, which replaces a system of regular syllabic feet with a system of stresses governing irregular syllabic patterns. Like the use of sound in Tennyson, Browning and Swinburne, sprung rhythm results in a music that impresses itself on the reader as an independent element of the poem's experience.

Yet Hopkins's theology ultimately makes his poetics unique. He shares the dilemmas of his contemporaries and their interest in exploring the expressive possibilities of what Ruskin calls the Gothic style. However, Hopkins's ability to comprehend the universal in the particular depends upon his belief in the Word, both as founding divine principle and as the organic relationship of language to the universe. This belief allows his poetry a cognitive density unique among his contemporaries. The balance that Hopkins's theology enabled him to maintain between what he calls mortal beauty and God's better beauty, grace, is a fragile one. He was haunted by the possibility of a universe in which one could not escape the unique particularity of one's own experience – in the words of one of the 'terrible sonnets', the 'selfyeast' of a spirit that a dull dough sours. Hopkins commits himself to the most daring and difficult poetic project of his contemporaries, for he places in a theological framework the most radical assumptions of what Pater called the Aesthetic movement.

Just as Matthew Arnold was the dominant critical voice at mid-century, Walter Pater provided the philosophical framework for the poetics of the century's final decades. Pater had personal associations with the major poets writing then. He was one of Hopkins's tutors at Oxford, he was a friend of Oscar Wilde, and he defended the work of the Pre-Raphaelites. Pater introduced the term 'aesthetic poetry' for the work of the Pre-Raphaelites in a review, first published in 1868, of Morris's poetry. He argues that aesthetic poetry develops from Romanticism. It is an art in which 'the forms of things are transfigured' (Pater 1919: 1). He finds his model for transfiguration in medieval art and literature, although his description of it is remarkably similar to Hallam's description of the poetry of sensation in emphasizing the way in which the sensation of nature conveys mood:

> Of the things of nature the medieval mind had a deep sense; but its sense of them was not objective, no real escape to the world around us. The aspects and motions of nature only reinforced its prevailing mood, and were in conspiracy with one's own brain against one. A single sentiment invaded the world: everything was infused with a motive drawn from the soul. (Pater 1919: 8)

Pater departs from Hallam in his abandonment of any belief that such aesthetic emotion provides knowledge of the real appearance of nature. In the poetry of D. G. Rossetti, Pater writes, the sense of lifeless nature 'is translated to a higher service, in which it does but incorporate itself with some phase of strong emotion'.

The original conclusion to 'Aesthetic Poetry' became the conclusion to *The Renaissance*, in which Pater defines the solipsism that is the basis for his poetics. He first reduces experience to a group of impressions – colour, odour, texture – in the mind of the observer. He then reduces the scope of experience yet further:

> Experience, already reduced to a group of impressions, is ringed round for each one of us by that thick wall of personality through which no real voice has ever pierced on its way to us, or from us to that which we can only conjecture to be without. Every one of those impressions is the impression of the individual in his isolation, each mind keeping as a solitary prisoner its own dream of a world. (Pater 1910: I, 235)

Although we might describe Browning's or Tennyson's characters in the way in which Pater describes the conditions of consciousness, Browning and Tennyson both create a dramatic frame that enables the reader to analyse and judge such solitary imaginings. Although D. G. Rossetti, Morris, Swinburne and Hopkins in different ways share the poetics that Pater articulates, none of them abandons with such emphasis the possibility of meaning beyond a purely subjective impressionism. Pater has given up the project that motivated earlier Victorian aesthetics: that of finding the conjunction between individual sensation and knowledge of objects. He revises Arnold's advice to the critic to see the object as in itself it really is; the aesthetic critic must 'know one's impression as it really is'.

Having reduced experience so radically, Pater asserts that intensity of experience is the only success to which one can aspire. The love of art for its own sake offers the best way to achieve the 'quickened, multiplied consciousness' that Pater desires. Aesthetic poetry provides a distillation of a transfigured world, an artificial or earthly paradise. Although Pater describes this poetry with fine discrimination, he makes more radical claims on its behalf than the poets would themselves. Swinburne, for example, refused to accept a narrow view of art for art's sake as an adequate basis for aesthetics, claiming that the artist must have the liberty of bringing within his range any subject, including moral or religious passion. Pater limits the significance of such subjects to the intensity of aesthetic experience they can provide. In a later essay, on the School of Giorgione, Pater asserts that all art aspires towards the condition of music. The mere matter of a poem – its subject, its incidents, its situation – 'should be nothing without the form, the spirit, of the handling'. This form, Pater goes on to state, 'should become an end in itself'.

Pater's work develops directly from earlier Victorian aesthetics, but it marks a radical departure. Oscar Wilde celebrated the subversiveness he found in Pater. For Wilde, art never expresses anything but itself; it has an independent life. It is, accordingly, indifferent to subject matter and to fact. It keeps between itself and reality 'the impenetrable barrier of beautiful style, of decorative or ideal treatment'. Thus, lying – the telling of beautiful untrue things – is the proper aim of art, for the liar tries simply 'to charm, to delight, to give pleasure'. Revising both Arnold's and Pater's instructions to the critic,

Wilde praises the effort 'to see the object as in itself it really is not'. Art should not be held to any external standard; its only motive is the creation of beauty. Because such a definition of art ignores the utilitarian concerns of society, the artist is necessarily alienated. Life drives art into the wilderness, a situation that to Wilde is the true decadence.

Wilde's importance as a critic stems not only from his provocative formulation of Pater's poetics but also from his use of them to define a pose and a culture. For Wilde, aestheticism is not the melancholy attenuation of Romanticism that it appears to be in Pater but a rebellion and liberation. The artist creates a personal style that itself constitutes a criticism of society. The homosexual identity that both men and women writers of the 1890s embrace – among them Wilde, Michael Field, Vernon Lee – is the profoundest expression of the separate and subversive identity they create. Artists develop a subculture in which the aesthetic becomes the point from which society's banality, hypocrisy and repression are revealed. It is one of the interesting ironies of the history of Victorian poetics that the embrace of art for art's sake at the end of the century, which had developed from the poetics of late Romanticism as articulated by Hallam and practised by Tennyson, expresses a radical social criticism.

The poetry of the Decadence illustrates a similar irony. Although many poems of the 1890s are exactly what Wilde's poetics would lead you to expect – evocative, richly patterned lyrics that present images and moods – a number of the most important poetic innovations have to do with subject matter – the use of details of modern urban life, like make-up, street girls, trains and cigarettes. The liberation of subject matter in Decadent poetry makes it seem less distant from other poetic voices of the late nineteenth century who were bringing a new realism to the lyric and who are usually thought of as an extreme contrast to the Decadents – W. H. Henley, Thomas Hardy, Rudyard Kipling.

In many ways the best guide is Arthur Symons, whose critical prose acutely describes the poetry of the end of the century in ways that anticipate the development of modernism. Symons was the most important connection between French and British writers of the 1890s. He introduced the work of Verlaine, Mallarmé and Huysmans to his British contemporaries, and provided a name for a literary movement that could encompass poetry on both sides of the Channel in his book, *The Symbolist Movement in Literature*. Writing in 1893, Symons asserts that the best term to describe the new movement in European literature is 'Decadence', because current art and literature share all the qualities that mark the end of great periods: 'an intense self-consciousness, a restless curiosity in research, an over-subtilizing refinement upon refinement, a spiritual and moral perversity' (1893: 858–9). He goes on to argue that impressionism and symbolism define the two branches of the Decadent movement and that the two have more in common than either supposes. Although one works with the visible world, the other with the spiritual, both try to flash upon you in a sudden way a new and perfect sense of the artist's intuition, rejecting all ready-made impressions and conclusions. Symons's linking of impressionism to symbolism recalls how close throughout the Victorian period, from Tennyson to the Pre-Raphaelites, were a poetics centring upon visual impressions as a way of communicating an emotional landscape and a poetics evoking emotion through language distanced from its immediate referents. Impressionism develops from the poetry of sensation, as it evolves through the Victorian period. Symbolism has analogues in the poetry of the Pre-Raphaelites, as Yeats recognized. The way in which the work of the Pre-Raphaelites encompasses both the poetry of sensation and a proto-symbolism supports Symons's argument that impressionism and symbolism are closely related branches of modern poetics.

Symons dedicated *The Symbolist Movement in Literature*, which he originally wanted to entitle 'The Decadent Movement in Literature', to Yeats. Yeats's own essay, 'The Symbolism of Poetry', begins with a tribute to Symons's book and then proceeds to define symbolism in a way remarkably similar to Hallam's poetry of sensation:

> All sounds, all colours, all forms, either because of their preordained energies or because of long association, evoke indefinable and yet precise emotions, or, as I prefer to think, call down among us certain disembodied powers, whose footsteps over our hearts we call emotions; and when sound, and colour, and form are in a musical relation, a beautiful relation to one another, they become, as it were, one sound, one colour, one form, and evoke an emotion that is made out of their distinct evocations and yet is one emotion. (1973: 156–7)

Although Yeats does not mention Hallam in this essay, he says specifically in 'Art and Ideas' that he developed the poetics of his early work from Hallam's essay on Tennyson, rejecting only the element of detailed description. He finds the exemplar of Hallam's poetics not Tennyson, however, of whom he is repeatedly critical, but D. G. Rossetti. Elsewhere he expresses his debt to Pater. In describing the 1890s in his autobiography, he writes, 'If Rossetti was a subconscious influence, and perhaps the most powerful of all, we looked consciously to Pater for our philosophy' (1965: 201). When Yeats edits *The Oxford Book of Modern Verse* in 1936, he opens it with Pater's description of da Vinci's La Gioconda.

These relationships are important because they demonstrate what modernist polemics often obscure: the roots that modernism has in the poetics at the end of the century, poetics that in turn developed from earlier strands in the century. Eliot's concept of the objective correlative, the set of objects which 'must terminate in sensual experience' that evokes a given emotion, resembles Hallam's idea of the poetry of sensation. Pound's idea of the image also develops from nineteenth-century impressionism and shares with it the project of connecting a precise and objective visual language with a poetry of mood and reverie. Similarly, the idea of persona, which became a cardinal principle in modern poetics, develops from Browning's conception of the dramatic monologue, as Pound acknowledged.

As the continuity between Victorian and modern poetics demonstrates, the history of poetics is not a succession of distinct, reified totalities, each coinciding with a literary-historical period. Rather, it is an evolution in which elements of previous practice and theory are assimilated and developed by succeeding generations of writers. Critics have spent much time debating whether writers whose work spans the centuries like Hardy are Victorian or modern. The question is a false one. There is no point at which one literary period ends and another begins. However, the continuity of literary history results in a retrospective influence as well as a prospective one. The choices that succeeding generations of writers make shape our understanding of the significance of the past. Victorian poetry is extraordinarily various; it has many contradictory strands. The achievement and influence of high modernism has paradoxically given more prominence to Tennyson, the Pre-Raphaelites and the Decadence than to other elements of Victorian poetics.

The Victorians were the first generation of poets to think of themselves as modern in Mill's sense of occupying a present distinguished in a remarkable way from the past. As each succeeding generation of writers defines itself as modern in a never-ending regression towards the present, the challenge of writing an evolutionary literary history increases. How do we write a history of modern literature if each generation asserts its modernity by insisting on its difference from the past? Writing a history of the modern will require us to question its repeated sense of its own uniqueness.

References and Further Reading

Armstrong, Isobel (1972) *Victorian Scrutinies: Reviews of Poetry, 1830–1870*. London: Athlone Press.

Armstrong, Isobel (1993) *Victorian Poetry: Poetry, Poetics, and Politics*. London: Routledge.

Arnold, Matthew (1932) *The Letters of Matthew Arnold to Arthur Hugh Clough*. Ed. Howard Foster Lowry. London: Oxford University Press.

Arnold, Matthew (1960–77) *Complete Prose Works*. Ed. R. H. Super. Ann Arbor: University of Michigan Press.

Arnold, Matthew (1965) *The Complete Poems*. Ed. Kenneth Allott. New York: Barnes & Noble.

Austin, Alfred (1869) 'Poetry of the Period: Mr. Swinburne.' *Temple Bar*, 26, 57–74.

Bagehot, Walter (1898). *Literary Studies*. Ed. Richard Holt Hutton. London: Longmans, Greene.

Browning, Elizabeth Barrett (1900) *Complete Works*. Eds Charlotte Porter and Helen A. Clarke. New York: Crowell.

Browning, Robert (1981) *The Poems*. Ed. John Pettigrew. New Haven: Yale University Press.

Buchanan, Robert (1871) 'The Fleshly School of Poetry.' *Contemporary Review*, 18, 334–50.

Carlyle, Thomas (1896–1901) *Works*. Ed. H. D. Traill. London: Macmillan.

Christ, Carol T. (1975) *The Finer Optic: The Aesthetic of Particularity in Victorian Poetry*. New Haven: Yale University Press.

Christ, Carol T. (1984) *Victorian and Modern Poetics*. Chicago: Chicago University Press.

Cunningham, Valentine (2000) *The Victorians: An Anthology of Poetry and Poetics*. Oxford: Blackwell.

Eliot, T. S. (1964) *Selected Essays*. New York: Harcourt, Brace & World.

Faas, Ekbert (1988) *Retreat into the Mind: Victorian Poetry and the Rise of Psychology*. Princeton, N.J.: Princeton University Press.

Hallam, Arthur (1943) *The Writings of Arthur Hallam*. Ed. T. H. Vail Motter. New York: MLA.

Hopkins, Gerard Manley (1956) *Further Letters of Gerard Manley Hopkins*. Ed. C. C. Abbott. London: Oxford University Press.

Hopkins, Gerard Manley (1959) *The Journals and Papers of Gerard Manley Hopkins*. Eds Humphrey House and Graham Storey. London: Oxford University Press.

Hopkins, Gerard Manley (1967) *The Poems of Gerard Manley Hopkins*. Eds W. H. Gardner and N. H. Mackenzie. London: Oxford University Press.

Jarrell, Randall (1953) *Poetry and the Age*. New York: Alfred A. Knopf.

Johnson, E. D. H. (1952) *The Alien Vision of Victorian Poetry: Sources of the Poetic Imagination in Tennyson, Arnold, Browning*. Princeton, N. J.: Princeton University Press.

Kermode, Frank (1964) *Romantic Image*. New York: Vintage.

Langbaum, Robert (1957) *The Poetry of Experience: The Dramatic Monologue in Modern Literary Tradition*. London: Chatto & Windus.

Mermin, Dorothy (1995) '"The Fruitful Feud of Hers and His": Sameness, Difference, and

Gender in Victorian Poetry.' *Victorian Poetry*, 33, 149–68.

Mill, John Stuart (1963–90) *Collected Works*. Eds Ann P. Robson and John M. Robson. Toronto: Toronto University Press.

Morley, John (1866) 'Mr. Swinburne's New Poems: *Poems and Ballads.' Saturday Review*, 22, 145–7.

Pater, Walter (1910) *Works*. London: Macmillan.

Pater, Walter (1919) *Sketches and Reviews*. New York: Boni and Liveright.

Rossetti, Christina (1979–90) *Complete Poems: A Variorum Edition*. 3 vols. Ed. R. W. Crump. Baton Rouge: Louisiana State University Press.

Rossetti, Dante Gabriel (1999) *Collected Writings*. Ed. Jan Marsh. London: J. M. Dent.

Ruskin, John (1904–12) *Works*. Eds E. T. Cook and Alexander Wedderburn. London: George Allen.

Shaw, W. David (1987) *The Lucid Veil: Poetic Truth in the Victorian Age*. Madison: University of Wisconsin Press.

Stodart, Mary Ann (1842) *Female Writers*. London: R. B. Seeley and W. Burnside.

Swinburne, Algernon Charles (1925–7) *Complete Works*. Eds E. W. Gosse and T. J. Wise. London: William Heinemann.

Symons, Arthur (1893) 'The Decadent Movement in Literature.' *Harper's New Monthly Magazine*, 87, 858–67.

Symons, Arthur (1958) *The Symbolist Movement in Literature*. New York: E. P. Dutton.

Tennyson, Alfred Lord (1987) *The Poems of Tennyson*. Ed. Christopher Ricks. Berkeley, Calif.: University of California Press.

Tucker, Herbert F. (1985) 'Dramatic Monologue and the Overhearing of Lyric.' In Chaviva Hosek and Patricia Parker (eds). *Lyric Poetry: Beyond New Criticism* (pp. 226–43). Ithaca, N. Y.: Cornell University Press.

Wilde, Oscar (1908) *Works*. Ed. Robert Ross. London: Methuen.

Wise, T. J. and Symington, J. A. (1934) *The Brontës: Their Lives, Friendships and Correspondence*. Oxford: Shakespeare Head Press.

Yeats, W. B. (1965) *The Autobiography of William Butler Yeats*. New York: Collier Books.

Yeats, W. B. (1973) *Essays and Introductions*. New York: Collier Books.

PART ONE
Varieties and Forms

1

Epic

Herbert F. Tucker

Readers of *Aurora Leigh*, *Idylls of the King* or *The Ring and the Book* rightly wonder that epic poetry persisted so long after notices of generic expiration had been clearly posted by Milton, then by Dryden and Pope, and then by several generations of public-spirited novelists. This was a reaction to which the Victorian poets themselves were no strangers. The Brownings and Tennyson repeatedly betray, and indeed incorporate into their masterworks, suspicion that the modern epic is a contradiction in terms, its traditional functions having been taken over by the newer narratives of science, history and above all realist fiction. That the great Victorian epics were written in spite of such suspicion surely has something to do with the emphasis their plots give to heroic faith in an era of doubt, be that era medieval (Tennyson), early modern (Browning) or frankly contemporary (Barrett Browning). The poet who contrived, against long odds, to pull another epic out of the hostile fire of modernity might well rank as a culture hero for that deed alone.

Yet it would be a mistake to regard such feats as solo performances. For one thing, these three epic virtuosi had each other's example to emulate or play against; for another, they worked their epic magic in a surprisingly numerous and diverse company. Stretch the frame of Victorian literary history beyond its ordinary dimensions and the canvas fairly swarms with poetical monuments of immense ambition, narrative and lexical daring, cultural and historical sweep, whose failure and success alike tell a tale that the student of nineteenth-century poetry needs, if not to know, then at least to know something about. What follows here, then, is a chance to make acquaintance with a surprisingly vigorous anachronism, as it was exemplified in many poems, running often to hundreds of pages, that even in their day were overshadowed by hardier literary species; some poems practically as tough to find as they are to read; even a few poems swallowed in deep night since the hour of their birth. This inventory of the obscure is offered less in the hope of finding converts than in blunt recognition that it is these works, with as many more unmentioned congeners, that make 'Victorian epic' more than a nonce label for a tribe of oversized freaks. Not only do these works bridge an otherwise mysterious gap between Blake's epic experiments and Pound's, shedding by the way a collateral light on Victorian literary kinds we know much better. The epics treated below were themselves episodes in the history of a coherent and durable idea about poetry's relation to culture, an idea in which it remains possible to take a lively interest today, and which the changing circumstances of Victorian Britain placed under extraordinary and revealing pressure.

The Whole Idea

For two centuries now a remarkably stable theory about epic poetry has been in place, to which commentators on the genre have confidently referred, and to which aspiring poets have either conformed or else conspicuously refused to conform. This theory arose during the later 1700s to supersede another one, also long-lived, which Renaissance neoclassicists had centred on the principle of *unity of design*. In the neoclassical view, Homer, Virgil and their early modern imitators had striven above all to unify the epic action, with special attention to its duration, setting and moral theme. These means of control and focus had let each poet frame a massively roomy structure and affix to it such refractory generic conventions as supernatural agents, celestial interventions and underworld descents, casts of clashing thousands and a hero's worldwide travels. So ran the established view, which the new epic theorists of the eighteenth century inherited only to recast it radically. Retaining unity as a key concept, they began to seek it not so much in the internal structure of epic as in the ambient culture for and about which epic spoke, looking less at the unified work a poem *was* than at the unifying work a poem *did*. Enlightened, self-respecting readers could not help being more impressed by the difference than by the similarity between the lives they led and the exploits of archaic, far-flung heroes; accordingly, they found traditional neoclassicist dogma about the timeless human universality of epic hard to believe. Rather than reject the dogma outright, however, they recuperated it by way of a paradox: they learned to regard epic's universality as a function entirely of its unique locality and moment. The authority of an epic was indeed a binding force for cultural unification, they conceded, but it was binding only on members of the historically specific culture that had produced and been reflected in it.

This migration of the unity criterion from formal to cultural premises was abetted by certain tendencies within neoclassicism itself, as curiosity about questions of textual design intensified to the point where the great antique epics started to crack under cross-examination. Towards the end of the eighteenth century textual scholars brought newly sophisticated analysis to bear on the Homeric poems and, gingerly but surely, on the books of the Bible as well. These efforts loosened the legendary grip of Homer and Moses while restoring the epic testaments to the collective possession of the ancient Greek and Jewish peoples. Neoclassicism had decried as artistic flaws the gaps and redundancies that dotted the text of the *Iliad* or Genesis. But these now became legible instead as fault lines witnessing to the work's durable history: the very imperfection of the palimpsestic text now gave evidence of the living tradition of its cultural reception, among successive generations whose earnest interference demonstrated how vital a stake they had in its meaning. The new ideal of cultural unity in one sense set Homeric and Hebraic (and, by increasingly evident implication, Norse and Persian – and of course Anglo-Saxon) peoples apart from one another, since each people was as unique as its founding epic text. In another sense, though, the new ideal furnished the ground of an enlarged understanding that complex wholeness as such was a property shared by all cultures, no matter how distant in space or time.

These ideas now possess the force of truism, a force that they have exerted for generations and that the Victorians felt if anything more strongly than we do. The international culturalist consensus that extends from Vico and Herder in eighteenth-century Italy and Germany to Lukács (Hungary), Bakhtin (Russia) and Frye (Canada) in the twentieth owes some of its plausibility and much of its stamina to the persistence among us of distinctive anxieties that the modern reconsideration of epic confronted from the first. Do we live in a unified culture, or want to? What does cohesion cost, when reckoned in terms of exclusivity? How much disorder are elasticity and diversity worth? It was when such questions would not go away two hundred years ago that literary intellectuals began rehearsing them in the newly culturalist theory of epic. Cultural unity became a working criterion for analysis only once it could no longer be taken for granted in practice. The vindication of cultural unity within the forms of epic first arose among scholars and poets who became modern intellectuals at the point where they realized that unity, as an intuitive and unconsidered cultural given, had disappeared from their world.

This troubled awareness was a precondition of the literary refinements of alienation and palliative nostalgia that we call Romanticism; and in Britain it emerged most clearly in the ballad revival of the later eighteenth century and in its epic analogue, the Ossian debate. The latter arose when in the 1760s James Macpherson published English translations of old epics whose Gaelic originals turned out not to exist, and it riveted British literary attention for decades. It did so because Macpherson's experiment on the public hunger for recovered origins revealed to his attackers and champions alike the extent to which whatever is recovered from the past must be *recreated* before it can be received in the present. The same principle also emerged as the collectors of old ballads quarrelled over editorial procedures and fumed over hoaxes: the unity of an epic text was at bottom an imaginative matter. Not only that, so was the unity of the culture that the epic text spoke for. This dawning consensus made of the poet – imaginative shaper *par excellence* – a legislator with a national mandate. The stage was thus conceptually set for the shattering events that closed down the century, when the French Revolution swiftly elevated the imagination of national identity from a contemplative possibility into a practical crisis of European proportions. The spectacular unification of a people around the idea of their own sovereignty was infectious; the shock waves of revolution traversed Europe in a few years and the world in a few decades, producing a pandemic of nationalist constitutionalism from which we have yet to recover.

In nearby Britain the French germs of revolution bred contagion in some quarters and allergy in others. But both the radical vanguard and the reactionary establishment formulated their positions in nationalist terms, and the most pronounced literary symptom of this insurgent nationalism was an outbreak of epic. Ambitious verse narratives of every ideological stripe poured from the British press, as the genre that had slumbered since Milton reclaimed in practice a prestige it had held only in theory for more than a hundred years. Nearly every major Romantic poet projected an epic; and the loss of those projects that failed, like Coleridge's and Keats's, was more than compensated by the multiple epics of Southey, Blake and a constellation of lesser lights now utterly dimmed but notable in their time. Our still rather Victorian habituation to anthologies of lyric poems masks from us the literary-historical fact that the epicizing long poem was not anomalous for British Romanticism but paradigmatic. When Wordsworth called his lyrics 'little cells' and 'adjuncts' to the cathedral of social renovation he meant to edify, he did no more than utter the dream of his generation. The serious poet's task at the start of the nineteenth century was to show the people of Britain their destiny through an archetypal history in which they were included and defined.

Such was the generic bequest that descended from the Enlightenment through the Romantic era to the Victorian poets. They received it, understandably, with ambivalence. On one hand gleamed an irresistibly flattering challenge: the construction of a lofty tale whose artistic coherence and affiliation with the greatest of poetic traditions should assert at once Britain's fitness to lead the world and the continuity of such national promise with the glory of the past. On the other hand loomed an invincibly discouraging tangle of intelligent doubts: about the state of the national health, about the direction or even existence of the national mission, and thus about the viability of any master narrative presuming to vindicate them. Epic came to the hardiest Victorian poets as a problem, and those who took it up did so as a compound *trial*. They had to try the resources of the genre, submitting its antique conventions to the stress of an accelerating modernity, and they had conversely to test the worth of modern experience by the standard which was held up for emulation by the formidable virtues of epic grandeur, comprehensiveness and permanence.

As a result the Victorians' epic performances were extraordinarily tentative: sometimes guardedly hesitant, more often impelled by a bravado that hid an else crippling self-consciousness; at their best, more inventively experimental than all but a few of the big fictional and historical narratives in prose that dominated the age. (The more a prose narrative practised formal innovation, the likelier it was to be discussed in epic terms, as were Carlyle's *French Revolution*, Dickens's *Tale of Two Cities*, Eliot's *Daniel Deronda*.) The apologetic burden under which Victorian epic laboured also generated a comic impulse shading into self-raillery, which had been perfected by Dryden and Pope as mock-epic survivalists in the aftermath of Civil War and Glorious Revolution, and lately reprised by Byron once victory over Napoleon had left the nation, its war machine unharnessed, wondering what on earth it was supposed to be next. The risqué, flamboyantly unfinished *Don Juan* (1819–24), making no secret of the generic pretensions it also made fun of, expressed the unsettled state of the epic art before sober Reform dawned around 1830; and Byron's cheeky nerve would persist, if only as nervousness, in epicizing poems across the century. At the same time, such generic satire was parasitic by nature and could subsist only so long as straightforward epic retained enough vitality to prop it up – as *The Excursion* (1814) by Wordsworth had done for *Don Juan*. While the Victorians naturally looked to Tennyson as their pillar of epic state, those who read *Idylls of the King* with care realized what a willowy and often self-parodic performance that long-evolving work actually was. Like their laureate, the best poets learned to rescue epic from its own excess by playing

high seriousness and abundantly grounded scepticism against each other. Shifting, disso-
nant intervals of faith and doubt give epic its curious tone during the Victorian decades,
as alternating affirmation and subversion of an ideal of cultural coherence recapitulate the
ambiguous reception of a legacy felt to be ennobling and embarrassing in roughly equal
measure.

In State

Not the least embarrassing feature of the epic legacy was the clarity of its call for a great
national poem. Such a poem, seizing on a prestigious action from the past and showing
how the values it exemplified had persisted for good into the present, should carry forward
the tradition that led through Virgil's *Aeneid* to Camoens's *Lusiads*, and that originated –
so argued the chief Victorian statesman W. E. Gladstone in the no fewer than five books
he devoted to the subject – in Homer's ur-patriotic feat of imagining the archaic Greeks
into civilized unity. In the Revolutionary and Napoleonic years shoals of epic poets had
answered the national muster; *Alfred* (Joseph Cottle, 1800; James Pye, 1801), *Richard the
First* (James Bland Burges, 1801; also Eleanor Porden, 1822), *Wallace* (Margaret Holford,
1809) and many another worthy stalked the pages of Romantic epic during Britain's hour
of need. But once peace had ushered in the 1820s, and certainly once the point of First
Reform had been gained circa 1830, the long burst of patriotic inspiration was spent and
the sails of poetry flapped among inglorious trade winds. Was the national poem dead in
the water? *Beowulf* was dusted off after long cold storage in an Oxford library, equipped
with new Anglo-Saxonist scholarship in a parting salvo against the French and their puny
Song of Roland, and circulated among general readers by 1835. The very outlandishness of
this thawed-out epic's Geatish glory must have made readers wonder, though, where the
British epic of the future was to come from.

Apparently from outlands more outlandish still. With few exceptions Victorians wrote
their national poems about nations other than England. The Gaelic fringes of Great Britain
continued to attract epic notice, and not just in *Idylls of the King*, which, as Tennyson's
scheme crystallized during the 1860s, increasingly withdrew into Welsh sources and
Cornish headlands. William Allingham's *Lawrence Bloomfield in Ireland: A Modern Poem*
(1864) was half a verse novel but half an epic too, while Ulsterman Samuel Ferguson's
five-book *Congal* (1872) was the thing itself; Irish traditions of heroic verse remained sufficiently vital to bring the young W. B. Yeats into the lists with *The Wanderings of Oisin*
(1889). Emily Pfeiffer's *Glân Alarch: His Silence and Song* (1877) returned to medieval
Wales for a plot that united Gael with Saxon as it blent epic with novel; the Scottish
Highlands, seemingly confiscated by Macpherson and Scott, enjoyed a late-blooming but
genuine glory in *The Bothie of Toper-na-fuosich* (1848), Arthur Hugh Clough's wittily sturdy
dactylic hexameter romp in and out of just enough seriousness to keep its epic pretences
real. With remarkable consistency the epic impulse of these works flags as their scene
approaches England, whose Victorian account evidently had to be rendered in the coin of
the novel. This generic geography becomes unmistakable in Barrett Browning's *Aurora*

Leigh (1856), which is the greatest of verse novels while its heroine resides in England, and which is obliged – for precisely that reason – to quit the country for France and Italy in order to consummate its marriage plot in a way that leaves Aurora free to fulfil her epic potential.

Aurora Leigh's flight abroad stands for the Victorian national poem's. The travails of Italy furnished the plot for Robert Browning's two major achievements in the genre, each of which sought to do for Italy what could not – or need not – be done for Britain. *Sordello* (1840) went back behind Dante into the pre-Renaissance, to pursue Browning's characteristic interest in the problematics of transition: although the troubadour hero squanders his political opportunity, the contribution he makes to an emergent vernacular literature helps lay the ground for the Italian emancipation from papal, French and German power that was under way in Browning's lifetime. Then from the apex of that emancipation *The Ring and the Book* (1868–9) looked back to another twilight historical zone, the late seventeenth century. Here Browning's prismatic vision of multiple narratives shows the swirl of decadent authoritarianism and liberal modernity stirring up forces that will project, through the Risorgimento, a new united Italy. Each epic showcases a problem of national identity, each was written in London, yet neither evinces more than passing interest in the condition of England. Nor were the emigrant Brownings alone in the epic export trade. *Sordello* was scarcely published (and forgotten) when Thomas Babington Macaulay hit the jackpot with an 1842 collection of national poems in foot-tapping stanzas that were not the British ballads they sounded like but *Lays of Ancient Rome* instead. At just the time when Browning was looking past the Second Reform Bill agitation at home and towards the Continent, so was George Eliot, who would novelize her own nation's crisis in *Middlemarch* only after epicizing another's in *The Spanish Gypsy* (1868), a work whose generic experimentation complements a theme of ethnic hybridity. When Robert Lytton (under the pseudonym of Owen Meredith) took most seriously the epic pretensions of his verse novel *Lucile* (1860), he whisked the action off to a Crimean battlefield. Alfred Austin, on his way to becoming the century's last poet laureate, set the high point of his much-revised epic *The Human Tragedy* (1876) in Rome with Garibaldi and moved its disillusioned catastrophe to the barricades of the Paris Commune, which is where the socialist William Morris, before refusing the laureateship Austin would accept, set his red idyll *The Pilgrims of Hope* (1886).

Poets from the most powerful state on earth thus repeatedly apprehended the greatness of nation-making as a literally alienated majesty, just as they relegated home affairs to the novel or 'domestic epic' (Matthew Arnold, Preface to *Poems*, 1853). Victorians who noted this oddity customarily explained it with reference to the unheroic nature of contemporary British life – a theory advanced by Thomas Love Peacock as early as 1820, spurned as cliché in book 5 of *Aurora Leigh*, yet still dear to Austin in the preface he wrote for the final edition of *The Human Tragedy* (1889). But the centrifugal force of Victorian national poetry admits of an explanation closer to home. It was a response to the challenge that burgeoning empire poses to national identity. When a nation's extent is fixed by global coordinates rather than landed borders, when administration supersedes conquest as the national mission, the nation will learn to regard itself as *post-national*. It will conceive its identity as a back-formation, to be grasped primarily in contrast to the diversity of tribal or pre-nationalist others that it has to manage – and that it therefore must not too closely resemble. Nationalism being other peoples' affair, it was the business of imperial Britain to train a surveillant eye on them and, by knowing them, to know itself above and beyond the limits of the merely national. For such training the fugitive, exported Victorian epic of state proved a highly eligible instrument. On one hand it indulged hot blood and the confused alarms of struggle abroad; on the other hand, the linguistic and mannerly Englishness that brought it home made it into something like state intelligence. Disinterestedly attentive supervision of an alien strife became the content of a comprehensive epic form at just the time when it was becoming the official posture of empire. In this sense no Victorian narratives so well captured the mind of Britain as those that fled its shores, like the Brownings' cosmopolitan *chefs-d'oeuvre*, like William Morris's intransigently Icelandic *Sigurd the Volsung* (1876), and like Swinburne's *Tristram of Lyonesse* (1882), a work set not so much abroad as afloat, on the open (but Britannia-ruled) sea that was the century's highway. Through commerce with a larger world these works diversified a British experience that had been made prosaically dull by the very commercial and executive virtues to which Britain's hegemony in that larger world was due.

Of this shift towards a post-national identity the cannier poets who did stick to home-grown epic took due note. Failure to do so led to productions like Alexander Smith's *Edwin of Deira* (1861), four books of generically correct blank-verse narrative devoted to the seventh-century Anglo-Saxon king who first embraced Christianity and gave his name to Edinburgh. Here was a subject that fit the national epic formula perfectly, only to show that epic nationalism of the Romantic sort had become suddenly, firmly parochial, its inlandishness unmistakably outmoded. A scrappier domestic example was set by Edward Bulwer-Lytton in *King Arthur* (1849), which flaunts the skittery ambivalence that epic duties could prompt in even a seasoned Victorian author and turns that ambivalence into jaunty amazement at what a complicated affair Britishness has lately become. Veering between romance and epic modes, Bulwer-Lytton cannot decide where to get a purchase on his Arthurian materials, or where to put an Arthur who will obviously not stay at home. Destined by a Virgilian fate to fuse by marriage the Welsh and Saxon stocks that will breed a British future, Bulwer-Lytton's Arthur first must make a Grand Tour over the Alps and back into Tuscany and Scandinavia, and before the end he is dealing for good measure with Aryan Druids and Odin-worshippers from the Caucasus. The whole miscellany seems bent on proving from what a multicultural midden Britain's favourite legend has sprung, and proving too how auspicious it is, for purposes of empire, that the national hero should turn out to know his way around the map so well.

Between Bulwer-Lytton's promiscuity and the probity of Smith stands Tennyson's sustained public performance (1842–85) in what was by virtual royal commission *the* Victorian national epic. *Idylls of the King* wielded the matter of Arthur with utmost decorum and minimal foreign traffic of the Bulwer-Lytton sort; yet the poem's impressive array of styles, tones and narrative modes is there to enact a set of themes – cultural translation, systemic corruption, political collapse – whose contemporary referent could only be the dynamics of Victoria's distended empire. For the island realm of Camelot knows sorrows of imperial scope; Arthur's experiment in administrative organization is doomed by the splendid logic of its own ambition. Harried at every outpost by subcivilized barbarians, the Arthurian regime of elective discipline and invisible knightly bonds succumbs not to these but to failures that are internal to its system: treason, espionage, and the sheer fatigue that besets an overextended network of intelligence and abstracted trust. Saddest of all Victorian epics, the *Idylls* in their gloomy analytic coherence shadow with equivalent plangency the losses that empire exacts and the downfall that awaits it.

A radically different nationalist subgenre, the working-class epic, took root in England during the first Victorian decades by turning the problematics of mainstream epic inside out. To the voiceless constituency of a poet disenfranchised by the First Reform Bill's property thresholds, the epic ideal of social totality offered precious leverage on the still open question of national identity. How was British society as a whole to be constituted, for whose benefit and at whose behest? No less a politician-in-waiting than Disraeli staged the question for debate between allegories of Order and Progress in his aborted *Revolutionary Epick* (1834). As the diffident orthographic flourish of its title may suggest, this poem conceded but did not applaud the inevitability of reform, focusing its suspended judgement on the problematic conquest/liberation of Italy by Napoleon – a test case whose selection looked inspired indeed by the time of the 1864 revised edition, once a second Napoleon had invaded Italy again, and under democratic banners of even more ambiguous stripe. Disraeli's dilettantism of the 1830s was meanwhile put to shame by contemporaries who had more at stake than self-promotion. Ebenezer Elliott's *The Village Patriarch* (1829) was 'in its nature and unconscious tendency, Epic', declared Carlyle in an essay of 1832; yet not much seems 'unconscious' about the long memory of Civil War insurgency that embeds its vision of 1820s agrarian hardship. By the hungry 1840s Chartism was raising consciousness of and about the working class at a fast clip, and during these years poets across the political spectrum had recourse to long narratives that invoked the social whole from an avowedly partisan perspective.

Sarah Stickney Ellis in *The Sons of the Soil* (1840) traces for twelve books the fortunes of a propertied farming family, explicitly linking their rise and decline to the effect exerted on local prices by the geopolitical economies of war- and peace-time. As Ellis disapprovingly notes the way inflated expectations of gentility damage a wider agrarian community, the poem lives up to the epic implication of its title and offers a conservative assessment of the national basis that is Eng*land*. One would call W. J. Linton's *Bob Thin or the Poorhouse Fugitive* (1845) an epic only after calling it other things like a doggerel tract or comic book. Still, the stark contrast it draws between alternative social systems – an industrially displaced weaver escapes London's degrading parish workhouse to join a utopian rural commune of mutual help – enlists for propaganda purposes a cogently epicizing grasp of those systems as wholes (imaginatively facilitated by abundant graphics, in the *Gesamtkunstwerk* spirit in which Blake had laboured a generation before). Between Ellis and Linton, in *The Vale of Caldean; or, The Past and the Present* (1844) William Dearden lashes out evenhandedly to right (workhouses) and left (Owenite socialism), certain only that commercial recklessness has reduced his Yorkshire home to a sink of factory waste and urban sprawl, his dalesmen neighbours to wage slaves. All three works represent downtrodden and neglected people as victims of a circumstance that, because it is national in character, entitles its victims to national attention and concern – a political correlative of the coherentist epic vision. All three tap epic's power to project historical, diachronic continuity onto the present as active, synchronic value; and they do so in order to mobilize nostalgia into a plan for the nation.

For progressives impatient with such a retrofit there was *Orion: An Epic Poem in Three Books* (1843), which R. H. Horne priced for the people in its first edition at a mere farthing per copy and billed as 'an experiment upon the mind of a nation'. An *Endymion* for the age of industry, Horne's farthing epic takes Orion through puppy love and trials of giant strength to establish the dignity of the body, the virtues of free trade, and above all the salvation that lies in hard work. Honest toil is where the thinking 'mind of a nation' merges with its labouring body in this allegorical epic, 'Divine with human blending'; and the 'higher consciousness' with which in the last book Orion looks out on Mount Epos (!) implies a technological vision of all nations as one gigantic working class. A more advanced working-class epic was written by the more politically advanced author who signed himself 'Thomas Cooper, the Chartist' on the title page of *The Purgatory of Suicides* (1845). Seasoning ten books of Byronized Spenserian stanzas with remarks on his condition as a political prisoner in Stafford gaol, staring down despondency after a decade's effort on behalf of the now-stagnant People's Charter, Cooper finds his theme in a high consultation among shades of the eminent kings and revolutionaries, poets and sages, who saw fit to take their own lives. Their discourses on religion, science and politics present an unsurprising compendium of radical thought; what requires notice is the way Cooper suspends narrative interest in favour of theoretical debate – an odd strategy for epic, but oddly appropriate to his theme. The narrative meaning of suicide being *ipso facto* nihilistic, it poses a worst-case scenario for the storytelling impulse that ordinarily belongs to epic: the faith in posterity that upholds an individual hero has precious little to hope for in the company Cooper keeps. What is needed is not new stories but fresh perspective on the old ones. Accordingly Cooper the Chartist converts the infernal Dantesque dead-endedness of his suicides into a 'purgatory' where there is a job to do. The name of that job is theory, and its aim is to cast out despair by recasting apparent lost causes (like the People's Charter) as stalled causes instead. Taken up into dialectic and debate, the life-story episodes of *The Purgatory of Suicides* become weighty chapters in the one story, longer than lifetimes and radically epic in import, of winning broad participation in a just commonwealth.

In Faith

Religion may seem an implausible option for compassing an epic totality, yet it was an option that Victorian poets repeatedly exercised. That their motives for doing so were not altogether fanatical can be hard for anyone who reads their interminable poems to bear in mind. Still, those motives were important, and they lead to the heart of one principal conception of British identity: membership in the established Anglican church. As the passing decades disentangled church membership from the rights (and spoils) of state, the bitterly contested process of secularization produced repercussions noisy enough to direct attention to the historically national dimensions of religious life. Since Tudor times the Protestant island had defined itself denominationally, and during the nineteenth century the materials of the Bible still had much to offer an epic aspirant. Possessing the gravest dignity, Biblical narrative at the same time extended to poetic fancy a sublime range of great practical flexibility. To the Bible stories, broadly familiar for longer than anyone could remember, the true believer brought a still-Miltonic conviction of personal implication in the still-unfinished story they told: as the American poet James McHenry explained in introducing *The Antediluvians, or the World Destroyed* (1840), in the Flood he had a subject 'not only great in its character, but *universal* in its effects, that all men might feel an interest in its details'. Geology and ethnology gave increasing cause to doubt such a claim to universality, yet in the patriarchal Genesis stories even the sceptic confronted narratives of primitive origins whose relevance as sheer secular ancestry lay beyond dispute. Believer and infidel alike could be expected to find in the Biblical thematics of election, sacrifice and redemption a deep structural paradigm for the destiny which they shared as Britons, and which the Victorian religious epics' favourite scenery of revelation and judgement repeatedly staged.

The definitive version of epic apocalypse was *The Course of Time* (1827), published by the evangelical admirers of young Robert Pollok in the year of his death. This ten-book immersion *in ultimas res* begins after Doomsday and flashes back from eternal Paradise, through the song of a 'Bard of Earth', to embrace Old and New Testament history (one book), a moralized satire on the nineteenth century (two books), the Millennium and the corrupt age that follows (one book each), and the Last Judgement (four whole books). Pollok's preter-Miltonic sweep commits him to a fast-forward narrative preferring pageantry to incident, masses to persons and, where persons do come into play, moral exemplars to developed individuals. These features distinguish *The Course of Time* from the more earthbound epics that had appeared during earlier waves of evangelical revivalism. Richard Cumberland's *Calvary* (1792), its interpolated two-book prequel *The Mount of Olives* (1814) by Charlotte Dixon, and James Montgomery's well received *The World Before the Flood* (1813) look like ploddingly humane character studies next to Pollok's righteous overdrive.

The features that set Pollok apart from his Romantic precursors were widely gratifying to the rising Victorian generation. Not only did his epic have a prominent place by mid-century on the missionary syllabus in India, but it was also regularly imitated at home. When Montgomery's antediluvian theme recurred in John Abraham Heraud's self-describedly 'gigantick' *The Judgement of the Flood* (1834) and Jean Ingelow's 'semi-epic' *A Story of Doom* (1867), both manifested Pollok's influence. The latter kept the faith with regimental severity and a tendency to archaic diction, while the former inflamed piety by every means not forbidden to the orthodox; and both epitomized their shared evangelical cultural formation by the moral satisfaction they took – and trumpeted in their titles – in the delivery of summary verdicts on the panorama of history. The anonymous poet of

The Last Judgment (1857) hails Pollok by name among the Righteous Bards but outdoes him too, by beginning at 'the end of Time' and staying there for twelve books of unremitting eschatology in the present tense. In a better instance of the genre, Edward Henry Bickersteth's *Yesterday, To-Day, and For Ever* (better-selling, too, with twenty-three printings between 1866 and 1893), our protagonist dies in book 1, only to be reunited a book later in a 'suburb of the New Jerusalem' with the loved ones he has left behind, all of them to be regaled for six books by the history of the universe in review and then four more of participant observation of Doomsday and the Apocalypse.

No lover of Milton and Blake can reject such epic topics out of hand, although the flabbergasting badness of their routine execution exhaustively demonstrates the difference between transfiguring imagination and pedestrian fancy. But then it is the very interplay between the flat-footedness of these religious epics and their will to soar that engenders their literary-historical interest. Their vast ambition makes them studies in the dynamics of omniscience, a narrative convention which is so widespread in the Victorian realist novel that we overlook its peculiarity, but which the Biblical epics flush out into the open by floodlighting its literal, theological origins. This ambition is, at the same time, typically pursued by the timidest of means, approximations of epic cleanliness to godliness that have everything to do with the administrative zest attending each work's climactic division of the wicked from the blessed. At the micro-level triumphantly correct versification and routinized grandiloquence; at the macro-level a tidy, task-oriented symmetry careful to match beginnings with ends, and pleased to install a smooth narrative hinge smack at mid-poem – all bespeak a bureaucratic confidence in regularity which Max Weber was not the first observer of nineteenth-century Protestantism to note. This drive to classify and dispose inevitably lands the subgenre of the Victorian religious epic in contradiction: its will to segregation within an ark or New Jerusalem defeats the epic purpose of summoning a culture-wide congregation. The more fervently Heraud or Bickersteth invokes divinely omniscient sanction for his sectored vision, the more he denominates that vision's partiality to a single sect. The formidable cohesiveness of the Victorian Biblical epic is purchased by trading the uncertain promise of a culture for the sure communion of a cult.

This result was, while not forestalled, at least forecast by a different epic subgenre, one that packed up the Bible and ventured abroad to imagine one or more foreign cultures as experienced from within a holistic belief system other than Christianity. Southey had pioneered such epic tourism among the Arabs of *Thalaba the Destroyer* (1801), the Aztecs of *Madoc* (1805) and the Hindus of *The Curse of Kehama* (1810). While emergent British interests in Asia Minor, Latin America, and India gave a distinct colonial timeliness to this first Victorian laureate's projects of poetic penetration, their overriding aim was not conquest but sympathy: the grasp of another culture by acknowledging, and imaginatively inhabiting, the independent totality comprised by its customs and beliefs. Sympathy being a two-way street, Southey and such immediate successors as Byron and Thomas Moore (*Lalla Rookh*, 1817) travelled it with strong misgivings. The extensive annotation that accompanies their oriental narratives cushions the journey east or south – north, too, if we include Scott's verse narratives – with plenty of insurance, in the form of ethnocentric scholarship that by turns certifies unlikely wonders and removes the mask from a modern Western poet who remains ultimately superior to his stunt of cultural ventriloquism. Such a cleft response to alterity reprised a familiar, age-old feature of epic reception: witness the efforts of urbane antiquity to civilize barbaric Homer and of early Christianity to convert pagan Virgil. It was something else, though, for the Romantic bard to serve as his own commentator. His anxious escape into the notes registers modern epic's problem of how to go forth into otherness without going native, how to render, without surrendering to, an alien cultural whole.

Among Victorian poets who took up the challenge of the ethnic epic, ambivalence yielded to polyvalence, intercultural confrontation to multicultural diffusion. As fresh versions of both the canonical European classics and world epics poured from British presses – the Finnish *Kalevala*, the Persian *Sháhnámeh*, the Indian *Mahabharata* – the reader's access was nearly always made easier, and safer, by editorial introductions and interventions. Yet these accessories, and the cognitive dissonance they had fostered in so many Romantic texts, disappeared from original poetry in Victorian years. What took their place was a kind of archival epic, a gathering of tales representing diverse peoples, faiths and outlooks. This tourist's or collector's subgenre was comparable in some respects to the fellow-travelling political epic of state we considered in a previous section, but it was even freer of overtly self-interested agenda. Here the principle of unity was anthological, which is to say based on the motives of acquisition, classification and display that typified the Victorian museum and exhibition. The bestselling pathbreaker in this kind was *The Earthly Paradise* by William Morris (1868–70), an enormous tapestry of two dozen leisurely tales from the northern and southern streams of European narrative; lesser performances included his namesake Lewis Morris's *Epic of Hades* (1877), Owen Meredith's *Chronicles and Characters* (1868) and Arthur O'Shaughnessy's *Epic of Women* (1870). In each of these works a medley of storied voices is brought to choral order by a conducting intelligence, which bespeaks at one and the same time a world-weary sophistication and a zeal for world-historical universalism. All faiths are relative, these many-sided epics confess, but in such a way as to constitute a new confession of faith in faith itself, a free-trade mysticism without duties. Their comparativist creed looks through systems of mythology to a cluster of pan-cultural absolutes: the divine mystery that myth can only shadow forth, the collective human power that shapes myth in its myriad local forms, the progressive history of the cultural endeavour to approximate the ultimate. The French had a word for it – *l'épopée humanitaire* – though it was the British who erected its visible symbol in the Albert Memorial (1872), where the frieze of poets at the progressive royal's sculpted feet is crowned by none other than Homer.

Before century's end this new faith inspired modern bards to reintegrate and consolidate what Morris and others had exhibited in profusion, and to weld the earlier samplings of culture into an evolutionist narrative whole. In the central canto of *Balder the Beautiful: A Song of Divine Death* (1877), Robert Buchanan had expressly universalized his Nordic twilight-of-the-gods theme by introducing the sacrificed Balder, through his 'brother' Christ, to a fraternity of slain gods that includes Prometheus and Buddha among others. The same comparativist universalism structures Buchanan's allegorical *The City of Dream*,

An Epic Poem, published the same year (1888) as Mathilde Blind's yet more ambitious *The Ascent of Man*. This latter work, an avowedly Darwinian epic by a poet of radical sympathies, surveys planetary history from the primeval earth through human prehistory to the vaunts and sorrows of empire whereby Rome brought forth Waterloo, the whole poem being keyed to an essentially erotic mythology of humanity's ongoing self-redemption, scheduled for completion in aeons to come.

It would be hard to find, or even imagine, a more panoramically liberal scope for total action than Mathilde Blind's. What strikes the student of Victorian epic, nevertheless, is the structural resemblance her freethinking opus bears to Pollok's monument to evangelical orthodoxy sixty years before in *The Course of Time*. Taking the two poets' titles together, we might say that the Course of Time and the Ascent of Man prove to be two names for the same process. We find in both epics not only a cosmologically sweeping embrace of all ages, bound for ultimate redemption by the power that subtends all nature, but also a preference for ecstatic overview that discounts human will and action, to the point where traditional epic heroism and responsible agency drop from sight. Whether scripturally or scientifically derived, providential or promethean, a common fate attends the epic of religious totality: a fate, moreover, that ironically dooms the genre to record the ideology of its moment with crisp fidelity. Heraud and Ingelow, as we have seen, were preaching in spite of themselves to the Victorian choir; yet so were Blind and Buchanan haranguing the Victorian lecture hall. For the ethnic-anthological epic itself presupposed and catered to an intellectual audience of mobile bourgeois privilege that came into its own during the last, imperial third of the century. The gallery of evolving epic worldviews fell into coherence when regarded from a perspective that was quite historically and culturally specific: that, namely, of a managerial and leisured class of educated, comfortable, anglophone whites. This class beheld in its own deliverance from creed and system the last, logical step in religious history. Their comparativism crowned the pageantry of bygone myths it saw through, in confident expectation that the utopian harmonies of a liberal-spirited future would ratify exactly the position which the emancipated reader occupied already. In this sense the post-sectarian epic of graduated myth constituted a religious counterpart to the post-nationalist epic that Victorian poets were concurrently outsourcing to foreign parts: the claim that each subgenre made to disengaged summary overview now seems in hindsight the most historically distinctive thing about it.

In Person

We have seen how the epic drive towards a comprehensive vision of cultural integrity, pursued by way of either state or church, incurred a certain risk of grandiose dissipation. Where political imperialism or ecumenical universalism tempted the Victorian imagination to feats of self-transcendence, the result usually looks in historical hindsight like self-gratification instead. Call it the transcendental fallacy: left to their own devices, the unattached, freethinking British intelligentsia who undertook epics tended to reshape the histories of nation and spirit from the vantage of the present and in their own image.

The most resourceful poets anticipated this liability by incorporating it into the stories they told. Tennyson allegorizes the collective anomie of obsessive self-culture in the *Idylls* with the vanishing knights of 'The Holy Grail' (1869), Browning imputes a tincture of needy idealism to his admirable and complicated pope in *The Ring and the Book*, and Barrett Browning averts a like risk in *Aurora Leigh*, or tries hard to, by making visionary idealism the ruling passion of her (blind and fallen) leading man Romney. These diversionary defences were necessary because the transcendental fallacy came with the territory of modern epic, and indeed had done so since Macpherson decked out a sentimental Man of Feeling around 1760 as an ancient Celt. The unity of culture might have a life of its own, and it might not, but the standpoint from which poets imagined such unity had to be built afresh every time. Nor was there any way, under a modern dispensation, to keep the scaffolding from impinging on the panorama.

One could, of course, make a virtue of necessity by focusing on the scaffolding itself, which is exactly what the most wholeheartedly transcendentalist school of Victorian epic poets did. This was the Spasmodic school, so called as it flared up during the early 1850s under immodest critical encouragement and then was extinguished by the mockery of an inspired parodist. W. E. Aytoun's hilarious *Firmilian* (1854) made eclectic fun of three works in particular: Philip James Bailey's *Festus: A Poem* (1839, revised and colossally expanded 1845, 1864, 1889), Alexander Smith's *A Life-Drama* (1853) and Sydney Dobell's *Balder* (1854). At their ridiculous worst these productions defy parody by pre-empting it; what made them nevertheless worth the attention of a conservative critic like Aytoun was the serious challenge their Romantic constructivism posed to any essentialist faith in cultural norms. Everything about these loosely framed, roughly joined, insistently extemporized poems is in flux – indeed, in convulsive spasm. Their mode is rapturous, their narrative opportunistic, their worldview up for grabs. This effect proceeds from the completely unstageworthy yet still pointedly dramatic form that they all share, wherein the poet does not narrate action from a fixed position at variable speed but projects it, never mind how plausibly, at the real-time rate of consciousness itself, one moment per moment. Spasmodic action, furthermore, is largely coextensive with the poet's creative activity: the protagonists are all poets, and when not reciting or discussing their verses they are likely to sound just as if they were, converting the now-wild, now-mundane experience that comes their way into tropes whose headlong originality earned the wondering accolades of contemporaries like Tennyson and Browning, Arnold and D. G. Rossetti, who eclipsed them but learned from them first.

It was the saturation of the poetic product by the poetic process that made the Spasmodic epics significant in their day, and that claims our attention here. These poems found their epic totality in the wholeness of a creative psyche whose perception of the world was unapologetically reflective of itself. The plot is programmatically engrossed by the instant, Blake's 'pulsation of an artery' wherein the poet does his work: the moment impulsively lived becomes analogically equivalent to the fullness of time, all history being a God-sized pattern of humanity's instantaneously creative interval. Smith's title *A Life-Drama* thus denotes both sheer vitality and the *Bildung* design of a biography conceived as the succession of sheerly vital moments. The same holds for Bailey, England's counterpart to

Victor Hugo in France and Walt Whitman in America (whom Bailey in fact helped to inspire). The uninhibited dilation that is Bailey's hallmark not only pervades *Festus* thematically but sponsored its elephantine growth into a jubilee edition, five times its already hefty original size, that dwarfs *Leaves of Grass*. The reader who has toured the solar system with Bailey's hero, and girded for scenes set 'Anywhere' and 'Everywhere', learns to think nothing of pausing for a 2,000-line disquisition on the joint mission of the eminences of world humanity. That such an interpolation might be redundant or irrelevant is a judgement ruled out in advance by the poem's expressly 'omnist' ethos of plenary indulgence, its glad omnium-gatherum embrace of epic's traditional function as cultural encyclopedia and warehouse of genres, and its plot of total forgiveness: at the close even Lucifer is redeemed, on an epic understanding that *Tout comprendre c'est tout pardonner*. Dobell shares this transcendentalism – 'As God contains the world', his Balder declares, 'I will contain / Mankind, and in the solvent of my soul / The peopled and unpeopled ages' – but he conveys it in a punitively severe mode that renders spasm as cramp. Balder's shamed failure to live up to the totalizing ideal he repeatedly imagines makes in a negative way much the same point that Bailey's super-Faustian euphoria and Smith's improvisation affirm. The ordered wholeness of world or psyche or plot is not a given but a project under construction, thrown together on impulse and held together by ever-ready, fast-dissolving analogies. This makes the traditional heroic simile an essential part of the epic action, and indeed makes non-stop assimilation the working logic of a narrative structure comprising nearly interchangeable episodes.

Bailey exulted in this logic when he wrote for his second edition (1845) a long scene in which Festus summarizes, under flimsy cover of rehearsing the long poem of an unnamed 'friend', the action of the long poem that he is in. 'It hath a plan, but no plot. Life hath none.' Maybe so, but what follows is a scene-by-scene recapitulation of Bailey's *Festus*, right up to the very scene in progress, and then straight on to a preview of coming attractions including the plump finale. Set at 'Home', the scene occurs at about the point where in classical epic the hero goes to ground zero, descending to the underworld to learn the future from ghosts of the past. Bailey's version of this convention is extravagant in its navel-gazing panache yet not atypical of Spasmodism, and it illustrates the dumbfounding candour with which the Spasmodics produced their own creative procedures for inspection. Laying all their cards on the table, they in effect called in the immense bet that cultural coherentism had placed on epic a century before; and they almost broke the bank. It took Aytoun's brilliant intervention – fortified by Arnold's ostentatious 1853 rejection of his own introspective drama of vocation *Empedocles on Etna*, and by the conservative philippics evoked by what savoured of Spasmodism in Tennyson's *Maud* in 1855 and Barrett Browning's epic poem about an epic poet the year after – to stigmatize as inflationary counterfeit the Spasmodic currency of self-awareness raised to cosmic pitch.

Spasmodism may have been overpowered by the critical establishment, but its hunch about the grounds of epic coherence in modern culture was not thereby falsified. What an official literary culture pronounced against in the 1850s the poets continued to harbour, assess and replay. The Victorian epics worthiest of the name would incorporate into their speaking on behalf of national and spiritual identity a sharp sense of who it was that spoke, and how 'he that tells the tale' (Tennyson's formula in the *Idylls*) occupied a subject position that constrained, even as it enabled, whatever comprehensiveness the poem might pretend to. And no wonder: an epic whose terms were not also lyrical would not have represented the nineteenth century very satisfactorily, while conversely the sense of civic duties that never deserted epic kept visible (what lyric forms tended to conceal) the abidingly political implications of poetic perspectivism. That Victorian Calliope took up the lyre and strung it with the gut of an irresistible self-consciousness is an observation consonant with much that the study of other genres has shown about the heyday of the British middle classes: not least, how their prickly individualism was codependently related to their unslaked thirst for political and cultural communion.

See also: NATIONHOOD AND EMPIRE; POETRY IN THE FOUR NATIONS; DOMESTIC AND IDYLLIC.

REFERENCES AND FURTHER READING

Bakhtin, M. M. (1981) *The Dialogic Imagination: Four Essays*. Austin: University of Texas Press.

Colley, Linda (1992) *Britons: Forging the Nation, 1707–1837*. New Haven: Yale University Press.

Curran, Stuart (1986) *Poetic Form and British Romanticism*. New York: Oxford University Press.

Foerster, Donald M. (1962) *The Fortunes of Epic Poetry: A Study in English and American Criticism 1750–1950*. N. p.: Catholic University of America Press.

Frye, Northrop (1957) *Anatomy of Criticism: Four Essays*. Princeton, N. J.: Princeton University Press.

Gibson, Mary Ellis (1995) *Epic Reinvented: Ezra Pound and the Victorians*. Ithaca, N. Y.: Cornell University Press.

Griffiths, F. T., and S. J. Rabinowitz (1990) *Novel Epics: Gogol, Dostoevsky, and National Narrative*. Evanston: Northwestern University Press.

Graham, Colin (1998) *Ideologies of Epic: Nation, Empire, and Victorian Epic Poetry*. Manchester: Manchester University Press.

Harvey, A. D. (1976) 'The English Epic in the Romantic Period.' *Philological Quarterly*, 55, 241–59.

Herbert, Christopher (1991) *Culture and Anomie: Ethnographic Imagination in the Nineteenth Century*. Chicago: University of Chicago Press.

Kelly, Van (1994) 'Criteria for the Epic: Borders, Diversity, and Expansion.' In Steven M.

Oberhelman, Van Kelly and Richard J. Golsan (eds). *Epic and Epoch: Essays on the Interpretation and History of a Genre* (pp. 1–21). Lubbock: Texas Tech University Press.

Lucas, John (1990) *England and Englishness: Ideas of Nationhood in English Poetry*. London: Hogarth Press.

Lukács, Georg (1920) *The Theory of the Novel*. Trans. Anna Bostock (1971). London: Merlin Press.

Merchant, Paul (1971) *The Epic*. London: Methuen.

Moretti, Franco (1994) *Modern Epic: The World-System from Goethe to Garcia Marquez*. Trans. Quentin Hoare (1996). London: Verso.

Mori, Masaki (1997) *Epic Grandeur: Toward a Comparative Poetics of the Epic*. Albany: SUNY Press.

Preyer, Robert (1961) 'Sydney Dobell and the Victorian Epic.' *University of Toronto Quarterly*, 30, 163–79.

Richards, Thomas (1993) *The Imperial Archive: Knowledge and the Fantasy of Empire*. London: Verso.

Roberts, Adam (1999) *Romantic and Victorian Long Poems: A Guide*. Aldershot: Ashgate.

Scholes, Robert E., and Robert Kellogg (1964) *The Nature of Narrative*. New York: Oxford University Press.

Shaffer, Elinor S. (1975) *'Kubla Khan' and The Fall of Jerusalem: The Mythological School in Biblical Criticism and Secular Literature 1770–1880*. Cambridge: Cambridge University Press.

Tillyard, E. M. W. (1958) *The Epic Strain in the English Novel*. London: Chatto and Windus.

Trumpener, Katie (1997) *Bardic Nationalism: The Romantic Novel and the British Empire*. Princeton, N. J.: Princeton University Press.

Wheeler, Michael (1990) *Death and the Future Life in Victorian Literature and Theology*. Cambridge: Cambridge University Press.

Wilkie, Brian (1965) *Romantic Poets and Epic Tradition*. Madison: University of Wisconsin Press.

2

Domestic and Idyllic

Linda H. Peterson

The Rise of Domestic Poetry

Domestic poetry lost currency in the last century as a genre for scholarly analysis, but the Victorians recognized it as a kind of poetry both popular among readers and esteemed by critics. The domestic ideology that dominated Victorian culture – the set of beliefs that located moral value and psychological health in the home, that sanctified the Victorian hearth as a domestic altar and the woman as an 'angel in the house', and that praised the 'domestic affections' as the source of the nation's strength – emerged in the work of early Victorian poets, male and female alike, in descriptive scenes of home, narratives of family life, and verses on the domestic affections. 'Upon the sacredness of home life', Alfred, Lord Tennyson, maintained, 'the stability and greatness of a nation largely depend', and according to his son Hallam, 'one of the secrets of his power over mankind was his true joy in the family duties and affections' (Tennyson 1897: I, 189). If this dominant ideology was eventually questioned, challenged and rejected or revised by later Victorian writers, and the genres associated with it similarly rejected or revised, the culture of domesticity none the less left its mark on the poetry of the period, including its predilection for the 'idyll' and development of the hybrid 'domestic idyll'.

Domestic poetry was predominantly a phenomenon of the 1830s, 1840s and 1850s, but it had its roots in Romantic poetry and its influence extended well beyond the close of the century. As Herbert Tucker has argued, English poetry underwent a 'domestication' in the 1820s as the surviving Romantics 'called in their foreign investments for domestic conversion' or, in less metaphorical terms, created a 'mystic fusion of piety with domesticity upon the unassailable ground of instinctual feeling' (Tucker 1994: 525, 531). The original balance in the *Lyrical Ballads* (1798) between natural and supernatural, familiarity and wonder, ordinariness and excitement gave way to an increasing emphasis on the familiar, the familial and the *heimlich* – as in the domestic vignettes of Wordsworth's *Excursion* (1814), his *Ecclesiastical Sketches* (1822) and his 1825 lyric 'To a Skylark', which reimagines this Shelleyan avatar as 'True to the kindred points of Heaven and Home!' According to Tucker, this process of domestication was the literary counterpart of a 'maturation of British colonial trade into a global empire' that 'precipitat[ed] homesick Britons by the thousands across the seven seas' (1994: 522).

The phenomenon can be linked to other cultural and historical influences as well. As Madame de Staël noted in 1803, in a comparison of German and English literature, 'Domestic affections holding great sway over the hearts of the English, their poetry is impressed with the delicacy and solidarity of those affections' (I, 224). In such georgic poems as Cowper's *The Task*, which begins 'I sing the SOFA' and celebrates domestic life – 'Domestic happiness, thou only bliss / Of Paradise that has survived the fall!' (III, 41–2) – in Coleridge's conversation poems set in familiar, homely places, and, more generally, in the emergence of Romantic women's poetry from 'the private sphere of unheroic domestic life' (Ross 1989: 238), Victorian poetry found ample precedent for its domesticity. An increasing sense of loss resulting from the urbanization and industrialization of English life, the disappearance of small English villages and rural landscapes, the removal of work from cottage industries to factories, and the return to domestic peace after the era of the Napoleonic wars – these historical changes further contributed to a felt need for domestic poetry. It was nostalgic verse, lamenting what had been lost as much as celebrating what remained.

The early Victorian poet most readily associated with domestic poetry is Felicia Hemans, largely because of her widely acclaimed volumes *Records of Woman* (1828) and *Songs of the Affections* (1830), and such popular anthologized verses as 'The Homes of England' and 'The Graves of a Household'. In *Records* Hemans recounts the heroism of women in times of social and political crisis, linking their brave deeds to their strong domestic ties and feminine sense of duty; the poems of this volume valorize the affections of husbands and wives, mothers and children, and especially mothers and daughters, as in 'Madeline: A Domestic Tale', which celebrates a mother's love as she rescues a daughter dying in exile and restores her to health in a sunny homeland, 'beneath our vines once more'. In *Songs of the Affections* Hemans expands the range to include all household members in scenes of joy and sorrow, pleasure and grief, whether emigrants singing farewell to their 'homesteads, warm and low', or soldiers dying with memories of home and 'a blessing on that holy hearth', or prodigals returning home with a vision of 'scenes of those blessed years' that have the power to 'soften and atone' (see 'Song of Emigration', 'The Soldier's Death-Bed' and 'The Return').

Hemans's most widely reprinted poems link domestic to civic virtues, in Tennyson's terms 'the sacredness of home life' with 'the stability and greatness of a nation'. Her 'Homes of England' catalogues English domestic types – the 'stately', 'merry', 'blessed' and 'cottage' homes – in an order that stabilizes the English class system from aristocratic hall to peasant hut, but that also affirms the source of national greatness as the domestic hearth and 'hallowed wall'. Taking its epigraph from Walter Scott's *Marmion* – 'Where's the coward that would not dare / To fight for such a land?'– the poem offers an alternative view of heroism. It locates English freedom in the home, particularly in the woman's voice that 'flows forth in song, / Or childhood's tale', and suggests that the nation will remain 'fair' and 'free' if it roots its children's affections in a domestic(ated) space, in 'groves' and 'flowery sod', 'Where first the child's glad spirit loves / Its country and its

God!' Hemans's 'The Graves of a Household' extends this civic vision into the colonial and imperial realm. What severs the children of a household is also what binds them together as a family: their domestic life, tended by 'the same fond mother', motivates them to colonize the West, serve in the navy, fight in Spain, or produce art in Italy – all actions that eventually lead to foreign graves.

Hemans's domestic economy – her fusion of domesticity with piety rooted in a cultivated feeling or sentiment – influenced her contemporaries and the next generation of Victorian poets. Whether in verses about the home or, more specifically, about rooms or objects within the household, the poetry of the 1830s and 1840s was homely stuff. In 1846, for example, Anne Brontë included a poem titled simply 'Home' in the *Poems* of Currer, Ellis and Acton Bell; like many of Hemans's verses, it dwells more on the loss of home, on nostalgia for the 'barren hills' and 'little spot', than on any particularized household space. The domestic affections emerge sharply as the speaker roams among the grand landscapes of a mansion:

> Though all around this mansion high
> Invites the foot to roam,
> And though its halls are fair within –
> Oh, give me back my home!
>
> (ll. 25–9)

The generalizations common in such domestic poetry – what Tucker calls the 'poetic abstention from concrete details of home life' (1994: 537) – made possible its universal appeal; readers empathized with the speaker's loss of home or happy memories of family life, having experienced similar emotions, and supplied the details for themselves.

Even domestic poetry that seemingly fixes its attention on an object or room works on this principle. Eliza Cook's enormously popular 'The Old Arm-Chair' describes not the chair itself, but the mother who sat in it and the moral sentiments associated with her:

> I love it, I love it; and who shall dare
> To chide me for loving that old Arm-chair?
> I've treasured it long as a sainted prize;
> I've bedewed it with tears, and embalmed it with sighs.
> 'Tis bound by a thousand bands to my heart;
> Not a tie will break, not a link will start.
> Would ye learn the spell? – a mother sat there;
> And a sacred thing is that old Arm-chair.
>
> (ll. 1–8)

As the speaker records her memories, they combine visions of her mother ('Her eye grew dim, and her locks were grey') and the feelings evoked then and now ('the scalding drops start down my cheek'). Sight and sentiment remain general; readers participate – and bind their own affections – by calling up similar memories of a sacred childhood object or scene.

Within this sentimental nexus, virtually any space in the house might become the subject of a poem, though some were privileged spaces: certainly the hearth, as in Alaric A. Watts's 'My Own Fireside', which envisions mother and babe at the hearth, 'Shrine of my household deities; / Bright scene of home's unsullied joys', but also the bedroom, as in Thomas Hood's 'Lines on Seeing my Wife and Two Children Sleeping in the Same Chamber', which imagines earth in 'its so spacious round' and sky in 'its blue circumference above' condensed and contained within 'this little chamber' (MacKay 1858: 260, 343–5). If such poems seem conventional in their scenes and sentiments, that was part of the point. Domestic poetry reflected, even as it helped formulate, the conventions of Victorian home life. Poems that neglected or departed from conventionality were often less successful, as the example of Tennyson's 'O Darling Room', published in his 1832 *Poems*, attests. Unquestionably about a domestic space:

> O darling room, my heart's delight,
> Dear room, the apple of my sight,
> With thy two couches soft and white,
> There is no room so exquisite,
> No little room so warm and bright,
> Wherein to read, wherein to write
>
>   (ll. 1–6)

the poem associates strong sentiment with a bedroom without supplying the object of attachment. If, as biographers have argued, that object was Arthur Hallam, Tennyson's friend who had shared the room during a recent visit, then the object was unnamable. If instead, as the lines suggest, Tennyson meant to substitute the abstract 'reading' and 'writing', then the object was too vague – and the descriptive details too strong – to evoke a sympathetic response. John Wilson Croker, unduly severe in his criticism, none the less understood the inadequacy of this piece as domestic poetry:

In such a dear *little* room a narrow-minded scribbler would have been content with *one* sofa, and that one he would probably have covered with black mohair, or red cloth, or a good striped chintz; how infinitely more characteristic is white dimity – 'tis as it were a type of the purity of the poet's mind. (Jump 1967: 81)

The invocation of purity in a young man's bedroom – rather than in a more conventional familial space – leads to suspicion about what might really be in 'the poet's mind'. Moreover, the inclusion of specific decorative description (like white dimity for 'purity') works against the principle of generalization.

As these examples suggest, domestic poetry was less about the home *per se* than about the 'domestic affections', those ties that bound the Victorian husband and wife, mother and child, brother and sister in a network or net (the noun depends upon one's perspective) of love and duty. In an anthology entitled *The Home Affections Pourtrayed by the Poets* (1858), the editor Charles MacKay explains that 'the one great affection of the heart, that binds the family together' is 'LOVE'; it plays a prominent part 'in the literature of every nation' but 'to poetry more especially belongs the duty of celebrating the beauty and purity of the Affections' (MacKay 1858: v). As if to prove poetry's celebratory power, MacKay compiled nearly 400 pages of verse about domestic love, including Hemans's 'The Graves of a Household', Cook's 'The Old Arm-Chair' and Watts's 'My Own Fireside'. His arrangement, from childhood to youth, maturity and age, suggests that Victorian domestic poetry was meant to be not merely descriptive or epideictic but developmental and disciplinary, aiming at the cultivation of 'the heart' of all family members, at every stage of life.

For all the high-minded apologetics, we should note that volumes like *The Home Affections* were commercial objects: 'I hope it will be found worthy to be the GIFT-BOOK OF ENGLISH LITERATURE', MacKay concludes his introduction. Indeed, the rise of the literary annual and the lady's giftbook, as much as the rise of Victorian domestic ideology, accounts for the increase in domestic poetry. With the appearance in the late 1820s of the annual, a publishing innovation that combined visual and verbal texts, an almost insatiable commercial need developed for poetry to complement the lavish engravings of innocent romance and domestic life. Samuel Taylor Coleridge may have composed 'Domestic Peace' (1795) in democratic celebration of the 'cottaged vale' in contrast to the 'sceptered state', but when George Croly composed 'Domestic Love' in the late 1820s, a poem reminiscent of Coleridge's –

> Domestic Love! not in proud palace halls
> Is often seen thy beauty to abide;
> Thy dwelling is in lowly cottage walls,
> That in the thickets of the woodbine hide
>   (ll. 1–4)

– his eye was on the commercial market as much as political reform (Watts 1829: 227; MacKay 1858: 3). Not just minor male poets like Croly, T. K. Hervey and Alaric Watts, or poetesses like Felicia Hemans, Mary Howitt and Eliza Cook, but major (or soon-to-be major) poets like Wordsworth, Tennyson and the Brownings came under the literary influence of giftbooks and annuals in the 1830s.

Alaric Watts, credited with inventing the literary annual, drew in his friends Felicia Hemans, Letitia Landon and Mary Howitt to supply verses for his *Literary Souvenir* and *Poetical Album*; Howitt later contributed to and edited *Fisher's Drawing-Room Scrap-Book* and published her own *Hymns and Fire-side Verses* (1839), a poetical fusion of religious and domestic piety (Watts 1884: I, 167–77). T. K. Hervey, the editor of *The Poetical Sketch Book* (1829) and *The English Halcyon: A Selection of Modern Poetry* (1841), was best known, according to fellow editor Rufus Griswold, for his ' "poems of the affections", descriptive of domestic incidents and feelings, upon which he writes with taste, simplicity, and tenderness' (1848: 416). Eliza Cook, with her prolific versifying on rural and working-class domestic life, became a literary phenomenon, 'the rage of London' (Leighton and Reynolds 1995: 175–7). Writing simple poems, many with the adjective *old* in the title, as in 'The

Old Arm-Chair', 'The Old Farm-Gate' and 'The Old Barn', she capitalized on the nostalgic aspect of domestic verse, and made herself into a much-sought-after contributor to literary journals and annuals; in 1849 she launched an independent *Eliza Cook's Journal*, a combination of stories, poems, moral editorials and practical essays on domestic life.

Perhaps because so many domestic poets were so obviously minor versifiers, the two major Victorian women poets, Elizabeth Barrett and Christina Rossetti, eschewed domestic poetry throughout their careers. Turning instead to heroic, philosophical and religious verse, Barrett agreed with her friend Mary Mitford that 'Cook' was a suitable name for the writer of such stuff as 'The Old Arm-Chair', and Rossetti told her brother to just call her 'Eliza Cook' if he thought her verses were quite that bad (Raymond and Sullivan 1983: I, 170; Rossetti 1903: 88).

Rossetti occasionally invoked a domestic scene, as in 'Goblin Market', to validate the bonds of sisterly love and warn against the rapacity of the outside world. But most often when she writes of 'home', it is to contrast an earthly 'house' with the heavenly 'home' for which all Christians should strive or to correct the Victorian overemphasis on material domesticity. Her allegorical 'From House to Home' (1858), written in response to Tennyson's 'The Palace of Art', moves from a false 'earthly paradise supremely fair / That lured me from the goal' – a place utterly domestic with its 'undulating green', 'stately trees', 'smooth garden beds' and gentle animals – to a true home among the blessed. The poem ends with the admonishment and resolution:

> Therefore, O friend, I would not if I might
> Rebuild my house of lies, wherein I joyed
> One time to dwell: my soul shall walk in white,
> Cast down but not destroyed.

Rossetti's later devotional poetry, especially the verses grouped as 'Songs for Strangers and Pilgrims' in her 1893 *Verses*, continues this High Anglican refusal to sacralize the domestic space; instead, the poems insist that piety must be (re)directed to the eternal realm.

Elizabeth Barrett's poetry, despite the heroic direction of her early verse, was more amenable to Victorian domesticity, and some of her occasional verses found their way into literary annuals and household collections, most frequently 'The Deserted Garden' (Griswold 1848: 431–2). A reverie of happy days spent in an old garden, the poem can be read as a lament for lost childhood. It none the less subtly suggests that, by the 1830s when it was written, the domestic garden, conventional site of a young maiden's thoughts of love, had become an anachronism. Barrett's garden, now a place of 'wilderness', has better uses as a 'hermit-home' for the modern female child, in whose secret nooks she can read 'minstrel stories' and exercise her imagination. When Barrett Browning returned to the garden in *Aurora Leigh* (1856), it was to register her dismay at the overdomestication of English landscape and life:

> All the fields
> Are tied up fast with hedges, nosegay-like;
> The hills are crumpled plains, the plains parterres,
> The trees, round, woolly, ready to be clipped,
> And if you seek for any wilderness
> You find, at best, a park. A nature tamed
> And grown domestic like a barn-door fowl.
>
> (I, 629–35)

Aurora, the young poetess, seeks an alternative landscape in Italy, where she may rekindle her imagination amidst its 'grand nature' of 'multitudinous mountains', 'palpitating pines' and 'headlong leaps of waters' (I, 617–21). The final books of *Aurora Leigh* offer a revised version of domestic space in their description of Aurora's Florentine house, with its view not only of nature but of the city as well (VII, 515–41), thus extending the woman poet's vision beyond the home or the simple pastoral scene to encompass the civic life of the nation.

Robert Browning was less wary of domestic verse. Before his marriage to Elizabeth Barrett, he published two versions of the garden poem as 'Garden Fancies' in *Hood's Magazine* (1844), and later included them in the seventh number of *Bells and Pomegranates*, his bid for poetic popularity. The first, 'The Flower's Name', tells of a lover's return to a garden where he walked with his beloved and monologizes his reverie on a flower with a 'soft meandering Spanish name', which she singled out for special attention. The second, a less conventional poem, 'Sibrandus Schafnaburgensis', recounts a reader's revenge on a pedantic book, left in the crevice of a plum tree to blister and rot. Browning's combination of conventional and counter-conventional in this pair would be repeated in *Men and Women* (1855), many of whose lyrics begin as domestic poems, only to be inverted or revised in order to question the conventions of domesticity itself.

'Love among the Ruins', for example, the lyric that opens the first volume of *Men and Women*, contrasts the heroic and the domestic, the landscape of imperial conquest 'Where the domed and daring palace shot its spires / Up like fires' with the quiet pastoral of 'the solitary pastures where our sheep / Half-asleep / Tinkle homeward through the twilight'. The poem ends with the embrace of lovers and the speaker's rejection of heroic ambition in the assertion: 'Love is best'. Yet if this poem celebrates love in a 'little turret', the opening monologue of the second volume questions the influence of the domestic affections. Andrea del Sarto desires domestic bliss, a quiet evening with his wife 'by the window with your hand in mine / . . . as married people use', but his desire, as much as his wife's faithlessness, hinders him in his painterly ambition to achieve greatness 'in the New Jerusalem, / Meted on each side by the angel's reed, / For Leonard, Rafael, Agnolo, and me'. Another pair in the volume, 'A Lover's Quarrel' and 'By the Fire-side', juxtaposes domestic love broken and fulfilled. In the first, three months of bliss are severed by 'a word', a 'shaft from the devil's bow'; in the second, an ageing husband recalls his happy domestic life, the joy he felt (and still feels) as he watches his wife:

> as you mutely sit
> Musing by fire-light, that great brow
> And the small spirit-hand propping it,
> Yonder, my heart knows how!
> (ll. 257–60)

If Victorian readers tended to identify the speaker of 'By the Fire-side' with Browning himself and 'my perfect wife, my Leonor' with Elizabeth Barrett, that was less because of descriptive details in the poem than because of the myth of domestic bliss that the Brownings embodied and encouraged. With tales of their romantic elopement from London and married life in Italy, the Brownings represented the domestic ideal in life even if they did not always choose to represent it in their art.

They were not the only poets to cultivate the myth of domesticity. As literary collaborators, William and Mary Howitt embodied a version of Victorian domestic ideology that associated literary production with a peaceful home life; in William's *The Boy's Country Book* (1847), Mary's books for children, and their columns and poems in the jointly edited *Howitt's Journal* (1847–9), the pair drew upon and reproduced their own home life in poems and tales celebrating middle-class domesticity. For Tennyson, too, domesticity was 'one of the secrets' of his poetic power; his 'true joy' lay 'in the family duties and affections' (Tennyson 1897: I, 189). The epitome of this association of domestic life and poetry appeared in Coventry Patmore's *The Angel in the House* (1854–6), a poetic sequence celebrating married love and domestic bliss. Inspired by his first wife Emily, who died just after its completion, Patmore traces the courtship and marriage of a fictional Felix and Honoraria in a poem meant to be the modern culmination of the heroic tradition:

> In these last days, the dregs of time,
> Learn that to me, though born so late,
> There does, beyond desert, befall
> (May my great fortune make me great!)
> The first of themes, sung last of all,
> In green and undiscover'd ground,
> Yet near where many others sing,
> I have the very well-head found
> Whence gushes the Pierian Spring.
> (I, 28–36)

If later Victorian poets responded with a 'sneer at the "domesticities"', including Swinburne and Gosse, who referred to Patmore as the 'laureate of the tea-table, with his humdrum stories of girls that smell of bread and butter' (Drabble 1995: 29), others like Alice Meynell defended the virtues of Patmore's verse: 'There are some things in both English and French domestic life that lack courtesy and grace, but it would be better done to restore these qualities than to deride the hearth in general' (Meynell 1903: 19). What the debate over *The Angel in the House* reminds us, quite apart from its signal that the fortunes of domestic poetry were waning by the mid-1850s, is that Patmore believed he had found in domestic life the subject of modern poetry and the making of his literary fame. He was not alone, as the long, successful career of the poet laureate, Alfred Tennyson, reveals.

Idyllic Poetry and the Domestic Idyll

Tennyson experimented with domestic verse early in his career, as in the ill-fated 'O Darling Room', the unpublished 'Home' and the more successful 'lady poems' of the 1830 volume. His serious work in the domestic tradition began, however, with the 'English Idyls' (spelt by Tennyson with one *l*), a few written for the 1832 *Poems*, more written or extensively revised for his 1842 volume. These idylls, as much as *In Memoriam* (1850), staked Tennyson's claim for public stature and the laureateship. As Robert Pattison has argued, 'Tennyson's poetic career is a history of the idyll in miniature': his poetry begins by being acutely self-conscious and eclectic; it develops a certain self-assurance and confidence that allows it to become simpler and more direct; and, finally, as had occurred with Virgil and Ovid, it fulfils its epic inclinations in *Idylls of the King* (1979: 46).

The idyll form that Tennyson adopted had an illustrious history in Greek poetry. (Indeed, it is possible to argue that Tennyson evoked this history, particularly in his allusions to Theocritus, in order to avoid the association of his 'English Idyls' with the more common domestic verse of his female contemporaries.) The idyll was an Alexandrian form – that is, a late Greek poetic development appearing after the heyday of the epic and after Greek poets had become self-conscious, sophisticated and eclectic. As a belated form, the idyll appealed to Tennyson, who had epic ambitions but believed that the era of heroic verse had ended. 'Why take the style of those heroic times?', the poet Everard Hall asks in Tennyson's 'The Epic', 'For nature brings not back the Mastadon.' The Alexandrian dispute over the future of poetry – with Apollonius arguing for imitation of the Homeric epic and Callimachus arguing against further epic production and turning instead to the idyll – illumined Tennyson's thinking about his own career, including his turn to the domestic idyll.

Like their Alexandrian counterparts, Tennyson's 'English Idyls' are short poems, usually short narratives that capture (or recapture) a single, significant episode in a man or woman's life; in 1838 Tennyson felt that if he wanted to make his mark, it would be 'by shortness, for the men before me had been so diffuse, and most of the big things except King Arthur had been done' (Tennyson 1897: I, 166). Like the Alexandrian idyll, too, Tennyson's idylls focus on psychological states, on the representation of the mind under the influence of an overmastering passion; according to Robert Pattison, 'Whereas the epic had sought to depict unity in the human community and the forces governing it, the idyll turned to the heart to search for its generalities' (1979: 23). Finally, like the classical idylls, Tennyson's versions are set in the countryside; this typically occurs because the idyll is essentially an urban poetic form, one that emerges in nostalgia for a pastoral way of life. As Walter Houghton noted in *The Victorian Frame of Mind*, 'In the recoil from the City, the home was irradiated by the light of the pastoral imagination. It could seem a country of peace and innocence where life was kind and duty natural' (1957: 344).

'The Miller's Daughter', Tennyson's first experiment with the domestic idyll and central to his 1832 *Poems*, incorporates these features. In a reverie told in old age, it narrates the tale of a 'late-left orphan of the squire' who falls in love with a miller's daughter. By concentrating on the moment that the young man first sees his Alice, the poem is able to capture both the young man's joy in love –

> I loved, and love dispelled the fear
> That I should die an early death:
> For love possessed the atmosphere,
> And filled the breast with purer breath
> (ll. 89–92)

– and the old man's happiness in 'the settled bliss' of domestic life, 'the comfort I have found in thee'. The poem is retrospective in multiple senses: at the level of story, it looks back on a long life of tranquillity and contentment in love; at the level of allusion, it looks back to Theocritus's seventh idyll, *Harvest Home*, and to Mary Russell Mitford's prose idyll, *The Queen of the Meadow* (1827), the latter a nostalgic reminiscence of a village way of life disappearing from England even as it was being recorded.

Donald Hair has observed that 'Victorian readers often thought that the idyl ought to deal with the idyllic; that is, with the pastoral landscape which offered the possibility of a contented human existence. But such expectations ignored a good part of the pastoral tradition in poetry, for some of Theocritus' idyls were bitterly critical of actual social conditions' (1981: 76). Following Theocritus, Tennyson expanded his range in the 1842 *Poems* to create an idyllic sequence that moves from the pastoral ideal to modern disillusionment. After the introductory poems, 'The Epic' and 'Morte d'Arthur', which turn away from the Homeric tradition, Tennyson offers a sequence of five idylls: 'The Gardener's Daughter', a happy tale of romantic love and art inspired in a garden; followed by 'Dora', an idyll recalling the Biblical story of Ruth with the power of familial love, for good or ill, at its center; 'Audley Hall', a classical idyll modelled on the singing contests of Theocritus with friendship and same-sex love as its subject; 'Walking to the Mail', still in the classical mode but with a failed marriage and fallen house as its subject; and finally 'Edwin Morris', a satirical idyll of faithless love and the bitter reality of the Victorian marriage market, a topic Tennyson would take up again in *Maud* (1855). To these five poems, which demonstrate the power and range of the idyllic form, he added seven others in 1842 and, in his 1884 collected works, labelled them 'English Idyls'. Throughout his career he published idyllic verse, not all labelled as such, as in 'Enoch Arden' (1864) and 'Locksley Hall, Sixty Years After' (1886).

Tennyson's sequence within the 'English Idyls' demonstrates the flexibility of the genre both to embody and to reflect critically upon Victorian pastoral and domestic ideologies. Because the idyll embeds lyrics within a frame, rather than presents the speaker's voice directly, as did much women's domestic verse, Tennyson was able to express, yet distance himself from, domestic sentimentality. Because, moreover, his idylls use dialogue and conversation, as did his Theocritan models, the poems have the effect of presenting multiple perspectives, within which the reader is encouraged to find an ideal. Like the dramatic monologue that Browning developed, the Tennysonian idyll became a characteristically Victorian form in its self-consciousness and removal from Romantic lyricism.

Tennyson's development of the idyll culminates in the *Idylls of the King* (which he spelled with two *l*s to distinguish them from his 'English Idyls'). Often classified as 'epic', these poems in fact capitalize on the eclecticism of the idyll tradition by incorporating features of various literary modes: romance from Malory's *Morte d'Arthur* and the Welsh *Mabinogion*; epic and allegory from Virgil, Spenser, Milton and Tasso; lyric and domestic poetry; and the Victorian domestic novel. To account for this variety, critics have debated the generic classification and described the *Idylls* in different terms: Donald Hair as 'an heroic treatment of domestic themes, images, and actions'; Jerome Buckley as 'not a single unified narrative but a group of chivalric tableaux . . . [that] move through a series of sharply visualized vignettes toward a pictured climax'; Robert Pattison as 'an Arthurian romance composed of twelve idylls so arranged as to form an allegorical, cyclical epic' (Hair 1981: 122; Buckley 1960: 172–3; Pattison 1979: 135). All these possibilities could be contained within the idyll, which with its eclecticism and epic ambition allowed Tennyson an opportunity for adaptation and amalgamation.

In a sequence recalling the movement of the 'English Idyls' from early domestic harmony to discord and disruption, the *Idylls of the King* narrate the progress of Arthur's kingdom – and, by analogy, the Victorian empire – in the rise and fall of the Round Table and in the faith and faithlessness of Arthur's wife Guinevere and friend Lancelot. Taken as a whole, they are meant to be an English national epic. As Tennyson suggests in his 'Dedication: To the Prince Consort', they redefine masculine heroism for the modern age:

> And indeed He seems to me
> Scarce other than my king's ideal knight,
> 'Who reverenced his conscience as his king;
> Whose glory was, redressing human wrong;
> Who spake no slander, no, nor listed to it;
> Who loved one only and who clave to her[.]'
> (ll. 5–10)

Yet the twelve books remain individually *idylls* – that is, each is an *eidyllion*, a 'framed picture' or 'little picture' of a character or pair of characters coloured (or obsessed) by a single, dominant emotion. In keeping with the idyllic (as opposed to epic) tradition, the emphasis falls on the psychology (rather than the actions) of the characters.

The *Idylls of the King*, published serially between 1859 and 1885, provoked diverse responses in kind and in criticism, including new versions of the idyll. Perhaps to capitalize on Tennyson's success, perhaps to counter or correct his fusion of classical and modern traditions into the 'domestic idyll', other poets published their own versions of idyllic verse in the 1860s and 1870s. Austin Dobson, a minor poet, regrouped poems from his 1873 and 1877 volumes into *Old World Idylls* (1880) in order to ride the popular wave and perhaps, in poems like 'An Autumn Idyll', which parodies the singing contests of Theocritus, to suggest the impossibility of a pure idyll in the modern age. More significantly, Walter Savage Landor, a classical scholar and poet, brought out *Heroic Idyls* in 1863. Framed as the last tales of Homer, told to an aged Laertes and his simple helper, Agatha, these idylls return to their classical roots. They retell mythical stories or imagine dialogues among Greek figures – the tale of Atalanta and the golden apples, the trial of Aeschylos for revealing the Eleusian mysteries, a debate between Hippolyta and Theseus, a conversation among Sappho, Alcaeus, Anacreaon and Phaon – in pure *eidyllia*, 'little pictures' of classical life, without the moralizing about heroism or domestic faithfulness so dominant in Tennyson's *Idylls*. Landor's poems may have been a reminder to other neo-Hellenists, including Tennyson, of what the genre was originally meant to be.

A more serious poetic challenge came from Robert Browning, who published two series of *Dramatic Idyls* in 1879 and 1880. As Clyde de Ryals notes, Browning was invading Tennyson's poetic terrain, hoping for a popular success like the laureate's after a period of depression and imaginative drought (1975: 167–8). The *Dramatic Idyls* fulfilled his hopes in that they were well received by the critics and his reading public. After their publication, Tennyson complained to his friend William Allingham: 'I wish Browning had not taken my word Idyll' (1897: 291). Tennyson's complaint involved more than a sense of territoriality in that Browning's idyls, however uneven in quality, implicitly critique the work of his fellow poet.

Browning's poems recover the range of the idyll: from imaginative redactions of Greek sources in 'Pheidippides' (the runner who brought the news of victory from Marathon to Athens) and 'Echetlos' (meaning 'holder of the ploughshare', an unnamed warrior who killed many Persians at the battle of Marathon), to an old Russian folktale in 'Ivàn Ivànovitch' and an old Arabian tale in 'Muléykeh', to expansions of episodes from Bunyan's *Life and Death of Mr. Badman* in 'Ned Bratts' and from contemporary gossip in 'Clive'. Browning draws attention to his sources in epigraphs or opening lines that remind the reader of the derivative, if also highly learned and sophisticated, nature of the idyll. In contrast, Tennyson often obscured the sources of his 'English Idyls', particularly when they derived from contemporary novelists or fellow poets – as in 'The Miller's Daughter', derived from Mary Russell Mitford's *The Queen of the Meadow* (1827), 'Dora', derived from Mitford's *Dora Cresswell* (1828), 'Locksley Hall', derived from Sir William Jones's translation of the *Moallakát*. Browning was insistent that renewal, not originality, was the basis of idyllic verse.

Perhaps most important, Browning, in his best dramatic idyl, 'Pan and Luna', resists the domesticating of sexual love and the moralizing of older sources that characterize the *Idylls of the King*. 'Pan and Luna' has its origin in Virgil's *Georgics*, in three lines in the midst of advice to sheep-farmers that retell the myth of the moon's eclipse: ' 'Twas with gift of such snowy wool, if we may trust the tale, that Pan, Arcadia's god, charmed and beguiled thee, O Moon, calling thee to the depths of the woods; nor didst thou scorn his call' (III, 391–3, trans. Fairclough). Browning describes the lush Arcadian landscape and naked beauty of the 'Maid-Moon with limbs all bare', imagines the growing consciousness and fright of Luna pursued, even gives a scene of ravishment when Luna, 'of unmatched modesty betrayed', was:

> Bruised to the breast of Pan, half god half brute,
> Raked by his bristly boar-sward while he lapped
> – Never say, kissed her! that were to pollute
> Love's language – which moreover proves unapt
> To tell how she recoiled.
>
> (ll. 83–7)

Yet Browning finally refuses to explain Virgil's enigmatic tale, particularly the phrase 'nor didst thou scorn his call', suggesting that such explanation ill befits the idyl ('Love's language . . . proves unapt to tell') and spoils the Virgilian gift:

> Explain who may! Let all else go, I keep
> – As of a ruin just a monolith –
> Thus much, one verse of five words, each a boon:
> Arcadia, night, a cloud, Pan, and the moon.
>
> (ll. 101–4)

As Betty Flowers observes, this is the antithesis of Tennyson's treatment of the Arthurian myth, where the loss of modesty and purity becomes a tragedy, a woman's 'downfall'; 'in "Pan and Luna" the narrator's dramatic reading of Virgil's text seems designed to lead Victorian readers to a conclusion that they might otherwise resist: that the high and the low, the body and the soul, are not created to be at war, but are in fact necessary to each other' (1987: 157).

The Waning of Domestic and Idyllic Verse

Browning's gentle critique of Tennyson's idylls was part of a larger movement away from the domestication of English poetry, a rebellion against what Herbert Tucker has called 'house arrest' (1994). In perfecting the domestic idyll, Tennyson created a form suited to Victorian domestic ideology but restrictive in the kinds and qualities of love it could represent. By the end of the 1850s, when domestic poetry reached its peak and the first four *Idylls of the King* appeared in print, a counter-movement had set in.

Some writers had, of course, always resisted domestic verse. Thomas Hood's 'Domestic Poems' (1837), for example, humorously re-envision the domestic affections in parodies of their more serious counterparts. As if in response to Burns's 'John Anderson, My Jo' or Tennyson's 'The Miller's Daughter', the speaker of Hood's 'Hymeneal Retrospections' recalls his wedding day and the changes that have ensued:

> O Kate! my dear partner, through joy and through strife!
>   When I look back on Hymen's dear day,
> Not a lovelier bride ever changed to a wife,
>   Though you're now so old, wizened, and gray! . . .
> Your figure was tall, then, and perfectly straight,

> Though it now has two twists from upright –
> But bless you! still bless you! my partner! my Kate!
> Though you be such a perfect old fright!
>
> (ll. 1–4, 33–6)

So, too, Hood de-idealizes the parent–child bond and nineteenth-century paeans to childhood in 'A Parental Ode to My Son, Aged Three Years and Five Months' (a parody of Wordsworth's 'To H. C. Six Years Old' and more famous 'Ode: Intimations of Immortality'):

> Thou happy, happy elf!
> (But stop, – first let me kiss away that tear) –
> Thou tiny image of myself!
> (My love, he's poking peas into his ear!)
> Thou merry, laughing sprite!
> With spirits feather-light,
> Untouched by sorrow, and unspoiled by sin –
> (Good heavens! the child is swallowing a pin!)
>
> (ll. 1–8)

Yet Hood's uneven juxtapositions did not seriously disrupt the Victorian domestic ideal, in that the poems remind the reader of it even as they point to a more common reality.

Two decades after Hood's parodies, however, we can trace a visible waning of domestic verse and the domestic idyll on several fronts: the diminishing presence of domestic verse in anthologies of poetry after mid-century; the quiet refusal of second- and third-generation Victorian women poets to write domestic verse; and an impatience with, or outright rejection of, domestic sentimentality by literary reviewers.

Whereas poetic anthologies published in the 1830s to 1850s included a fair share of domestic verse, by 1860, when Francis Palgrave published *The Golden Treasury*, such verse had virtually disappeared. In T. K. Hervey's *The English Helicon* (1841) and the anonymously collected *Book of the Poets* (1842), both editors had located the strength of contemporary English poetry in the turn from epic to lyric and, specifically, in the turn to domestic virtues, to 'a home scene of domestic virtue and happiness [that] outshines a Roman triumph' (see Peterson 1999: 198). Their anthologies included a variety of women writers known for their domestic verse: Anna Barbauld, Felicia Hemans, Joanna Baillie, Mary Mitford, Mary Howitt and others. By 1860, Palgrave's *Golden Treasury of the Best Songs and Lyrical Poems* offered a different interpretation of the strength of English lyric. As William Brewster notes in his 1928 edition of this Victorian classic, after love lyrics (thirty-seven in number) the most important group of poems in the *Golden Treasury* (fifteen in number) 'might be called martial or heroic' (1928: xi). By eliminating domestic verse and instead anthologizing martial lyrics, many from the Napoleonic era, Palgrave remasculinized, reheroicized and redirected the course of English poetry.

Mid- and late-Victorian women poets participated in the redirection, though not in Palgrave's terms. Not only did Christina Rossetti reject the ideological grounds of domestic verse, Barrett Browning also challenged the cultural assumptions that identified it as a feminine domain. In *Aurora Leigh* (1856), the eponymous heroine debates with her cousin Romney whether women's verse can move beyond the pastoral, domestic and sentimental. Romney insists that women poets, limited in scope, cannot do so:

> Therefore, this same world
> Uncomprehended by you, must remain
> Uninfluenced by you. – Women as you are,
> Mere women, personal and passionate,
> You give us doting mothers and perfect wives,
> Sublime Madonnas, and enduring saints!
> We get not Christ from you – and verily
> We shall not get a poet, in my mind.
>   (II, 218–25)

Aurora vows to produce more than 'doting mothers and perfect wives', or as Romney later puts it, 'happy pastorals of the meads and trees' (II, 1201), and aims at a more comprehensive oeuvre. Her successors followed – as a comparison of early and late Victorian women's poetry in recent anthologies reveals (see Leighton and Reynolds 1995; Armstrong and Bristow 1996). When some women, like Alice Meynell, engaged the older tradition of domestic verse, it was with ironic distance, as in 'The Modern Mother' and 'Cradle-Song at Twilight', which portray women fallen from or faithless to the domestic ideal.

The reaction against domestic verse can be seen most clearly, however, in slighting responses to *Idylls of the King* and Swinburne's vehement attack on Tennyson in his 'Notes on Poems and Ballads' (1866). While most reviews of the *Idylls* were favourable, with critics like Walter Bagehot and William Gladstone positively glowing with admiration for Tennyson as the greatest poet of the age and the *Idylls* as the nineteenth-century's greatest literary work, some reviewers began to characterize Tennyson as 'a drawing-room Wordsworth' (Jump 1967: 236) and question the effect of his repetitive use of the idyllic form. When Alfred Austin re-evaluated Victorian poets in *The Poetry of the Period* (1870), he pointed to 'those blank verse English Idyls which sounded the key-note' of Tennyson's career and attributed his popularity to the dominant ideology: 'he does not ask men to give up their newly-found idol, the cherished poetical god of their narrow domestic hearth' (Jump 1967: 298, 310). Across the Channel, in his *History of English Literature* (1871) the French critic Hippolyte Taine characterized English verse in general, and Tennyson in particular, as 'confined within a sort of flowery border':

> Does any poet suit such a society better than Tennyson? Without being a pedant, he is moral; he may be read in the family circle by night; he does not rebel against society and life; he speaks of God and the soul, nobly, tenderly, without ecclesiastical prejudice; there is no need to reproach him like Lord Byron; . . . he will pervert nobody. (Jump 1967: 272)

By the 1860s and 1870s, domestic poetry had begun to seem narrow and confining rather than ennobling.

Swinburne's reaction, which came in defence of his badly received *Poems and Ballads* (1866), a volume depicting more ardent passions and less ideal forms of love than those allowed in domestic poetry, attacked the reigning ideology. Crediting (and thus blaming) Tennyson for setting a trend that 'would turn all art and literature "into the line of children"', he pointed to 'the idyllic form' as the source of the problem:

Thus with English versifiers now, the idyllic form is alone in fashion. The one great and prosperous poet of the time has given out the tune, and the hoarser choir takes it up. . . . We have idyls good and bad, ugly and pretty; idyls of the farm and the mill; idyls of the dining-room and the deanery; idyls of the gutter and the gibbet. (Peckham 1970: 339)

Swinburne posed the question for Victorian poetry as this:

whether or not the first and last requisite of art is to give no offence; whether or not all that cannot be lisped in the nursery or fingered in the schoolroom is therefore to be cast out of the library; whether or not the domestic circle is to be for all men and writers the outer limit and extreme horizon of their world of work. (Peckham 1970: 338)

His answer was a resounding 'No', with a call to make poetry 'noble and chaste in the wider masculine sense'.

How accurate was Swinburne's assessment of the state of poetry in the mid-1860s? Swinburne certainly had a point about the influence of the domestic idyll on poetic fashion. The numerous publications styling themselves idylls – *Drift: A Seashore Idyl* (1866), *The Angel: An Idyl* (1870), *Snowbound: A Winter Idyl* (1872), *A Sussex Idyll* (1877), *An Idyl of Work* (1875), to list only a sample – support his point about 'the hoarser choir'. Yet Swinburne exaggerates the dominance of the form among the major Victorian poets. Virtually every classically trained poet experimented with idyllic verse at some moment in his career, including Swinburne's friend and mentor Walter Savage Landor in *Fiesolan Idylls* (1831), later in *Heroic Idylls* (1863); Arthur Hugh Clough in three *Idyllic Sketches* (*c.* 1847); Matthew Arnold in 'Thyrsis' (1866); and Browning in *Dramatic Idyls* (1879–80). But these poems, as well as the varieties of non-idyllic forms used by the same poets, give evidence against the claim that the 'domestic circle' was 'the outer limit and extreme horizon' of mid-Victorian poetry. The surging of erotic desire in Clough's 'Natura Naturans', the love of man for man in 'Thyrsis', the imagining of sexual violence in 'Pan and Luna', the range from devoted to jealous and destructive love in the *Heroic Idyls* – these suggest that the Tennysonian domestic idyll was only one of several Victorian reincarnations.

Swinburne's attack does, however, provide evidence of a turning away from early Victorian domestic ideology and its poetic forms, and a looking outward to other literatures and cultures. Whether the turn was that of the Pre-Raphaelites to medieval culture, of Pater to the Renaissance, or of neo-Hellenists like Swinburne, Hardy and Michael Field to ancient Greece, the later Victorian poets seldom wrote domestic verse.

See also: Arthurian Poetry and Medievalism; Nationhood and Empire.

REFERENCES AND FURTHER READING

Allingham, William (1907) *A Diary*. Eds H. Allingham and D. Radford. London: Macmillan.

Armstrong, Isobel, and Virginia Blain (eds) (1999) *Women's Poetry, Late Romantic to Late Victorian: Gender and Genre, 1830–1900*. London: Macmillan.

Amstrong, Isobel, and Joseph Bristow (eds) (1996) *Nineteenth-Century Women Poets*. Oxford: Clarendon Press.

Brewster, William Tenney (1928) *The Golden Treasury, Selected from the Best Songs and Lyrical Poems in the English Language, by Francis F. Palgrave*. New York: Macmillan.

Buckley, Jerome Hamilton (1960) *Tennyson: The Growth of a Poet*. Cambridge, Mass.: Harvard University Press.

De Staël, Madame (1803) *Germany*. 3 vols. London: John Murray.

Drabble, Margaret (ed.) (1995) *The Oxford Companion to English Literature*. Oxford: Oxford University Press.

Edmond, Rod (1988) *Affairs of the Hearth: Victorian Poetry and Domestic Narrative*. London: Routledge.

Fairclough, H. Rushton (trans.) (1940) *Virgil's Works*. Cambridge, Mass.: Harvard University Press.

Flowers, Betty S. (1987) 'Virtual and Ideal Readers of Browning's "Pan and Luna": The Drama in the Dramatic Idyl.' *Browning Institute Studies*, 15, 151–60.

Griswold, Rufus W. (ed.) (1848). *The Poets and Poetry of England in the Nineteenth Century*. Philadelphia: Carey and Hart.

Hair, Donald S. (1981) *Domestic and Heroic in Tennyson's Poetry*. Toronto: University of Toronto Press.

Hervey, T. K. (ed.) (1841) *The English Halcyon: A Selection of Modern Poetry*. London: A. H. Baily.

Houghton, Walter E. (1957) *The Victorian Frame of Mind 1830–1870*. New Haven: Yale University Press.

Jump, John D. (ed.) (1967) *Tennyson: The Critical Heritage*. London: Routledge and Kegan Paul.

Leighton, Angela, and Margaret Reynolds (eds) (1995) *Victorian Women Poets*. Oxford: Blackwell.

Lootens, Tricia (1994) 'Hemans and Home: Victorianism, Feminine "Internal Enemies," and the Domestication of National Identity.' *PMLA*, 109, 238–53.

MacKay, Charles (ed.) (1858) *The Home Affections Pourtrayed by the Poets*. London: George Routledge.

Meynell, Alice (ed.) (1903) *The Angel in the House, Together with The Victories of Love*. London: George Routledge and Sons.

Mitford, Mary Russell (1832) *Queen of the Meadow* and *Dora Cresswell*. In *Our Village*. London: Geo. B. Whittaker.

Pattison, Robert (1979) *Tennyson and Tradition*. Cambridge, Mass.: Harvard University Press.

Peckham, Morse (ed.) (1970) *Swinburne: Poems and Ballads, Atalanta in Calydon*. Indianapolis: Bobbs-Merrill.

Peterson, Linda H. (1999) 'Anthologizing Women: Women Poets in Early Victorian Collections of Lyric.' *Victorian Poetry*, 37, 193–209.

Raymond, Meredith B., and Mary Rose Sullivan (eds) (1983) *The Letters of Elizabeth Barrett Browning to Mary Russell Mitford, 1836–1854*. Winfield, Kans.: Wedgestone Press.

Ross, Marlon B. (1989) *The Contours of Masculine Desire: Romanticism and the Rise of Women's Poetry*. Oxford: Oxford University Press.

Rossetti, W. M. (1903) *Rossetti Papers: 1862 to 1870*. London: Sands.

Ryals, Clyde de L. (1975) *Browning's Later Poetry, 1871–1889*. Ithaca, N. Y.: Cornell University Press.

Tennyson, Hallam (1897) *Alfred Lord Tennyson: A Memoir by his Son*. London: Macmillan.

Tucker, Herbert F. (1994) 'House Arrest: The Domestication of English Poetry in the 1820s.' *New Literary History*, 25, 521–48.

Watts, Alaric A. (ed.) (1829). *The Poetical Album; or Register of Modern Fugitive Verse*. London: Hurst, Chance.

Watts, Alaric Alfred (1884) *Alaric Watts: A Narrative of his Life*. London: Richard Bentley.

3

Lyric

Matthew Rowlinson

I

In a large view, the most distinctive characteristics of Victorian lyric are those it shares with much Western lyric of the last two centuries, but with few other lyric traditions. These are, first, its status as the product of print culture, and second, the predominance in it of the dramatic and descriptive modes. The literary lyric from the nineteenth century on is a printed form that understands itself variously as preserving, succeeding, incorporating or remaking earlier lyric forms with other modes of circulation and reception. Of course, innumerable lyrics had previously entered print, but only in the nineteenth century does print become for lyric the hegemonic medium, with the result, on the one hand, that all lyric production takes place with a view to print, and on the other, that lyrics which had previously been circulated and received in other media are now remediated through print.

Print's long rise to its nineteenth-century dominance of lyric poetry took a crucial turn in the second half of the preceding century, when volumes collecting traditional songs and ballads became a recognized and increasingly popular genre. The earlier of these collections, like Thomas Percy's *Reliques of Ancient English Poetry* (1765) and Joseph Ritson's *Ancient Songs* (1792), relied on prior manuscript and printed sources; later collections, like Walter Scott's *Minstrelsy of the Scottish Border* (1802–3), included material transcribed for the first time from oral sources. By the second decade of the nineteenth century, a vogue had appeared for lyric poems adopting the forms of traditional songs, most visibly in the poems of Byron and Thomas Moore. Byron and Moore's poems, in turn, were swiftly adopted by a new popular song culture whose materials were printed texts and music. Each of the figures I have named played an important role in mediating oral culture through print; in English poetry, the most influential – though frequently oblique – meditation on this role is that of William Wordsworth. The explicit project of Wordsworth's poetry was to assimilate into literary language the rhetoric and diction of everyday rural speech. His poems repeatedly allegorize this project by dramatizing encounters between the poet and marginal, illiterate figures whose utterances both challenge him and provide the basis for his poetry. 'The Solitary Reaper' (1807), for example, records its speaker's encounter in the Scots Highlands with a reaper singing at her work. The song is in Erse, and hence certainly part of an oral tradition; the speaker does not understand it, but none the less claims to bear its music away with him. The printed poem has for topic its own relation to the alien utterance that provoked it.

Wordsworth's poetry, like Scott's and Moore's, and Burns's before them, is in part the printed mediation of current non-print cultures. In the period covered by this volume, however, the situation is somewhat different. Popular song, for instance, had by the 1830s become a form disseminated and preserved predominantly in print. In earlier periods of literary history, print was for lyric only one circuit of transmission among others, coexisting not only with practices of oral performance but also with the manuscript circulation of lyrics within coteries. But in the Victorian era for the first time virtually all sites of manuscript production and oral performance existed within a culture of print, which thus organized the entire field of composition and reception. So organized, the genre of lyric poetry is in Victorian Britain for the first time fully implicated in the production of printed text as a commodity, rather than, as for Wordsworth, Scott and Moore in the first decades of the nineteenth century, occupying a liminal position between commodity production, a patronage system and traditional society.

For Victorian poets, lyric appears as a genre newly totalized in print. The anthologies and critical editions of the period aimed in principle to incorporate into print the various lyrical modes that print itself superseded. Victorian print-lyric does not confront song cultures that exist independently of it, and, unlike Burns, Moore or Wordsworth, its authors do not understand themselves as located on the border between print and oral culture. In Victorian poetry, it would be hard to know where such a border existed. Matthew Arnold was the most Wordsworthian of the major Victorian lyricists, and for him as for Wordsworth the encounter with a figure excluded from print or even literate culture is a recurrent topic. But in Arnold these figures are mute, like the addressee of 'To a Gypsy Child by the Sea Shore' (1849). This poem contrasts both with 'The Solitary Reaper' and more directly with earlier Wordsworthian poems representing a dialogue between child and adult. The child's muteness in Arnold's lyric, and its identification as a gypsy, suggest how lyric now belongs to a discursive system that has no external border. The gypsy does not appear as a figure with a home outside England, or outside modernity, but rather as an emblem of exclusions internal to both. Arnold's poem thus imagines no other utterance confronting its own, but only a mute presence whose non-response structures the very utterance it records.

II

Lyric is the most dialectical of Victorian genres. Two of its central undertakings are to incorporate models it has itself superseded and to define itself by negation. The motivation of lyric utterance by the silence of an auditor or addressee is a generic convention and long predates the nineteenth century; it is a characteristic device of Victorian poets, however, to incorporate these silent figures into the representational frame of their poems, for instance by making their silence a dramatic response to the utterance the poem records. The fullest development of this tendency occurs in dramatic monologue, but the power of a silent other to complete, modify or subvert an utterance dialectically is a pervasive topic in every kind of Victorian poetry.

Robert Browning's seminal experiments in dramatic monologue from 1836 on systematically explore this topic's formal possibilities. In 'Porphyria's Lover' (1836), he writes a poem that from its title on insists that the speaker's identity, and the meanings both of his utterance and of the action it narrates, are given by the mute woman in whose presence he speaks. The speaker is only identified as Porphyria's lover, and the only motive he states for the act he narrates is Porphyria's will. The act, however, is that of strangling her. The mode of Porphyria's murder emphasizes that death has silenced her; the poem is thus built around the contradiction between the speaker's claim that his act is the pure expression of Porphyria's will, liberated from the circumstances that had prevented her from expressing it herself, and the ironic implication that it was on the contrary only the last and most catastrophic of those circumstances. The moment when Porphyria's 'utmost will' (l. 53) appears is also the moment when it disappears beyond recovery. There is no interpretation that will reconcile this contradiction; hence Robert Langbaum's widely influential claim of a generation ago that the reader of dramatic monologue is forced to oscillate between two responses, which he termed sympathy and judgement (1971: 85).

The rejection of totalization that Browning stages in his dramatic monologues, however, should be understood as a mediation and critique of lyric. Victorian poetics, following Kant, distinguishes rigorously between the aesthetic use of language and the instrumental. Pure art for Kant has no aim external to itself (1952: 62–3); this doctrine underlies, for instance, J. S. Mill's influential distinction of poetry from rhetoric. In Mill, for whom lyric is the original and most authentic genre of poetry, poetic utterance is characterized by its interiority. Taking lyric as his exemplar, Mill writes of poetry in general that it is 'feeling, confessing itself to itself in moments of solitude' (1981: 348), having no aim to persuade and showing no awareness of any audience. On this view, as Kant proposed, the poem's aim would be achieved in the very act of its utterance. Browning thus wrote his dramatic monologues in the context of a widespread assumption that in poetry, and *a fortiori* in lyric, the instrumental use of language is excluded; it is this context that determines the significance of his poems of the 1840s, which collectively mount a formal experiment aimed at undoing this exclusion and foregrounding the operation of rhetoric in poetry.

In the major dramatic monologues of the forties and fifties, then, Browning characteristically represents utterances that not only imply a dramatic context, but are also spoken with specific persuasive or apologetic intent. The meanings of these utterances are in each case mediated by a mute audience, whose relation to the speaker and whose historical character we must understand in order to understand the utterance at all. Fra Lippo Lippi, for instance, in the monologue that bears his name (1855), speaks while under arrest by the night watch in fourteenth-century Florence: his utterance is in the first instance a plea to be released. The very circumstance that prompts his utterance also prevents him from speaking freely; at the poem's outset one of the watch is literally gripping his throat. As in 'Porphyria's Lover', strangulation allegorizes the pressure of mediation to which the poem submits speech. Neither in 'Fra Lippo Lippi', nor in 'The Bishop Orders his Tomb in St Praxed's Church' (1845) or 'Bishop Blougram's Apology' (1855) – to name only a few of many possible examples – is there any question of unmediated access to the inner life of the speaker. Indeed, the way speech conceals inner life from others and arguably from the speakers themselves becomes an increasingly prominent theme of the monologues.

In this respect, then, Browning's monologues are designed as antithetical to lyric. The dialectical character of Victorian lyric, though, is nowhere clearer than in the way this antithesis itself becomes the medium in which lyric appears. As Herbert F. Tucker has shown, within the dramatic monologue the antithesis of dramatic and lyrical utterance is itself a theme; 'Fra Lippo Lippi' provides his initial example (1985: 232–3). There the blank verse text of Lippo's discourse, printed in Roman type, is repeatedly interrupted by rhymed fragments in a Tuscan lyric form, the *stornello*, printed in italics: '*Flower o'the pine, / You keep your mistr . . . manners, and I'll stick to mine!*' (ll. 238–9). These fragments comment obliquely on Lippi's narrative, but do so from no specifiable position in the poem's dramatic frame. They neither address Lippi's interlocutors, nor are they in every case necessarily Lippi's utterances. They locate lyric in the poem as a mode of utterance alien to its dramatic form, and perhaps even one that it suppresses. Such a suppression is implied in the fragment I have just given as an example, where even as he quotes the *stornello*, Lippi amends 'mistress' to 'manners', staging in two words the suppression of desire by 'manners' that is a major topic of the poem's narrative, and implicitly aligning it with the suppression or censorship of lyric utterance.

'Fra Lippo Lippi' is not alone among Browning's dramatic monologues in incorporating fragments of song. Other poems that do so include 'Caliban upon Setebos' and – in a rather different way – '"Childe Roland to the Dark Tower Came"'. Robert Langbaum argues more generally that, for all their dramatic character, the speakers' utterances in Browning's monologues invariably tend towards song in that they are always in some way excessive in relation to their dramatic situation, which is to say that there is always something about them in excess of pure instrumentality. Browning's characters, in Langbaum's view, always reveal more of themselves than a purely dramatic reading can account for; this excess of self-revelation he identifies with lyric (1971: 182–200).

Browning's dramatic monologues afford a useful introduction to the dialectical character of Victorian lyric because they manifest their underlying affiliation with lyric only antithetically. Dramatic in form, historicist in theme, and generally unmusical in diction, these poems constitute a medium in which lyric appears as an unassimilated fragment or as an excess that frames the whole. The era does offer, however, other ways of mediating lyric than through dramatic form. The writing of Alfred Tennyson in the years 1830 to 1850 includes probably the most influential lyrics of the first half of Victoria's reign. His first solo volume, *Poems, Chiefly Lyrical* of 1830, was as the title suggests largely comprised of lyrics; subsequent volumes in 1832 and 1842 also included many lyrics, though Tennyson's experiments in the genre increasingly tended towards hybridization with varieties of narrative and dramatic poetry, such as the ballad, the idyll, and the epyllion or little epic.

In the 1830 volume, four of the poems were simply entitled 'Song'; this title refers literally to one of the poems' main topics – they are poems *about* song – and figuratively to the poems themselves: metaphorically, the poems *are* songs. The quality of self-reflexivity, by which the poem discusses the conditions of its own existence, recurs throughout Tennyson's early lyrics. The poems appear to frame themselves, which is also to say that they are framed by themselves – a formal trait that corresponds to the way lyric in Browning's more antithetical treatment becomes a genre that is both contained by and contains the dramatic monologue. Both poets are responding to the historical situation in which they at once write as the privileged inheritors of a newly totalized genre, and write what might be called post-lyrics, as members of the first generation of poets for whom print has fully colonized the fields of manuscript and song production.

The best known of the 1830 'Songs' is thus at once a lyric and an allegory of lyric production. The kernel of 'A spirit haunts the year's last hours' is the utterance that closes the second stanza: 'My very heart faints and my whole soul grieves / At the moist rich smell of the rotting leaves, / And the breath / Of the fading edges of box beneath, / And the year's last rose' (ll. 16–20). The sentence might well be taken as an exemplar of lyric utterance; in it a first-person speaker expresses a consciousness entirely given over to a single emotion, to which the utterance itself is equally given over. It contains no hint of narrative, for instance in any suggestion that the speaker's grief might have a cause prior to the moment of its expression, or that this expression might have a purpose to be accomplished in the future. The cause of the speaker's grief is indeed so proximate to the utterance expressing it that the poem metaphorically identifies them by personifying the box and endowing it with breath in which to expire its fading life – a personification that implicitly identifies it with the speaker and the speaker's utterance with the figural breath that is supposedly its cause. The garden breathes out its life as the speaker breathes out a grief whose cause and expression thus virtually collapse into one.

The lines I have quoted, however, are the last of the poem's second and last stanza. The opening stanza is a description of the garden whose decay occasions the speaker's grief and of the grieving spirit that haunts it: 'A spirit haunts the year's last hours / Dwelling amid these yellowing bowers: / To himself he talks; / . . . / Earthward he boweth the heavy stalks / Of the mouldering flowers' (ll. 1–8). The whole poem thus displays a marked recursiveness at the level of meaning: the speaker grieves at the smell of the dying garden, which is itself the work of a grieving spirit. There is no indication that there is anything outside the garden, or outside the poem, to account for the grief they equally express. The only motive for the grief is the decay of the garden, and if we take the enclosed garden as a figure for the enclosed space of the poem itself, then we can read the poem as an expression of grief at its own decay. (The analogy between the poem and the garden is strengthened by a long prior tradition of figuring poets as gardeners and their utterances as flowers; to this convention we owe the word 'anthology', whose Greek roots mean 'a gathering of flowers'.)

The terminal, self-mourning, self-reflexive qualities of this poem are in different and often more complex ways apparent throughout Tennyson's poems of the 1830 and 1832 volumes. Especially in the latter, Tennyson's exploration of lyric is often not, as in 'A spirit haunts the year's last hours', purely lyrical in form, but rather encloses a lyric voice or a personification of lyric voice in a narrative frame. 'The Hesperides' (1832) thus comprises the song of the three daughters of Hesperus – a song whose main theme is the need to keep on singing – and a fragmentary opening narrative. The poem stages the mutual exclusion of lyric and narrative; indeed, it constitutes lyric as a defence against narrative, a defence in the form of an utterance that does nothing but circle back on itself.

I have argued that the elaborate framing devices of Tennyson's early poems correspond to the development of dramatic form in Robert Browning; both register the novel historical function of print-lyric as a totalizing form that at once preserves and supersedes its multiple predecessors. Though the poem is not strictly a lyric, this claim is particularly relevant to 'The Lady of Shalott' (1832), a poem that centrally concerns its own relation to song. The poem narrates the death of an aristocratic woman who has spent her life in a tower singing and weaving; in life – though she could be heard from outside – she remained unseen, but in death her mute corpse appears to the public gaze. The poem thus narrates the substitution of a visible (indeed legible, as the viewers of the Lady's corpse read her name beneath it) sign for a voice. And it aligns the dead voice with forces that were at the date of the poem suffering major historical defeats. These are landowning aristocrats, the poem having been published in the year of the first Reform Bill, and artisanal weavers: textiles were the first commodity whose production shifted to the factory system, with the result that during the 1830s 100,000 weavers were thrown out of work in cotton alone. An aristocratic woman weaving and singing was in 1832 a deeply topical object of nostalgia.

That the poem's summary figure for these defeats should be the silencing of a singing voice suggests the force that song had in the nineteenth century as a synecdoche for traditional society, and hence lyric's importance in the period as the principal genre in which traditional song was mediated. The modernity of 'The Lady of Shalott', however, is that unlike the work of Wordsworth, Scott or Moore, it does not claim to be such a mediation; the topic of its narrative is indeed mediation's impossibility. The Lady's corpse at the close does not in any sense preserve or make legible her song or her mode of life; these are on the contrary represented as irrecoverable. The poem's claim to continuity with the objects of its nostalgia is considerably more equivocal, and can be located by a certain generic instability.

Although 'The Lady of Shalott' is a narrative poem, lines 1–68 unfold in a continuous present tense; they verge, therefore, on descriptive lyric, and indeed the narrative is slowed by description throughout the poem. Here are the opening lines as Tennyson revised them for a second edition in 1842:

> On either side the river lie
> Long fields of barley and of rye,
> That clothe the wold and meet the sky;
> And through the field the road runs by
> To many-towered Camelot;
> And up and down the people go,

Gazing where the lilies blow
Round an island there below,
The island of Shalott.

(ll. 1–9)

These lines, like most of the poem's first two parts, describe the landscape around the Lady's tower on the island of Shalott. In the poem's supernatural plot, the Lady will fall under a curse if she looks out of her tower at this landscape. Her defence against the curse is to remain in her tower, observing the outside world only in a mirror, and weaving continuously – the 1832 version specifies that the weaving itself defends against the curse. Passages of description like the one I have just quoted thus refer in the first instance to a sight forbidden to the Lady.

What the Lady weaves, however, is what she sees in her mirror – which means that these lines, like all of the descriptive passages in the first two parts of the poem, refer not only to the world as it exists outside the tower but also to its reflection inside, and to the representation of that reflection in the Lady's web. They thus refer at once to a frame and to its contents, to objects and to their mediation, in a recursiveness I have characterized as typical of Tennyson's work. The significance of that structure here is that in representing at once the image and its frame, this poem at once represents the Lady's defence – her web – and the forbidden sight against which it defends her. As there is a structural analogy between the poem's mimetic work and that of the Lady's weaving, we can see the poem's tendency to descriptive lyric, like the Hesperides' song, as itself embodying a defence. Like that song, lyric here defends against narrative, or, to eschew formalism, against historical change. But the double reference of the poem's lyrical descriptions to the Lady's web *and* to the object whose sight it wards off suggests that the antithesis between the defence and the object is not secure. These descriptions aim at once to make the object present and to make it absent: a contradiction whose historical meaning is the ambiguity of Victorian print-lyric's relation to the earlier lyric modes it mediates.

III

I have already noted the unique prominence of descriptive lyric in European and American lyric poetry from the late eighteenth century on. In English, this prominence appears in retrospect to have been determined by the overwhelming influence of Wordsworth, though his 'Lines Written a Few Miles Above Tintern Abbey . . .' (1798), the most influential descriptive lyric in English, was historically part of a larger cultural trend in which other poets such as William Lisle Bowles, Coleridge and Charlotte Smith also participated. By the Victorian era, however, Wordsworth's influence on descriptive lyric was paramount, both in its own right and as refracted through Keats, Shelley, and the Byron of *Childe Harold's Pilgrimage* and 'The Prisoner of Chillon'.

A crucial test for my claim that Victorian lyric is best understood as belonging to a first moment of total mediation by print is posed by the case of John Clare. Clare's greatest celebrity predates our period, coming in the early 1820s, after the publication of his hugely successful *Poems Descriptive of Rural Life and Scenery* (1820). Clare's early models were found in eighteenth-century Georgic, beginning with James Thomson, and he appeared in print as himself a Georgic figure, identified on his title page as 'A Northamptonshire Peasant'. During the 1820s and early 1830s, however, Clare read and met his poetic contemporaries; by 1832 he had assembled a collection entitled *The Midsummer Cushion*. Largely made up of descriptive lyrics, the collection was a critical departure both from his own earlier practice and from that of Wordsworth and Keats. *The Midsummer Cushion* as Clare wrote it remained unpublished until 1972, though in 1835 his publishers brought out a heavily edited selection under the title *The Rural Muse*.

As a self-educated field labourer, Clare was closer than any other poet I will discuss in this chapter to an oral culture of ballad and lyric, as references in his poetry, correspondence and prose writing demonstrate. But his poetry does not either in its models or in his ambitions for it belong to this culture. Clare's reading – indeed the fact that he could read at all – and his brief celebrity were equally phenomena that depended on print. The difficulties of Clare's entry into print, however, demonstrate with particular clarity the limits governing the field of print-lyric in the nineteenth century. The most salient of these is that it was organized around the figure of the author: witness F. T. Palgrave's *Golden Treasury* (1861), in which the totality of lyric up to the Victorian age was divided into the 'Books' of Shakespeare, Milton, Gray and Wordsworth (1964: xi). To achieve the dignity of print in 1861, a lyric needed, if only in retrospect, to be suffused by the spirit of an author.

The central fact of Clare's life as a writer is that he was excluded by his class position from endowing his works with the full dignity of authorship. He was denied, on the one hand, the privilege of *withdrawal* from his text, and, on the other, that of presumptive *control* over it. Hence the particularity of Clare's identification in his first book as a 'peasant poet'; hence also his publisher's normalization throughout his career of grammar, spelling, versification and, most particularly, regional dialect and nomenclature. The contradictions that follow from the conditions of Clare's original entry into print remain today: to be true to what Clare wrote, modern editions print transcriptions of his manuscripts. In thus presenting his text unmodified by the print conventions of either his time or ours, Clare's editors treat him, as Hugh Haughton and Adam Phillips note, as if he were 'not "of" print' (1994: 20). Even as it rectifies it, this presentation ratifies the exclusion his writing suffered in his lifetime.

The 1835 volume was the last Clare published. From 1837 for all but a few months until his death in 1864, he was confined at the expense of his patrons to institutions for the insane. Even more than in his earlier poetry, Clare's capacity to endow his writing with authorship is in these years starkly open to question. Much of the poetry he wrote while institutionalized survives only in transcripts by the superintendent of the Northamptonshire General Asylum. Some of it, like the rambling medleys *Child Harold* and *Don Juan*, may have been written while Clare believed himself to be Byron. His output includes lyrics in Scottish dialect in the manner of Burns. Other poems, including perhaps his best-known lyric 'I am', have as their explicit theme the hidden, minimal nature of the identity they represent. Though all of these are chronologically Victorian poems, they were for historically specific reasons unpublishable as such during the Victorian era.

The characteristic topic of lyric in the nineteenth century is mediation; in the case of descriptive lyric it is the mediation of the visual image. The pattern is set by 'Tintern Abbey', whose topic is the mediation of the sights confronting the poet by other terms – memory, consciousness, language and finally another person, the poem's addressee. The descriptive lyrics composed by Clare in the 1820s and 1830s, however, have different concerns. They aim above all at minute fidelity to visual detail; here, for instance, are some lines from 'The Nightingales Nest' (1832):

> How curious is the nest no other bird
> Uses such loose materials or weaves
> Their dwelling in such spots – dead oaken leaves
> Are placed without and velvet moss within
> And little scraps of grass . . .
> The nest is made an hermits mossy cell
> Snug lie her curious eggs in number five
> Of deadend green or rather olive brown
> And the old prickly thorn bush guards them well.
>
> (ll. 76–80, 88–91)

Though the nightingale is celebrated as a songbird, in this poem she falls silent precisely because the poet has come close enough to see her eggs and nest so clearly:

> How subtle is the bird she started out
> And raised a plaintive note of danger nigh
> Ere we were past the brambles and now near
> Her nest she suddn stops – as choking fear
> That might betray her home.
>
> (ll. 57–61)

There is in this poem no claim, as in 'Tintern Abbey', to totalize a 'mighty world / Of eye, and ear' (ll. 105–6); the poem does not claim to work as a mediator in which sight and sound coexist as forms of a single whole. The bird's fame as a singer is belied by her appearance; the poet marvels that she has 'no better dress than russet brown' (l. 21). More generally, the poem dramatizes the discontinuities, first of speaking and hearing – one must 'hush' to hear the nightingale – and finally of hearing and seeing: the nest and eggs can be seen only at the cost of silencing the bird. The poem itself appears sometimes to represent speech and sometimes to represent an image, incorporating the discontinuity of sight and sound as a discontinuity in its own mode.

Clare's poem is thus not organized by the topics of mediation and totalization that dominate nineteenth-century lyric; this fact is historically determined by the inassimilable quality of his work to the medium of commodified print in which lyric actually was undergoing totalization when he wrote. As the nineteenth century progressed, lyric came with increasing self-consciousness to reflect on its own mediated character; as we have seen in 'The Lady of Shalott', representation of the mediation of visual images is one form of this reflection. 'The Lady of Shalott' also offers an early example of how in Victorian poetry *un*mediated visual experience is increasingly represented as petrifying or shattering.

Even when the images represented in Tennyson's early descriptive poetry do not – as in 'The Lady of Shalott' – turn out already to be representations, they can be so overloaded with detail as to draw attention to the mediating artifice of the poem and so also function to represent representation. When Tennyson compares the waterfalls in 'The Lotos-Eaters' (1832) to 'Slow-dropping veils of thinnest lawn' (l. 11), the simile at once mediates the object and refers to its own work of mediation. The tendency to represent the image as already a mediation, or as self-veiling, is in general deeply characteristic of Victorian lyric. A central instance is Matthew Arnold's 'Dover Beach', probably written between 1849 and 1851, though not published until 1867. More than Tennyson's poetry, Arnold's looks back to Wordsworth for its formal models. Like 'Tintern Abbey', 'Dover Beach' describes a place it specifies by name – a poetic commonplace in 1798, but more unusual fifty years later; also like 'Tintern Abbey', it combines the descriptive and dramatic modes. Most crucially, it derives from Wordsworth its organizing antithesis of sight and sound – rendered more acute here than in the earlier poem – with the recurring Wordsworthian term 'gleam' appearing and vanishing at the outset to signal the extinction of Wordsworth's visionary project.

'Dover Beach' begins with the description of a view:

> The sea is calm tonight.
> The tide is full, the moon lies fair
> Upon the Straits; on the French coast the light
> Gleams and is gone; the cliffs of England stand,
> Glimmering and vast, out in the tranquil bay.
>
> (ll. 1–5)

But it turns on a line of invitation – 'Come to the window, sweet is the night air' – to describe instead the sound by which the view is accompanied: 'the grating roar / Of pebbles which the waves draw back, and fling, / At their return, up the high strand', a sound which the first stanza closes by describing as an 'eternal note of sadness' (ll. 6–14). At the heart of the discontinuity between the view of the calm sea and the sound of the waves is the contrast between the sound's continuity and the periodicity of the full tide, caused by the moon whose equally periodic light it reflects. To these contrasting elements of the scene the poem's speaker attaches contrasting affective responses, suggesting that the luminous calm it presents to the eye is only a temporary appearance that masks the sadness suggested by the perpetual sound of the pebbles grating on the beach.

The claim that the calm of the poem's setting is an illusion becomes the dominant strain of its argument. By its last lines the calm sea and the moonlight are merely forms of appearance that make the world *seem* 'like a land of dreams' (l. 31) and so conceal a reality in which we see nothing at all. The poem's relation both to the visual image with which it begins and to visual images in general is thus profoundly antithetical: in its culminating figuration of the world as it really is, though there are sounds to hear, there is despite appearances no light to see by: 'we are here as on a darkling plain / Swept with confused alarms of struggle and flight' (ll. 35–6).

The force of this argument is not simply to prefer sound to sight; it is more accurately to prefer an allegorical scene to the one in which the poem is set and which it begins by describing. In this sense, 'Dover Beach' is an anti-descriptive lyric; it is also anti-descriptive in the sense that it works to allegorize the description with which it began. This work is clearest at the opening of the third stanza, where the sea actually confronting the speaker suggests an allegorical image: 'The Sea of Faith / Was once, too, at the full, and round earth's shore / Lay like the folds of a bright girdle furled' (ll. 21–3). These lines touch on one of Arnold's recurring themes, the historicity of religions. In the Catholic church of the Middle Ages, despite its belief in its own permanence and universality, the forces of historical change were constantly at work; faith is thus not only a social phenomenon that appears and disappears on a periodic basis, but also one that, even when at the full, conceals the real conditions of its own existence. Hence the refiguration of the sea as a garment. The most striking feature of this movement of the poem is that it uses the allegorical image to demystify the literal one. The seductions of the visual image are exposed to critique when the image is made into an allegory of religion; only as allegory does its real nature appear.

I began my reading by noting the antithesis of sight and sound in 'Dover Beach', and have suggested that up to a point the poem privileges sound over the visual image. While the poem's third stanza is devoted to demystifying its own initial presentation of a visual image, its initial presentation of the accompanying sound as an 'eternal note of sadness' is not subjected to the same kind of critique. Rather, it is echoed by a response attributed to Sophocles, whose tragedy is by no means so decisively relegated to the past as the faith of the third stanza. Hellenic Greece, tragedy and sound are thus aligned in the poem as privileged terms in a series of binary oppositions; their derogated counterparts are the Christian Middle Ages, comedy and the visual image. The series can be extended to include masculinity (Sophocles, the pebbles) as a further privileged term and femininity (the moon, the sea, the church) as a derogated one. By making this extension we see the logic of the poem's dramatic situation, in which a male speaker interprets the scene to a silent addressee, presumably a woman.

That said, however, the privilege granted the first terms in these oppositions is only relative; the argument of the poem as a whole subordinates both the visual and the aural elements of the description with which it opens to an allegorical schema. The sights and sounds of the poem's setting are discovered to be forms of appearance that allegorize the real conflicts organizing the scene of its utterance; space does not permit a full account of these here, but they certainly include the conflict of a man and a woman hinted at by the poem's dramatic situation as well as the conflict of pagan and Christian philosophy. Its final lines aim to mediate these conflicts by framing them in a single allegorical image. Here, sound is not privileged over sight; rather, the antithesis of sight and sound is resolved into unintelligibility on both sides, and so allegorizes the poem's final view of all the other conflicts it stages. The final image of the poem, the negative mediation of all the conflicting terms it has previously invoked, subordinates them all to an ironic view of history. It derives from a passage in Thucydides' *History of the Peloponnesian War*, one that for Arnold had associations with his father, Thucydides' translator, with John Henry Newman, who had been received as a Catholic in 1845, and with his Radical friend Arthur Clough. The concluding image of 'Dover Beach' signifies among other things Arnold's equivocal rejection of the various commitments these men represented to him.

Matthew Arnold belonged to the last generation of British poets for whom poetic learning necessarily meant learning in the classical languages. The poetry of his somewhat younger contemporaries D. G. Rossetti and William Morris also makes self-conscious displays of learning, but principally in the literature of the European vernaculars. One reason for this innovation is the incorporation into print of this literature's historical archive, which only in the nineteenth century becomes a systematic project. Rossetti's and Morris's poetry was made possible by this project, to which they also contributed. Both poets were influenced at a very early age by reading Malory, who received his first modern edition in 1816. In the sphere of the lyric, Rossetti's influential translations of fourteenth-century Italian poetry (1861) included a bibliography of the modern editions he had used; his equally influential translations of Villon relied on the first complete edition of the French poet's works, published in 1849.

The appearance during the nineteenth century of critical editions and translations of vernacular poetry and the erosion in the latter part of the century of the special distinction accorded to classical models should both be recognized as aspects of a single development: the invention of secular, vernacular literature as an object of critical and historical study, with editorial and pedagogical practices initially modelled on those which since the Renaissance had governed study of the classics. Literary lyric in English at mid-nineteenth century had for four hundred years been a field organized by the mediation into print of Greek and Latin lyric on the one hand, and on the other of vernacular song. The poem's staging of its relation to these antithetical models became the most basic level of its meaning. After mid-century, however, this organizing antithesis appears to collapse, both its terms having been fully incorporated into print. The rise in status that vernacular lyric undergoes in the nineteenth century is thus accompanied in Britain by its decisive separation from practices of oral invention and performance with which it had hitherto been print culture's major point of contact.

By the 1860s, British lyric poetry displays a new sense of confronting the prior history of lyric as a totality, a sense which I have argued results from confronting it in print. Perhaps the most compelling evidence for this shift is provided by the poetry of Swinburne, which like D. G. Rossetti's seeks models in European lyric and in English song forms, while adding to these influences systematic reference to the Greek lyric poets, Sappho above all. Even the return to what might be called folk-motifs which appears in the poetry of the 1880s and 1890s unfolds with frequent ironic reference to the same motifs' appearance in classical poetry. Thomas Hardy's poems afford a case in point, but the most salient instance is the poetry of A. E. Housman.

Housman's lyrics collected in *A Shropshire Lad* (1896) adopt the persona of a Shropshire yeoman, and frame in a series of lapidary utterances a tissue of allusions that includes folk-songs, the entire literary tradition of English lyric including dialect poets like William Barnes, and Latin lyric, especially that of Horace and Propertius. The lyrics are often descriptive in mode, but the landscapes they describe are thoroughly allegorical: Housman's poems do not, like 'Dover Beach' or 'Tintern Abbey', stage a dialectic of image and mediation; here the image is already fully mediated. One could no more visit the places named in Housman's Shropshire than one could visit Horace's Sabine farm; Housman stages in his poems the obliteration by time of places and things that names refer to, leaving behind a world that exists only in books. When he began composing the poems he had never been to Shropshire; a major source for the entire cycle was Murray's *Handbook of Shropshire and Cheshire* (1879).

The drama of poem 31, as of many in the cycle, is the relation of present and past; the poem begins by presenting a series of images of named places at a particular moment and season:

> On Wenlock edge the wood's in trouble;
> His forest fleece the Wrekin heaves;
> The gale, it plies the saplings double,
> And thick on Severn snow the leaves.
>
> (ll. 1–4)

On the one hand, the autumn gale that blows through this scene signifies change and the approach of winter. It blows down the leaves that constitute the medium in which its effects appear; it is so violent that it will itself not last long: 'The gale, it plies the saplings double, / It blows so hard, 'twill soon be gone' (ll. 17–18). It signifies not merely change of what is present, but something in the present that is not fully present; that is why the poem is set in autumn, a liminal season, constituted by the recollection of summer and the anticipation of winter: already, the leaves are falling like snow. On the other hand, though it brings change, the autumn gale has returned in the same way to Wenlock and the Wrekin since before they bore their names, and before these woods were standing:

> 'Twould blow like this through holt and hanger
> When Uricon the city stood:
> 'Tis the old wind in the old anger,
> But then it threshed another wood.
>
> (ll. 5–8)

The wind signifies something that recurs in the same way from one era to another, but that cannot appear in a visual image. What the poem assigns to the field of the visual belongs strictly to the particular moment of its utterance in the present tense. As a descriptive lyric, it excludes from representation the very thing that is none the less its topic: the wind whose recurrence from the past is the ground of the speaker's ultimate identification with a Roman who might have stood in the same place and the same wind centuries earlier. This identification generates the *memento mori* with which the poem ends: 'Today the Roman and his trouble / Are ashes under Uricon' (ll. 19–20).

The crux of Housman's poem is thus to identify this trace from the past that recurs in the present, and so is never either fully past or sufficiently present to become an object of representation. The solution to this crux is found not in the poem's images, but in the language that mediates them. Its germ appears to have been the account in Murray's *Handbook* of the Wrekin, in whose name, Murray writes, 'the name of Vr-ikon, "City of Iconium", whose ashes smoulder beneath its slopes, is virtually enshrined' (quoted by Archie Burnett in Housman 1997: 342). Though everything in the visual image is transient, the landscape is none the less haunted by the past through the names it bears. Other words in the poem also emphasize the temporal existence of language; 'holt' and 'hanger' of line 5 both survive unchanged from Old English; 'holt' according to the *OED* in 1899 had passed out of standard usage into dialect and poetry. 'Ply' as a verb (ll. 3, 17) is similarly marked as surviving only rarely or in dialect from a history that extends back to Middle English. Housman's poem is thus rich in dialect words which, rather than marking a geographical location, effect a temporal dislocation and stage the haunting of the present by the traces of the past.

This dislocated time and not the evanescent time of the visual image is in fact the poem's setting. In so far as it is one where past and present coexist, the place the poem represents cannot be seen in Shropshire or anywhere else, but is embodied only in the lexicon. Housman's dialect words, in dramatic contrast to Clare's sixty years earlier, appear in his poems not as the token of a specific regional origin – and hence of a marginal class identity – but rather as a form of scholarship. Far from setting his poetry at the margins of print culture, they locate it at one of its centres.

IV

In my earlier discussion of lyric and print I read the Victorian convention by which lyric utterance comes into being in dialectical relation to or as the memorial of a silent voice as an historical allegory. In this allegory the silenced characters are typically women, like the singer whose alien music Wordsworth recalls in 'The Solitary Reaper'. We should not interpret the proliferation of women who are mute, dead or exist only as images in Victorian lyric as reflecting a reality in which women did not write lyric. Throughout the nineteenth century women's entry into the whole field of print remained fraught with difficulty, but the general trend was to increased participation. This is particularly true of poetry, where from the end of the Napoleonic wars women attained new visibility as authors, editors and members of the reading public. This new visibility is most importantly ratified with respect to lyric poetry by the vogue for illustrated annuals that extended from the late 1820s to the 1850s. The annuals had lyric as their principal literary component, and were produced with a female readership in mind, predominantly by women authors and editors (Reynolds 1995: xxv–xxvii).

That said, the self-understanding in terms of gender that structures much of Victorian lyric posed distinct problems – as well as offering certain affordances – to women who wrote in the genre. If in this self-understanding lyric utterance comes into being in relation to a mute woman, the female poet writing lyric may experience an identification that makes this muteness in some sense her own. Victorian lyrics by women constitute a distinct sub-genre from those written by men in part because they respond to different precursors – most notably Felicia Hemans and Letitia Landon (L. E. L.), the major women poets of the 1820s and 1830s – and in part because, even in so far as they entered the same generic field as male-authored lyrics, they did so from a different position. In the gendered allegory that structures the field, the unmediated song of which the print-lyric is the mediated effect or trace is characteristically figured as a woman's. This convention affected the position actual women were understood to occupy in relation to lyric when they appeared as writers, and in so doing also affected the kinds of lyric they actually produced.

Consider for instance Christina Rossetti's early lyric 'When I am dead, my dearest':

> When I am dead, my dearest,
>   Sing no sad songs for me;
> Plant thou no roses at my head,
>   Nor shady cypress tree:
> Be the green grass above me
>   With showers and dewdrops wet;
> And if thou wilt, remember,
>   And if thou wilt, forget.
>   (1850; ll. 1–8)

A reading of this poem must proceed by a series of reversals. To begin with, it is best understood as a pointed response to the male lyricism that takes its stand over a woman's grave; in asking that she not be memorialized by songs or flowers, the poem's speaker rejects what we have seen to be recurring Victorian figures for lyric production. To reject these figures, however, Rossetti has herself written a lyric; the double-sided character of this gesture is most apparent in the second stanza, with the appearance of another conse-crated figure for lyric in the speaker's anticipation that, in death, she 'will not hear the nightingale / Sing on, as if in pain' (ll. 10–11). Here the poem mentions the nightingale only to deny that the speaker will hear it; and invokes the anthropomorphism that makes its song an expression of pain, only to demystify it.

The double gesture of repeating and rejecting lyric's organizing figures, especially those having to do with gender, is at the centre of this poem. As much as any other I have con-sidered, it constitutes itself in relation to a mute woman; rather than figuring itself as a man's utterance for or about a woman after her death, this poem figures itself as a woman's proleptic speaking for her dead self. In a more concentrated way than any other lyric we have discussed it at once represents an utterance and its memorial; its double temporal-ity is emphasized by the fact that the poem's manuscript includes three opening stanzas framing it as the utterance of a girl now dead.

In Christina Rossetti the general character of Victorian print lyric as a form with a double relation to its own past is given a particularly literalizing turn. 'When I am dead, my dearest' is the representation at once of a voice and of the memory of a voice. A similar and in some ways stranger effect is produced by lyrics like the sonnet 'After Death' (1849), which represent themselves as actually spoken by dead women. These utterances embody an impossible temporality, in which a voice belonging to the past appears in the present to describe its own passing. Even Rossetti's many devotional lyrics, though they do not usually present such complex dramatic situations as those on erotic themes, often take up eschatological topics in ways that produce striking temporal dislocations.

The dialectics of past and present, of speech and silence, that organize much Victorian lyric thus assume a particularly subjective form in Rossetti's poems, where they are often staged by the double positioning of a female speaker. Precisely because for Victorian lyric in general, the figuration of a mute woman is so characteristic an allegory of the poem's mediating work, in lyrics by women the relation of the poem to speech or song is a problem very often posed in relation to a single subject, rather than for instance in a dramatic mode. To close this section, I will consider some of the political possibilities this tendency opened up, with reference to the work of Elizabeth Barrett Barrett (E. B. B., as she continued to sign herself after becoming Elizabeth Barrett Browning).

E. B. B. was the most various and experimental of the major Victorian poets. Even in the genre of lyric, her output resists generalization. It includes for instance the early descriptive lyrics 'The Deserted Garden' and 'A Sea-Side Walk', both published in 1838 and showing the influences of Wordsworth and early Tennyson. I will focus here, however, on two of her most distinctive lyrics (outside the *Sonnets from the Portuguese*), the political poems 'The Cry of the Children' (1843) and 'A Curse for a Nation' (1856). Both of these lyrics, particularly the latter, explicitly dramatize the poet's struggle to give utterance, and both have as a central question the power of poetic utterance to produce real effects. In this respect, they are the principal Victorian successors to the Romantic odes, especially Shelley's 'Ode to the West Wind'. Only Swinburne's *Songs Before Sunrise* (1871), itself strongly influenced by E. B. B., takes up as effectively the legacy of Shelley's Radical poetics.

The central problem of both poems is to represent a group whose oppression has excluded them from effective political utterance. To speak on behalf of such a group is to claim a privilege from which they are excluded. To represent the specificity of the kind of oppression with which these poems are concerned is to represent a silence, a place in political discourse where something is missing. This is in fact the movement of both poems, in which spoken utterances are in different ways self-undoing. 'The Cry of the Children' is addressed to the speaker's 'brothers' (l. 1) – and there is reason to think the speaker is male as well as the poem's addressees – exhorting them and us to listen to the child factory-workers whose exploitation was at the time a major public scandal. As the poem progresses, the children do speak – but they speak without hope, longing for death, and refusing to pray to a God whom they imagine in the image of a factory-owner. Only in the final stanza does the children's speech point beyond itself, and also beyond the utterance in which it is framed, to another wordless utterance that is the true burden of the poem: 'the child's sob in the silence curses deeper / Than the strong man in his wrath' (ll. 155–6). The result of the speech represented in the poem is at length a silence in which a child's sob can be heard.

The gendering of the dialectic of speech and silence is only implicit in 'The Cry of the Children', where the speaker and auditors appear to be male and the only figure specifically gendered as female is the dead child Alice. In the later 'A Curse for a Nation', however, the question of whether a woman can speak in a lyric is explicitly at issue. The poem is an attack on American slave-owners, and was written at the request of Boston abolitionists to be published in their journal the *Liberty Bell* in 1856. In a strict sense, this is a poem without a speaker, since it presents itself as a text written to be sent away for publication, so that 'all may read' (l. 50). As a written text, however, it incorporates transcriptions of a series of spoken utterances, beginning with the very command to write:

> I heard an angel speak last night,
> And he said 'Write!
> Write a Nation's curse for me,
> And send it over the Western Sea.'
> (ll. 1–4)

Moreover, when it appears, the curse itself is from beginning to end one that falls on speech:

> Ye shall watch while strong men draw
> The nets of feudal law
>   To strangle the weak,
> And, counting the sin for a sin,
> Your soul shall be sadder within
> Than the word ye shall speak.
>   This is the curse. Write.
>
> When good men are praying erect
> That Christ may avenge his elect
>   And deliver the earth,
> The prayer in your ears, said low,
> Shall sound like the tramp of a foe
> That's driving you forth.
>   This is the curse. Write.
> (ll. 85–98)

Addressed to the American people, these stanzas recognize that as a republic the United States has broken what E. B. B. represents as the feudal net of hereditary and clerical privilege in which Britain and much of Europe remain enmeshed. But the curse they impose is that, because of slavery, the new republic can neither speak nor hear clearly. Though its people can see the oppression of the weak in Europe, their speech will be muted by the shame of slavery. And owing to slavery, the prayers of good people will sound in American ears like a threat.

The curse culminates in a stanza enjoining Americans from seeking themselves to curse the ill-deeds of others:

> Recoil from clenching the curse
> Of God's witnessing Universe
> With a curse of yours.
> THIS is the curse. Write.
>   (ll. 116–19)

As Dorothy Mermin has written, the curse on Americans is that they must recoil from cursing, as any curse they uttered would only clench the curse on them (1989: 234). The curse thus silences those on whom it falls by transforming every utterance they make, and indeed every utterance they hear, into its own reiteration.

The curse of slavery – and indeed of oppression in general – as E. B. B. represents it here is that it corrupts and hollows out the language that might be used to denounce it. In this respect, the end of the poem is foreshadowed by the beginning. If Americans are at the end of the poem prevented from cursing 'ill-doers' abroad, it is because the curse would recoil on their own ill-deeds. So at the outset of the poem, the poet herself refuses the injunction to write the curse – first, because Americans are her brothers, and second, because, seeing the injustices practised in her own nation, she cannot curse another. These grounds of refusal imply E. B. B.'s awareness that the curse she pronounces recoils on her, both as an American sympathizer in politics and as a Briton. This awareness is represented in the poem's very form: if, as we have seen, the burden of the curse is that those on whom it falls will hear it in the voices of others, and will themselves be bound to repeat it, then we can see why the action of the poem is precisely the hearing and repeating of the curse by the poet herself. No more than those to whom she transmits it does she claim to escape it.

Except that, as I have said, the curse is throughout represented as bearing on speech. And the poem does not represent E. B. B. as speaking the curse, or even properly as uttering it, but rather as its mute transcriber. The refrain of the curse itself repeatedly recalls this: 'This is the curse. Write.' For the task of transcription, the poet is selected above all because she is a woman: 'To curse, choose men', she protests, 'For I, a woman, have only known / How the heart melts and the tears run down.' To which the angel's response comes, '"Therefore," the voice said, "shalt thou write / My curse tonight"' (ll. 38–42). The poem thus aligns the silent work of transcription with a femininity that is characterized not by cursing or by any other form of speech but by melting and tears. While this work mediates the utterance of a male voice, an utterance that for all its power knows that it cannot escape its own critique, it does not do so without leaving on it a trace. While the angel refers to the curse he speaks as 'my curse' he also describes it as coming 'from the depths of womanhood / . . . very salt, and bitter, and good' (ll. 47–8). Even as the poem mediates a man's spoken utterance, it figures its work of mediation as producing a text with a taste – of tears, or of blood: of the body's unmediated expression. This taste is the poem's summary figure for the place of a mute, female grief that works in this utterance while remaining distinct from it. It is also the basis of the identification E. B. B. claims with the slave women whose part she takes, whose own weeping and cursing remains unheard in the public discussion her poem both joins and critiques.

V

I close with E. B. B.'s 'A Curse for a Nation' because it provides a critical instance of my thesis in this chapter and also marks its limit. The allegorical nature of this poem's references to voice – and, consequently, to its antithesis, writing – is clearer than in any other I have discussed. The voices that speak in this poem enter a circuit of lyric address that crosses the Atlantic and appears in the last stanza to be literally universal. In this circuit, speakers in widely distinct places hear one another, and respond to what they hear by modifying their own utterances out of fear, shame or anger. In the nineteenth century such a circulation of addresses can only be an allegory for utterances mediated by print; it is thus the argument of E. B. B.'s poem that print lyric (or at least, lyric in the elevated, public mode of her own) constitutes a single totality – in effect, that it can in its entirety be reduced to the reiteration of a single utterance, which she names a curse.

This totality is a curse because it is constituted by a single systematic set of exclusions. These are allegorized as writing, which here figures a silent work of mediation, whose property is itself to elude mediation, to disappear. It is a work aligned with women's work, and slaves'; if the poem exposes its traces, it none the less does not bring it into its field of representation.

For my purposes, then, the double force of 'A Curse for a Nation' is, first, that it provides an image for what I have been arguing is the newly totalized field of print lyric, and second, that it defines this field's limits. I will not pursue any further E. B. B.'s political version of this argument; I will rather close with a literary-historical note on the appearance of totality newly offered by print-lyric in the Victorian era. In this appearance, print-lyric was able to incorporate the totality of its own antecedents, becoming the medium for a coherent summing up of its own history. Such an appearance can only be sustained by innumerable omissions and forgettings, as we can see by the prominence of fragments in the lyric canon.

This prominence reflects the uniquely central role anthologies have played in lyric canon formation. The obverse of the anthology's power to constitute a genre as a totality by establishing the shared traits of the texts it incorporates is precisely its tendency to make them into fragments even as it does so. The anthology's work of historical recovery is also a work of erasure; the connections it promotes among its texts are not established in a vacuum, but more or less deliberately overwrite the traces in those texts of other contexts in which they have already circulated. Palgrave's *Golden Treasury* thus prints songs from Shakespeare's plays as separate lyrics, supplying them with titles to reinforce their appearance as distinct, complete poems. Similarly, an address to Asia from Shelley's *Prometheus Unbound* appears on its own, retitled 'Hymn to the Spirit of Nature'.

As soon as we step outside the field of lyric itself, we can see that its character as an assemblage of fragments was clear in perspectives available to the Victorians. Matthew Arnold's career as a serious lyric poet came to an end in the early 1850s; subsequently, he wrote narrative poetry and tragedy and eventually largely gave up poetry for criticism. The crucial document of this development is the preface Arnold wrote for the 1853 edition of his *Poems*; though it does not frame its case in these terms, the preface is a polemic against lyric's dominance in the Victorian hierarchy of poetic genres. To make this polemic Arnold goes to Aristotle's *Poetics* for his definition of poetry as the imitation of an action. From this definition it follows that his examples of good poetic practice largely come from tragedy; to the excellence of Greek tragedies considered as wholes, Arnold contrasts the poetry of his own day, whose incoherence he attributes to a criticism that values the fragment over the totality:

> We have poems which seem to exist merely for the sake of single lines and passages; not for the sake of producing any total impression. We have critics who seem to direct their attention merely to detached expressions, to the language about the action, not to the action itself. . . . They will permit the poet to select any action he pleases, and to suffer that action to go as it will, provided he gratifies them with occasional bursts of fine writing, and with a shower of isolated thoughts and images.

Arnold's horror of the isolated and the fragmentary in literature is of a piece with a life-long view only developed in his later criticism: that a coherent literary tradition at the centre of a common culture could counteract what he saw as the class conflict and subjective isolation characteristic of modernity. Even in the 1853 preface it is clear that for Arnold a fragmented poetry reflects a fragmented society, expressing what is personal and peculiar about the poet and not the 'elementary feelings' shared by all. His view of the atomizing effect of a poetics privileging the brilliant isolated thought or expression finds an echo in a very different literary register. From the beginning of the Victorian era to the present, a certain kind of picaresque hero in prose fiction is characterized by a facility in quotation – particularly from lyric poetry – so extreme that it amounts to a discursive pathology. Dick Swiveller, in Dickens's *The Old Curiosity Shop* (1840–1), might be the first of the type; distinguished twentieth-century instances are Dorothy L. Sayers's Peter Wimsey and P. G. Wodehouse's Bertie Wooster. All of these characters belong to the landed gentry or aristocracy, but they are none the less at odds with their class and family, of which they might be described as more or less severed limbs. They all live in the metropolis; two of them appear to have no relations but aunts. The class loyalties of each are significantly complicated by a style of life that includes working-class pastimes like music hall – in the cases of Wooster and Wimsey – and social relations, like Swiveller's engagement and marriage to a scullery-maid. Each of these characters, in short, is constructed on a principle of the comic conjunction of incongruous loyalties, habits and identifications. And in each case this principle finds expression in thinking and conversation represented as confused, fragmentary and arbitrarily associative – particularly when they involve quotation. All of these characters quote compulsively from a wide range of sources, but often from lyric. Bertie Wooster refers most often to Burns and Shakespeare, Wimsey to a more various and more recondite canon, extending at least through Housman. Dick Swiveller's references are for the most part to texts that had been set to music, some of them anthologized in collections of glees and drinking-songs, some found in the works of popular poets of the eighteenth and early nineteenth centuries – Byron, Moore, Anna Barbauld, among others.

In the fragmentary and heterogeneous citations of lyric that clutter these characters' discourse we can see a comic but none the less critical account from the novelist's point of view of print-lyric as a cultural phenomenon. In this account, lyric belongs, not to an entire society, but to a particularly conflicted male class fraction. And, far from imagining print-lyric as mediating the past, these novels represent their characters' compulsive recollections as signs of a disordered memory – one that 'does those things which it ought not to do and leaves undone the things it ought to have done' (Sayers 1978: 62), as Wimsey puts it, instantiating the fault he describes. None the less, lyric remains one of the two genres in which Victorian print culture claimed to mediate a social totality, incorporating all classes and a history from which nothing needed to be erased. It seems appropriate to close with a critique of that claim from the other such genre, that of the novel.

See also: SONNET AND SONNET SEQUENCE; THE MARKET.

REFERENCES AND FURTHER READING

Arnold, Matthew (1960) 'Preface to the First Edition of *Poems* (1853).' In R. H. Super (ed.). *The Complete Prose Works of Matthew Arnold* (I, 1–15). Ann Arbor: University of Michigan Press.

Arnold, Matthew (1979) *The Poems of Matthew Arnold*. Eds Kenneth Allott and Miriam Allott. London: Longman.

Browning, Elizabeth Barrett (1988) *Selected Poems*. Ed. Margaret Forster. Baltimore: Johns Hopkins University Press.

Browning, Robert (1981) *The Poems*. Eds John Pettigrew and Thomas J. Collins. New Haven: Yale University Press.

Clare, John (1984) *John Clare*. Eds Eric Robinson and David Powell. Oxford: Oxford University Press.

Haughton, Hugh, and Adam Phillips (1994) 'Introduction: Relocating John Clare.' In Hugh Haughton, Adam Phillips and Geoffrey Summerfield (eds). *John Clare in Context* (pp. 1–27). Cambridge: Cambridge University Press.

Housman, A. E. (1997) *The Poems of A. E. Housman*. Ed. Archie Burnett. Oxford: Oxford University Press.

Kant, Immanuel (1952) *The Critique of Judgment*. Trans. J. C. Meredith. Oxford: Oxford University Press.

Langbaum, Robert (1971) *The Poetry of Experience: The Dramatic Monologue in Modern Literary Tradition*. Third edition. New York: Norton.

Mermin, Dorothy (1989) *Elizabeth Barrett Browning: The Origins of a New Poetry*. Chicago: University of Chicago Press.

Mill, John Stuart (1981) 'Thoughts On Poetry and its Varieties.' In J. M. Robson and Jack Stillinger (eds). *Collected Prose Works of John Stuart Mill* (I, 342–65). Toronto: University of Toronto Press.

Palgrave, Francis Turner (ed.) (1964) *The Golden Treasury of the Best Songs and Lyrical Poems in the English Language*. Fifth edition. London: Oxford University Press.

Reynolds, Margaret (1995) 'Introduction I.' In Angela Leighton and Margaret Reynolds (eds). *Victorian Woman Poets: An Anthology* (pp. xxv–xxxiv). Oxford: Blackwell.

Rossetti, Christina (1994) *Poems and Prose*. Ed. Jan Marsh. London: J. M. Dent.

Sayers, Dorothy L. (1978) *Gaudy Night*. London: NEL.

Tennyson, Alfred (1987). *Tennyson's Poems*. Ed. Christopher Ricks. Berkeley and Los Angeles: University of California Press.

Tucker, Herbert F. (1985) 'Dramatic Monologue and the Overhearing of Lyric.' In Chaviva Hosek and Patricia Parker (eds). *Lyric Poetry: Beyond the New Criticism* (pp. 226–43). Ithaca, N. Y.: Cornell University Press.

Wordsworth, William (1981). *The Poems*. Ed. John O. Hayden. New Haven: Yale University Press.

4

Dramatic Monologue

E. Warwick Slinn

The dramatic monologue is arguably the flagship genre of Victorian poetry. Widely regarded as the most significant poetic innovation of the age, it gained widespread use after the 1830s by an overwhelming range of poets, both male, from Alfred Tennyson to Algernon Swinburne, and female, from Felicia Hemans to Augusta Webster. Its use continued throughout the twentieth century, influencing poets, both British and American, from T. S. Eliot and Ezra Pound to Peter Porter and Richard Howard. It has been the focus for discussions about continuities, and discontinuities, between Victorian poetry and what went before (Langbaum 1957) or came after (Christ 1984); and it continued to attract scholarly attention when other forms of Victorian poetry were being neglected (Sessions 1947; Fuson 1948; Langbaum 1957). Being thoroughly immersed in the cultural conditions of its time – philosophical, psychological and political – it may also provide the best guide to what is Victorian about Victorian poetry. At the same time, while the poems were written in the nineteenth century, and talked about then as retrospective or psychological drama, the dramatic monologue is effectively a twentieth-century concept. Victorian poets used names such as 'dramatic lyrics', 'dramatic romances', 'lyrical monologues' or 'monodramas'. While, therefore, the term 'dramatic monologue' was first used by a poet, George Thornbury, in 1857, by a few reviewers in 1869 and 1871, and by Tennyson in 1886 (Culler 1975: 366), it was not until books on Tennyson in 1894 (Brooke) and Robert Browning in 1908 (Curry) that the form gained substantial recognition as a named genre. To contemplate the dramatic monologue is consequently to engage in a conscious act of critical retrospection, where the study of a historical phenomenon is concomitant with the constructions of modernist and postmodernist understanding. The result is a growing awareness in recent decades of the cultural significance of this generic explosion, of the ways in which it provided a medium, whether witting or unwitting, for multiple forms of cultural critique.

Genre

The dramatic monologue is a lyrical-dramatic-narrative hybrid. It absorbs an emotional expressiveness from lyrics, a speaker who is not the poet from drama, and elements of mimetic detail and retrospective structuring from narrative. This particular hybrid, which developed its recognizable features during the early Victorian period in the 1830s, followed several decades of destabilizing generic categories. In one sense, it was simply a natural development from the refashioning of old hybrids that Romantic poets had already begun, in the lyrical ballads of Wordsworth and Coleridge, or the lyrical drama of Byron and Shelley. In another sense, however, the move towards a poetry that overtly separated speaker from poet was a step away from the Romantic tendency to emphasize lyrical modes that indulged solitary self-expression – the ode, the hymn, the sonnet. A dramatized speaker is a way of avoiding the excesses of authorial self-absorption – or eluding gender constraints.

This triple mixing of genres almost guarantees a poetry of disjunctive effects. Narrative or mimetic detail, for instance, produces a sense of immediacy, of specificity in space and time, that undercuts the atemporal quality of pure lyricism, the illusion that a lyrical utterance takes place outside historical limits (Tucker 1985: 227). Also, while the dramatic monologue deliberately exploits the emphasis in lyrical writing upon a speaker's internalized and isolated subjectivity, it disrupts that isolation by placing the speaker in relationship to an auditor (an audience in the poem), whether actually present, or absent and imagined – or present and at the same time imagined. Acknowledged in most accounts of the form, and fundamental to the dramatic aspect of the hybrid (along with the 'drama-tized' speaker), the auditor is a key aspect of the Victorian contribution to monologues. Indeed, the term *auditor*, while accurately defining the non-speaking role of the audience as listener, suggests a passivity that belies the active agency of that presence. To the extent that speakers in monologues respond to the auditors, anticipating their objections, responding to their gestures or attempting to persuade them of the speaker's own efficacy and truth, the auditors play an active, if literally silent, role in the monologue. Obvious examples are Lucrezia in Robert Browning's 'Andrea del Sarto' (1855), whose wish to leave Andrea in order to join her lover focuses the whole occasion of the poem, and Gigadibs in Browning's 'Bishop Blougram's Apology' (1855), whose critical journalism is a sore provocation to the Bishop's intellectual sophistication. Better, I think, to refer to the audience as an *interlocutor*, a term that is also used and that acknowledges this active presence, pointing to the inherently intersubjective feature of what is otherwise too easily read as a merely intrasubjective drama. Even in a poem where there is no literal auditor, Browning's 'Soliloquy of the Spanish Cloister' (1842), Brother Lawrence dominates the speaker's mind to such an extent that he functions as a defining other, as an external presence who affects and shapes the speaker's every waking thought. Interlocutors may be represented by some form of functional substitute (a mirror in Webster's 'By the Looking-Glass', 1866, or self-images in 'A Castaway', 1870), and they are constituted more by the speaker's perceptions than by any separate reality. Nevertheless, they are a key element of the dramatic aspect of monologues that directs attention outwards to speakers' social contexts. Interlocutors provoke the paradox that dramatic monologues may not be mono-logues at all, but rather versions of what we have come to know, through the work of the Russian theorist Mikhail Bakhtin, as dialogism, where supposedly single voices are the repository of a plurality of voices, of conflicting interdiscursive practices (Nichols 1990). This cultural pluralism gives the genre a decidedly political edge.

The mixed features of the form (self-interested eloquence, verbal immediacy, mimetic detail, interlocutory intrusion) are rarely present in equal proportions. Nor are there any set structural – metrical, rhyme, stanzaic – requirements. Hence the genre is confounded by uncertain parameters, and attempts at tight formalist definition have usually foundered on a series of necessary qualifications. Ina Sessions provides the classic example. For her, a 'perfect' dramatic monologue contains 'speaker, audience, occasion, revelation of character, interplay between speaker and audience, dramatic action, and action which takes place in the present' (1947: 508), but her list is based on the three examples thought by most scholars to be generically pure – Robert Browning's 'My Last Duchess' (1842), 'Fra Lippo Lippi' and 'Andrea del Sarto' (1855). She then has to distinguish among others which are 'imperfect', 'formal' and 'approximate' (see also Sinfield's rejection of a similar list, 1977: 7–8). In 1957, Robert Langbaum's seminal study of monologues sought to elude the limits of such formalist taxonomy by emphasizing the genre's affective qualities, shifting attention from content to reader response, where he located a disequilibrium of sympathy and judgement as a distinguishing feature.

This attention to the reader's role is significant, since the genre's hybrid nature places extra demands on readers. Whereas most lyrical writing asks readers to play a relatively passive role, identifying with the poet, or in John Stuart Mill's famous formulation, 'overhearing' the speaker (Tucker 1985), the dynamic characteristics of the dramatic monologue, particularly those which separate speaker from poet and thence reader from speaker, demand that the reader be mentally active. The reader is required to stand back while being imaginatively engaged, to assess the speaker's qualities and arguments while simultaneously empathizing with the speaker's predicament. That double action on the part of the reader may lead to dramatic irony, understanding more than the speaker understands (realizing discrepancies or ethical lapses, or determining a moment when the implications of meaning confound rhetorical intent), as well as to Langbaum's tension of sympathy and judgement. 'Our interest's on the dangerous edge of things', says Browning's Bishop Blougram (l. 395), and that goes for readers of dramatic monologues as well. As speakers perform delicate balancing acts of verbal persuasion and self-display, readers watch transfixed, themselves balancing their admiration of an audacious quip with their disturbed sense of moral equivocation (or, in the case of stranglers and poisoners, worse). Langbaum has been criticized for overemphasizing sympathy (readers have complained that no one can sympathize with the wife-murdering Duke of Ferrara in 'My Last Duchess'), but while it is clear that Langbaum's universalizing of the reader requires qualification, his point is closer to sympathetic imagination, understanding unfamiliar perspectives, than to sympathy as fellow-feeling or moral support. Without understanding, speakers may be too easily dismissed, and the poem with them: 'My Last Duchess' as merely a poem about a repressive male aristocrat who murders spontaneity, both literally and figuratively. With sympathy and no analytical judgement, on the other hand, cultural critique or ironic limits may be missed: how nine hundred years of class decorum have forged a behavioural brittleness that becomes dependent on strict protocols and rigid control; how the Duke himself, and not just his painted Duchess, stands there 'as if alive'. Some critics have thought sympathetic imagination means an identification with the interlocutor rather than the speaker, substituting the reader for the internalized audience. But, taken literally, that would be to acquiesce in the limits of an auditor, to be absorbed (and silenced) by the speaker's rhetorical network. The reader's role is yet more complex, becoming the locus for an active and conscious production of meaning that delineates the qualities and limits of several layers of textual action – interlocutor, as well as author, speaker and language. In that process, the dramatic monologue is a form that requires the reader's discernment as a participating element, and Langbaum's humanist tension of sympathy and judgement may also be reconceived as a deconstructive tension between rhetoric and logic.

If Langbaum firmly established the dramatic monologue as a major genre for literary studies, he also confirmed earlier approaches which stressed the dramatization of character. That emphasis, however, had been attached to tacit humanist belief in the unmediated nature of human subjectivity, and this view was increasingly questioned during the late 1970s and 1980s, when monologue critics shifted attention from judgements about moral culpability to questions about the constructions of textual artifice. Ralph Rader in 1976 and Alan Sinfield in 1977, for example, almost simultaneously focus on the fiction–reality nexus. Sinfield argues that the dramatic monologue is an authorial 'feint' that 'sets up a fictional speaker whilst claiming for him, by use of the first person, real-life existence' (1977: 25). He then accounts for varying forms of monologues by claiming that they may rest anywhere between the extremes of confession, on the one hand, and drama, on the other – that is to say, between the authenticity of personal utterance, or authorial expression, and the artifice of fiction, or simulated character. Rader approaches this same continuum by dividing it among expressive lyrics, dramatic lyrics, dramatic monologues and mask lyrics. But Harold Bloom best highlights the problem of explaining how monologues could be both real and artifice, where all is finally artifice, when in 1979 he stresses the role of rhetoric in Robert Browning's poetry. His definition of the 'true center' in reading Browning remains a provocative beginning for any discussion of monologue theory: 'The problems of rhetoric – of our being incapable of knowing what is literal and what is figurative where all, in a sense, is figurative – and of psychology – is there a self that is not trope or an effect of verbal persuasion? – begin to be seen as one dilemma' (1979: 2). This claim by Bloom for the inseparability of character and language became part of a general move by critics to view speakers as invented selves, not just in the sense of poetic fictions, but in the sense that the fictive selves in monologues represent the fictive inventions and rhetorical processes that constitute selves in real life. As the speaker notes in one of Browning's extended monologues, *Fifine at the Fair* (1872), 'The histrionic truth is in the natural lie' (section lxxxv) – the guarantor of truth in fiction (histrionic truth) is that it parallels the fiction in life (the natural lie). By emphasizing the role of rhetoric, Bloom formulated character as a semiotic event, and since then scholars, fuelled by post-structuralist theories of subjectivity, have increasingly attended to the way dramatic monologues foreground the role of language in the construction of subjectivity (Tucker 1984, 1985; Martin 1985; Slinn 1991, 1999; Armstrong 1993).

The display of discursive or rhetorical practices is true of all poetry, where the increased intensity of figuration in poetic artefacts draws attention to itself as specifically linguistic. Dramatic monologues, however, combine that intensity of figuration with an overt representation of speaking subjects that focuses attention on the semiotic basis for identity, on the interdependence of self (as known) and signs. The older emphasis on monologues as the dramatization of character, as if 'character' is an essential self separate from representation, thus becomes less apparent since the 1970s. But critics do not reject character: they redefine it. Hence they redefine the nature of the dramatic in monologues as the effort of speaking subjects to maintain an identity within the disseminations of discourse, within the fluid mobility of signifiers. Loy Martin, for example, defines the genre as a 'struggle between the subject as homogeneous "true person" and as heterogeneous and "disappearing" moment of speech or signification' (1985: 31). Speakers, that is to say, are both determinate and indeterminate, and for Martin the dramatic monologue is 'a form that can never resolve the contradiction at its center' (1985: 31). Speakers are tied to speech, to the limits and transience of utterance, in order to produce their role as subject; consequently they are tied to both the disjunctions and the social dimensions of language. Victorian dramatic monologues expose a terrifying prospect for poets and speakers. Monologists speak in order to affirm their authority; they argue for the validity of their position and perceptions in order to establish the self, if nothing else, as a viable centre in which to locate meaning and value. Yet the moment they speak, they commit the self to a social or dialogical intrusion, to an inevitable division, that ironically undermines their single sovereignty in the very act of attempting to establish it. That is not to say that subjects do not exist in dramatic monologues, but the nature of the form exposes the way subjectivity is constituted through discourse, through the exigencies and processes of language (Tucker 1984: 125–6; Slinn 1991: 1–3, 33–7).

Identity in these processes may be diffused, dispersed, less secure. Early Victorian readers assumed a subjective authenticity in Romantic lyrics, but dramatic monologues tend rather to disrupt the authority (and hence the authenticity) of speaking voices, whether authorial or fictive. They problematize questions about who speaks, putting the self into question (Tucker 1984: 136). They do this in terms of both the author–speaker–reader relationship and the poem's dramatized content. Elisabeth Howe stresses the distance between speaker and poet in a dramatic monologue. Arguing that the speaker's 'otherness' is felt as a difference from reader as well as author, she notes how this otherness is established through a variety of means: name, dates, place, morality, history, mythology, irony (1996: 6–7). That distance is crucial to distinctions between lyrics and dramatic monologues, as Howe suggests, but it also provokes questions about alterity, about whether the otherness of speakers is entirely separate from poet and reader, or whether it is complicit within structures of writing and reading, inseparable from authorial or readerly projections. Who speaks? Poet, speaker, dialect, reader? All four? In terms of content, dramatic monologues notoriously display acts of self-objectification or self-analysis. Sometimes that is in order to confirm the speaker's righteousness (Browning's 'Johannes Agricola in Meditation', 1836), to justify proposed action ('Ulysses'), or to determine the nature of a threatening power (Browning's 'Caliban Upon Setebos', 1864). Sometimes it is to escape punishment ('Mr Sludge, "the Medium" '), to instigate a subtle revenge (Barrett Browning's 'Bertha in the Lane', 1844), to pursue an erotic spirituality (Christina Rossetti's 'The Convent Threshold', 1858), or to represent the injustices of cultural denial (Amy Levy's 'Xantippe', 1881). Sometimes the self-scrutiny is inadvertent or unconsciously ironic, and sometimes it is linguistically self-conscious, as it is for Bishop Blougram or Webster's castaway courtesan (discussed below). Invariably, however, such representations involve shifting patterns of division and separation, diffusing the sense of determinate subjects, problematizing the self as author of its own utterance. Hence, as speakers construct themselves and are at the same time constructed by their speech and attempts at self-representation, dramatic monologues typically display an endlessly dynamic process of subjectivity in discourse. Numerous borders are tested or transgressed as speakers proffer various versions of 'the dangerous edge of things', Blougram's liminality where our fascination follows verbal balancing acts, interplay, process, a dynamic of discursive restlessness.

Clearly the dramatic monologue is a dynamic, unfixed genre. Varying combinations of lyric, drama and narrative allow an array of shifting relationships between speaker and author, or between speaker and interlocutor, and thence between reader and poem. Nicholas Shrimpton, for instance, making use of Rader's formalist distinctions, observes that 'Swinburne writes dramatic lyrics, monodrama, mask lyrics, and dramatic monologues, and mixes them without warning' (1993: 61). When confronted with that degree of fluid formalism it may seem less than useful to insist upon generic specificity, and one of the fascinating features of the dramatic monologue as a mobile hybrid is that it almost perversely exposes the limits of any attempt to pin it down. Nevertheless, what-ever the level of fluid process or *post hoc* generic determination, the fact remains that something happened to Victorian poetry that the poets themselves named as 'dramatic'. The massive Victorian production of poems where the speaker is not the poet, or where personal expressiveness is placed in a context which objectifies its process (Arnold's 'Stanzas from the Grande Chartreuse', 1855), or where a speaker objectifies herself for self-scrutiny (Webster's 'By the Looking-Glass', or 'Faded', written 1870), marks a liter-ary phenomenon that amounts to a virtual paradigm shift. Obviously conventional lyri-cism never disappears, but during the nineteenth century the ascendancy of lyrical forms became supplanted by monologues that are in varying degrees 'dramatic'. While this process culminated eventually in the modernism of Pound and Eliot (Christ 1984; Howe 1996), the shift to the dramatic is wonderfully illustrated by Tennyson's revision of his early poem, 'Tithon'. Written first in 1833, it was rewritten twenty-six years later as 'Tithonus' (1860).

In 'Tithon', Tennyson offers this expression of the terrible dilemma of a human figure who was given immortal life, but without immortal youth or beauty:

> Ay me! ay me! what everlasting pain,
> Being immortal with a mortal heart,
> To live confronted with eternal youth:
> To look on what is beautiful nor know
> Enjoyment save through memory.
>
> (ll. 11–15)

This is conventional expressive lyricism, where the assertion of a personal emotional state is couched as a definitive statement of a universal condition, outside language. After the initial self-pitying lament, the passage seeks, through rhythmic regularity and repeated infinitives, to transcend the individual predicament, depicting an ahistorical condition of mythic suffering. This is an idealist poetry of nomination and abstraction. In 'Tithonus', however, Tennyson changed all that. He still portrays the torment of the speaker's suffering self-consciousness, aware of the predicament of everlasting decay, but now he represents this state through direct utterance, replacing the previous lines with a brief personal history:

> Alas! for this gray shadow, once a man –
> So glorious in his beauty and thy choice,
> Who madest him thy chosen, that he seemed
> To his great heart none other than a God!
> I asked thee, 'Give me immortality.'
> Then didst thou grant mine asking with a smile,
> Like wealthy men who care not how they give.
> But thy strong Hours indignant worked their wills,
> And beat me down and marred and wasted me,
> And though they could not end me, left me maimed
> To dwell in presence of immortal youth,
> Immortal age beside immortal youth,
> And all I was, in ashes.
>
>   (ll. 11–23)

This is no longer the poetry of atemporal abstraction. It remains decidedly rhetorical and euphonious, but it is nevertheless the poetry of enactment, of immediate verbal action. The interlocutor is Aurora herself and the utterance enables Tithonus to locate the source of his predicament squarely within the historical bounds of his relationship with her. Through the consequential structures of narrative sequence ('Who madest him . . . that he seemed'), he blames Aurora for his ambition and for thoughtlessly and irresponsibly granting his wish for immortality. At the same time, his utterance ironically draws attention to the defensive self-interest of his representation: if Aurora too easily gave him immortality, he sought it because she flattered his vanity. The technical formalism – alliteration, assonance, sibilants, the emphatic stress of (virtually) monosyllabic pentameters – produces an effect of self-enclosed frustration and bitterness, drawing attention to the means by which Tithonus structures both his perception of Aurora and her culpability. Hence Tithonus's performance, his narrative of anger and despair, enacts (as opposed to illustrates) the relationship between personal predicament and mythic consciousness. The passage brings into being both individual subjectivity (the shift from Tithonus's human vanity to betrayed and stricken im-mortal) and social or mythic authority (he constructs Aurora as morally responsible). The aesthetic effect of 'Tithonus' is quite different therefore from the expressive claim of 'Tithon' to represent a generalized condition. The cited passage from 'Tithonus' provides the combination of lyricism (personalized eloquence), narrative (personalized history) and external relationship (a distinctively separate or 'other' speaker addressing an interlocutor whose assumed presence shapes his or her speech) that denotes the poem as a monologue that is dramatic.

Contexts

The earliest Victorian versions of dramatic monologues are usually noted as Tennyson's 'St Simeon Stylites' (written 1833, published 1842) and Robert Browning's 'Porphyria's Lover' (1836). But monologues or lyrical poems with an imagined persona have very ancient origins. The *prosopopoeia*, or impersonation, is a longstanding rhetorical form where a historical or imaginary person is presented as actually speaking; the idylls of Theocritus and Ovid's *Heroides* contain dramatic speeches and epistles; and the tradition of complaint often imitates specified speakers other than the poet (Culler 1975; Sinfield 1977; Howe 1996). Philip Hobsbaum (1975) relates the rise of monologues to the fall of stage drama, noting a growing tendency in the early nineteenth century to applaud scenes as set pieces or to anthologize extracted speeches, such as Charles Lamb's *Specimens of English Dramatic Poets* (1808), and Dwight Culler (1975) suggests a relationship between dramatic monologues and monodrama, an eighteenth-century mode that was flexible in structure, depicting sequential phases of varying mood and passion. The best-known adaptation of monodrama is *Maud*, although Hemans's 'Arabella Stuart' (1828) provides an earlier example. Many men and women poets in the early nineteenth century used dramatic voices, or speakers other than the poet – Hemans, Letitia Landon, John Clare, Leigh Hunt, Walter Savage Landor. Much of this writing, however, tends to be sentimental or melodramatic, and more subtle precursors for dramatic monologues may be Romantic 'conversation' poems, such as Coleridge's 'Frost at Midnight' (1798) or Wordsworth's 'Tintern Abbey' (1798). While these poems do not separate speaker from poet, they move towards a form of self-enactment, incorporating a distinctive location, a silent interlocutor, elements of narrative, the speaker's responses to changing circumstances, and a covert appropriation of the interlocutor.

In terms of social contexts, however, there was, by the time Victoria came to the throne in 1837, a widespread cultural obsession with self-scrutiny (Shaw 1987: 47–74; Faas 1988: 57–62). No doubt fuelled in aesthetic terms by the self-absorption and expressiveness of much Romantic writing, this obsession most notably emerged from the growing desire among philosophers and psychologists at the turn of the century to define the nature of selfhood. Figures such as Locke, Hume, Hartley, Reid and Priestley had established self-analysis as a prerequisite for studying the mind. Indeed, the stated need by psychologists in the early part of the century to treat their own mind as an object to be observed parallels Romantic and idealist emphasis on knowing oneself by looking within – objectifying the self in order to experience it as a subject. So widespread was this rage for self-knowledge that many Victorians reacted against its excesses, notably Thomas Carlyle, who in his essay 'Characteristics' (1831) rejected self-contemplation as 'the symptom of disease'. Some critics have claimed that dramatic monologues developed as part of this reaction. While, however, the distancing of speaker from poet may be a means of gaining some perspective on a speaker's emotional state, or in the case of a woman writer of being 'in control of her objectification' (Armstrong 1993: 326), the genre predominantly develops as a means of representing or displaying subjectivity and self-consciousness, not avoiding it.

Carlyle's metaphor of disease reminds us, for instance, that accompanying this cultural introspection were nascent stages in modern psychology. Whereas pre-nineteenth-century approaches had separated the human soul or mind from the body, mental studies were now including body as well as mind, incorporating the pathology of mental aberrations and illness. There were three main areas of activity that the early Victorians would have understood under the name of mental science: 'introspective psychology', mainly concerned with normal consciousness, but expanding its attention to the study of dreams and unconscious mental activity; 'mesmerism', which became widely publicized in the late 1830s until reinterpreted as hypnotism in the middle of the century; and 'psychological medicine', which focused on mental patients and asylums. Mesmerism attracted interest from literary figures – Dickens, Thackeray, the Carlyles, in addition to Arnold, Clough, Tennyson and the Brownings – clearly fascinating the widespread Victorian desire to probe boundaries between flesh and spirit. But it was the shifting concept of insanity that most relates to what reviewers hailed as the dramatic-psychological nature of new forms in poetry. Changing theories about mental illness represented a more compassionate view of lunatics and particularly an expanded sense of their rationality. An understanding of insanity was broadening from simple loss of reason, to deluded imagination, and then to what British psychologists called 'moral insanity', or the French, following Philippe Pinel, called 'rational lunacy' (*folie raisonnante*). After J. C. Prichard's *A Treatise on Insanity* (1835), moral insanity became known in England as a 'morbid perversion of the feelings, affections, and active powers' which often coexisted with 'an apparently unimpaired state of the intellectual faculties' (Prichard, cited Faas 1988: 45). This less determinate distinction between madness and sanity, and the notion of an apparently rational, yet dangerously destructive, or comically excessive, mental state, clearly fascinated both Tennyson ('St Simeon Stylites', *Maud*) and Robert Browning ('Porphyria's Lover', 1836; 'My Last Duchess', 1842; 'Too Late', 1864).

Some early psychologists argued that the only way to understand the insane was to identify with their plight, to imagine what it must be like to see with their eyes. But empathic self-projection is also a technique of the dramatic or narrative artist, and powers of sympathetic identification were employed by poets writing their monologues as much as by psychologists contemplating their patients. There may have been a coincidence of mutuality rather than any demonstrable cross-influence between these two cultural activities, but their parallels continue until the end of the century, when the role of monologues as a portrayal of obsessive, one-sided talk that exposes a speaker's subjectivity to public scrutiny anticipates the famous talking cure of psychoanalysis. The dramatic monologue depends on active reading, and the reader's engagement makes her effectively an analyst, listening to the talk of the analysand (the speaker as patient), and weighing its psychological, political and social significance. Still, if psychoanalysis takes over where the monologue leaves off, turning the role of the reader into that of a mental health professional, it all began with a broadly based culture of introspection at the beginning of the nineteenth century, out of which emerged the dramatic monologue as a culturally consonant form.

In the realm of philosophy, introspection was encouraged by the dominating influence of the Cartesian *cogito* (I think therefore I am), which taught that the mind is its own place and that truth may be known simply by looking within. This notorious formula has reinforced the metaphysical assumptions of idealist philosophy for nearly four hundred years and underpinned what we now think of as the logocentrism of conventional lyricism – where the lyrical form assumes a speaker who is discrete, uniform, self-enclosed, male, and yet universal, manifesting an absolute or transcendent truth. If, however, lyricism as a genre privileges the mind in private and introspective moments, the dramatic monologue as a genre challenges the singularity and universality of that private meditation. Cartesian philosophy encourages the dualistic belief in a self that is separate from the cultural and political world outside. The dramatic monologue challenges that dualism by showing the self is not a discrete whole; it is part of an open system. The dramatic quality of the monologues, where speakers address an interlocutor and are located in a specific political or historical context, exposes the way in which speakers are always mixed with what is outside themselves – with other persons, times, cultures. The individual exists not as a separate entity, but as a part of human history. Most obviously true for monologues with named historical speakers ('St Simeon Stylites', 'Fra Lippo Lippi', 'Xantippe'), the point is also true for monologues without named speakers that nevertheless specify social contexts (Barrett Browning's 'The Runaway Slave at Pilgrim's Point', 1847; D. G. Rossetti's 'Jenny', 1870; 'A Castaway').

A concern with social contexts also points towards the politics of the form. In one sense tying the dramatic monologue to a culturally and personally specific speech act is to tie it to point of view. It would then be easy enough to read the genre as a post-Kantian celebration of the singular self: in a world where all is as I perceive it to be, I make my own reality. But that view encourages the self-centred bias of pure lyricism to the point potentially of deluded excess, allowing the tyranny of self-indulgence to prevail as much as the passionate sublime of transcendent desire – in other words, a lover of Porphyria (or strangler of women) as much as an admirer of the river Wye (or worshipper of nature). And that is Browning's point, as through irony he exposes both the limits to point of view and the uncertain boundaries of selfhood. Isobel Armstrong, for example, has brilliantly explained how Browning derived a Benthamite poetics from the liberal milieu he shared with John Stuart Mill and William Johnson Fox. During the 1830s, Mill's theory of poetry as solitary expressionism, as 'overheard' lyricism, amounts, as Armstrong explains, to a 'poetics of exclusion' (1993: 137). It denies poetry the validity of public knowledge, abolishing externality, time, agency and the reader – everything to do with the political (1993: 141). Browning's early monologues 'Porphyria's Lover' and 'Johannes Agricola' (later called 'Madhouse Cells', 1842) parody Mill's private poetry, showing how the effective solipsism of internalized and personal feeling leads to delusion and visions of omnipotence (see also Tucker 1984: 124–6). Fox's theories, by contrast, drew on the features of drama (dialogue, relationship, objectification), stressing the externalized aspects of represented speech and thus allowing for political critique. Browning added these dramatic features to lyrical form, grounding psychological conditions in social history. At the same time, Fox's account of realism and representation remained deficient, being unable to conceive the crucial function of constitutive fictions (crucial, that is, for a fictional art form), and for that Browning turned to Jeremy Bentham's utilitarian ideas about legal fictions. Bentham viewed fictional constructs as the product of social institutions such as the law: they are potentially iniquitous, and yet indispensable; essential to language and conceptualizing, they intervene substantively in the world, affecting choices and actions. Bentham's theory of fictions thus provided Browning with a way of understanding how personalized or imaginative constructions are political, entering and affecting the world of social interaction (Armstrong 1993: 148–51). Through absorbing all three views (expressive, dramatic, fictive), Browning makes possible the politics of the dramatic monologue. The expressive subject becomes a matter of psychological process, objective drama becomes a matter of public representations, and poetic fiction becomes a matter of cultural construction and discursive practices.

Cultural Critique

Victorian dramatic monologues encompass a vast range of topics, many of which allude to contemporary controversies. 'The Runaway Slave at Pilgrim's Point', for example, was published in a Boston anti-slavery annual (in 1847 for 1848), with relevance not only for the American abolition debate, but also for the aftermath of moral imputation and financial consequence that followed the British abolition bill in 1833 (enacted in 1834). Dramatizing the protest speech of a female slave who smothers her own child, it also questions Victorian assumptions about motherhood and emerging views about infanticide. Two decades later, 'Caliban Upon Setebos' hints again at issues related to slavery (Caliban is Prospero's slave from Shakespeare's _The Tempest_), this time alluding to the triple arena of Darwinism, colonialism and theology. Many readers have taken Caliban as a mediating figure in the evolutionary development from prehuman to human beings, but the figure of Caliban was also widely used in Victorian journals and cartoons as an example of the bestiality and primitivism of native peoples that justified the supposedly civilizing intrusions of British colonization. Browning's subtitle to the poem ('Natural Theology on the Island'), on the other hand, points to debate about anthropomorphism, to the epistemological dilemma about how to know God. Other monologues also refer to religious disputes, to antinomianism ('Johannes Agricola'), faith ('Bishop Blougram's Apology'), immortality and death ('Tithonus', 'The Bishop Orders His Tomb at St Praxed's Church', 1845), or Biblical authenticity ('A Death in the Desert'). Others again refer to male celibacy and manliness ('Fra Lippo Lippi'), to art and creativity ('Andrea del Sarto', 'Cleon', 1855, 'Abt Vogler', 1864), and to spiritualism ('Mr Sludge, "the Medium"'). Many refer to the Woman Question, whether in terms of redundant women ('Bertha in the Lane'), fallen women (Dora Greenwell's 'Christina', written 1851), repressed women ('Xantippe') or prostitution ('Jenny', 'A Castaway'), the last being published in the context of the Contagious Diseases Acts of the 1860s. And I have already alluded to monologues that portray 'moral insanity' or mental aberration: examples range among delusion ('St Simeon Stylites'), murder ('Porphyria's Lover', D. G. Rossetti's 'A Last Confession', 1870), revenge (Browning's 'The Laboratory', 1845, and 'A Forgiveness', 1876), necrophilia (Swinburne's 'The Leper', 1866) and suicide (Levy's 'A Minor Poet', 1884).

Such a list suggests a formidably close relationship between dramatic monologues and cultural debate. It provides a clear sense of the way in which monologues were used as a means of exposing the limits and assumptions surrounding areas of contestation. While the poems invariably dramatize these issues in terms of individual perceptions and desires, according to the fundamental focus of the genre on subjectivity, they imply, albeit in varying degree, an external dimension that relates directly back to cultural process. The strength of assertiveness, for example, that is a feature of the genre is also a feature of its political dimension, since the energy of direct address allows speakers to make claims that exhibit the relationship between personal subjectivity and political consequences. Hence poems expose the tyranny of control and negation ('Porphyria's Lover', 'My Last Duchess'), the means of ideological gender construction ('Jenny'), the potential for repression to provoke resistance and rebellion ('The Runaway Slave'), the commodification of women through the fusion of economic and female worth ('A Castaway'), and the terrible waste of female intellect in a world where cultural power rather than ability determines recognition and responsiveness ('Xantippe').

At the same time, thematic allusiveness and an aggressive tone are not the main points to note about the way in which monologues provide a cultural critique. In observing that Robert Browning becomes a political poet because he realized 'the possibility of making a cultural critique in terms of the structure of the monologue itself', Isobel Armstrong offers a clue about how the genre may enact cultural criticism (1993: 141). By representing speakers talking about themselves and how they construct their perceptions, the dramatic monologue seems an ideal form to expose these subjective processes and how they relate to cultural beliefs. But the point is the process and enactment that are features of the form rather than just the allusiveness of content and theme. It is not a matter of writing directly about cultural problems, which might as easily be done in polemical prose, but of displaying the fundamental act of utterance that grounds subjectivity and speech in cultural contexts and processes. When Fra Lippo Lippi announces his presence – 'I am poor brother Lippo, by your leave' (l. 1) – the ingratiating gesture to his audience immediately grounds the utterance in the circumstances of his discovery: a monk, found by the night-watch where monks ought not to be, in the local red-light district, 'Where sportive ladies leave their doors ajar' (l. 6). Lippo's speech is direct and social: 'Aha, you know your betters!' (l. 12); 'But you, sir, it concerns you that your knaves / Pick up a manner nor discredit you' (ll. 21–2); 'He's Judas to a tittle, that man is!' (l. 25). Immediate verbal enactment is fundamental, therefore, and because the form's structure draws attention to subjectivity as a social event, readers are able to observe the means by which cultural contexts impose themselves on speakers and by which speakers attempt to impose themselves on cultural contexts. As a painter-monk, Lippo's life is dominated by the economic power of Cosimo de' Medici and by his prior's liturgical power, but Cosimo's patronage allows him to escape arrest, and the monologue asserts Lippo's sensual energy and artistic credo against the aesthetic ignorance and theological abstractions of his monastic superiors: 'Come, what am I a beast for?' he asks, both ingenuously and ingeniously (l. 80). As Lippo inserts himself ('I'm a beast, I know', l. 270) into the dualistic language of his godly culture ('"Your business is to paint the souls of men"', l. 83), he simultaneously flouts and conforms to monastic structures. For Lippo that tension sustains a dynamic creativity, although for a different painter, Andrea del Sarto, the conflict between the politics of beauty (including his wife's beauty that is admired by all: 'My face, my moon, my everybody's moon', l. 29) and aesthetic ambition (to be recognized beside Raphael and Michelangelo) produces a capitulation that is sadly inhibiting: 'I'm the weak-eyed bat no sun should tempt / Out of the grange whose four walls make his world' (ll. 169–70). Hence a dramatic monologue generically displays a radically political as well as psychological event – that moment when the forces of social discourse and the claims of personal utterance meet in the construction and dissolution of individual identity and power.

Two recent conceptual issues that might assist in understanding these points and thence the cultural significance of the genre are performativity and agency. These concepts relate to earlier attempts to define the 'dramatic' in monologues and to questions about the portrayal of ethical choice and individual freedom. It has been obvious enough to many readers that monologues incorporate a dramatic model, portraying the verbal performance of their speakers – Robert Browning's 'histrionic truth'. While, however, attending to 'performance' recognizes the monologue as drama, as a rhetorical 'display' of beliefs and perceptions, this approach also tends to tie understanding of performance to the assumptions of humanist subjectivity, to self as the author of all action, to an essential self that controls the display. The performative point about dramatic monologues, on the other hand, is not performance in that conventional sense; it is more to do with the reciprocal relations between verbal action and social process. Performativity focuses attention on 'the reciprocal and discursive means by which normative structures and personal subjectivities are shown to invade and constitute each other through acts of speaking' (Slinn 1999: 69). A performative is literally a verb (such as 'promise' or 'dare') whose referential action is its own utterance; it does not describe an event, but acts that event. It *is* the event. Loosely, therefore, a poem is a performative to the extent that it produces its own event – not just the event of which it speaks, but the event which is its speaking. In performing itself, a performative also brings new reality into being – the social existence of the promise, the dare, or the poem as artefact. In order to effect this reality, however, performatives cannot occur without recognizable specifications and a defined situation, such as the repetition of certain formulae and an audience to bear witness, as when getting married, swearing to tell the truth, or naming a ship. So the concept of performativity also recognizes the complex of relationships between speaker, utterance, text, audience and context that allows speech to constitute (not just reflect or report) social meaning. Hence it provides a way of theorizing the relationship between rhetorical utterance and cultural reality (Slinn 1999). In terms of dramatic monologues, it becomes, for example, a way of accounting for the combination of lyric expressiveness and representational mimicry, of explaining how the idealism of personal expressiveness is inseparable from the materialism of social and historical imitation. Performativity helps us to understand how verbal acts and gestures in dramatic monologues, far from being empty fictions or merely the idealisms of atemporal lyricism, are continuous with the same verbal acts and gestures in everyday life that perform identities as if real. Performativity, that is to say, focuses attention on a dramatic monologue as in all senses a verbal 'act' – uttering, displaying, persuading, citing, fabricating, textualizing – in conjunction with the social conditions that allow that act to occur – speaker, audience, language, convention, practice.

The practical consequence for reading dramatic monologues is that we can attend to the way in which verbal enactment within the poem intertwines both personal speech and cultural process. Sometimes this is a matter of attending to the way speech structures enact cultural structures. Early in 'The Bishop Orders His Tomb at St Praxed's Church', for instance, the Bishop, while addressing his sons, alludes first to his mistress, their mother, and then to a rival bishop who is now dead: 'She, men would have to be your mother once, / Old Gandolf envied me, so fair she was!' (ll. 4–5). During these lines, the pronoun ('She'), which begins as an active subject for a statement about the boys' mother, transforms, through the sideways injection of Gandolf, into a passive object of male rivalry ('so fair she was'). That is to say, the grammatical incompletion and shift in grammatical subject show how the value of the Bishop's mistress is measured by Gandolf's envy – when he thinks of her, he thinks of Gandolf's defeat. Here, anacoluthon enacts the cultural process whereby a woman's significance is defined not by her role as mistress or mother, but by homosocial rivalry, and we are thus given a sense very early in the poem of the way in which the cultural structures of homosocial conflict underpin the Bishop's discourse. Such an example is relatively clear, but sometimes passages are more complex. Consider the famous account of the Eucharist in this poem, when the Bishop imagines lying on his tomb after his death:

> And then how I shall lie through centuries,
> And hear the blessed mutter of the mass,
> And see God made and eaten all day long,
> And feel the steady candle-flame, and taste
> Good strong thick stupefying incense-smoke!
>
> (ll. 80–4)

The sensory emphasis and obvious materiality of this scene have been taken by readers as an indication of the Bishop's notorious carnality. But if we read the passage as a provocative statement about the Catholic doctrine of transubstantiation, it enacts an absorption of institutional discourse into personal expression that displays the workings of doctrinal systems, problematizing Catholic and non-Catholic views alike about the Eucharist. The contest of spirit with matter was always a favourite Victorian obsession, and Protestant, usually dualist, views of the Eucharist treat it as a material symbol of a spiritual truth (the wafer 'represents' Christ's body), instead of regarding the wafer, once transformed, as the thing itself, as actually being Christ's body. Through the miracle of transubstantiation, the material is indeed the divine, and vice versa. They are undifferentiated. Hence the Bishop's apparently crude materialism as he imagines himself watching 'God made and eaten all day long' is not, in terms of transubstantiation, materialism, but simply religious truth, where distinctions between figurative and literal language disappear. Since there is only the thing itself (the God/wafer), and no longer 'representation' (a symbolic substitute), there is no longer any demarcation between sign and referent, between material and ideal. In the Bishop's enunciation, therefore, he is less travestying Catholic doctrine than taking it for granted, absorbing it into his everyday speech. The grounding of his imagined afterlife in sensory images simply suggests the extent to which he identifies, albeit unthinkingly, with doctrinal teaching. Institutional discourse and personal utterance thus intertwine.

In a more secular example, Webster's high-class prostitute in 'A Castaway' plays consciously with the cultural value assigned to modesty, seizing upon a witty irony:

> A wanton I, but modest!
>   Modest, true;
> I'm not drunk in the streets, ply not for hire
> At infamous corners with my likenesses
> Of the humbler kind; yes, modesty's my word –
> 'Twould shape my mouth well too, I think I'll try:
> 'Sir, Mr. What-you-will, Lord Who-knows-what,
> My present lover or my next to come,
> Value me at my worth, fill your purse full,
> For I am modest; yes, and honour me
> As though your schoolgirl sister or your wife
> Could let her skirts brush mine or talk of me;
> For I am modest.'
>
>   (ll. 47–58)

The second half of this extract is a practice performance, a proposed claim to recognizable social value. As a command ('Value me'; 'honour me'), it is a literal performative, a self-referential enactment that would ground her cultural worth in her personal worth: 'For I am modest.' The justification for her command is the cultural coin of modesty, which she can justifiably claim in so many respects: not excessive or ostentatious, she is moderate and decorous. Yet despite these personal qualities, her trade means she lacks the moral dimension that pervades the public function of the term – she lacks decency. She knows therefore that the performative would fail: 'Well, I flout myself', she continues (l. 58). 'But yet, but yet', she immediately adds, suggesting her protest that despite her awareness of the irony in being a modest wanton, she still clings to the truth of her modesty. So she locates herself on a cultural fault line, on a rift between personally defined respectability and publicly defined wantonness. Hence this practice performative and wordplay exposes the way contemporary (Victorian) values impose public morality on personal quality. The courtesan may indeed be modest in all personal behaviour and private habits, but at the political level the moral dimension of the term would be denied her, not because of any intrinsic quality, but simply because of a moral judgement about her social practice, her means of earning a livelihood. The difference that determines 'honour' between the speaker and her lover's wife is not therefore to do with intrinsic worth, but with public practice. She is denied modesty on a public level because of the patriarchal and capitalist hypocrisy that will not, when it comes to women, separate economic practice from sexual morality. Women who ply a trade, of whatever kind, will find that their private modesty is always overlaid by a subtly imposed gender prejudice. Hence in this passage the word 'modesty' functions as a site of cultural contestation, where bourgeois morality displaces personal respectability. Again, personal utterance merges with cultural process.

Agency is also a metaphor that models the relationship between self and world. It arises from recent debate in cultural studies about the ability of an individual to act outside the control of public institutions or external social forces. In general, agency is a contemporary version of the old freedom of choice versus determinism debate: can we choose our own actions or are they determined for us by cosmic or providential powers? Agency, however, focuses more intently on the secular and political interrelationship between individual and society. Loosely used, it may simply refer to individual action. But agency is a more complex metaphor than that usage allows. It represents a double action – acting on behalf of another while acting as oneself. Travel agents sell tickets for another company while at the same time making a profit for themselves; secret agents act for themselves in the field but also on behalf of an authorizing power (who may deny their existence). Hence agency is an appropriate metaphor for recent theories of subjectivity that explain how it is not possible to be an independent subject free from the structuring processes of cultural contexts. Being a subject, like being an agent, is always to be subject to (an external authority) as well as being subject of (individual action). In dramatic monologues, this double action represents the interconnection between speakers acting or speaking for themselves as active subjects, and some other force that drives or authorizes them – unconscious desire perhaps, or institutional or hegemonic power.

An obvious example of this double action can be found in 'Bishop Blougram's Apology'. Blougram clearly acknowledges his role as agent for the church and how the church in turn is the earthly agent for God, manifesting through faith His ultimate power. Christianity, Blougram claims, is 'The most . . . precise / And absolute form of faith in the whole world' (ll. 306–7), and consequently the 'most potent of all forms / For working on the world' (ll. 308–9). Acting on behalf of a power such as this, he is able to assert with some satisfaction to the journalist Gigadibs that even the Bishop's 'shade' is 'so much more potent' than Gigadibs' 'flesh' (l. 932). Through this agency Blougram also advances his personal cause, fulfilling his desire for '*Status, entourage,* worldly circumstance' (l. 26). This double role, acting for himself while acting for the church, is directly indicated by his verbal shift of the possessive when describing how people pay obeisance to the divine through kissing the hand of its representative: 'now folk kneel / And kiss my hand – of course the Church's hand' (ll. 335–6). In this moment of provocative conjunction, the ambivalent ownership of the hand indicates the correlation of person and institution that grounds the Bishop's identity. Each gains from the other through a relationship of mutual appropriation. The Bishop gains influence and status (l. 904) and the church gains a devoted servant, one who affirms his task as making 'the absolute best of what God made' (l. 355). Perhaps a less obvious example of agency occurs in Rossetti's 'Jenny', where the urbane male speaker, contemplating the sleeping prostitute, Jenny, thinks of himself as an agent for liberal idealism and male sensitivity towards women: he comes from a room 'full of books' (l. 23) and hopes that Jenny might be glad he is 'not drunk or ruffianly' (l. 65). But the politics of liberal idealism turn out to be the politics of gender ap-propriation and covert capitalism. He figures Jenny as 'a volume' to be read (l. 158), thus absorbing her into a world of knowledge where men are the active readers of passive, feminized texts; and when he gratuitously leaves gold coins in Jenny's hair (ll. 337–9), he signals his complicity in the economic structures that maintain her circumstance. Perhaps there is a telling irony when he wonders if he might be 'the subject' of her 'dreams' (l. 338), for while that might mean he is an object of Jenny's dreaming, it is as 'subject' that he figures himself, not as the subjected. It is as male subject – a male agent, acting out his masculine identity under the ultimate authority of patriarchal culture – that he constitutes Jenny as the object of his musing.

The condition of being subjected, 'subject to' a power, is most apparent within the con-ditions of slavery. In 'The Runaway Slave at Pilgrim's Point', the speaker exists within a slave-justifying ideology that divides the world into a colour code of black and white. As black female slave, she is repressed as the negation of all that is white and valuable; thus she is raped, disallowed the human emotion of grief (l. 100), denied subjectivity, allowed only the state of being subjected, and denied therefore the double role of agent. But by killing her own child she rebels against this repression, and by flaunting her blackness she uses that very negation as a means of establishing agency. Her actions and identity are defined by the slave-owning culture that appropriates her colour, class and gender, and yet she is able to employ those very acculturated features to act in rebellion. Labelled black, she becomes black: 'I am black, I am black' is her continuing refrain. As the black opposite that defines the power of her masters, she becomes at the same time an agent for blackness, confronting the slave-owners with their political contradictions, showing the way to other slaves, and prophesying the dialectical reversal of the master–slave relationship: 'We are too heavy for our cross, / And fall and crush you and your seed' (ll. 244–45). Her speech is necessarily structured by the matrices of hegemonic language, but it is through her very utterance, directly addressing the slave-owners and forcing them to 'see' her, to recognize her, that she establishes her agency. Barrett Browning's poem thus shows how the appropriations of a hegemonic class may in turn be appropriated and used against them. As these examples suggest, then, dramatic mono-logues, in the hands of skilled practitioners, may become a potent means of exposing the politics of agency – the moral appropriations and cultural interdependence of self and other.

See also: VERSE DRAMA; LYRIC.

References and Further Reading

Armstrong, Isobel (1993) *Victorian Poetry: Poetry, Poetics and Politics*. London: Routledge.

Berardini, Claire M. (1996) 'Tennyson and the Poetic Forms of Resistance.' In Ruth Robbins and Julian Wolfreys (eds). *Victorian Identities: Social and Cultural Formations in Nineteenth-Century Literature* (pp. 81–96). London: Macmillan.

Bloom, Harold (1979) 'Introduction: Reading Browning.' In Harold Bloom and Adrienne Munich (eds). *Robert Browning: A Collection of Critical Essays* (pp. 1–12). Englewood Cliffs, N. J.: Prentice-Hall.

Brooke, Stopford (1894) *Tennyson: His Art and Relation to Modern Life*. London: Isbister.

Christ, Carol T. (1984) *Victorian and Modern Poetics*. Chicago: University of Chicago Press.

Culler, A. Dwight (1975) 'Monodrama and the Dramatic Monologue.' *PMLA*, 90, 366–85.

Curry, Samuel S. (1908) *Browning and the Dramatic Monologue: Nature and Interpretation of an Overlooked Form of Literature*. Boston: Expression.

Faas, Ekbert (1988) *Retreat into the Mind: Victorian Poetry and the Rise of Psychiatry*. Princeton, N. J.: Princeton University Press.

Flint, Kate (1997) '". . . As a Rule, I Does Not Mean I": Personal Identity and the Victorian Woman Poet.' In Roy Porter (ed.). *Rewriting the Self: Histories from the Renaissance to the Present* (pp. 156–66). London: Routledge.

Fuson, Benjamin (1948) *Browning and his English Predecessors in the Dramatic Monologue*. Iowa City: State University of Iowa Press.

Hobsbaum, Philip (1975) 'The Rise of the Dramatic Monologue.' *Hudson Review*, 28, 227–45.

Howe, Elisabeth A. (1996) *The Dramatic Monologue*. New York: Twayne.

Hughes, Linda K. (1987) *The Manyfacèd Glass: Tennyson's Dramatic Monologues*. Athens, Ohio: Ohio University Press.

Langbaum, Robert (1957) *The Poetry of Experience: The Dramatic Monologue in Modern Literary Tradition*. New York: Random House.

Martin, Loy D. (1979) 'The Inside of Time: An Essay on the Dramatic Monologue.' In Harold

Bloom and Adrienne Munich (eds). *Robert Browning: A Collection of Critical Essays* (pp. 59–78). Englewood Cliffs, N. J.: Prentice-Hall.

Martin, Loy D. (1985) *Browning's Dramatic Monologues and the Post-Romantic Subject*. Baltimore: Johns Hopkins University Press.

Mason, Michael (1974) 'Browning and the Dramatic Monologue.' In Isobel Armstrong (ed.). *Robert Browning* (pp. 231–66). London: Bell.

Maynard, John (1992) 'Reading the Reader in Robert Browning's Dramatic Monologues.' In Mary Ellis Gibson (ed.). *Critical Essays on Robert Browning* (pp. 69–78). New York: Hall.

Mermin, Dorothy (1983) *The Audience in the Poem: Five Victorian Poets*. New Brunswick, N. J.: Rutgers University Press.

Nichols, Ashton (1990) 'Dialogism in the Dramatic Monologue: Suppressed Voices in Browning.' *Victorians Institute Journal*, 18, 29–51.

Rader, Ralph W. (1976) 'The Dramatic Monologue and Related Lyric Forms.' *Critical Inquiry*, 3, 131–51.

Rosmarin, Adena (1985) *The Power of Genre*. Minneapolis: University of Minnesota Press.

Scheinberg, Cynthia (1997) 'Recasting "Sympathy and Judgment": Amy Levy, Women Poets, and the Victorian Dramatic Monologue.' *Victorian Poetry*, 35.2, 173–91.

Sessions, Ina Beth (1947) 'The Dramatic Monologue.' *PMLA*, 62, 503–16.

Shaw, W. David (1987) *The Lucid Veil: Poetic Truth in the Victorian Age*. London: Athlone.

Shaw, W. David (1999) *Origins of the Monologue: The Hidden God*. Toronto: University of Toronto Press.

Shires, Linda M. (ed.) (1984) 'The Dramatic "I" Poem.' Special Issue. *Victorian Poetry* 22.2.

Shrimpton, Nicholas (1993) 'Swinburne and the Dramatic Monologue.' In Rikky Rooksby and Nicholas Shrimpton (eds). *The Whole Music of Passion: New Essays on Swinburne* (pp. 52–72). Aldershot: Scolar Press.

Sinfield, Alan (1977) *Dramatic Monologue*. London: Methuen.

Slinn, E. Warwick (1991) *The Discourse of Self*

in Victorian Poetry. London: Macmillan; Charlottesville: University Press of Virginia.

Slinn, E. Warwick (1999) 'Poetry and Culture: Performativity and Critique.' *New Literary History*, 30, 57–74.

Tucker, Herbert F. (1984) 'From Monomania to Monologue: "St. Simeon Stylites" and the Rise of the Victorian Dramatic Monologue.' *Victorian Poetry*, 22.2, 121–37.

Tucker, Herbert F. (1985) 'Dramatic Monologue and the Overhearing of Lyric.' In Chaviva Hosek and Patricia Parker (eds). *Lyric Poetry: Beyond New Criticism* (pp. 226–43). Ithaca, N. Y.: Cornell University Press.

Wagner-Lawlor, Jennifer A. (1997) 'The Pragmatics of Silence, and the Figuration of the Reader in Browning's Dramatic Monologues.' *Victorian Poetry*, 35.3, 287–302.

5

Sonnet and Sonnet Sequence

Alison Chapman

Wordsworth had a dramatic conversion to the sonnet in 1802, after his sister Dorothy read aloud to him Milton's sonnets. The genre's post-Renaissance rehabilitation had been under way since at least 1750, but Wordsworth's enthusiasm gave the revival a new intensity. His admonition to 'Scorn not the sonnet' addresses contemporary critics and, indeed, Victorian essayists and anthologizers follow his lead in being uniformly outspoken in their defence of the genre. This defence does, however, come at a price. While the amatory and subjective sonnet is praised, particularly in the Petrarchan or Italian form (characterized by an octave followed by a sestet, with a turn or volta at line 9, and usually rhymed *abbaabba cdecde* or *cdccdc*), other varieties are denigrated. What emerges is a constrictive sonnet ideology that disparages the political sonnet, the Shakespearean or English sonnet, or any other 'illegitimate' form. (The Shakespearean or English sonnet is characterized by three quatrains followed by a turn at the couplet, usually rhyming *abab cdcd efef gg*, although there are many other combinations, particularly in the Spenserian sonnet, which has the more intricate rhyme scheme *ababbcbccdcdee*.) Although these critics implicitly and explicitly claim to be following Wordsworth's lead in the promotion of the sonnet, then, they do so at the expense of the sonnet's variety and heterogeneity, which were, ironically, characteristic of the form practised by Wordsworth and his precursor Milton.

In Wordsworth's two sonnets on the sonnet, the relationship between form and content is figured in a way that was to be repeated by subsequent commentators. In 'Scorn not the sonnet', the form is compared to a catalogue of items – key, lute, pipe, myrtle leaf, lamp, trumpet – which are shown to transcend their smallness. The genre, it is suggested, is innately material, but it has a materiality capable of exceeding its formal limitations and, furthermore, flouting attempts to police the genre. The sonnet, in other words, transcends its own space. In another sonnet on the sonnet, Wordsworth makes explicit the sonnet's transformative power: 'the Sonnet's scanty plot of ground' gives solace to the poet and, although a 'narrow room', it is no prison.

Essays on the Sonnet

An important essay on the sonnet by James Ashcroft Noble makes clear the overwhelming influence of this precursor: '[Wordsworth's sonnet] possesses us, pervades us, transfuses his spirit into our spirit, and makes us feel with him. He does this in virtue of his strong humanity' (1896: 39). In Noble's terms, it is as if the 'spirit' of Wordsworth is a transcendent energy like his very sonnets, which allows the Victorian sonneteers to continue in his tradition. Sonnet criticism, however, also reaches back farther than Wordsworth. The Victorian critic Charles Tomlinson's study, *The Sonnet: Its Origin, Structure, and Place in Poetry*, is significant for the detailed attention paid to the early sonnets by Dante and Petrarch and the summary dismissal of the Shakespearean form:

> I seek to prove that while the Italian Sonnet of the best writers, taking Petrarch as their exponent, is made up of several organic parts, each of which has its determinate function, and the result of the whole is a logical, consistent structure, the English form is generally more loose and inaccurate. (1874: vii)

The sense that only a Petrarchan form can be 'legitimate' (1874: 27) is repeated by most of the sonnet commentators from the 1790s (Curran 1986) and throughout the Victorian period. Victorian poets, in particular Hopkins and Meredith, did often resist the strict formula of Petrarchanism, but they did so from within this sonnet ideology. In this sense, the small space of the sonnet becomes a contested site for debates about generic and ideological purity. Tomlinson, for example, laments any deviation from the 'legitimate':

> The object of the regular or legitimate Italian sonnet is to express one, and only one idea, mood, sentiment, or proposition, and this must be introduced in appropriate language in the first quatrain, and so far explained in the second, and this may end in a full point; while the office of the first tercet is to prepare the leading idea of the quatrains for the conclusion, which conclusion is to be perfectly carried out in the second tercet, so that it may contain the fundamental idea of the poem, and end, as it were, with the point of the epigram. In short, the quatrains should contain the proposition and proof; the tercets its confirmation and conclusion. It must be obvious that such conditions exclude the final couplet of the English sonnet, and are also opposed to the practice so common with Wordsworth and other celebrated English sonnet-writers, of running the second quatrain into the first tercet. If the English had followed the Italian practice of printing the sonnet – that is, with such an arrangement of type as to distinguish each separate part, and show that it really is a structure made up of four distinct members or organs – the defect alluded to would probably have corrected itself by the eye as well as by the ear. (1874: 28–9)

It is notable that the debate about the sonnet's form takes on associations of national and racial purity. Any example of a sonnet which is a hybrid of types, or which flouts the sonnet laws and conventions, is condemned as irregular, illegitimate, or a 'violation' (Noble 1896: 5). The Petrarchan sonnet is represented, according to this formula, as natural, eternal, transcendent, rather than part of a complex European tradition (1896: 123–8). The sonnet is thus defined as a perfect organic space. It must have 'impressive unity', be 'thoroughly homogeneous', have a 'vital organism' and an 'imaginative completeness', according to Noble. Sonnets are, Noble adds, 'flawless pearls of poetry' (1896: 22).

William Sharp similarly places great importance on the sonnet's conciseness and density. He makes clear that the aesthetic value also has a commercial counterpart: '[the sonnet's] conciseness is an immense boon in these days when books multiply like gossamer-flies in a sultry June' (1886: xxv), and so, 'it is realised that if good a sonnet can speedily be read and enjoyed, that if exceptionally fine it can with ease be committed to memory, and that if bad it can be recognised as such at a glance, and can be relegated to oblivion by the turning of a single page' (1886: xxv). In this way, sonnets as aesthetic objects have a commodity value in the literary marketplace, although an examination of sonnet anthologies suggests that, paradoxically, the Victorian sonnet ideology also insists that the sonnet is an anti-commodity, beyond monetary value.

Sharp's sonnet analysis, like that of most other commentators, argues that the sonnet laws are natural and not constructed. In particular, he argues that a sonnet's subject matter will naturally fit its form, for 'poetic impulse that arises out of the suddenly kindled imagination may generally be trusted to instinctively find expression through the medium that is most fitting for it' (1886: xxvii). This ideology may be fruitfully read against the grain, for a reading of the sonnets discloses their cultural and generic overdetermination; the sonnet becomes a hyper-reflexive form that repeatedly comments on its own construction.

Sonnets on the Sonnet

James Ashcroft Noble concludes his essay on the sonnet with a final definition of the form: '[a sonnet is] a literature within a literature, a domain within a domain' (1896: 62–3). It might be fair to state that the sonnet is the supremely meta-textual form, a genre which inherently comments on itself and, implicitly, on its small size. Certainly the many sonnets on the sonnet testify to a self-consciousness about the genre as exemplified by the paradigmatic poems discussed above by Wordsworth. Many of the sonnets on the sonnets discuss and exemplify the rules of the genre, unleashing a host of analogies: the sonnet is a bell, a gem, a dew-drop, a tear, a berry, a diamond, a pearl, a star, a sound, a wave, a shell, or a flower. (See, for example, Eugene Lee Hamilton's 'What the Sonnet Is', Edward Brownlow's 'The Sonnet', Symonds's 'The Sonnet (III)', Richard Watson Gilder's 'The Sonnet', and Poe's parody 'An Enigma'.) All the analogies set up the sonnet as akin to a material space, a small concrete thing, and an aesthetic object. Furthermore, the insistence repeated throughout the period that the sonnet is analogous to the small and the beautiful, and yet that it transforms and transcends its small size, incorporates the Romantic categories of the beautiful and the sublime.

This paradox of the genre is the subject of Elizabeth Barrett Browning's sonnet 'The Soul's Expression', which communicates both the inadequacy of the sonnet to articulate and breathe (ex-press) the poet's meaning and also the dangers of the transcendental sublime:

With stammering lips and insufficient sound
I strive and struggle to deliver right
That music of my nature, day and night
With dream and thought and feeling interwound,
And inly answering all the senses round
With octaves of a mystic depth and height
Which step out grandly to the infinite
From the dark edges of the sensual ground!
This song of soul I struggle to outbear
Through portals of the sense, sublime and whole,
And utter all myself into the air.
But if I did it, – as the thunder-roll
Breaks its own cloud, my flesh would perish there,
Before the dread apocalypse of soul.

Barrett Browning is cautious of the cost of the sonnet epiphany. She describes it here as a self-immolation, in an implicit critique of Wordsworth's sonnet on the sonnet that figures the genre as an unproblematical expression of the poet ('with this key / Shakespeare unlocked his heart'). As a vehicle of self-expression, the 'mystic' octaves and the 'sublime whole' that the commentators had praised in the form are an impossible and dangerous ideal. Instead, this sonnet suggests that the genre for Barrett Browning represents a frustrating but self-protecting work in progress. The failure of language to articulate meaning fully is also explored in her sonnet 'Insufficiency'. Although her 'soul throbs audibly / Along my pulses, yearning to be free', 'what we best conceive, we fail to speak'. Pure expression is only found in her body, in the pulsing of her blood, or after death, the 'dread apocalypse of soul' in which the 'broken strains' will be perfected.

Conventionally, as many commentators on the sonnet explore (Spiller 1992; Montefiore 1987), Petrarchan sonnets are spoken by a male, who addresses an ideal female beloved who is absent, unattainable or dead. In this way, the male speaker predicates his identity on the absence of the female addressee. When women poets write from within the convention, they are faced with its inexorable code that counsels them to silence. Many of Christina Rossetti's sonnets ironically speak from the position of the dispossessed, marginalized, silenced and excluded. Rossetti's only sonnet on the sonnet, however, astutely transforms this Petrarchan ideology through the figure of her mother:

Sonnets are full of love, and this my tome
    Has many sonnets: so here now shall be
    One sonnet more, a love sonnet, from me
To her whose heart is my heart's quiet home,
    To my first Love, my Mother, on whose knee
I learnt love-lore that is not troublesome;
    Whose service is my special dignity,
And she my lodestar while I go and come.
And so because you love me, and because
    I love you, Mother, I have woven a wreath

> Of rhymes wherewith to crown your honoured name:
> In you not fourscore years can dim the flame
> Of love, whose blessed glow transcends the laws
> Of time and change and mortal life and death.
>
> (Rossetti 1979–90: II, 59)

In this sonnet, Rossetti fashions her mother, rather than a beloved, as her muse. The sonnet suggests that Petrarchan love is 'troublesome' as 'love-lore', and the sonnet gladly exchanges amatory love for maternal love. In addition, the speaker positions the mother as more important than sexual love and also its archetype, her 'first love'. This love, unlike the love in Petrarchan ideology, is reciprocal, requited, and associated with plenitude and fulfilment. In fact, one might argue that, through the material presence of the mother, Rossetti exposes the sonnet tradition's investment in its formal materiality over the deanimated or absent female addressee.

Christina Rossetti's brother, the painter-poet Dante Gabriel Rossetti, was perfectly placed to comment on the sonnet's inherent meta-textual ekphrasis. Langbaum comments that he 'defined the modern sonnet stemming from Wordsworth' (1982: 340). Dante Gabriel Rossetti is the author of perhaps the most famous Victorian sonnet on the sonnet, which serves as the introduction to his sequence *The House of Life*. This sonnet he dedicated to his mother. On her eightieth birthday (27 April 1880), he presented her David Main's *Treasury of English Sonnets*, into which he inserted an illustrated manuscript of his introductory sonnet. While the poem's composition history is thus associated with his mother, it eschews Christina's maternal presence for a double comparison of the sonnet form to loss as well as presence:

> A Sonnet is a moment's monument, –
> Memorial from the Soul's eternity
> To one dead deathless hour. Look that it be,
> Whether for lustral rite or dire portent,
> Of its own arduous fulness reverent:
> Carve it in ivory or in ebony,
> As Day or Night may rule; and let Time see
> Its flowering crest impearled and orient.
>
> A Sonnet is a coin: its face reveals
> The soul, – its converse, to what Power 'tis due: –
> Whether for tribute to the august appeals
> Of Life, or dower in Love's high retinue,
> It serve, or, 'mid the dark wharf's cavernous breath,
> In Charon's palm it pay the toll to Death.

This poem is another example of the subversion of the Petrarchan form to introduce a concluding couplet more familiar in the Shakespearean or English type. Such a blurring of generic forms neatly parallels the other paradoxical doublings in the sonnet: love and death, dead and deathless, day and night, monument and coin. In comparison with Barrett

Browning's sense of the impossibility of articulation within the sonnet, Dante Gabriel Rossetti motivates the paradoxes to serve the sonnet's inherent divisions between octave and sestet throughout his sequence (or, here, between octave and quatrain/couplet). It is important to note, in fact, that Rossetti always represented a clear stanzaic gap between divisions of the sonnet. As Hall Caine comments, such a deliberate separation was not unique, 'but he was the first who obeyed throughout a series of sonnets the canon of the contemporary structure requiring that a sonnet shall present the two-fold fact of a single thought or emotion' (1882: 31). Rossetti's exploitation of the sonnet's inherent bifurcated organicism is characteristic of his 'two-sided' aesthetic, which typically plays with generic and interartistic differences. In his sonnet on the sonnet, Rossetti embraces the fact that the genre is an inherently conflicted space, and although its 'arduous fullness' might be pregnant with erotic meaning, he insists that the sonnet is always in thrall to something else besides itself and its writer.

A manuscript version of the poem in the Fitzwilliam Museum, University of Cambridge, reveals that 'arduous' was originally 'intricate', which conveys Rossetti's sense of the sonnet as a work of art and an aesthetic object. The sonnet instructs that the form must be 'impearled', 'carved'. Furthermore, it must bear the stamp of its origin, whether the power of love or death inspired the poem. In an introductory note in the manuscript to the sequence *House of Life*, in the Fitzwilliam Museum, Rossetti insists that the sonnet is not directly experiential:

> To speak in the first person is often to speak most vividly; but these emotional poems are in no sense 'occasional'. The 'Life' involved is life representative, as associated with love and death, with aspiration and foreboding, or with ideal art and beauty. Whether the recorded moment exist in the region of fact or of thought is a question indifferent to the Muse, so long as her touch can quicken it.

The sequence of oppositions set up in this explanatory note again instructs us that the fullness and wholeness of the sonnet belie its conflicted doubleness. Furthermore, as the sonnets are not directly experiential, the narrative will be neither directly autobiographical nor progressive. The complicated composition and publication history of *The House of Life* affirm its state as a sequence in progress, capable of multiple forms and narratives. Barrett Browning's double-bind, in which she desires full expression in a sonnet and yet also fears its self-destructive consequences, is transformed by Rossetti into a troubled acceptance of the genre's divisions and contradictions, despite his contemporary commentator's insistence upon the sonnet's perfect unity and coherence.

Perhaps the most compelling paradoxical figure in Dante Gabriel Rossetti's sonnet on the sonnet is his comparison of the poetic form to a monument and a coin. The double image invokes the sonnet as an art object that has a monetary value. The sonnet anthologies that appeared in the Victorian period also encoded the genre as both capable of and yet also resisting commodification. Sharp's 1886 *Sonnets of this Century*, in many ways exemplary of Victorian sonnet anthologies, illustrates the genre's relationship to the literary and economic marketplace. Sharp's edition is intended, he notes in the introductory essay, for those readers 'whom Editions-de-luxe or even comparatively moderately priced books are more or less difficult of attainment' (1886: xxiv). The anthology is thus specifically marketed to maximize the potential readership and bring the pleasure of sonnet to those normally financially prohibited from purchasing editions. Everything about the anthology, however, from its diminutive size to the design of the page layout, emphasizes the sonnet's aesthetic value. Each sonnet, alphabetically arranged by author, has a page to itself, with the poet's underlined name at the top and the whole page bordered by a red line. The spatial effect of the large margins is to emphasize the form's small and compact size, its inherent coherence and organicism, corresponding with the sonnet ideology shaped by Victorian commentators.

In an article on sonnet anthologies and cultural value, Natalie Houston also notes that this spatial layout of sonnets is typical of the sonnet editions of the nineteenth century. For her, it makes a significant impact on reading: 'considering that poems in general poetry anthologies were frequently printed over two or more columns or pages, these sonnet anthologies offered nineteenth-century readers a more focused and reflective reading experience than did the large general anthologies' (1999: 249). It manoeuvred readers, Houston continues, into treating sonnets as 'an object of study' and 'cultural capital' in a bite-size chunk, capable of being memorized and exchanged (1999: 249). The page layout, however, serves two paradoxical functions overlooked by Houston. First, the design has the effect of positioning the sonnet as a valuable aesthetic object of the reader's gaze, contained and commodified ready for the reader's consumption. But the generous expanse of white margin surrounding each poem also figures it as an anti-commodity, beyond economic value, separated from the poems preceding and following, isolated and removed from cultural exchange. In a significant way, therefore, sonnet anthologies repeat the conflicted discourse of the genre produced by the sonnet critics. The prescriptions encoded into the sonnet – from its metrics to its content – were, however, frequently flouted by the sonnet writers themselves.

Sonnet Sequences

Arguably the most significant contribution of the Victorians to the sonnet renaissance was the revival of the sonnet sequence. Almost all of the sequences are part of the aesthetic and amatory strand of the sonnet history, influenced by the Petrarchan form and amatory ideology of Spenser's *Amoretti* and Sidney's *Astrophil and Stella* (notable exceptions are Emily Pfeiffer's 'Peace to the Odalisque' and William Michael Rossetti's *Democratic Sonnets*). The major sequences are: Barrett Browning's *Sonnets from the Portuguese*, Christina Rossetti's *Monna Innominata: A Sonnet of Sonnets* and *Later Life*, Dante Gabriel Rossetti's *The House of Life*, Augusta Webster's *Mother and Daughter* and George Meredith's *Modern Love*.

Elizabeth Barrett Browning's sequence has, since the early 1990s, been rediscovered by feminist literary critics as a turning point for nineteenth-century women poets. *Sonnets from the Portuguese* is a semi-autobiographical sequence of forty-four Petrarchan sonnets which describe the poet's courtship with Robert Browning. Barrett Browning took the manuscript with her when she eloped to Italy after her secret marriage, but only showed it to her husband by way of consolation when his mother died. Thus, the sequence was not originally intended for publication. Barrett Browning only consented to publish at the insistence of Browning and on the condition that their private and personal nature be disguised by representing the poems as a translation from the Portuguese (a reference to her poem 'Catarina to Camoëns', which had been much admired by Browning). Translation is in many ways the most important rhetorical trope of the poems, for they translate the amatory discourse of Petrarchanism into a vehicle for a female poet speaking from an active subject position. The result is to transform both the sonnet sequence and the sentimental tradition of women's poetry into a more muscular and dynamic poetics. For Barrett Browning, the sonnet becomes a transformative space, capable of moving between a host of fundamental oppositions such as speaker/addressee, life/death, love/grief.

Recently there has been a welcome shift of critical attention away from explaining the autobiographical nature of the sequence and its perceived sentimentality, towards accounts of the different ways in which agency and authorship are put into question. For example, in the very first sonnet, the speaker makes it clear that another power or agency is structuring the sequence. The poem begins with the speaker thinking of her past life, and those melancholy years that have cast a shadow over her:

> Straightway I was 'ware,
> So weeping, how a mystic Shape did move
> Behind me, and drew me backward by the hair,
> And a voice said in mastery while I strove, . . .
> 'Guess now who holds thee?' – 'Death,' I said. But, there,
> The silver answer rang, . . . 'Not Death, but Love.'
>
> (ll. 9–14)

The 'mystic shape' with its powerful agency forces her to begin to exchange death for love, figured autobiographically as respectively her dead brother Bro (for whose death at sea she held herself responsible) and Browning. In addition, the 'mystic shape' takes on a striking physical form in the pulling of hair, the signifier of transgressive feminine strength, in one of her two sonnets, to George Sand, whose shorn hair is depicted as uncannily and grotesquely floating back to her. Throughout the sequence, images of the desiring female body, and specifically the body of the woman poet, are figured as part of the translation of the genre into one accommodating an active woman's voice. But, significantly, such physical, material figures are part of an intersubjective exchange with the beloved, Robert Browning. In other words, the sequence neither rejects Petrarchanism nor simply feminizes it, but is a process of translation.

The two sonnets which most effectively display the transformative troping of the female body are numbers 18 and 19. These again invoke the speaker's hair, as locks are exchanged for love tokens:

I never gave a lock of hair away
To a man, dearest, except this to thee,
Which now upon my fingers thoughtfully
I ring out to the full brown length and say
'Take it'. My day of youth went yesterday;
My hair no longer bounds to my foot's glee,
Nor plant I it from rose or myrtle-tree,
As girls do, any more. It only may
Now shade on two pale cheeks, the mark of tears,
Taught dropping from the head that hangs aside
Through sorrow's trick. I thought the funeral-shears
Would take this first, but love is justified, –
Take it, though, . . . finding pure, from all those years,
The kiss my mother left here when she died.

The soul's Rialto hath its merchandise;
I barter curl for curl upon that mart
And from my poet's forehead to my heart,
Receive this lock which outweighs argosies, –
As purply black, as erst, to Pindar's eyes,
The dim purpureal tresses gloomed athwart
The nine white Muse-brows. For this counterpart, . . .
Thy bay-crown's shade, Belovèd, I surmise,
Still lingers on thy curl, it is so black
Thus, with a fillet of smooth-kissing breath,
I tie the shadow safe from gliding back,
And lay the gift where nothing hindereth,
Here on my heart, as on my brow, to lack
No natural heart till mine grows cold in death.

The gift of a lock of hair is traditionally a courtly synecdoche for the consummation of a sexual relationship. In sonnet 18, the lock of hair is specifically a reminder of the speaker's age and loss of youth. The speaker represents herself as aged, faded and, against Petrarchan tradition, an unaesthetic object of exchange. The curl, however, as a synecdoche of her body and her desire, participates in a new kind of exchange for the Petrarchan tradition: the economy of the gift. (This new economy is also apparent in the courtship correspondence; Kintner 1969: 288–93, 300.) As Judith Still (1997) argues, the gift is an exchange that subverts the capitalist marketplace, for, ideally, it suspends obligation and laws of ownership. In the *Sonnets from the Portuguese*, the act of exchanging gifts is a reciprocal exchange. It is a personal gift, to be hidden away from others' eyes 'here on my heart'. As a figure for the bodies of subject and addressee, the locks of hair express what language fails to do in Barrett Browning's 'Insufficiency': an articulation of female desire in a way that potentially threatens to singe the laurels and the hair on Browning's head with the 'red wild sparkles' of sexual passion (sonnet 5).

Judith Still's analysis of the gift economy concedes that it may only be a utopia, for the market cannot be so easily evaded. Indeed, sonnet 19 suggests as much, with the reciprocal gift of Browning's lock taking place on the Rialto, the centre of Venice's marketplace and synecdoche for its thriving mercantile economy. The lock also bears a further significance: it stands figuratively not only for the bodies and desires of the lovers, but also for the sonnets themselves, which are eventually gifted in manuscript to Browning. The association of the sonnet sequence with the speaker's lock of hair suggests that poetry cannot exist completely outside the marketplace, even published poetry that is originally written in private and exchanged as a gift. Furthermore, the poet/speaker, whose body and desire are represented by the lock and the poem, is also inherently part of the mercantile exchange. Indeed, as Gitter (1984) demonstrates, the Victorian fascination with locks of hair encoded both the aesthetic and the mercantile body (represented most famously by Dante Gabriel Rossetti's 'Jenny').

While Elizabeth Barrett Browning revives the Petrarchan sonnet to forge a complex new dynamics between active and passive, subject and object, speaker and addressee, Christina Rossetti's *Monna Innominata: A Sonnet of Sonnets* speaks from the position of the other and the silenced. This sequence has a highly overdetermined structure of a macro-sonnet, comprising fourteen sonnets divided to replicate an octave and sestet (Harrison 1988). The sequence's preface suggests that it is a challenge to Rossetti's precursor. The unnamed lady gives a voice to the Beatrices and Lauras whose silence makes them 'resplendent with charms, but (at least to my apprehension), scant of attractiveness'. The preface continues ironically:

> [H]ad the Great Poetess of our own day and nation only been unhappy instead of happy, her circumstances would have invited her to bequeath to us, in lieu of the 'Portuguese Sonnets', an inimitable 'donna innominata' drawn not from fancy but from feeling, and worthy to occupy a niche beside Beatrice and Laura. (Rossetti 1979–90: II, 86)

Such comments are 'elusive' (Harrison 1990: 110), and indeed, Rossetti felt it necessary to clarify her oblique reference to Barrett Browning in a letter to Dante Gabriel, after a reviewer questioned her meaning (Rossetti 1997: II, 299). Harrison summarizes the differences between the poetics of the two women poets: '[Rossetti's poetic strength] in opposition to Elizabeth Barrett Browning's, lies, not in assertive outspokenness, but rather in a baffling and defiant, sometimes ostensibly self-contradictory, sometimes masochistic, and sometimes riddling, silence' (1990: 110).

Although *Monna Innominata* is an oblique if self-conscious corrective to the *Sonnets from the Portuguese*, its ending with 'The longing of a heart pent up forlorn / A silent heart whose silence loves and longs' has been accepted by at least one feminist critic as poetic failure (Montefiore 1987). But within a hyperconsciousness of restrictive poetic space, and the repeated emphatic staging of closure at the end of each sonnet, the sequence voices the position of loss, absence and longing both specifically as a sequence addressed to Rossetti's close friend Charles Cayley and generically as the unnamed lady of sonnet tradition. Within these formal constraints, Rossetti dematerializes the sonnet and speaks out of the interstice, the in-between: 'Come back to me who watch and wait for you: – / Or come not yet, for it is over then', 'My hope hangs waning, waxing, like a moon / Between the heavenly days on which we meet', 'If only now I could recall that touch, / First touch of hand in hand', 'Thus only in a dream we are at one'. The sequence's most important rhetorical figures, furthermore, are those of substitution, doubling and exchange:

> For verily love knows not 'mine' or 'thine';
> With separate 'I' and 'thou' free love has done,
> For one is both and both are one in love.
>
> (sonnet 4)

> Yea, as I apprehend it, love is such
> I cannot love you if I love not Him,
> I cannot love Him if I love not you.
>
> (sonnet 6)

Whereas *Sonnets from the Portuguese* employed tropes of exchange as intersubjective, such as the lock of hair, Rossetti's doublings and substitutions eschew the sonnet's traditional synecdoche for metonymy. Thus, where for the Wordsworthian sonnet the synecdoche allows the sonnet's small space to contain the ineffable, *Monna Innominata* suggests that the speaker's erotic and spiritual desire exceeds form *and* language in an endless play of desire. W. David Shaw (1990) argues that Rossetti often means more than she can say. In her sonnet sequence, both the form and the articulation exceed the genre's closure.

Rossetti's play of language produces liminal sonnets which both perfect the Petrarchan form on a micro- and macro-level and yet also dissolve the norms of the genre. *Later Life: A Double Sonnet of Sonnets* similarly contains a chain of substitutions as the speaker explores the frustrations and fears of mortality and materiality: 'We lack, yet cannot fix upon the lack: / Not this, nor that; yet somewhat, certainly' (sonnet 6). Her uncanny dematerialization, as her troubled desire for the afterlife is expressed, positions the subject outside the sonnet form altogether in another revision of Wordsworth's sonnet ideology: 'I have dreamed of Death: – what would it be to die / Not in a dream, but in the literal truth' (sonnet 27). In comparison, Dante Gabriel Rossetti's sonnet sequence *The House of Life* attempts to reify and materialize language and the space of the genre, as suggested in the introductory sonnet. As William Sharp suggests, these sonnets are aesthetic objects in themselves: 'his imagination is so concrete that its creations always present themselves to him as things of form and colour, and his sonnets spread themselves out like fair paintings on the walls of the gallery of the mind' (1886: 57).

It is not only Dante Gabriel Rossetti's sonnets on pictures which express the form as an aesthetic object. In his sequence, the formal constraints of the genre are highlighted by the stanzaic gap between octave and sestet, dramatizing spatially the material shape of the poem. The sequence's materiality is, however, uncanny, for it preserves in tension an experiential and aesthetic 'moment's monument' that commemorates both the moment and its passing. For Dante Gabriel Rossetti, then, the sonnet is somewhat taxidermic or, in Wagner's words 'a kind of death in life, a formalised stasis' (1996: 133). Its record of the moment represents a poetic texture of materiality and immediacy which is illusory (1996: 132). The very density of language, the weight of figurality, Rossetti's 'fundamental brain-work' (as he put it), contributed to the effect. Thus, as much as the sonnet is reified

as an aesthetic object and an experiential moment, mortality and loss shadow the sequence.
For example, 'The Portrait' (sonnet X):

> O Lord of all compassionate control,
>   O Love! let this my lady's picture glow
>   Under my hand to praise her name, and show
> Even of her inner self the perfect whole:
> That he who seeks her beauty's furthest goal,
>   Beyond the light that the sweet glances throw
>   And refluent wave of the sweet smile, may know
> The very sky and sea-line of her soul.
>
> Lo! it is done. Above the enthroning throat
>   The mouth's mould testifies of voice and kiss,
>   The shadowed eyes remember and foresee.
> Her face is made her shrine. Let all men note
>   That in all years (O Love, thy gift is this!)
>   They that would look on her must come to me.

Implicitly, the ekphrastic sonnet is the picture of the beloved which testifies to and immor-
talizes her beauty. The description is, however, curiously elusive. As the 'perfect whole'
of both the beloved and the sonnet are announced, both are nevertheless fractured. The
lady has the traditional Petrarchan sweet glance and smile, but the inner landscape of her
soul, its 'sky and sea-line', undermines the representation of her presence. The sestet,
indeed, suggests that the moment of the portrait's wholeness and completion has already
become the past and the future. The moment has dissolved. The sonnet, in capturing the
portrait of the beloved's soul, has de-animated it so that 'her face is made her shrine' at
the moment of completion. Its purpose is to signify to the future her beauty and wholeness. 'The Portrait' is haunted by its own temporality.

The House of Life, with its complex history of composition and publication, and its
complex figurality, dramatizes the genre's fractured investment in its own materiality.
Other sonnet sequences play out that drama rather differently. Meredith's *Modern Love*,
the narrative of a failing marriage and marital jealousy, contributes an important innovation to the sonnet with its sixteen lines, made up of four quatrains. The extra two lines
attempt to delay the sonnet's traditional volta and closure, just as the tortured speaker
attempts to postpone the final dissolution of his marriage. The sequence is, like Dante
Gabriel Rossetti's, haunted: 'I claim a phantom-woman in the Past. / The hour has struck,
though I heard not the bell!' (sonnet 3). The ghost is love (sonnet 6), who haunts the
speaker with the memory of marital content: 'Shall I, unsustained, / Drag on Love's nerveless body thru' all time?' (sonnet 10). *Modern Love* is a sustained and tortured parody of
Petrarchanism (see in particular sonnet 30), which mourns figuratively and literally the
fruitless, barren marriage. In sonnet 11, the couple's marital strife is represented as a dead
infant, slain by the speaker's wife in her betrayal (compare also sonnet 50).

A different concern with physical materiality and the sonnet's space is shown in Augusta Webster's unfinished *Mother and Daughter* sequence, posthumously published by William Michael Rossetti in 1895. In her sonnets, Webster insists on maternal plenitude and presence as, following Christina Rossetti, 'the passion of maternity' which subverts Petrarchanism (sonnet 26). Even to be haunted is to experience the presence of love (sonnets 8 and 12). The sequence, then, self-consciously deconstructs the deanimation of the genre at the hands of such sonneteers as Dante Gabriel Rossetti, whose sonnet space is the vehicle for the dissolution of the aesthetic object. The start of *Mother and Daughter* celebrates the inter-subjective dynamics between speaker and addressee. In the beginning of the sequence, the daughter represents presence and materiality: her voice, in sonnet 1, for example, intimates the present moment and plenitude. Even in her dreams, as in sonnet 5 during a thunder storm, the daughter, in her 'unconscious grace', speaks out 'Mother'. As the sonnets progress, however, and as the child grows up, the speaker begins to fear the loss of her relationship with the daughter. The remarkable sonnet 11 translates this fear into a demystification of the Petrarchan image of woman's sexual love which does not withstand betrayal and pain. Marital love is displaced by the love between mother and daughter, which is represented as far more dynamic. In sonnet 15, the speaker anticipates her own absence in death, in the 'voiceless mould', as 'no strangeness, but Death's natural hest'. In contrast, however, and whereas Wordsworth momentarily and painfully forgets the death of his daughter in his sonnet 'Surprised by joy', Webster refuses to acknowledge the mortality of her child in the sestet: 'looking on the dawn that is her face / To know she too is Death's seems misbelief.' In sonnet 25, the speaker defends her decision to have only one child by declaring that their love has a unity and wholeness which transcends the smallness of their family: 'Love's most priceless things / Have unity that cannot be undone', and 'None takes the strong entireness from her: none', for 'she is one, she has the whole'. The following sonnet makes clear that this oneness extends triumphantly to their relationship. Both make the other whole, beyond the fear of mortality and dissolution:

> Oh! Child and mother, darling! Mother and child!
> And who but we? We, darling, paired alone?
> Thou hast thy mother; thou are all my own.
> Thy passion of maternity which sweeps
> Tideless 'neath where the heaven of thee hath smiled
> Has but one channel, therefore infinite deeps.
>
> (sonnet 26)

For Webster, the traditional materiality of the sonnet form is the perfect vehicle in which to express her theory of the maternal. Indeed, the unity expressed in sonnet 25 sounds similar to the ideal unity and wholeness of the Petrarchan sonnet form required by Victorian genre ideology. Webster thus closely allies the genre's organic form and content in a new configuration, to refuse the sonnet's associations with dissolution and mortality.

That this genre, with such rigid rules encoded into its small space, can repeatedly subvert the sonnet ideology is remarkable. Belying its highly wrought fourteen lines, the Victorian sonnet does indeed surpass its formal limitations. The Indo-Anglian Toru Dutt's 'Sonnet – Baugmaree' offers another example of its potential for dramatic cultural negotiation and is perhaps the most flamboyantly self-conscious Victorian example of the subversion of the sonnet form:

> A sea of foliage girds our garden round,
> But not a sea of dull unvaried green,
> Sharp contrasts of all colours here are seen;
> The light-green graceful tamarinds abound
> Amid the mangoe clumps of green profound,
> And palms arise, like pillars gray, between;
> And o'er the quiet pools the seemuls lean,
> Red, – red, and startling like a trumpet's sound.
> But nothing can be lovelier than the ranges
> Of bamboos to the eastward, when the moon
> Looks through their gaps, and the white lotus changes
> Into a cup of silver. One might swoon
> Drunken with beauty then, or gaze and gaze
> On a primeval Eden, in amaze.

Dutt begins her sonnet with a traditional Petrarchan octave, rhyming, conventionally, *abbaabba*. The content of the octave, however, subverts the ideology of the Victorian sonnet and of Petrarchanism, for it situates the speaker in an Indian garden which is, paradoxically, excessively abounding in sensuous Pre-Raphaelite tropes of exuberance and excess. This is a clear challenge to the racial purity insisted on by Victorian commentators on the sonnet. The bowered garden, furthermore, is represented with a defined boundary, girded by foliage, but the contents exceed its size. In implicit contrast to a traditional English garden, the greens are varied and profuse, yielding division and contrast rather than unity, wholeness and organicism. The tamarinds, mango clumps, palms and seemuls remind us that the speaker is not in England. At the end of the octave, at what is traditionally the Petrarchan sonnet's turn, the sound of the seemuls is compared to both an intensely doubled red and the sound of the trumpet. In his 'Scorn not the sonnet', Wordsworth compares Milton's sonnets to trumpets. The synaesthesia of Dutt's trumpet, however, displaces the Miltonic and Wordworthian tradition in favour of Madame de Staël's Corinne, who (as Jane Stabler has pointed out to me) is positioned at the centre of the Indian garden. In her famous improvisation at the Capitol, which gave women poets a paradigm of the inspired, spontaneous artist, the voice of Corinne is compared to 'the sound of victorious trumpets, which has been likened to scarlet amongst the colours' (de Staël 1807, 1998: 33). Thus, Dutt subtly and coyly reminds us of the sonnet's racial hybridity and the subversive nationhood of the prototypical woman artist, as she parodies the Victorian anglicization of Petrarchanism.

The sestet contains another surprise, for it reverts to the Shakespearean sonnet form of a quatrain followed by a couplet. While earlier sonneteers such as Wyatt and Sidney and

Donne had favoured the form of Italian octave followed by Shakespearean sestet, in the context of Victorian sonnet ideology, which prized the Petrarchan form as the ideal, Dutt implies that neither form can contain the speaker's desire. Her use of the hybrid sonnet form flouts all the Victorian sonnet's rules of legitimacy and purity. The sestet, further-more, insists that the content exceeds the form, but this is no mere reiteration of the Wordsworthian sonnet sublime. Indeed, for Dutt, the sonnet goes beyond its restrictive patriarchal and Petrarchan space through figurality, as the moon, that potent symbol of the feminine and of changeableness and mutation, shines through the gaps of the bamboos. Like Christina Rossetti, Dutt locates her desire in the in-between, the space left open by the bamboos and silvery luminosity of the lotus. The turn, again subverting any norm of the sonnet by coming in the middle of line 12, suggests that one can either be overcome with beauty in a loss of consciousness, or accept the presence and plenitude of the garden's excesses and (adopting a Spenserian term that encompasses both verb and noun) enter into its exuberance 'in amaze'. These last lines, furthermore, suggest that her Indian garden is the original garden, the 'primeval Eden', which both surpasses and precedes Western traditional literary forms and figures.

Dutt's extraordinary poem serves as a fitting reminder that the Victorian sonnet form, despite its 'scanty plot of ground' and rigid metrics, is capable of multiple transforma-tions. Its intense and self-conscious meta-textuality means that any reading of the sonnet should take into account the complex relationship between form and content. In its record of a moment, the sonnet's insistence on its own space and materiality encodes it generi-cally as both aesthetic object and commodity. That moment's inevitable dissolution, and the form's transcendence of its miniature size, ensure that the sonnet is, furthermore, an anti-commodity, escaping its own temporality and concreteness. That transcendence, and its terrible potential cost, mean that the post-Wordsworthian sonnet is not a place of 'brief solace', but of cultural negotiation, painful loss and radical subversion.

See also: ANTHOLOGIES AND THE MAKING OF THE POETIC CANON; VERSE NOVEL; LYRIC.

REFERENCES AND FURTHER READING

Caine, Hall (1882) *Recollections of Dante Gabriel Rossetti.* London: Elliot Stock.

Chapman, Alison (1999) 'Uncanny Epiphanies in the Victorian Sonnet.' In Wim Tigges (ed.). *Moments of Moment: Studies in the Literary Epiphany* (pp. 115–35). Amsterdam: Rodopi.

Chapman, Alison (2000) *The Afterlife of Christina Rossetti.* Basingstoke: Macmillan.

Cooper, Helen (1988) *Elizabeth Barrett Browning. Woman and Artist.* Chapel Hill and London: University of North Carolina Press.

Curran, Stuart (1986) *Poetic Form and British Romanticism.* New York and Oxford: Oxford University Press.

Feldman, Paula R., and Daniel Robinson (1999) *A Century of Sonnets: The Romantic-Era Revival 1750–1850.* New York and Oxford: Oxford University Press.

Gill, Stephen (1998) *Wordsworth and the Victorians.* Oxford: Clarendon Press.

Gitter, Elisabeth G. (1984) 'The Power of Women's Hair in the Victorian Imagination.' *PMLA*, 99, 936–54.

Going, William T. (1976) *Scanty Plot of Ground:*

Studies in the Victorian Sonnet. The Hague: Mouton.

Harrison, Antony H. (1988) *Christina Rossetti in Context.* Brighton: Harvester.

Harrison, Antony H. (1990) *Victorian Poets and Romantic Poems.* Charlottesville: University Press of Virginia.

Houston, Natalie M. (1999) 'Valuable by Design: Material Features and Cultural Value in Nineteenth-Century Sonnet Anthologies.' *Victorian Poetry*, 37.2, 243–72.

Kintner, Elvan (ed.) (1969) *The Letters of Robert Browning and Elizabeth Barrett Browning: 1845–46.* Cambridge, Mass.: Harvard University Press.

Langbaum, Robert (1982) 'The Epiphanic Mode in Wordsworth and Modern Literature.' *New Literary History*, XIV, 335–58.

Leighton, Angela (1986) *Elizabeth Barrett Browning.* Brighton: Harvester.

Lysack, Krista (1998) 'The Economics of Ecstasy in Christina Rossetti's *Monna Innominata*.' *Victorian Poetry*, 36.4, 399–416.

Mermin, Dorothy (1989) *Elizabeth Barrett Browning. The Origins of a New Poetry.* Chicago and London: University of Chicago Press.

Miller, J. Hillis (1985) *The Linguistic Moment: From Wordsworth to Stevens.* Princeton, N. J.: Princeton University Press.

Montefiore, Jan (1987) *Feminism and Poetry: Language, Experience, Identity in Women's Writing.* London: Pandora Press.

Noble, James Ashcroft (1896) *The Sonnet in England and Other Essays.* Second edition. London: John Lane; Chicago: Way and Williams.

Rossetti, Christina (1979–90) *The Complete Poems of Christina Rossetti.* Ed. R. W. Crump. 3 vols. Baton Rouge and London: Louisiana State University Press.

Rossetti, Christina (1997) *The Letters of Christina Rossetti.* Vol. I. Ed. Antony H. Harrison. Charlottesville: University Press of Virginia.

Russell, Matthew S. J. (1898) *Sonnets on the Sonnet: An Anthology.* London: Longman, Green.

Sharp, William (ed.) (1886) *Sonnets of this Century.* London: Walter Scott.

Shaw, W. David (1990) *Victorians and Mystery: Crises of Representation.* Ithaca, N. Y.: Cornell University Press.

Spiller, Michael R. G. (1992) *The Development of the Sonnet: An Introduction.* London and New York: Routledge.

Staël, Madame de (1807, 1998) *Corinne, or Italy.* Trans. Sylvia Raphael. Oxford: Oxford University Press.

Still, Judith (1997) *Feminine Economies: Thinking Against the Market in the Enlightenment and the Late Twentieth Century.* Manchester: Manchester University Press.

Tomlinson, Charles (1874) *The Sonnet: Its Origin, Structure, and Place in Poetry.* London: John Murray.

Wagner, Jennifer Ann (1996) *A Moment's Monument: Revisionary Poetics and the Nineteenth-Century English Sonnet.* London: Associated University Presses.

6
Elegy
Seamus Perry

As literary classifications go, 'Victorian' is more arbitrary even than most; but the label does, fortuitously, associate a body of writing with the most famous modern act of devoted mourning. 'She herself felt that her true life had ceased with her husband's', Lytton Strachey wrote, in a surprisingly tender stretch of his normally spry biography of Victoria, 'and the remainder of her days upon earth was of a twilight nature – an epilogue to a drama that was done' (1921: 218). Each night, Albert's clothes were laid out with hot water and a clean towel, which was remarkable even by prevailing standards of morbid ceremony. All the same, the queen's display of bereavement feels somehow representative, for Victorians, not least the poets among them, have often been seen as particularly disposed to elegiac feelings, and not least by the Victorians themselves. Max Beerbohm's cartoon of a Browning Society gathering, for instance, winningly portrays a dismal room of long faces; but then the poet himself in their midst beams inscrutably to himself, stirring his cup of tea, so the message of the full portrait is more intricate than pervasive gloom. That twinkling eye obliges a chapter like this one to begin with customary noises about generalizing: of course, many Victorian poems are as blithely remote from elegiac sentiment as any; anyway, death has always been a favourite subject; and even those many Victorian poets who did find their most telling voices weighing kinds of loss were, naturally, no more single-minded about the practice of elegizing than Victorians were about anything else. Still, for all that, the occasion of elegy does seem to have drawn some of the century's most powerful imaginations. Tennyson's *In Memoriam A. H. H.* (1850) presides over the literary age: an extraordinary public success (it sold 5,000 copies in weeks), the poem interweaves a private loss with more epochal anxieties, as though seeking in bereavement a route to the spirit of the age. Critics sometimes call it the most representative Victorian work of art, part of which exemplary feel doubtless comes from its close involvement with Victoria herself: it was Albert's admiration for the poem that led to Tennyson's appointment as laureate; and, after Albert's death, Tennyson was evidently flattered as well as touched to learn that the widowed queen found 'much on which she loves to dwell in your "In Memoriam" . . . how many were the passages she had marked' (Lang and Shannon 1982–90: II, 297n.2).

The term 'elegy' initially referred to a particular metrical form, not a subject; but, by the nineteenth century, the word had acquired its modern meaning, referring to poems that responded particularly to a death. The final stage in any adequate response to loss is persuading yourself, and perhaps others too, that the attenuated world is still worth persisting with: this is the recuperation that Freud (1953–66: 245, 246) calls the 'work of mourning', which, once completed, sets 'the ego . . . free and uninhibited again', as 'respect for reality gains the day'; and elegies, typically anyway, enact this important piece of psychology, as though to educate the tribe. Freud's account might make a successful recovery seem very complete and single-mindedly healthy, but poets, as William Empson observed (1953: xiii), are often most at home when writing from a background of conflicting impulses; and the greatest elegiac poetry (like most actual grief I suppose) doesn't exhibit merely a recuperative return to the world, but rather a kind of double-heartedness, which recognizes the need to move on, while staying true to the dead.

There is an obvious paradox in writing pleasurable verses about loss, but the emotional paradox underwriting the best elegy is an altogether more intricate association, of recol-lection back and movement forward, of memory and expectation. Milton's 'Lycidas', for a prominent example, is at once a lament and a consolation, setting the dwelling sadness of recollection very honestly against the necessary recovery of prospect: the poem begins with bare devastation ('Lycidas is dead, dead ere his prime / Young Lycidas, and hath not left his peer'), but modulates into something like serenity ('So Lycidas sunk low, but mounted high, / Through the dear might of him that walk'd the waves') and ends with a famous case of pressing on ('To-morrow to fresh Woods, and Pastures new'). Milton registers his spirit's transition in the shifting life of the phrase *no more*: the sadly contrastive, backward-looking 'no more' of the poem's opening lines ('The Willows, and the Hazle Copses green, / Shall now no more be seen, / Fanning their joyous Leaves to thy soft layes') moves quietly into the progressive 'no more' of its close ('Weep no more, woful Shepherds weep no more'). The device is marvellous because it insinuates a continuity within a change: the demands of life push the poet on to pastures new, but the memory of the past lingers irremovably in the poem's auditory existence, as though a single thing were the heart of both a perennial loss and a new kind of future; which is the situation of someone mourning.

So then, an elegy is not, traditionally, merely a lament; nor yet is it an unchecked yowl of outrage at the wrongness of the universe; but rather a dealing with despair, spoken from the other side of grief; and the feeling that it moves towards, or around, is consola-tory, though (in the best elegies) not simply consolatory. This often involves an immense effort of the mind to think well of death – often by denying that it is, strictly, death at all. That obviously finds an important precedent in Christ, who died but did not die, and who raised Japhet's daughter: 'the damsel is not dead, but sleepeth' (Mark 5:39); but the elegiac turn need not be Christian. In his elegy for Keats, the atheist Shelley summons the scriptural allusion only to decline it, in favour of Platonic reasons to be cheerful: 'Peace, peace! he is not dead, he doth not sleep – / He hath awakened from the dream of life.' Adonais overcomes death by being 'made one with Nature'; and this is another common feature of elegy: to think of the death as somehow intended by, or implicated within, a persisting natural order, which is why classical elegies, as well as more recent elegies con-scious of their ancestry, tend to be written as pastoral: that is, as in 'Lycidas', the words are placed in the mouths of grieving shepherds.

A modern writer is likely to regard with great suspicion both those kinds of consoling discovery – the supernaturalism of the afterlife as much as the naturalism of pastoral: to see them as a con or a trick, 'That vast moth-eaten musical brocade', as Philip Larkin called religion, 'Invented to pretend that no one dies'. (Zeiger's 1997 book about modern elegy is exemplarily entitled *Beyond Consolation*, and locates the origin of the tradition of disenchantment it describes firmly within the Victorian period.) Historians have often described the 'secularization' of the Western Mind, and gathered the more devastating nineteenth-century aspects of it under the rubric 'Victorian Doubt': a clumsy idea, if only for its implication of untroubled centuries before the queen. But of course traditional kinds of Christian faith were indeed being tested with increasing severity during the century, and many Victorians were dreadfully self-conscious about living through a spiritual catastrophe. 'We are most hopeless, that had hoped most high', wrote Clough, 'And most beliefless, that had most believed' ('Easter Day', ll. 88–9).

Summoning such vast cultural movements to account for any particular poem feels very ham-fisted; but it is not difficult to make out the general connection in our Victorian case. For naturally enough, along with the authority of Scripture, the Prayer Book's 'sure and certain hope of the resurrection to eternal life, through our Lord Jesus Christ', and its whole attendant repertoire of consolation, got badly shaken: a deepening uncertainty that underlay the age's often obsessive arts of death and commemoration – not only elegies, but also innumerable deathbeds and graveyards in paintings and novels, collections of 'last words', grand necropolises, and elaborate mourning rituals. And if appeals to transcendent immortality were much less obviously to hand, then nature had changed too, from a magical view to a scientific one, with similarly immense consequence. That it should be a Victorian sage, Ruskin, who (in *Modern Painters*, 1856) regarded the grounds of pastoral consolation as a *fallacy* is no coincidence: any lingering atavistic trust in nature's interested connection with human life was unpicked by the progress of nineteenth-century science and finished off by Darwinism. *In Memoriam* is, in some sections, as much a lament for the old benevolent idea of nature's fellow-feeling as it is one for Hallam; and among the strong emotions at work in Housman is outrage that nature should be so negligent of his feelings. As the hero of Mallock's account of the *Zeitgeist*, *The New Republic* (1877), complains: 'Life stares at us now, all blank and expressionless, like the eyes of a lost friend, who is not dead, but who has turned an idiot.' The impulse to console was not forgone, of course: the speaker in 'Prospice', a rare elegy by Browning, refuses despair ('Fear death?') with pugnacious confidence ('I shall clasp thee again, / And with God be the rest!', ll. 1, 27–8); but the best Victorian elegies reach out for it more tentatively.

Victorian elegy emerges not only within a particular episode in the history of religious feeling, but also at a specific, late Romantic moment in literary history. One of the most telling Romantic elegies is the one that Wordsworth *didn't* write (despite encouragement) about the master of his college, on the grounds that 'I felt no interest in the deceased person': that invokes the poetic standard which Keats would later call 'the true voice of feeling'. If a classical poem seeks to describe what Dr Johnson termed 'general nature', then a Romantic poem will characteristically appeal to the reality of a particular 'I', emphasizing not the universality of its sentiments but their uniqueness. The testing new criterion, then, is often *sincerity*: 'when a Man is treating an interesting subject', Wordsworth writes in his 'Essays upon Epitaphs', 'no faults have such a killing power as those which prove that he is not in earnest, that he is acting a part, has leisure for affectation' – the poet should, rather, exude the 'charm of sincerity' and an 'inward simplicity' (Wordsworth 1988: 345, 346). So the testing point for post-Romantic elegy is about the eloquence or the inwardness of poetic language: its public efficacy and address or personal authenticity. This all-important distinction in possible poetic voices might first be heard in the difference between Gray's lapidary and handsomely generalizing 'Elegy Written in a Country Churchyard' (1751) and the stifled intimacy of his sonnet in memory of Richard West (1742), which concludes by lamenting the impotence of its poetry: 'I fruitless mourn to him that cannot hear, / And weep the more because I weep in vain.'

Wordsworth (the most important Romantic presence in Victorian elegy) thought those lines among the very few in Gray's poem that were any good: they shed the literary refinement that, as Wordsworth saw things, corrupted the feelings in most of the sonnet, and lapse savingly into a human voice; and it is no coincidence that they admit poetic incapacity, for one of Wordsworth's most effective (and paradoxical) bequests was his discovery of the expressive power of inarticulacy. When this power exerts itself, an accomplished public voice falters beneath a private pressure, as in his muted elegy for the obscure Lucy:

> She *lived* unknown, and few could know
>   When Lucy ceased to be;
> But she is in her Grave, and, Oh!
>   The difference to me.
>
> ('Song', ll. 9–12)

The reticent virtues of that are just the opposite of Milton's grand performance: Wordsworth's is quite as much a performance, but, so to say, of a very private sort; and it gives rise to a paradoxical understanding of the lyrical voice. J. S. Mill, a good Wordsworthian, makes the point: 'eloquence is *heard*, poetry is *over*heard. Eloquence supposes an audience; the peculiarity of poetry appears to us to lie in the poet's utter unconsciousness of a listener. Poetry is feeling, confessing itself to itself in moments of solitude' (1981: 348).

Publishing confessions made to yourself is about as introspective as you can get while communicating at all; and Romantic poems often give the impression that they're reluctant to yield up their innermost privacies: a Romantic distrust of the publicity of language, which distorts and corrupts the integrity of inner feeling, importantly shapes the Victorian practice of elegy. For elegy is duty-bound to turn a private experience into a public meaning: its whole function, you might say, is to relate the one to the other; but, after the Romantics, the public and private inflections of the voice often show themselves at odds. Tennyson (reportedly) said of *In Memoriam* that the poem was more hopeful than he was himself (Ricks 1989: 339, headnote): the public voice and the private experience failed to coincide. In the case of *In Memoriam*, it is as though the classical work of elegy is not being completed properly: the conditions are not propitious; and this is something which the poem's poignant double-life of wandering irresolution and wilfully steadying optimism must surely communicate even to readers who have never come across Tennyson's remark.

The subject of *In Memoriam A. H. H. Obiit MDCCCXXXIII* is Arthur Hallam, Tennyson's Cambridge friend. He was a fellow Apostle ('The Apostles' is the undergraduate society in section LXXXVII; Hallam was its brightest star), a poet and the fiancé of Tennyson's sister; and Tennyson was clearly much in love with him (and loved in return). Hallam died, suddenly, from a blood vessel burst in his brain, at the age of twenty-two, in September 1833; the body was brought back to England by boat – the episode which features in an early sequence of the poem. The first sections of *In Memoriam* date from the month Tennyson learned of Hallam's death; it grew and grew over the next seventeen years, haphazardly: 'I did not write them with any view of weaving them into a whole, or for publication, until I found that I had written so many' (Hallam 1897: I, 304). Rearranged into a fictive chronological order spanning nine years, it was finally published (with important revisions on the eve of its appearance) in 1850.

The most striking discovery in the poem, as critics have often noted, is its stanza, about which many things have been beautifully said. Here is Charles Kingsley:

> The poems seem often merely to be united by the identity of their metre, so exquisitely chosen, that while the major rhyme in the second and third lines of each stanza gives the solidity and self-restraint required by such deep themes, the mournful minor rhyme of each first and fourth line always leads the ear to expect something beyond. (Jump 1967: 183)

Some first stirrings of the poem were rhymed *abab* (see Ricks 1989: 347), and the difference makes clear the inspired rightness of the final choice, *abba*: the *In Memoriam* stanza is one of the great formal responses to the occasion of elegy, acknowledging the necessity of trying to move on, but insistent too about the compulsion to look back – a paradoxical matter of 'loiter[ing] on' (XXXVIII). The verse entwines a moment of confirmation (in its middle couplet) with a lingering return (in its outer rhyme), so that each verse, whatever the sense of purpose with which it sets out, ends acoustically haunted by the thought with which it began: 'the perfect embodiment', as Christopher Ricks says finely, 'of the true relationship of faith to faintness in the poem' (1989: 216). 'Rhyme has been said to contain in itself a constant appeal to Memory and Hope', wrote Hallam, in an essay Ricks quotes (Ricks 1984: 77, quoting Hallam 1943: 222): a new rhyme looks forward hopefully to its completion, and a completing rhyme recalls its partner; and if each *In Memoriam* stanza begins with expectation, it soon relapses again into recollection – the texture is self-enfolding, as though seeking to protect a memory of Hallam, as much as the bruised being of Tennyson himself, from change ('that large grief which these enfold': V). Tennyson himself announces, quite near the end, what might serve as motto for the whole: 'though my lips may breathe adieu, / I cannot think the thing farewell' (CXXIII) – which allows a note of tenacious return to sound ('I try to persuade myself forward, but I am unable to move my thoughts on from this thing') beneath a necessary assertion of hope ('I cannot conceive that this parting is really absolute or complete, that he is *really* dead').

For example:

> Behold, we know not anything;
>   I can but trust that good shall fall
>   At last – far off – at last, to all,
> And every winter change to spring.
>
> So runs my dream: but what am I?
>   An infant crying in the night:
>   An infant crying for the light:
> And with no language but a cry.
>
>   (LIV)

The hesitancy and self-undoing of the verse are terrible but marvellous: 'trust' can seldom have been invoked so doubtfully, a last resort; nor the remoteness of 'At last – far off – at last' made so falteringly emphatic. 'Fall' dwindles audibly to the reduced rhyme of 'all'; 'spring' circles back forlornly, as with seasonal inevitability, to find the bleak 'anything' which the stanza had begun gathering its strength to overcome. Even this scant trust is promptly undone by the next verse, with its stymied internal repetitions, and its extraordinary freezing-up of rhyme – 'I / night / light / cry' – as near as matters to the helpless immobility of *aaaa*. Repetition and return were always among Tennyson's most potent poetic resources, and in the history of a grief they found one of their most natural occasions; for repetition is the stuff of mourning: thoughts that return insistently to the dead, anniversaries which unforgivingly recur. T. S. Eliot (1951: 333–4) likened the poem to a diary, implying the sense of passing months and years which is so important a part of the poem's life: three Christmases pass; seasons change; the poem has its uninsistent but unmistakeable 'internal chronology' (Bradley 1901: 22). And that sense of duration is all-important, because one of the great themes of *In Memoriam* is time passing, its impact on grief: the dreadful proximity of its necessary power to heal and its heartless inducement to forget ('the victor Hours': I).

The question of the poem's unity, which once occupied critics a good deal, seems much less pressing now; but it is not a redundant question, because it responds accurately to an anxiety at work in the poem itself. The rival titles which Tennyson contemplated nicely imply the division of feeling that unsettles any firm sense of the poem's shape. At one point he was considering *Fragments of an Elegy*, which, like his description of the work in section XLVIII as 'Short swallow-flights of song' that evade 'a larger lay', frankly concedes incompleteness; at other times, he called it *The Way of the Soul*, implying a greater spiritual resolve – while, at his most positive, he compared the poem's progress to that of 'a kind of *Divina Commedia*, ending with happiness' (*Memoir*, I, 304). Certainly, the story begins with grief, the poem turning about the starting point of all elegy ('He is not here': VII), and it ends with an auspicious marriage (Tennyson's sister's). In its bluff way, the remark of his friend FitzGerald testifies to his outward success: 'it is about three years before the Poetic Soul walks itself out of darkness and Despair into Common Sense' (quoted Ricks 1972: 203). But both men exaggerate the final victory of common life: when Bradley worried the poem for a structure that would accomplish the business of true elegy as 'Lycidas' or 'Adonais' did – 'the transition from gloom to glory' – he found it oddly unwilling to oblige (Bradley 1901: 23–30). Just as Tennyson's stanzas read like Petrarchan sonnets never reaching the turn of the sestet, so the poem as a whole never quite achieves its return to life. True, there is a very beautiful section (XCV) describing a numinous communion, apparently between Tennyson and Hallam: 'The living soul was flashed on mine', originally '*His* living soul'; and some critics have seen it as the elegy's requisite turning point. But (as Kennedy 1977 has said well) the verses oddly invert the normal turn of elegy by insisting on Hallam's terribly real *removal* from Tennyson's life ('The dead man touched me from the past'); and even this tenuous relief is checked by a counter-voice: 'At length my trance / Was cancelled, stricken through with doubt.' Tennyson's genius was for irresolution – 'undulations to and fro' (CXIII) – which is why the more firm-hearted moments of hope in the poem seem so unfirm: the essayist's 'we' hardly ever rings true ('And yet we trust it comes from thee, / A beam in darkness: let it grow': 'Prologue'), while the personal 'we' can be devastating ('We cannot hear each other speak': LXXXII). That, presumably, is what Eliot meant when he praised the poem for the quality of its doubt, rather than of its faith (1951: 336).

The shock at Hallam's death was general among the circle, and intensified by a sense of national bereavement, not lost on Tennyson. Hallam himself had written distrustingly of 'that return of the mind upon itself, and the habit of seeking relief in idiosyncrasies rather than community of interest' which he saw as characteristic of modern poetry (Jump 1967: 41); and much of the uneasy progress of *In Memoriam* (which repeatedly returns upon itself) is marked by the difficult transition between private feeling and public responsibility, leaving the poem 'anonymous but confessional', as Ricks says, 'private but naked' (Ricks 1972: 209). Tennyson shares Wordsworth's paradoxical inclination towards a wordless emotional privacy in a way which insistently obstructs the poem's fluency : 'I sometimes hold it half a sin / To put in words the grief I feel' (V). The universality of the theme (' "I" is not always the author speaking of himself', Tennyson said, 'but the voice of the human race speaking thro' him' (Hallam 1897: I, 305)) is recurrently inhibited by the incommunicably personal nature of the poem's feeling: 'That loss is common would not make / My own less bitter, rather more: / Too common!' (VI).

One of the most powerful things in the work is its evocation of reticence: as when a thought slips into view, giving the sense of something that had been in mind all along, but not publicly acknowledged. Section CVIII is a good example: the poem's bracing and general rhetorical questions maintain a brave face; but, in a last turn of the verse, the final word – 'thee' – brings abruptly to light a terrible personal closeness, always present but unmentionable. For all Tennyson's marvellous verbalism, the poem repeatedly professes itself merely a sort of sketch or ghost of the thing it should be – 'given in outline and no more' – let down by its language's inability to do anything like justice to the loss in hand. Doubt characterizes more than the poem's religious opinions; the poem itself is a sad, self-disparaging thing, a 'sad mechanic exercise', a sequence of 'wild and wandering cries', inspired only by 'an earthly Muse . . . owning but a little art' (V, 'Prologue', XXXVII). Such honest equivocations give the poem a faltering self-consciousness: it is, in good part, a poem about the business of elegy, about the kind of poem it should be, or the kind it finds itself to be instead; it quotes itself (LVI) and mulls its own procedures and progress, or lack of progress – all of which sounds tiresomely self-knowing, but such self-awareness here is a mark of diffidence, not aggrandizement, and anyhow possesses an important kind of psychological truth, for self-consciousness is not the least burdensome part of grief.

Part of Hallam's promise lay in the resolve with which he faced the age's crisis of faith; and, indeed, the poem's religious speculations often draw on Hallam's writings. The connection between Hallam's death and the interests of the epoch are what licenses the widening circle of the poem's reference to include the impact of the new geology: 'O earth, what changes hast thou seen! . . . The hills are shadows, and they flow / From form to form, and nothing stands' (CXXIII). The poem is preoccupied with 'change', as any elegy is: by the mysterious alteration that has turned Hallam 'to something strange' (XLI), but also by the changes working within the poet himself, which have left him feeling 'The same, but not the same' (LXXXVII). Unlike 'Lycidas', where the attentive permanence of pastoral nature marries happily enough with the eternity of heaven, Tennyson's 'nature' herself comes to exemplify this frightening new universal principle of flux and impermanence.

Tennyson thought 'Lycidas' 'a test of any reader's poetic instinct' (Hallam 1897: I, 152); and *In Memoriam* includes many elements of the earlier poem's pastoral mode, especially in the earlier sections, Tennyson casting himself as a mourning shepherd ('I take the grasses of the grave / And make them pipes whereon to blow': XXI), and portraying Hallam's reabsorption into nature as a Wordsworthian homecoming ('And from his ashes may be made / The violet of his native land': XVIII). He tenderly enjoins the elements to bring his beloved's corpse across the sea, as though addressing an attentive universe ('Sleep, gentle heavens, before the prow; / Sleep, gentle winds, as he sleeps now': IX), and momentarily feels the hushed Wye to be in tune with his 'deepest grief' (XIX); while the death is said at one point to have 'sickened every living bloom, / And blurred the splendour of the sun' (LXXII). But the undeluded heart of the poem, shockingly alert to 'Nature, red in tooth and claw' (LVI), recognizes the deep fallacy of the old conventions, and the kinds of needily egotistic distortions of nature's heedlessness that grief may incite: 'The wild unrest that lives in woe / Would dote and pore on yonder cloud' (XV). Sorrow tells him, early on, that 'The stars . . . blindly run' (III); that the only constant is change (a paradox which Tennyson found very compelling): the seasons' unaffected succession, lurking in the background of *In Memoriam*, is itself tacit testimony to nature's unstartled indifference. Toward the end of the poem, Tennyson attempts to think well even of this starkly anti-pastoral nature: the flux that governs all things, he speculates, may have a direction after all, and Hallam be by some mysterious dispensation the next stage of evolution, 'Appearing ere the times were ripe' (Epilogue); but this is as poignantly fantastic as the pastoral conventions it seeks to replace.

The pastoral elements have made some readers uneasy about their formulaic feel; but this is rather the point: the pastoral moves are a part of the sad mechanic exercise (not unlike Dr Johnson doing long division sums to stave off madness). 'Don't you think the world wants other notes than elegiac now?' FitzGerald asked in a letter, when he learnt of moves to publish, 'Lycidas is the utmost length an elegiac should reach' (Ricks 1989: 334): the comparison is an irresistible one, and in his unimpressed but shrewd way FitzGerald puts his finger on the strange kind of experiment that makes *In Memoriam* – the genius of the thing is just in the way the poem meanders, aspiring to a purposeful 'way' but guiltily aware of the thought of 'aimless feet' (LIV), alluding to a pastoral consolation that it cannot bring itself to fulfil, nor for which it can abandon all hope. The incongruity of the pastoral ingredients suggests the more generally oblique relationship that *In Memoriam* instinctively strikes with the traditions of elegy, inventing itself *sui generis* as it goes along ('Still onward winds the dreary way; / I with it': XXVI), wandering indecisively between the therapeutic success of elegy's properly healing form and the unfinished business of confessed '*Fragments*'. The poem's power lies in its special kind of failure, even its professed incompetence: it is a masterpiece of uncertainty, enabled by the honesty of its diffidence, the progressive and consolatory duties of the poem's genre embarrassed by the eddying movements of its unquiet heart.

Matthew Arnold's elegies also enjoy an enabling inability to do things by the book; but where Tennyson is inclined to blame himself, Arnold reproaches the conditions of the age. The difficulty in fulfilling the elegiac norms is not so much the burden of loss as a reluctance to move on, given the unpromising prospects of life: modern elegy is stymied before it begins. In 'The Scholar-Gipsy', Arnold says:

> amongst us one,
>   Who most has suffered, takes dejectedly
> His seat upon the intellectual throne;
>   And all his store of sad experience he
>   Lays bare of wretched days;
> Tells us his misery's birth and growth and signs,
>   And how the dying spark of hope was fed,
>   And how the breast was soothed, and how the head,
> And all his hourly varied anodynes.
>
> (ll. 182–90)

The poet in question might be Goethe, as Arnold later said; but it sounds more like Tennyson: *In Memoriam* appeared two or three years before Arnold wrote his poem. Either way, even that tenuous flicker of hope is denied to the majority of Arnold's generation: 'This for our wisest! and we others pine, / And wish the long unhappy dream would end.' The impulse behind a good deal of Arnold's poetry is the irresistible attraction of withdrawing from the unpoetic world – 'the brutal world' ('Immortality'): 'world', like 'life', does a lot of sad work in Arnold's verse, both words meant to invoke the same epochal fret, 'The hopeless tangle of our age' or 'this strange disease of modern life' ('In Memory of the Author of "Obermann"', 'The Scholar-Gipsy'). It was Wordsworth's gift momentarily to redeem the world from its modern confusion of 'doubts, disputes, distractions, fears' and return us to 'The freshness of the early world', so making life worth living (no less): 'Memorial Verses', Arnold's unconsoling elegy for him, laments the passing of such power from the earth.

At the same time, though, the yearning to quit is obviously something that a manly spirit should firmly resist. Arnold's elegy for his father, Thomas Arnold, headmaster of Rugby, memorializes the 'radiant vigour' of his public virtues as positively Christ-like ('Rugby Chapel'), which has a fraught air to modern ears; and yet, after all, the virtues were indeed noble and life-consuming; and such high-minded engagement with the details of the world – Arnold himself spent his career as a school inspector and tireless pedagogue, as well as a campaigning man of letters – looked with justified disapproval, though wistfully, at the charmed, reclusive and solitary alternative to 'life'. Arnold often identified, in a slightly nebulous way, that alternative existence of inward singleness and sureness of purpose (not modern uncertainty and self-doubt) with Poetry: a charmed release into unfretful being. Given the abiding theme, the recurrence of death in the poems is scarcely odd, though it does cast death in a peculiar way: as a way of getting removed from the 'world', it certainly avoids 'life' very successfully; and Arnold's elegies (collected together in the edition of 1881) invest it with the full force of his mixed feelings.

'In Memory of the Author of "Obermann"' – the author is de Senancourt, for whose work Arnold's note claims a 'profound inwardness' – memorializes a death that only confirms the pre-existing tenor of its subject's genius. 'Immovable . . . still / As death, composed to bear', Senancourt watched the strife of the world with blithe disinterest: 'He only lives with the world's life, / Who hath renounced his own' – a curious adaptation of Jesus's advice (Matthew 26:25). Arnold tries to hurry himself out of such deathly pleasures and back towards life again ('Away the dreams'), announcing with a strange kind of heroism, 'I in the world must live', as though this were a peculiar cross; but, though the poem ends with 'A last, a last farewell', it keeps saying 'farewell', as though unwilling to leave. The wonderful poetic hero of 'The Scholar-Gipsy', a delightfully non-elegiacal elegy, is happily free *never* to get back to the business of life, but to roam the Oxfordshire countryside forever like a wood-spirit; and while the poem stops to ponder whether he is marvellously immortal or, more prosaically, deceased, it winningly insinuates that really it amounts to much the same: 'early didst thou leave the world, with powers / Fresh, undiverted to the world without'. Either way, the Scholar-Gipsy is free of modern disease, living the ideal life that Arnold cannot. The poem might have been wearisomely regretful, but the unconcealed pleasure of the fantasy has a sprightliness qualifying the global woe: tables are spryly turned when the long-dead Gipsy is warned off the infectious alive ('fly our paths, our feverish contact fly!').

Still, you might say the poem embraces the Gipsy's fantastic world-free world and life-evading life a little too single-heartedly: for there is more to be said for the world than that. Arnold himself thought so, anyway, as he wrote to his friend, the poet Clough:

. . . the Gipsy Scholar at best awakens a pleasing melancholy. But this is not what we want.

> The complaining millions of men
> Darken in labour and pain –

what they want is something to *animate* and *ennoble* them. (Lowry 1932: 146)

When he came to elegize Clough, a few years later, in 'Thyrsis', his most ambitious attempt at full-blown pastoral elegy, 'The Scholar-Gipsy' returned to mind. (Pastoral elegy, like 'Lycidas', often took as its subject a dead poet.) Like the earlier poem, 'Thyrsis' is set in the hills outside Oxford: a few months after Clough's death, Arnold wrote to thank his widow for the gift of some of her husband's verses, explaining 'I shall take them with me to Oxford, where I shall go alone after Easter; – and there, among the Cumner hills where we have so often rambled, I shall be able to think him over as I could wish' (Lowry 1932: 160). The poem is rooted in autobiographical fact, then; but it is also very bookish and artificial, drawing not only on Arnold's own verses, but also on Virgil's *Eclogues* and Theocritus; and the actual and the literary get interestingly tangled.

For a start, the setting is, as it were, secondary pastoral – as though, like a good deal of Arnold's most distinctive poetry, written somehow against the odds, the best shot at pastoral that a belated modern poet might manage. Much of the poem's charm comes from the details of Oxfordshire and Berkshire ('I know what white, what purple fritillaries / The grassy harvest of the river-fields, / Above by Ensham, down by Sandford, yields'), local and unidealized. Proserpine may have 'loved the Dorian pipe . . . / But ah, of our poor Thames she never heard'; so there is something a little academic about the elegiac exercise: 'wind-dispersed and vain the words will be, / Yet, Thyrsis, let me give my grief its hour / In the old haunt'. And if the landscape wobbles between Arcadia and England, then Thyrsis doesn't turn out to be a very securely pastoral character either; in fact he's a *failed* pastoral figure: the burden of the poem is to blame Clough for his own ruin, for he abandoned the shepherd's life (= resigned his fellowship at Oriel) to enter the world 'outside our happy ground', which, unsurprisingly, de-tuned his 'piping' (= his poetry).

Arnold's poem is a curious kind of elegy, more reproachful than eulogistic, and concludes that Clough's life was a disappointment: he never realized his Oxonian potential, his poetry went off the boil. In a poem ostentatiously based on one omen, the signal tree, Clough himself is surreptitiously the most profound omen: an exemplary figure of a life gone wrong, as Arnold's own might too, or might have already. The comparison with the properly ideal figure is unhesitating, and in its way quite unforgiving – 'Our Gipsy-Scholar haunts, out-living thee!': the Scholar-Gipsy knows that the light worth pursuing is not to be found in 'the world's market', where Thyrsis found himself waylaid. Arnold knows it as well ('I seek it too'), and he obviously yearns to associate himself with the Gipsy's destiny, rather than with the purposefully worldly Thyrsis's; but the poem is frank enough to admit that life is taking Arnold away from the scene of poetry too ('Too rare, too rare, grow now my visits here!'), and Arnold ends the poem just as far from pastoral reassurances as his dead friend – amid 'the great town's harsh, heart-wearying roar'.

Confirmation that Arnold's Gipsy still remains about the hills, happily dead and well, comes in 'Thyrsis' through the oddly arbitrary 'evidence' that the signal-elm still stands: Arnold finally sights it (but doesn't reach it) in line 160. The tree is a figure of some controversy, as it happens; the best researches suggest that it was actually an oak. It is the sort of discrepancy that wouldn't be possible in a more whole-heartedly pastoral affair like 'The Scholar-Gipsy'; but here the irreality is a clue to wider discontents. The arbitrary attachment of a private meaning to a single tree is a bit of childlike magic, poignantly wilful; but the habit of appropriating elements of the world within a private symbolism is more troubling when it turns on Clough himself. Arnold misrepresents Clough's motives in leaving Oxford very badly: he didn't leave to throw himself into public affairs at all, but for private, high and noble reasons, unable to subscribe to the Articles of the Church of England; nor did his poetry grow noticeably more strident or fretful once he had. To be fair, Arnold himself quickly saw that the real Clough had somehow slipped from the poem: 'one has the feeling, if one reads the poem as a memorial poem, that not enough is said about Clough in it' (Russell 1895: I, 327); which is typically engaging and frank. A similarly wobbly relationship with actuality occurs in Arnold's curiously misjudged elegy for the Brontës, 'Haworth Churchyard', which equivocates awkwardly between the matter-of-fact and the self-consciously literary. Arnold had the details of the graves wrong, keen to see the doomed siblings clustered in the harsh moorish ground, like the characters at the end of *Wuthering Heights*, when in fact they are buried quite respectably in a vault within the church (and Anne is buried elsewhere). 'I am almost sorry you told me about the place of their burial', he wrote to Elizabeth Gaskell, who had told him the truth, 'It really seems to me to put the finishing touch to the strange cross-grained character of the fortunes of that ill-fated family that they should even be placed after death in the wrong, uncongenial spot' (Allott 1979: 442 headnote) – which is to say, not the spot that he chose for them.

To call such small readjustments of truth 'egotistical' would be tiresome; but that would invoke something like Arnold's own criterion, for no one speaks more stirringly of the need to see 'the object as in itself it really is' than he does, or criticizes more tellingly poets who write *'without their eye on the object'* (Arnold 1965: 35, 150). Self-regard is the danger always attending a poet elegizing another poet, especially where, as in 'Thyrsis', the dead poet becomes identified with concerns or dangers too close to the elegist's heart: 'The strength of the poem', says Bernard Richards, 'lies partly in the fact that it is a lament for Arnold's own lost, romantic youth' (1988: 160), which generously accepts Arnold's own romanticism as a poetic advantage, but might as well describe the poem's imaginative limits. Harold Bloom once claimed the self-attending turn to 'Thyrsis' as typical of all major elegies for poets, which (he said) 'do not express grief but center upon their composer's own creative anxieties' (1973: 151), but such identification need not exclude a more selfless attentiveness to the dead. One of the unannounced triumphs of *In Memoriam*, a triumph at once poetic and ethical, is the way it allows Hallam (for all the idealization that he obviously enjoys) to retain a kind of independent reality, even when death has transformed him into a pure object of consciousness. 'Mine, mine, for ever, ever mine', claims Tennyson of Hallam towards the poem's close, which is true of any memory; but goes on, most beautifully, to imply that his ownership is very different from the self-serving re-creation of the grieving sentimentalist: 'Strange friend, past, present, and to be; / Loved deeplier, darklier understood' (CXXIX). 'Strange friend' lucidly finds a difference as well as an intimacy; 'darklier understood' gently concedes an obscurity as well as a lasting familiarity.

Christina Rossetti provides one of the period's sharpest satires on the self-interest that shadows elegy. The hero of 'The Fate of a Frog' leaves the privacy of his pond for the public highway, only to be crushed by a passing cart: 'My road to Fame turns out a wry way', he laments as he perishes, 'I perish on this hideous highway.' As it happens, the driver is singing a poignant song about a frog; and Rossetti's contrast between the frog of art and the real frog is unforgiving and polemical about the kinds of fantasy that are always ready to distort the practice of elegy:

> O rich and poor, O great and small,
> Such oversights beset us all:
> The mangled frog abides incog,
> The uninteresting actual frog;
> The hypothetic frog alone
> Is the one frog we dwell upon.

To elegize a real frog might seem an odd assignment, of course, though there is a rather mirthless spoof 'Ode to an Expiring Frog' in *Pickwick Papers* (chapter xv); but, as it happens, dead animals inspired Arnold to some very good elegies, written about his pets, which quite avoid the co-opting symbolism of 'Thyrsis', or treat it with affectionate satire. 'Geist's Grave', about his dachshund, knowingly sketches the right sort of affecting deathbed scene ('A meek last glance of love didst throw, / And humbly lay thee down to die'), but the dog is far too much of a dog to fulfil such human requirements for long ('lending half an ear / To travellers on the Portsmouth road'). Kaiser, a mongrel, died seven years later, leaving only Max (another dachshund): 'Full well Max knows the friend is dead / Whose cordial talk, / And jokes in doggish language said, / Beguiled his walk' ('Kaiser Dead'). The privacy of their doggish language is charmingly absolute; the creatures are so incorrigibly different; and if that is true of dogs, it is even truer of a bird, as Arnold says in the sprightly elegy for canary Matthias:

> Birds, companions more unknown,
> Live beside us, but alone;
> Finding not, do all they can,
> Passage from their souls to man.
> Kindness we bestow, and praise,
> Laud their plumage, greet their lays;
> Still beneath their feathered breast,
> Stirs a history unexpressed.
>   ('Poor Matthias', ll. 95–102)

Matthias keeps his secrets: the poem conjures the bleak, incommunicable isolation of Arnoldian Man into something humane and deft.

The threat of posthumous appropriation which Matthias jokily resists, and *In Memoriam* avoids so profoundly, can never be more pressing than when the impulses behind the elegy are religious or evangelical; for then the whole pressure of the poem's conception works to make its subject exemplary or representative. Hopkins was certainly aware of the way in which elegies for others could be thin disguises for deeper concerns with oneself. The poem that begins 'Margaret, are you grieving / Over Goldengrove unleaving?' resolves itself into a bleaker underlying truth, 'It is Margaret you mourn for'; and, in a different way, you sometimes sense the dominant presence of Hopkins himself displacing the notional subject of his elegiac pieces: the sheer wordy inventiveness of his poems, and his own absorbing interest in their technical challenges and opportunities, can take over. No one could claim much individuality for 'the tall nun' and her five sisters in 'The Wreck of the Deutschland'; they have been transformed into religious symbols: within the world of the poem, she is tall really because she 'rears herself to divine / Ears', and they are five in number to emulate the 'cipher of suffering Christ'. But perhaps the great set piece is not wholly representative; anyway, Hopkins's whole theology was, in principle, preoccupied with the individuality of other selves: the distinction of his elegy for 'Felix Randall', for example, is its demonstration of an unthinking response to an unexceptional death ('Felix Randall the farrier, O is he dead then? my duty all ended') finding itself surprised by sudden feeling for an individual, to whom he discovers an unexpected debt ('Thy tears that touched my heart, child, Felix, poor Felix Randall').

Hopkins's friend, Coventry Patmore, represents a quite different kind of experiment in elegy: the domestic elegy. Interspersed among his sequence, *The Unknown Eros*, Patmore has a number of poems written after the death of his wife, many addressed to her. Patmore strives for a speaking voice, with an extremely variable line; and the result is a good deal more palatable than the stickily mystical portrait of marriage in *The Angel in the House*, though not without some bad swerves, especially when reaching for God or mulling kisses. Patmore's description of betraying his dead wife in dreams of 'sordid streets and lanes / And houses brown and bare' ('Eurydice') is horrid and candid, and his self-reproach when he finds himself attracted to another woman ('Tired Memory') is honestly memorable; but the verse is never altogether happy with its speaking line and stumbles ill-advisedly on occasion into something more wilfully literary: 'Thy Sister sweet, / Who bade the wheels to stir / Of sensitive delight in the poor brain, / Dead of devotion and tired memory . . .'.

Patmore was a champion of William Barnes, whose Dorset dialect poems speak a domestic voice with a surer success, as in 'The Wife A-Lost':

> Since I noo mwore do zee your feäce,
> Up steäirs or down below,
> I'll zit me in the lwonesome pleäce,
> Where flat-bough'd beech do grow:
> Below the beeches' bough, my love,
> Where you did never come,
> An' I don't look to meet ye now,
> As I do look at hwome.
>
> (ll. 1–8)

The poem's quiet brilliance lies in the way it brings things home: 'noo mwore do zee your feäce' is not a poeticism for 'not here any more'; it really is her face that he is missing and which he instinctively looks for. The dialect announces a poetry of homeliness, opting out of the heroic gestures: Barnes once said he wrote in it because he could not help it; but he wrote a good deal in standard English too. What really mattered was the way the dialect could free the poetry from the duty of certain kinds of accomplishment; so that here, for instance, the willed provincialism of the idiom allows the poem to evade the recuperative models of high elegy, and offer instead an heroically understated portrait of day-to-day coping:

> Since now bezide my dinner-bwoard
>   Your vaïce do never sound,
> I'll eat the bit I can avword,
>   A-vield upon the ground;
> Below the darksome bough, my love,
>   Where you did never dine,
> An' I don't grieve to miss ye now,
>   As I at hwome do pine.
>
> (ll. 17–24)

What is not said is everything: the level-toned patience of the rationalizing, and the determination to maintain that things are just about all right, are beautifully observed, as though keeping darkness down; while the numbness of bereavement registers in the insistent return to a few unshiftable points of reference – 'hwome', 'love', 'now'.

Swinburne thought the 'Thyrsis' one of the language's great elegies, alongside 'Adonais' and 'Lycidas', and Arnold's finest single poem: he liked the 'English-coloured verse' that it shared with 'The Scholar-Gipsy', with its offerings of 'field-flowers and hedgerow blossoms'. Nothing could seem more emphatically uninterested in such possibilities than his own most ambitious exercise in pastoral elegy, 'Ave Atque Vale', a poem about Baudelaire; but, though its paraphernalia is quite different to Arnold's, it similarly sets itself at a modern distance from the classical norms. Swinburne's poem is just as absorbed by the dilemmas of its own proceeding as was *In Memoriam* ('Shall I strew on thee rose or rue or laurel, / Brother, on this that was the veil of thee?'); but quite unguiltily. On the contrary, it is a self-consciously gorgeous performance, and spends much of its time mulling over the gaudy possibilities that it might have pursued, piling them up in languid, verb-deferring questions:

> Now all strange hours and all strange loves are over,
>   Dreams and desires and sombre songs and sweet,
>   Hast thou found place at the great knees and feet
> Of some pale Titan-woman like a lover,
>   Such as thy vision here solicited,
>   Under the shadow of her fair vast head,
> The deep division of prodigious breasts,
>   The solemn slope of mighty limbs asleep,
>   The weight of awful tresses that still keep
> The savour and shade of old-world pine-forests
>   Where the wet hill-winds weep?
>
> (ll. 56–66)

There is the ghost of the *In Memoriam* rhyme scheme in that, with a couplet between and a truncated line to complete: so you feel the verse pausing doubly to admire its ruminative beauty, a good deal too exquisite to bring itself to the falsity of a resolution. The oddly preludial feel to it all is the secret of the poem's peculiar success, as though it were treading gingerly but with immense style about an unspeakable emptiness: it is not a coincidence that the idea of hollowness crops up several times ('What ails us with thee, who art wind and air? / What ails us gazing where all seen is hollow?').

Swinburne could be boisterously secular ('Glory to Man in the highest! for Man is the master of things': 'Hymn of Man'); 'Ave Atque Vale' is actually very hard-headed about Baudelaire's plain extinction. True, the tenth stanza offers a brief flash of communion with the lasting life of Baudelaire's poetry; but the poem ends frankly professing the irrelevance of its own fine words: 'There is no help for these things; none to mend / And none to mar; not all our songs, O friend, / Will make death clear or make life durable.' The best that one can summon up, in place of the normal turn of elegy, is the lean thought that at least life is over ('Nor sight nor sound to war against thee more'): 'That no life lives for ever; / That dead men rise up never', as Swinburne bouncily put it in 'The Garden of Proserpine'. All that remains is the self-sufficing formalism of uncommitted ritual to go through ('I stand, and to the gods and to the dead / Do reverence without prayer or praise'), exemplifying what John Bayley (1974: 86) once described as 'the dilemma of art in a Godless age, its need to search for and reveal salvation while showing that no such thing existed'. Unlike the more orthodox 'Memorial Verses' for Gautier – which protest too much, 'the music of thy living mouth / Lives' – the Baudelaire poem really claims nothing very much: it embraces its existence as a piece of ravishing antiquarian nonsense, as though the sort of thing that might once have meant something. The sense of distracted purpose can even give rise to uncertain moments of humour, as when the repeated questions grow practically jocular ('What of life is there, what of ill or good? / Are the fruits grey like dust or bright like blood?'), but it would be left to other poets in the period properly to realize the droll potential in elegy conducted quite without hope.

Humorous elegiac verse has some claim to being one of the most original of Victorian innovations; it comes, very often, from the same sort of amalgam of heartlessness and sentiment that you find in the best deaths in Dickens; but it is not his unique property. Thackeray, for instance, has a real tear-jerker of a poem about an old cane chair where dead Fanny once sat, the whole success of which stems from its unsteadily facetious alliance of mournfulness and domestic paraphernalia ('Old armour, prints, pictures, pipes, china (all crack'd), / Old rickety tables, and chairs broken-backed'). The poems of Edward Lear also come at death through incongruous jokes, though scarifying ones:

> There was an Old Man of Whitehaven,
> Who danced a quadrille with a Raven;
> But they said – 'It's absurd, to encourage this bird!'
> So they smashed that Old Man of Whitehaven.

Many of the best limericks embark, like this, on elegiac acts of commemoration (as though emulating Wordsworth's 'There was a Boy'), but promptly stumble into violence, described by the collapsed internal rhyme of line three; and then return brokenly, with unrhyming lassitude, to the terms of the first line once again. It is not unlike the *In Memoriam* stanza, though darkly absurd rather than measured, describing a nonsensically brutal world while sounding eminently rational about it ('There was . . . But . . . So').

'The Pobble Who has no Toes' reimagines 'Lycidas' as a swimming accident: the Pobble is not wafted off by dolphins, but his toes are carried away by mermaids (or possibly crawfish); and, back home, his Aunt is sturdily consolatory about the naturalness of loss: 'Pobbles are happier without their toes.' (Eric Partridge dates 'To turn up your toes', meaning 'to die', to 1860; the poem was written in 1867.) That, like the limericks, pursues a dark joke about the elegiac convention; which takes me to my last figure here, perhaps the greatest exponent of Victorian humorous death poetry: A. E. Housman.

Housman (in his lecture on 'The Name and Nature of Poetry') provocatively championed 'nonsense' as the condition under which poetry could exist most freely and purely, unhindered by the bothersome duty to communicate thoughts; and while his own verse doesn't reach very far towards the world of Lear's brand of 'nonsense', it thrives on a not dissimilar background awareness of poetry's ultimate irrelevance, and on the sense of the comic redundance of mournful ceremony, faced with the meaningless unkindness of the universe, that occasionally flashes out from Swinburne (whom Housman admired):

> The time you won your town the race
> We chaired you through the market-place;
> Man and boy stood cheering by,
> And home we brought you shoulder-high.
> To-day, the road all runners come,
> Shoulder-high we bring you home,
> And set you at your threshold down,
> Townsman of a stiller town.
> ('To an Athlete Dying Young', ll. 1–8)

The adroitly managed pairing of the funereal and the celebratory mirrors the simultaneous mordancy and drollness of Housman's own verse, his remarkable mixture of black glee and genuine plangency. Louis MacNeice once said that Housman 'used his tripping measures to express the profoundest pessimism' (1967: 140); and the humour of incongruity can sometimes be brisk as that implies. But at other times, the rich, self-conscious comedy of pulling out all the old stops creates something more subtly *sui generis*:

> When the eye of day is shut,
> And the stars deny their beams,
> And about the forest hut
> Blows the roaring wood of dreams.
> (*Last Poems*, XXXIII, ll. 1–4)

That, faithful to the old conventions which it sees through, describes an imaginary Shropshire – a place which featured in Housman's verse, he said, like 'the Cambridge of Lycidas'. This poem turns to a watery grave, as 'Lycidas' does, but Shropshire quite refuses the pastoral consolations that Milton entertains; and, in their place, all that remains is the world as bleak joke, death as arbitrary as a pun:

> In gross marl, in blowing dust,
> In the drowned ooze of the sea,
> Where you would not, lie you must,
> Lie you must, and not with me.
> (*Last Poems*, XXXIII, ll. 13–16)

See also: LYRIC; POETRY AND RELIGION.

REFERENCES AND FURTHER READING

Allott, Miriam (ed.) (1979) *The Poems of Matthew Arnold*. Second edition. London: Longman.

Arnold, Matthew (1965) *Essays on English Literature*. Ed. F. W. Bateson. London: University of London Press.

Bayley, John (1974) *The Uses of Division*. London: Chatto and Windus.

Bloom, Harold (1973) *The Anxiety of Influence: A Theory of Poetry*. New York: Oxford University Press.

Bradley, A. C. (1901) *A Commentary on Tennyson's In Memoriam*. London: Macmillan.

Chadwick, Owen (1975) *The Secularization of the European Mind in the Nineteenth Century*. Cambridge: Cambridge University Press.

Eliot, T. S. (1951) 'In Memoriam'. In T. S. Eliot, *Selected Essays*. Second edition. London: Faber.

Empson, William (1953) *Seven Types of Ambiguity*. Third edition. London: Chatto and Windus.

Freud, Sigmund (1953–66) 'Mourning and Melancholia.' In *The Standard Edition of the Complete Psychological Works of Sigmund Freud*, trans. James Strachey et al., 24 vols (XIV, 243–58). London: Hogarth Press/Institute of Psycho-Analysis.

Hallam, Arthur (1943) *The Writings of Arthur Hallam*. Ed. T. H. Vail Motter. New York: Modern Language Association of America.

Hallam, Lord Tennyson (1897) *Alfred, Lord Tennyson: A Memoir*. 2 vols. London: Macmillan.

Jump, John D. (ed.) (1967) *Tennyson: The Critical Heritage*. London: Routledge and Kegan Paul.

Kennedy, Ian H. C. (1977). *In Memoriam* and the Tradition of Pastoral Elegy.' *Victorian Poetry*, 15, 351–66.

Lang, Cecil Y., and Edgar F. Shannon (eds) (1982–90) *The Letters of Alfred Lord Tennyson*. 3 vols. Oxford: Clarendon Press.

Lowry, Howard Foster (ed.) (1932) *The Letters of Matthew Arnold to Arthur Hugh Clough*. Oxford: Clarendon Press.

MacNeice, Louis (1967) *The Poetry of W. B. Yeats*. London: Faber.

Mill, J. S. (1981) 'Thoughts on Poetry and its Varieties'. In J. S. Mill, *Autobiography and Literary Essays* (*Collected Works of J. S. Mill*, vol. I). Eds John M. Robson and Jack Stillinger. Toronto: University of Toronto Press; London: Routledge and Kegan Paul.

Richards, Bernard (1988) *English Poetry of the Victorian Period, 1830–1890*. London: Longman.

Ricks, Christopher (1972) *Tennyson*. London: Macmillan.

Ricks, Christopher (1984) *The Force of Poetry*. Oxford: Clarendon Press.

Ricks, Christopher (ed.) (1989) *Tennyson: A Selected Edition*. Harlow: Longman.

Russell, George W. E. (ed.) (1895) *Letters of Matthew Arnold 1848–1888*. 2 vols. London: Macmillan.

Sacks, Peter M. (1985) *The English Elegy: Studies in the Genre from Spenser to Yeats*. Baltimore: Johns Hopkins University Press.

Shaw, W. David (1994) *Elegy and Paradox: Testing the Conventions*. Baltimore: Johns Hopkins University Press.

Strachey, Lytton (1921) *Queen Victoria*. London: Chatto and Windus.

Wordsworth, William (1988) *Selected Prose*. Ed. John O. Hayden. Harmondsworth: Penguin.

Zeiger, Melissa F. (1997) *Beyond Consolation: Death, Sexuality, and the Changing Shapes of Elegy*. Ithaca, N. Y.: Cornell University Press.

7

Hymn

J. R. Watson

'Victorian England was religious.' With these words, Owen Chadwick began his study of the Victorian church (1971: 1). In one sense this is correct, but in one sense only: another book could be written, beginning 'The sea of faith / Was once, too, at the full.' The two, of course, are not incompatible: religious zeal can be intense at a time of difficulty, and there certainly was a great deal of both in the Victorian period, not only in England but in Wales, Scotland and Ireland, and throughout the British Empire. That religious activity took place, almost defiantly, against a background of uncertainty and doubt, and of social problems which stubbornly resisted the ministrations of religious reformers such as William Booth, or the visits of evangelists such as Dwight L. Moody and Ira D. Sankey. Belief and unbelief coexisted uneasily: geology and natural history, together with textual criticism, threatened the authority of the Bible, and undermined the traditional belief in life after death. The result is seen in the sensitive speculations of *In Memoriam*, the poem which, more than any other, reflects the struggling of hope – the same hope that, in George Frederick Watts's 1886 painting, holds over the world a damaged lyre.

In Memoriam began with a prologue, 'Strong Son of God, immortal Love', which is hymn-like in tone and form, so much so that it has been included in some hymn books. And the Victorian hymn was an expression, as Tennyson's poem was, of the cultural and spiritual preoccupations of the age. Hymns were evidence of faith and hope, but also of other things: weariness, unease, fighting, danger – 'Oft in danger, oft in woe / Onward, Christians, onward go.' They reflected an intense activity in church and chapel, trying to assert the centrality of religion in a world which was increasingly aware of uncomfortable truths.

That world changed through the decades. Hardy looked back to a rural church which slumbered in its old ways:

> On afternoons of drowsy calm
>   We stood in the panelled pew,
> Singing one-voiced a Tate-and-Brady psalm
>   To the tune of 'Cambridge New'.
>   ('Afternoon Service at Mellstock', ll. 1–4)

The congregation in the village church in 1850 (Hardy gives the date) were using *A New Version of the Psalms of David*, Tate and Brady's version of 1696; looking back, Hardy found himself wondering if he had gained 'by subtle thought on things / Since we stood psalming there'. His nostalgia for the certainties of a rural backwater may be contrasted with D. H. Lawrence's memory of going to school in a Nottinghamshire mining community at the end of the century. He quotes:

> Sun of my soul, thou Saviour dear,
> It is not night if Thou be near –

That was the last hymn at the board school. It did not mean to me any Christian dogma or any salvation. Just the words, 'Sun of my soul, thou Saviour dear', penetrated me with wonder and the mystery of twilight. (Beal 1967: 9)

Hardy was singing a metrical psalm in a village church; Lawrence was singing a hymn at the end of the day at school. The hymn was by John Keble: it was one of the poems from *The Christian Year* which encouraged others to try their hands at religious verse. At another time, Lawrence remembered, the hymn was 'Fair waved the golden corn / In Canaan's pleasant land' – which filled him with 'the wonder of "Canaan" which could never be localised'.

That hymn, by John Hampden Gurney (1802–62), was one of those which was once well known but has now disappeared. When Lawrence was a child at school, in the 1890s, hymn singing was part of the day's routine, although he also sang hymns in the Congregational chapel at Eastwood. Rural Dorset, in Hardy's youth, was very different. Instrumentalists led the music from the west gallery of the church. Accounts which survive of their performances are usually hostile, probably because the writers of those accounts were liturgical reformers with a mission to make the church more dignified (Robert Druitt, editor of the *Parish Choir* from 1846 to 1851, was a consistent denigrator of west gallery music). At their best, however, the musicians must have been lively and competent, and being members of the band certainly kept the men players in the church. Hardy's sympathy for them is seen in *Under the Greenwood Tree* and 'Absent-Mindedness in a Parish Choir', in both of which the old west gallery musicians are replaced by an organ. This was part of a general sense, encouraged partly by the Oxford Movement, that church services ought to be more decorous: and there is evidence that during the Victorian period the performance of church music improved steadily. Organists such as Samuel Sebastian Wesley, John Goss and Philip Armes raised the standards of cathedral music, and Sir Frederick Gore Ouseley, a wealthy baronet, even endowed a college at Tenbury in Worcestershire to encourage the proper singing of choral services.

A great step forward for congregations was the provision of a tune for each hymn, printed with the words. It has been ingeniously described by Ian Bradley as ranking alongside the penny post and the railway system 'as a great Victorian invention embodying the quest for order, efficiency and ease of communication' (Bradley 1997: 53). It must have helped towards the great success of *Hymns Ancient and Modern* (*A&M*) when it was published in 1861, for the hymns in that book were provided with strong tunes which have, in some cases, become inseparable from the words. The musical editor, William Henry Monk, was remarkable in his ability to find suitable matches of words and music, and his composers, such as John Bacchus Dykes, rose to the occasion. Monk's tune 'Eventide', to 'Abide with me', is an example; so is Dykes's 'Nicaea' to 'Holy, holy, holy' and 'Melita' to 'Eternal Father, strong to save'. Monk's name was the only one to appear on the title page, which meant that *A&M* was sometimes called 'Monk's book'; its great rival, the SPCK's *Church Hymns*, which appeared in 1871, was reprinted as *Church Hymns with Tunes* in 1874, with the name of Arthur Sullivan as musical editor on the title page.

Hymns Ancient and Modern signalled the acceptance of hymns by the Church of England. Indeed, its subtitle was 'for use in the Services of the Church', and its success swept away certain suspicions that had remained from the early years of the century – that hymn singing, in John Ellerton's words, 'came to us from an unwelcome source': 'from the Dissenters, eminently from the Methodists; it was first adopted by those of the clergy who sympathized most with them; for many long years it was that dreaded thing, a "party badge"; but it held its ground until wise men of all parties began to recognize its value' (1896: 185). Ellerton was quite correct. Hymns in the eighteenth century had been extensively used by the Methodists, and by other Dissenters; they had additionally been written by Calvinists such as Augustus Montague Toplady ('Rock of Ages, cleft for me') and evangelicals such as John Newton and William Cowper. The emphasis on individual salvation, and on the power of the blood of Christ, gave this evangelical hymnody a strong character which was not always welcomed by those in authority in the church. In 1820, for example, the bishop of London refused Reginald Heber, later the saintly bishop of Calcutta, permission to publish a book of hymns.

There were, however, many hymn books before *A&M*. Some of them were local selections, made for a particular church by a clergyman who wanted to have hymns available for use in worship. Heber's own collection was published in 1827, after his death; others with a wide circulation included Edward Bickersteth's *Christian Psalmody* (1833, enlarged 1841), W. J. Hall and Edward Osler's *Psalms and Hymns adapted to the Services of the Church of England* (1836), and *The Hymnal Noted*, by John Mason Neale and Thomas Helmore (1852, 1854). The nonconformists had their own books, too: in 1836 Josiah Conder edited *The Congregational Hymn Book*, designed to include and supplement the hymns of Isaac Watts, while the Methodists continued to rely on supplements to John Wesley's *Collection of Hymns for the use of the People called Methodists* of 1780. In 1854, the Primitive Methodists produced their own new book, described by Julian's *Dictionary of Hymnology* (1892) as 'the worst edited and most severely mutilated collection of hymns ever published'. At the other extreme was the refined Unitarian collection, *Hymns for the Christian Church and Home*, edited by James Martineau (1840). F. W. Faber, at the Oratory in London, produced his *Hymns* (1849, 1862) with the aim of giving Roman Catholics hymns to sing, noticing the hold upon Protestants of Wesley's hymns or of Newton and Cowper's *Olney Hymns*.

In addition to these inclusive and general collections, there were many with specific aims, or designed for specific audiences. As Ian Bradley (1997) has pointed out, these included hymn books for all kinds of good causes, such as *Hymns for Anti-Slavery Prayer*

Meetings (1838), *Social Hymns for the use of the Friends of the Rational System of Society* (1840) and the Chartists' *Democratic Hymns and Songs* (1849). There were hymn books to encourage temperance, hymns for children, hymns for invalids, hymns for missions, hymns for schools (each of the major public schools had its own hymn book) and hymns for individual denominations. Indeed, the success of *Hymns Ancient and Modern* and of *Church Hymns with Tunes* galvanized the nonconformists into action, and a series of major books appeared in the 1870s and 1880s; while a new style of preaching and singing was brought from America by Moody and Sankey, and resulted in the many editions of *Sacred Songs and Solos*.

The Church in Difficulty

Dwight L. Moody, whose mission to Britain in 1873–5 was assisted by Ira D. Sankey, preached, as he proudly claimed, 'the blood', that is the power of the blood of Jesus Christ to save sinners. The hymns which came out of that movement were strident and assertive, boldly setting the love of Jesus for the individual against the hostile world of the flesh and the devil:

> I am so glad that Jesus loves me,
> Jesus loves me,
> Jesus loves me, even me.
>
> . . .
>
> Satan, dismayed, from my soul now doth flee
> When I just tell him that Jesus loves me.

The pattern was one of trouble and temptation in this world – 'Dare to be a Daniel / Dare to stand alone' – followed by the reward in heaven:

> When the mists have rolled in splendour
>   From the beauty of the hills,
> And the sunlight falls in gladness,
>   On the river and the rills,
> We recall our Father's promise
>   In the rainbow of the spray:
> We shall know each other better
>   When the mists have rolled away.

Sankey's *Sacred Songs and Solos* is an extreme example of a response to doubt and difficulty. It threatens and cajoles, while at the same time emphasizing the love of Jesus for the individual sinner, and the certain hope of meeting our loved ones again in heaven: 'In the sweet by-and-by, / We shall meet on that beautiful shore.'

Tennyson's hesitations have been swept away, just as his flexible and expressive stanzas have been replaced by a crude rhetoric of repetition. But it is worth pausing for a moment over Moody and Sankey, because the patterns which they reproduce in such glaring obviousness are present in much Victorian hymnody. Again and again, those hymns end with a vision of heaven; and they often accommodate an awareness of the problems of this life. A hymn such as 'The Church's one foundation', written in 1866 by Samuel John Stone, a Berkshire vicar, takes this pattern into the corporate life of the church. It begins with confidence:

> The Church's one foundation
> Is Jesus Christ, her Lord;
> She is his new creation
> By water and the Word.

But the assurance gives way to an admission that there are problems:

> Though with a scornful wonder
>   Men see her sore opprest,
> By schisms rent asunder,
>   By heresies distrest,
> Yet Saints their watch are keeping,
>   Their cry goes up, 'How long?'
> And soon the night of weeping
>   Shall be the morn of song.

In the next verse ('And the great Church victorious / Shall be the Church at rest') Stone holds out the great hope of a final victory, in spite of the schisms and heresies: he was thinking in particular of the controversy between Bishop Colenso of Natal and the orthodox Bishop Gray of Capetown. Colenso's questioning of the historical accuracy of the Pentateuch, and the ensuing attempts to depose him, were just one of the many crises which rocked the Church of England during this period: the Gorham case of 1847–50 (in which Bishop Philpotts of Exeter refused to accept a clergyman because of his questioning of baptismal regeneration), the publication of *Essays and Reviews* in 1860, the defections to Roman Catholicism which followed each wrangling controversy, all of these disturbed the peace and were reflected in the writing of hymns. Philip Pusey (brother of E. B. Pusey, the Tractarian leader) wrote 'Lord of our life, and God of our salvation', with a prayer to God to 'Hear and receive thy Church's supplication':

> See round thine ark the hungry billows curling;
> See how thy foes their banners are unfurling;
> Lord, while their darts envenomed they are hurling,
>   Thou canst preserve us.

Pusey was writing during the controversy over church rates in the 1830s, but the image of the church under attack was common throughout the Victorian period. It was divided within itself, and the subject of scorn from without: it was particularly concerned by the way in which matters of controversy were decided by legal means, often in ways which offended one or other of the principal parties (so that the decision in the Gorham case, for example, dismayed the Tractarians).

In contrast, the Roman Catholic church offered a welcome certainty and authority, which is found in Newman's hymn from *The Dream of Gerontius* (1865):

> Firmly I believe and truly
> God is Three, and God is One;
> And I next acknowledge duly
> Manhood taken by the Son.
>
> . . .
>
> And I hold in veneration,
> For the love of him alone,
> Holy Church as his creation,
> And her teachings as his own.

The adverbs are important: 'firmly . . . duly'. Newman is insisting on firmness of belief and the duty of obedience. This was one way out of the turmoil and difficulty of the doctrinal differences of other churches, so often represented in hymns as 'darkness':

> Through many a day of darkness,
> Through many a scene of strife,
> The faithful few fought bravely
> To guard the nation's life.

This hymn, 'Thy hand, O God, has guided', was written by Edward Hayes Plumptre, who was appointed dean of Wells in 1881. It prompts the question 'Who were the "faithful few" who "fought bravely"?' It would depend on where you stood in any of the fierce controversies, and in the light of those disagreements the last line of each verse, 'One Church, one Faith, one Lord', reads almost like a plea for an unattained ideal.

The reality was much more like the vision of John Mason Neale:

> Christian, dost thou see them
> On the holy ground,
> How the troops of Midian
> Prowl and prowl around?
> Christian, up and smite them.

Who the troops of Midian were is never made clear, so that they may stand for the forces of evil generally, as they do in 'Fight the good fight with all thy might', by John Samuel Bewley Monsell, from his *Hymns of Love and Praise for the Church's Year* of 1863. But they may, in Neale's mind or in the minds of the singers, have stood for those within the church whose views were different.

Ancient Hymnody and German Hymnody

Neale's translations made him the most prolific author of *Hymns Ancient and Modern*, and this is itself significant: the book (with 'Ancient' in its title) was recognizing, as Neale himself had done, the great treasury of hymnic devotion to be found in medieval hymns, in the Latin hymns of the early church, and in the hymns of the Eastern church. He turned away from the controversies of his own time to breathe a purer air. The old hymns, he wrote in *A Short Commentary on the Hymnal Noted*, the *Hymnal* being the book which he published with Thomas Helmore in 1852 and 1854, 'have consoled thousands of God's faithful servants in all kinds of circumstances, almost from the days of the Apostles to our own: – and if on this account only, they ought to be dear to us' (1852, 1854: v). Neale was appealing to antiquity, away from what Matthew Arnold called 'this strange disease of modern life' – as surely as nineteenth-century architects such as Barry and Pugin and Waterhouse were subscribing, in the new Houses of Parliament and Manchester Town Hall, to ancient ideals of national pride and civic virtue.

So Neale translated a simple hymn of the Greek islands:

> The day is past and over:
>   All thanks, O Lord, to Thee!
> I pray Thee that offenceless
>   The hours of dark may be.
> O Jesu! keep me in Thy sight,
> And save me through the coming night!

This hymn, wrote Neale, 'is to the scattered hamlets of Chios and Mitylene, what Bishop Ken's Evening Hymn is to the villages of our own land' (1862: xli). He was trying to broaden the outlook of his countrymen, lift their eyes from the problems of the day to the 'huge treasure of divinity' of ancient hymns. He did so with a confident simplicity:

> Jerusalem the golden,
>   With milk and honey blest,
> Beneath thy contemplation
>   Sink heart and voice opprest.
> I know not, O I know not
>   What social joys are there,
> What radiancy of glory,
>   What light beyond compare.

The theme of the joys of heaven is one which is found in thousands of Victorian hymns, but it here acquires a force and nobility that comes from the effortless use of the 76.76. metre. It was for this hymn that Samuel Sebastian Wesley wrote the splendid 'Aurelia' (now generally used for 'The Church's one foundation') with its expressive minims (also found in 'Ewing', the tune to which the hymn is now most frequently sung).

Neale found the theme once more in Peter Abelard:

> O what their joy and their glory must be,
> Those endless sabbaths the blessèd ones see;
> Crown for the valiant, to weary ones rest;
> God shall be all, and in all ever blest.

Rest for the weary occurs again in Neale's versification of 'Come unto me, all ye that labour and are heavy laden, and I will give you rest' (Matthew 11: 28):

> Art thou weary, art thou languid,
>   Art thou sore distrest?
> 'Come to me' – saith One – 'and coming,
>   Be at rest!'

When writing such hymns Neale could forget his quarrels with the local bishop (who denounced his decorating of the chapel at Sackville College as 'spiritual haberdashery'), and forget his own weak health:

> O how glorious and resplendent,
>   Fragile body, shalt thou be,
> When endued with so much beauty,
>   Full of health, and strong, and free,
> Full of vigour, full of pleasure,
>   That shall last eternally!

His awareness of pain and sickness (he published *Hymns for the Sick* in 1843) links him with the women hymn writers of the nineteenth century, and is part of the pattern of trouble on earth followed by bliss in heaven. This contrast occurs again and again:

> Brief life is here our portion;
>   Brief sorrow, short-lived care;
> The life that knows no ending,
>   The tearless life, is *THERE*.

Neale was the greatest of the hymn translators. Another was Edward Caswall, who was an Anglican vicar who followed Newman into the Roman Catholic church and published *Lyra Catholica* in 1849, in the first flush of his convert's enthusiasm. His 'Jesu, the very thought of thee' is a moving translation of 'Jesu, dulcis memoria'. Neale and Caswall and others took the great treasures of Greek and Latin hymnody, and made them available to English-speaking congregations, enriching their worship and their spiritual life.

The translators of German hymns did the same, from Thomas Carlyle onwards. 'A safe stronghold our God is still', his translation of Luther's 'Ein' feste Burg', dates from 1831; it was followed by Frances Elizabeth Cox's *Sacred Hymns from the German* (1841) and

Richard Massie's *Martin Luther's Spiritual Songs* (1854). The greatest of German translators was the young Catherine Winkworth, who published *Lyra Germanica* in 1855 and *Lyra Germanica: Second Series* in 1858. Winkworth translated Luther, notably his 'Aus tiefer Noth' paraphrase of psalm 130, and also Joachim Neander ('Praise to the Lord, the Almighty, the King of Creation'), Paul Gerhardt ('Now all the woods are sleeping') and Martin Rinkart ('Now thank we all our God'). Her hymns subsequently appeared with tunes in *The Chorale Book for England* in 1863, with German chorale music edited by two distinguished musicians, William Sterndale Bennett and Otto Goldschmidt. In that title, the words 'for England' were important: not only was the tradition of great hymnody being brought over from Germany, but Germany was also the cradle of the Reformation, so that in the swaying tug of war between Tractarians on the one hand and evangelicals on the other, these hymns provided a counterbalance to Neale's advocacy of the pre-Reformation tradition. In the preface to *Lyra Germanica*, Winkworth described the way in which Luther had translated Latin hymns into the vernacular, 'thus enriching the people, to whom he had already given the Holy Scriptures in their own language, with a treasure of sacred poetry which is the precious inheritance of every Christian Church' (1855: viii). This unequivocal approval of Luther, which would have horrified Tractarians and Roman Catholics, was matched by her very Protestant remark, in a letter to Edward Herford, that 'nothing can supersede that inner sense of right and wrong, which I believe to be the voice of the Holy Spirit in the heart' (Shaen 1908: 175).

The new German hymns, therefore, made a significant contribution to the life of the Victorian church. Their source in German Protestantism was itself an ideological counter to the Catholic imagery of Neale's translations. It was clear to all that 'Now thank we all our God' was from a different tradition to Neale's 'The royal banners forward go' or 'The day of resurrection'. And one of the strengths of *Hymns Ancient and Modern* was that it included both.

Missions

If there was one topic on which all parties could agree, it was the importance of missionary activity. This was of two kinds: among the poor at home, and among 'the heathen' abroad. The consciousness that there were large numbers who never went to church and who were untouched by religion, especially in London and the great industrial cities, was a motive for the often heroic efforts to put churches into the poorest districts, and for some devoted labours by clergymen such as W. W. Champneys at Whitechapel; but hymns do not seem to have celebrated this kind of mission except incidentally (perhaps because the problem itself seemed so intractable, and was the subject of so much effort). Foreign missions were another matter. Only ten years before Queen Victoria's accession, Reginald Heber's widow had published his missionary hymn 'From Greenland's icy mountains', with its second verse ending 'The heathen in his blindness / Bows down to wood and stone', and it was taken for granted that throughout the British Empire, and beyond if possible, the benefits of Christianity should be made available to all. The missionary was a nineteenth-century hero: young men made selfless efforts in Africa and India, often going out to countries where they knew that their life-expectancy could be measured in months rather than years. They went in the spirit of the hymn by Sarah Geraldina Stock (1838–98), 'Let the song go round the earth':

> Let the song go round the earth,
>   From the eastern sea,
> Where the daylight has its birth,
>   Glad, and bright, and free;
> China's millions join the strains,
> Waft them on to India's plains.
>
> Let the song go round the earth,
>   Lands where Islam's sway
> Darkly broods o'er home and hearth,
>   Cast their bonds away;
> Let His praise from Afric's shore
> Rise and swell her wide lands o'er.

The image of dispelling darkness and bringing light is a common one:

> O'er heathen lands afar
>   Thick darkness broodeth yet:
> Arise, O morning Star,
>   Arise, and never set!

This was by Lewis Hensley (1824–1905), a Fellow of Trinity College, Cambridge. The first line of this, the last verse, is now usually amended, as in the *BBC Hymn Book* of 1951, to the innocuous 'O'er lands both near and far'. Similarly amended, by the editors of *English Praise* in 1975, has been Charles Oakley's 'Hills of the North, rejoice', with its original (written before 1865):

> Lands of the East, awake,
>   Soon shall your sons be free;
> The sleep of ages break,
>   And rise to liberty.

The assumption of superiority over other religions and other races that seems to underlie these hymns has led to their abolition or to their rewriting. But other hymns, on similar themes, have survived because they preached the coming of the kingdom without referring to the darkness of the heathen. They looked forward, quite legitimately, to a time of universal peace and joy, in which the whole world would rejoice in the coming of the New Jerusalem. John Ellerton's masterpiece, 'The day thou gavest, Lord, is ended', concludes with a final vision of the whole world at one:

> So be it, Lord: thy throne shall never,
> Like earth's proud empires, pass away;
> Thy kingdom stands, and grows for ever,
> Till all thy creatures own thy sway.

That hymn, written in 1870 for *A Liturgy for Missionary Meetings*, takes the singers of the first verse, where they are singing in church ('To thee our morning hymns ascended'), and launches them on a ride through space, watching the world as it turns:

> We thank thee that thy church unsleeping,
> While earth rolls onward into light,
> Through all the world her watch is keeping,
> And rests not now by day or night.

The journey continues, looking down at the land forms below:

> As o'er each continent and island
> The dawn leads on another day,
> The voice of prayer is never silent,
> Nor dies the strain of praise away.

The comma at the end of line two comes exactly in the middle of the five verses: that middle verse is beautifully pivoted on it, and that verse is the central poise of the hymn. For after three verses of imaginative vision, Ellerton brings us back again to earth with his final 'So be it, Lord'. I have likened it elsewhere (Watson 1997: 39) to a bridge, with abutments on either side and three leaping arches in the middle: and the abutments are made the stronger by referring (in verse 1) to the account of the creation in Genesis ('the day . . . the darkness') and by turning (in verse 5) to Revelation – as though Ellerton has neatly incorporated the beginning and end of the Bible.

'The day thou gavest' is a deeply satisfying hymn to sing, not least to the waltz-like tune by Clement Scholefield (which is only disturbing if the first beat of each bar is overstressed). Scholefield's tune was written for Ellerton's words, and printed in *Church Hymns with Tunes* (1874), with the name 'St Clement' as a little joke by Arthur Sullivan as music editor. The combination of words and music has made this one of the best loved of Victorian hymns, first brought into prominence by being chosen for the service at Queen Victoria's Diamond Jubilee in 1897; its warning against 'earth's proud empires' in the final verse suggests that Victoria was aware of the dangers of pride in her role as queen-empress, and should be enough to acquit the hymn of being a piece of cultural imperialism, as Susan Tamke has suggested it is (Tamke 1978). Nevertheless, Ellerton, like other writers of missionary hymns, was clearly hoping for a world in which 'all thy creatures own thy sway', without being explicitly dismissive of other religions; while his art, so beautifully organizing the hymn into a beginning, a middle and an end, is elegant and persuasive.

Children's Hymns

One of the chief concerns of the Victorian churches was the education of children, both in the weekday school and in the Sunday school; and just as Sunday-school teaching was seen as appropriate for women (or even girls: Charlotte Yonge taught a class of tiny children when she was seven), so the writing of hymns for children seems to have been a particular preserve of women. As Mrs E. R. Pitman put it, in *Lady Hymn Writers* (1892: 281–2), 'Women – and especially women who were mothers – have excelled in the art of writing hymns for children. Somehow it needs mother-love to interpret divine love to the little ones.'

The hymns do this in the simplest language:

> Jesus, who lived above the sky,
> Came down to be a man and die;
> And in the Bible we may see
> How very good he used to be.

This is the opening of a pre-Victorian hymn by Ann Gilbert (1782–1866), who with her sister Jane Taylor produced *Hymns for Infant Minds* in 1809 (another of their books contains 'Twinkle, twinkle, little star'). That book, together with Isaac Watts's *Divine and Moral Songs for Children*, was a model for later writers. One of the first was Frances Mary Yonge, mother of the novelist Charlotte Yonge, who published *The Child's Christian Year* in 1841: she was evidently trying to produce a book for children along the lines of Keble's immensely successful *Christian Year*, although she made few concessions to the children's minds. More accessible was the single hymn known to be by Jemima Luke (1813–1906), who wrote it for a village school near Bath in the same year, 1841:

> I think, when I read that sweet story of old,
>   When Jesus was here among men,
> How he called little children as lambs to his fold,
>   I should like to have been with them then:
> I wish that his hands had been placed on my head,
>   That his arms had been thrown around me,
> And that I might have seen his kind look when he said,
>   'Let the little ones come unto me.'

Keble himself produced in 1846 *Lyra Innocentium*, subtitled 'Thoughts in Verse on Christian Children, their Ways and their Privileges': as this subtitle implies, it is not strictly a hymn book for children, although Keble tried to unbend on occasion, but a book about children.

It was not until Cecil Frances Alexander (then still Miss Humphreys) published *Hymns for Little Children* in 1848 that the Victorian children's hymn really became successful:

> All things bright and beautiful,
>> All creatures great and small,
> All things wise and wonderful,
>> The Lord God made them all.

At her best, Alexander has a plainness of speech and a neatness of phrase that are admirable. She was also a good storyteller, incorporating a narrative line into the verse with unobtrusive skill, and beginning 'Once' (for 'Once upon a time . . .'):

> Once in royal David's city
>> Stood a lowly cattle shed,
> Where a mother laid her baby
>> In a manger for his bed:
> Mary was that mother mild,
>> Jesus Christ her little child.

This is the story of the Nativity as told to children for the first time, and fresh with simplicity. In the same way, Alexander explained the Crucifixion:

> We may not know, we cannot tell,
>> What pains he had to bear,
> But we believe it was for us
>> He hung and suffered there.
>
> He died that we might be forgiven,
>> He died to make us good.

Alexander at her best has a quality of innocence which makes her verses attractive, even though she is inclined to overdo the words 'little' and 'tiny', and some of the images seem dated, such as the rural children in 'All things':

> The tall trees in the greenwood,
>> The meadows where we play,
> The rushes by the water
>> We gather every day.

She also had a serene acceptance of inequality, which led to what Percy Dearmer (1933: 239) called 'the appalling verse':

> The rich man in his castle,
>> The poor man at his gate,
> God made them high or lowly,
>> And ordered their estate.

Alexander's other difficulty was that she did not know how to deal with naughty children. This was a common problem. Isaac Watts's *Divine and Moral Songs* faced it head-on, and threatened them with hell. Ann and Jane Taylor, in 'For a child who has been very naughty', were more gentle, allowing the child to ask for forgiveness ('Lord, I confess before thy face, / How naughty I have been'). Alexander threatens them with the withdrawal of love:

> Little children must be quiet,
>   When to Holy Church they go,
> They must sit with serious faces,
>   Must not play or whisper low.
>
> For the Church is God's own Temple
>   Where men go for praise and prayer,
> And the Great God will not love them
>   Who forget his presence there.

The result is the overriding concept, throughout Victorian children's hymnody, of the child who is obedient: 'Christian children all must be / Mild, obedient, good as he.'

If children were good on earth, they would go to heaven, often (in the days of high infant and child mortality) as children: portrayals of heaven frequently suggest that the angels have the faces of innocent children. So Alexander ends her Christmas hymn: 'When like stars his children crowned / All in white shall wait around.' In the same way, a hymn by Anne Shepherd (1809–57) begins

> Around the throne of God in heaven
>   Thousands of children stand,
> Children whose sins are all forgiven,
>   A holy, happy band,
>   Singing Glory, glory, glory!

The best known of these hymns, 'There's a friend for little children/ Above the bright blue sky', was written (unusually) by a man, Albert Midlane (1825–1909), and given a wonderful skipping tune, significantly (and sadly) called 'In Memoriam', by John Stainer. It must have been a consolation to grieving parents and to sick children to visualize 'a home for little children':

> No home on earth is like it,
>   Or can with it compare;
> For every one is happy,
>   Nor could be happier, there.

These simple patterns of obedience on earth followed by a reward in heaven were common in Sunday-school hymns:

> Father, lead me day by day
> Ever in thine own sweet way.
>   (John Page Hopps,
>   1834–1912)

> Looking upward every day,
> Sunshine on our faces;
> Pressing onward every day
> Toward the heavenly places.
> (Mary Butler, 1841–1916)

These are two of hundreds of hymns which imparted a simple code of precepts, followed by an equally simple set of rewards, to the nation's children.

Perhaps the most celebrated of children's hymns is Sabine Baring-Gould's 'Onward! Christian soldiers', a hymn which is still going strong. It was written in 1864 for a Sunday-school procession in Yorkshire, and later given the famous tune by Sullivan, 'St Gertrude'. It is a hymn which is based on the children's pleasure at 'playing soldiers', for the battle here is an easy one: 'At the sign of triumph / Satan's host doth flee'; and Baring-Gould was capable of writing absolute nonsense:

> We are not divided,
> All one body we,
> One in hope, in doctrine,
> One in charity.

However detached from the scrabbling divisions of the Victorian church this was (or perhaps because it allowed people to forget them for a moment), 'Onward! Christian soldiers' was one of those many popular hymns which seeped into the Victorian consciousness. It was a hymn of a just war (Tennyson saw Gordon of Khartoum as the 'Warrior of God'). It helped to suggest that war could, and should, be fought against evil, and it took its place, alongside hymns of dedication and service, in another kind of children's hymnody, that of the public schools.

Usually, each of these schools had its own hymn book, containing substantial and serious hymns which helped to foster a certain set of attitudes and principles. Lionel Adey, who has studied these books in *Class and Idol in the English Hymn*, charts the difference between classes in hymn books, finding evidence that while 'children from order-giving classes sang into their systems an expectation of responsible service, those from order-receiving classes [sang] one of subservience here and triumph hereafter' (1988: 133). Adey noted that in the public schools, while singing hymns in chapel in the nineteenth century, 'the future English establishment enjoys its sense of mission, its belief in the consecration of its class and country'. The dedication implied in these hymns led eventually to the Great War, where the young officers set an example to the private soldiers, the order-receivers, as they walked across the fields of the Somme to their deaths.

Women's Hymns

There had been hymns by women before the Victorian age, most famously by Anne Steele, the eighteenth-century Baptist writer who published under the name 'Theodosia'. In the nineteenth century, many more women became very successful hymn writers, often taking on the role of comforters to the sick and lonely. Charlotte Elliott, for example, published *The Invalid's Hymn Book* (1834) and *Hours of Sorrow Cheered and Comforted* (1836). Her best-known hymn, 'Just as I am, without one plea', is an eloquent plea for acceptance, and the subtext of worthlessness (she was an invalid for many years, living with her active clergyman brother) is characteristic of some women's hymnody. Elizabeth Cosnett, a distinguished contemporary hymn writer, has acutely pointed out, for example, that the last verse of Christina Rossetti's 'In the bleak mid-winter' shows 'the shepherd as someone with a trade or profession who can offer to Christ the material fruit of his daily work and the wise man as someone whose access to education gives him a role in society' –

> What can I give him,
>   Poor as I am?
> If I were a shepherd
>   I would bring a lamb;
> If I were a wise man
>   I would do my part;
> Yet what I can I give him –
>   Give my heart.

– whereas 'when a woman wrote these words women were largely excluded from the professions and from higher education' (1995: 178).

Christina Rossetti had no job and no degree. Her situation was typical of that of many intelligent women in the Victorian age, and the hymns which they wrote reveal their frustration. 'And art thou come with us to dwell', by Dora Greenwell (1821–82), for example, describes the coming of Christ into the world, 'God present with his world restored':

> Thou bringest all again; with thee
>   Is light, is space, is breadth, and room
> For each thing fair, beloved, and free,
>   To have its hour of life and bloom.
>
> Each heart's deep instinct unconfessed;
>   Each lowly wish, each daring claim;
> All, all that life hath long repressed
>   Unfolds, undreading blight or blame.

Greenwell lived with her tyrannical mother for eighteen years. In her verses the images of light, space, breadth and room, the idea of the flower unfolding to the sun, all show her longing to escape from the stifling role that life had given her, to be free from 'blight or blame', from the repression (the word 'repressed' is pre-Freud, and very insightful) of the 'heart's deep instinct'. With the coming of an ideal world, 'The humblest flower hath leave to blow, / And spread its leaves to meet the sun, / And drink within its soul the dew.' What lies behind this vision is the awareness of the crushed flower, of the wasted life.

It is not surprising, perhaps, that so many of these women hymn writers should have been what Ian Bradley, accurately but perhaps a little unkindly, calls 'sickly spinsters' (1997: 91). They saw themselves as struggling through life:

> Nearer, my God, to Thee,
> Nearer to Thee!
> E'en though it be a cross
> That raiseth me.

This is by Sarah Flower Adams (1805–48), a Unitarian: her imagery is that of darkness and stones, hoping for a dream like that of Jacob at Bethel:

> Out of my stony griefs
> Bethel I'll raise;
> So by my woes to be
> Nearer, my God, to Thee,
> Nearer to Thee!

The idea of coming 'nearer' to Christ becomes unhealthy when it is overemphasized, as it is by writers such as Fanny Crosby (Frances Jane van Alstyne, 1820–1915), the American evangelical who is said to have contracted with a publisher for thirty years to write three hymns each week (including 'Blessed assurance, Jesus is mine'):

> Draw me nearer, nearer, nearer blessed Lord,
> To Thy precious, bleeding side.
>   . . .
>
> O my Saviour, love me,
> Make me all Thine own.

Crosby's cloying and sickly verse is presumably the result of her own struggle and frustration, made more difficult for her because she was blind almost from birth.

At the opposite extreme is the writing of Frances Ridley Havergal (1836–79), an exception to the rule that these women writers were prone to invalidism. Havergal was an enthusiast for life: a poet, a fine musician, a mountain climber, a swimmer, whose enthusiastic energy comes out in the heartiness of:

> Who is on the Lord's side?
> Who will serve the King?
> Who will be his helpers
> Other lives to bring?
> Who will leave the world's side?
> Who will face the foe?
> Who is on the Lord's side?
> Who for him will go?

Havergal was picking sides in the great game of life: she acted out her own part, giving away the money she earned from writing, and putting her very considerable talents to work for God. Her most celebrated hymn records this: 'Take my life, and let it be / Consecrated, Lord, to Thee.' Successive verses enumerate her blessings: take my hands and feet (as an athlete), my voice (as a musician), my lips (as a speaker), my silver and my gold (as a comparatively well-off woman), my intellect, my will and my heart; and finally:

> Take my love; my Lord, I pour
> At Thy feet its treasure-store;
> Take myself, and I will be
> Ever, only, all for Thee!

Havergal's hymns are rare in that they dedicate to God her health and happiness (rare, too, in the mention of the intellect).

More often, in the women's hymnody of the age, their hymns look beyond the troubles of this life to a better world. Anna Laetitia Waring (1820–1910), who almost certainly suffered because of her publicly undeclarable love for another woman, described her heart as 'abiding' in heavenly love: 'In heavenly love abiding, / No change my heart shall fear.' She looked forward to a better time, with images of weather, linked with those of the twenty-third psalm:

> Green pastures are before me,
> Which yet I have not seen;
> Bright skies will soon be o'er me,
> Where the dark clouds have been;
> My hope I cannot measure,
> My path to life is free;
> My Saviour has my treasure,
> And he will walk with me.

With that hope, women hymn writers accepted their place, endured their lot, and looked forward longingly to their final reward.

The Individual and God

The finest women's hymnody is that which expresses, often in an oblique or disguised form, the longings of the human heart. The same can be said of the best Victorian hymn writing. And while some of it is banal, self-indulgent and manipulative, some of it takes its place as poetry because it is written, with skill and due attention to form, in praise of God and in true consideration of the spiritual life. It has as its subjects the Bible, the world, the church, the hopes and fears of men and women; but above all, it attempts to understand the serious questions of life. It does so in a public and accessible form, which sometimes sets it apart from Tennyson, or Browning, or Hopkins, or Emily Brontë. But that form, rigid within its stanzas and circumscribed by its need to be orthodox, has been a poetry that many people have known and loved for well over a century. The reasons are clear: the best Victorian hymns are not only well written, but they deal with important topics: the battle between good and evil ('For all the saints, who from their labours rest'); the keeping of promises ('O Jesus, I have promised'); danger ('Eternal Father, strong to save'); gratitude ('Come, ye thankful people, come'); beauty ('For the beauty of the earth'); and divine love ('O love that wilt not let me go'). They explore these things through an examination of the relationship between human beings and God:

> I heard the voice of Jesus say:
>   'Come unto me and rest;
> Lay down, thou weary one, lay down
>   Thy head upon my breast.'
> I came to Jesus as I was,
>   Weary and worn and sad,
> I found in him a resting-place,
>   And he has made me glad.

This hymn by Horatius Bonar (1808–89) taps into the familiar sense of the world as a difficult place, but placates the unease in the second half of each verse. This is helped in the singing by the remarkable tune by John Bacchus Dykes, 'Vox Dilecti', which moves halfway through the verse from G minor to G major (in the *English Hymnal*, Vaughan Williams, reacting against Victorian music, replaced it with an English folk tune, 'Kingsfold'). Bonar's hymn has survived into the twenty-first century because, I think, it understands the different moods, the inner weather (Aldous Huxley's phrase) of the soul.

In the same way, a hymn such as 'Abide with me', by Henry Francis Lyte (1793–1847), is moving because it carries within itself a recognition of human need as well as human hope. It is also beautifully written: the long lines allow the mind to feel its way into the emotion, while the chiasmus ('Abide with me . . . with me abide') gives a sense of restraint and order. The content is discovered through the form:

> Abide with me; fast falls the eventide;
>   The darkness deepens; Lord, with me abide;
> When other helpers fail, and comforts flee,
>   Help of the helpless, O abide with me.

The sense of evening, as the darkness deepens, is linked with 'eventide', the evening tide: Lyte, who was a clergyman at Brixham, knew the importance of the movements of the sea. This is made explicit in the next verse:

> Swift to its close ebbs out life's little day;
>   Earth's joys grow dim, its glories pass away;
> Change and decay in all around I see;
>   O thou who changest not, abide with me!

Human life has become as short as a little day, the brief space of time between one tide and another: as the tide ebbs, so life itself drifts away. It is into this powerfully realized sense of human transience that Lyte introduces his prayer: so that the hymn acknowledges both the shortness of life, and its dependence on God. 'Abide with me' is a cry of a child in need: 'stay with me'. So that at the end of the hymn, the vision of heaven – 'Heaven's morning breaks, and earth's vain shadows flee' – is accompanied still by a sense of need. There is no 'blessed assurance' here; just the confrontation with the reality of death, and the need for some kind of help – 'Help of the helpless, O abide with me.'

'Abide with me' is an outstanding example of the Victorian hymn. But the form is never less than interesting to the student of the period. It demonstrates many of the problems of the time, not only within the churches, but also within the hearts of men and women, faced as they were with the particular circumstances of their own lives. We should respect their efforts to understand the important questions, and to engage with the world around them; they are a cloud of witnesses, who, being dead, yet speak.

See also: TRACTARIAN POETRY; POETRY AND RELIGION.

REFERENCES AND FURTHER READING

Adey, Lionel (1986) *Hymns and the Christian 'Myth'*. Vancouver: University of British Columbia Press.

Adey, Lionel (1988) *Class and Idol in the English Hymn*. Vancouver: University of British Columbia Press.

Beal, Anthony (1967) *D. H. Lawrence: Selected Literary Criticism*. London: Heinemann.

Bradley, Ian (1997) *Abide with Me: The World of Victorian Hymns*. London: SCM Press.

Chadwick, Owen (1971) *The Victorian Church*. Third edition. London: A & C Black.

Cosnett, Elizabeth (1995) 'A (Female) Book-worm Reads Some Hymns.' *Bulletin of the Hymn Society of Great Britain and Ireland*, 205, 172–84.

Davie, Donald (1978) *A Gathered Church*. London: Routledge and Kegan Paul.

Davie, Donald (1982) *Dissentient Voice*. Notre Dame, Ind.: University of Notre Dame Press.

Davies, Horton (1961) *Worship and Theology in England from Watts and Wesley to Maurice, 1690–1850*. Princeton, N. J.: Princeton University Press; London: Oxford University Press.

Davies, Horton (1962) *Worship and Theology in England from Newman to Martineau, 1859–1900*. Princeton, N. J.: Princeton University Press; London: Oxford University Press.

Dearmer, Percy (1933) *Songs of Praise Discussed*. London: Oxford University Press.

Drain, Susan (1989) *The Anglican Church in Nineteenth-Century Britain: Hymns Ancient and Modern (1860–1875)*. Lewiston, Queenston, Lampeter: Edwin Mellen Press.

Ellerton, John (1896) *Being a Collection of His Writings on Hymnody*. London: SPCK.

Havergal, Maria V. G. (1880) *Memoirs of Frances Ridley Havergal*. London: James Nisbet.

Horder, William Garrett (1889) *The Hymn Lover: An Account of the Rise and Growth of English Hymnody*. London: J. Curwen & Sons.

Jay, Elisabeth (1979) *The Religion of the Heart: Anglican Evangelicalism and the Nineteenth-Century Novel*. Oxford: Clarendon Press.

Julian, John (1892) *A Dictionary of Hymnology*. London: John Murray.

Kent, John (1978) *Holding the Fort: Studies in Victorian Revivalism*. London: Epworth Press.

Litvack, Leon (1994) *John Mason Neale and the Quest for Sobornost*. Oxford: Clarendon Press.

Maynard, Constance L. (1926) *Dora Greenwell, A Prophet For Our Own Times On The Battleground of Our Faith*. London: H. R. Allenson.

Neale, John Mason (1852, 1854) *A Short Commentary on the Hymnal Noted*. London: J. Masters.

Neale, John Mason (1862) *Hymns of the Eastern Church*. London: Hayes.

Pitman, E. R. (1892) *Lady Hymn Writers*. London: T. Nelson & Sons.

Prickett, Stephen (1976) *Romanticism and Religion*. Cambridge: Cambridge University Press.

Shaen, Margaret J. (1908) *Memorials of Two Sisters, Susanna and Catherine Winkworth*. London: Longmans, Green.

Tamke, Susan S. (1978) *Make a Joyful Noise unto the Lord: Hymns as a Reflection of Victorian Social Attitudes*. Athens, Ohio: Ohio University Press.

Temperley, Nicholas (1979) *The Music of the English Parish Church*. Cambridge: Cambridge University Press.

Tennyson, G. B. (1981) *Victorian Devotional Poetry: The Tractarian Mode*. Cambridge, Mass., and London: Harvard University Press.

Watson, J. R. (1997) *The English Hymn*. Oxford: Clarendon Press.

Watson, J. R., and Kenneth Trickett (1988) *Companion to Hymns and Psalms*. Peterborough: Methodist Publishing House.

Wheeler, Michael (1990) *Death and the Future Life in Victorian Literature and Theology*. Cambridge: Cambridge University Press.

Winkworth, Catherine (1855) *Lyra Germanica*. London: Longmans.

Woods, Rollo G. (1995) *Good Singing Still: A Handbook to West Gallery Music*. Ironbridge: West Gallery Music Association.

8

Nonsense

Roderick McGillis

A quick glance through Walter Houghton's (1957) examination of the Victorian frame of mind turns up references to anxiety, worry, fatigue, doubt, rigidity, earnestness, loneliness, work and seriousness. But nowhere in either the table of contents or the index in Houghton's book do words such as play, humour, high jinks, gaiety, comedy, laughter or nonsense appear. The Victorians carried until quite recently the weight of a reputation for a seriousness as dour as it was sometimes dark. Something of a corrective appears in Richard Altick's *Victorian People and Ideas* (1973). Altick cautions that we not assume 'the Victorian spirit was devoid of humour . . . Indeed, everywhere one turned, the seriousness and earnestness of Victorian life were balanced by the comic impulse' (1973: 178–9). However, we had to wait until 1975 for a study of Victorian wit and humour, Ronald Pearsall's *Collapse of Stout Party*. Clearly, as J. Don Vann points out, the many Victorian periodicals devoted to humour testify that the Victorians had a sense of humour (1994: 290). And at least two famous Victorian bachelors show us that this sense of humour could veer towards the zany and the absurd. The work of Edward Lear and Lewis Carroll that has acquired the generic title 'Nonsense' serves as a source for a distinctive type of British humour we might now identify with the Goons, Monty Python, Mr Bean and Blackadder.

Lear and Carroll have become synonymous with Nonsense, but they were neither the creators of the genre nor the only practitioners of it during Victoria's reign. Both Stephen Prickett (1979) and Valentine Cunningham (2000) credit the Victorians with the creation of the Nonsense genre, but Noel Malcolm, in *The Origins of English Nonsense*, traces nonsense poetry back to the Middle Ages, and he also illustrates just how self-conscious a genre it had become by the mid-seventeenth century. According to Malcolm, nonsense 'existed only in a literary culture' (1997: 52); it did not come 'bubbling up from below', a manifestation of the folk spirit's drive to anarchy and excess (1997: 110). Rather than expressing a people's drive to shake off political yokes, nonsense is a deeply literary activity. If it has any political significance, then this may be purely personal; Malcolm cites the case of John Taylor, who 'stood some way outside the privileged socio-literary circles of his day', and who 'used nonsense poetry partly as a way of ironizing from a distance at the expense of the more elaborate poetic conventions' (1997: 124).

This view fits with the integral place of parody within nonsense; parody has as one of its obvious purposes an 'ironizing' of the works it takes for its subjects. Since most parodies target canonized works, the parody has a political function in that it makes fun of high art and its claim to privilege. So yes, nonsense verse is deeply self-conscious of form. It foregrounds such formal features as language, onomastics, rhythm, rhyme, stanza shapes and rhetorical devices – especially paradox, prosopopoeia, repetition, alliteration and paronomasia. In this type of verse, form subsumes subject. Travelling to sea in a sieve, hunting a snark, confessing an attraction to a passing gentleman, slaying a monster with a vorpal blade all become silly subjects in nonsense verse.

The Romantic penchant for finding subjects anywhere is both apparent and parodied in this verse. Take for example Henry S. Leigh's *Songs of the Sick Room* (1869). The first of these songs concerns the poet's dislike of cod-liver oil. Here's the last stanza of this four-stanza poem:

> There are few deeds of daring from which I should quail –
> There are few things I should tremble to do –
> But there's one kind of tonic that makes me turn pale,
> And quite spoils my appetite, too;
> But, you see, just at present, I've got none to spoil –
> So I don't mind alluding to cod-liver oil!
>
> (Cunningham 2000: 773)

The subject is both silly and realistic. Like much nonsense verse, this one has fun with the Victorian desire to capture reality, to get close to the things of the earth. This poem deals with something familiar from the everyday world, something that introduces health and food and desire and the stemming of desire. Deeds of daring and the taking of a vitamin supplement here come into conjunction; the elevation of a common-enough subject turns it towards the absurd. We can find sense here, but it is sense without import. What impresses the reader more than the sense of this poem are its formal features: the alliteration, the diction, the hint of chiasmus. Words threaten to detach themselves from context: 'quail' conjures up a feathered game bird even as it serves a verbal function; 'to do' might remind us that the poem we are reading is a to-do, a bustle and stir signifying little or maybe even nothing. In the final line, the poet says he does not mind 'alluding to cod-liver oil'. He means, of course, that he doesn't mind speaking of the tonic he detests; but he also means that he doesn't mind playing with this tonic. Indeed, the poem 'spoils' cod-liver oil, that is, spills it, and in doing so has ludic fun.

Nonsense is all ludic. The play's the thing in which to catch the portentousness of poetry. Nonsense verse serves to remind us that reality can be too much with us, and when it is we might well realize that its presence is something of a chimera. The questioning of reality is a well-known feature of Lewis Carroll's Alice books. But the same question-ing is part and parcel of the nonsense genre. Nonsense draws attention to the inevitable slippage between signifier and signified, the arbitrary connection between which has become standard currency in critical circles. Language has difficulty stating what is real precisely because what is real eludes precise statement. Here's a poem from Christina Rossetti's *Sing-Song* (1872) that illustrates the imprecision of language, its inability to capture reality:

> The peacock has a score of eyes,
>   With which he cannot see;
> The cod-fish has a silent sound,
>   However that may be;
>
> No dandelions tell the time,
>   Although they turn to clocks;
> Cat's-cradle does not hold the cat,
>   Nor foxglove fit the fox.

To say that Rossetti's poem registers language's inability to capture reality is not quite accurate. Each of the five assertions in the poem makes sense, even if we might wish to agree with Michael Heyman that the kind of sense a poem such as this makes is 'nonsense'. One of Rossetti's points is precisely that words such as 'foxglove' or 'cat's-cradle' signify by alluding to that which they are not. The words are in themselves paradoxical. Paradox is central to this poem and to nonsense generally.

We might say, drawing on Lecercle, that paradox is a manifestation of nonsense's polyphony; paradox defines the 'chronotope' of nonsense (1994: 168ff). The time and space of nonsense are both somewhere and nowhere, sometime and no time. The Rossetti poem has no discernible setting; its time and place are missing. We might follow Michael Holquist's lead and say that Rossetti's poem can 'be perceived only as what it [is], and not some other thing'. Nonsense delivers an 'immaculate fiction' (1969: 147). And yet this poem situates itself precisely in the nineteenth century, drawing on such familiar nineteenth-century items as cod-fish, cat's-cradles, and foxgloves, and parodying both Wordsworth and the Victorian mania for classifying. It does have significance beyond itself. The list of paradoxes in Rossetti's poem draws attention to a slippage between signifier and signified. They contradict each other – the foxglove doesn't 'fit' the fox, dandelions turn to clocks but they are not clocks. As Lecercle suggests, nonsense 'is structured by the contradiction . . . between over-structuring and destructuring, subversion and support' (1994: 3).

The language of nonsense both overdetermines meaning and deconstructs it; to put this the other way, it both carries meaning and subverts it. Here is an instance, the first three stanzas of C. S. Calverley's 'Lovers, and a Reflection' (1872):

> In moss-prankt dells which the sunbeams flatter
> (And heaven it knoweth what that may mean;
> Meaning, however, is no great matter)
> Where woods are a-tremble, with rifts atween;

Thro' God's own heather we wonn'd together,
I and my Willie (O love my love):
I need hardly remark it was glorious weather,
And flitterbats wavered alow, above:

Boats were curtseying, rising, bowing,
(Boats in that climate are so polite),
    And sands were a ribbon of green endowing,
And O the sundazzle on bark and bight!
                                    (Cunningham 2000: 682)

The speaker states outright that meaning is unimportant here, thus preparing the reader for the apparent absurdities of trembling woods with rifts between, lovers abiding or dwelling (wonn'd) through God's heather, boats curtseying, and the possibility of green sand. The language, although not nonsense coinage, is often archaic ('prankt', 'atween', 'wonn'd', 'alow') or deliberately unfamiliar ('bight'). This is hyberbolic language. The effect is to convince the reader that he or she enters here a nonsense chronotype, a time and space of non-meaning or of what Heyman terms 'non-sense' (1999–2000: 187). In this 'climate' (wherever this may be), bats flitter beneath the sun and wooden structures curtsey and bow. The tone is playful, drawing attention to alliterative and syntactic effects. In this context the word 'prankt' carries with it a suggestion of a practical joke. But if we pursue this notion, we begin to discern meaning. The joke here has to do with an undoing of a traditional love lyric. Who are the lovers? Who is Willie? Is the speaker a man or a woman? Is the name Willie meant to suggest an autoerotic theme? Once we move into such questions, we next have to question the import of the poem's language: woods, a-tremble, rift, wonn'd, curtseying, rising, bowing. Even that archaic word 'bight' can mean not only a bend in the land or a bay, but also a bend or fork in the human body. The language may not be as innocent as we might first suspect. But then again, it may be.

Whether we find the poem sexually naughty or sexually innocent, we can be certain that it expresses a certain self-consciousness. It sets out to lampoon the seriousness of the traditional love lyric; in fact, this poem is a parody of Jean Ingelow's 'Divided' (1863). The point is that no matter what the origin of nonsense verse, its very existence functions as a challenge to high art. It may be that the heirs of Lear and Carroll, the postmodernists, have transformed nonsense and parody until they become themselves the conditions of the high art that they once functioned to challenge. But this does not mean that the nonsense verse written by many Victorian writers fails in its challenge to the canon.

Victorian nonsense poetry takes aim at the high seriousness of canonized poetry, and it does so by linking itself with the tradition of popular poetry associated with the ballad, the nursery rhyme and children's chants. Children's literature itself has a history of duality, a canonized tradition of texts and a popular tradition mostly frowned upon by keepers of the canonical works. Despite this, children's literature has never, except for a very few exceptions, found a place in the adult canon. So the drift of nonsense towards children's literature seems a natural expression of nonsense's conscious challenge to canonical works. The most obvious example of this is the nonsense writing of Lewis Carroll. His nonsense verse chooses canonical works for adults as well as canonical works for children as the source for its parodic energy. In Carroll's verse we have parodies of Wordsworth, Tennyson and other mainstream poets for adults, and parodies of Watts, Taylor, Howitt and others known for their children's poetry. Lear too targets canonized works in his various forms of parody; his nonsense alphabets, his lyric effusions, his zany versions of nature poetry, his nonsense botany, his travel verses and prose stories puncture the seriousness and even portentousness of didactic children's literature and works by such Romantic luminaries as Wordsworth, Coleridge and Byron. Lesser-known versifiers such as Thomas Hood the Younger, William Brighty Rands and D'arcy W. Thompson take the Pre-Raphaelites, canonized children's works, and Romantic poetry generally as sources for their fun. The very form of nonsense poetry is a snub to the high-toned inflections of iambic pentameter and blank verse that came to dominate mainstream poetry from the seventeenth century on (see Easthope 1983: 64–9).

A glance through any anthology of nonsense verse will indicate that the formal features of this poetry include: an insistent accentual line, usually a succession of four-stress lines or alternating four- and three-stress lines, blunt rhymes that at times chime internally and are punctuated with off-rhymes and half-rhymes, a lightsome but perhaps lumpen use of alliteration, a love of exotic names, and a delight in neologisms. Some of these features are apparent in the opening of Swinburne's 'Nephelidia' (1880):

> From the depth of the dreamy decline of the dawn through a notable
>   nimbus of nebulous noonshine,
> Pallid and pink as the palm of the flag-flower that flickers with fear
>   of the flies as they float,
> Are the looks of our lovers that lustrously lean from the marvel of
>   mystic miraculous moonshine,
> These that we feel in the blood of our blushes that thicken and
>   threaten with sobs through the throat?

Swinburne parodies his own poetic mannerisms, but in doing so he turns nonsense's four-stress line into a double-length eight-stress line, and he emphasizes the silly allure of alliteration while throwing up a language that threatens to dislocate from meaning ('a notable nimbus of nebulous noonshine'). Again, we have language which is hyperbolic, over the top, as if the language itself were parodying the human desire to communicate precisely and fully. The very fullness of this verse signifies its emptiness.

Fullness and emptiness are themselves signs of desire, and desire is perhaps the secret of nonsense. The Victorians spoke of desire all the time, as writers such as Michel Foucault and James Kincaid have shown, but they did so often in a deeply coded manner. Perhaps they learned something from the folk imagination in their use of fairy-tale and nursery-rhyme discourse to express the unspeakable. This is the argument of Maureen Duffy's *The Erotic World of Faery* (1972). Already we have seen that Calverley's 'Lovers, and a Reflection' may code masturbation in its parodic language. But take a look at a familiar limerick by Edward Lear (1872):

> There was a young person of Janina,
> Whose uncle was always fanning her;
> When he fanned off her head, she smiled sweetly, and said,
> 'You propitious old person of Janina!'

Lear himself remarked that writing for children should be 'clear & bright, & incapable of any meaning but one of sheer nonsense' (cited Rieder 1998: 47). And so this limerick is clear and bright: in sprightly rhythm we read of a young woman who enjoys being fanned by her uncle. The uncle carries out his task so enthusiastically that he fans off the young woman's head. As often in Lear's limericks, the clarity of the brief narrative clouds in the final line. Does the young woman thank her uncle for fanning off her head? Her statement merely asserts that her uncle is an 'old person' and that he is 'propitious'. He is an old person; she is a young person. He serves (services?) her with his fan and she responds with a remark that he is propitious. Captain Grose's *Dictionary of the Vulgar Tongue* (1811) defines the verb 'to fan' as: 'To beat anyone. I fanned him sweetly; I beat him heartily.' But why, we might ask, should the young lady use a word – 'propitious' – that suggests advantage, favour and sweetness? According to the young woman, her uncle is a gracious person; she is pleased with his fanning. His fanning, she suggests, is a propitiation, an offering to her. So far we can say that the limerick expresses the physical pleasure the young woman receives from her uncle's propitiatory fanning. In this context, her detached head might well suggest excitement, pleasure in extremis, profane pleasure. This is clear enough.

But Lear's work, like much nonsense, comes with a visual aid, and his illustration significantly complicates what may be coded here. The young person of Janina reclines on a couch or divan in a position reminiscent of several paintings, most notably Goya's two pictures of *La Maja* (1798) and Edouard Manet's *Olympia* (1865). Manet's work especially links with Lear's depiction of the young person of Janina, but the intertextual reference goes back to Goya's depiction of La Maja dressed and La Maja *sans habille*. The clothed Maja wears an empire dress with the high waistline tucked snugly under her breasts. So too does the young person of Janina. Edouard Manet's Olympia echoes Goya's Maja 'Desnudo', with the addition of a black servant. Manet draws attention to a Greek-named female attended by a subaltern. Lear picks this up by showing his young person of Janina (a city in Greece) fanned by an uncle who looks distinctly 'other', a Turkish or Greek wearing later nineteenth-century costume. In fact, the face of the uncle looks more oriental than Turkish or Greek. What is going on here?

Lear's limerick with accompanying illustration codes both sexual pleasure and the relationship between colonizer and colonized. The woman in imperial dress receives pleasure from her subaltern uncle. The young woman's hair, with its topknot and feather, looking distinctly like an ink bottle and quill pen, lends her a masculine significance, while the old person's fan and distinctive dress feminize him. The visual discourse here maintains colonial stereotypes. From the perspective of nineteenth-century poetry, this limerick with its illustration expresses a familiar Victorian narrative of British colonial activity. However, from a psychoanalytical perspective, the limerick is far more complicated and ambiguous. As well as communicating desire, this limerick communicates fear: fear of women, of the other, of sexuality. These themes of desire, sexuality, fear and colonization are a regular feature of Lear's nonsense, turning up in the limericks ('There was an old man of the Cape', 'There was an old man of Jamaica', 'There was an old man of Peru', 'There was an old man who when little', 'There was an old man whose despair'), and in the longer lyrics such as 'The Pobble Who Has No Toes', 'The Dong with the Luminous Nose', 'The Owl and the Pussy-cat, and 'The Jumblies'.

To read Lear's work in the context of both desire and colonialism is, if we accept what Lear says, to be 'silly'. He writes that 'critics are very silly to see politics in such bosh' (cited in Rieder 1998: 47). But when a writer wishes to speak that which must not be spoken, denial seems an appropriate claim. The various old persons of Lear's limericks register frustration, anxiety, anger, passivity and eccentricity. Their collective behaviour must surely reflect Lear's sense of the world as a place where we are better off remaining in a kettle or a jar, or up a tree or in a bush, than we are trying to express individuality in a world of hard knocks (see for example that 'disgusting' old man of Breem). Lear's work can hardly avoid being 'political'. It may not be political in the sense of referencing topical political figures and issues directly, as W. S. Gilbert does or Carroll may do in the Alice books (see Thomas 1996: 166–7), but throughout Lear's writing he reveals a concern for the politics of community. For example, many limericks deal with the individual in conflict with his or her community or family. 'The Quangle Wangle's Hat' presents a vision of communal harmony, whereas 'Mr. And Mrs. Discobbolos' is a tale of family discord and violence. Lear's work may be seen as a strategy for dealing with unpleasant realities of both a social and a psychological kind. In an age of spiritual doubt and social injustice, nonsense becomes a means of survival, a way of dealing with unpleasant social, economic and political realities.

Perhaps this function of nonsense goes some way to explain why Lewis Carroll takes an interest in the British courts; like Dickens, he has fun with Britain's justice system. It may also explain something of the occasional nature of nonsense poetry. It appears not so much in book-length collections by one writer (Lear and Carroll are the exceptions here) as it does in scattered appearances in the periodical literature (sometimes later collected into single volumes, as in the case of W. S. Gilbert's various collections of 'Bab Ballads'), or tucked away in an author's otherwise serious volume of verse, or interpolated into prose fiction as we find in Carroll's work or that of his friend George MacDonald. In a volume of poems largely concerned with the poor of Victorian London, George R. Sims includes the poem 'Undertones' (1880), which carries the subtitle, 'By a Lunatic Laureate'. In this poem, nonsense fuses with social concern:

> There's a feeling that comes with the daze of joy
> And goes with the knights of grief –
> That stands on the top of a baby buoy,
> And floats with an anchor chief.
> It rides on the back of a noted Bill,
> And fights where your collars fray;
> It whispers in accents loud and shrill –
> To-morrow succeeds to-day.
>   (Cunningham 2000: 896)

The run of puns offers a message of hope for what the poem later refers to, in a suitably ambiguous way, as 'a new decayed'.

Ambiguity runs deep in nonsense. This sprightly and even joyous type of verse has its melancholy side. Take a brief example, the younger Thomas Hood's 'How Singular':

> Though pleasures still can touch my soul,
> Though sorrow's fountain still is open –
> Yet smile I not as erst I smole,
> Nor weep I as I erst have wopen.
>
> Some years ago, in my belief,
> Life was a pudding, earth its platter;
> I've pluck'd my plums of joy and grief –
> And all the rest is only batter.
>   (Grigson 1979: 143)

Mark West has commented on Lear's 'frustrations and sadness' (1987: 155), and Carroll's work too has its poignant reminders of loss (see Jackson 1981: 142). At its best, nonsense can even have fun with death, as the many jokes concerning death in the work of both Carroll and Lear indicate. As good an example as we could look for of nonsense's willingness to combine the comic with the morbid is Theo Marzial's doleful call to death, 'A Tragedy' (1873). Hear the song of a jilted lover:

> DEATH!
> Plop.
> The barges down in the river flop.
> Flop, plop,
> Above, beneath.
> From the slimy branches the grey drips drop,
> As they scraggle black on the thin grey sky,
> Where the black cloud rack-hackles drizzle and fly
> To the oozy waters, that lounge and flop
> On the black scrag piles, where the loose cords plop,
> As the raw wind whines in the thin tree-top.
> Plop, plop.
> And scudding by
> The boatmen call out hoy! and hey!
> And all is running in water and sky
> And my head shrieks – 'Stop',
> And my heart shrieks – 'Die.'
>   (Cunningham 2000: 942)

Is this poetry aspiring to the condition of nonsense or is it simply poetic excess? However we judge this, 'A Tragedy' displays many of nonsense's features. What we see here is a serious poetry trying, unsuccessfully but enjoyably, to employ the poetic gestures of nonsense. A more successful use of nonsense hyperbole is evident in lines such as, 'I caught this morning morning's minion, king-/dom of daylight's dauphin, dapple-dawn-drawn Falcon, in his riding' (Hopkins's 'The Windhover', ll. 1–2).

But nonsense avoids the overtly serious. It expresses in its very nature irony, an irony most evident in its insistence on paradox. This is a poetry both meaningless and meaningful, silly and serious, detached and engaged, timely and timeless. One aspect of nonsense's paradoxical nature is its appeal to a dual audience. The majority of the examples cited up to now in this chapter have as their target audience adults. However, the tendency is for us to think of nonsense as a genre specifically aimed at children. The two best-known practitioners of the genre – Lear and Carroll – created their most successful work for children, and yet this work has always found admiring adult readers. Like much writing for children, nonsense speaks to a dual audience.

U. C. Knoepflmacher reminds us that the 'notion that "adult" and "juvenile" texts should be kept apart did not become prevalent until the end of the nineteenth century' (1998: xiii). Writers for children had from the beginning known that their work would necessarily have to find approval with both children and the adults who cared for these children. If their work contains the kind of coding that we found in 'There was a young person of Janina', then the cracking of this code is more likely to be something an adult will accomplish. The child is more likely to clap for decapitation than to try and understand it in some psychoanalytic or symbolic way. The removability of body parts is something children encounter in folk tale and nursery rhyme; this fantasy that the body might come apart without dire consequences serves a deeply reassuring function. Carroll too plays on this fantasy in *Alice's Adventures in Wonderland*, although in this book 'they never executes nobody, you know' (1960: 125). Nonsense's appeal to a dual audience, both adult and child, is a crucial aspect of its subversive appeal. Nonsense thus breaks the barriers of high art, art that through sophistication and complexity speaks only to a learned and urbane audience. Nonsense punctures false urbanity. In nonsense, the adult and child reader share a laugh at pretension and high seriousness.

The absurdities of nonsense approach the carnivalesque in their delight in things of the body, including food and drink.

> 'In my youth', said the sage, as he shook his grey locks,
> 'I kept all my limbs very supple
> By the use of this ointment – one shilling the box –
> Allow me to sell you a couple?'
>
> (Carroll 1960: 70)

> Then fill up the glasses with Treacle and ink,
>   Or anything else that is pleasant to drink:
> Mix sand with the cider, and wool with the wine –
> And welcome Queen Alice with ninety-times-nine!
>
> (Carroll 1960: 330)

> A pin has a head, but has no hair;
> A clock has a face, but no mouth there;
> . . .
> A watch has hands, but no thumb or finger;
> A boot has a tongue, but is no singer.
>
> (Rossetti 1968: 54–5)

> There was an Old Man of Nepaul
> From his horse had a terrible fall;
> But, though split quite in two, by some very strong glue,
> They mended that Man of Nepaul
>
> (Lear 1951: 27)

These examples all suggest the pleasures of bodily existence. Inanimate objects cannot speak or eat or hold things or sing. Age need not bring decrepitude. Exotic fluids are fine for drinking the health of young queens. And even bodily breakage need not prove fatal. Perhaps the best example is Carroll's 'You are old Father William', in which William cavorts with glee despite his advanced age. Lear's work too has its active and energetic elderly characters. Something carnivalesque springs from the antics of these elderly characters and their younger counterparts.

To speak of the carnivalesque as an aspect of nonsense, we do not need to connect this poetry with the sanctioned, and hence safe, transgressions of the disenfranchised. It is true that much of this poetry derives from a tradition of anonymous nursery rhyme, doggerel and street verse, but much of it also derives from a parodic relationship with the productions of high art. By subverting sense and the depth of thought in the poetic canon, by standing sense on its head in order to draw attention to it, nonsense challenges a thoughtless acceptance of reality and a language that purports to reflect reality. Sense tells Alice that she is real, but Tweedledee informs her that she is 'only a sort of thing in his [the Red King's] dream' (1960: 238). Alice's common sense tells her that she is; Tweedledee's uncommon sense tells her that she is a figment of another's imagining. To be self and yet the creation of another is to be self and other. Paradox. And paradox, as Deleuze remarks, is the affirmation of two things (propositions, directions, senses) at the same time (1990: 1–3). Paradox creates movement, but movement along the surface. Deleuze identifies paradox as a 'dismissal of depth', and he argues that Alice's adventure amounts to a 'climb to the surface . . . and her discovery that everything happens at the border' (1990: 9). The border is the border between sense and no sense, sanity and madness, propriety and impropriety, seriousness and humour, reason and imagination, reality and fantasy.

For the Victorians, nonsense poetry served as an outlet for their frustrations and desires, while it also allowed them to indulge their interest in tangibles, the thingness of this world. The poetry is chock-a-block with things such as cod-liver oil, clothes, animals and birds, tables and chairs, food, curling-irons, combs, brushes, baskets, clocks, nutcrackers, sugar tongs, ships, foreign lands, caravans, lace, musical instruments, but mostly words, words exotic and strange, substantives and adjectives that 'begin to dissolve' (Deleuze 1990: 3). In fact, the very thingness of the world as we know it begins to dissolve in nonsense. This aspect of nonsense is apparent in some of the arcane lists Kingsley includes in *The Water Babies* (1863). For another example, here is Christina Rossetti's *Sing-Song* again:

> If a mouse could fly,
> Or if a crow could swim,
> Or if a sprat could walk and talk,
> I'd like to be like him.
>   (Rossetti 1968: 72)

Nonsense conditionals tease us into accepting a time and place in which impossible conditions are possible. After all, in the age of the locomotive and the telegraph anything did indeed seem possible. Nonsense reminds us that the world we know is perhaps less tangible than we might like to believe.

As part of the thingness of words, names are important in nonsense verse. Jumblies, Jabberwocky, Snark, Lady Jingly, Giant Frodgedobbublum, Buffalant, Professor Noctutus, Ahkond of Swat, and Cummerbund are a few of the names we meet in this verse. The last two, as Sumanyu Satpathy shows, are indications of Orientalism. Satpathy's concern is with Edward Lear, but as Samuel Foote's 'The Grand Panjandrum' (1755) indicates, Lear's Orientalist use of names is not unique. The names listed also echo a number of other aspects of nonsense. Those beginning with 'J' point to the nature of nonsense language, its jumbling of letters in unfamiliar combinations, its jabbering and jingling. 'Buffalant' and 'Noctutus' are examples of the portmanteau, the first being a combination of buffalo and elephant and the second being a Latin mix of *noctu* (by night) or *noctua* (the owl) and *tutus* (out of danger). (It is worth noting parenthetically that Latin has proved a useful vehicle for nonsense.) And 'Snark' is an example of a neologism; it has come down to North Americans in the word 'snarky'.

This interest in the thingness of words is perhaps a manifestation of the Victorian love of classifying and collecting. Kingsley's *The Water Babies* again comes to mind. We can also see this delight in accumulation in poetry that borders on nonsense. The collection of fruits in Rossetti's 'Goblin Market' (1862) shows a desire to move into a use of language for its own sake. So too does the description of the goblins as they approach the second sister, Lizzie:

> Laughed every goblin
> As they spied her peeping:
> Came towards her hobbling,
> Flying, running, leaping,
> Puffing and blowing,
> Chuckling, clapping, crowing,
> Clucking and gobbling,
> Mopping and mowing,
> Full of airs and graces,
> Pulling wry faces,
> Demure grimaces,
> Cat-like and rat-like,

> Ratel- and wombat-like,
> Snail-paced in a hurry,
> Parrot-voiced and whistler,
> Helter skelter, hurry skurry,
> Chattering like magpies,
> Fluttering like pigeons,
> Gliding like fishes.
>
> (Cunningham 2000: 669)

Language aspiring to the condition of pure sound is a feature of such nonsense. Here's a second example from chapter 20 of George MacDonald's fantasy, *At the Back of the North Wind* (1870):

> Householder snails, and slugs all tails,
> And butterflies, flutterbies, ships all sails;
>
> And weasels, and ousels, and mice, and larks,
> And owls, and rere-mice, and harkydarks,
>
> All went running, and creeping, and flowing,
> After the merry boy fluttering and going;
>
> The dappled fawns fawning, the fallow-deer following,
> The swallows and flies, flying and swallowing
>
> Cockchafers, henchafers, and cockioli-birds,
> Cockroaches, henroaches, cuckoos in herds.
>
> (1967: 162)

These passages aim to mimic a natural language, language as sound or song. After an earlier example of this kind of poetry in MacDonald's novel, an exasperated mother says what she's been reading is 'such nonsense', and her little boy responds by saying that the poetry sounds just like the song of the river (1967: 119–29). Like nursery-rhyme jingles – 'higgledy-piggledy', 'hoddley poddley', 'nieve nieve nick nack', 'wisky wasky weedle', are just a sample – nonsense poetry intensifies the focus on words as sound. Here's an example from W. S. Gilbert:

> Sing for the garish eye,
> When moonless brandlings cling!
> Let the froddering crooner cry,
> And the braddled sapster sing.
> For never and never again,
> Will the tottering beechlings play,
> For bratticed wrackers are singing aloud,
> And the throngers croon in May!
>
> (Wells 1958: 13)

This bit of nonsense contains a mixture of strange but identifiable words and words that appear to have no lexical meaning. Gilbert takes his verse to a region of non-meaning, and yet we know the stanza speaks of song, loss, and the necessity of continued song. The syntactical arrangement is familiar and the theme of music is also familiar; after all, this is a lyric. So we expect the sound of the words and rhythm to make sense. And more often than not sound does make sense, and, as the examples from Rossetti and MacDonald illustrate, sound can take patterns. Rossetti's similes speak to language's figuration and her run of participles draws attention both to alliterative effect and to the notion of action, energy and captivation. As for MacDonald, he can't resist using antimetabole utterance to go along with his familiar and unfamiliar creatures. Such devices do more than add sound patterns to a rhythmic scutter; they draw attention to language itself as both a communicative and an incantatory force. As in nursery rhyme and fairy tale, ritual is a typical feature of nonsense.

In addition to their sensitivity to sound, Rossetti and MacDonald parody anacreontic verse (MacDonald more so in the earlier verse from *At the Back of the North Wind*), and in doing so they are true both to nonsense's subversive treatment of canonic poetry and to its challenge to conventional modes of thought and communication. This is poetry that asks the reader to take notice and even to think, and to have fun while doing so. This explains the various nonsense modes: riddles, fables, parody, ballads, and didactic forms such as the cautionary rhymes of Heinrich Hoffmann and Hilaire Belloc (see Anderson and Apseloff 1989). If we wish to teach the forms of poetry, then nonsense verse might well serve as a vade mecum, since its attention to form is so intense and clear. And if we require a vade mecum of nonsense itself, we need only carry about with us Lewis Carroll's 'Jabberwocky', perhaps the most famous nonsense poem in English. Martin Gardner suggests that 'Few would dispute the fact that Jabberwocky is the greatest of all nonsense poems in English', and he goes on to compare it with abstract painting in that both 'may suggest vague meanings . . . or they may have no meaning at all' (Carroll 1960: 192).

It should be clear by now that 'no meaning at all' is hardly possible in language. Words and forms communicate despite any effort to render them miscommunicative. As Preminger and Brogan state: it is 'naive to believe that nonsense verse does not "make sense"; much of it does in its own way' (1993: 839). Note that phrase 'much of it', a hedge that suggests a possibility of non-meaning, a possibility of what Cuddon refers to as 'gibberish' (1991: 589). But gibberish is not nonsense poetry; the ravings of a mad person may not take the form of nonsense poetry. That which partakes in the craft of nonsense will, perforce, communicate, even if only to make the kind of subversive statement regarding the pretensions of high art that we looked at earlier. 'Jabberwocky', like all nonsense poetry, is a highly self-conscious literary production that takes as its subject poetry itself. The first stanza (which is also the final stanza) appeared in the family periodical *Misch-Masch* in 1855 as a 'Stanza of Anglo-Saxon Poetry' (see Carroll 1960: 191). Following the stanza in *Misch-Masch* is Carroll's explanation, and the explanation along with the stanza itself form a parody both of poetic communication and of critical interpretation.

Once the stanza becomes the frame to the entire 'Jabberwocky' poem, the parodic element grows. The most famous Anglo-Saxon poem is, of course, *Beowulf*, a poem that chronicles the life of a hero who battles three monsters. Beowulf's fights with Grendel and then with Grendel's mother take place when he is, if not exactly a beamish boy, then a young man. The poem valorizes masculine strength, bravery and violence. Beowulf's world is one of action rather than word, and when words are used they come as boasts and challenges to action. 'Jabberwocky' inverts this heroic world by replacing Beowulf's heroic weapon with a 'vorpal sword'.

Carroll claimed not to be able to explain 'vorpal', but Alexander Taylor avers that the word 'seems to be concocted out of Verbal and Gospel by taking alternate letters from each'. Taylor further suggests the poem 'vaguely burlesques the dragon-slayer of *The Faerie Queene*, whose sword was the word of God' (1952: 81). Whether or not Carroll was as ingenious as Taylor suggests, the connection with words and power is appropriate here. This poem is about the power of the word. Another of Carroll's sources is relevant here: William Blake (for Carroll's connection with Blake, see Cohen 1995: 107–13). 'Jabberwocky', in some ways, parodies Blake's 'The Tyger'. Like 'The Tyger', 'Jabberwocky' begins and ends with the same verse. Also like 'The Tyger', 'Jabberwocky' is about a crea-ture with 'eyes of flame' who appears to inhabit a forest, called here a 'tulgey wood'. Carroll's reading of 'The Tyger' accepts the creature in the forests of the night as something that frightens and that is better beheaded. The question is not what hand or eye could frame such fearful symmetry, but 'hast thou slain the Jabberwock?' And the beamish boy has – with his vorpal blade which went snicker-snack. We can see Carroll's poem as an anti-heroic statement or perhaps more precisely as a revisioning of the heroic. In 'Jabber-wocky', heroism has something to do with words (vorpal swords), or with what Blake refers to as Mental Fight.

Responding to a class in a girl's Latin school, Carroll stated the meaning of 'Jabberwock' as 'the result of much excited discussion' (Carroll 1960: 195). The Jabberwock is a monster of words; it comes through the tulgey wood 'whiffling' and 'burbling', two words that Gardner, drawing on nineteenth-century usage, glosses as words that refer to blustering, perplexing and evading. In short, these words suggest a speaker who huffs and puffs, a Bounderby in language. This is the monster the beamish boy beheads. 'Jabberwocky' is a poem about the power of poetry to cut through evasion, bluster and huffery-puffery in lan-guage. The same might be said of nonsense as a genre. The Victorians' delight in nonsense, then, fits with their delight in things simple and straightforward. In an age of uncertainty and difficult questions concerning faith and the future, in a time when armies clashed on a darkling plain, the certainties of fun and nonsense were a breath of fresh air, a connection with a pastoral tradition that some feared was in danger of being buried beneath the smoke and stir of dimness and doubt. Nonsense for the Victorians was, paradoxically, a means of staying grounded, of returning to shore after sailing the dark, broad seas:

> There was an old man of Dunluce,
> Who went out to sea on a goose:
> When he'd gone out a mile, he observ'd with a smile,
> 'It's time to return to Dunluce.'
>
> (Lear 1951: 178)

Carroll, or rather the Mock Turtle, utters a not dissimilar sentiment when he invites Alice to join the dance:

'What matters it how far we go?' his scaly friend replied.
'There is another shore, you know, upon the other side.'
(Carroll 1960: 134)

Susan Stewart points out that nonsense has been relegated to second-class citizens: the child, the servant, the mad (1979: 5). This may be true of the genre's fate in the twentieth century, but the Victorians did not relegate nonsense below stairs or to the nursery only. A central magazine such as *Punch* included nonsense in its pages, and many writers both for adults and for children used nonsense to poke fun at a variety of pretensions. Subjects included in nonsense verse included world travel, the empire, sex, fashion, standards of beauty, politics, nature, domestic life, the Woman Question, Darwinism, faith and doubt, and art itself. Nonsense looks both inward and outward. Deeply self-conscious on the one hand, and expressive of the unconscious on the other, this eminently loony genre of poetry kept the Victorians sane.

See also: DOMESTIC AND IDYLLIC; LYRIC; POETRY AND ILLUSTRATION; NATIONHOOD AND EMPIRE.

REFERENCES AND FURTHER READING

Altick, Richard D. (1973) *Victorian People and Ideas*. New York: Norton.

Anderson, Celia Catlett, and Marilyn Fain Apseloff (1989) *Nonsense Literature for Children*. Hamden, Conn.: Library Professional Publications.

Carroll, Lewis (1960) *The Annotated Alice*. Notes by Martin Gardner. New York: Bramhall House.

Cohen, Morton N. (1995) *Lewis Carroll: A Biography*. New York: Vintage.

Cuddon, J. A. (1991) *A Dictionary of Literary Terms and Literary Theory*. Oxford: Blackwell.

Cunningham, Valentine (ed.) (2000) *The Victorians: An Anthology of Poetry and Poetics*. Oxford: Blackwell.

Deleuze, Gilles (1990) *The Logic of Sense*. Trans. Mark Lester. New York: Columbia University Press.

Duffy, Maureen (1972) *The Erotic World of Faery*. New York: Avon Books.

Easthope, Anthony (1983) *Poetry as Discourse*. London, New York: Methuen.

Grigson, Geoffrey (ed.) (1979) *The Faber Book of Nonsense Verse with a Sprinkling of Nonsense Prose*. London, Boston: Faber and Faber.

Heyman, Michael (1999–2000) 'A New Defense of Nonsense; Or, Where Then is His Phallus? And Other Questions Not To Ask.' *Children's Literature Association Quarterly*, 24, 187–94.

Holquist, Michael (1969) 'What is a Boojum? Nonsense and Modernism.' In Peter Brooks (ed.). *The Child's Part* (pp. 145–64). Boston: Beacon Press.

Houghton, Walter (1957) *The Victorian Frame of Mind*. New Haven, London: Yale University Press.

Jackson, Rosemary (1981) *Fantasy: The Literature of Subversion*. London, New York: Methuen.

Kincaid, James (1992) *Child Loving: The Erotic Child and Victorian Culture*. New York, London: Routledge.

Knoepflmacher, U. C. (1998) *Ventures into Childland: Victorians, Fairy Tales, and Femininity*. Chicago, London: University of Chicago Press.

Lear, Edward (1951) *The Complete Nonsense of Edward Lear*. Collected and intro. Holbrook Jackson. New York: Dover.

Lecercle, Jean-Jacques (1994) *Philosophy of Nonsense: The Intuitions of Victorian Nonsense*. London, New York: Routledge.

MacDonald, George (1967) *At the Back of the North Wind*. First published 1870. London: J. M. Dent.

Malcolm, Noel (1997) *The Origins of English Nonsense*. London: HarperCollins.

Pearsall, Ronald (1975) *Collapse of Stout Party: Victorian Wit and Humour*. London: Weidenfeld and Nicolson.

Preminger, Alex and T. V. F. Brogan (eds) (1993) *The New Princeton Encyclopedia of Poetry and Poetics*. Princeton, N. J.: Princeton University Press.

Prickett, Stephen (1979) *Victorian Fantasy*. Bloomington, London: Indiana University Press.

Rieder, John (1998) 'Edward Lear's Limericks: The Function of Children's Nonsense Poetry.' *Children's Literature*, 26, 47–60.

Rossetti, Christina (1968) *Sing-Song: A Nursery Rhyme Book*. First published 1872. New York: Dover.

Satpathy, Sumanyu (1999) 'Lear's India and the Politics of Nonsense.' Unpublished paper delivered at the Children's Literature and the Fin de Siècle conference, Calgary.

Stewart, Susan (1979) *Nonsense: Aspects of Interte-xtuality in Folklore and Literature*. Baltimore: Johns Hopkins University Press.

Taylor, A. L. (1952) *The White Knight: A Study of C. L. Dodgson (Lewis Carroll)*. Edinburgh, London: Oliver & Boyd.

The 1811 Dictionary of the Vulgar Tongue: Buckish Slang, University Wit and Pickpocket Eloquence (1994). London: Senate.

Thomas, Donald (1996) *Lewis Carroll: A Portrait with Background*. London: John Murray.

Vann, J. Don (1994) 'Comic Periodicals.' In J. Don Vann and Rosemary T. VanArsdel (eds). *Victorian Periodicals and Victorian Society* (pp. 278–90). Toronto: University of Toronto Press.

Wells, Carolyn (1958) *A Nonsense Anthology*. First published 1902. New York: Dover.

West, Mark (1987) 'Edward Lear's A Book of Nonsense: A Scroobius Classic.' In Perry Nodelman (ed.). *Touchstones: Reflections on the Best in Children's Literature* (II, 150–6). West Lafayette, Ind.: Children's Literature Association Publications.

9

Verse Novel

Dino Felluga

Here is the story as it has been told so far: in the middle of the nineteenth century, at the very heart and height of the Victorian period, a peculiar and peculiarly perverse genre, the verse novel, arose in England only to disappear again by the 1870s. By the late 1860s, the form had achieved enough cohesion and visibility to be parodied in Edmund C. Nugent's *Anderleigh Hall: A Novel in Verse* (1866), a sure sign of a genre's ossification and imminent obsolescence. The verse novel took rather different forms in the two decades of its emergence, from the straightforward plot of Elizabeth Barrett Browning's *Aurora Leigh* (1856, dated 1857) to the epistolary fiction of Arthur Clough's *Amours de Voyage* (1858), from the sonnet sequence of George Meredith's *Modern Love* (1862) to the dramatic monologues of Robert Browning's *Ring and the Book* (1868–9). None the less, each work could be said to respond to the increasing marginalization of poetry that occurred after the collapse of the poetry market in the 1820s. As Lee Erickson (1996) has argued, whereas the publishers of Sir Walter Scott and Lord Byron enjoyed huge profits because of conditions that supported a luxury market for poetry in the Romantic period, by 1825 conditions were in place for the emergence of a mass market that oriented itself to the middle classes and their preference for novelistic forms. After this date, and perhaps even more clearly after the bank panic and financial crisis of 1826, publishers simply stopped publishing first editions of poetry, until by the thirties and forties Edward Moxon was virtually the only publisher in England of new collections of poetry by individual writers; and his firm survived, Erickson explains, because he required poets to underwrite part of the costs of publishing (1996: 36). Because of these conditions, poetry was forced into one of two apparently incompatible positions. On the one hand, it could embrace its marginalization as a virtue and explore increasingly rarefied forms that self-consciously rejected the dictates of the market: 'A poet may write poetry with the intention of publishing it', John Stuart Mill writes in 1833, 'he may write it even for the express purpose of being paid for it; that it should be poetry, being written under any such influences, is far less probable' (1833: 12–13). On the other hand, poetry could attempt to play to that market as best it could by exploring those characteristics that made the novel such a popular success (narrative sequentiality, realistic description, historical referentiality, believable characters, dramatic situations, fully realized dialogism and, above all, the domestic marriage plot). As the conventional wisdom goes, each of the verse novels I have mentioned followed the accommodating route to varying degrees and yielded to the nineteenth century's emergent mass market, a market that eagerly bought up domestic novels but for the most part shunned the previously dominant form of the lyric poem.

And yet the coincidence of verse and the novel is by no means so localized, and its relationship to the market is not as simple as that. Even the term 'verse novel' is surprisingly difficult to define given the sheer heterogeneity of the examples one can point to in the nineteenth century. The verse novel almost inevitably engages, overlaps or appropriates other poetic subgenres, including the sonnet sequence (George Meredith's sixteen-line version of the form in *Modern Love*), the dramatic monologue (Robert Browning's *Ring and the Book*) and the epic romance (Alfred Lord Tennyson's *Idylls of the King*). Indeed, one problem with discussing the question of the 'verse novel' is that poetry had for centuries before the rise of the novel valued various forms of fictional narrative, from the epic and the romance to the pastoral and the ballad. The moment of convergence between verse and the novel is further complicated by the fact that some critics, particularly the highly influential scholar Mikhail Bakhtin, have proposed that the novel can trace its emergence through the carnivalesque Rabelaisian satires of *Pantagruel* (1532) and *Gargantua* (1534) all the way back to the Menippean satires of ancient Greece (Bakhtin 1984a, 1981). The verse novel, it can be argued, has an equally amorphous genealogy. Indeed, one of the interesting aspects of Menippus' satires is precisely that they mixed elements of prose and verse in their overturning of what Bakhtin might call 'monological, centripetal, authoritarian discourse'. One could also point to other candidates. One critic, W. M. Dixon (1912), has claimed that William Chamberlayne's obscure 1659 *Pharonnida* is 'our first, and perhaps still our best novel in verse' (1912: 234). Other scholars have pointed to candidates ranging from Chaucer's *Canterbury Tales* to Byron's *Don Juan*. Well before the rise of the Victorian verse novel one can find critics like John Stuart Mill, despite his anti-market prejudices, admitting that 'Many of the finest poems are in the form of novels, and in almost all good novels there is true poetry' (1833: 6). Certainly, one can point to those poetical works that towards the end of the eighteenth century began to be termed 'poetical novels'. One popular work, *Louisa: A Poetical Novel in Four Epistles* (1784) by Anna Seward, had enough influence for Wordsworth in his 'Preface of 1815' to cite the 'metrical novel' as one example among many of narrative poetry, 'including the Epopœia, the Historic Poem, the Tale, the Romance, [and] the Mock-heroic' (III, 27).

However, it was not until the 1850s and 1860s that the 'verse novel' really came into its own as a distinct hybrid between two arch-generic forms that had, until this point, been considered as irreconcilable and even antagonistic. Prior to the Victorian period, educated poets who experimented with popular narrative forms tended to define themselves against 'vulgar literature', which is to say the literature of the *vulgus* – the common people. Wordsworth is a good example since he experiments with narrative forms in both his *Lyrical Ballads* (1798) and the *Prelude* (1850). The *Prelude*, in particular, is not only arguably one of the very first true autobiographies but also one of the first *bildungsromane* and even *künstlerromane*, two novelistic subgenres that are integral to the development of the novel as a distinct form. However, despite the apparent coincidence of the poetic and the prosaic in his poetry, Wordsworth follows Coleridge in condemning narrative forms. It is not until the 1850s that you find Elizabeth Barrett Browning asking poets to represent 'common, ugly, human dust' (*Aurora Leigh*, VI, 163) and Clough in 'Recent English Poetry' (1853) unapologetically calling for the immediate incorporation of novelistic concerns and styles into modern poetry (with the explanation that a novel's 'plain tale' 'obtains one reading at any rate; is thrown away indeed tomorrow, but is devoured today' [1853: 397]).

Following Wordsworth's dismissal of narrative forms, few critics have explored the dynamic interplay that occurs in the nineteenth century between poetry and contemporary narrative genres like the novel. (One notable exception is Jay Clayton's *Romantic Vision and the Novel* [1987].) After all, Wordsworth and Coleridge helped to establish the very genre of literary criticism as a response to what they perceived as the threatening spectre of an emergent mass market. Wordsworth's concept of the 'People' as distinct from the 'Public' (III, 83–4), and Coleridge's juxtaposition between, on the one hand, a 'National Clerisy' comprised of 'the learned of all denominations' (Coleridge 1976: 46) and, on the other, landowners, merchants and manufacturers, established the very concept of a 'high culture' at the beginning of the nineteenth century, an idea that would legitimate the efforts of subsequent critics – the specialists of that high culture – to establish a separate, rarefied realm for the poetic.

Bakhtin, who provides us with some of the terms that might help us to understand the verse novel (dialogism, heteroglossia, speech genres), surprisingly skips over the genre entirely, arguing that 'not until the twentieth century is there a drastic "prosification" of the lyric' (1984b: 200). Instead, like so many other critics in the twentieth century, Bakhtin consistently defines the poetic against the novelistic:

> The poet must assume a complete single-personed hegemony over his own language . . . To achieve this, the poet strips the word of others' intentions, he uses only such words and forms (and only in such a way) that they lose their link with concrete intentional levels of language and their connection with specific contexts. Behind the words of a poetic work one should not sense any typical or reified images of genres (except for the given poetic genre), nor professions, tendencies, directions (except the direction chosen by the poet himself), nor world views (except for the unitary and singular world view of the poet himself), nor typical and individual images of speaking persons, their speech mannerisms or typical intonations. (1981: 297)

In such statements, Bakhtin is not far from John Stuart Mill, who argues that the true poet must 'succeed in excluding from his work every vestige of . . . lookings-forth into the outward and every-day world and can express his feelings exactly as he has felt them in solitude' (1833: 13). Bakhtin of course overstates his case, as he himself admits: 'It goes without saying that we continually advance as typical the extreme to which poetic genres aspire; in concrete examples of poetic works it is possible to find features fundamental to prose, and numerous hybrids of various generic types exist' (1981: 287n). Indeed, what is striking about Bakhtin's list of anti-poetic, novelistic attributes is that we find them all in Robert Browning's supremely dialogic *Ring and the Book*, a fact that would lead Oscar Wilde to exclaim:

> Yes, Browning was great. And as what will he be remembered? As a poet? Ah, not as a poet! He will be remembered as a writer of fiction, as the most supreme writer of fiction, it may be, that we have ever had . . . Meredith is a prose Browning, and so is Browning. He used poetry as a medium for writing in prose. (1975: 7–8)

If one buys Bakhtin's argument that novelistic dialogism by definition opposes those '*forces that serve to unify and centralize the verbal-ideological world*' (1981: 270), then the verse novel should offer us the same questioning of all ideological discourse that Bakhtin reads in the novelistic tradition, particularly his English favourites, Fielding, Smollett, Sterne and Dickens.

Or could it be that the verse novel offers us a form that is even more potentially subversive than the novel? After all, as a number of Foucauldian critics, such as John Bender (1987), Nancy Armstrong (1987) and D. A. Miller (1988), have argued by examining the very authors admired by Bakhtin, the novel may, in fact, be far from liberatory, since it helps to establish the patriarchal hegemony of middle-class, heterosexual, domestic ideology in the nineteenth century. Could it also be that the verse novel's potential subversiveness has remained largely ignored by critics precisely because of a literary specialization that was itself instituted in the nineteenth century to combat the market's perceived obliteration of generic hierarchies? Positions at research institutions are created for either the Victorian novel or Victorian poetry. Could it be that this specialization has made subsequent critics blind to the richness of hybrid forms like the verse novel? Because of its hybridity, the verse novel could be said to resist, on the one hand, the periodization and specialization of the very discipline of literary criticism and, on the other, both the monological tendencies of the Romantic lyric and the hegemonic ideologies of the bourgeois novel.

It is no coincidence that all the examples of the Victorian verse novel I have mentioned so far revolve around perverse or failed domestic relationships. Many critics have commented on the Victorian novel's instantiation and naturalization of separate spheres for men and women through that genre's pervasive ideology of middle-class domesticity. And the idyll of the Victorian 'angel in the house' found its preferred literary expression in the heart – and by the hearths – of the domestic novel. The verse novel, by contrast, seems intent to question that ideology on the level of both content and form.

Aurora Leigh

Elizabeth Barrett Browning attacks domestic ideology head on in what she called her 'novel-poem', even while the narrative trajectory of her work appears, on the surface, to conform most closely of all the verse novels to the traditional plot of the domestic novel (although with a good amount of sensationalism thrown in). The story follows Aurora

Leigh's growth as an author, including her youth, her initial rejection of her cousin Romney Leigh's proposal of marriage, her career in London, and then her entanglement in a sensationalist plot involving Romney's new choice of bride, the lower-class Marian Erle. Through the machinations of the aristocratic Lady Waldemar, who wants Romney for herself, Marian is taken to France on the eve of her marriage to Romney, drugged and then raped, leading to the birth of an illegitimate child. Seeing Marian by chance in Paris, Aurora decides to help her; they move to Florence, where Romney Leigh, now blind because of a workers' revolt at his estate, comes to propose once again to Marian, who rejects him. Once Aurora realizes that Romney is blind, she confesses her love for him and they decide to marry.

Despite the sensationalistic twists, the main plotline follows a trajectory similar to any domestic novel. Aurora and Romney Leigh must overcome their pride and prejudice, much as Elizabeth and Darcy must do in Jane Austen's *Pride and Prejudice*, a domestic novel that E. B. Browning is at once invoking and reworking. Only after an ideological rapprochement can Aurora and Romney be united in a transcendent vision of heavenly domestic perfection. As Romney puts it:

> 'First, God's love.'
> 'And next', he smiled, 'the love of wedded souls,
> Which still presents that mystery's counterpart.'
> (IX, 881–3)

Before we reach this closural apogee, however, we witness a consistent questioning of middle-class culture's indoctrination of women in the ideology of domesticity.

Two figures, Aurora's aunt and Romney Leigh, are made to represent the period's dominant hegemonic views about gender, particularly the notion that men and women inhabit naturally separate spheres. The passages that describe Aurora's education at the hands of her aunt are a striking example of poetic satire and utterly undercut the beloved Victorian image of the 'angel in the house'. One such passage is worth quoting at some length:

> I read a score of books on womanhood
> To prove, if women do not think at all,
> They may teach thinking (to a maiden aunt
> Or else the author), – books that boldly assert
> Their right of comprehending husband's talk
> When not too deep, and even of answering
> With pretty 'may it please you', or 'so it is', –
> Their rapid insight and fine aptitude,
> Particular worth and general missionariness,
> As long as they keep quiet by the fire
> And never say 'no' when the world says 'ay',
> For that is fatal, – their angelic reach

> Of virtue, chiefly used to sit and darn,
> And fatten household sinners, – their, in brief,
> Potential faculty in everything
> Of abdicating power in it.
>
> (I, 427–46)

Romney, following this same logic, questions the ability of women to be great authors, pointing out, for example, how periodical reviews are only able to praise a woman author in condescending terms:

> 'You never can be satisfied with praise
> Which men give women when they judge a book
> Not as mere work but as mere woman's work,
> Expressing the comparative respect
> Which means the absolute scorn.'
>
> (II, 232–6)

Of course, at the start of the plot, Romney himself subscribes to this view of woman's poetry, arguing, in much the same terms as Aurora's aunt, that women – because of their natural tendency to feel rather than reason – are only capable of succeeding in the domestic sphere:

> 'Women as you are,
> Mere women, personal and passionate,
> You give us doating mothers, and perfect wives,
> Sublime Madonnas, and enduring saints!
> We get no Christ from you, – and verily
> We shall not get a poet, in my mind.'
>
> (II, 220–5)

Having established domestic duties as the only option for a woman, Romney, a few lines later, proposes – and Aurora just as quickly declines, refusing, as she says, to be 'the complement of [man's] sex merely' (II, 435–6). Instead, arguing that 'I too have my vocation' (II, 455), Aurora pursues her art and soon finds herself in that melodramatic tale of sensationalist plot twists that ultimately leads to Italy, where she establishes an all-woman commune of sorts with Marian Erle and Marian's illegitimate child (a result, as you will recall, of forced prostitution). Deliberately confusing the angel/whore dichotomy of middle-class domestic ideology, Marian and Aurora for a time become the bastard child's 'two mothers' (VII, 124) in a matriarchal domestic idyll, in which, Aurora writes, 'I should certainly be glad, / Except, god help me, that I'm sorrowful / Because of Romney' (VII, 925–6).

The tale then ends conventionally enough in a heterosexual marital union, except that, as in Charlotte Brontë's *Jane Eyre*, we are presented with a now blind and beaten male protagonist, who must rely on the strength and vision (in both senses) of his mate. As my mention of *Jane Eyre* makes clear, the novel, as a genre, is by no means incapable of similarly questioning the ideology of middle-class domesticity. What distinguishes the verse novel's approach from novelistic critiques is an ability to question domestic ideology not just at the level of content, or even of the form of the content, but at the level of, what Hayden White (1987), following Louis Hjelmslev, has dubbed 'the content of the form' – the ideologies that are inextricably connected to form. Elizabeth Barrett Browning brings to the fore this issue by superimposing a generic struggle onto the traditional domestic marriage plot. In so doing, Browning seeks to work out that most pervasive of Victorian dialectics, the real vs. the ideal, associating Romney with the real, the prosaic, the objective and the immanent while aligning Aurora Leigh with the ideal, the poetic, the subjective and the transcendent. As Aurora puts it:

> We were not lovers, nor even friends well-matched:
> Say rather, scholars upon different tracks,
> And thinkers disagreed: he, overfull
> Of what is, and I, haply, overbold
> For what might be.
>
> (I, 1106–10)

In her marriage of verse and the novel, of the ideal and the real, of Aurora and Romney, Browning seeks to have it both ways:

> Without the spiritual, observe,
> The natural is impossible – no form,
> No motion: without sensuous, spiritual
> Is inappreciable, – no beauty or power.
>
> (VII, 773–6)

This formulation highlights at once the complex generic hybridity of *Aurora Leigh* and the desire for a perfect reconciliation that leads Browning into some rather suspicious ideological manoeuvres of her own at the end of *Aurora Leigh* (Romney's transcendent vision of a New Jerusalem in the final lines, for example). The point is that Browning's self-consciousness about genre consistently leads her into an appreciation of the ideological nature of all formal choices, a fact that is perhaps best exemplified in her catalogue of various generic possibilities in book V of *Aurora Leigh*. Although she at times mouths Romantic commonplaces – 'Trust the spirit, / As Sovran nature does, to make the form' (V, 224–5) – she at other times comes close to a proto-Lacanian understanding of all symbolic form as ideological fantasy construction:

> O world, O world,
> O jurists, rhymers, dreamers, what you please,
> We play a weary game of hide-and-seek!
> We shape a figure of our fantasy,
> Call nothing something, and run after it
> And lose it, lose ourselves too in the search,
> Till clash against us comes a somebody

> Who also has lost something and is lost,
> Philosopher against philanthropist,
> Academician against poet, man
> Against woman, against the living the dead, –
> Then home, with a bad headache and worse jest!
>   (VI, 282–93)

Not only is Browning here showing her consciousness of (and frustration with) the various dialectical oppositions of the Victorian period, but she seems to be coming to a consciousness of the fact that either side of any dialectic is shaping world systems out of nothing (shaping 'a figure of our fantasy' and calling 'nothing something'). In other words, Browning is here arguing for the fantastical and ultimately groundless nature of all ideological positions. Perhaps driven by a new historical consciousness in the nineteenth century (an understanding that England's empire, like Rome's, will eventually fail, as will all ideals held dear in the present age), Browning here acknowledges that the philosopher-poet and the prosaic philanthropist ultimately betray the fact that they are both reliant on ideological mystification to proceed.

Amours de Voyage

Arthur Clough takes ideological self-consciousness yet one step further in his epistolary verse novel of 1858 (first published in the *Atlantic Monthly* of 1855). The poem presents the philosophical musings of Claude, who is travelling through Italy as a tourist and writing to his friend Eustace. Throughout, we follow Claude's failed attempts to establish an amorous connection with Mary Trevellyn, whom we also hear from in a handful of letters; as a backdrop to the narrative, the newly formed Italian Republic is threatened and then falls because of an invasion by French troops in the spring and summer of 1849.

Clough could be said to be exploring a very similar dialectic to Elizabeth Barrett Browning's in the intimated if not intimate plotted union of Claude and Mary. Much like *Aurora Leigh*, Clough's verse novel superimposes generic, gendered and general principles onto its two main protagonists: the prosaic, feminine, objective real on the one hand and the philosophico-poetic, male, subjective ideal on the other. Seeming to play out a separate-spheres argument, Claude argues that women are not capable of achieving his ideal of perfection: 'Ah, but the women, – God bless them! they don't think at all about it. / Yet we must eat and drink, as you say. And as limited beings / Scarcely can hope to attain upon earth to an Actual Abstract' (III, 130–2). What saves Clough from the charge of sexism is the fact that Claude is a superb early example of the modernist anti-hero, not to mention the decadent *flâneur*: feckless, selfish, 'discontented', as Claude himself admits, 'with things in particular, idle, / Sickly, complaining' (II, 311–12). As Claude states, after a truly surprising anti-climax that refuses the final marital closure of the conventional Victorian novel, 'I am more a coward than ever, / Chicken-hearted, past thought' (V,

144–5). Indeed, in the end Claude doubts the value of his own search for the ideal, which is again discussed in terms of his relationship with Mary:

> Utterly vain is, alas! this attempt at the Absolute, – wholly!
> I, who believed not in her, because I would fain believe nothing,
> Have to believe as I may, with a wilful, unmeaning acceptance.
> I, who refused to enfasten the roots of my floating existence
> In the rich earth, cling now to the hard, naked rock that is left me. –
> Ah! she was worthy, Eustace, – and that, indeed, is my comfort, –
> Worthy a nobler heart than a fool such as I could have given.
>
> (V, 63–9)

Playing the clod that is Claude's homonym and refusing to enfasten his roots into the rich earth of the real, of the body, and of the objective world, Clough's protagonist cannot but be read with a certain degree of critical distance even while we cannot help but acknowledge that he speaks many of Clough's own personal beliefs.

Unlike E. B. Browning, Clough in the end refuses to believe in anything but incommensurability between ideological positions; in so doing, he could also be said to come to an understanding of the ideological nature of all formal choices. The poem's epigraph from 'a French novel' is apt: '*Il doutait de tout, même l'amour*' ('he doubted everything, even love'). As Claude writes in response to a letter from his friend, Eustace,

> Juxtaposition is great, – but, you tell me, affinity greater.
> Ah, my friend, there are many affinities, greater and lesser,
> Stronger and weaker; and each, by the favour of juxtaposition,
> Potent, efficient, in force, – for a time; but none, let me tell you,
> Save by the law of the land and the ruinous force of the will, ah,
> None, I fear me, at last quite sure to be final and perfect.
>
> (III, 151–6)

Following in the footsteps of Marx and Hegel, who are writing at just this time, Clough makes a case for the ephemerality of all ideas and laws. Indeed, at times he even sounds like the neo-Marxist Louis Althusser in 'Ideology and Ideological State Apparatuses' (1970): '*Action will furnish belief,* – but will that belief be the true one?' (*Amours de Voyage*, V, 20). According to Clough, everything changes with time because of the great law of juxtaposition, or, to put it in Marxist terms, because of the dialectic. Once again, we are seeing here a self-consciousness among the Victorians about the contingency of all values (an anticipation that all beliefs will someday be replaced by new ones), an understanding that goes along with the rising new disciplines of history, palaeontology and archaeology, not to mention the theories of Charles Darwin. Whereas the eighteenth century believed that reason would lead men to ultimate truths, the nineteenth century began to reinterpret 'truth' as 'ideology', as but the belief of the moment. And it could be said that the verse novel, through its juxtaposition of opposing generic conventions and expectations, helped to foreground the contingency of all values and the ideological nature of all formal choices.

Modern Love

Whereas E. B. Browning seeks to have it both ways (both/and) in her effort to resolve the dialectic between the real and the ideal, the novelistic and the poetic, the objective and the subjective, and whereas Clough refuses to resolve the dialectic because of his love of juxtaposition (either/or), Meredith could be said to question either side of the dialectic in his turn to French-inspired novelistic naturalism (neither/nor), thus critiquing both the preciosity of traditional poetry and the preciousness of the Victorian novel. Rather than have a narrative that leads up to a final marital closure (which was common for the Victorian novel), Meredith explores what happens *after* the nuptial celebration: he explores the breakdown of a marriage between two unnamed protagonists. (The details of the breakup follow aspects of Meredith's own failed marriage to Mary Nicolls, who left him for the painter Henry Wallis.) After a sequence of events that includes adultery (by both wife and husband), prevarication, bitterness and regret, the narrative finally ends in the wife's suicide.

Although the representation of adultery was not new for the Victorian novel (Meredith himself explored the issue in *The Ordeal of Richard Feverel* [1859], and Barbara Leckie [1999] has recently discussed the centrality of adultery in the sensation-novel debates of the 1850s and 1860s), reviewers were shocked to find it in the 'high' generic form of the sonnet sequence. What is worse, the Victorian reader found Meredith picking apart what he represents in *Modern Love* as the sham of bourgeois domestic bliss. Finding violence hidden behind the 'game of Sentiment' (XXVIII, 3) and 'this wedded lie' (XXXV, 16), Meredith sees only hypocrisy in domestic duty: 'A world of household matters filled her mind, / Wherein he saw hypocrisy designed' (V, 2–3). The best example, perhaps, is the seventeenth sonnet, in which the couple play-acts domestic bliss: 'We waken envy of our happy lot/ Fast, sweet, and golden, shows the marriage-knot./ Dear guests, you now have seen Love's corpse-light shine.' In such sequences, Meredith seems to question at once poetry's unwillingness to step down into the muck of the sordid real and the Victorian novel's tendency to idealize the domestic sphere.

As with E. B. Browning and Clough, what distinguishes Meredith's treatment of adultery from the naturalist novel's depiction of the same is a superb self-consciousness about form that results from the hybrid nature of the verse-novel form. This becomes clearest in sonnet XXV, where Meredith feels the need to step outside of his work in order to remark upon his poem's generic status. As in the fifth book of *Aurora Leigh* or as in the italicized headers at the start of each of Clough's cantos, Meredith here is by implication remarking upon the generic mixing of his own work in a way that suggests a self-consciousness about the ideological implications of generic choice:

You like not that French novel? Tell me why.
You think it quite unnatural. Let us see.
The actors are, it seems the usual three:
Husband, and wife, and lover. She – but fie!
In England we'll not hear of it. Edmond,
The lover, her devout chagrin doth share;
Blanc-mange and absinthe are his penitent fare,
Till his pale aspect makes her over-fond:
So, to preclude fresh sin, he tries rosbif.
Meantime the husband is no more abused:
Auguste forgives her ere the tear is used.
Then hangeth all on one tremendous IF: –
If she will choose between them. She does choose;
And takes her husband, like a proper wife.
Unnatural? My dear, these things are life:
And life, some think, is worthy of the Muse.

What is at issue here is the opposition between the natural and the non-natural artificiality of laws or genres: 'You like not that French novel? Tell me why. / You think it quite unnatural. Let us see.' In broaching the question of 'naturalness', Meredith implicitly asks the same question of his own work. Are we being presented in *Modern Love* with 'life' and with what is natural to it? In asking an apparent question about nature, though, Meredith is, in fact, alluding to the designation of a generic form, of an artificial *techne*, *naturalism*, itself a subset of the genre designation 'novel'. In forcing us to consider such questions, Meredith demands ('Tell me', he writes) that we consider the question of naturalness and that we also justify our generic (and, therefore, arguably artificial) definitions *of* naturalness. In raising the question of the natural and of what one can properly call the natural, Meredith underscores precisely the artificiality of form, of the technical aspect of his own work. He also underscores his work's own arguably unnatural mixing of the genres of the novel and the lyric poem, since the narrative he then goes on to recount is precisely the narrative of the sonnet sequence we have been reading. We appear to have been reading a sequence of poems; however, sonnet XXV – the dead centre of the sonnet sequence – appears to step outside of poetic form to remark upon its surrounding poems as not, in fact, poetry at all, but a novel. Meredith thus opens up a law of contamination in the very act of naming, an act that is, according to Jacques Derrida in the 'Law of Genre' (1980), outside the law (the law of the law) and that underlines a certain undecidability in the very form of Meredith's poem.

The Ring and the Book

Robert Browning's *Ring and the Book*, by a different method, uncovers the prejudices and limitations of the novel's pretensions to objective realism, not to mention its reliance on a straightforward narrative. The story is based on what Browning in book I calls an 'old yellow Book', which in 1860 he bought in a second-hand market in Florence. The book contains a collection of documents produced during and after a sensational Roman murder trial in 1698. Based on these documents, Browning relates how Count Guido Franceschini murdered his wife, Pompilia, and her parents, following Pompilia's supposed adultery with Giuseppe Caponsacchi. Browning also gives us the details of the trial, including dramatic monologues in the voices of the opposing lawyers and a dramatic monologue in the voice of Pope Innocent XII, who decides to deny Guido any reprieve. As Browning illustrates by offering up in each dramatic monologue a different account of the events, any one narrative skews the 'whole story' of the events leading up to the murder. With each new speaker, one learns a little more about each character's motivations and the sometimes irreconcilably contradictory details of the case. In this way, Browning questions whether any objective, mimetic representation of events is ever possible.

The poem, in fact, begins with a question about referentiality: 'Do you see this Ring?' (I, 1) the narrator asks us in the very first line of the poem. Of course, the question itself is a provocation, a self-referential gesture, for its referent is, after all, missing. As Loy D. Martin's study of Browning's dialogism (1985) might put it, the poem offers up an opening deictic gesture ('*this* Ring') as well as an implied addressee (Do *you* see it?) and even the suggestion of a continuing temporal act (*seeing* something that has continued, does continue and will continue to exist), all of which forces us to assume a larger spatio-temporal universe preceding and surrounding the utterance. Browning's verse novel, from the start, thus also opens up the question of referentiality, which grounds his generic competitor, the novel proper. No, we are forced to answer, we do not, in actuality, see the ring, even less so since, as we learn, ''T is a figure, a symbol, say; / A thing's sign' (I, 31–2). Browning then offers us another implied promise of referentiality: 'now for the thing signified' (I, 32). Again, however, we are foiled, for what Browning then offers as the ring's signified is nothing but another sign:

> Do you see this square old yellow Book, I toss
> I' the air, and catch again, and twirl about
> By the crumpled vellum covers, – pure crude fact
> Secreted from man's life when hearts beat hard,
> And brains, high-blooded, ticked two centuries since?
> Examine it yourselves!
>
> (I, 33–8)

No, we are forced to respond again, we do not see this book either, although we do recognize it as a sign for the actual material book that we hold in our hands, one that was purchased, certainly, with the gold ring's simulacrum, coin, just as Browning bought his: 'I found this book, / Gave a *lira* for it, eightpence English just' (I, 38–9); and, again, 'a lira made it mine' (III, 83).

In short, Browning grants to the reader those things that the novel takes for granted – referentiality, 'pure crude fact' – and, as with the ring and the book Browning facetiously asks us to 'examine', he takes away with one hand what he offers up with the other. The entire twelve-volume poem, after all, is about the impossibility of having once and for all that 'pure crude fact'.

Through such manoeuvres, Browning is also questioning whether one can ever truly have the truth of the text, whether one can ever properly own a text through the exchange of coin: 'a lira made it mine'. How is one to understand this circulation and exchange, of text for gold? Once one gives away something – 'Examine it yourselves!' – can one be sure of a proper return: 'Give it me back!' (I, 89)? As it turns out, the narrative can only begin, for narrator and reader alike, with a market exchange, the purchase with coin of a material object, which then begins the *symbolic* exchange of signifieds – 'T is a figure, a symbol, say; / A thing's sign'. Like the gold ring, like money itself, after all, for money is nothing but a 'thing's sign', the book is nothing but a symbolic exchange, without practical use value, a luxury item, or so it is viewed by the criticism often directed at poetry over the course of the nineteenth century. Browning responds with the dialectically opposed critical reaction, by making a claim for the book's curative powers – 'The thing's restorative / I' the touch and sight' (I, 89–90) – yet he must also acknowledge a certain impurity, perhaps precisely because of the necessity of market exchange. The ring, once again, is the figure, the symbol of this impurity:

> the artificer melts up wax
> With honey, so to speak; he mingles gold
> With gold's alloy, and, duly tempering both,
> Effects a manageable mass, then works.
> But his work ended, once the thing a ring,
> Oh, there's repristination! Just a spirt
> O' the proper fiery acid o'er its face,
> And forth the alloy unfastened flies in fume;
> While, self-sufficient now, the shape remains,
> The rondure brave, the lilied loveliness,
> Gold as it was, is, shall be evermore:
> Prime nature with an added artistry –
> No carat lost, and you have gained a ring.
> (I, 18–30)

Herein is the figure for Browning's own book, a figure that encircles so many of the issues that are tied to poetry in the Victorian period: the alienated labour of the artist-producer ('the artificer . . . works'); the commodified value of the book (the implied question: how is one to find its equivalence in the gold standard?); the wished-for self-sufficiency of the poetic text ('self-sufficient now, the shape remains'); the impossibility of a perfect purity of form ('Prime nature with an added artistry'); the relation of art and artifice to nature.

What is at stake, after all, is the purity of *poetic* form, for Browning has chosen that most impure of genres, the verse novel, to present his 'pure crude fact'. He writes a narrative in verse to a public that spurns him – 'Well, British Public, ye who like me not' (I, 410) – to a public that mistrusts the lie that is poetic form because that public prefers the narrative realism of the novel. Indeed, when in book I Browning goes to Rome to try 'truth's power, / On likely people', the response he gets is mistrust about poetry's manipulation of narrative truth, of referential mimesis:

'Do you tell the story, now, in off-hand style,
Straight from the book? Or simply here and there,
(The while you vault it through the loose and large)
Hang to a hint? Or is there book at all,
And don't you deal in poetry, make-believe,
And the white lies it sounds like?'

(I, 451–7)

And Browning concedes as much, even as he denies it: 'Yes and no!' (I, 457). As Derrida points out, 'One can "make the truth" ["*faire la vérité*"] (the expression is Saint Augustine's) only to the extent that the possibility remains forever open of "counterfeiting it [*la "contrefair"*]' (Derrida 1992: 152n.). Browning could be said to go yet one step further; the truth can only come about *by way of* the counterfeit:

Well, now; there's nothing in nor out o' the world
Good except truth: yet this, the something else,
What's this then, which proves good yet seems untrue?
This that I mixed with truth, motions of mine
That quickened, made the inertness malleable
O' the gold was not mine, – what's your name for this?
Are means to the end, themselves in part the end?
Is fiction which makes fact alive, fact too?

(I, 698–706)

The Verse Novel's Reach

As I began by arguing, these four verse novels are certainly not the only ones that one might examine in the nineteenth century. One can make, and some have made, the case for other candidates. Herbert F. Tucker (1992) argues, for example, that Alfred Tennyson's hugely popular *Idylls of the King* subscribes to or, at the very least, engages novelistic conventions (and I make a similar argument in my article, 'Tennyson's *Idylls*, Pure Poetry, and the Market' [1997]). One could also mention Clough's earlier *The Bothie of Toper-na-fuosich*, Tennyson's *Maud* and Coventry Patmore's *Angel in the House*, among others; however, these works are arguably less self-conscious about their position between competing generic exigencies. Perhaps precisely for this reason, they tend also to be, and this is particularly the case in Patmore's work, less critical of nineteenth-century domestic ideology. There have, however, been a good number of works that have followed the lead of the four verse novels I have examined, works that have, in fact, explored similar issues: the ideology of genre, gender trouble, the impossibility of knowing objective truth, and the opposition between nature and artifice. Indeed, the inherent self-consciousness of the verse novel's hybrid form has made it a favourite of modernists and postmodernists alike. Many examples of the verse novel's influence exist, although it may be that the most notable and distinguished include Nabokov's *Pale Fire* (1962), itself influenced by Pushkin's Russian example of the nineteenth-century verse novel, *Eugene Onegin* (1833); Akira Kurasawa's film *Rashomon* (1950), which traces its influences to *The Ring and the Book* through Ryunosuke Akutagawa's Browning-inspired prose tale 'In a Grove' (1921); and the recent postmodern takes on the verse novel, Vikram Seth's *Golden Gate: A Novel in Verse* (1986) and Anne Carson's *Autobiography of Red: A Novel in Verse* (1998). What ties together these extremely diverse works is precisely their unflinching self-consciousness about ideological form and their suspicion that, as Browning puts it:

> Who trusts
> To human testimony for a fact
> Gets this sole fact – himself is proved a fool.
> (*Ring and the Book*, XII, 601–3)

See also: DRAMATIC MONOLOGUE; SONNET AND SONNET SEQUENCE; THE MARKET; MARRIAGE AND GENDER.

ACKNOWLEDGEMENT

I would like to thank those people who helped me with specific details of this article, including Shaun Hughes, Peter Hühn, Herbert F. Tucker, my Verse Novel and Nineteenth-Century Poetry classes at Purdue (spring and fall 2000), and, above all, Emily Allen and Marjorie Stone.

REFERENCES AND FURTHER READING

Althusser, L. (1970) 'Ideology and Ideological State Apparatuses.' *La Pensée*. Reprinted in H. Adams and L. Searle (eds) (1986). *Critical Theory Since 1965* (pp. 239–50). Tallahassee: University Presses of Florida.

Armstrong, Nancy (1987) *Desire and Domestic Fiction: A Political History of the Novel*. New York: Oxford University Press.

Bakhtin, M. (1981) *The Dialogic Imagination*. Trans. Caryl Emerson and Michael Holquist. Ed. Michael Holquist. Austin: University of Texas Press.

Bakhtin, M. (1984a) *Rabelais and His World*. Trans. Helene Iswolsky. Bloomington: Indiana University Press.

Bakhtin, M. (1984b) *Problems of Dostoevsky's Poetics*.

Trans. and ed. Caryl Emerson. Minneapolis: University of Minnesota Press.

Bender, John B. (1987) *Imagining the Penitentiary: Fiction and the Architecture of Mind in Eighteenth-Century England*. Chicago: University of Chicago Press.

Browning, Robert (2001) *The Ring and the Book*. Peterborough: Broadview.

Clayton, J. (1987) *Romantic Vision and the Novel*. Cambridge: Cambridge University Press.

Clough, Arthur Hugh (1853) 'Recent English Poetry.' *North American Review*, 77. Reprinted in W. E. Houghton and G. R. Stange (eds) (1968). *Victorian Poetry and Poetics* (pp. 395–403). Boston: Houghton Mifflin.

Coleridge, Samuel Taylor (1976) *On the Constitution*

of the Church and State. Ed. John Colmer. Princeton, N. J.: Princeton University Press.

Derrida, Jacques (1980) 'The Law of Genre.' *Critical Inquiry*, 7, 55–81.

Derrida, Jacques (1992) *Given Time: 1. Counterfeit Money*. Trans Peggy Kamuf. Chicago: University of Chicago Press.

Dixon, W. M. (1912) Reprinted in 1964 as *English Epic and Heroic Poetry*. New York: Haskell House.

Erickson, Lee (1996) *The Economy of Literary Form: English Literature and the Industrialization of Publishing, 1800–1850*. Baltimore: Johns Hopkins University Press.

Felluga, Dino (1997) 'Tennyson's Idylls, Pure Poetry, and the Market.' *Studies in English Literature*, 37, 783–803.

Leckie, B. (1999) *Culture and Adultery: The Novel, the Newspaper, and the Law, 1857–1914*. Philadelphia: University of Pennsylvania Press.

Martin, L. D. (1985) *Browning's Dramatic Monologues and the Postromantic Subject*. Baltimore: Johns Hopkins University Press.

Mill, John Stuart (1833) 'What is Poetry.' *Monthly Repository*, 7, 60–70. Reprinted in F. P. Sharpless (ed.) (1976). *Essays on Poetry* (pp. 3–22). Columbia: University of South Carolina Press.

Miller, D. A. (1988) *The Novel and the Police*. Berkeley: University of California Press.

Tucker, Herbert F. (1992) 'Trials of Fiction: Novel and Epic in the Geraint and Enid Episodes from *Idylls of the King*.' *Victorian Poetry*, 30, 441–61.

White, H. (1987) *The Content of the Form: Narrative Discourse and Historical Representation*. Baltimore: Johns Hopkins University Press.

Wilde, Oscar (1975) *Plays, Prose Writings and Poems*. London: Dent.

Wordsworth, William (1974). 'Preface of 1815.' In E. J. B. Owen and J. W. Smyser (eds). *The Prose Works of William Wordsworth*, 3 vols (III, 26–39). Oxford: Clarendon Press.

10
Verse Drama
Adrienne Scullion

In May 1837 William Bell Scott went to the Theatre Royal, Covent Garden, where he saw one of the five performances of Robert Browning's new verse drama, *Strafford*. Scott, later to emerge as a significant Pre-Raphaelite painter, was already an admirer of Browning's dramatic poem *Paracelsus* (1835) and his expectations for the new play were high. But, as his memoirs record, he was bitterly disappointed by what he saw on stage: 'The speakers', he wrote, 'had every one of them orations to deliver, and no action of any kind to perform. The scene changed, another door opened, and another half-dozen gentlemen entered as long-winded as the last' (Scott 1892: I, 124).

In his preface to the published edition of the same play, Browning described *Strafford* as attempting something new: it was a play of 'Action in Character, rather than Character in Action'. It seems that he and Scott had very different understandings of the idea and the role of 'action' in drama. This chapter is about some of these differences.

Scott's criticism is typical of responses to productions of the quixotic genre that is Victorian verse drama: that it is full of static scenes, of monotonous, repetitive and undramatic speeches, of events reported but not seen. Typically, Victorian verse drama is cast as a form caught between literary fashion and theatrical convention – in its particular balancing of action and character it is the very opposite of the sensation melodramas that came to dominate the contemporary popular theatre. It is a genre that is dramaturgically compromised by the conflicting demands of the nineteenth-century theatre industry – including restrictions imposed by censorship and other government legislation – and the rhetorical experimentation of contemporary belles-lettres. And, of course, it is situated historically between the ideas and practices of Romanticism at the start of the century and realism and modernism at the end.

Verse drama is a genre that theatre historians have, surprisingly, neglected: theatre historiography of the mid-nineteenth century has been dominated by class-based analyses, reinterpreting the appeal of the popular theatre – in particular melodramas but also music hall and pantomime – and recovering its political subtexts. In addition theatre historians have reassessed the role of women as writers, producers, actors and audiences. But, despite work on Joanna Baillie, Fanny Kemble, Augusta Webster and other women writers whose oeuvre includes verse drama, the form has not proved itself the richest of seams. Indeed the very fact that so few of these plays were ever performed tends to exclude them from the attention of the theatre historian. Most scholarly approaches to verse drama have, then, focused on its literary as opposed to its theatrical attributes. Here too, however, the genre struggles to establish its own terms of reference; here too the writing is often judged negatively, as worth attention only to the extent that it can reveal something of the process by which the poet developed towards more serious writings in a more 'appropriate' genre. Nevertheless, the form did attract the attentions of many of the nineteenth century's most celebrated novelists and poets: Charles Lamb, Samuel Taylor Coleridge, William Wordsworth, John Keats, Percy Bysshe Shelley, Lord Byron, Walter Scott, Leigh Hunt, Joanna Baillie, George Eliot and Charles Dickens all wrote dramas. But as Terry Otten comments, 'Never have so many major authors contributed so little of the history of English drama . . . How it was possible for such poets to produce a body of dramas so bad has baffled more than one critic' (1972: 3).

Wordsworth, for example, offered his play *The Borderers* (1796) to Covent Garden in 1796, but it was rejected. Coleridge's *Remorse*, a tragedy with elements of sentiment, melodrama and the supernatural, was performed at Drury Lane in 1813 (and revived as a one-night benefit in 1817). Although many of the speeches are over-long, and the plotting is rather conventional, it is none the less distinguished by the quality of the verse. Shelley's *The Cenci* (1819) was a play that the contemporary theatre could not accommodate: its subject, the rape of a woman by her father, excluded it from contemporary production. Nevertheless the play has had its champions amongst modern critics (see, for example, Ferriss 1998). Daniel P. Watkins (1982) has drawn attention to the plays written by Walter Scott, including *Halidon Hill* (1822), *Macduff's Cross* (written 1821, published 1823), *Auchindrane; or, The Ayrshire Tragedy* (1830) and *The Doom of Devoroil* (written 1817, published 1830). Indeed, Scott had a lively interest in the theatre: he played a major role in the management of the Edinburgh Theatre Royal and was a sponsor of Joanna Baillie. Byron was similarly engaged with the business of theatre. In 1815 he became a member of the committee of management of Drury Lane; he wrote the address which reopened that theatre in 1812; and he was a great admirer of the actor Edmund Kean. Byron also wrote several verse dramas – including *Cain* (published 1821), *Sardanapalus* (published 1821, produced 1834), *The Two Foscari* (published 1821, produced 1838) – but only one, *Marino Faliero*, was performed (seven times at Drury Lane in 1821) in his lifetime. Contemporary responses anticipate William Bell Scott's to *Strafford*; for John Genest, 'Lord Byron deserves the greatest credit for the beauty and spirit of his dialogue, and the just delineation of his characters – but here the praise ends . . . too much is said, and too little is done' (1832: IX, 91). Nevertheless William Charles Macready's 1830 adaptation of Byron's *Werner* became a standard piece in the mid-nineteenth-century repertoire, and even Byron's 'speculative drama' *Manfred* was produced at Covent Garden in 1834. But it was Joanna Baillie who has the best claim to be the progenitor of Victorian verse drama. Written over nearly four decades, *Count Basil* and *De Monfort* in *A Series of Plays* (1798), *The Family Legend* (1810), *The Bride* (1828), and *The Martyr* in her collection of *Dramas* (1836) exemplify the form's diversity. In recent years Baillie's contribution to Romantic drama has been recognized by criticism that has also encouraged a wider investigation of the contribution of other women playwrights in the late eighteenth and nineteenth centuries (see, for example, Burroughs 1997; Davis and Donkin 1999).

In the 1830s the period's leading young actress contributed two verse dramas of some interest – *Francis the First* (1832) and *The Star of Seville* (1837). Fanny Kemble's plays are well suited to the demands of her contemporary stage, although the production success of both plays (the former at Covent Garden and the latter at the Walnut Street Theatre in Baltimore) was perhaps predicated upon her fame as an actor rather than her skill as a writer. Nevertheless both are capable historical dramas with fine and poised roles for actors and ample opportunity for elaborate and lavish staging.

Sir Henry Taylor's contribution to the evolution of the Victorian verse drama was even more significant. His 1834 play *Philip van Artevelde*, and more particularly its challenging preface, are polemical declarations against the canons of Romantic drama: Isobel Armstrong describes his work as a 'directly moral and rational attack on a poetry of sensation' (Armstrong 1993: 97–8). *Philip van Artevelde*, published in two volumes, is impossibly long for production. It is theatrically rather stilted but there is at least some attempt at realism in its delineation of political ambition and its psychological consequences. The preface, however, is much more incendiary. In it Taylor describes his dissatisfaction with the 'indulgence in the mere luxuries of poetry' that he detects in Romanticism and, in particular, in the work of Byron (see Poston 1980, 1978). Taylor uses the dramatic form to emphasize his insistence that poetry should concern itself with actions rather than simply with the poet's subjective reflections, but, as Browning's description of *Strafford* indicates, the broad genre that is Victorian verse drama is preoccupied not with the choice between action and character but with the relation between the two. In this chapter, my purpose is not to rehabilitate Victorian verse drama as a neglected genre which, when read 'correctly', will prove rewarding, but to review the plays in the terms proposed in prefaces, introductions and dedications by their writers.

Writing in 1811 the essayist and critic Charles Lamb argued that Shakespeare's plays were better read than they were acted: 'it may seem a paradox', he wrote, '[but] I cannot help being of the opinion that the plays of Shakespeare are less calculated for performance on a stage, than those of almost any other dramatist whatever' (Lamb 1903: I, 99). It is a verdict that shockingly reverses current orthodoxies. Lamb argues that the subtlety, depth and sophistication of Shakespeare's plays can only be diminished in performance, and that the plays better reveal their themes, ideas, arguments, the richness and beauty of their poetry and, most significantly of all, the power of their characters when encountered in the reader's imagination. Lamb judged that Shakespeare's plays in performance afforded only 'juvenile pleasures' (I, 98) – the sets, the costumes, the appearances of the actors were mere surface distractions that had little to do with a deep understanding of the text. For Lamb the production and acting styles of the contemporary theatre were particularly detrimental because they distracted the attention from the ear to the eye. He criticized all aspects of the theatrical conventions of the day, including theatre architecture, scenography, design and acting styles, arguing that it was impossible for an actor:

> To know the internal workings and movements of a great mind, of an Othello or a Hamlet for instance, the *when* and the *why* and the *how far* they should be moved; to what pitch a passion is becoming; to give the reins and to pull in the curb exactly at the moment when the drawing in or the slackening is most graceful. (I, 98)

In Lamb's analysis, to enact Shakespeare's plays 'is to turn the medium of representation into an object of representation and so to present the audience, absurdly, with the doings of a group of people who all seem to be orators' (Shepherd and Womack 1996: 98). In contrast, reading the plays will focus attention on the potential humanity of the characters, as the drama is internalized and experienced in the reader's imagination.

For Lamb, Shakespeare's plays are not, then, blueprints for performance; they are not about representing people speaking; they are not, in fact, about externalized enactment at all; but instead they are a means to show 'the inner structure and workings of [the] mind' (Lamb 1903: I, 99). Lamb's appraisal of Shakespeare's plays, and his critical analysis of contemporary theatre production as a constraining and indeed unnecessary mediation between the audience and the text, remain a key statement of the 'wide-spread nineteenth-century anti-theatrical bias that placed poetry far above performance and elevated the author's art at the expense of the actor's' (Fulton 1997: 158). In criticizing theatre convention and practice, Lamb was equally keen to highlight the rather different pleasures of reading:

> what we see upon a stage is body and bodily action; what we are conscious of in reading is almost exclusively the mind, and its movements: and this I think may sufficiently account for the very different sort of delight with which the same play so often affects us in the reading and the seeing . . . [T]he reading of a tragedy is a fine abstraction. (Lamb 1903: I, 108, 111)

This seeming dichotomy of pleasures should frame any understanding of Victorian verse drama and usefully resets the rather reductive page/stage stand-off that imposes inappropriate critical demands on the genre of verse drama. Although writers may have been ambitious of theatre production, pleasure in reading was recognized as an appropriate and notably contemporary aesthetic. This affords the modern commentator grounds on which to reject false divisions between plays unsuited to representation upon the physical stage and those written for the 'ideal stage which all men erect in their own minds' (Mason 1974: 248). While recognizing the genre's inconsistent record in production, reference to the paradigm offered by Lamb might facilitate a more flexible approach to Victorian verse drama, in which 'action' is found in structure and organization, in 'internal' characterization and the subtleties of character relations, rather than in externalized display and enactment, and pleasure may be derived from reflective reading as much as from sensational production.

Robert Browning wrote eight plays in the decade between *Strafford* in 1837 and *A Soul's Tragedy* and *Luria* in 1846. Of these only two – *Strafford* and *A Blot on the 'Scutcheon* (1843) – were staged, both by William Charles Macready, the one senior actor-manager likely to promote and produce the work of a new young playwright like Browning. But neither *Strafford* nor *A Blot on the 'Scutcheon* succeeded. Despite this, several modern critics argue that Browning's dramas are 'daring', 'innovative' and even 'experimental'.

Strafford is a historical drama, set in the years immediately preceding the Civil War. It describes a crisis in English government, political manoeuvring at the court of Charles I and the growing antagonism between Parliament and monarchy. The play's narrative concerns this political rivalry. The five-act structure reflects shifts in the balance of power between Charles and the House of Commons through a series of parallel scenes switching between groups of each political faction. The play introduces each group – monarchists and Parliamentarians – as secure in its own public space: for one the Whitehall court of Charles, and for the other the political palaces of Westminster. Drama is produced by the migration of characters between the two groups, and by incursions of characters into the other group's spaces.

Michael R. Booth warns that 'early Victorian tragic authors were obsessed with historical fact', and adds that this is 'an over-indulgence which hopelessly clogs Browning's *Strafford*' (Booth et al. 1975: 148). *Strafford* is, however, a history play that directly engages contemporary debates about systems of government and democracy. The play's concern with issues of political representation and the role of the individual in relation to collective decision making, Parliaments and assemblies carried significant resonance for the nineteenth-century audience. After all, this was an audience already debating constitutional government and issues of representation in terms of suffrage, trade unionism and other forms of collective action. Set in this context, *Strafford* emerges as a political play that values modernizing democracy and the integrity of representative government.

But *Strafford* is perhaps more significantly about character: in Lamb's terms, it is also a drama of 'the inner structure and workings of mind' (Lamb 1903: I, 99). Browning's focus on 'Action in Character' allows the play to develop into a psychological drama tracing the conflict between two strong and complex characters. The play dramatizes the political and personal rivalry between the former friends Wentworth, later the earl of Strafford, and John Pym. The play's action contrasts the political and personal rivalries of these characters, and their emotional development. The focus of the action in *Strafford* is not the externalization of the political conflict on stage but the psychological trajectory of its principal characters. Seen in this way, the play is a scientific as much as a poetical and dramaturgical experiment, investigating the 're-action' of these characters and its impact on the audience. According to Otten, Browning 'rejected the classical theory of character as agent of plot and attempted to find a dramatic form which could retain the objectivity of drama and yet be a kind of equivalent to the subjective action in a lyric' (1972: 109).

It is important to qualify this idea: in investigating 'Action in Character' Browning does not wholly dispense with 'Character in Action'. *Strafford* enacts meetings, confrontations and collusions, and the play certainly has the potential to be spectacular: there are heroic entrances involving numerous characters, lavish tableaux and much stage business (although, as Donald S. Hair neatly puts it, these function merely to 'give the impression of action' [1972: 49]). The play also contrasts public drama with domestic drama, the national stage with the intimate and personal one. In this Browning demonstrates a clear understanding of the dynamic potential of both diegetic and performance space in the drama that is one aspect of the play's meta-theatricality.

Browning has a distinctive response to the key dialectic of character and action. For Ryals, Strafford and Pym represent 'two equal and opposite points of view' set against each other and 'brought into hostile collision [with] no possible reconciliation and in which good and ill are so blended that each demands equal sympathy from the audience' (1993: 36). Ryals argues that this is a particular feature of the play's innovation, for not only is each character understood more completely in relation to the other, but the structural, thematic and narrative interaction of the two characters establishes the key moral dialectic of the drama. The better character promotes the worse cause, while the worse character stands for the better cause.

Neither Strafford nor indeed Pym is to be understood as a conventional hero. In their different ways both characters offer studies of psychological crisis and of obsession, principally political monomania: Strafford is unwaveringly devoted to monarchism; Pym is an equally unquestioning Parliamentarian. But neither character's politics is completely motivated by ideology or principle. Rather, both are driven by more subjective and unpredictable emotions: by love, jealousy, anger and desire. For each character these emotions are compromised, uncertain, flawed and frustrated. In addition, neither character is a conventional romantic protagonist. Although, in narrative terms at least, Strafford's sacrifice might cast him as more nearly the tragic hero, there is enough in the text (in his former relationship with Pym, his devotion to Charles and his patronage of Carlisle) to unsettle his heroism.

Almost the first thing we know about Strafford and Pym is their former devotion: according to Vane 'Pym and he [Strafford] were sworn, 'tis said, / To live and die together' (I.i.110–11). When Strafford's love of Charles supplants his friendship for Pym, Pym becomes the betrayed object of Strafford's affections. Certainly Pym's account of his feelings at Strafford's trial suggest something of the spurned lover:

> at the Trial, as he gazed, my youth,
> Our friendship, divers thoughts came back at once
> And left me, for a time . . . 'Tis very sad!
> (IV.ii.189–91)

Strafford denies prior friendships, rejects former politics and devotes himself wholly to Charles. His politics becomes individualized, focused on the person. By contrast, Pym's reaction is to deny the personal and to focus merely on the institutions of power. But while Pym may be cast as the more measured politician, he is no rationalist. His Parliamentarianism becomes maniacal and he too is motivated by failed and frustrated passion: the Parliament becomes for him an end in itself, not a potentially democratic means to justice and equity.

It is Strafford's love of the person of the king, even more than the institution of the monarchy, that alienates his one-time friends, compromises his social and political position, his judgement and his political acumen, and leads inevitably to his execution.

Strafford's love for the king, which has replaced his love of Pym, is described by Browning in conventionally romantic ways. Strafford wants to be with the king, to spend time with him, to be physically close to him: there are several scenes of him waiting to see the king, hoping for an audience with or even just a glimpse of Charles. He talks of and to the king in speeches full of sighs and longings and heady foolishness:

CHARLES:	You shall rule me. You were best
	Return at once: but take this ere you go!
	Now, do I trust you? You're an Earl: my Friend
	Of Friends: yes, while . . . You hear me not!
WENTWORTH:	Say it all o'er again – but once again:
	The first was for the music: once again!
CHARLES:	Strafford, my friend, there may have been reports,
	Vain rumours. Henceforth touching Strafford is
	To touch the apple of my sight: why gaze
	So earnestly?
WENTWORTH:	I am grown young again,
	And foolish. What was it we spoke of?

(I.ii.239–48)

Against a public backdrop of wars in Ireland and Scotland, factions in the Commons and the Lords, and politicking at court, the private aspect of the emotions to which Strafford gives voice exposes his vulnerability in his relationship with Charles:

STRAFFORD:	My liege . . . I am yours,
	Yours ever: 'tis too late to think about:
	To death, yours . . .
	But here! But here! I am so seldom here,
	Seldom with you, my King! I, soon to rush
	Alone upon a giant in the dark!
CHARLES:	My Strafford!

(II.ii.35–41)

In a play of passion, loyalty and division amongst men, the character of Strafford stands out against the social and political fraternity of the Parliamentarians. He is certainly enamoured of Charles and, when seen in parallel with his failed relationship with Pym, one might argue that the language of his love verges intriguingly on the homoerotic. He describes Charles as his 'Friend of Friends', repeating the phrase like a charm; he refuses to listen to the warnings of the politicians or of the devoted Carlisle; and his descriptions of the king become ever more sensual:

> What, do they [the Parliamentarians] beard the King,
> And shall the King want Strafford at his need?
> Am I not here?
>
> . . .

> Curse nothing to-night! Only one name
> They'll curse in all those streets to-night. Whose fault?
> Did I make kings? set up, the first, a man
> To represent the multitude, receive
> All love in right of them – supplant them so,
> Until you love the man and not the king –
> The man with the mild voice and mournful eyes
> Which sends me forth.
>   – To breast the bloody sea
> That sweeps before me: with one star for guide.
> Night has its first, supreme, forsaken star.
>
>   (II.ii.279–81, 287–96)

Browning shows Charles to be a foolish and indecisive monarch, one undeserving of the good man's loyalty. Panic, short-term opportunism and naivety mark Charles's political immaturity. The other characters cast Strafford's loyalty as blind and deluded, but he does demonstrate a measure of self-awareness: he acknowledges that his image of the king is romantic and idealized; he recognizes that Charles is flawed; but finally he knows that this is part of the reason why he must be loyal. The implicit irony of this situation only confirms that Strafford is no tragic hero: he is not caught unawares by his fall from author-ity; he recognizes what is happening; he understands the context for and the ramifications of his choices; but this self-awareness cannot deter him from his chosen path. As he puts it himself, 'God put it in my mind to serve, die / For Charles, but never to obey him more!' (III.ii.156–7)

However, late in the play (in act IV, scene iii) we learn that Strafford is a father and that it is partly to protect his children that he agrees to sacrifice his own life. This fact is revealed in an unexpected scene at the opening of act V, scene ii, which, although it is set in the Tower, begins as a small and intimate moment of domesticity, wherein Straf-ford talks with and says farewell to his children. It is a scene that moderates and even revises the previously internalized action of the play. Contemporary theatregoers would have found the scene less surprising than the modern reader does. In the context of nineteenth-century drama the scene fulfils generic expectations, sentimentalizing the heroic and introducing pathos where there had previously been moral dilemma. But for the modern reader the shift in tone that comes with the two children appearing on stage seems to run counter to the characterization that Browning has established. In this, the final act of the play, and close to its climax, Browning introduces a very different moti-vation for Strafford's sacrifice: not just his love of Charles but his love for his children:

> 'tis for my children! 'Twas for them
> I first consented to stand day by day
> And give your Puritans the best of words,
> Be patient, speak when called upon, observe
> Their rules, and not return them prompt their lie!
> What's in that boy of mine that he should prove

> Son to a prison breaker? I shall stay
> And he'll stay with me. Charles should know as much,
> He too has children!
>
> (V.ii.124–32)

This intervention unsettles the play's focus from the close analysis of character to an externalized (and sympathetic) justification of that character's action. His self-sacrifice is reset as 'a father's proud and rather stubborn attempt to leave to his children a reputation for honour' (Hair 1972: 50). This perhaps also hints at Browning's lack of confidence in the potential of his distinctive critical project to work on his contemporary stage. At this late point in the drama, pathos and sentiment unexpectedly shift Strafford more towards the figure of the traditional tragic hero, a figure which the rhetorical experimentation that characterizes the rest of the play seems to disallow.

In addition to commenting on *Strafford* as a history play and as a drama concerned with the nature of action, Browning's preface also highlights a concern with character and characterization. The playwright describes all but one of his characters as 'faithful' to their historical original. He states, however, that 'My Carlisle . . . is purely imaginary' (Browning 1970–: II, 9). Of course, all Browning's characters are to some degree imaginary, revised and reset for dramatic expediency and poetic effect rather than for historical accuracy. It is interesting, therefore, to consider why Browning singled out the figure of Carlisle as working in a significantly different way.

Carlisle's distinctive function in *Strafford* is to highlight the play's meta-theatricality. The play is self-reflexive – it is about deception, disguise and masking, it is about characters playing roles, donning new or opportunistic identities and deceiving themselves and others. Carlisle is the figure who most frequently refers to the idea of performance: 'there's a masque on foot' (II.ii.260), she says of the events around her (Ryals 1982: 32). Like Pym, Carlisle is frustrated in her love for Strafford by the presence of the king. She sacrifices herself so that Strafford might think better of the weak and foolish king, crediting Charles with her own initiatives to free the imprisoned Strafford, assuming the role of friend and confidante as opposed to lover: 'One must not lure him [Strafford] from a love like that! / Oh, let him love the King and die!' (II.ii.243–4). Carlisle's function is to offer a commentary on plot and characterization. Her unspeaking presence within key scenes (including the final one) highlights the artifice of performance within the narrative and within Browning's conception of the theatre event itself.

Other characters too can use irony to highlight the play's dialectic of action and character. Strafford, for example, foretells his story being retold in fanciful song and being played by ciphers, perhaps even in some fictionalized history play:

> What, the common songs will run
> That I forsook the People? Nothing more?
> Ay, Fame, the busy scribe, will pause, no doubt,
> Turning a deaf ear to her thousand slaves
> Noisy to be enrolled, – will register
> The curious glosses, subtle notices,

> Ingenious clearings-up one fain would see
> Besides that plain inscription of The Name –
> The Patriot Pym, or the Apostate Strafford!
>
> (V.ii.50–8)

Strafford's identification of the characters as actors fulfilling assigned roles – 'Patriot Pym' and 'Apostate Strafford' – is another example of the complex manner in which the play focuses and refocuses on the idea of the dramatic agent and on the dynamic nature of character.

The fact that this seemingly rather staid, ponderous and even highly conventional play can incorporate self-reflexivity, meta-theatricality and even the homoerotic suggests the extent to which Browning's first play is indeed innovative. While formal experimentation and structural innovation are somewhat easier to detect in the later work *Pippa Passes* (1842) – in which separate scenes are connected only by the figure of Pippa, whose over-heard song affects each character in different ways – it is important to note that in an ostensibly conventional and arguably 'unsuccessful' Victorian verse drama there is still potential for dramaturgical risk-taking and political commitment.

In the mid-century George Eliot wrote the dramatic poem *Armgart* and *The Spanish Gypsy* (begun 1864, completed 1868). The latter was composed during and after travels in Spain, particularly in the south of that country and around Granada. Although Eliot was ambitious to write a play, she offers her work as a 'dramatic poem', and, though she makes use of an extraordinary variety of poetic and prose forms, there is no attempt to make the play performable. Scenes of dramatic dialogue are interspersed with long narrative sections of blank verse delivering a mixture of plot, character motivation and 'stage directions'; there are scenes written in prose and some lyrics and ballads to be sung by Juan, the play's poet-musician figure. Eliot's biographer Rosemary Ashton describes the piece as 'a hybrid creature, more a narrative poem with some of the dialogue set out as in a play than a verse drama, and divided not into acts but into five books of irregular length' (1996: 292); a conclusion very similar to that of Sylvia Kasey Marks, who describes the play as 'a hybrid work which does not successfully blend the various forms contained in it' (1983: 185).

The play is set in the late fifteenth century, when Catholic Spain used the Inquisition to cleanse the state by expelling from the country the Moors and the gypsies, a group cast as a similarly 'alien' and indeed inferior race. The heroine is Fedalma. She believes herself to be a Spanish-Catholic noble but her true heritage is shockingly revealed: she is the daughter of Zarca, the king of the gypsies. According to the Prior:

> She bears the marks
> Of races unbaptised, that never bowed
> Before the holy signs, were never moved
> By stirrings of the sacramental gifts.
>
> . . .
>
> That maiden's blood
> Is as unchristian as the leopard's.
>
> (I)

Fedalma is faced with a dilemma over her identity and, in particular, her publicly perceived identity and her moral obligations to whatever cultural heritage she claims. Her dilemma is cast in personal and indeed psychological terms as a choice between the father and her lover, the duke Silva. Her decision is predicated on a sense of destiny, of duty and of a clear sense of community with the gypsies (this is hinted at early in the play when, to the disquiet of Silva, she dances in public). But even as she assumes a new, rebellious, transgressive and potentially active identity she rather stoically describes herself as the victim of fate:

> Vengeance! She does but sweep us with her skirts –
> She takes large space, and lies a baleful light
> Revolving with long years – sees children's children,
> Blights them in their prime
>
> . . .
>
>   For me –
> I am but as the funeral urn that bears
> The ashes of a leader.
>
>   (V)

Fedalma's crisis precipitates the tragedy of her father's death, an event which presents her with a new political role, to lead the gypsies out of Spain to a new freedom in Africa. But this must also result in her inevitable alienation from Silva:

> SILVA: [a] deep dark gulf
>   Divides us.
> FEDALMA: Yes, for ever. We must walk
>   Apart unto the end. Our marriage rite
>   Is our resolve that we will each be true
>   To high allegiance, higher than our love.
>   Our dear young love – its breath was happiness!
>   But it had grown upon a larger life
>   Which tore its roots asunder. We rebelled –
>   The larger life subdued us. Yet we are wed;
>   For we shall carry each the pressure deep
>   Of the other's soul. I shall soon leave the shore.
>   The winds to-night will bear me far away.
>   My lord, farewell!
>   He did not say 'Farewell.'
>   But neither knew that he was silent. She,
>   For one long moment, moved not. They knew nought
>   Save that they parted.
>
>   (V)

Marks (1983) compares Fedalma and her dilemma to the heroines of Eliot's novels and traces allusions to Euripides' *Iphigeneia*, to Orestes in Aeschylus' *The Oresteia*, to the stories of Faust and Rigoletto, and to Shakespeare's *Othello*. James Krasner (1994) modifies this view by reading *The Spanish Gypsy* in relation to Eliot's own perception of public and private responsibility, her conception of the role of the artist and her response to Christian belief and iconography, in particular the iconography of the Annunciation. Eliot presents a distinctive and intriguing work that mixes linguistic forms. But it is much more of a literary exercise than an engagement with the idea of theatre or performance or, rather, performativity. The tension between action and character is thereby minimized and the piece works exclusively on the page.

A slightly more convincing response to the purpose of theatre is achieved by Augusta Webster. She published translations of Greek tragedies as well as a collection of *Dramatic Studies* (1866), the five-act dramas *The Auspicious Day* (1872) and *Disguises* (1879), and the three-act *In a Day* (1882) and *The Sentence* (1887). Of these, *Disguises* is the most appealing. It is an historical romance, suggestive in both setting and tone of Shakespeare's comedies of youthful love, for example *As You Like It* and *Love's Labour's Lost*. With a range of characters adopting assumed and secret identities, its plot is complicated but also engaging and the characterizations appear fresh and energetic. But Webster's strongest creations are the women of the play: the politically aware and shrewd Claude, queen of Aquitaine, and the youthful and loving Gualhardine are dynamic and active heroines; while Bertrade, the sister of the count, is a complex and demanding creation.

In pointed contrast to Browning's monarch in *Strafford*, Claude is thoughtful and pragmatic, but she is also a passionate and sexual figure. This results in some of her most heartfelt and difficult choices, as she is deeply aware of her political role and the demands placed upon her as queen:

> Oh, I know a queen is never loved.
> We are lauded, sworn by, prayed to, died for, even;
> For a smile, a greeting, men will stake their souls . . .
> And all the while be so indifferent
> As the cold waters that wait upon the moon.
>
> (IV.i)

Webster seems particularly interested in the demands made on women and on the choices they make. Claude, Gualhardine and Bertrade must all make both moral and pragmatic choices that expose them to significant social and even sexual danger. The political dealings between the camps, the courtly games of disguise and hidden identity, as well as the revelation of another legitimate heir for De Peyriac place significant obstacles between the lovers. And it is the women who facilitate the happy resolution.

The play concludes with peace assured and a plea from Gualhardine to put away the disguises of the drama:

> Hush! we'll feign no more
> We have, in turns, all played disguiseful parts,
> Been life's forced actors, puppets to ourselves:
> The masque is ended.
>
> (V.ii)

Disguises makes Victorian verse drama's typical reference to the Elizabethan drama, but what distinguishes Webster's play is that she draws from that context more than thematic or poetic references. Instead she generates a dynamic and readable plot. The play's narrative and characters are appealing, the mountain setting distinctive, and the verse both readable and also speakable. In its particular balance of character and action *Disguises* is perhaps more suited for production than some better-known Victorian verse dramas.

Appearing towards the end of the century Alfred, Lord Tennyson's *Becket* (begun 1876, first published 1884, produced 1893) is a verse drama that certainly differs from Browning's *Strafford* in many ways. Whereas *Strafford* had only limited production success, *Becket* was a great hit – albeit a decade after its initial publication and shortly after the play-wright's death. Whereas *Strafford* can be recovered as dramaturgically bold and challenging, *Becket* is politically conventional and seems to demonstrate none of the earlier play's formal experimentation. But then *Strafford* is the work of a young man, testing himself, willing to try new ideas and genres; *Becket* was the work of the most senior of the Victorian poets, written towards the end of his career. Thematically, however, *Becket* has much in common with *Strafford*. Both are plays of crisis and drama between men, although among the *dramatis personae* of both plays there is a somewhat marginalized young woman. Both plays idealize just government, dramatizing the relationship between a good man and his king. Like *Strafford*, *Becket* is concerned with ideas of Englishness, and both plays focus on key moments from English history. But unlike *Strafford*, *Becket* is a play written by a conservative: the play's politics, representations and sense of history are all fixed, and there are none of the frictions and fissures that allow the unsettling readings of dramaturgical experimentation, political relevance and sexuality that reveal themselves in Browning's play.

But *Becket*, like *Strafford*, is still a Victorian verse drama, and the shadow of Lamb and the conventions and prejudices of the contemporary stage loom large. Tennyson's dedication of the published text makes it clear that the play is 'not intended in its present form to meet the exigencies of our modern theatre'. This is a neat evasion: it suggests that the play is to be judged on literary terms (that it is a play to be read); but it also suggests that the play has something of a higher function, a more timeless purpose quite apart from the commercial and prosaic demands of the theatre. In the event, it took the intervention of Henry Irving, an enormously skilled contemporary producer and expert script editor, to prepare the text for production. Irving's adaptation reduced the play's length by nearly one third with a series of cuts – a mixture of bold editing and judicious trimming – which included excising all of Walter Map's role (substantially choric and comedic in a laboured and really rather unfunny way) and further reducing the role of Rosamund (Henry's two visits to her are distilled into one). The revisions were all designed to strengthen the central role of Becket, which was, of course, to be played by Irving. According to the poet's son, Hallam Tennyson:

> Irving's arrangement has been criticised as too episodical; but the thread of human interest remains strong enough for its purpose, as from first to last it holds the audience in an atti-

tude of rapt attention. Assuredly Irving's interpretation of the many sided, many-mooded, statesman-soldier-saint was as vivid and as subtle a piece of acting as has been seen in our day. (1897: II, 195)

Like Tennyson, Irving was a figure at the heart of establishment Victorian culture and his production of *Becket* aspired to represent the best of mainstream Victorian theatre. Irving was certainly attracted to *Becket* as a history play, and as a play about English politics. The heroic tone of the piece suited his acting style and the historical and geographic settings afforded the Lyceum the opportunity to display its high production values in both staging and costuming. In addition the timing of the production, in February 1893, capitalized on the public outpouring of affection following the death of the poet laureate on 6 October 1892. All these elements frame the initial production as an example of the prestigious cultural product that Irving's theatre promoted, but so too does the play's use of history, which also fits neatly into this conservative context.

Hallam Tennyson insists on the playwright's sensitivity to the religious as well as historical ramifications of his hero's life. He writes that his father was indeed interested 'to learn the impression made upon Roman Catholics by his work' and tested the play on W. G. Ward:

> What struck Ward in my father's play was the clear and impressive manner in which he had brought out Becket's feeling that in accepting the Archbishopric he had changed masters, that he was not simply advanced to a higher service of the same liege lord, but that he had changed his former lord paramount . . . ; and had become a power distinct from and it might be antagonistic to the King. (1897: II, 193, 194)

Ward's comments highlight the key drama of the play, Becket's crisis of loyalty, split between friendship and faith, secular and religious hierarchies:

> I served King Henry well as Chancellor;
> I am his no more, and I must serve the Church
>
> . . .
>
> The worldly bond between us is dissolved,
> Not yet the love. Can I be under him
> As Chancellor? as Archbishop over him.
>   (I.i.81–2, 189–91)

But the play focuses more on the personal, character-specific ramifications of this extra-ordinary crisis rather than widening its relevance and application to contemporary politics. In this regard Tennyson's history play has less immediacy and relevance than Browning's investigation of democracy. This is a play (and an initial production) that understands and uses the past more as heritage than history; it is a play that substantially resists using the past to comment on and parallel contemporary society. Nevertheless, one can still see in the conflict between Henry and Becket a version of the tension between establishment and dissenting religion that was certainly current in nineteenth-century society. But the push towards heritage culture means that Becket's identity as Catholic martyr is effectively reduced in favour of his more secular role, constructing a new version of Englishness based on morally aware and active citizenship, and the effective consensus of church, monarch and people. Becket's martyrdom is thereby cast as the consequence of his character and his political position as much as of his faith.

The play follows Becket's evolution from friend and confidante of Henry, from soldier and politician, to religious leader and moral voice. The transformation is charted in scenes that shift from close dialogues and subtle plottings in private chambers to set-piece tableaux and grand entrances in monumental cathedrals and grand halls; scenes shift from French castles to English bowers; and, of course, the climax is a bloody assassination in Canterbury cathedral, played out during a great thunderstorm. But for all its potential spectacle and dynamic staging, *Becket* has a distinctive approach to action that, like *Strafford*, focuses on character in drama. For Tennyson's play does more than dramatize Becket's assassination; what it describes is the character trying to understand the circumstances of and reasons for his tragedy. This focus is clear from the very first scene, in which Becket and Henry play chess:

BECKET: My liege, I move my bishop.
            . . .
            Look to your king.
            . . .
            Well – will you move?
HENRY: There. (*Moves.*)
BECKET: Check – you move so wildly.
HENRY: There then! (*Moves.*)
BECKET: Why – there then, for you see my bishop
            Hath brought your king to a standstill.
            You are beaten.
HENRY: (*kicks over the board.*) Why, there then – down go bishop and king together.

                                        (Prologue, ll. 15–23)

Admittedly the scene appears as a laboured metaphor, with the two protagonists debating the moves of their pieces, the 'bishop' and the 'king', but it does foreshadow exactly the course of the narrative. Everything about the plot is revealed, so that by the end of the scene the audience knows what will happen. The rest of the play, then, replays this chess game focusing not on the action of the characters but on their motivation and psychology and, as in *Strafford*, charting the emotional, political and indeed physical separation of two friends. The externalized action, the plot, the elements of 'Character in Action' are described (and perhaps are even dispensed with) in the prologue, while the rest of the play focuses on the real meat of the Victorian verse drama, that is, 'Action in Character'.

A significant dramaturgical debate in Victorian verse drama is the dialectic of character and action. The genre is also marked by the tension inherent in writing for two types of consumption, two types of audience: theatregoers and the private reader. Only rarely did writers produce plays that could successfully satisfy both markets. But at the height of Victorian England the two markets could coexist. Describing the first night of *Iolanthe* at the Savoy Theatre in 1882, Clement Scott wrote that:

> I was so interested in the book that I could scarcely attend to the stage, except with my ears, and this feeling was general, for the whole audience was plunged into the mysteries of the libretto, and when the time came for turning over the leaves of the book there was such a rustling as is only equalled when musicians are following a score at an oratorio. (Shepherd and Womack 1996: 228)

The undimmed house lights that allowed the audience to read their copies of the printed libretto while simultaneously attending to the stage also illuminate an odd moment of consumption. The pleasures of reading and the pleasures of performance are perceived as complementary rather than mutually exclusive and the odd schizophrenia of the Victorian verse drama and its audience is revealed.

See also: DRAMATIC MONOLOGUE; THE SPASMODICS.

REFERENCES AND FURTHER READING

Armstrong, Isobel (ed.) (1969) *The Major Victorian Poets: Reconsiderations.* London: Routledge and Kegan Paul.

Armstrong, Isobel (1993) *Victorian Poetry: Poetry, Poetics and Politics.* London and New York: Routledge.

Ashton, Rosemary (1996) *George Eliot, A Life.* London: Hamish Hamilton.

Booth, Alison (1995) 'From Miranda to Prospero: The Works of Fanny Kemble.' *Victorian Studies,* 38, 227–54.

Booth, Michael R., et al. (1975) *The Revels History of Drama in English, volume 6, 1750–1880.* London: Methuen.

Brown, Susan (1995) 'Determined Heroines: George Eliot, Augusta Webster and Closet Drama by Victorian Women.' *Victorian Poetry,* 33, 89–109.

Browning, Robert (1983–) *The Poetical Works of Robert Browning.* Eds Ian Jack and Margaret Smith. Oxford: Clarendon Press.

Burroughs, Catherine (1997) *Closet Stages: Joanna Baillie and the Theater Theory of British Romantic Women Writers.* Philadelphia: University of Pennsylvania Press.

Burroughs, Catherine (ed.) (2000) *Women in British Romantic Theatre: Drama, Performance and Society,* 1790–1840. Cambridge: Cambridge University Press.

Davis, Tracy C., and Ellen Donkin (eds) (1999) *Women and Playwriting in Nineteenth-Century Britain.* Cambridge: Cambridge University Press.

DeVane, William Clyde (1995) *A Browning Handbook.* New York: Appleton-Century-Crofts.

Donoghue, Denis (1952) *The Third Voice: Modern British and American Verse Drama.* Princeton, N. J.: Princeton University Press.

DuBois, Arthur (1936) 'Robert Browning, Dramatist.' *Studies in Philology,* 33, 626–55.

Ferriss, Susan (1998) 'Percy Bysshe Shelley's *The Cenci* and the Rhetoric of Tyranny.' In Terence A. Hoagwood and Daniel P. Watkins (eds). *British Romantic Drama: Historical and Critical Essays* (pp. 208–28). London: Associated University Presses.

Fulton, Lynn M. (1997) 'The Standard of Flesh and Blood: Browning's Problems with Staged Drama.' *Victorian Poetry,* 35, 157–72.

Genest, John (1832) *Some Account of the English Stage From the Restoration in 1660 to 1830.* 10 vols. Bath: Carrington.

Hair, Donald S. (1972) *Browning's Experiments with Genre.* Edinburgh: Oliver & Boyd.

Jordan, John O. (1973) 'The Sweet Face of Mothers: Psychological Patterns in *Atalanta in Calydon.*' *Victorian Poetry*, 11, 101–14.

Krasner, James (1994) '"Where No Man Praised": The Retreat from Fame in George Eliot's *The Spanish Gypsy.*' *Victorian Poetry*, 32, 55–74.

Lamb, Charles (1903). *The Works of Charles and Henry Lamb.* Ed. E. V. Lucas. London: Methuen.

McCormick, James Patton (1953) 'Robert Browning and the Experimental Drama.' *PMLA*, 68, 982–91.

Marks, Sylvia Kasey (1983) 'A Brief Glance at George Eliot's *The Spanish Gypsy.*' *Victorian Poetry*, 21, 184–90.

Mason, Michael (1974) 'Browning and the Dramatic Monologue.' In Isobel Armstrong (ed.). *Writers and their Background: Robert Browning* (pp. 231–66). London: G. Bell.

Mullin, Donald (1987) *Victorian Plays: A Record of Significant Productions on the London Stage, 1837–1901.* New York: Greenwood.

Otten, Terry (1972) *The Deserted Stage: The Search for Dramatic Form in Nineteenth-Century England.* Athens, Ohio: Ohio University Press.

Poston, Lawrence (1973) 'Browning's Political Skepticism: *Sordello* and the Plays.' *PMLA*, 88, 260–70.

Poston, Lawrence (1975) 'Browning's Career to 1841: The Theme of Time and the Problem of Form.' *Browning Institute Studies*, 3, 79–100.

Poston, Lawrence (1978) 'Wordsworth among the Victorians: The Case of Sir Henry Taylor.' *Studies in Romanticism*, 17, 293–305.

Poston, Lawrence (1980) '*Philip van Artevelde*: The Poetry and Politics of Equipoise.' *Victorian Poetry*, 18, 383–91.

Ryals, Clyde De L. (1982) 'Browning's Irony.' In Richard A. Levine (ed.). *The Victorian Experience: The Poets* (pp. 23–46). Athens, Ohio: Ohio University Press.

Ryals, Clyde De L. (1984) 'Irony in Browning's *Strafford.*' In H. W. Matalene (ed.). *Romanticism and Culture: A Tribute to Morse Peckham and a Bibliography of his Work* (pp. 147–57). Columbia, S. C.: Camden House.

Ryals, Clyde De L. (1993) *The Life of Robert Browning: A Critical Biography.* Oxford: Blackwell.

Scott, William Bell (1892) *Autobiographical Notes of the Life of William Scott.* 2 vols. Ed. W. Minto. London: James R. Osgood, McIlvaine.

Scrimgeour, Gary J. (1968) 'Nineteenth-Century Drama.' *Victorian Studies*, 12, 91–100.

Shepherd, Simon, and Peter Womack (1996) *English Drama: A Cultural History.* Oxford: Blackwell.

Tennyson, Hallam (1897) *Alfred, Lord Tennyson: A Memoir.* 2 vols. London: Macmillan.

Trewin, J. C. (1955) *Mr Macready: A Nineteenth-Century Tragedian and his Theatre.* London: George G. Harrap.

Watkins, Daniel P. (1982) 'Scott the Dramatist.' In Terence A. Hoagwood and Daniel P. Watkins (eds). *British Romantic Drama: Historical and Critical Essays* (pp. 182–207). London: Associated University Presses.

11

Working-Class Poetry

Florence Boos

Nineteenth-century working-class poetry comprised a broad range of verse written and read by 'the poor': manual labourers, autodidacts and other members of 'the working classes', as well as their natural political allies, radical activists and editors such as William James Linton and Ernest Jones.

This genre's forms and venues included songs, chants, ballads, broadsides, newspaper-poems and religious and political hymns, verse in dialects or regional languages, and works sold by subscription or for charity by their working-class authors, as well as books undertaken by publishers for sale to middle- and working-class audiences. Despite stultifying obstacles to publication and a near-universal absence of formal education beyond the earliest years until after the passage of the Education Acts of 1870 and 1872, many of these works are anything but formulaic, and a few manifest dramatic power, reflective complexity and haunting beauty.

A genuinely representative Victorian poetic 'canon' would therefore include a wide range of 'primitive' verse forms, as well as poetry in regional languages such as Scots, 'Doric', Scots Gaelic or Lancashire dialect, and other traditional modes of expression of the desires of everyday life and hopes for democratic 'reform'. In this chapter, I will survey some of these desires and their realizations under four (rough, and not entirely disjoint) rubrics based on genre, thematic preoccupations and modes of publication: 'Ballads and Broadsides', 'Dialect and Regional Language Poetry', 'Chartist and Other Political Poetry' and 'Introspection and "the Poet's Mission"'.

In *The Making of the English Working Class* (1963), E. P. Thompson characterized 'working-class' and 'class-consciousness' in terms of an evolving cluster of political attitudes. Subsequent revisionists, however, questioned whether such a consciousness could be identified by the 1830s, as Thompson claimed, and focused on more diffuse and apolitical continua of attitudes and motivations (e.g. Joyce 1991). Whatever the nuances and gradations of wealth, poverty, privilege and deprivation for those who experienced them, the view expressed in this chapter will be that 'working-class poetry' was a preferred literary form for the expression of collective protest as well as oral narration, humour, satire and individual inspiration, and offered as such a uniquely valuable mirror of the imaginative life and aspirations of 'ordinary' Victorian writers, as well as their often more middle-class readers, editors and potential patrons.

The boundaries between Victorian 'working-class' and middle-class literature were indeed shifting and sometimes traversable. Writers of middle-class origins could face distinctly 'proletarian' ends, and, conversely, rich, poor and middle class alike heard and transmitted rural and 'folk' ballads, edited by such conspicuously aristocratic patrons as Lady Caroline Nairne. Literary 'hacks' of working-class origins wrote a wide variety of original broadside 'ballads', but the printers of such works also bought and published the texts of music-hall songs, and pirated works by middle-class authors such as 'The Song of the Shirt' by Thomas Hood. Middle-class journal editors such as William and Mary Howitt and W. J. Fox printed the poems of many working-class poets, but so also did 'working-class' counterparts such as Thomas Cooper, John Bedford Leno, and (the only woman in this category) Eliza Cook. Middle-class patrons and anthologizers such as George Gilfillan and D. E. Edwards published hard-cover collections of working-class poetry (and sometimes straitened the gates of what they would collect), but so also did John Cassell, Ben Brierley and others who began their careers as artisans or factory workers.

Urban ballads, hymns and music-hall songs had an especially complex class audience, and dialect and Chartist poems were directed both to working-class audiences (who read them for the most part in newspapers) and their middle-class counterparts (who were more likely to encounter them in book form). Most working-class poets lived markedly uncertain lives. Not only did they suffer swift reversals when sales faltered or publishers refused adequate payment, but harsh responses to their political activities sometimes imprisoned them and destroyed their families' means of subsistence overnight.

Many were also driven in mid-career or old age to seek small grants of subsistence from the Royal Literary Fund, whose archives now contain some of the best records we have of the lives and fortunes of indigent authors and the families left even more destitute at their deaths. Almost all, once again, were (literally) self-educated, and most bore memories that made them critical observers of their peers and 'betters' – whose indulgence they often had to seek. These complex allegiances and cross-purposes merged into a vast continuum of individual fates that underlay the complex braid of nineteenth-century popular poetry.

These patterns also evolved, of course, over time. Traditional ballads retained their rural audiences throughout the century, and other forms of popular poetry flourished in ephemeral mass-press publications, but self-identified 'working-class' poetry began to ebb towards the end of the century, in the wake of the modest reforms effected by the Education Acts and the Electoral Acts of 1867 and 1884. This change was also accelerated by the rise of other, more manipulable forms of mass culture and entertainment in the decades that followed.

Ballads and Broadsides

The several attractions of 'folk' ballads included their rural origins, generally high quality, distinctive forms of musical accompaniment, and apparent capacity to transcend class divisions. Members of all social classes sang them, and their characteristic tetrameter/trimeter quatrains ('ballad stanza') provided a template for varieties of 'popular' literature that have survived to this day. Prototypes of many well-known 'traditional' ballads dated from the Middle Ages and Renaissance, of course, but they continued to evolve throughout the eighteenth and nineteenth centuries, and middle-class and aristocratic collectors, such as Thomas Percy (*Reliques of Ancient English Poetry*, 1765), Walter Scott (*Minstrelsy of the Scottish Border*, 1802) and to a lesser degree Lady Caroline Nairne (*Life and Songs of the Baroness Nairne*, 1869), freely emended or 'improved' the versions they printed. Later collectors such as Francis Child (*English and Scottish Popular Ballads*, 1883–98) and Gavin Greig and James Duncan (*Last Leaves of Traditional Ballads*, 1925) sought to apply more scrupulous methods of reconstruction to the ballads' imaginative and linguistic origins, and Alexander Carmichael's ten-volume *Carmina Gadelica* (1900) carefully mined a well-preserved oral tradition of Gaelic lyrics, sung at birthings, marriages, cloth-softenings and funerals, which memorialized vanished love, wandering spirits and assorted acts of individual heroism and clan villainy.

For all their textual scruples, most nineteenth- and early twentieth-century editors of ballads tended to interpret away any political or social commentary they found. Despite their ministrations, however, class tensions continued to glow in the embers of the 'Robin Hood' cycle, for example, and in other works such as the macabre 'Lammikin', in which a mason murders an aristocratic family who refuse to pay him for the construction of their castle. Many other ballads – such as 'Lord Lovell', 'Sweet William', 'Fair Janet', 'Burd Helen' and 'The Brown Maid' – decried the ironies and hypocrisies of seduction, desertion, and marriage for gain across class divides, and racism appeared as an explicit plot element in 'The Brown Maid'. Critics interested in literary confrontations with gender, class and race have not yet given such works and their evolution the attention they warrant.

In 'Auld Robin Grey', for example, one of Nairne's dramatic monologues, the ballad's speaker is a young woman whose starving family has pressed her into marriage with a better-situated old man. When a former lover thought to have died at sea survives and returns hopefully to offer his hand, 'O sair did we greet, and meikle did we say: / We took but ae kiss, and I bade him gang away.' The woman's struggles to honour her love and dutiful intentions are unself-pitying and unadorned, and her stoic resignation expresses the transparent effects of rural poverty on the circumstances and emotions of 'ordinary' people.

More explicit forms of political advocacy appeared in the Gaelic 'songs' of Mary Macdonald Macpherson (Mairi Nic a'Phersain, 1821–98), who simplified and refined elaborate poetic formulae of traditional heroic Gaelic verse to protest the forced emigration of the Highland 'Clearances', of which she was a bitter opponent. 'Big Mary of the Songs' was born in Skye, and married and lived with Isaac Macpherson in Inverness until his death in 1871, then managed to train herself as a midwife and support herself and her four surviving children with this skill until she returned to Skye in 1882. She had already begun to compose and recite her oral denunciations of the 'enemies of her people' in 1872, and sang them on the stump in vigorous support of a local land-reform candidate in 1874. Her verse-chants and recitations helped elect land-reformers throughout the Highlands when the Voting Act of 1884 widened the franchise to include many crofters. 'The Incitement of the Gaels', the best-known and perhaps the most widely circulated of her 'songs', celebrated armed resistance by Skye crofters in the 1884 'Crofter's War', and 'incited' her hearers to demand the return of their land. Among other things, she also declaimed her contempt for the 'turncoats' and traitors among her fellow Gaelic singers:

> I could name them one by one,
> who sang against the owners of the land
> and turned their coats upon their backs
> and ate the words which had been their art.
> (Kerrigan 1991: 93)

Macpherson claimed to be unable to write either English or Gaelic, but she is said to have composed more than 12,000 lines of Gaelic verse, about two-thirds of them preserved through the good offices of a scribe. (A brief description of her career appears in Boos 1998. A full edition of the 'Incitement' in the original appears in Meek 1977.)

Many shorter ballads appeared in 'broadsides', single sheets sold by printers such as James Catnach and John Pitts in the disreputable Seven Dials district of London, and hawked by charity-seekers, street singers and itinerant salespeople for a few farthings. Hepburn (2000) estimates that poor readers bought about 65 per cent of these urban broadsides, and he comments in detail on the desperation and deprivation that wove the ragged fabrics of their satiric and 'sensational' plots. Some published works also reappeared in broadside form, as I mentioned earlier (e.g. Henry Kirk White's 'The Wandering Boy' and Eliza Cook's 'God Speed the Keel of the Trusty Ship'), but Hepburn has identified many writers who wrote specifically for broadside publication, among them 'J. H.', Jane Harvey, George Brown and John Morgan, who devoted hundreds of ballads to issues such as bribed elections, ruinous taxation and workhouse labour. Morgan himself died in poverty sometime after 1876 (Hepburn 2000: 53).

One view of unequal justice appeared in the anonymous 'The Grand Dissolving Views':

> The next was a police court, two prisoners in were led,
> The one a well-dressed swindler, and a boy who was ill fed,
> He'd stolen food, confessed his guilt, for pardon did entreat,
> He said he was an orphan, and nothing had to eat;
> Three months hard labour was his doom, I thought it a disgrace,
> While he who swindled many got off with a good grace,
> He paid for counsel with the spoil, 'twas money pulled him through,
> And justice blind, in silence smiled, in that grand dissolving view.
> (Hepburn 2000: 139)

Other broadside parodies of the smugly callous appeared in 'The Women Flogger's Lament of Marylebone Workhouse!' and 'The Fat Old Parish Vestryman', and satires of sentimental and patriotic verse in works such as 'The Happy Land!! Comic Version'. The speaker of William Billington's 'Friends are Few When Foak are Poor' observed the soul-destroying effects of poverty on human ties:

> even my own brother Jim
> He swears aw'm nowt a-kin to him!
> 'Bi gum', thout aw, 'thad is a thower,
> A mon's *a boggart* [ghost]when he's poor.'
>
> . . .
>
> Sooa, th' world wags on, fro' day to day,
> An still it ses or seems to say, –
> 'This poverty's a deadly sin,
> Wod banishes both friends and kin –
> An stinks i'every nobel nooas!
>
> (ll. 29–32, 41–5)

More widely circulated inexpensive newspapers, magazines and books gradually displaced broadsides over the last three decades of the nineteenth century.

Dialect and Regional Language Poetry

As several of the examples already cited make clear, many working-class authors wrote in regional dialects or languages – partly because these were the natural vehicles of their everyday speech, and partly because they saw in them threatened embodiments of the independent cultures and intrinsic values of the working poor. Lancashire dialect poetry, in particular – unusually well-preserved and well-studied – flourished from the late 1850s to the 1870s in the published work of Samuel Laycock, Edwin Waugh and others, but Brian Hollingworth has observed that the oral antecedents of this phenomenon went back several generations (1977: 3). Like many of their exemplars and predecessors – Robert Burns, for example – mid-nineteenth-century dialect poets celebrated fairs, courting and other pleasures. But they also sought to find narrative frames for the hardships and beleaguered ideals of working-class life, battered and eroded in a new industrialized environment of alcoholism, unemployment, destitution and the gradual obliteration of extended family structures.

Many early dialect poems, recited or circulated in broadsides, bore no record of their authorship. John Harland, for example, remarked in an 1839 *Manchester Guardian* article that 'half literary, half oral' poetry was frequently 'exhibited in rows upon the dead walls of our large towns, where a few yards of twine, and here and there a nail driven into the mortar of the wall, form the bookstand and reading desk of the lover of song amongst our industrious population'. 'Th' Owdham Weyver', a durable example of this genre, reached a broader audience when Elizabeth Gaskell included it in *Mary Barton* (1847), but Gaskell purged several traces of class confrontation from her text for middle-class readers. In the anonymous original (preserved in Hollingworth 1977: 11–12), the Oldham weaver recalled his brutal reduction to near starvation, mocked clerical enjoinders to patience, and recalled his bitter response to a boss who withheld his already meagre wages ('In a mind as I'm in I'll ne'er pick o'er again, / For I've woven mysel' to th' fur end'). Later, when the police had already carried away most of his family's furniture to pay his debts, they returned to snatch a final stool from under him and his wife:

> And we both went wack upo' th' flags . . .
> I sed to our Margit as we lay upo' th' floor,
> We shall never be lower in this world, I'm sure,
> But if we alter I'm sure we mun mend,
> For I think in my heart we are both at far end, . . .
> Our Margit declared if hoo'd cloas to put on,
> Hoo'd go up to Lundun an' see the big mon,
> An' if things didn't alter when hoo had been,
> Hoo swears hoo'll feight blood up to th' e'en.
> Hoo's nought again th' King, but likes a fair thing,
> An' hoo says hoo can tell when hoo's hurt.

It might have been a wise choice even for an anonymous author to have Margit, not the speaker, threaten to 'feight blood up to th' e'en' if her demands were not met, for the last six lines (modified to refer to the queen after 1837) evoked the Chartist movement's crushed efforts to present their Charter to Parliament. The original monologue's anger, raw misery, bitter sense of the grotesque aspects of destitution, and complete absence of 'edifying' or 'uplifting' sentiments effectively conveyed the stark indignities of the old couple's poverty, but Gaskell – anticipating perhaps her middle-class readers' reactions – simply glossed the expurgated version of the poem as an expression of 'that humour which is near akin to pathos'.

Samuel Laycock (1826–93), one of the best Lancashire-dialect poets, composed 'Lyrics of the Cotton Famine' when he was laid off work at a Stalybridge woollen mill in the early 1860s. In addition to several 'Owdham-Weyver'-like monologues ('The Shurat Weaver's Song', 'Aw've Turned my Bit o' Garden O'er' and 'It's Hard to Ceawer i' th' Chimney Nook'), he included in it a verse description of himself and the other inhabitants of his back alley in 'Bowton's Yard', part of a genre of expressions of local poetic solidarity which included Waugh's 'Eawr Folk' and 'Tum Rundle' and Samuel Fitton's 'Cotton Fowd'.

In 'What! Another Crack'd Poet?', another dramatic monologue, Laycock dramatized the marginal circumstances and demanding audiences working-class poets such as himself faced. Having learned that a younger friend writes verse, he advises him to try quack medicines instead:

> Heaw would t'loike goin' reawnd wi' a bag full o' books?
>   Heaw would t'loike to go hawkin' thi brains?
> Or, when tha's bin tryin' to do some kind act,
>   To be towd thar't a foo' for thi pains.
> Aw can tell thi this, Jim, it's aboon twenty year',
>   Sin' aw wur set deawn as a foo';

An', tho' it's a charge 'at one doesn't loike t'own,
　　Aw'm beginnin' to think 'at its true . . .

But aw'll drop it, owd friend, for aw'm gradely fagg'd eawt;
　　Booath mi brain an' mi hon 'gin to tire;
Iv tha loikes tha can stick these few loines i' thi book;
　　Or – iv tha prefers it – i' th' fire.

The poem's reflexive characterizations of the poet's lot prompt certain obvious questions – how its 'few loines' were preserved, for example; whether the poem originated in a phantom dialogue with a younger self; and what, if anything, made the speaker change his mind.

Strikingly many dialect poems memorialized personal or familial ties: parents' love for each other and their children (Joseph Ramsbottom's 'Sorrowin''; J. W. Mellor's 'Eawr Jack'); fond memories of other kindly relatives (Laycock's 'Mi Grondfeyther'); and the heavy burdens poor parents of many children assumed (Sam Fitton's 'Th' Childer's Holiday'; Joseph Ramsbottom's 'Philip Clough's Tale'; Joseph Burgess's 'There's Nowt Loike Spinnin' Shoddy'; and Laycock's 'Welcome, Bonny Brid!').

Edwin Waugh (1817–90), the best-known Lancashire dialect poet, also wrote one of the period's most popular 'sentimental' songs, 'Come Whoam to Thi Childer an' Me', widely promoted by the philanthropist Angela Burdett-Coutts and circulated in thousands of broadside copies. In its internal dialogue, a wife and her children anxiously wait for her husband's belated arrival, and he responds to their anxieties in the poem's last stanza:

'God bless tho' my lass; aw'll go whoam
An' aw'll kiss thee an' the childer o' round;
Thae knows that wheerever aw roam,
Aw'm fain to get back to th' owd grown;
Aw can do wi' a crack o'er a glass;
Aw can do wi' a bit of a spree;
But aw've no gradely comfort, my lass,
Except wi' yon childer an' thee.'

Some contemporaries may not have credited the poem's facile assurances, for several wrote parodies (among them Ben Brierley's 'Go Tak Thi Ragg'd Childer an Flit'), and Waugh's readers may have been more moved by the poem's saccharine reconciliation because of its carefully glossed hints at alcoholism, desertion and other betrayals. Waugh himself separated from his wife and children, and his poems included verse reconstructions of bitter marital quarrels ('Dinner Time') and an angry wife's wrath ('Margit's Coming').

All the known Lancashire poets seem to have been men, but several went out of their way to write about the crushing labours of poor women (e.g. James Standing's 'Wimmen's Wark Es Niver Done [As if bi a Woman Hersel]', and Sam Fitton's 'Th' Childer's Holiday'). The speaker of Joseph Burgess's 'Neaw Aw'm a Married Mon' even expressed concrete intentions to help his new wife do the inevitable housework:

> Soo aw'st help to mop un stone,
> Help to scrub un skeawr,
> Un do everythin aw'm shown,
> If it lies within mi peawer;
> Fur, neaw aw'm a married mon,
> Aw'm beawn to be soa good,
> Un do the best aw con
> To be o'a husbant should.

In retrospect, Burgess's touchingly didactic and hortatory aims seem clear.

Other Lancashire dialect poems wavered between angry despair and impassioned appeals for resolution and resignation. Shame at his debts, dependence on charity and fear of the workhouse have driven the speaker of Joseph Ramsbottom's 'Frettin" to consider suicide ('A sudden plunge, a little blow, / At once ud eend mi care an' pain!'), but:

> it ill ud tell
> O' thoose wur left beheend, aw fear:
> It's wrong at fust to kill mysel,
> An' wrong to lyev mi childer here.
> One's like to tak some thowt for them –
> Some sort o' comfort one should give;
> So one mun bear, an' starve, an' *clem* [go hungry],
> An' pine, an' mope, an' fret, an' live.

Matthew Arnold's readers were unlikely to follow the example of 'Empedocles on Aetna' and throw themselves into a volcano, but readers of 'Th' Owdham Weyver' and William Billington's 'The Surat Weyver' had less 'philosophical' reasons to question the purpose of their existence.

At their best, these dialect poems preserved examples of regional speech the educational establishment sought to eradicate, and their irony, humour and transparent appeals for empathy and solidarity gave concrete expression to universal human desires for a modest measure of dignity and worth. The reflective equilibrium of poems such as Laycock's 'Thee and Me' or Richard Bealey's 'My Piece Is o bu' Woven Eawt' defied condescension, and their clarity and immediacy offered plain-spoken counterweights to the diffuse epiphanies and sublimations of middle- and upper-class Victorian verse.

As linguists know, differences between 'dialect' and language have no sharp boundary. 'Lallans', for example – lowland Scots – was the mother tongue of many nineteenth-century working-class poets. Janet Hamilton (1795–1873), born in Langloan near Glasgow, was a tambourer (embroiderer), shoemaker's wife and mother of ten children. She read poetry from early childhood, committed her own first poems to memory as a married teenager (her husband helpfully transcribed them), left off poetry for a number of years after the birth of her third child in 1814, taught herself to write around 50, lost her sight in her 60s, and continued to compose verses in her head and dictated them to her son James until she died at 78. Quick dialogue, mercurial humour and a strong sense of satiric *réplique* characterized the distinctive oral quality of her work, and her publication of four volumes of essays and poems in old age (consolidated after her death in *Poems, Sketches and Essays* [1880]) was a doubly unique achievement for a woman of her class and time.

Hamilton published her first poems and temperance essays in standard English in the early 1850s, and later dedicated her third book 'lovingly and respectfully . . . to her Brothers, the Men of the Working Class' in 1868, when she was 73. She lived her entire life in Coatbridge, at mid-century one of the most blighted and polluted agglomerations in all of Great Britain, and she drafted poetic tributes to the neglected insights of older women, and detailed memoirs in 'Doric' prose of the early nineteenth-century village life she had known there as a child. Her 'Ballads of Memorie', for example, provide excellent evocations of the attitudes and aspirations of a lost early nineteenth-century village culture.

She was also a natural satirist, who could chronicle the moral and familial cost of these changes with swingeing force. In 'Oor Location', for example, she canvassed a grittily detailed cityscape of toiling workers and tavern-frequenters in a brilliant set piece of Doric rant:

> A hunner funnels bleezin', reekin',
> Coal an' ironstane, charrin', smeekin';
> Navvies, miners, keepers, fillers,
> Puddlers, rollers, iron millers;
> Reestit, reekit, raggit laddies,
> Firemen, enginemen, an' Paddies;
> Boatmen, banksmen, rough and rattlin',
> 'Bout the *wecht* [weight] wi' colliers battlin',
> Sweatin', swearin', fechtin', drinkin',
> Changehouse bells an' *gill-stoups* [mugs] clinkin',
> Police – ready men and willin' –
> Aye at han' when stoups are fillin',
> Clerks, an' counter-loupers plenty,
> Wi' trim moustache and whiskers dainty,
> Chaps that winna staun at trifles,
> Min' yet they can han'le rifles . . .
> Frae whence cums misery, want, an' wo
> The ruin, crime, disgrace an' shame,
> That quenches a' the lichts o' hame,
> Ye needna *speer*[ask], the *feck* [bulk] ot's drawn
> Out o' the change-house and the pawn.

In the midst of 'A Wheen Aul' Memories', a wistful late autobiographical poem in which she revisited the vanished precincts of her youth, she evoked once again the coal-dust, clamour and eerie sublimity of nearby Gartsherrie, this time in a pounding, four-beat balladic chant:

> Noo the bodies are gane an' their dwallin's awa',
> And the place whaur they stood I scarce ken noo ava,
> For there's roarin' o' steam, an' there's reengin o' wheels,
> Men workin', and sweatin', and swearin' like deils.
>
> And the flame-tappit furnaces staun' in a raw,
> A' bleezin', and blawin', an' smeekin' awa,
> Their eerie licht brichtein' the laigh hingin' cluds,
> Gleamin' far ower the loch an' the mirk lanely wuds.

Contemporary reviewers predictably admired more conventional accounts of seduction and abandonment in works such as 'Effie, A Ballad', but these satirical poems revealed her deepest analytical gift, which also flourished in her defences of regional cultural integrity. In 'A Plea for the Doric', for example, she apologized for 'Parnassian' efforts 'to busk oot my sang wi' the prood Southron tongue', and heaped scorn on the long line of Scottish journalistic expatriates who had literally, as well as figuratively, gone south:

> I'm wae for *Auld Reekie* [Edinburgh]; her big men o' print
> To Lunnon ha'e gane, to be nearer the mint;
> But the coinage o' brain looks no a'e haet[whit; bit] better,
> Though Doric is banish'd frae sang, tale, and letter.

These wonderfully blunt 'apologies' for the Scottish vernacular may have helped encourage later working-class poets – Jessie Russell, Ellen Johnston, John Young and Joseph Wright – to explore more deeply the tonal eloquence of their native tongue.

The span of Hamilton's preoccupations matched her chronological age. Like the Lancashire poets, she published her poems in the 1860s and 1870s, but she was born twenty-two years before Waugh, and thirty-one before Laycock. The Lancashire dialect poets, who wrote from the geographical centres of Chartism, northern industrial radicalism, and 'the Cotton Panic', naturally saw their fellows as members of a distinct class of suffering workers. Hamilton – who also developed strong interests in science, education and international politics – saw hers as fellow inheritors of a proud hyperborean culture of labouring Scots, whose fiercely independent traditions may have made them the more accountable for their faults. In 'A Lay of the Tambour Frame', for example, her speaker vigorously denounced working-class opponents of better pay for needlewomen:

> Selfish, unfeeling men!
>   Have ye not had your will?
> High pay, short hours; yet your cry, like the leech,
>   Is, Give us, give us still.
> She who tambours – tambours
>   For fifteen hours a day –
> Would have shoes on her feet, and dress for church,
>   Had she a third of your pay.

Contemporary reviewers tolerated Hamilton's mild feminism, appeals for women's education and celebration of women's roles as storytellers and co-curators of autochthonous Scottish traditions. Some of them may have done so because they could also find 'respectable' expressions of these attitudes in her religious poems and ardent support of temperance movements. Others may simply have been impressed by her unusual combination of wit, fluency, Scottishness, autodidacticism and great age:

> *Punch* acknowledges what he is glad to own as a debt, and not his debt only but all his readers', and all English and Scotch working men's, to an old woman – a poor old woman – Janet Hamilton of Coatbridge. After the stories (so well told by Samuel Smiles) of Robert Dick and Thomas Edwards, there are few records, even in the annals of the Scottish poor – so rife, to their honour, in lives of self-devotion and self-culture – than that of this poor old woman. (*Punch*, cited in the 1885 edition of *Poems*)

Hamilton's essays and poems deserved better than 'Lunnon''s faint praise, however sincere and well-intended it may have been, for they preserved the meditations of a trenchantly clear-headed working-class observer of the cataclysmic social changes in the Europe of her time.

Political and Chartist Poetry

The Chartist movement emerged from protest movements of the 1830s and the drafting of a six-point 'Charter' for electoral reforms by the London Working Men's Association in 1838, and survived through Parliament's many rejections of the Charter until imprisonment or transportation of many of its leaders obliterated what was left of the movement in the early 1850s. Even in betrayal and defeat, however, Chartism raised the consciousness of many working- and middle-class Britons, and a few aged survivors saw partial extensions of the suffrage they sought passed through Parliament in 1867 and 1884. Songs and poetry obviously provided Chartist public meetings with forms of expression and inspiration, but they also bore witness to the ability of working people to sustain an alternative culture. Chartist verse was indeed sung and recited as secular hymnody at meetings, demonstrations, marches and presentations of the Charter, but its calls for action, social criticism, and appeals to populist history and communitarian ideals also appeared in newspapers such as the *Chartist Circular* and the *Northern Star*. Chartist poetry evolved with the movement whose utopian aspirations it expressed, from early confidence to embittered revolutionary protest and final evocations of a still-visionary future. All these qualities may be traced in the work of the movement's best-known poets, among them Ernest Jones, W. J. Linton and Thomas Cooper.

Ernest Jones (1819–69) turned his back on an aristocratic ancestry and legal career to devote his life to populist and revolutionary causes, and published a number of novels, essays and books of verse, which included *Chartist Poems* (1846) and *The Battle-Day and Other Poems* (1855). His active work as an editor of Chartist newspapers and his public support of 'physical force' led to imprisonment for alleged sedition, and illnesses contracted or aggravated in prison later contributed to his relatively early death. As co-editor of the *Labourer*, he vigorously defended the great tradition of honourable defiance:

> Chartism is marching into the fields of literature with rapid strides . . . Its poetry is, indeed, the freshest and most stirring of the age . . . Yet, from many we have expected more . . . What is Robert Browning doing? . . . Has he nothing to say for popular rights? Let him . . . ascend into the cottage of the poor. (*Labourer*, 1848: 96)

Jones's impassioned verse was enlivened by personal as well as speculative meditations and an exact sense of the political events of his day. In it he analysed the underlying motives of widespread social injustice ('Labour's History', 'A Song for May', 'The March of Freedom', 'The Age of Peace'); defended the ideals of political poetry ('The Better Hope', 'The Poet's Death', 'The Poet's Mission'); and blended acerbity with his own personal version of Blake's 'Jerusalem' ('England['s] Greatness', 'The New Moral World').

One of Jones's chants was 'The Song of the Low', sung at Chartist gatherings and the most openly parodic of several working-class hymns to 'lowness':

> We're low, we're low – we're very very low
>   Yet from our fingers glide
> The silken flow – and the robes that glow,
>   Round the limbs of the sons of pride.
> And what we get – and what we give,
>   We know – and we know our share.
> We're not too low the cloth to weave –
>   But too low the cloth to wear.
>   (followed by refrain, 'We are low . . .')

In other stanzas, Jones indicted the theft of labour in all its forms – on the farm, in the mines, in domestic labour and in war – and culminated in a final call for revolutionary redress ('The thrust of a poor man's arm will go / Through the heart of the proudest king!'). As in all radical movements, the incantatory rhetoric of mass meetings clearly sharpened the 'tensions between verbal militancy and (usually) moderate behavior' Timothy Randall identified as 'a recurring feature of Chartist verse' (1999: 175).

Other, quieter poems bore immediate witness to the two years Jones spent in jail ('The Prisoner to the Slaves', 'Prison Bars', 'The Silent Cell'):

> Troublesome fancies beset me
>   Sometimes as I sit in my cell,
> That comrades and friends may forget me,
>   And foes may remember too well.
>
> That plans which I thought well digested
>   May prove to be bubbles of air:
> And hopes when they come to be tested,
>   May turn to the seed of despair.
>   ('Prison Fancies')

'The Silent Cell' also concludes with a Lovelace-like exhortation and expression of hope that:

> [t]hey'll find me still unchanged and strong
>   When breaks their puny thrall;
> With hate – for not one living soul –
>   And pity – for them all.

Jones, like Hamilton, was interested in science and technology, and the benefits he hoped it might bring a more enlightened world. His epic *The New World: A Democratic Poem* celebrated in heroic, almost socialist-realist couplets the uncertain wonders of the balloon, the train, the steam-driven hammer and the telegraph:

> Then, bold aspiring as immortal thought,
> Launched in the boundless, mounts the aeronaut;
> While o'er the earth they drive the cloudy team,
> Electric messenger, and car of steam;
> And guide and govern on innocuous course,
> The explosive mineral's propelling force; . . .
> Mechanic power then ministers to health,
> And lengthening leisure gladdens greatening wealth;
> With steely fingers on twin dials placed,
> The thoughts of farthest friends are instant traced.

In other, comparably rhapsodic passages, he predicted cloud-seeding, efforts to formulate universal languages and searches for extraterrestial intelligence. The man who could write these lines deserves a twenty-first century literary biography.

William James Linton (1812–97) was a poet, journalist and engraver, who drew illustrations for Howitt's *People's Journal* in the 1840s and 1850s and published *Thirty Pictures by Deceased British Artists* (1860) before he emigrated to the United States in 1866. In 'The Dirge of the Nations', a series of *Prometheus Unbound*-like verses which appeared in the *Republican* in 1848, Linton deplored English workers' endurance of the 'peace of hounds in their kennel, awed / And scourged', and invoked a countervailing realm of democratic ends in Shelleyan cadences:

> Let us bear, and let us toil!
> Though the Future hide our spoil.
> We have wrung the secret out
> From the Inscrutable; our shout
>   Hath o'er-ridden Fate's decree;
> And the thunder of our glee
> Yet shall roll through Heaven's gates
>   On the western clouds of Doom:
> Lo! the morrow, past the gloom
> Of the midnight grief, awaits
> The clear dawning of our fame!

In *Rhymes and Reasons Against Landlordism*, first published in his journal, the *English Republic*, in 1851, Linton denounced state violence ('War! – War!'), espoused the cause of Irish labourers ('Landlordism'), and attacked the institution of private property both in practice ('Emigrants', 'Irish Harvest Song') and in theory ('Property'):

> But earth, its mines, its thousand streams,–
>   And air's uncounted waves,
> Freighted with gold and silver beams
>   To brighten lowliest graves, –
> The mountain-cleaving waterfall, –
>   The ever-restless sea, –
> God gave, not to a few, but all,
>   As common Property.

In other poems, he dramatized sporadic efforts at resistance by contemporary farmers. In 'Revenge', for example, bystanders who have refused to identify the slayer of a hated rent-collector have their reasons:

> Who sold the farm above his head?
> Who drove the widow mad?
> Who pull'd the dying from her bed?
> Who rob'd the idiot lad?
> Who sent the starv'd girl to the streets?
> Who mock'd grey Sorrow's smart?
> Yes! listen in thy blood. His heart
>   Yet beats.

Two Chartist poets provided models for middle-class novels that later became part of the nineteenth-century canon. George Eliot took her prototype for the title-figure of *Felix Holt* from the life and career of Gerald Massey (1828–1907), a youthful revolutionary who later became a mystically inclined Christian socialist, and Charles Kingsley modelled the tailor-hero of *Alton Locke* on Thomas Cooper (1805–72), a self-educated shoemaker who later became a lecturer and journalist. Cooper's most ambitious poetic work was *The Purgatory of Suicides: A Prison Rhyme in Ten Books* (1845), which Martha Vicinus (1974) and others have criticized for its 'Parnassian' qualities, but he also wrote quite singable ballads ('The Lion of Freedom') and 'smaller prison rhymes' ('A Song for the Free', 'The Time Shall Come When Wrong Shall End'), as well as elegiac and dedicatory sonnets ('Sonnets on the Death of Allen Davenport', 'Dedicatory Sonnet to Thomas Carlyle').

In *Purgatory*, Cooper rewrote conventional history and religion in the service of agnostic idealism, Miltonic defiance, Dantean exhortation, and a deeply chiliastic vision of a secular paradise. Stephanie Kudick (Boos 2001:165–71) has observed that the poem's opening lines recapitulate the speech that led to Cooper's imprisonment in 1843–5:

> Slaves, toil no more! Why delve, and moil, and pine,
> To glut the tyrant-forgers of your chain? . . .
> Shout, as one man, – 'Toil we no more renew,
> Until the Many cease their slavery to the Few!'

In subsequent sections, Cooper brooded on poverty, class-exploitation, the execution of a fellow prisoner, his widowed mother's struggles to raise him, and the deaths of poor people in endless cycles of senseless wars, before he evoked a counter-vision of enlightenment and working-class autonomy – 'The Change', William Morris called it – that would surely come. Then at last:

> The sinewy artisan, the weaver lean,
> The shrunken stockinger, the miner swarth,
> Read, think, and feel; and in their eyes the sheen
> Of burning thought betokens thy young birth
> Within their souls, blithe Liberty! . . .
> Ay, they are thinking, at the frame and loom;
> At bench, and forge, and in the bowelled mine;
> And when the scanty hour of rest is come,
> Again they read – to think, and to divine
> How it hath come to pass that Toil must pine
> While Sloth doth revel: how the game of blood
> Hath served their tyrants; how the scheme malign
> Of priests hath crushed them; and resolve doth bud
> To band, and to bring back the primal Brotherhood.
>   (X: 16, 18)

The Purgatory of Suicides found its worthy place in a tradition of nineteenth-century radical epics which ranged from *Prometheus Unbound* through Ernest Jones's *New Moral World* and Mary Smith's 'Progress' (reviewed below), to William Morris's poetic tribute to the Paris Commune in *The Pilgrims of Hope* (1886). Cooper's intricate frame and wide erudition are as accomplished as anything one can find in other marginally canonical poems of the period (Swinburne's *Mary Stuart*, for example), and *Purgatory* is genuinely graced by its epic aspirations and vivifying democratic ideals.

The Wider Nets of Radical Verse

Chartists were of course not the only working-class authors of significant political verse, and many writers of such poems were anonymous. One of them was the 'Manchester operative' who assimilated textile-factory workers to 'nature red in tooth and claw' in sixteen concise and brilliant lines:

> Keen hawk, on that elm-bough gravely sitting,
>   Tearing that singing-bird with desperate skill,
> Great Nature says that what thou dost is fitting –
>   Through instinct, and for hunger, thou dost kill . . .

> O, natural Hawk, our lords of wheels and spindles
> Gorge as it grows the liver of their kind:
> Once in their clutch, both mind and body dwindles –
> For Gain to Mercy is both deaf and blind.
> O, instinct there is none – nor show of reason,
> But outrage gross on God and Nature's plan,
> With rarest gifts in blasphemy and treason,
> That Man, the souled, should piecemeal murder man.
> ('Just Instinct and Brute Reason', *Howitt's Journal*, i, 132)

William and Mary Howitt published this poem in 1847, but added the somewhat distancing gloss, 'Our operative is severe, but perhaps his sufferings are, and for misery we must make ample allowance.' The voice of the 'operative' was not heard again, to my knowledge, in the forests of mid-nineteenth-century poetry.

As I have already remarked, some of the period's best poetic accounts of deprivation were also the most concrete. Consider, for example, the spare, almost-Pre-Raphaelite concision of the following lines, from *Songs and Lyrics* (1892) by the coal-miner poet Joseph Skipsey (1832–1903):

> 'Get up!' the caller calls, 'Get up!'
>   And in the dead of night,
> To win the bairns their bite and sup,
>   I rise a weary wight.
>
> My flannel dudden [coarse clothes] donn'd, thrice o'er
>   My brids are kiss'd, and then
> I with a whistle shut the door,
>   I may not ope again.
>
>   ('Get Up')

Women were categorically barred from positions of active engagement or leadership in the Chartist movement, as they were from any such roles in the mass political movements of mid-nineteenth-century Britain (except the few focused specifically on women's causes). This did not mean, of course, that they were politically unaware. Ellen Johnston, for example, an impoverished Scottish textile worker, managed with help and great effort to publish her 1854 *Autobiography, Poems and Songs* by subscription in Glasgow in 1867, and one of the poems reproduced in this modest volume was 'The Last Sark', in which a distraught wife cries out to her husband in pain and helpless rage:

> Gude guide me, are you hame again, an' ha'e yet got nae wark?
> We've naething noo tae put awa' unless yer auld blue sark;
> My head is rinnin' roon about far lichter than a flee –
> What care some gentry if they're weel though a' the puir wad dee! . . .

It is the puir man's hard-won cash that fills the rich man's purse;
I'm sure his gowden coffers they are hit wi mony a curse.
Were it no for the working man what wad the rich man be?
What care some gentry if they're weel though a' the puir wad dee?

My head is licht, my heart is weak, my een are growing blin';
The bairn is faen' aff my knee – oh! John, catch haud o' him,
You ken I hinna tasted meat for days far mair than three;
Were it no for my helpless bairns, I wadna care to dee.

Other working-class women poets vigorously advocated women's education (Janet Hamilton) as well as legal efforts to curb domestic violence (Jessie Russell, Agnes Mabon, Marion Bernstein) and 'temperance' – protest against what we would probably call 'substance abuse' (all of the above, especially Hamilton).

Mary Smith, for example, an ardently self-educated servant who became a newspaper contributor, school aide and schoolmistress in Carlisle, campaigned for many social causes – against the Contagious Diseases Acts, for example (laws which empowered police to pull women off the street at will and examine them for venereal diseases), and for the Married Women's Property Acts (which curbed husbands' 'rights' to their wives' earnings and property). In *Progress, and Other Poems . . . Including Poems on Life and Labour* (1863), Smith argued in periodic octameters that:

'Women's Rights' are not hers only, they are all the world's beside,
And the whole world faints and suffers, while these are scorn'd, denied.
Childhood, with its mighty questions, Manhood with its restless heart,
Life in all its varied phases, standing class from class apart,
Need the voice, the thought of woman, woman wise as she shall be,
When at last the erring ages shall in all things make her Free.

Eliza Cook, the eleventh child of a tinsmith and brazier, published *Melaia, and Other Poems* (1838), *Poems, Second Series* (1845) and *New Echoes* (1864), and managed to find the financial and other resources to edit *Eliza Cook's Journal* as a penny-biweekly from 1849 to 1854. In didactic but broadly humanitarian poems such as 'A Song for the Ragged Schools', Cook commented on the factory conditions, the dignity of labour and working-class education ('Better build schoolrooms for the boy, / Than cells and gibbets for the man'), as well as the 'simple' democratic virtues of popular art:

Who scorns the 'common' sculpture art that poor men's pence can buy,
That silently invokes our soul to lift itself on high?
Who shall revile the 'common' tunes that haunt us as we go?
Who shall despise the 'common' bloom that scents the market-row?
Oh! let us bless the 'Beautiful' that ever lives and greets
And cheers us in the music and the flowers of the 'Streets'.

('The Streets')

Introspection and 'the Poet's Mission'

Driven by pressing needs for solace and consolation, many working-class poets wrote introspectively to recall joy, redress faults, assuage despair, and find some meaning in the omnipresence of death, especially the deaths of young children. I will focus in this section on working-class expressions of beleaguered hope, and countervailing assertions of pride in the poet's role.

'Marie', for example (her last name is not known), was a dye-worker from Chorley who published several poems in William and Mary Howitt's *The People's Journal* and *Howitt's Journal* beginning in 1847, and in assorted journals for a few years thereafter (*The People's Journal*, *Eliza Cook's Journal*, *Cassell's Family Magazine*). Flashes of persuasive wit appeared in her expressions of faith in personal autonomy, the poet's vocation and the dignity of all 'labour', and the stoic philosopher Epictetus might have admired her love of beauty and calm expressions of lyric self-abnegation:

> Though ignored our lowly lot,
> Scornful glances harm us not;
> We accept our homely fate:
> And a beauteous life create; –
> From earth's bosom, brown and bare,
> Flowerets draw their colours rare;
> And, though we are seeming stinted,
> All our days are rainbow-tinted
> > By our noble will!
> > ('The Indomitable Will')

One of her later poems set 'earnest hope' against the spectre of death ('To Liberty', 1852), and I cannot find her name or pseudonym in print after.

In her *Autobiography of Mary Smith, Schoolmistress and Nonconformist: A Fragment of a Life*, published posthumously in 1892, the stalwart servant, schoolmistress and feminist activist regretted bitterly her failure to realize 'the inner cravings of my soul after literary pursuits' (1892: 192), and traced this failure to the constraints imposed on her as a woman as well as to her personal inadequacies and the meagre economic circumstances of her youth.

As others before her (and after), Smith sought solace in solidarity with other humble under-labourers of human history, who have struggled – perhaps in vain – to envision a kind of ethical and aesthetic kingdom of ends. In 'Progress', for example, a 116-page historical epic she may have modelled in part on Cooper's *Purgatory of Suicides*, she expressed this elusive ideal in an ardent memorial tribute to the myriad 'spirits of dead centuries' (p. 71) – a community of unremembered secular saints, whose struggles for solidarity and enlightenment might encourage us in our own:

Ye have no name nor place in all our lore,
    Forgot by e'en tradition's garrulous tongue,
But ye – oh could we know you! – evermore
    War with us against evil foes of wrong;
Your breath is still upon us, still we feel
Faint whispers of your glories through us steal;
Faint whispers of your thinkings; your great heart
With time still blending, still its noblest part.

And when our hearts, unresting, seek pure peace;
    When the tide overflows them of pure thought;
When the world's noisy tongues that hold us cease,
    And all the troubled soul to rest is wrought:
'Tis then your spirit, greater than our own,
Which thrills us with a sense of things unknown,
Which folds us in a glory, that makes bright
Our fleeting moments, with Eternal Light.
                                        (pp. 72–3)

A distinct but related subgenre can be identified in working-class poets' expressions of
pride in the fact that they *were* working-class poets. Comfortably situated Victorian poets
also celebrated their craft, of course – in Tennyson's 'The Poet's Vow', for example, or
Robert Browning's 'One Word More'. But their poorer brothers' and sisters' intensity
and persistence bore witness to the strength of a sustaining but deeply threatened life-
ideal. Examples of such tributes include Ernest Jones's 'The Poet's Mission' and 'The
Poet's Death', Charles Cole's 'The Poet's Love of Liberty', Allen Davenport's 'The Poet's
Hope', John Rogerson's 'The Minstrel's Lot', John Critchley Prince's 'To Poesy', James
Waddington's 'Genius', Joseph Skipsey's 'The Brooklet' and John Nicholson's relatively
conflict-ridden 'Genius and Intemperance', as well as Laycock's 'What! Another Cracked
Poet?', quoted earlier.

    Working-class poets also went out of their way to pay tribute (sometimes posthumous)
to their fellows. Examples of such authorial solidarity included Cooper's 'Sonnets on the
Death of Allen Davenport', Alexander Wilson's 'The Poet's Corner', William Billington's
'Gerald Massey' and Richard Furness's 'To the Memory of Ebenezer Elliott'. In his prose
preface to *Hours With the Muses* (1841), the Manchester operative John Critchley Prince
expressed the poet's pride in unusually pointed terms:

> It is almost impossible to take too extended a view of the nature and characters of Poetry
> . . . Above all, if [the poet] had the will to devote his God-like energies to the good of his
> fellow-men, his existence would be a blessing and a benefit to the age in which he lived
> . . . A few such mighty spirits would effectively regenerate the human race . . . I have been
> indebted to poetry, as a source of intellectual enjoyment, during years of many sorrows, many
> baffled hopes, and many vain endeavours to rise above the evils of my condition.

The city poet, deprived of appeal to a rural populist tradition, faced special problems and
earned special rewards. In 'The City Singers' (1873), for example, the Manchester
working-class poet John Lawton Owen claimed:

> This dower of song is manna to the city,
>   It is the dew upon a crowded field;
> Broadcast it scatters life, and love, and pity,
>   And e'en the reapers cannot tell the yield . . .
> So shall street children, playing in the gutter,
>   And toilers sweating at the busy loom,
> Instinctively your lyric-lesson utter
>   While they shall steal like fragrance through the room.

Other forms of gratitude were even more immediate and more intense. When Ellen Johnson thanked the socialist Alexander Campbell for his support for her work in the *Penny Post*, she drew on a personal history of discouragement, desertion, sexual abuse and numbing toil:

> My life's young years were spent in dark repining,
>   In persecution, falsehood, and envy;
> But now a world of love is round me twining –
>   My fame is soaring upwards to the sky.
>   ('Lines to Isabel from the Factory Girl')

Fanny Forrester, a Manchester textile-factory worker and the last writer to be considered in this section, managed to publish her work in *Ben Brierley's Journal* for a few years in the 1870s. In one of these poems, 'The Lowly Bard', she portrayed the working-class poet as a harried and exhausted angel of mercy, who perceived and recorded human suffering and endurance in stifling factories and foetid slums, as well as chronic illness and early death. In the poem's final scenes, for example, a poet hovering in a garret at the side of a dying and delirious man hears his last anguished wish – to support and sustain his children:

> 'Mine, only mine, to toil for and to cherish!
>   Lay your cool hand, sweet Mary, on my brow!
> Children plead more, they must not, shall not perish!
>   There, do not hold me – I am stronger now!
> I've much to do, and precious time is fleeting.'
>   The priest bends lower o'er the ragged bed –
> No banner waves, nor muffled drum is beating;
>   Yet, 'tis a hero that lies still and dead.

Such heroism was clearly one of the marks of Mary Smith's community of secular saints, who comfort the distraught writer, in turn, in the poem's conclusion:

> The great may flaunt their pampered bards above him,
>   But when *their* laurels shall be sere and brown,
> Kind heaven will grant, because the lowliest love him,
>   To the poor rhymester an *eternal crown*.

The resonance of this view did impel some of those who held it to 'rise above the evils of [their] condition', and make a unique collective contribution to an understanding of the sorrows of the dispossessed.

Conclusion

We have ranged briefly through some of the verse poor Britons wrote and sang in the nineteenth century, religious, anti-clerical, inspirational, instructive, humorous, meditative, reflective and reflexive poems in almost all their registers – 'traditional' and narrative ballads, urban broadsides, regional satires and political protests. Not all working-class literature was 'anti-establishment', of course, or 'self-improving', or oral and traditional in character, or composed in quatrains, couplets or Spenserian stanzas. But its allusions were 'political' in a wider sense as well as 'literary', and many of the registers and tonalities they found would resonate deeply if they could be seen and understood by writers in the 'third world' today.

That might in some cases be difficult, for as Martha Vicinus (1974) and others have remarked, Victorian working-class poetry also appealed to specifically *British* traditions, shaped by its public nature and antecedents in ballads and popular songs, and influenced by the eighteenth-century pastoralism of Cowper, Ferguson, Gray or Crabbe, as well as the reformist romanticism of Burns, Byron, Shelley and the early Wordsworth. The populist and reformist tradition these poets adapted and extended, moreover, has also estranged them from other paradigms that have generally guided *academic* taste, in the later twentieth century and beyond – *l'art pour l'art*, symbolism, imagism, modernism, 'new criticism', structuralism, deconstruction, 'postmodernism' and the like. Taken together, these divergences from nineteenth-century working-class poets' models and exemplars have ironically made their works less 'popular', for they have rendered their recovery and interpretation more difficult, more historicist and therefore more 'academic'.

Readers of nineteenth-century working-class poetry should also keep in mind that the extant works we have may be a partial and somewhat biased sample. The British class system was brutally effective, and the testimonies of almost all published working-class poets to the difficulties they encountered strongly suggest that it interdicted the 'Parnassian' and non-'Parnassian' efforts of many more unschooled manual labourers (see Ashton and Roberts 1999). What middle-class editors were willing to publish, moreover, was clearly constrained not only by their own personal canons of taste, and the forms and sentiments they deemed appropriate for 'humble' authors, but also by the more arbitrary preferences of middle-class purchasers and other market constraints. A good body of evidence, for example, suggests that many publishers and anthologists selected women poets' blandest effusions, and repressed aberrant expressions of inappropriately 'strong' thought.

Given these circumstances, it should be said that the preservation of the working-class poetic corpus we *do* have is a testimony to the dedication and (basically) good offices of William and Mary Howitt, John Cassell, Alexander Campbell, George Gilfillan, W. J. Linton, Ernest Jones, Eliza Cook, Ben Brierley and other committed working- and middle-class editors, who printed and edited works most other editors refused to consider. Behind or at the side of every poor poet whose work has survived stood at least one more or less sympathetic patron or editor, a genuine blessing, occasionally mixed, which only a few aspiring poor writers could hope to have.

Finally, little or nothing is known about most working-class authors' lives. Very few posthumous manuscripts of poor writers have been preserved, and it is likely therefore that many poems and other writings left uncompleted or unpublished at death were destroyed. Not only they, but the contexts which sustained them, are now therefore irrecoverable.

Despite the distinctive contribution working-class authors made to mid-Victorian romanticism and reformism, it also became harder to identify a distinct body of working-class poetry as the century waned. In part at least, this diminution may have been an ironic consequence of improved educational and literary opportunities, as well as the expansion of mass culture into other channels (music-hall performances, fiction and eventually films). Be that as it may, it was still possible at the turn of the century to identify a few poets with clear working-class backgrounds (Fred Henderson, Ethel Carnie, Lizzie Smith and even D. H. Lawrence), and a few middle-class poets strongly identified themselves with radical-democratic and/or socialist ideals (William Morris, Edward Carpenter and, in some moods and periods of his life, Oscar Wilde). But conscious cultivation of working-class poetry as a category had begun to fade. The raw, early industrial rapacity that created some of its most anguished tensions had begun to recede, however slowly and painfully, and the passions and interest which sustained it in mid-Victorian Britain found new forms of expression – in radical political poetry, poetic indictments of the losses of two world wars, and fictional and memoir representations of settled aspects of working-class life.

A few characteristics of working-class poetry also found indirect or collateral descendants, sometimes in unlikely places: in certain aspects of aestheticism (especially its use of ballads, refrains and folk metres; consider D. G. Rossetti's 'The King's Tragedy', for example, or Wilde's 'Ballad of Reading Gaol'); in populist and reformist literature associated with the arts and crafts movement; and in folk accompaniments to political radicalism in various parts of the English-speaking world (one lineage might be traced in North America, for example, from the European prototype of Morris's 'Chants for Socialists' through Joe Hill, Woody Guthrie, Pete Seeger and Paul Robeson to Joan Baez, Bonnie Raitt and beyond). Still other linguistic and thematic registers of nineteenth-century working-class poetry have also found successors in the thematic choices, dialect usages and self-consciously demotic focus of British modernist poetry (Hardy's Wessex poems, for example; Edith Sitwell's 'bucolic lyrics'; A. E. Housman's 'A Shropshire Lad'; and the work of Jessie Anderson, Marion Angus, John Buchan, Violet Jacob and other poets of the Scots vernacular revival).

As a whole, then, Victorian 'people's poetry' in its many forms – ballads, broadsides, dialect and regional poetry, Chartist verse, and the vast array of poems on political and personal themes – responded in revealing ways to the conditions of its time, and served as the matrix of many dramatically rendered works of lasting merit. Its several facets therefore merit closer study, better preservation, and the benefit of modern reprints and scholarly editions, before their sources in manuscripts, historical records and copies of ephemera and periodicals are slowly but irrevocably lost. Many would still read the poems of Cooper, Hamilton, Jones and Linton, I believe, if editors made them accessible in critical and/or annotated form. Many more would gain a sense of the depth of working-class poetry if it were given the attention it deserved in anthologies of Victorian poetry, or better yet, a carefully edited anthology of nineteenth-century working-class literature.

In their thematic choices and affiliations, these works blended protest, reformist politics, self-assertion and moral reflection in complex ways. The ideals and aspirations which animated them could be integrated, up to a point, with generalized appeals to traditional faith, on the one hand, and with autodidactic variants of a classical or 'polite' education (as in Thomas Cooper's *Purgatory*) on the other. But the imaginative possibilities they sought were fundamentally opposed to many 'elite' traditions, and their oral, musical and affective roots neither needed nor would have been likely to bear an extensive admixture of artistic framing, textual ambiguity and high-cultural allusions.

Many imbricated intents and attitudes could nevertheless be found in the variety of working-class cultural expression, and the very complexity of these interrelations makes sense of a commentator's remark that it is 'the broad uniformity of condition and outlook in the culture of the labouring poor that is striking, [for] power and powerlessness, hope and fatalism, aspiration and accommodation, were not opposites but different sides of the same coin of poverty' (Joyce 1991: 228). Because of these complex interrelations, it would also be unreasonable if not impossible to try to separate 'political' from 'non-political' strands in working-class poetry, for the aims of literature are intrinsically aesthetic and expressive as well as argumentative. The deepest 'political' poetry may convey the worldview of an underclass more effectively than any sociological analysis, and politics and economics may inflect not only poetic subjects and forms, but the most fundamental imaginative conceptions of morality and emotion, pathos and transcendence itself.

Working-class verse, in short, was a repository of anger, humour and utopian hopes. It embraced individual poems which were sonorous, witty, trenchant, lyrical and reflective, and genres and traditions which were as complex, in their ways, as middle-class poets' and editors' elaborate framing devices and modes of collection were in theirs. It remains one of our most valuable sources of information about the nineteenth-century popular imagination, and the deepest hopes and unfulfilled aspirations of not-so-'ordinary' people.

See also: THE MARKET; ANTHOLOGIES AND THE MAKING OF THE POETIC CANON; POETRY AND SCIENCE.

REFERENCES AND FURTHER READING

Alves, Susan (1996) 'A Thousand Times I'd Rather Be a Factory Girl: The Politics of Reading American and British Female Factory Workers' Poetry 1840–1915.' Diss., Northeastern University.

Armstrong, Isobel (1993) *Victorian Poetry: Poetry, Poetics and Politics*. London: Routledge.

Ashraf, Phyllis M. (1978, 1979) *An Introduction to Working-Class Literature in Great Britain*. Part I,

Poetry. Part II, Prose. East Berlin: Lehrmaterial zur Ausbildung von Diplomlehrern Englisch.

Ashton, Owen, and Stephen Roberts (1999) *The Victorian Working-Class Writer*. London: Mansell.

Bold, Alan (1979) *The Ballad*. London: Methuen.

Boos, Florence (1995) 'Cauld Engle-Cheek: Working Class Women Poets in Victorian Scotland.' *Victorian Poetry*, 33.1, 53–74.

Boos, Florence (1996) ' "Oor Location": Victorian Women Poets and the Transition from Rural to Urban Scottish Culture.' In Debra Mancoff and Dale Trela (eds). *Victorian Urban Landscapes* (pp. 133–56). New York: Garland Press.

Boos, Florence (1998) ' "We Would Know Again the Fields": The Rural Poetry of Elizabeth Campbell, Jane Stevenson, and Mary Macpherson.' *Tulsa Studies in Women's Literature*, 17.2, 325–77.

Boos, Florence (1999) 'Janet Hamilton.' In William Thesing (ed.). *Victorian Women Poets: Dictionary of Literary Biography* (pp. 149–58). Detroit: Bruccoli, Clark, Layman.

Boos, Florence (2000) 'Ellen Johnston.' In Abigail Bloom (ed.). *Nineteenth-Century Women Writers* (pp. 231–4). Westport, Conn.: Greenwood Press.

Boos, Florence (ed.) (2001) 'The Poetics of the Working-Classes.' *Victorian Poetry*, 39, 2. This volume contains essays on Chartist rhetoric by Mike Sanders and Kelly Mays; on Thomas Cooper by Stephanie Kudick; on Ernest Jones by Ronald Paul; on Eliza Cook by Solveig Robinson; on Ebenezer Elliot by Alexis Easley; on Ellen Johnston by Judith Rosen; on execution ballads by Ellen O'Brien; on women poets in the periodical press by Florence Boos; and on dialect poetry by Lawrence McCauley.

Colls, Robert (1977) *The Collier's Rant: Song and Culture in the Industrial Village*. London: Croom Helm.

Friedman, Albert (1961) *The Ballad Revival: Studies in the Influence of Popular on Sophisticated Poetry*. Chicago: University of Chicago Press.

Gerould, Gordon (1957, 1974). *The Ballad of Tradition*. Oxford: Oxford University Press; New York: Gordian Press.

Hepburn, James (2000) *A Book of Scattered Leaves: Poetry of Poverty in Broadside Ballads of Nineteenth-Century England*. Vol. 1. Lewisberg: Bucknell University Press.

Hollingworth, Brian (ed.) (1977) *Songs of the People: Lancashire Dialect Poetry of the Industrial Revolution*. Manchester: Manchester University Press.

James, Louis (ed.) (1976) *English Popular Literature, 1819–51*. New York: Columbia University Press.

James, Louis (1988) 'Working-Class Literature.' In Sally Mitchell (ed.). *Victorian Britain: An Encyclopedia* (pp. 874–5). New York and London: Garland.

Janowitz, Anne (1998) *Lyric and Labour in the Romantic Tradition*. Cambridge: Cambridge University Press.

Journes, Hugues (1991) *Une Litterature Revolutionnaire en Grande-Bretagne: La Poesie Chartiste*. Paris: Publisud.

Joyce, Patrick (1991) *Visions of the People: Industrial England and the Question of Class, 1848–1914*. Cambridge: Cambridge University Press.

Joyce, Patrick (1994) *Democratic Subjects: Studies in the History of the Self and the Social in Nineteenth-Century England*. Cambridge: Cambridge University Press.

Kerrigan, Catherine (ed.) (1991) *An Anthology of Scottish Women Poets*. Edinburgh: Edinburgh University Press.

Klaus, H. Gustav (1997) *Factory Girl: Ellen Johnston and Working-Class Poetry in Victorian Scotland*. New York: Peter Lang.

Kovalev, Y. (1956) *An Anthology of Chartist Writing*. Moscow: Foreign Languages Publishing House. The introduction, trans. J. C. Dumbrick and Michael Beresford, appeared in *Victorian Studies*, 2.2 (1958), 117–38.

Maidment, Brian (1985) 'Poetry in Victorian Manchester.' In Alan J. Kidd and K. W. Roberts (eds). *City, Class and Culture* (pp. 148–66). Manchester: Manchester University Press.

Maidment, Brian (ed.) (1987) *Poorhouse Fugitives: Self-Taught Poets and Poetry in Victorian Britain*. Manchester: Carcanet.

Meek, Donald (1997) *Mairi Mhor Nan Oran: Taghadh d'a h-orain le eachdraidh a beatha is notaichean*. Gairm: Glaschu.

Randall, Timothy (1999) 'Chartist Poetry and Song.' In Owen Ashton, Robert Fyson and Stephen Roberts (eds). *The Chartist Legacy* (pp. 171–95). Woodbridge: Merlin Press.

Rose, Jonathan (1988) 'Working-Class Poets and Poetry.' In Sally Mitchell (ed.). *Victorian Britain: An Encyclopedia* (pp. 877–8). New York: Garland.

Rose, Jonathan (2001) *The Intellectual Life of the British Working Classes*. New Haven, Conn: Yale University Press.

Schwab, Ulrike (1993) *The Poetry of the Chartist Movement: A Literary and Historical Study*. Dordrecht: Kluwer Academic.

Scheckner, Peter (ed.) (1989) *An Anthology of Chartist Poetry: Poetry of the British Working Class, 1830s–1850s*. Rutherford, N. J.: Fairleigh Dickinson University Press.

Vicinus, Martha (1974) *The Industrial Muse: A Study of Nineteenth-Century British Working-Class Literature*. London: Croom Helm.

Zlotnick, Susan (1991) ' "A Thousand Times I'd Be a Factory Girl": Dialect, Domesticity, and Working-Class Women's Poetry in Victorian Britain.' *Victorian Studies*, 35.1, 7–27.

Zlotnick, Susan (1998a) 'Lowly Bards and Incomplete Lyres: Fanny Forrester and the Construction of a Working-Class Woman's Poetic Identity.' *Victorian Poetry*, 36.1, 17–36.

Zlotnick, Susan (1998b) *Women Writing and the Industrial Revolution*. Baltimore: Johns Hopkins University Press.

12

The Classical Tradition

Richard Jenkyns

Like much else in the culture of the Victorian age, the classical element in Victorian poetry needs to be seen in relation to the Romantic period that preceded it. But the issue is clouded by the fact that the word 'classical' is used in two quite different senses. In one usage, 'classical' denotes the civilizations of ancient Greece and Rome, from the time of Homer to the period of late antiquity. In another sense, 'classical' is applied to an aesthetic tendency, and is seen as the antithesis of 'romantic': classicism represents a stress upon perfection of form, balance, control, the conscious use of traditional shapes and motifs, as distinct from the primacy given by romanticism to passion, spontaneity, originality, excess and the uninhibited expression of the self. In this second sense Romanticism, and those Victorian poets who carried on the Romantic aesthetic, may seem necessarily opposed to classicism. But in the first sense there need not be any conflict at all: many nineteenth-century writers celebrated the romantic qualities in the literature of Greece and Rome. And even in the second sense the division between the classical and the Romantic may prove not to be as stark as at first sight appears. For there is a subtle complication: the classical ideals of purity and chaste perfection could themselves be admired by the Romantics, adored with a romantic extravagance of passion. Classicism, after all, could seem close to the Romantic cult of primitive simplicity, untrammelled by the artifices of civilization, of the noble savage and the natural man. And indeed it is in the Romantic age that the worship of Hellas reaches its height, with the ancient Greeks being idolized for what was seen as the radiance, harmony and serenity of their art and literature.

Most of the Victorian poets, like their predecessors, were educated chiefly in the literature and civilization of Greece and Rome, and we should expect to find these things bred into their bones. But they were also the inheritors of a shift in taste and attitudes that began in the second quarter of the eighteenth century and gathered pace in the century's second half. In social and political terms this change is exemplified in Rousseau's noble savage, and in the ideas behind the French Revolution and the foundation of the American republic. In terms of visual art, it takes the form of a reaction against the baroque, now seen as licentious, self-indulgent and artificially overelaborate, and a preference for the honesty of a plainness not tricked out with fancy adornments – if for grandeur, then for the grandeur of a bare austerity. In terms of the classical world, this revolution in taste is marked by some devaluation of the Roman achievement, sometimes seen now as derivative and overcivilized in comparison with the freshness, force and directness of the Greeks.

It is difficult to describe these matters without misleadingly simplifying some multiform and diverse phenomena. The literature of ancient Greece alone extends over a period of a thousand years or more, and is immensely varied in character. Moreover, the response of Romantics and Victorians to this complexity was itself complex. Even a single phenomenon could be viewed in a complex way. Take Greek Doric architecture, for example, unknown to western Europe until the later eighteenth century. It could be seen as nobly simple, in contrast to the elaboration of Roman architecture and the modern baroque; or as rudely, ruggedly grand, in contrast to the tameness of modern style. Homer might seem primitive, natural and direct, in contrast to the sophisticated obliquities and romantic half-lights of Virgil; but when Keats first looked into Chapman's Homer and breathed the Greek poet's 'pure serene' he was romantically liberating himself from the classicism of Pope's translation. Part of the fascination of Hellenism, perhaps, lay in this ambivalence.

J. J. Winckelmann famously declared, in his *Reflections on the Painting and Sculpture of the Greeks* (1755), that the characteristics of Greek art were 'a noble simplicity and a calm greatness'. G. E. Lessing retorted, in *Laocoön* (1766), that while Greek sculpture might rightly be so described, Greek tragedy was not: Sophocles' wounded hero Philoctetes does not bear his sufferings calmly; he shrieks and howls. The German debate about Hellenism was introduced to a wider audience by A. W. Schlegel in his *Lectures on Drama* (1809), soon translated into English and much drawn upon by Coleridge for his own lectures. The consequence of Schlegel and other writers who picked up his themes was that the relationship of classical antiquity, and particularly of the Greeks, to the modern world was commonly seen in terms of a series of contrasts or dichotomies: between past and present, classical and romantic, whiteness and colour, south and north, pagan and Christian, the definite and the indefinite, objective and subjective, perfection within limits and a yearning for the infinite. Sculpture was the master art of the Greeks, Schlegel suggested, as music of the moderns. Metaphors of light, radiance and clarity were constantly applied to Greek art and literature. Such imagery interacted in the British imagination with two other kinds of consciousness; living in a nation which was industrialized in a way that was quite new in human history, and aware of how different their climate was from that of the Mediterranean, English authors developed a further contrast: between a smoky, dun modernity, absorbed in getting and spending below grey skies, and the luminous brightness of Hellas.

The idealization of ancient Greece, originating in German Romanticism, became a recurrent tendency running through Victorian literature and thought right to the end of the century; indeed, it gained new impetus from the aestheticism of Walter Pater and his disciples, manifested, for example, in the verse of Oscar Wilde. Classical Greece was used as a yardstick against which the modern world was measured and found wanting. Its utility for the modern spirit lay in its sheer distance, in time and space and character: it was seen as a refuge for the spirit oppressed by romantic *Weltschmerz* or a corrective for certain tendencies of the modern mind. But this use of classical antiquity coexisted with another: Latin and Greek texts, still the basis of a gentleman's education, continued to provide much of the furniture with which an educated person's mind was equipped; the corpus of Latin and Greek literature formed the stock of a curiosity shop peddling all sorts of different goods. In terms of the classics, therefore, the historian of Victorian literature has two stories to tell: one about a self-conscious Hellenism, the other about the continuance of a broad classical tradition. In the latter case, the use of classical themes by earlier English poets may be as important an influence as the classical sources themselves: the tradition is a mixed and evolving one. In the one case the classical is a model or an aspiration; in the other, a quarry, a store of themes, ideas and values to be drawn upon from time to time, when they happen to prove serviceable.

'The human mind', Shelley wrote in the preface to his verse drama *Hellas*, 'attained to a perfection in Greece which has impressed its image on those faultless productions, whose very fragments are the despair of modern art.' The idealization of Greece encouraged a feeling of inferiority in the nineteenth-century poet, and a sense of secondariness, of the burden of the past, became itself a theme for verse. This sense connected itself especially with the idea of epic, which by the common consent of critics from the Renaissance onwards was the highest form of poetry. Two conceptions came together: that the ancient poets had realized the possibilities of epic so consummately well as to leave nothing for the modern poet to do (this was what Goethe, who had begun and abandoned an *Achilleid*, told J. P. Eckermann (*Conversations with Goethe*, 1847: 5 July 1827)); and that heroic verse could not be made out of the prosaic, commonplace conditions of modern life.

The prevalence of such attitudes may be gauged from the protest which Elizabeth Barrett Browning put into the mouth of the poetess heroine of her *Aurora Leigh* (V, 139ff):

> The critics say that epics have died out
> With Agamemnon and the goat-nursed gods –
> I'll not believe it. I could never dream . . .
> That Homer's heroes measured twelve feet high.
> They were but men! – his Helen's hair turned grey
> Like any plain Miss Smith's, who wears a front . . .
> All men are possible heroes: every age . . .
> Looks backward and before, expects a morn
> And claims an epos.

But every age, Aurora Leigh continues, appears unheroic to those who live in it. The present age, for instance, is belittled by thinkers, 'and the poets abound / Who scorn to touch it with a finger tip'. There are two ideas here: that any period, including the present, can successfully be given the heroic treatment; and that all periods seem commonplace at the time. Aurora Leigh puts these two ideas together as she argues (V, 204ff) that 'this live, throbbing age':

> spends more passion, more heroic heat
> Betwixt the mirrors of its drawing rooms
> Than Roland with his knights, at Ronscesvalles.

> To flinch from modern varnish, coat or flounce,
> Cry out for togas and the picturesque,
> Is fatal – foolish too. King Arthur's self
> Was commonplace to Lady Guenever;
> And Camelot to minstrels seemed as flat
> As Regent Street to poets.

As it happens, the nineteenth century did see the 'heroization' of the joys and sorrows of ordinary life in modern times – not in verse, however, but in prose fiction. George Eliot, who may be termed the Aurora Leigh of the novel, was indeed to compare and contrast her characters with the protagonists of Homer and Greek tragedy; but that is another story.

It is not true, in fact, that all ages seem flat to themselves; a belief in the 'poetrylessness' of the present time was a distinctive characteristic of the nineteenth century, and imparts its own flavour to the Victorians' attitudes to the past, not least to classical antiquity. But even if the claim of Aurora Leigh (or her creator) had been true, the argument might seem to point to the opposite conclusion: if the present age always appears flat, a poet might as well turn to the past. The charms of Camelot certainly drew Tennyson. As a young man, he wrote 'Morte d'Arthur', a fragment of an imaginary, unwritten epic, and presented as such; for he prefaced it with a curious poem, called simply 'The Epic', set on a Christmas Eve at the present day. One of the guests at the Christmas party is a poet who has recently burnt his epic on King Arthur in twelve books (the same number as in the *Aeneid*). The poet is asked his reason (ll. 34ff):

> 'Nay, nay,' said Hall
> 'Why take the style of those heroic times?
> For nature brings not back the Mastodon,
> Nor we those times; and why should any man
> Remodel models? these twelve books of mine
> Were faint Homeric echoes, nothing-worth,
> Mere chaff and draff, much better burnt.'

However, a friend has rescued the eleventh book from the flames; and this (it is pretended) is 'Morte d'Arthur'.

Many years later Tennyson incorporated 'Morte d'Arthur' into his *Idylls of the King*. But although the *Idylls* bears the subtitle 'in twelve books' and has more lines than the *Aeneid* – above 10,000 – the work is not presented as a unified whole, handling a single action – Aristotle's definition of epic, based upon Homer's example – but as a collection of stories, loosely linked. Tennyson knew that the meaning of the Greek *eidullion*, anglicized as 'idyll' – as in the Idylls of Theocritus – was 'little picture' or 'little sketch'. He knew too that the pastoral mode, to which some of Theocritus' idylls belong, was traditionally considered the lowliest of the poetic genres, as epic was the highest. There is thus in his conception a paradoxical blending of two antithetical classical influences. The idea of the work also expresses the 'anxiety of influence': the poet cannot hope to match Homer or

Virgil, but offers fugitive sketches of an epic theme. Or to put the matter another way, the poem embodies an aesthetic that delights in the fragmentary, the hesitant, the incomplete, like that romantic taste for the picturesque which prized a ruined abbey or temple more than the building entire. The imaginary poet scorned his 'faint Homeric echoes', but another person might find in those evanescent sounds a peculiar charm, like that 'Passion of the Past' evoked by Tennyson in another poem ('The Ancient Sage', ll. 219, 223ff):

> A height, a broken grange, a grove, a flower
> Had murmurs 'Lost and gone and lost and gone!' . . .
> Desolate sweetness, far and far away.

In 'Morte d'Arthur' the King describes Avilion, the blessed isle to which he will be borne in death (ll. 260ff):

> Where falls not hail, or rain, or any snow,
> Nor ever wind blows loudly; but it lies
> Deep meadowed, happy, fair, with orchard lawns
> And bowery hollows crowned with summer sea.

The classically educated reader will recognize in this both an imitation and the imitation of an imitation: it is modelled on the description of Olympus, home of the gods, in the *Odyssey*, on which in turn Lucretius modelled his picture of the gods' philosophic calm, according to the doctrine of Epicurus. But Tennyson's own notes on these four lines cite not only these two passages but another from the *Odyssey*, one from the *Iliad*, and one from Pindar. We can see two processes here. There is a conscious intertextuality, in which the relationship to the classical model is an intended part of the meaning; and there is also the use of classical poetry as a quarry, stimulating a happy expression from time to time, fortuitously, as the occasion arises. We may also feel that part of Tennyson's effect comes from the fusion of classical inspiration with elements that are quite unclassical: as the work blends epic and idyll, so it also medievalizes the classical.

Comparing 'Morte d'Arthur' to his own *Sohrab and Rustum*, Matthew Arnold suggested that 'the likeness, where there is likeness . . . , proceeds from our both having imitated Homer'. Like Tennyson, he blends classical elements into a story taken from another age, culture and religion, in this case from Persian legend. Like Tennyson again, he offers a fragment: despite its epic machinery, *Sohrab and Rustum* is less than nine hundred lines long and bears the subtitle 'An Episode'; it begins, 'And the first grey of morning filled the east', as though it were a piece torn from some larger work. Yet it represents a substantially different relation to classical precedent from Tennyson's. Arnold selects a single model as deliberately as Pope chose Horace for his Epistles or Johnson Juvenal for 'London' and 'The Vanity of Human Wishes': the poem is continuously close to the *Iliad* both in its details and in its general design. Thus Arnold bends the plot to bring it nearer to Homer's. The story is essentially simple: a great warrior kills on the battlefield an opponent who turns out to be his son. But Arnold makes some additions: Rustum is angrily unwilling to fight, like Homer's Achilles (ll 178f): 'aloof he sits / And sullen, and has pitched his tents apart'. There is even an embassy to Rustum, to urge him to change his mind and enter battle, like the embassy to Achilles in the ninth book of the *Iliad*, with the sage counsellor Gudurz corresponding to Homer's Odysseus. Even in such a detail as the ambassador's arrival and Rustum's reaction Arnold keeps Homer steadily in mind. These are Arnold's lines (ll. 199ff):

> and there Rustum sate
> Listless, and held a falcon on his wrist,
> And played with it; but Gudurz came and stood
> Before him; and he looked, and saw him stand,
> And with a cry sprang up and dropped the bird,
> And greeted Gudurz with both hands, and said: –
> 'Welcome! these eyes could see no better sight.
> What news? but sit down first, and eat and drink.'

And this is Homer (*Iliad* IX. 186ff, tr. M. Hammond):

> They . . . found Achilles giving pleasure to his heart with a clear-voiced lyre . . . He was delighting his heart with this, and singing tales of men's glory . . . They walked further forward, with godlike Odysseus leading, and stopped in front of him. Achilles left his seat and jumped up in astonishment . . . And swift-footed Achilles showed his greeting and said to them: 'Welcome! Oh, you are dear friends that have come!' [Achilles then offers food and drink.]

Arnold imitates many features of Homeric style: the repetition of words and phrases, the arming scene, and, most conspicuously, the formal epic simile (though thanks to Milton, this last can be considered to belong to an English tradition too). Several of these are obvious variants on Homeric similes, one or two on similes in Virgil, who had himself adapted some of Homer's images to his own purposes. Even the most oriental of Arnold's similes has a Homeric inspiration. Sohrab reveals the mark of identity pricked upon his arm (ll. 672ff):

> as a cunning workman, in Pekin,
> Pricks with vermilion some clear porcelain vase,
> An emperor's gift – at early morn he paints,
> And all day long, and, when night comes, the lamp
> Lights up his studious forehead and thin hands –
> So delicately pricked the sign appeared
> On Sohrab's arm, the sign of Rustum's seal.

The apparently irrelevant digression, breaking up the syntax ('at early morn he paints', etc.), mimics Homer's practice in general, but Arnold has a more particular inspiration for the idea in a simile also describing a handsome warrior's blood (*Iliad*, IV, 141ff, tr. Hammond):

> As when a woman stains ivory with crimson dye, in Maeonia or Caria, making a cheek-piece for horses. It lies there in her room, and many horsemen yearn to have it for the wearing: but it waits there to be a treasure for a king, both horse's finery and rider's glory. Such, Menelaus, was the staining with blood of your sturdy thighs, and your legs, and your fine ankles below.

Here we can see original talent making creative use of the tradition; significantly Arnold modifies his source, in which Sohrab has a gemstone or seal attached to his arm, so that he can adapt Homer's image.

Ironically, it could be said that Arnold in patterning himself so much on Homer is not so much Homeric as Virgilian, since it is Virgil who invents the idea of what has since been called secondary epic, shaping his plot to parallel those of the *Odyssey* and *Iliad*, and sustaining throughout the entire work a complex intertextual relationship with his Homeric models. In terms of tone and spirit, however, it is Tennyson who has often been seen as a very Virgilian poet, one whose belief in a providence which governs the world is clouded by an all-suffusing sense of sadness. The idea of Virgil as a man of tentative faith shadowed by melancholy, haunted by the tears that lie at the heart of the things, the *lacrimae rerum* (a phrase that actually means something rather different in its original context in the *Aeneid*), may owe a certain amount to Tennyson himself ('To Virgil', stanza 6), who hails the great man as:

> Thou that seëst Universal
>   Nature moved by Universal Mind;
> Thou majestic in thy sadness
>   at the doubtful doom of humankind.

Yet Tennyson's idea of Virgil is not as wholly Tennysonian as is sometimes supposed: he recognizes in the Roman poet the proclamation of imperial power, as well as a voice of grace and grief. 'Roman Virgil', he begins, and returns to the 'ocean-roll of rhythm' that will 'sound for ever of Imperial Rome' (stanzas 1, 8). He is also conscious of Virgil as the contributor to a continuing and developing tradition: the address to 'Roman Virgil' at the poem's start is answered in the last stanza by 'I salute thee, Mantovano'. In part this is a just response to Virgil himself, whose *Georgics* and *Aeneid* deeply explore the interplay between three overlapping forms of patriotism, the Roman, the Italian, and an affection for locality which in Virgil's case is expressed through the evocation of his native Mantua. But 'Mantovano' also takes us to Dante, who addresses the master by this title, and to modern Italy (the poem was, as its subtitle declares, 'Written at the Request of the Mantuans for the Nineteenth Centenary of Virgil's Death'). Tennyson tells the Italians of the Risorgimento that Virgil, the classic figure of a vastly distant age, is also their fellow-countryman. At the same time he evokes the contrasts between past and present, Italy and England, north and south (stanzas 9, 10):

> I, from out the Northern Island
>   sundered once from all the human race,
>
> I salute thee, Mantovano.

This alludes to a line in Virgil's first Eclogue, which speaks of the 'Britons utterly separated from all the world'. Tennyson's paraphrase adds the little word 'once': with a consciousness of both change and continuity, he implies that Britain has now entered into the family of European civility and indeed that it is now the dominant imperial power that Rome had been.

Tennyson's relation to classical names and motifs is often momentary, eclectic and mingled with other overtones. 'Now lies the Earth all Danaë to the stars', he writes in one of the lyrics in *The Princess* (section 7, l. 167). This line uses our common inheritance of Graeco-Roman mythology wonderfully to evoke voluptuous beauty, passivity, receptivity. But this is the classical carried into the mainstream of the European tradition and absorbed within it: the whole lyric is richly and imaginatively pictorial, and the reader is likely to think not of some Greek poet but of the paintings of the Italian Renaissance, and indeed it has been noted that Hallam's last letter to Tennyson praised Titian, adding 'I wish you could see his Danaë. Do you just write as perfect a Danaë!' Tennyson contrasts an outer and an inner world: 'Now lies the Earth all Danaë to the stars, / And all thy heart lies open unto me.' The comparison between the first of these lines and the next is a comparison between inanimate nature and human emotion, between the universe and the individual, between myth and actuality, between the art of the past and the immediate moment, experienced in the here and now. The classical is one element in all of this, woven into its complexity.

Tennyson drew upon classical mythology for several of his monologues, for example 'Tithonus' and 'The Lotos-Eaters'. But in these cases the myth provides little more than the starting idea: in the former case, immortality without immortal youth, in the latter, the temptations of an idle, druggy hedonism. Indeed, the essence of these pieces is to take a piece of Greek tale and suffuse it with modern, romantic sentiment: the reader who turns, fuddled with the sprawling, sensuous swoon of 'The Lotos-Eaters', to the passage in the *Odyssey* on which it draws may be surprised to find it so brisk and brief. 'Ulysses' is a more complicated case. Odysseus (to give the hero his original Greek name) had already gone through diverse mutations in antiquity – Sophocles alone can depict him, in different works, as the cynical advocate of expediency and as the type of wise submission to the gods – and Tennyson plays his own variation on the Ulysses theme. His principal source is Dante's *Inferno*, in which Ulysses tells his story, but his knowledge of Homer, which Dante lacked, enables Tennyson to comment, as it were, upon both poems, and even to play them off against each other. Tennyson's Ulysses, looking to his final voyage of exploration, offers in effect two alternative endings, one from Dante, who has the hero sucked down by a vortex beyond the Pillars of Hercules, and one from ancient Greece (ll. 62ff):

> It may be that the gulfs will wash us down:
> It may be we shall touch the Happy Isles,
> And see the great Achilles, whom we knew.

The *Odyssey* contains elements of the *Bildungsroman*: we watch the growing up of Odysseus' son, Telemachus, a sensible young man. Tennyson gives this an ironic twist, as he has Odysseus, the restless adventurer, praising his son rather faintly for his blameless attention to common duties, being 'decent not to fail / In offices of tenderness', respectful in his adoration of the household gods (ll. 33ff). Arnold wrote of a passage in *Ulysses*: 'It is no blame to their rhythm, which belongs to another order of movement than Homer's, but it is true that these three lines by themselves take up nearly as much time as a whole book of the *Iliad*' (*On Translating Homer*, on *Ulysses*, 19ff). But that, in a way, is the point: the purpose is to illuminate and transform a classical model through the application of a modern and personal sensibility. Tennyson said that there was more of himself in *Ulysses* than in *In Memoriam*. The classical myth is an object against which the poet's subjectivity can play; it licenses an indirect exploration of private emotion which, given directly, might seem too raw or self-regarding.

Tennyson's invitation poem 'To the Rev. F. D. Maurice', bidding the addressee visit the author on the Isle of Wight, indicates how subtle and complex the use of the classical tradition could still be in Victorian poetry. These are the opening lines:

> Come, when no graver cares employ,
> Godfather, come and see your boy:
> Your presence will be sun in winter,
> Making the little one leap for joy.

The genre of invitation poem at once suggests Horace, who was much in Tennyson's mind, even in the construction of the metre. A few months before, Tennyson had written another poem, 'The Daisy', in what he himself called 'a metre which I invented, representing in some measure the grandest of metres, the Horatian Alcaic'. The invitation to Maurice is even closer to Horace's form (though one must bear in mind one essential difference, that Latin verse is scanned by quantity – that is, in accordance with the varying length of syllables – whereas English verse is scanned by stress accent). The Horatian Alcaic, itself a modification by the Roman poet of a Greek lyric form, is a four-line stanza of especially impressive form, its shapeliness deriving largely from the contrast between the weightiness of the third line, with three long syllables in succession, and the rippling, dactylic rhythm of the last. The last two lines of Tennyson's stanza are pretty close to Horace. It is unusual in English to produce three stresses in succession (the equivalent of Horace's three long syllables), but in a couple of stanzas Tennyson does even that (ll. 11, 27): 'Yet one lay-hearth would give you welcome'; 'And on through zones of light and shadow'.

In the English tradition the invitation poem suggests such pieces as Jonson's 'Inviting a Friend to Supper' or Milton's sonnet, 'Lawrence of virtuous father virtuous son', whose first line is itself an echo of one of Horace's odes. Tennyson's closest model is one of Horace's odes to his patron Maecenas, both in general conception and in a few more particular allusions, but he also includes a stanza which recalls Milton's imitation, in the sonnet to Lawrence, of Horace's first spring ode. At such a point to ask whether Tennyson's lines are after Horace or after Milton is to put a question that hardly has an answer. Tennyson slips himself into the current of an Augustan tradition, descending through the English poets, that can give the illusion of being almost uninterrupted.

He also understood the Latin poets' practice of *aemulatio*, 'emulation'. The lyric from *The Princess*, 'Come down, O maid, from yonder mountain height', puts itself into the pastoral tradition which goes back ultimately to Theocritus, though Tennyson himself said that there was no real likeness to Theocritus 'except perhaps in the Greek Idyllic feeling' (the landscape in the poem was apparently inspired by Switzerland). But at the end of the poem, just as Virgil had displayed his virtuosity by paraphrasing some especially melodious passages of Theocritus, so Tennyson emulates some word music in Virgil's first Eclogue:

> Myriads of rivulets hurrying through the lawn,
> The moan of doves in immemorial elms,
> And murmuring of innumerable bees.

It is worth comparing Virgil's almost humorous mimicking of the sounds of bees and doves, which can be pretty well recognized even without knowledge of Latin (ll. 53ff):

> hinc tibi, quae semper, vicino ab limite saepes
> Hyblaeis apibus florem depasta salicti
> saepe levi somnum suadebit inire susurro: . . .
> nec tamen interea raucae, tua cura, palumbes
> nec gemere aëria cessabit turtur ab ulmo.

[Here, as ever, the hedge at your neighbour's boundary where the bees of Hybla feed full on the willow blossom will often by its gentle humming invite sleep to come . . . , nor meanwhile will the hoarse wood-doves, your delight, nor the turtle-dove cease to moan from the lofty elm.]

Here is pure sensuousness, with no purpose beyond its own beauty: both poets yield to the pleasure of onomatopoeia and the uncomplicated charm of surface.

Among Victorian poets Matthew Arnold is the one most associated with Hellenism, but although he discussed his doctrine in his prose works of literary and social criticism, he remains oddly elusive. He can seem to be a revivalist, imitating classical forms and recasting classical mythology in a modern language, rather as contemporary architects were imitating the Gothic buildings of the thirteenth and fourteenth centuries. Or he can seem to express his irremediable alienation from the ancient world, conscious of his historical situation as a post-Romantic in an industrial society. Arnold the revivalist is most conspicuously seen in his longest poetical work, *Merope*, a verse drama modelled upon Greek tragedy. No one has been able to think very highly of this piece. It is at its best when it is most like a Victorian novel, in the portrayal of Polyphontes, who like Bulstrode in George Eliot's *Middlemarch* has done a bad deed for which he hopes that subsequent good may atone. But the work is lifeless, and with its lack of theatrical sense and static, functionless chorus, quite un-Greek.

The attempt to revive Greek verse drama is a curious, usually forgotten corner of Victorian literary history. Robert Bridges wrote several such pieces, including a *Prometheus the Firegiver* praised, at least by his friends, for its fidelity to the Greek spirit. Swinburne's *Atalanta in Calydon* is remembered for its choruses; he followed it with *Erechtheus*, which he aimed to make more 'purely genuine in its Hellenism of form and thought', claiming that even the lyrics were rigidly obedient to the musical rule of Greek tragedy, and consulting an Oxford professor to make the poem 'impregnable' from a scholarly point of view. Because these works lie mostly unread, we can easily be unaware of this dutiful, revivalist streak in Victorian poetic life, but it is part of the story, and it is interesting that it can affect as antinomian a spirit as Swinburne. If these works were all we had to judge by, we should be likely to conclude that the classical influence upon the Victorian poets was deadening. Hopkins made the point: when his friend Robert Bridges sent him a copy of his verse drama *Ulysses*, he was sharply critical of the decision to put a goddess into the piece: the Greek gods, he argued, were 'the merest frigidity, which must chill and kill every living work of art they are brought into'. But Hopkins's answer to the dilemma, as we shall see, was not to throw aside the Greek spirit but to distil it more thoroughly.

Arnold, for his part, was aware that his practice did not always match his principles. In 1852 he published *Empedocles on Etna*, the longest work of his earlier poetic career, but a year later he suppressed it on the grounds, as he explained in the preface to *Poems* (1853), that the subject was 'morbid' because the sufferings of the central figure 'find no vent in action'. Into the feelings of a man in Empedocles' situation, he argued, 'there entered much that we are accustomed to consider as exclusively modern'. From his surviving fragments the 'calm, the cheerfulness, the disinterested objectivity' which mark the great monuments of early Greek genius have disappeared: 'the dialogue of the mind with itself has commenced; modern problems have presented themselves; we hear already the doubts, we witness the discouragement, of Hamlet and of Faust'. On this account Greek literature, at its highest, stands as the antithesis of modern, romantic unease and introspection; yet in an essay of 1857, paradoxically entitled *On the Modern Element in Literature*, Arnold argued that Athens in the fifth century BC was the only truly modern age in literature: Thucydides was a modern, scientific historian as Raleigh was not; Sophocles was modern and 'adequate' (a peculiarly Arnoldian word) as no subsequent poet has been.

So were the Greeks modern or were they not? A good deal of Arnold's verse is intriguingly entangled in this equivocation. Despite his suppression of *Empedocles* he continued to explore the dialogue of the doubting, discouraged mind with itself, the angst of modern existence; indeed the essence of his verse, to most of his readers, is a troubled, melancholy agnosticism, restless and ill at ease. In his sonnet 'To a Friend', he had declared that the men who propped his mind 'in these bad days' were Homer, the Stoic philosopher Epictetus and above all Sophocles, 'Who saw life steadily, and saw it whole' (a famous line, which he was to quote himself in *On the Modern Element*). This is to see the value of antiquity for the present age in its sheer unlikeness, to find in classical completeness and perfection an antidote to modern mess and muddle. But elsewhere, more ambivalently, he combines this sense of distance with a sense of kinship, of experience shared. In 'Dover Beach' the sound of waves grating on an English shore leads to this reflection (ll. 15ff):

> Sophocles long ago
> Heard it on the Aegaean, and it brought
> Into his mind the turbid ebb and flow
> Of human misery; we
> Find also in the sound a thought,
> Hearing it by this distant northern sea.

Here are some familiar contrasts – in time between now and 'long ago', in space between the Aegean and the distant north – but the sea's 'eternal note of sadness' is unchanged. With the words 'this distant northern sea' Arnold plays the game that Tennyson was to play in his poem 'To Virgil' of viewing oneself through other eyes: he describes his position in space from Sophocles' standpoint rather than his own. This kind of self-consciousness has a characteristically nineteenth-century flavour. John Stuart Mill observed, in his essay *The Spirit of the Age* (1831), that the idea of comparing one's own age with past ages or with those yet to come was now for the first time the dominant idea of the age. But Arnold's phrase goes a step beyond comparing two ages: it compares them from the viewpoint of the other age. This practice of self-awareness, of observing oneself from the outside, is expressed in Macaulay's famous fantasy, in his 1840 review of Ranke's *History of the Popes*, of the New Zealander, in some future epoch, coming to look upon the ruins of St Paul's; it was to be a leading idea in Pater's *Marius the Epicurean* (1885) and in several of James Elroy Flecker's poems in the early years of the twentieth century. And thus the evocation of classical antiquity could come to serve a distinctively modern end.

In 'Stanzas from the Grande Chartreuse' Arnold played a variation on some of these themes. The poet asserts his dissociation from the faith to which the Carthusian monks have devoted their lives (ll. 79ff):

> Not as their friend or child, I speak!
> But as, on some far northern strand,
> Thinking of his own Gods, a Greek
> In pity and mournful awe might stand
> Before some fallen Runic stone –
> For both were faiths, and both are gone.

Here, curiously, he claims both a contrast and a likeness between himself and a Greek.

Though Arnold is the most obvious practitioner among Victorian poets of what one might call a hard-edged classicism, he too could sometimes be blurrier, most notably in 'Thyrsis', his pastoral lament in memory of his friend Clough. The pastoral threnody for a dead poet has a Greek precedent in the anonymous *Epitaphium Bionis*, but it is also a distinctively English tradition, thanks to Spenser's 'Astrophel', Milton's 'Lycidas' and Shelley's 'Adonais', with 'Thyrsis' the last in the sequence. At first the poem seems to be another exploration of the contrasts between past and present, south and north (Clough had died in Italy). Arnold sets the 'easy access to the hearer's grace / When Dorian shepherds sang to Proserpine', who had herself 'trod Sicilian fields' and known the roses and lilies of Enna, against the humble landscape of 'our poor Thames' and the Cumner cowslips (ll. 91ff). The white evening mist on an English hillside is contrasted with the 'broad lucent Arno-vale' and the here and now with a more poetic age (ll. 161ff, 81ff):

> Alack, for Corydon no rival now!
> But when Sicilian shepherds lost a mate,
>   Some good survivor with his flute would go,
> Piping a ditty sad for Bion's fate.

The first allusion is to Virgil's seventh Eclogue, in which Corydon and Thyrsis have a singing competition with each other. But this, instead of separating Clough from the literary, Graeco-Roman world of pastoral, puts him into it: he is the dead Thyrsis whom the poem commemorates, as the dead Daphnis is commemorated in Virgil's fifth Eclogue, or Bion in the *Epitaphium*. Two senses of loss become blurred – one for a beauteous, god-haunted Grecian past and the other for Clough's life and his Oxford companionship with the poet. The land of lost content, haunted by pastoral echoes, is in the end not only Italy but even more the English landscape of 'sweet spring-days', bluebells and hawthorn, to be followed by the pomps of high midsummer (ll. 61ff). The effect of the poem is thus strangely ambivalent, with an elusiveness not unlike that which is so characteristic of Virgil's own pastoral.

Robert Browning is radically unlike all other Victorian poets in his use of the classical world, as in so much else. Though the nineteenth century was a great age for the historical novel, rather few of these novels were set in the ancient world, and most of those few were set in the period of the high or later Roman Empire: Edward Bulwer-Lytton's *The Last Days of Pompeii*, Charles Kingsley's *Hypatia*, John Henry Newman's *Callista*, Wilkie Collins's *Antonina*, Pater's *Marius the Epicurean*. It was partly that these writers were interested in depicting the life of the early Christian church, partly that the world of late antiquity, already looking back upon the zenith of classical Greece from a great distance, could be seen to have a strange likeness to the Victorian age. Novels set in classical Greece itself barely existed at all. Walter Savage Landor's *Pericles and Aspasia* can hardly be called a novel: this short book of imaginary letters, cool and high-minded, aspires to the condition of sculpture, presenting its figures as in marble on a frieze. The idealization of Athens made it unpromising territory for a novelist; for novels do not deal in perfection.

For a sense of the ordinary life of classical Greece in Victorian literature we must turn not to prose but to Browning's two long, discursive poems, *Balaustion's Adventure* and its sequel, *Aristophanes' Apology*. Even so there is little narrative in the first of these pieces and even less in the second; they are, so to speak, 'novels of ideas', like *Marius the Epicurean*. In the later poem the young poetess Balaustion champions her hero Euripides, while Aristophanes protests the value of his rough, exuberant comedy; a translation of Euripides' *Heracles*, entire, is embedded within the narrative. In the earlier poem Balaustion paraphrases Euripides' *Alcestis*, analysing it as she goes, with particular stress on the play's supposed psychological realism – a unique and fascinating experiment in practical criticism and close reading done in verse.

In treating the ancient world Browning stands apart from other Victorian poets in seeming to have an interest in what it was like to be there; even so, and perhaps not altogether wisely, he puts allusions to modern times into these pieces. Aristophanes is made to prophesy Shakespeare – that is, a poet from the remote Tin Islands who will combine tragedy and comedy into a single art of universal scope (*Aristophanes' Apology*, ll. 5140ff). Balaustion knows of a 'great Kaunian painter' who has depicted Heracles wrestling with Death for Alcestis' life; but Browning is clearly thinking of a picture by Frederic Leighton (*Balaustion's Adventure*, ll. 2672ff). She also knows of a poetess who described Euripides as 'the human, with his droppings of warm tears' (ll. 2671, 2412); this is Browning's tribute to his wife, who used the phrase in 'Wine of Cyprus', in which she compared and contrasted the three great Greek tragedians, Aeschylus being 'the thunderous' and Sophocles 'the royal' (stanzas 11, 12) (Swinburne, who purported to dislike Euripides, chortled at the thought of his 'droppings'). So even when making ancient Greece his setting, Browning is thinking about the modern experience of reading Greek literature. He investigated this theme more directly in two other poems, 'A Grammarian's Funeral' and 'Development', in which the speaker contrasts his father reading Homer to him as a child with his adult experience of reading Aristotle's *Ethics* in the original. Like some other of Browning's works, these poems seem unlike anything much else in Victorian literature.

The subject of 'A Grammarian's Funeral' is a professional scholar, something Browning was not; but curiously, two poets active in the later part of the Victorian period ended up as professors of classics, Hopkins as professor of Greek in Dublin and Housman in the chair of Latin at Cambridge. It is true that we do not immediately think of Housman as a Victorian poet, but *A Shropshire Lad* is in fact a product of the 1890s. In Housman the dissociation between his verse and his professional studies is extraordinarily strong: the little lyric 'The weeping Pleiads wester' is a paraphrase of a Greek poem often attributed to Sappho, but that apart, there is almost nothing classical, in any of the word's senses, to be found in his verse at all. It seems likely that he found in antiquity a value system which satisfied his bleak agnosticism, but he does not (like Swinburne, say) let classical allusion colour his austere picture of the human situation. The case of Hopkins is more complicated. We have heard him, in a letter to Bridges, arguing the impossibility of successfully reviving a pagan deity in modern verse; but he went on to contrast his own use of the Greek treasure-store: 'I sent you a sonnet . . . in which a great deal of early Greek thought was distilled; but the liquor of the distillation did not taste very Greek, did it? The effect of studying masterpieces is to make me admire and do otherwise' (Abbott 1935: 210). This last sentence may make us aware how fully absorbed and invisible the classical influences upon Victorian poetry can sometimes be. There is much conscious allusion to classical predecessors in Victorian verse: the intertextuality is a part of the effect. But in other cases though the classical influence may be part of the poem's 'archaeology', it can hardly be considered as necessary to its final meaning.

Hopkins's work is pervaded by a Platonist idea of nature. The grand paradox of Platonism is that it both exalts and belittles the physical world as perceived by our senses. On the one hand, the highest reality is the ideal world of forms, of which the various beauties of the perceptible world are at best imperfect copies; on the other, the perceptible world is not only indeed beautiful but our way of access to the eternal reality which, however imperfectly, it expresses. Hopkins's vision is of this kind: he glorifies the 'pied beauty' of the world both because it is inexhaustibly lovely in itself and because God is to be found within nature's 'inscape'. The germ of these ideas was planted in Hopkins by his undergraduate studies of Plato, though he attributed them himself to the influence of the medieval philosopher Duns Scotus – that is, to Plato at several removes. Hopkins claimed that his sprung rhythm was based upon the lyrics of Pindar and Greek tragedy. He also acknowledged the presence of Pindar behind *The Wreck of the Deutschland*. Like many of Pindar's odes, this poem begins with a prayer to deity, combines moral and reflective lyric with narrative, and contains some account of the poet's own circumstances. Like Pindar too, Hopkins might be said to have written a victory ode, the narrative being a story of triumphant martyrdom. On the poem's surface, however, there is nothing classical at all.

By contrast, Swinburne, as rhapsodical as Hopkins, decorated a romantic effusiveness with a fair amount of classical gloss; names of Graeco-Roman gods or taken from Greek mythology are sprinkled liberally across his verse. He had an especial passion for Sappho, once declaring, in an extravagant moment, that she was 'the greatest poet who ever was at all' (Lang 1959–62: IV, 124). (He was distinguishing her from Shakespeare, 'the greatest dramatist that ever was also a poet', and Aeschylus, 'the greatest poet who ever was also a prophet'.) This passion stimulated some of the best and the worst in him. 'Anactoria' – the title is taken from the name of one of the beloved girls whom Sappho addresses – comes close at times to self-parody in its thick, lush eroticism; and though fragments of Sappho's verse are embedded in its self-indulgent length, its perfervid overstatement is far from her limpidity. Yet in his 'Sapphics' the discipline of writing in the accentual form of her metre, imitating her craft as well as her content, led him to a restless, original beauty:

> All the night sleep came not upon my eyelids,
> Shed not dew, nor shook nor unclosed a feather,
> Yet with lips shut close and with eyes of iron
>   Stood and beheld me.

Swinburne may also illustrate the way in which the ancient world could provide an alternative source of value for rebels of various kinds against conventional morality and belief. His hostility to Christianity led him to the opinion that even Dante was the lesser poet for his beliefs, but he could declare the *Oresteia* of Aeschylus to be the greatest spiritual work of man. Despite its title, 'The Garden of Proserpine' has not much that is classical to show in its externals; the significant classical influence lies in its outlook upon life and death and humanity's relation to the world's eternal order:

> From too much love of living
>   From hope and fear set free,
> We thank with brief thanksgiving
>   Whatever gods may be

> That no life lives for ever;
> That dead men rise up never;
> That even the weariest river
>   Winds somewhere safe to sea.

This is not exactly Homer or Sophocles, not exactly Stoicism or Epicureanism, though it seems to owe something to all these sources. In its echoes of the bleak, brave disillusionment that the *Iliad* and much of Greek tragedy express, and in its use of vaguely conceived pagan gods to dignify a gauntly grand agnosticism, this is not far from Thomas Hardy.

The ancient world, or parts of it, could also be depicted as a realm of unrestrained sensuality, a sort of fleshly paradise supposedly innocent of the anxieties imported by Christianity. This tendency is recurrent and obvious in Swinburne; and it is not surprising that Dowson should have associated with classical verse his swooning lyric of lust and regret, 'Non Sum Qualis Eram Bonae Sub Regno Cynarae', even though the classical element goes no further than the title, a quotation from the first ode of Horace's fourth book. More unexpected is to find a turbid eroticism in the poetry of the establishment:

> Then, then, from utter gloom stood out the breasts,
> The breasts of Helen, and hoveringly a sword
> Now over and now under, now direct,
> Pointed itself to pierce, but sank down shamed
> At all that beauty . . .

> The mountain quickens into Nymph and Faun;
> And here an Oread – how the sun delights
> To glance and shift about her slippery sides,
> And rosy knees and supple roundedness,
> And budded bosom peaks.

These passages are from Tennyson's 'Lucretius' (ll. 60–4, 187–91). The laureate's portrayal of the Roman poet as torn between his Epicurean philosophy, which taught the attainment of pure serenity, and his passionate fantasies, induced by a love potion, might be seen as dramatizing the conflict between two versions of the classical: an ideal of calm and balance, and a total immersion in the sensual.

Less overtly sensual, though in another way perhaps more risky, was the efflorescence of homoerotic (usually pederastic) verse in the later nineteenth century, written by authors who except for Wilde are now uniformly and deservedly forgotten. These poems were commonly given a Hellenic colouring, sometimes through reference to the beautiful youths in Plato's dialogues, more often through allusion to the Idylls of Theocritus. Turning from *The Ballad of Reading Gaol* to the rest of Wilde's verse, the modern reader may be struck by how derivative it is, and how thick with classical reference. This may remind us that throughout the nineteenth century classical myth remained an easy refuge for the poet without a great deal to say – a refuge to which resort was often made. We might be tempted to conclude from this that what Philip Larkin was to call the myth-kitty was already in the nineteenth century something a good poet should avoid. That would be a hasty judgement, however. In almost every age, after all, most of the poetry written is unoriginal, and what the character of lesser verse suggests, right to the end of the Victorian era, is that these poets in some respects had more in common with their predecessors across some centuries before than with their successors only half a century later: the classical inheritance, in all its variety, was still a storehouse to which one might naturally turn.

Pater, in his essay on Winckelmann later incorporated into *The Renaissance*, distinguished between the absorbed elements in our intellectual life and Hellenism, which he saw as not only an absorbed element but also a conscious attitude, deliberately revived from time to time to clarify and correct a culture. The story of the classical in Victorian poetry is one both of conscious Hellenism and of the broad classical legacy, of an inheritance absorbed into contemporary culture and of a classicism that advertises its distinctiveness. Some of the best Victorian poets are caught up in both these aspects of the classical tradition, and in the interplay between them. And while minor poets might be predictable in their use of classical themes, their more gifted contemporaries were diverse in their handling of the tradition. The story of the classical tradition in Victorian verse is not simple, therefore; but that lack of simplicity suggests how multifariously stimulating that tradition might still be to the inventiveness of some of the best talents of the time.

See also: Epic; Elegy; Poetry in Translation; Domestic and Idyllic; Marriage and Gender; Sexuality and Love.

References and Further Reading

Abbott, C. C. (ed.) (1935) *The Letters of Gerard Manley Hopkins to Robert Bridges*. London: Oxford University Press.

Anderson, W. (1965) *Matthew Arnold and the Classical Tradition*. Ann Arbor: University of Michigan Press.

Cruzalegui Sotelo, P. (1998) *L'Experiencia Platonica en l'Anglaterra del Dinou*. Barcelona: PPU.

Highet, G. (1949) *The Classical Tradition: Greek and Roman Influences on Western Literature*. London: Oxford University Press.

Jenkyns, R. (1980) *The Victorians and Ancient Greece*. Oxford: Blackwell.

Jenkyns, R. (1991) *Dignity and Decadence: Victorian Art and the Classical Inheritance*. London: Harper-Collins.

Jenkyns, R. (ed.) (1992) *The Legacy of Rome: A New Appraisal*. Oxford: Oxford University Press.

Lang, C. Y. (ed.) (1959–62) *The Swinburne Letters*. New Haven. Conn.: Yale University Press.

Redpath, T. (1981) 'Tennyson and the Literature of Greece and Rome.' In H. Tennyson (ed.). *Studies in Tennyson* (pp. 105–30). London: Macmillan.

Rudd, N. (1991) 'Two Invitations: Tennyson *To the Rev. F. D. Maurice* and Horace to Maecenas (*Odes* III. 29).' *Hermathena*, 150, 5–19.

Super, R. H. (ed.) (1960) *Matthew Arnold: On the Classical Tradition* (*The Complete Prose Works of Matthew Arnold*, vol. 1). Ann Arbor: University of Michigan Press.

Thomson, J. A. K. (1951) *Classical Influences on English Poetry*. London: Allen and Unwin.

Turner, F. (1989) 'Why the Greeks and not the Romans in Victorian Britain?' In G. W. Clarke (ed.). *Rediscovering Hellenism: The Hellenic Inheritance and the English Imagination* (pp. 61–81). Cambridge: Cambridge University Press.

Vance, N. (1997) *The Victorians and Ancient Rome*. Oxford: Blackwell.

13

Arthurian Poetry
and Medievalism

Antony H. Harrison

Studies since 1970 – by Alice Chandler, Mark Girouard, Raymond Chapman, R. J. Smith, Jerome Mitchell, and others – have demonstrated that the term 'Victorian medievalism' describes more than a widespread social phenomenon. From the late eighteenth century onward, a strong interest in medieval history and all things medieval, in fact, generated a multivalent cultural discourse that had permeated the conceptual life and practical behaviour of English men and women well before the debacle of the Eglinton Tournament in 1838, and continued to do so at least until the end of World War I. By the early Victorian period a reified language of medievalism was current and visible in politics, literature, art, architecture, theology, love-making and popular entertainments. It was characterized by a specialized vocabulary, a distinctive iconography and the use of particular literary genres (historical novels, ballads, narrative romances, love lyrics), and it involved a network of value-laden associations. This coded discourse was especially attractive to many writers, and their adaptations or appropriations of it can be seen to have generated particular ideological effects. Well before mid-century, medievalist discourse was universally understood and commonly employed by educated individuals. It was in this respect comparable, perhaps, to the discourses of political economy and evangelical Protestantism. Medievalist discourse employed an array of conceptual terms that denoted particular belief systems and modes of conduct wholly integrated into middle- and upper-class culture: chivalry, manliness, selflessness, gallantry, nobility, honour, duty and fidelity (to the crown as well as to a beloved). This discourse also promulgated a belief in the spiritual power of love and in the positive moral influence of women. Such ideals were either formulated explicitly or understood implicitly in terms of medieval literature, mythology and iconography. As Mark Girouard has demonstrated, they are everywhere embedded in Victorian literature, painting, architecture and religious documents, which frequently employ the language of chivalry, courtly love and Gothicism, as well as materials from Arthurian mythology and pre-Reformation Catholicism.

We may begin to enter the field of social relations in which Victorian medievalism participated by analysing the settings, form, style, content and ideological effects of much Victorian poetry. Verse that can be viewed as 'medievalist' was written and published by nearly every canonical poet of the era (and by many non-canonical figures as well), from

Alfred, Lord Tennyson, Robert Browning and Matthew Arnold to the central Pre-Raphaelite poets – Dante and Christina Rossetti, William Morris and A. C. Swinburne – and even to Thomas Hardy (e.g. 'Copying Architecture in an Old Minster') and Elizabeth Barrett Browning, who often none the less deprecated the use of archaic settings by contemporary poets.

A good deal of medievalist poetry written relatively early in Victoria's reign – E. B. Browning's ballads 'The Romaunt of Margaret' and 'The Romaunt of the Page', for instance, or Tennyson's 'Morte D'Arthur' and 'The Lady of Shalott' – can be seen to emerge from the medievalist revival begun during the late eighteenth century and carried into the Romantic period in the fiction of Sir Walter Scott, in popular ballads, and in poems such as Keats's 'The Eve of St Agnes' or Coleridge's 'Christabel'. Yet what distinguishes much Victorian medievalist verse (even the early work) from poetry that preceded it is the social and political force of its ideological operations.

One of the greatest (and longest) Arthurian poems of the period serves as a useful initial example. The first version of Tennyson's *Idylls of the King*, consisting of 'Enid', 'Vivien', 'Elaine' and 'Guinevere', was published by Moxon & Co. in July of 1859. Forty thousand copies of the first edition were issued. Ten thousand copies sold within six weeks, and the demand was so great that a second edition was needed within six months. By the time the second series of *Idylls* came out in 1869, six more editions had been produced (Hagen 1979: 109–10). The extraordinarily wide dissemination of this poem may be explained by the convergence of a popular author and popular subject matter in a cultural project that benefited from the public's engagement with both. As a thus notable specimen of medievalist discourse in mid-Victorian England, the *Idylls* provides a text against which we can graph the ideological operations of other poetry that appropriates medieval settings, language or literary forms over a period of a quarter century, from the publication of Matthew Arnold's *Tristram and Iseult* (1852) to the appearance of Swinburne's 'Ballad of Francois Villon' in 1878.

Tennyson's work best illustrates what might be described as a traditionalist and conservative engagement with medievalist discourse in mid-Victorian England. Like so many poets who were his contemporaries, including Arnold, Browning, Swinburne, Morris and the Rossettis, Tennyson discovered the usefulness of medievalist topoi early in his career, having written by 1833 important poems like the 'Morte d'Arthur' (published in 1842) and 'The Lady of Shalott' (1832, revised 1842). (In this respect he resembles earlier prose writers as diverse as Sir Walter Scott, Richard Hurd and Kenelm Digby.) For the next forty years Tennyson continued to deploy the discourse of medievalism. From 1833 to 1885 he wrote Arthurian poems, most of them finally assembled into his Arthurian epic, *Idylls of the King*, which appeared in its 'completed' form in 1888. Setting this long and immensely popular work by the poet laureate against other poetic manipulations of medievalist motifs, vocabulary and iconography in mid-Victorian England affirms Michel Foucault's assertion that any ostensibly unified discursive formation, such as medievalism, is actually a colloquy of 'irruptive' voices. Analysis of medievalist works by William Morris, Matthew Arnold, Dante Rossetti and A. C. Swinburne further demonstrates how these poets, like Tennyson, employ a culturally pervasive discourse so as to achieve varied ideological effects through which their work acquires cultural power.

In 1862 Tennyson dedicated the newest edition of his first four *Idylls* to the memory of Victoria's beloved Prince Albert, setting up specific political and ideological contexts for the poem as a whole. The laureate resurrects Albert as an incarnation of Arthurian perfection: 'He seems to me / Scarce other than my [Arthur's] ideal knight':

> modest, kindly, all-accomplish'd, wise,
> With what sublime repression of himself,
> And in what limits, and how tenderly;
> Not swaying to this faction or to that;
> Not making his high place the lawless perch
> Of wing'd ambitions, nor a vantage-ground
> For pleasure; but thro' all this tract of years
> Wearing the white flower of a blameless life,
> Before a thousand peering littlenesses.

This description, with its emphasis on Albert's selflessness, presents Victoria's influential consort as a politically neutral ideality. 'A lovelier life, more unstained than his', the narrator claims, is unimaginable. Albert, father of England's future kings, is harbinger of an 'ampler day' in Tennyson's perfectibilian system of beliefs. 'Laborious for [the land's] people and her poor', he is seen as the 'Far-sighted summoner of War and Waste / To fruitful strifes and rivalries of peace', possessing a 'Sweet nature gilded by the gracious gleam / Of letters'. He is therefore 'dear to Science, dear to Art, / Dear to thy land and ours, a Prince indeed, / Beyond all titles.'

In this dedication and throughout the *Idylls* Tennyson presents an array of positive values that he associates with Arthur's Camelot as natural, inevitable, unquestionable and absolute – as non-ideological, in fact. None the less, the sentimental and romantic image of Albert he foregrounds here and the idealizations of Arthur deployed throughout the body of his poem operate as ideology usually does: the systems of value and belief they support are assumed to be valid, generally accepted and, in the case of this poem, divinely sanctioned. Tennyson could succeed with such an assumption because the ideological formulae that operated as subtexts for medievalist discourse in Victorian England were fundamental to the process of middle- and upper-class socialization. Tennyson directly articulates these formulae in 'Guinevere'.

In this stridently anti-feminist idyll, Arthur comes to the nunnery at Glastonbury where Guinevere had retreated after her public exposure as an adulteress. War (between the king and Lancelot, as well as the king and Modred's forces) is destroying Camelot. Arthur ostensibly makes this journey to affirm his love for Guinevere despite events, but he first upbraids her mercilessly, reminding her that she has ravaged 'that fair Order of my Table Round, / A glorious company . . . To serve as model for the mighty world'. Rehearsing the oaths his knights swore, Tennyson through Arthur ventriloquizes a system of values and a code of conduct so prevalent in Victorian England that varied forms of medievalist discourse automatically elicited them. These values and behaviours constituted an essential horizon of

expectations for educated readers, and Arthur reinscribes them in a litany of infinitive constructions that point towards the ideal of a perfected (albeit amorphous) sociality. Arthur's
knights promised, as all true, strong and good Englishmen presumably should:

> To reverence the King, as if he were
> Their conscience, and their conscience as their King,
> To break the heathen and uphold the Christ,
> To ride abroad redressing human wrongs.
> To speak no slander, no, nor listen to it,
> To honour his own word as if his God's,
> To lead sweet lives in purest chastity,
> To love one maiden only, cleave to her,
> And worship her by years of noble deeds,
> Until they won her; for indeed I knew
> Of no more subtle master under heaven
> Than is the maiden passion for a maid,
> Not only to keep down the base in man,
> But teach high thought, and amiable words
> And courtliness, and the desire of fame,
> And love of truth, and all that makes a man.

This passage is worth quoting at length because it so visibly adapts the discourse of
medievalism to advocate an historically particular, that is, mid-Victorian, network of values
widely accepted by the middle and upper classes. Quite obviously, it valorizes Christianity
as, implicitly, the exclusive domain of truth and honour. In the political arena it promul-
gates an alliance between monarchy and religion (conscience) that sanctions imperialism
('to break the heathen'). By association with Christianity and by means of authoritative tes-
timonial (Arthur's), it asserts the ultimate value of desexualized love in the service of self-
reformation (keeping down 'the base in man') and summons a host of abstract, politically
manipulable ideals: 'high thought', 'amiable words', 'love of truth' and, most strikingly,
'all that makes a man'. Here women exist as chaste ciphers to serve the patriarchy in its
pursuit of goals ('courtliness' and 'the desire of fame') that will sustain and reaffirm an elitist
power structure in society. In this passage, but also throughout *Idylls of the King*, Tennyson
adopts medievalist discourse in the service of Tory social, political and religious values.

   William Morris's 'The Defence of Guenevere', from *The Defence of Guenevere and Other
Poems* published in 1858, provides an apposite contrast to the laureate's highly popular epic
because it is fraught with ideologically emergent elements. 'The Defence of Guenevere'
manipulates the dramatic monologue form and plays upon typical Victorian expectations
of medievalist discourse, including those Tennyson's poem sanctions, in order to challenge them. The poem is both formally and – by the dominant mid-Victorian standards – morally 'impure'. Its dramatic monologue form is 'sullied' by the insertion, at
strategic moments during Guenevere's speech, of a narrator who serves to clarify and
enforce the explosive ideological effects of both her self-presentation and the poet's
presentation of her as a physically, emotionally and intellectually seductive icon. The

elements of Morris's poem thus constitute a series of irruptions in the dominant values attached to medievalist discourse by mid-Victorian audiences, as these might be measured by the ideological effects of Tennyson's first four *Idylls of the King*.

'The Defence of Guenevere' is an epiphanic poem that draws readers into it through the use of a culturally familiar discourse, only to awaken them to the illusory idealizations purveyed in that discourse. The poem counters Victorian ideals of manliness (derived from medieval codes of chivalry) by making Guenevere a genuine heroine. About to be burned at the stake, she delivers a monologue that sanctions sexual passion rather than chastity. She distracts her audience of knights with blatant sexual displays, denies the authority of kingship, interrogates divine justice, and exposes the self-interested hypocrisy of 'chivalrous' behaviour and 'respectable' public morality.

Unlike Tennyson's Arthur, Morris's narrator sees Guenevere as both heroic and victimized. Her monologue displays her bravery, admired at every turn: 'Though still she stood right up, and never shrunk, / But spoke on bravely, glorious lady fair!' Guenevere perceives her own performance in chivalric terms, as well: '"So, ever must I dress me to the fight"', she murmurs at one turning point in the poem. As a uniquely female combatant, however, her best weapon is her beauty, which she flaunts, playing upon the traditional medievalist equation of beauty with virtue. Standing at the stake, wet and apparently naked, she repeatedly taunts her audience (both the knights and Victorian male readers) with the irony of that equation, 'passionately twisting . . . her body there'. Recalling the day of her first meeting with Lancelot, she confides seductively, '"I dared not think, as I was wont to do, / Sometimes, upon my beauty"', which she invites her audience to enjoy. '"[I]f I had / Held out my long hand up against the blue"', she gestures:

> 'And, looking on the tenderly darken'd fingers,
> Thought that by rights one ought to see quite through,
> There, see you, where the soft still light yet lingers,
> Round the edges; what should I have done,
> If this had joined with yellow spotted singers,
> And startling green drawn upward by the sun?
> But shouting, loosed out, see now! all my hair.'

She continues the seduction relentlessly, often interrupting her own argument that she is 'better than innocent'. Near the conclusion of the poem, she performs onanistically:

> 'See my breast rise,
> Like waves of purple sea, as here I stand;
> And how my arms are moved in wonderful wise . . .
> See through my long throat how the words go up
> In ripples to my mouth.'

The poem's explicit challenge to the Victorian equation between virtue and medievalist discourse appears at this crux in her monologue: 'will you dare . . . / To say this thing is vile?' she rhetorically asks the mesmerized knights.

Not once does Morris's Guenevere deny her infidelity. Rather she portrays all sexual passion as natural and irresistible, comparing its effect to slipping '"slowly down some path worn smooth and even, / Down to a cool sea on a summer day"'. Reaching that haven, one feels 'strange new joy' and a sense of purgation. The 'worn head' lay:

> 'Back, with the hair like sea-weed; yea all past
> Sweat of the forehead, dryness of the lips,
> Washed utterly out by the dear waves o'ercast.'

Through her seductive performance, Guenevere compels her auditors' awareness of their own irrepressible sexual energies. She makes a special example of her accuser, Gauwaine, whose 'dear pity' for her, she observes, '"creeps / All through [his] frame, and trembles in [his] mouth"'. Moreover, he is guilty, too, of moral and sexual hypocrisy, she insists, through association with his mother, whose infidelity elicited '"Agravaine's fell blow"' – '"her head sever'd in that awful drouth / of pity"' called revenge.

Guenevere further deflates the self-righteous behaviour of her accusers and the chivalric code they follow with the example of Mellyagraunce, the 'stripper of ladies' who discovered blood from Lancelot's tourney wounds on Guenevere's sheets and publicly denounced the adultery. This timid knight, however, would accept Lancelot's challenge of a trial by arms only when Lancelot agreed to fight 'half-arm'd' and with his 'left side all uncovered'. Divine justice reduced Mellyagraunce to 'a spout of blood on the hot sand.' Guenevere has, none the less, already challenged and perplexed accepted notions of such justice. At the beginning of her monologue she compares her choice between Arthur and Lancelot to an arbitrary but forced decision between two deceptively symbolic cloths: trying to be dutiful – choosing the blue cloth of 'heaven's colour', rather than the red one – leads to her damnation. This is in part because of Arthur's inadequacy as a husband. Unlike Tennyson's would-be saviour of the world, Morris's Arthur is a philistine, out of touch with animating and salving natural passions, who 'bought' Guenevere with 'his great name and his little love'.

'The Defence of Guenevere' thus appropriates the dramatic monologue form and transposes the standard materials of medievalist discourse to undercut the conservative, patriarchal ideology typically identified with it. Here Christian values are supplanted by erotic ones, chivalry is a fraud, and Christian ideals of virtue are displaced by ideals of amoral beauty, sexual indulgence and political subversiveness as these are displayed in the heroic person of Guenevere and in her adulterous relationship with Lancelot, who predictably comes to the rescue in the poem's final lines.

'The Defence of Guenevere' failed as cultural intervention at the time of its publication. Most of those who read the poem and the volume in which it appeared in 1858 found it so radical, both ideologically and formally, that they simply did not know what to make of it. The *Saturday Review* spoke for such readers in describing Morris's work as 'not like anything we ever saw'. Only the reviewer for the *Tablet* found in it what later readers did: 'power everywhere' (Lindsay 1975: 97). For subsequent generations this first poem of Morris's first volume became his best-known and most influential work, and eventually the collective efficacy of his writings led to his canonization among Victorian poets.

The ideological strategies of work by such poets becomes institutionalized in the apparatuses that perpetually reinforce and reconstruct cultural values: it is memorized in classrooms, anthologized in textbooks and display books, discussed in periodical literature and strategically positioned in political speeches, for example. Effective poets *are* seen, as Thomas Carlyle insisted on seeing them, as heroes and visionaries. Great claims are made for their value in the social world, as W. B. Yeats demonstrates in the case of Morris, and such claims are largely based on the ideological effects of their poetry. In his essay 'The Happiest of the Poets', Yeats insists that Morris's 'mind was illuminated from within and lifted into prophecy in the full right sense of the word, and he saw the natural things he was alone gifted to see in their perfect form' (Yeats 1961: 62). In Yeats's commentary on Morris we also come to understand how the ideological effects of poetry (through its embeddedness in a variety of media) can be practical and immense: in ways rarely applicable to writers of fiction, the ideals poets promulgate are seen to transcend, but also to *overtake*, the realities those ideals challenge. As Yeats asserts, Morris 'knew as Shelley knew . . . that the economists should take their measurements not from life as it is, but from the vision of men like him' (Yeats 1961: 63).

As I have attempted to demonstrate, in the Arthurian works of Morris and Tennyson such amatory and religious, or erotic and spiritual, impulses as often dominate both medieval and Victorian medievalist poetry are reconcilable. In Tennyson's work the suppression of lust facilitates Christian virtue and 'civilized' behaviour. In Morris's poem, passionate self-expression enables psychological health, 'joy' and personal fulfilment. A number of other important Victorian poets, however, employ medievalist discourse in a manner that argues for the opposition between love and religion. Among them are Matthew Arnold, Christina and Dante Rossetti, A. C. Swinburne, E. B. Browning and Thomas Hardy, for example, whose works' various manipulations of the topoi, iconography and terminology of medievalism result in special ideological effects when they appropriate this traditional dialectic.

Poems by three of these writers (Arnold, D. G. Rossetti and Swinburne), all published between 1852 and 1870, demonstrate how medievalist discourse appears to have set the terms for a mid-century dialogue among Victorian poets concerning the vexed relations, and difficult choices to be made, between love and faith. Significantly, the poems I will discuss by Arnold (*Tristram and Iseult* and 'Dover Beach') and Rossetti ('The Blessed Damozel') were conceived and initially composed during or soon after a period in Europe characterized by near political chaos, and in Britain by great social turmoil reflected in the highly public debates surrounding the franchise and the cause of improved conditions for the working classes. Such debates were often focused on the Chartist Movement (1838–48). In poems by Arnold and Rossetti that exploited the language and iconography of Victorian medievalism, however, the political discourse surrounding events in England and the conflicts in Europe became either refocused (in Arnold's work) or altogether elided (in Rossetti's) so as to privilege a concern with spiritual and aesthetic matters (love, faith, art). The ideological effect of such strategies was to devalue activity in the sociopolitical world and open up discursive spaces through which readers might achieve the illusion of transcending that world (as was the case with Yeats's response to Morris).

In a letter to Herbert Hill written on 5 November 1852, Arnold acknowledged that his plan for *Tristram and Iseult*, published in 1852, had been conceived during one of his two trips to Thun in September 1848 and September 1849. Arnold explains:

> I read the story . . . some years ago at Thun in an article in a French Review on the romance literature: I had never met with it before, and it fastened upon me: when I got back to England I looked at the Morte d'Arthur and took what I could, but the poem was in the main formed, and I could not well disturb it. (Lang 1996: 247)

This episode from 'romance literature' clearly provided a distraction for Arnold from the explosive political events going on around him.

In the months prior to Arnold's first visit, Europe was politically chaotic: revolutionary activity had broken out in Sicily in January, in Paris on 24 February, and in Germany and Italy in March. With the fall of Metternich, Austria was in the throes of political disintegration, and the Russians were preparing for war. In April war broke out between Germany and Poland. By the spring of the following year, matters had not improved. In March 1849, Sardinia renewed its war against Austria. By 30 April, French forces had clashed with Garibaldi's republican troops. (Although Louis Napoleon's true intentions remain uncertain, on 31 May the Roman republic accepted French protection.) In April, as well, Austrian and Hungarian forces became embattled, and in July Russian troops moved to occupy Moldavia and Wallachia to quash the stirrings of a revolutionary movement there. Russia's actions precipitated the reopening of the Eastern question and resulted in negotiations for an alliance between England and France, which were concluded in October 1849. On 6 October Britain ordered its Mediterranean fleet to proceed to the neighbourhood of the Dardanelles.

For Matthew Arnold, at the time secretary to Lord Lansdowne, who, as Whig elder statesman, was in the thick of English political activity, these events would have been of great moment. From Thun on 23 September Arnold wrote a letter to Arthur Hugh Clough expressing a fear that, on his return to England, he would be unable to maintain any distance from the chaotic swirl of political activity surrounding him: 'When I come to town', he laments, 'I tell you beforehand I will have a real effort at managing myself as to newspapers and the talk of the day' (Lang 1996: 156). Arnold's poetry composed during this period, in fact, became a vehicle for the repudiation of 'the talk of the day' and the sociopolitical issues privileged by such discourse.

Typically, Arnold's verse is elegiac, a poetry of lost love or lost faith. But uniquely for his personae love and faith often appear to be interchangeable spiritual impulses: in Arnold's work love is drained of its eroticism and faith of its asceticism. Much of his poetry laments the permanent loss of both, as does the plaintive narrative voice in an ideologically central passage from *Tristram and Iseult*:

> 'tis the gradual furnace of the world,
> In whose hot air our spirits are upcurl'd
> Until they crumble, or else grow like steel –
> Which kills in us the bloom of youth, the spring –
> Which leaves the fierce necessity to feel,
> But takes away the power – this can avail,
> By drying up our joy in everything,
> To make our former pleasures all seem stale.
> This, or some tyrannous single thought, some fit
> Of passion, which subdues our souls to it,
> Till for its sake alone we live and move –
> Call it ambition, or remorse, or love –
> This too can change us wholly, and make seem
> All which we did before, shadow and dream.

As is common in Arnold's poetry of this period, this passage employs generalized metaphors which at once suggest and disguise an array of urgent public issues and refocus the discourse that would normally attach to them. These lines employ a notably industrial metaphor – 'the gradual furnace of the world' that either chars spirits or refines them as 'steel' – so as to condemn involvement in the external world of economic competition and labour that metaphor suggests. But his narrator's acknowledgement that a single (internal) obsession – ambition, love, remorse – can equally destroy us implies through an ironic reversal that the prepossession with escape from social (and implicitly political and economic) reality may have the power to reduce that reality to illusion – 'shadow and dream' – and thereby restore the spirit's access to 'joy'.

Arnold's *Tristram* is a formally hybrid medievalist poem about the fatality of love, but ultimately about the inevitability of spiritual unfulfilment. As we have seen, Arnold's central metaphor – the 'furnace of the world' – locates his critique historically. The experience of spiritual debility he deplores, like 'this strange disease of modern life' lamented in 'The Scholar-Gipsy', is uniquely the effect of the industrial revolution.

Tristram and Iseult, like Morris's 'Defence of Guenevere', is ideologically oppositional, and in a variety of ways. From its opening, where we find Tristram already on his deathbed, the poem formally undercuts traditional versions of the Tristram myth. He is fading in and out of consciousness, taunted by memories and yearning for the irrecoverable past while tenuously hoping for the arrival of Irish Iseult. This 'peerless hunter, harper, knight' is no longer heroic but pathetic. The story Arnold narrates is Iseult of Brittany's tragedy, not Tristram's, and it is one that altogether challenges the value of romantic love. The 'spring-time' of Tristram's fatal passion:

> Is already gone and past,
> And instead thereof is seen
> Its winter, which endureth still.

He is tormented by 'a secret in his breast / Which will never let him rest' – unable even in his dreams of the past 'to get free / From the clog of misery'. And in the present, when

Irish Iseult arrives, no joy resurges. We find only that 'both have suffer'd / Both have pass'd a youth consumed and sad', and 'both have brought their anxious day to evening, / And have now short space for being glad!' Like Tristram, Irish Iseult has been tortured rather than fulfilled by her love, described as a 'longing' that 'dogg'd by fear and fought by shame / Shook her weak bosom day and night', devouring 'her beauty like a flame'.

Arnold none the less does not use this medieval story of victimized lovers to illustrate the evils of erotic indulgence or to advocate self-suppression and chastity, as Tennyson would do a few years later in his *Idylls*. Iseult of Brittany, for all her wholesomeness, fares no better than the lovers united by the fatal draught: 'Joy has not found her yet, nor ever will'. Her noble and selfless devotion to Tristram has produced a 'fatigued' woman 'dying in a mask of youth'. Love, variously idealized in medievalist discourse, is here denounced and repudiated altogether, presumably in favour of emotional detachment from experience, a philosophical approach to life that Arnold promotes everywhere in his major poems and prose works. His narrator is vitriolic in attacking amatory ideals because they exemplify 'tyrannous single thoughts' that ruin human lives:

> And yet, I swear, it angers me to see
> How this fool passion gulls men potently;
> Being, in truth, but a diseased unrest,
> How they are full of languor and distress
> Not having it; which when they do possess,
> They straightway are burnt up with fume and care,
> And spend their lives in posting here and there
> Where this plague drives them.

Thus, Arnold's *Tristram* exploits a medieval topos and setting to disparage in generalized but absolute terms the 'furnace' of a world in which fulfilment is unattainable through the usual channels. The pursuit of love (like Tristram's) is as fruitless as the pursuit of fame (illustrated by the examples of 'bald Caesar' and 'Alexander, Philip's peerless son'). Religious faith is, similarly, not available as a source of fulfilment. Although described as 'The sweetest Christian soul alive', Britannic Iseult remains unrewarded for her devotion. This poem implicitly adopts a stance of secular nihilism, and that stance is patently ideological. Its deep pessimism requires a repudiation not only of the materialist, utilitarian, perfectibilian, amatory and Christian values embraced by many middle- and upper class Victorians of the period (including Tennyson), but also of the spiritual illusions proffered by the Romantics, especially Wordsworth, as alternatives to those values. This poem in fact propounds a transvalued Byronic ideology of defiant martyrdom, a self-assertive 'ideology against ideology' that is also central to Arnold's other major compositions of the late 1840s and early 1850s, including 'Dover Beach', a work seldom thought of as medievalist.

Probably composed about the same time as *Tristram and Iseult*, this dramatic monologue more directly acknowledges its political subtexts: these are suggested by the famous concluding image of its speaker hearing 'confused alarms of struggle and flight, / Where ignorant armies clash by night' across the English channel. But this image signals a retreat from the political world, rather than engagement with it, and Arnold appropriates the dramatic monologue form here to assault other frameworks of value dominant in mid-Victorian England than those challenged in Morris's 'Defence of Guenevere'. A lament for lost spiritual certainties, 'Dover Beach' presents as its central metaphor the medieval 'Sea of Faith', which was once 'at the full, and round earth's shore / Lay like the folds of a bright girdle furl'd' – a reference to the widespread Victorian belief that spiritual life in pre-Reformation Europe was harmonious. (By 1867, when 'Dover Beach' was first published, Victorian audiences would be able to recall at least two familiar touchstones for such a belief in Carlyle's *Past and Present* and Ruskin's 'The Nature of Gothic'.) The speaker in 'Dover Beach', whose voice is more forceful than that of the narrator of *Tristram and Iseult*, employs this metaphor to decry the intellectual, moral and spiritual chaos of the modern world mirrored in political conflicts also rendered metaphorically. He does so – cleverly – by feinting to idealize the religious harmony of medieval Europe ('a land of dreams'). However, this move serves primarily to explode ideals – 'joy', 'love', 'light', 'certitude', 'peace' – that Victorians like Carlyle and Ruskin ascribed to medieval culture and then attempted to transpose onto their own.

According to this poem, whatever spiritually unifying and redemptive effects the medieval church may have had are long gone, existing in idealized histories only to highlight the modern world's pervasive insufficiencies. The withdrawal of the Sea of Faith, re-enacted here as the poem exposes illusions among its Victorian audience that medievalist idealities can recur, horribly reveals 'the vast edges drear / And naked shingles of the world'. The only ideal that remains for Arnold's persona turns out to be intellectual commitment: to a realistic view of the world to be mutually held as a bond between himself and his auditor, his 'love' (and implicitly, between Arnold and his reader). The monologue's dramatic situation, with its manipulation of the props of traditional romantic liaisons, is employed strictly in the service of such a worldview:

> Ah, love, let us be true
> To one another! for the world, which seems
> To lie before us like a land of dreams,
> So various, so beautiful, so new,
> Hath really neither joy, nor love, nor light,
> Nor certitude, nor peace, nor help for pain;
> And we are here as on a darkling plain
> Swept with confused alarms of struggle and flight,
> Where ignorant armies clash by night.

'Dover Beach' here brings two prominent Victorian discursive formations – medievalist and amatory – into collision so as, ultimately, to oppose both and to affirm one variety of anti-social solipsism. As in Arnold's *Tristram*, self-affirmation in defiance of the illusory optimisms propagated by 'the world' (whether under the sign of love or under the sign of faith) is an ideological stance, specifically a reversion to the iconoclastic impetus behind Romanticism, but one that disallows the ultimately compensatory ideologies formulated by all the major English Romantic poets except Byron.

Like Arnold, Dante Rossetti in his most famous poem, 'The Blessed Damozel', is concerned with the relations between love and faith. Originally drafted in 1847, when Rossetti was 19, the poem was not widely read until its publication in his *Poems* (1870). Unlike Arnold's work of the late 1840s and early 1850s, 'The Blessed Damozel' (like the other medievalist poems of the 1870 volume) fully elides the historical contexts of its composition, focusing its action, image patterns and emotional field in the discourses of medievalism and romantic love. These discourses in the poem engage, subsume and usurp Christianity, implicit as an alternate discursive formation, and they generate Rossetti's well-known, literal conceptualization of a Heaven of Love. The poem thus creates an imaginative space that challenges the sociopolitical space in which he (and Arnold and every European of the era) actually lived.

During the course of Rossetti's early career, his fervent interest in international politics gave way to an obsession with art in which struggles for power are none the less implicated. The formation of the Pre-Raphaelite Brotherhood, with its own aesthetic manifesto (espoused in the poems and prose of the *Germ*, in which Rossetti first published 'The Blessed Damozel'), for instance, self-consciously challenged the dominant, official schools of art in England, especially the Royal Academy. But increasingly for Rossetti, art became the site of the only variety of power worth having in the world, because it allowed access to and provided mirrors of human psychological and emotional realities that he believed were of ultimate interest to all people, fully engaged in the sociopolitical world or not. That is, Rossetti as an eminently modern artist appears to have understood the necessity of estrangement from industrial society to survive life in it meaningfully. The ideological effects of his work demonstrate that a kind of social power can be accrued through an art of defamiliarization, and he was able to produce such art by developing highly complex strategies of parody.

In 'The Blessed Damozel' of 1870, for instance, Rossetti appropriates medievalizing language and iconography parodically. The poem interrogates the relations between erotic and religious impulses, using a tone that fluctuates between the serious and the ludicrous. In appropriating specific semiotic features of medievalist discourse the poem destabilizes the language, image patterns and conceptual frameworks of both conventional courtly love literature and traditional Christianity, especially orthodox concepts of the afterlife. Such features include numerological symbolism (the 'three lilies' in the Damozel's hand, the 'seven stars' in her hair, the 'lady' Mary's 'five handmaidens'); linguistic archaisms ('damozel' and 'aureole'); emblematic image patterns (the 'white rose of Mary's gift'; the 'Dove' whose 'plumes' touch 'every leaf' of 'That living mystic tree'); direct references to medieval musical instruments ('citherns and citholes'); and mention of 'God's choristers' that recalls medieval concepts of the music of the spheres. But as these elements of the poem become focused exclusively on its erotic drama, rather than on the spiritual values implicit in the language employed to 'decorate' that drama, they are drained of traditional Christian meaning.

In effect the poem presents a Heaven which exists only in the language of physical desire. But even the credibility of amatory impulses that dominate the poem is undercut, because their value is so exaggerated that they overtake the religious system of beliefs they normally subserve in familiar medieval literature, from the *Romance of the Rose* to Dante's *Vita Nuova*. Rossetti's parodic procedures in this poem are not primarily iconoclastic, however; they do not serve to subvert serious Christian and Petrarchan values that might be held by his audience. Rather, they draw attention to the conceptual silliness of the poem itself, which must be viewed, ultimately, as a hyper-artificial construct, a seductive and ornate bricolage and conflation of pre-existing ideologies. In the final analysis, 'The Blessed Damozel', like Rossetti's painting on the subject, presents itself as an aesthetic object that refuses any ideological commitment – to courtly love values or to medievalizing religious belief – that a reader might normally expect of such a work. Appropriation of these traditions in the poem instead projects an aesthetic ideal in whose service other value systems and varied modes of discourse might be exploited.

If Rossetti's poetry aestheticizes medievalist discourse, Swinburne's, by contrast, manipulates it iconoclastically, both to counter what he perceived as false idealizations of the Middle Ages in his contemporary culture and to attack the 'respectable' – that is, Christian, politically conservative and materialist – values he saw as dominant in Victorian society. Typically in Swinburne's poetry, relations between faith and love break down. In familiar works from his *Poems and Ballads* (first series, 1866) that privilege medieval contexts or motifs – such as 'In the Orchard', 'The Triumph of Time', the 'Hymn to Proserpine', 'Laus Veneris' and 'The Leper' – an elegiac faith in the supreme power and value of erotic love in human lives supplants all varieties of traditional Christian religious faith, whose hostility to eros Swinburne consistently reviles. In many of these poems the only indications that devotees of eros live in a world dominated by Christianity are profane and even sexually suggestive uses of God's, or the Virgin Mary's, name.

'In the Orchard', for example, imitates the Provençal alba or aubade, a medieval lyric form in which two illicit lovers lament the approach of dawn and their imminent parting. But the poem is also a dramatic monologue, a form comfortingly familiar to Victorian audiences by 1866. Swinburne's strategy of formal hybridization is deceptive, however; the poem employs both the form and the topos to ideologically oppositional ends, extolling the power of erotic love as a challenge to love of God, while appropriating and transvaluing the imagery of romantic naturalism in the service of that exaltation. The poem further compels Victorian readers viscerally to confront the power of sexuality in human lives, and it does so both explicitly and through the use of puns. All this is accomplished in the space of fifty lines.

Initially the poem overturns traditional gender roles: the entire lyric is spoken by a woman who commands her 'fair lord' to 'take . . . my flower, my first in June, / My rose, so like a tender mouth'. In her refrain this woman – clearly a medieval chatelaine, rather than a Victorian angel in the house – not only invokes God's name blasphemously, but also suggests a belief that God is a force opposed to her passion, like the implacable dawn: 'Ah God, ah God, that day should be so soon'. Otherwise in the work, the operations of nature are analogous to the operations of human passion, and its elements appear to exist solely to serve lovers' needs:

> The grass is thick and cool, it lets us lie.
> Kissed upon either cheek and either eye,
> > I turn to thee as some green afternoon
> Turns toward sunset, and is loth to die.

At the heart of the poem – and at its structural centre – is an apotheosis of erotic love's inescapable power: passion is ultimately insatiable, and can be quelled only in death. 'Ah', the speaker sighs:

> > my heart fails, my blood draws back; I know,
> > When life runs over, life is near to go;
> > > And with the slain of love love's ways are strewn,
> > And with their blood, if love will have it so.

'Do thy will now; slay me if thou wilt', she concludes, but not without a punningly explicit thrust at a prudish audience, designed to raise their sexual consciousness: 'Yea, with thy sweet lips, with thy sweet sword; yea, / Take life and all, for I will die, I say'. Despite such playfulness, the poem's framework of values is clear and serious: 'Love, I gave love, is life a better boon?' the chatelaine rhetorically asks.

Swinburne's use of medievalist discourse is usually more complex, scholarly and sophisticated than that of his contemporaries. In addition to writing many medievalist lyrics and composing two long Arthurian narratives in the epic tradition (*Tristram of Lyonesse*, 1882, and *The Tale of Balen*, 1896), Swinburne produced ideologically skewed translations of works by the single medieval poet he acclaims as the equal of Sappho and as the pre-eminent balladist of the period, François Villon. In these translations, as well as his elegiac celebration of Villon's genius in 'The Ballad of François Villon' (1878), common high Victorian uses of medievalist discourse are turned against themselves, everywhere undercutting the moral values and ideological expectations of his audience. Swinburne idealizes Villon on the grounds of both his skill as a poet and his unsavouriness as a character: what most Victorian readers would have seen as the scandalousness of his work is for Swinburne in part the source of its greatness. In the '*Envoi*' to his ballad, Swinburne eulogizes the 'Prince of sweet songs made out of tears and fire' whom 'Love reads out first at head of all our quire'. Yet Villon could succeed as the 'poor perfect voice' of medieval love poetry only because, according to Swinburne's mythography, 'A harlot was thy nurse, a God thy sire', that is, because of the depth and height of his amatory experience. Just as in the infamous 'Dolores' Swinburne parodies the Victorian revival of medieval hymns (in translations and editions generated by high Anglican churchmen such as R. C. Trench and J. M. Neale), so in his canonization of Villon he affronts respectable bourgeois values and sensibilities that Victorian medievalist discourse such as that employed by Tennyson most often served to reaffirm. He had done much the same thing earlier, albeit with tongue in cheek, in his poem 'The Leper', supposedly based on a medieval event recorded in the *Grandes Chroniques de France*, 1505. (The medieval French excerpt from the *Chroniques* that accompanies the poem was, however, an invention of Swinburne himself.) In 1866 the ideological shock value of this monologue, spoken by a necrophiliac lover caressing the body of his 'lady' (dead from leprosy) and chanting the praises of eros ('Nothing is better, I well think, / Than love'), would have been considerably greater than it is even today.

Thus, like Arnold's and Rossetti's poems, Swinburne's often deployed Victorian medievalist discourse to definable ends. While in Arnold's poetry medieval allusions and settings enabled defiant self-assertion in a chaotic and meaningless world, and Rossetti's poems exploited medievalist props to draw attention to the power and beauty of artistic surfaces, Swinburne's appropriated medieval literary genres and settings to extol erotic love – rather than the repressive Christian God – as the ultimate power in the human world.

Analysis of Victorian medievalist poems, whether by Tennyson, Morris, Arnold, Rossetti or Swinburne, supports Michel Foucault's claim that a text 'constructs itself only on the basis of a complex field of discourse'. That is, 'the frontiers of a book are never clear-cut . . . [I]t is caught up in a system of references . . . it is a node within a network' (Foucault 1972: 23). Like so many of his contemporaries, from Gerard Genette to Julia Kristeva, Foucault understood how the intertextual operations of discursive formations such as Victorian medievalism serve to communicate subtle or overt ideological positions. Such discourses are often employed in ways that influence or alter the field of social relations in which ideologies invariably compete for dominance. On the battlefield of Victorian poetry, conservative and elitist values – Christian, materialist and imperialist like those of the poet laureate – were often under siege by emergent or competing systems of belief such as those here discussed in the work of Morris, Arnold, Rossetti and Swinburne, who can be seen to have marshalled medievalist discourse in the immediate service of cultural criticism.

See also: DOMESTIC AND IDYLLIC; POETRY IN TRANSLATION; NATIONHOOD AND EMPIRE; MARRIAGE AND GENDER.

REFERENCES AND FURTHER READING

Armstrong, Isobel (1993) *Victorian Poetry: Poetry, Poetics and Politics*. London: Routledge.

Browning Institute Studies 8 (1980).

Chandler, Alice (1970) *A Dream of Order: The Medieval Ideal in Nineteenth-Century English Literature*. Lincoln, Nebr.: University of Nebraska Press.

Chapman, Raymond (1986) *The Sense of the Past in Victorian Literature*. New York: St Martin's Press.

Eagleton, Terry (1991) *Ideology*. London: Verso.

Foucault, Michel (1972) *The Archaeology of Knowledge and the Discourse on Language*. Trans. A. M. Sheridan Smith. New York: Pantheon Books.

Girouard, Mark (1981) *The Return to Camelot: Chivalry and the English Gentleman*. New Haven: Yale University Press.

Hagen, June Steffensen (1979) *Tennyson and his Publishers*. University Park: Pennsylvania State University Press.

Harrison, Antony H. (1988) *Swinburne's Medievalism: A Study in Victorian Love Poetry*. Baton Rouge: Louisiana State University Press.

Harrison, Antony H. (1990) *Victorian Poets and Romantic Poems: Intertextuality and Ideology*. Charlottesville: University Press of Virginia.

Kiernan, Victor (1982) 'Tennyson, King Arthur, and Imperialism.' In Raphael Samuel and

Gareth Stedman Jones (eds). *Culture, Ideology and Politics: Essays for Eric Hobsbawm* (pp. 126–48). London: Routledge and Kegan Paul.

Lang, Cecil Y. (1996) *The Arnold Letters*. Vol. 1. Charlottesville: University Press of Virginia.

Lindsay, Jack (1975) *William Morris: His Life and Work*. London: Constable.

Mitchell, Jerome (1987) *Scott, Chaucer, and Medieval Romance*. Lexington: University of Kentucky Press.

Pater, Walter (1868) *Appreciations, with an Essay on Style*. London: Macmillan.

Sinfield, Alan (1986) *Alfred Tennyson*. Oxford: Blackwell.

Smith, R. J. (1987) *The Gothic Bequest: Medieval Institutions in British Thought, 1688–1832*. Cambridge: Cambridge University Press.

Spectator, 11 June 1870. Review of Dante Rossetti's *Poems*, 1870 (724).

Staines, David (1978) 'Swinburne's Arthurian World: Swinburne's Arthurian Poetry and its Medieval Sources.' *Studia Neophilologica*, 50, 53–70.

Tucker, Herbert (1988). *Tennyson and the Doom of Romanticism*. Cambridge, Mass.: Harvard University Press.

Yeats, William Butler (1961) *Essays and Introductions*. New York: Macmillan.

14

Poetry in Translation

J.-A. George

Linguistic Nationalism

George Washington Moon, an American Fellow of the Royal Society of Literature, spoke to the linguistic nationalism of the age when, in 1868, he declared that 'I can believe that the English language is destined to be that in which shall arise, as in one universal temple, the utterance of the worship of all hearts' (Dowling 1986: 44). Moon's quasi-religious discourse proved surprisingly accurate, for it anticipates the time when English would fulfil its 'destiny' of becoming a 'universal' language. At the same time, this sentiment reflects what Linda Dowling identifies as the Victorian awareness 'of the conventional and ennobling equation between the English nation and the language of Shakespeare and Milton' (1986: 67). In the light of this 'ennobling equation', it is hardly surprising that one of the major literary projects of the period involved the translation of classical, medieval and contemporary European poetry into 'the language of Shakespeare and Milton'. As Denis Donoghue argues, 'Translations were crucial . . . as [a] means of getting for English society the best that had ever been thought in the world' (1995: 161).

Before the nineteenth century, English verse translation was dominated by the ambition to translate into English verse the major works of Greece and Rome. Particularly popular were Douglas's *Aeneid*, Chapman's Homer, Dryden's Virgil, Pope's *Iliad* and Cowper's *Odyssey*. Classical translations continued to be produced throughout the nineteenth century, by amateurs, such as Elizabeth Barrett and Augusta Webster, and by a new breed of professional scholars such as Benjamin Jowett, master of Balliol College. But in the Victorian period the importance of classical translation was rivalled by translation of other kinds. Lady Charlotte Guest's *Mabinogion* and Morris's *Beowulf*, for example, fed the interest that Victorians took in their cultural origins; translations from non-European languages, particularly the languages of the east, enhanced the Victorian sense of Britain as the centre of a global empire; translations of Villon and of Dante and his contemporaries nurtured the medievalism that marked so much of Victorian culture; and women poets found that they could conduct complex negotiations with the established literary tradition via translation. The body of verse translation produced in the period is far too large to be surveyed in detail. In this chapter I shall simply give examples of each of the major kinds.

Classical Poetry

Matthew Arnold's *On Translating Homer* (1860), an attack on the allegedly 'quaint' translation of the *Iliad* produced by F. W. Newman, one of Cardinal Newman's brothers, was provoked, as Donoghue suggests, by a belief that Newman's version 'tended to undermine the *Iliad* as a force in English cultural life' and thus ran counter to Arnold's own attempts 'to bring over from Greece, Rome, Germany, and France, the particular values which modern Britain lacked, notably sweetness and light' (1995: 161). The lecture itself, however, offers more than just a negative assessment of Newman, for Arnold also interrogates the unstable nature of translation itself:

> My one object is to give practical advice to a translator; and I shall not the least concern myself with theories of translation as such. But I advise the translator not to try 'to rear on the basis of the *Iliad*, a poem that shall affect our countrymen as the original may be conceived to have affected its natural hearers'; and for this simple reason, that we cannot possibly tell *how* the *Iliad* 'affected its natural hearers'. It is probably meant merely that he should try to affect Englishmen powerfully, as Homer affected Greeks powerfully; but this direction is not enough, and can give no real guidance. For all great poets affect their hearers powerfully, but the effect of one poet is one thing, that of another poet another thing: it is our translator's business to reproduce the effect of Homer, and the most powerful emotion of the unlearned English reader can never assure him whether he has *re*produced this, or whether he has produced something else. (Culler 1961: 218)

According to Arnold the translator's success can be judged only by 'scholars; who possess, at the same time with knowledge of Greek, adequate poetical taste and feeling' (Culler 1961: 218), that is, by figures like 'the Provost of Eton, or Professor Thompson at Cambridge, or Professor Jowett here in Oxford'. Two issues emerge from Arnold's lecture that are central to all Victorian translation. First, translation is an import, and imported goods are valuable precisely in so far as they supply a lack, that is, when similar articles of domestic manufacture are unavailable. Second, a crucial question to ask of any verse translation is, who is its proper audience?

I begin with a translation of Homer that would have offended Arnold even more than Newman's. Morris ranked the Greek poet's work at the top of his own personal list of Great Books, stating: '[These are] the kind of book which Mazzini called "Bibles"; they cannot always be measured by a literary standard, but to me are far more important than any literature' (MacCarthy 1994: 562). Morris's translation of the *Odyssey* was published in 1886–7 and had been preceded some dozen years earlier by Morris's rendering of the major epic of the Roman Empire, the *Aeneid*. As the *Odyssey* was a major source for the *Aeneid*, the poems obviously have many points in common. They are both concerned with a victorious quest and address the nature of heroic action. Such heroism was highly

appealing to Morris and he filtered it through his own particular ideological lens: the
poet's commitment to socialism is evident in his translation of the Latin epic. In the *Aeneid*
the political triumphs over the personal; the hero, Aeneas, ultimately abandons his lover
Dido in favour of his quest to found the New Troy.

Morris's prefatory argument for book IV states 'Herein is told of the great love of Dido,
Queen of Carthage, and the woeful ending of her' (1900: 89). Crucially, it is revealed in
this book that Dido, like the city she reigns over, signifies a feminine (and anti-social)
world of private desire which has seduced Aeneas away from his greater, public destiny.
The Latin reads:

> venisse Aenean, Troiano sanguine cretum,
> cui se pulchra viro dignetur iungere Dido;
> nunc hiemem inter se luxu, quam longa, fovere
> regnorum immemores turpique cupidine captos.
>
> (IV, 408)

and Morris translates:

> How here was come Aeneas now, from Trojan blood sprung forth,
> Whom beauteous Dido deemed indeed a man to mate her worth:
> How winter-long betwixt them there the sweets of sloth they nursed,
> Unmindful of their kingdoms' weal, by ill desire accursed.
>
> (1900: 96, IV, 191–4)

Of particular interest is the way in which Morris renders the final two lines of this passage.
In line 193 he refuses the disapproving tone of the original, for the adjective 'longa' (from
'longus') can be defined as 'too long' or 'tedious'. When Virgil states that Dido and Aeneas
spent the winter ('hiemem') luxuriating together ('inter se luxu') and then adds that they
did so 'quam longa' – for far too long – he is passing judgement. The longer Aeneas stays
in the hermetically sealed world he and his lover have created, the longer it will take him
to get back to his real purpose – the pursuit of his greater destiny. The pitfalls of this are
further illustrated in the phrase 'regnorum immemores' or, to use Morris's phrase, they
became 'Unmindful of their kingdoms' weal'. The addition of 'weal' here is also noteworthy, subliminally suggesting as it does the more democratic image of a common-
weal(th). In line 194, Morris translates 'captos' as 'accursed', rather than 'captured or
hunted'. Thus, Virgil's Dido and Aeneas have become imprisoned by, and prey to, their
desire; the rulers have become the vanquished; whereas for Morris they remain victims,
star-crossed lovers.

Eventually there is a price to be paid for being unmindful for too long of the wider
obligations to country and kin. In Dido's case, the punishment is a double one: she is
abandoned by Aeneas and then chooses to die by her own hand, 'decrevitque mori, tempus
secum ipsa modumque exigit' (l. 428). In Morris she 'doomed her death, then with herself
she planned its time and guise' (1900: 106, IV, 475). The use of a word such as 'doomed'
here (from Old English 'dōm', or 'judgement') is typical of Morris's tendency to archaize

the vocabulary of his translations of classical (and medieval) texts. Morris's translation becomes a means of appropriating a Latin poem of the first century BC for Victorian England, but through his archaisms he resists the act of appropriation in which he seems to be engaged.

In book VI Aeneas meets with his father, Anchises, in the underworld. After a highly charged reunion ('His face was wet with plenteous tears e'en as the word he spake, / And thrice the neck of him beloved he strove in arms to take' [Morris 1900: VI, 699–700]), Anchises prophesies his son's (and his son's descendants') future: 'And sure to teach thee of these things, and show thee and their press, / And of mine offspring tell the tale, for long have I been fain, / That thou with me mightst more rejoice in thine Italia's gain' (Morris, 1900: VI, 716–18). He then develops an imperial image of 'hic rem Romanam' (l. 857), translated by Morris as 'the Roman weal' (l. 183), which is portrayed as an agent of justice: 'But thou, O Roman, look to it the folks on earth to sway; / For this shall be thine handicraft, peace on the world to lay, / To spare the weak, to wear the proud by constant weight of war' (ll. 853–5). In such passages Morris remakes Aeneas in the image of a far more contemporary hero, the Italian patriot Mazzini. Thus, Morris's translation attests to two impulses. Through his archaisms he pushes Virgil's poem back into the past, but in his politics he ushers it into the present.

Virgil composed the *Aeneid* to honour both the emperor Augustus and Rome itself, and the patriotic impulse behind the writing of the epic was not lost on Morris. Indeed, he reflected upon the personal nature of his own patriotism in 'Early England' (a lecture delivered to the Hammersmith Socialist League in 1886, around the same time as Morris's translation of the *Odyssey* was published):

> I am not a patriot as the word is generally used; and yet I am not ashamed to say that as for the face of the land we live in I love it with something of the passion of a lover: that is to say more than its beauty or interest in relation to other parts of the earth warrants. Perhaps that is because I am in the habit of looking at things that pass before my eyes; (which I think has now ceased to be a common habit) and connecting their present outward seeming with times gone by and times to come. (Lemine 1969: 158)

Morris's passion is determined by a vision of the nation in which its past, present and (projected) future merge. So, in Morris's *Aeneid* he looks back at the antique, celebrates a current political movement, the Italian Risorgimento, and prophesies the future establishment of a just commonwealth, in which peace will be universal, and the strong will no longer oppress the weak.

For Morris, translation is a political activity, but it could be said that the merging of past and present is also crucial to the relationship between another great Victorian poet-translator and his antique subject matter. As Yopie Prins has argued, 'Swinburne's own poetic corpus . . . is . . . constituted on a Sapphic model, as Swinburne is increasingly cast – by himself as well as by his readers – in the role of Sappho' (1999: 116). This is confirmed by Swinburne's own admission, in 'Notes on Poems and Reviews' (published as a pamphlet in 1866), that 'I have striven to cast my spirit into the mould of hers, to express and represent not the poem but the poet' (Peters 1961: 225). But whereas Morris turns back to Virgil as a way of insisting on the poet's public responsibility, Swinburne turns to Sappho as a way of insisting that the poet's one responsibility is to himself and his art.

Swinburne's utilization of a 'Sapphic model' is most explicit in his dramatic monologue 'Anactoria', which initially appeared in his *Poems and Ballads* of 1866 (in 1889 Michael Field would also produce a version of Sappho, titled *Long Ago*). The two main sources of this poem, Sappho and Catullus's Latin translation of her work, are discussed by Swinburne in 'Notes on Poems and Reviews':

> Catullus 'translated' – or as his countrymen would now say 'traduced' – the 'Ode to Anactoria' – a more beautiful translation there never was and will never be; but compared with the Greek, it is colourless and bloodless, puffed out by additions and enfeebled by alterations. Let any one set against each other the first two stanzas, Latin and Greek, and pronounce. (This would be too much to ask of all my critics; but some may be capable of achieving the not exorbitant task.) Where Catullus failed I could not hope to succeed; I tried instead to reproduce in a diluted and dilated form the spirit of a poem which could not be reproduced in the body.

> Now the 'Ode to Anactoria' (as it is named by tradition) – the poem which English boys have to get by heart – the poem (and this is more important) which has in the whole world of verse no companion and no rival but the 'Ode to Aphrodite', has been twice at least translated or 'traduced'. I am not aware that Mr. Ambrose Phillips, or M. Nicolas Boileau-Despréaux, was ever impeached before any jury of moralists for his sufficiently grievous offense. By any jury of poets both would assuredly have been convicted. Now, what they did I have not done. To the best (and bad is the best) of their ability, they have 'done into' bad French and bad English the very words of Sappho. Feeling that although I might do it better I could not do it well, I abandoned the idea of translation.

> I tried, then, to write some paraphrase of the fragment which the Fates and the Christians have spared us. (Peters 1961: 224–5)

Swinburne, it seems, presents his 'paraphrase' as embodying his own version of Oscar Wilde's Decadent manifesto that 'There is no such thing as a moral or immoral book. Books are well written, or badly written. That is all' (1990: 11). Swinburne's own Decadent leanings were, of course, on show for all to see in 'Anactoria', 'a poem vehemently attacked by the critics . . . and [a poem which was] a deliberate attempt to scandalize Swinburne's readers' (Prins 1999: 117).

For many Victorians the most scandalous aspect of this poem was its 'sublime sadomasochism' (Prins 1999: 117), as demonstrated in the following passage:

> I would my love could kill thee; I am satiated
> With seeing thee live, and fain would have thee dead.
> I would earth had thy body as fruit to eat,
> And no mouth but some serpent's found thee sweet.
> I would find grievous ways to have thee slain,

> Intense device, and superflux of pain;
> Vex thee with amorous agonies, and shake
> Life at thy lips, and leave it there to ache;
> Strain out thy soul with pangs too soft to kill,
> Intolerable interludes, and infinite ill;
> Relapse and reluctation of the breath,
> Dumb tunes and shuddering semitones of death.
> (Lang 1975: 488, ll. 23–34)

There is an exhibitionistic quality to the sadomasochism of these lines, for 'interludes' (l. 32) and 'Dumb tunes and shuddering semitones of death' (l. 34) evoke images from the performing arts (drama and music respectively). As Cecil Y. Lang notes, 'Formally, "Anactoria" is a dramatic monologue; effectively and intentionally, it is a symphonic poem' (1975: 522). More importantly, to view the text as a type of performance establishes a vital link between it and the original oral poetry of Sappho, whose own monodies would have been sung aloud. This aspect of 'Anactoria', along with its explicit portrayal of homosexuality ('I charge thee keep thy lips from hers or his', l. 19) and its intensely personal nature, help to align Swinburne's poem closely with the Greek source. As Willis Barnstone argues, 'Much of Greek love poetry is about homosexual love . . . In the poems of Sappho hardly a whiff of politics appears. Her persistent subjects are family, private friends and foes, and love' 1972: (9–10). A greater contrast to the *Aeneid*, with all of its epic grandeur and patriotic discourse, would be difficult to find.

Indeed, in 'Notes on Poems and Reviews' it was the artistic not the ethical integrity of 'Anactoria' that Swinburne cited in his own defence against the charges of 'blasphemy' the poem generated:

> What is there now of horrible in this? The expressions of fierce fondness, the ardours of passionate despair? Are these so unnatural as to affright or disgust? Where is there an unclean detail? where an obscene allusion? A writer as impure as my critics might of course have written, on this or on any subject, an impure poem; I have not. And if to translate or paraphrase Sappho be an offence, indict the heavier offenders who have handled and re-handled this matter in their wretched versions of the ode. Is my poem more passionate in detail, more unmistakable in subject? I affirm that it is less; and what I affirm I have proved. (Peters 1961: 226)

The 'expressions of fierce fondness, the ardours of passionate despair' upon which 'Anactoria' is predicated are contextualized in the poem's epigraph, where Aphrodite asks Sappho: 'τίνος αὖ τὺ πειθοι / μαψ σαγηνεύσας Φιλότατα' (conventionally rendered as 'whom shall I create to provide you a place in her heart's love'). The goddess plays a fuller role in Swinburne's 'Sapphics' (like 'Anactoria', from *Poems and Ballads* of 1866) where she appears to the poem's sleepless speaker:

> Then to me so lying awake a vision
> Came without sleep over the seas and touched me,

> Softly touched mine eyelids and lips; and I too,
>   Full of the vision,
>
> Saw the white implacable Aphrodite,
> Saw the hair unbound and the feet unsandalled
> Shine as fire of sunset on western waters.
>   (Swinburne 1904: 204, ll. 1–7)

Next, Aphrodite herself views a procession of 'singing women' (l. 23), among whom is the 'tenth' muse. She, too, is singing, but in a different key as it were, of 'wonderful things they knew not. / Ah the tenth, the Lesbian!' (ll. 29–30). Aphrodite then beckons this additional muse by name, 'Turn to me, O my Sappho' (l. 41), though her command goes unheeded. The explicit reference to Sappho in 'Anactoria' stands as Swinburne's own form of public acknowledgement; for the Victorian poet voices his belief in the immortality of the classical poet in the lines 'I Sappho shall be one with all these things, / With all high things for ever . . . Yea, though thou diest, I say I shall not die' (ll. 276–7, 290). *This* is Swinburne's ultimate rebuttal to his critics.

Medieval Poetry

William Morris did not only try his hand at the 'best' that the classical world had to offer. In August of 1892 he began translating the Old English epic poem *Beowulf* (first edited by John Kemble, friend of Tennyson and sister of Fanny Kemble, in 1833), another one of his 'Bibles', into modern verse. Morris was not proficient in Old English, however. Therefore, to aid him in the task he used a 'crib' in the form of a prose paraphrase provided by the scholar A. J. Wyatt of Christ's College, Cambridge. The translation is unsuccessful, but not without interest. Here, for example, is Morris's rendering of lines 2247–66, the lines known as 'The Lay of the Last Survivor':

> 'Hold thou, O earth, now, since heroes may hold not,
> The owning of earls. What! it erst within thee
> Good men did get to them; now war-death hath gotten,
> Life-bale the fearful, each man and every
> Of my folk; e'en of them who forwent the life:
> The hall-joy had they seen. No man to wear sword
> I own, none to brighten the beaker beplated,
> The dear drink-vat; the doughty have sought to else-wither.
> Now shall the hard war-helm bedight with the gold
> Be bereft of its plating; its polishers sleep,
> They that the battle-mask erewhile should burnish:
> Likewise the war-byrny, which abode in the battle
> O'er break of the war-boards the bite of the irons,
> Crumbles after the warrior; nor may the ring'd byrny
> After the war-leader fare wide afield

On behalf of the heroes: nor joy of the harp is,
No game of the glee-wood; no goodly hawk now
Through the hall swingeth; no more the swift horse
Beateth the burg-stead. Now hath the bale-quelling
A many of life-kin forth away sent.'
(Morris 1966: 246–7)

Though Morris seems unaware of the alliterative principles of Old English verse, he carefully preserves the compounds, sometimes even contriving to retain their sound: 'hall-joy' (*sele-dream*), 'drink-vat' (*drince-fæt*), 'battle-mask' (*beado-griman*), 'war-byrny' (*here-pad*), 'war-leader' (*wig-fruman*), 'glee-wood' (*gleo-beames*), 'burg-stead' (*burh-stede*), 'bale-quelling' (*bealo-cwealm*) and 'life-kin' (*feorh-cynna*). On two occasions Morris even supplies a compound where one is not found in the original: thus, 'heardra helm' (comparative adjective + noun, l. 2255) becomes 'hard war-helm' and 'borda' (l. 2259) is translated as 'war-boards'. Interestingly, Hopkins was already showing how such compounds could be introduced into modern English poetry.

Morris was attracted in part to *Beowulf* because he shared its cult of heroism, but in his translation the heroism loses much of its Germanic character. Morris absorbs *Beowulf* into his own medievalism. It is almost as if his translation displaces the poem by about five centuries and at least one culture. In other words, his *Beowulf* owes more to Malory and the conventions of Old French romance than it does to the Germanic warrior society that inspired the original poem. Accordingly, Hroðgar's hall is rendered as a 'court' and arriving at its entrance Beowulf declares that he has come to bid a 'boon' (l. 352, from OE '*ben*') of Hroðgar, 'if to us he will grant it / That him who so good is, anon we may greet' (ll. 346ᵇ–7). In lines 350ᵇ–5 the messenger answers this genteel speech with equal courtesy:

I therefore the Dane's friend
Will likely be asking of the lord of the Scyldings,
The dealer of rings, since the boon thou art bidding,
The mighty folk-lord, concerning thine errand,
And swiftly the answer shall do thee to wit
Which the good one to give thee aback may deem meetest.
(Morris 1966: 189)

The tensions implicit in the Old English poem between Beowulf's opposing army and Hroðgar's sentinel disappear from Morris's version. They are replaced by courtly benevolence, chivalric courtesy and fair speech – all typical components of Morris's own original medievalist texts.

Morris's tendency to romanticize the world of the Old English epic is particularly apparent in the final third of the poem. Admittedly *Beowulf* becomes more elegiac in mood towards its close but in Morris the poem becomes sentimental, for instance, in the lines where Beowulf, now an old man on the brink of his last (and fatal) battle, bids farewell to the people he has reigned over for fifty years. The Old English reads:

gesæt ðā on næsse   nīð-heard cyning,
þenden hǣlo ābēad   heorð-genēatum,
gold-wine gēata.   Him wæs geōmor sefa,
wǣfre ond wæl-fūs.
(Wyatt 1948: ll. 2417–20ª)

Morris translates:

Sat then on the ness there the strife-hardy king
While farewell he bade to his fellows of hearth,
The gold-friend of the Geats; sad was gotten his soul,
Wavering, death-minded.
(Morris 1966: 252, *v.* 10)

Morris's medievalism was his weapon against modernity, *Beowulf* part of his artillery. To Morris's way of thinking, the Anglo-Saxons were 'anti-modern' partly because they were anti-urban. As he observed in his lecture 'Early England': 'Their want of sympathy with the city life in the first years of their occupation [of this country] was almost as marked as that of the gypsy or Bedouin for house life' (Lemine 1969: 165). He also respected what he perceived to be the Anglo-Saxons' strong sense of community, 'in which every free man had to take his share of responsibility for carrying on the business of the Community' (Lemine 1969: 165). William Morris not only idealized *Beowulf*, he also idealized the culture that had engendered it. The effect is at once to recognize the pastness of that culture, and to assert its authority as a blueprint for an as yet unrealized future.

D. G. Rossetti's medievalism seems rather different. Medievalism, as Antony H. Harrison argues in this volume, was a discourse that 'promulgated a belief in the spiritual power of love and in the positive moral influence of women'. Such a belief is at least partly responsible for Dante Gabriel Rossetti's decision to translate the medieval Dante's autobiographical *Vita nuova* (described by Pater as a 'little book [that had] early become a pattern of imaginative love' [Phillips 1986: 55]). Rossetti was the son of a famous Dante scholar, and so devoted to Dante himself that he insisted on inverting the order of the names his parents had given him. His interest in Dante is, then, unsurprising, but its character is distinctive. David Wallace believes, in fact, that Rossetti's engagement with Dante facilitates 'a shift from a public and political Dante to a private and subjective one':

Rossetti's early poem 'Dante at Verona' (*c.* 1848–52) portrays the exiled poet as a moody and isolated individual who thinks of nothing but the death of Beatrice. This prepares the way for Matthew Arnold's characterization of Dante as 'essentially aloof from the world, and not complete in the life of the world', as 'the grand, impracticable Solitary'. (Jacoff 1993: 248)

This is quite different from the Dante invoked in Byron's *Prophecy of Dante*, Barrett Browning's *Casa Guidi Windows* and Swinburne's *Songs before Sunrise*, who is, first and foremost, a poet of Italian nationhood, and hence a powerful inspiration in Italy's struggle for independence. Rossetti seems uninterested in Dante as a public poet, and turns instead to the *Vita nuova*, a prose text, composed after Beatrice's death in 1290, interspersed with sonnets explicated by the unnamed narrator, the 'I', of the work who recounts eleven remembered meetings, either real or imaginary, with Beatrice. (Interestingly, but unknown to Rossetti, the *Vita* had already been translated into English by Arthur Hallam, but the translation was destroyed by his father after Hallam's early death.)

William Michael Rossetti implicitly acknowledges this 'private and subjective Dante' who emerges from D. G. Rossetti's *The Early Italian Poets* (later retitled *Dante and his Circle*):

> [these] versions have taken rank as a sort of cross between translated and original work. They have been accepted as bringing the English reader as close to the medieval Italians as he is ever likely to be brought; and also as introducing him to the tone and quality of Rossetti's own mind and hand in poetic production . . . If he had not undertaken the translations, and had not given them the development which they here assume, some substantial traits in his own poetry would be less intelligibly marked and less securely recognisable. (Rossetti 1892: v–vi)

For Rossetti, as his brother recognized, the practice of translation and of original composition were scarcely distinct. 'Rossetti's own mind and hand' are seen, for example, in his translation of the final sonnet of the *Vita nuova*:

> Beyond the sphere which spreads to widest space
>   Now soars the sigh that my heart sends above;
>   A new perception born of grieving Love
> Guideth it upward the untrodden ways.
> When it hath reached unto the end, and stays,
>   It sees a lady round whom splendours move
>   In homage; till, by the great light thereof
> Abashed, the pilgrim spirit stands at gaze.
> It sees her such, that when it tells me this
>   Which it hath seen, I understand it not,
>   It hath a speech so subtile and so fine.
> And yet I know its voice within my thought
> Often remembereth me of Beatrice:
>   So that I understand it, ladies mine.
>
>   (Harper 1930: 147–8)

Rossetti deviates from the original in a highly personal way on at least two occasions. As medieval Dante tells us, the 'pilgrim spirit' ('spirito peregrino') is 'acciò che spiritualmente va là suso, e sì come peregrino lo quale è fuori de la sua patria, vi stae'. Rossetti translates: 'because it goes up spiritually, and like a pilgrim who is out of his known country' (1968: 147). Accordingly, in the penultimate line of the original it is the pilgrim spirit, indicated by the third person verb form 'ricorda', who remembers Beatrice, 'però che spesso ricorda Beatrice'. Rossetti shifts the focus to the first person direct object ('Often remembereth me'), effectively making 'himself' the recorder of the image of the dead beloved, though the catalyst for the thought is still the pilgrim spirit.

The translation of lines seven and eight of the sonnet are also revealing. The Italian reads: 'e luce sì, che per lo suo splendore / lo peregrino spirito la mira'. Rossetti's version of these lines provides an intriguing addition: the pilgrim spirit (a personified abstraction belonging to the male speaker) is seen to be 'abashed' by 'the great light' of the lady. In the original, she simply engages the attention of the 'peregrino spirito' because of her splendour. Rossetti's insertion of 'abashed', a word from the literature of courtly love, makes the impact that Beatrice has on the male gaze even greater than is suggested in Dante. Rossetti's Dante seems, like Morris's *Beowulf*, to use translation to appropriate the medieval for 'medievalism', but Victorian medievalism, like Victorian classicism, might be either public and political or private and personal.

The world evoked by Dante is in stark contrast to the world evoked in another medieval poet, the Frenchman François Villon (1431–?65), whose poetry was translated by both Rossetti and Swinburne. Swinburne, in fact, seems to have had more of a fellow feeling for Villon than for Dante (the opposite might be said of Rossetti). As Antony H. Harrison notes: 'Although Swinburne has an appropriate critical respect for the greatness of Dante's work, Villon . . . is his favorite . . . because of his earthy and rebellious vigor' (Harrison 1988: 12). For this reason Swinburne described Villon as 'a singer of . . . the future; he was the first modern and the last medieval poet. He is of us' (Harrison 1988: 12). This is Swinburne's translation of the French poet's 'Fragment on Death':

> Death makes him shudder, swoon, wax pale,
>   Noses bend, veins stretch, and breath surrender,
> Neck swell, flesh soften, joints that fail
>   Crack their strained nerves and arteries slender.
>   O woman's body found so tender,
> Smooth, sweet, so precious in men's eyes,
>   Must thou too bear such count to render?
> Yes, or pass quick into the skies.
>   (Swinburne 1904: 139, ll. 9–16)

That the poem is 'earthy' and grounded in the physical is clear enough. In addition to this, however, this passage from 'Fragment on Death' has elements of the sadomasochism seen in 'Anactoria'. As McGann states, 'Swinburne regarded Villon as the first great lyrical voice of the Christian era, indeed, as the reincarnation of Sappho, the first great lyrical voice of the pagan era' (1972: 89). Like Sappho, though in a very different way, Villon allowed Swinburne to escape both the stylistic and ethical conventions of nineteenth-century verse, as, for example, in his 'Ballad of Villon and Fat Madge':

> When all's up she drops me a windy word,
>   Bloat like a beetle puffed and poisonous:
> Grins, thumps my pate, and calls me dickey-bird,
>   And cuffs me with a fist that's ponderous.

We sleep like logs, being drunken both of us;
Then when we wake her womb begins to stir;
To save her seed she gets me under her
  Wheezing and whining, flat as planks are laid:
And thus she spoils me for a whoremonger
  Inside this brothel where we drive our trade.

Oriental Poetry

Rossetti was instrumental in securing the place of Edward FitzGerald's rendering of the *Rubáiyát* of Omar Khayyám (1048–1131) as the most influential Victorian translation of a non-European poem. In 1861, two years after its publication:

> the Celtic scholar Whitley Stokes . . . gave a copy [of FitzGerald's translation] to Dante Gabriel Rossetti, who went with Swinburne to the shop [Quaritch's old shop on Castle Street] and bought more copies of the poem at a penny each. Soon the poem was read by William Morris, Edward Burne-Jones, and George Meredith. Beyond the Pre-Raphaelite circle, demand began to grow. (Decker 1997: xxxiv)

FitzGerald was continuing an interest in English translations of oriental poetry that began with Sir William Jones (1748–94), a noted scholar of Arabic, Persian and Sanskrit, who founded the Asiatic Society of Bengal and did much to improve the image of the Orient in Europe. In the Victorian period there were, for example, translations of the *Mahabharata* and of the Persian *Sháhnámeh*, but FitzGerald's is the only Victorian oriental verse translation that has established itself as an English classic. It is worth asking why. Most obviously the popularity of the poem seems to have rested on its blithe dismissal of all conventional Victorian ethical imperatives:

> Here with a Loaf of Bread beneath the Bough,
> A Flask of Wine, a Book of Verse – and Thou
>   Beside me singing in the Wilderness –
>   And Wilderness is Paradise enow.
>   (Decker 1997: 11)

In limpid quatrains, FitzGerald articulates the view of life that in a poem such as 'The Garden of Proserpine' Swinburne offers as a flaunting defiance of Victorian pieties:

> Oh, come with old Khayyám, and leave the Wise
> To talk; one thing is certain, that Life flies;
>   One thing is certain, and the Rest is lies;
> The Flower that once has blown for ever dies.
>   (Decker 1997: 13)

But, because these views are offered in the guise of a translation, FitzGerald was not felt to be subversive. Indeed, it was perhaps FitzGerald's perfect articulation of Khayyám's ambition rather to 'soothe the Soul through the senses into Acquiescence with Things as they were, than to perplex it with vain mortifications after what they *might be*' (Decker 1997: 6) that made his translation so appealing to the Victorians.

Women Translators

Elizabeth Barrett Browning's *Sonnets from the Portuguese* suggests how important the trope of translation is for Victorian women poets. The sonnet sequence was given this title on the suggestion of Robert Browning in an attempt (in vain, it transpired) to deflect attention from the autobiographical nature of the poems, which chart the development of the courtship. The title is also a reference to his favourite poem by Barrett Browning, 'Caterina to Camoens'. Writing to her sister Arabel after the surprise gift of the sonnets to Robert, who had not known of their composition, Barrett Browning explains that 'I felt shy about them altogether' because she had once heard Robert 'express himself strongly against "personal" poetry' (Forster 1993: 237). This anecdote is significant, because women poets found translation a screen against the charge of excessively personal and introspective poetry. Translation is, indeed, a metaphor for an alternative women's poetics: not only in the wider sense of an exchange and transformation of foreignness and the other (in, for example, women poets' obsession with Italy), but also in the sense of the imitation of poetry in a foreign language.

This is particularly the case with Sappho: throughout the period, women poets – Letitia Landon, Felicia Hemans, Barrett Browning, Christina Rossetti, Caroline Norton and Mary Coleridge – were drawn to Sappho's fragments more in gestures of absorption and imitation than in endeavours to translate. Most significant in this category, however, is 'Michael Field' (Katherine Bradley and Edith Cooper), whose volume *Long Ago* (1889), their first joint volume of poems, acknowledges the importance of Henry Wharton's 1885 edition of Sappho, which was the first to introduce in translation the female pronoun for Sappho's object of address. The Fields, who were termed by Robert Browning his 'two dear Greek women', both translate, absorb, elaborate and imitate Sappho's fragments. The erotic poetry of Michael Field, in fact, brings into sharp focus the long tradition of women poets' appropriation of Sappho's poetry, and her figure, in order to explore issues and anxieties concerning women's creativity (see Prins 1999). But the legacy of Sappho is a double bind, a 'bid for self-expression, physical passion and poetic power' over the body of a precursor who leapt to her death because of unrequited love (Leighton 1992: 36).

The scholarly act of translation, as well as imitation and the trope of translation, offered Victorian women the opportunity to participate in the culture of poetry while sidestepping vexed issues of female poetic creativity, issues that predicated women's poetry on the private sphere of emotions and affections. To translate poetry from another language, and another poet, in other words, was an ironic liberation that asserted women's intellectual and scholarly abilities while displacing the ideology of female creativity. The limitations of women's education, however, confined the activity of translation to the middle and upper classes. Translators such as Elizabeth Barrett, for example, enjoyed early lessons in the classics at home with their brothers, although their formal education was curtailed when those brothers moved on to school. Barrett was to have a close intellectual relationship with the blind classicist Hugh Stuart Boyd (see 'Wine of Cyprus') which compensated for the cessation of her brother Edward's lessons in Greek. Mary Coleridge, later in the century, was privately tutored with a group of other women by the classicist William Cory, who encouraged her interest in Sappho. Unless born into a bi- or multilingual house, such as the Rossettis', however, women had otherwise to rely upon self-tuition. All Rossetti children were sucked into what Christina termed the 'Dante vortex', thanks to their father's eccentric Italian scholarship, but only Dante Gabriel Rossetti translated from Dante and his circle. Maria was a respected Dante scholar, publishing her study on the *Divine Comedy*, *A Shadow of Dante*, in 1871. She also published *Exercises in Idiomatic Italian through Literal Translation from the English* (1867). Christina translated her *Sing-Song* into Italian as a linguistic exercise, and wrote poetry in Italian which was only published posthumously, suggesting that, for her, and despite her father's nationhood, Italian was a private 'mother tongue'.

Despite these limitations, Victorian women's translations cover a wide range of languages and poets. Little academic attention to date has been paid to the issue of Victorian women translators of poetry, and the following survey is intended as an outline of the breadth of translating activities which are yet to be fully uncovered. In the classics, most significant are Elizabeth Barrett's translation of *Prometheus Bound* (1833, revised edition 1850) and Augusta Webster's version, published in 1866, followed by a translation of *Medea* in 1868. Webster's confidence in her translating skills is evident in two remarkable essays published in the *Examiner* in 1877, which take issue with Robert Browning: 'We could wish nothing better for literature than that Mr. Browning, having translated the Agamemnon of Æschylus, should go on to translate the Agamemnon of Robert Browning' (Sutphin 2000: 366). In European languages, Margaret Oliphant's translations of Leopardi are notable. A. Mary F. Robinson, proficient in Greek, French and Italian, translated the work of her first husband, the French scholar and professor of Persian James Darmester. She also imitated popular European poetic forms, such as the *rispetto* and *stornello*. One of the most remarkable translators of the end of the period is Gertrude Bell, whose translations from Persian poetry, *Poems from the Divan of Hafiz* (1897), gives a flavour of her scholarly investment in eastern culture to which her travel writing also attests (see *Safar Nameh: Persian Pictures* [1894]).

Fascinating, if now little-known, translations from the Italian by a woman poet appeared in 1884 under the title *Roadside Songs of Tuscany*. Its translator (as well as illustrator) was Francesca Alexander (1837–1917). In 'The Author's Preface' Alexander discusses the contents of the volume and her reasons for collecting them together:

> These songs and hymns of the poor people have been collected, little by little, in the course of a great many years which I have passed in constant intercourse with the Tuscan contadini. They are but the *siftings*, so to say, of hundreds and hundreds which I have heard and learnt,

mostly from old people: many of them have never, so far as I know, been written down before, and others it would be impossible now to find . . .

It seems to me that there are others who will collect and preserve the thoughts of the rich and great; but I have wished to make my book all of poor people's poetry, and who knows but it may contain a word of help or consolation for some poor soul yet? However that may be, I have done my best to save a little of what is passing away. (1888: 1, 6)

John Ruskin furnished a preface to Alexander's book, making the modest claim that Alexander 'in her translation, aims only at rendering their meaning clear with a pleasant musical order and propriety of cadence' (Alexander 1888: 13). But it is clear that Ruskin found in these translations a confirmation of his aesthetic and his political principles. The translations preserved the thoughts and feelings of the poor, and they were free from the 'pathetic fallacy' that disfigured more sophisticated perceptions of the world. Hence he compares these Tuscan poems with ancient Greek verse: 'And they correspond . . . very closely to early Greek ballad in the lays of Orpheus and Hesiod, – and indeed to Greek epic verse altogether, in that such song is only concerned with the visible works and days of gods and men; and will neither stoop, nor pause, to take colour from the singer's personal feelings' (Alexander 1888: 14). The transpersonal, ballad quality Ruskin identified in these roadside songs is illustrated in the following example:

> Non vi maravigliaté, giovinetti;
> S'io non sapessi troppo ben cantare,
> In casa mia non c'eran maestri,
> Nè mica a scuola son ita ad imparare.
> Se volete saper dov'era la mia scuola,
> Su per i monti, all'acqua, – alla gragnuola.
> E questo è stato il mio imparare,
> Vado per legne, e torno a zappare.

Alexander's translation reads:

> You ask me for a song, then be content,
> With little grace, in all I sing or say;
> And judge me kindly, for I never went
> To school, and masters never came our way.
> The only school where ever I did go,
> Was on the mountain, in the hail and snow.
> And this, alas! was all they made me learn –
> To go for wood, and dig when I return.

The phrase 'in all I sing or say' (l. 2) indicates that this poem was initially forged in an oral tradition, as does the fact that the 'singer' never went to school, and hence, presumably, is illiterate. Through translating such songs Alexander allows access to a pre-literate culture that neither she nor her readers could ever experience directly.

Alexander acknowledges that a 'great many' of these verses 'were taught me by the celebrated improvisatrice, Beatrice Bernardi of Pian degli Ontani' (1888: 1). She recounts how Bernardi's talent had its origin in a miraculous event which took place on her wedding day: 'suddenly she felt in herself a new power, and began to sing the poetry which was then born in her mind, and having once begun, found it impossible to stop, and kept on singing a great while' (1888: 3). For Alexander, her relationship with Bernardi was similarly, if less dramatically, empowering. Through translation she found her own gift of song. In this she speaks for many of her contemporaries. Victorian translators may seem to have been involved in an imperial project, motivated by the desire, in Donoghue's words, of 'getting for English society the best that had ever been thought in the world' (1995: 161). But, as the Victorians knew very well, to export Englishness through empire is inevitably to admit the foreign into England. In the nineteenth century, verse translation became one of the most important means by which English poets challenged the orthodoxies of their own culture. For Rossetti, Morris and Swinburne translation made possible not simply new poetic styles but new modes of feeling, which might be public and political, as in Morris, or much more personal, as in Rossetti, who found in Dante and his contemporaries a mode of fashioning a new subjectivity.

See also: ARTHURIAN POETRY AND MEDIEVALISM; THE CLASSICAL TRADITION; THE PRE-RAPHAELITE SCHOOL.

REFERENCES AND FURTHER READING

Alexander, Francesca (1888) *Roadside Songs from Tuscany.* New York: John Wiley and Sons.

Arnold, Matthew (1906) *On the Study of Celtic Literature and On Translating Homer.* New York: Macmillan.

Barnstone, Willis (trans.) (1972) *Greek Lyric Poetry, including the Complete Poetry of Sappho.* New York: Schocken Books.

Bassnett, Susan (ed.) (1997) *Translating Literature.* Cambridge: D.S. Brewer.

Cervigni, Dino S., and Edward Vasta (eds) (1995) *Vita Nuova.* London: University of Notre Dame Press.

Colgrave, Bertram, and R. A. B. Mynors (eds) (1969) *Bede's Ecclesiastical History.* London: Oxford University Press.

Conlon, John J. (1982) *Walter Pater and the French Tradition.* London: Associated University Presses.

Culler, A. Dwight (ed.) (1961) *Poetry and Criticism of Matthew Arnold.* Boston: Houghton Mifflin.

Decker, Christopher (ed.) (1997) *Rubáiyát of Omar Khayyám.* London: University Press of Virginia.

Donoghue, Denis (1995) *Walter Pater: Lover of Strange Souls.* New York: Alfred A. Knopf.

Dowling, Linda (1986) *Language and Decadence in the Victorian Fin de Siècle.* Princeton, N. J.: Princeton University Press.

Forster, Margaret (1993) *Elizabeth Barrett Browning.* London: Flamingo.

Gosse, Sir Edmund, and Thomas James Wise (eds) (1968) *The Complete Works of Algernon Charles Swinburne.* Vol. III. New York: Russell and Russell.

Harper, Henry Howard (ed.) (1930) *Dante's New Life.* Boston: Bibliophile Society.

Harrison, Antony H. (1988) *Swinburne's Medievalism: A Study in Victorian Love Poetry.* London: Louisiana State University Press.

Jacoff, Rachel (ed.) (1993) *The Cambridge Companion to Dante.* Cambridge: Cambridge University Press.

Lang, Cecil B. (ed.) (1975) *The Pre-Raphaelites and their Circle*. London: University of Chicago Press.

Leighton, Angela (1992) *Victorian Women Poets: Writing Against the Heart*. Hemel Hempstead: Harvester Wheatsheaf.

Lemine, Eugene D. (ed.) (1969) *The Unpublished Lectures of William Morris*. Detroit: Wayne State University Press.

MacCarthy, Fiona (1994) *William Morris: A Life for Our Time*. London: Faber and Faber.

Mackail, J. W. (ed.) (1905) *The Earthly Paradise: A Poem by William Morris*. Vols 1 and 2. London: Longmans, Green.

McGann, Jerome J. (1972) *Swinburne: An Experiment in Criticism*. London: University of Chicago Press.

Morris, William (1900) *The Aeneids of Virgil*. Longmans, Green.

Morris, William (1966) *The Collected Works of William Morris: Volume X, Three Northern Love Stories, The Tale of Beowulf*. New York: Russell and Russell.

Peters, Robert L. (ed.) (1961) *Victorians on Literature and Art*. New York: Appleton-Century-Crofts.

Phillips, Adam (ed.) (1986) *The Renaissance: Studies in Art and Poetry*. Oxford: Oxford University Press.

Prins, Yopie (1999) *Victorian Sappho*. Princeton, N. J.: Princeton University Press.

Rossetti, Dante Gabriel (1968) *Poems and Translations, 1850–1870 Together with the Prose Story 'Hand and Soul'*. London: Oxford University Press.

Rossetti, William (ed.) (1892) *Dante and his Circle, with the Italian Poets Preceding him (1100–1200–1300)*. London: Ellis and Elvey.

Selver, Paul (1966) *The Art of Translating Poetry*. Boston: Writer.

Sutphin, Christine (ed.) (2000) *Augusta Webster: Portraits and Other Poems*. Peterborough, Ont.: Broadview.

Swinburne, Algernon Charles (1904) *The Poems of Algernon Charles Swinburne in Six Volumes*. London: Chatto and Windus.

Virgil (1933) *Eclogues, Georgics, Aeneid I–IV*. Loeb Classical Library Vol. 1. London: William Heinemann.

Wilde, Oscar (1990) *The Complete Stories, Plays and Poems of Oscar Wilde*. London: Tiger Books International.

Wolfe, Humbert (ed.) (1928) *Selected Poems of Algernon Charles Swinburne*. London: John Lane and Bodley Head.

Wyatt, A. J. (ed.) (1948) *Beowulf with the Finnsburg Fragment*. Revised edition. Ed. R. W. Chambers. Cambridge: Cambridge University Press.

15

Tractarian Poetry

Stephen Prickett

If we judge poetry in market terms it is hard to resist the conclusion that Tractarian poetry was (after Shakespeare's) the most successful ever written in English. The flagship volume, Keble's *The Christian Year*, was published in 1827, and sold an average of 10,000 volumes a year over the next fifty years – a figure only distantly challenged by that of Tennyson's *In Memoriam* (1850) and far greater than that ever achieved by the then poet laureate, William Wordsworth. Counting the lesser, but still substantial sales of *Lyra Innocentium* (1846) and his posthumous *Miscellaneous Poems* (1869), Keble alone must rank as the most popular English poet of his age. If we add the immediate popularity of *Lyra Apostolica* (1836) by Richard Hurrell Froude and John Henry Newman, together with the lasting impact of some of Newman's individual works, 'Lead Kindly Light' (1834) and *The Dream of Gerontius* (1866) (set to music by Elgar in 1900), with its great choral hymn 'Praise to the Holiest in the Height', we are clearly looking at one of the most widely known poetic movements of all time. In a poll published by the Congregational journalist W. T. Stead in 1896, asking what particular hymns had helped well-known figures in their lives, Newman's 'Lead Kindly Light' was mentioned more than any other. Amongst those who cited it were Thomas Hardy, the agnostic, W. E. Gladstone, the high churchman, Max Müller, the scholar of comparative religion, Justin McCarthy, the radical MP, the marquis of Ripon, a Roman Catholic, and Sir Evelyn Wood, a leading diplomat (Bradley 1997: 192).

Posthumous acclaim does not always follow contemporary popularity, and poems sung as hymns are, of course, valued for a variety of reasons other than strict poetic merit. But in the case of Tractarian poetry, praise has been more than usually muted. Wordsworth himself, who was appropriated by the Tractarians as their own unofficial 'poet laureate' from the 1830s, was ambiguous about their poetry in public and derogatory in private. *The Christian Year*, he once said, was so good that he wished he could rewrite it so as to make it even better (Battiscombe 1963: 104), adding off the record that though he admired Keble as a man, his poetry was greatly inferior to that of Isaac Watts, and positively 'vicious in diction' (Moorman 1965: 479–80).

Wordsworth's distinction between Keble the man and his poetry was not shared by all his contemporaries. Given that the Oxford Movement was born in controversy, and that many of its original adherents either went over to Rome, like Newman, Archdeacon Henry Manning and the Balliol Fellow W. G. Ward, confirming what its detractors had always known, or, like J. A. Froude and Mark Pattison, lost their faith altogether, it is hardly surprising that they were judged as much by personalities as by poetry. Subtexts were never very deeply submerged. Beneath Charles Kingsley's denunciation of what he saw as Newman's casuistical defence of lying was the unspoken but widely understood accusation that Newman's circle was basically a homosexual ring. Stories like that of Newman's final retreat from Oxford to Littlemore, wetting the hand of his companion Ambrose St John with tears, made one Oxford acquaintance of both E. B. Pusey and Newman say very pointedly, when asked in old age to compare them, 'Pusey was a *man.*'

Other criticisms were less concerned with Newman's sexuality than with his intelligence. Thomas Carlyle, with unusual viciousness (even for him), once commented that Newman had 'the brain of a moderate-sized rabbit'. Later critics have noted that Newman's understanding of his world was peculiarly limited. Eric Griffiths cites the extraordinary passage in the *Discourses to Mixed Congregations* (1849) implying that Newman thought that miners, like the pit ponies in *Black Beauty*, spent their entire lives underground (Griffiths 1989: 288). Even more extraordinary, perhaps, to modern ears is Newman's justification of Israelite massacres in the book of Joshua, which sound unfortunately close to Himmler's praise for the Waffen SS:

> Doubtless, while the servants of God executed His judgements, they could still bend in pity and hope over the young and the old whom they slew with the sword – merciful amid their severity – an unspeakable trial, doubtless, of faith and self-mastery, and requiring a very exalted and refined spirit to undergo. Doubtless, as they slew those who suffered for the sins of their fathers, their thoughts turned, first to the fall of Adam, next to that unseen state where all inequalities are righted, and they surrendered themselves as instruments unto the Lord, of mysteriously working out good from evil. (*Parochial Sermons* 13, 187)

The general question of whether writers' views can be separated from their aesthetics is complicated by the Tractarian poets' own confidence in an unshakeable link between them. Though later experience arguably made Newman more circumspect, in his Tractarian days he, like Keble, believed that good was produced by good men. Though in his Oxford *Lectures on Poetry* (1844) Keble admitted Byron and Shelley, despite their beliefs and lifestyles, into the poetic pantheon as 'Secondary poets', this was because they exemplified those mentally affected by the intolerable tensions of their art (Keble 1912: II, 339). These lectures, developed during his years as professor of poetry at Oxford from 1832 to 1841, provide Keble's most complete exposition of poetic theory. Appearing in 1844, as *De Poeticae vi Medica*, they remained virtually unknown to any wider audience because they were published, as delivered, in Latin – and remained untranslated until 1912.

Keble's aesthetics, starting from a Romantic sense of personal wholeness, offer the most complete exposition ever devised of poetry as the spontaneous overflow of powerful feelings. But whereas for Wordsworth that image suggested a spring of water gushing uncontrollably from the ground, for Keble, writing early in the railway boom when boiler explosions were common, the phrase irresistibly suggests the safety-valve of a steam engine. 'My notion', he wrote to J.T. Coleridge in 1832, 'is to consider poetry as a vent for overcharged feelings, or a full imagination, and so account for the various classes into which poets naturally fall, by reference to the various objects which are apt to fill and overpower the mind, so as to require a sort of relief' (Coleridge 1869: 199).

Poetry, for Keble, was the product of tension or repression. Someone who, under emotional stress, can find easy expression for their feelings is, by definition, no poet (Keble 1912: I, 36). Reviewing Lockhart's *Life of Scott* in 1828 he argues, 'Poetry is the indirect expression in words, most appropriately in metrical words, of some overpowering emotion, or ruling taste, or feeling, the direct indulgence whereof is somehow repressed' (Keble 1877: 6). Repression or reserve – tension between what is felt and what finally finds expression – is at the creative heart of 'the poetic', a quality, incidentally, not peculiar to poetry. All art forms, including not merely literature but music, sculpture, painting and even architecture, have a 'poetical' element. 'What is called the poetry of painting', says Keble, 'simply consists in the apt expression of the artist's own feeling' – feeling, of course, expressed under tension (Keble 1912: I, 38). In this radical 'expressionistic' reshaping of genres, the traditional categories that had dominated criticism ever since Aristotle become meaningless: 'there will be as many kinds of poems as there are emotions of the human mind' (I, 88).

For Keble there are two main classes of poets: Primary and Secondary. The Primary are 'those who, spontaneously moved by impulse, resort to composition for relief and solace of a burdened or over-wrought mind'; the Secondary 'those who, for one reason or another, imitate the ideas, the expression, and the measures of the former' (I, 53–4). The list of Primary poets is strictly classical, ending properly with Virgil – though Dante makes it as an afterthought (II, 471). There were problems with moderns. Despite the lectures being dedicated to him, Wordsworth remains unlisted. Though fulfilling the Primary criteria as a poet, as a man he suffered from the grave disadvantage of being neither ancient Greek nor Roman. Writing to J.T . Coleridge on 5 July 1844, Keble comments he would like 'to substitute modern examples for the Greek and Latin', mentioning also Byron and Shelley (Coleridge 1869: 205).

This theory takes to its logical conclusion Wordsworth's sleight-of-hand in the Preface to the *Lyrical Ballads*, whereby poetry was defined in terms of its author's characteristics ('what is a poem? . . . a poet is . . .'). Keble now classifies poetry by the writer's emotions, which seek relief and health by disguised utterance. In what M. H. Abrams calls nothing less than a 'radical, proto-Freudian theory, which conceives literature as disguised wish-fulfilment, serving the artist as a way back from incipient neurosis', poetry is equated with healing (Abrams 1953: 157). 'Each several one of the so-called liberal arts declares Keble, 'contains a certain poetic quality of its own, and . . . this lies in its power to heal and relieve the human mind when agitated by care, passion, or ambition' (Keble 1912: I, 53). Keble does *not* believe that one of the powers of 'the poetic' is that it can heal or give relief to the person under strain; he believes that we must *define* 'the poetic' by this healing power. *Ibi ars medica, ubi poesis*. Where there is healing, there is the poetic.

Here, too, is rooted Keble's belief in the 'soothing' power of poetry. In his 1827 advertisement to *The Christian Year* he drew attention to the poems on the occasional services of the Prayer Book, which, he tells us, 'constitute, from their personal and domestic nature, the most perfect instance of that *soothing* tendency in the Prayer Book, which it is the chief purpose of these pages to exhibit'. The title of the poem for the fourth Sunday after Epiphany gives us the full strength of this word for Keble: *The World is for Excitement, the Gospel for Soothing*. Though not immune to the search for an infantile dream-world that attracted so many Victorian writers, Keble gives the word much of its older meaning: 'to prove or show to be true; to assert or uphold a truth'; or 'to give support', 'encourage' or 'confirm'. As in Aristotelian catharsis, where tension is first built up and then released in tragedy through the emotions of pity and terror, Keble's 'poetic' involves an unresolved tension between private emotion and the restraints of public expression, finally finding utterance in veiled or even ironic form whose release brings with it a healing and soothing effect for poet and reader. But such healing rests on a much more profound process of 'asserting and upholding the truth' even in the hidden symbolic forms of poetry. The Prayer Book and the Gospels are essentially 'poetic' because they compellingly assert the truth. Once again, Keble's thought is grandly holistic. 'Health' is a matter not merely of a sound body, but of a well-adjusted psyche, and, finally, of right beliefs.

For Keble, the ultimate example of 'poetry' is the church itself. If poetry (including *The Christian Year*) shows the potentially sacramental nature of human experience, the Primary poets are analogous to the founders of the church: the prophets, apostles and early Fathers who have shaped our religious sensibilities. They, like such founders, bring soothing and catharsis out of the tensions of life. Secondary poets resemble the saints who have regenerated church tradition, perpetually cleansing and reforming. If such an analogy sometimes seems forced, for Keble it is *more* than an analogy: the apostles, Fathers and saints are the true Platonic types of the poets, making the unseen world visible to the faithful.

Such holism was easy for Lytton Strachey in his *Eminent Victorians* (1918) to satirize. Even for contemporaries, Keble's view of nature, based on an elaborate system of 'correspondences', seemed at once antiquated and mechanical – out of touch with both science and the earlier Romantics. What in Wordsworth, for instance, had been a real questioning of loss of joy in nature becomes in Keble a pious nostalgia resolved only by the putative joys of heaven:

> The distant landscape draws not nigh
> For all our gazing; but the soul
> That upwards looks, may still descry
> Nearer, each day, the brightening goal.
> ('Fourth Sunday in Advent')

In the poem for Septuagesima Sunday (a popular hymn), Keble famously opens the 'book of Nature' (foreshadowing 'Tract Eighty-Nine'), implying that the simple Christian need not worry about secular science:

There is a book, who runs may read,
Which heavenly truth imparts,
And all the lore its scholars need,
Pure eyes and Christian hearts.

The works of God above, below,
Within us and around,
Are pages in that book, to show
How God Himself is found.

The glorious sky embracing all
Is like the Maker's love,
Wherewith encompass'd, great and small
In peace and order move.

'Tract Eighty-Nine' details the mystical significance of the universe. The sky represents 'a canopy spread over the tents and dwellings of the saints'; birds are tokens of 'Powers in heaven above who watch our proceedings in this lower world'; and waters flowing into the sea are 'people gathered into the Church of Christ'. The smell of flowers is the 'odour of sanctity'; trees and weeds are 'false principles'; the tamarisk, 'the double mind'; the palm, 'eternal purity'. 'The Sun, the greater light, is our Lord; the Moon, the lesser light, the Church.' 'He appointed the moon for certain seasons, and the Sun knoweth his going down' – or, as he puts it in 'Septuagesima Sunday':

The Moon above, the Church below,
A wondrous race they run,
But all their radiance, all their glow,
Each borrows of its Sun.
. . . Two worlds are ours: 'tis only Sin
Forbids us to descry
The mystic heaven and earth within,
Plain as the sea and sky.

The Christian Year confines itself almost exclusively to nature and the cycle of the liturgical year. An appendix offers occasional poems on the sacraments and the special services of the Prayer Book (the Churching of Women, the Commination Service etc.), and a few on related Tractarian hobby-horses – King Charles the Martyr and the Gunpowder Plot. This very explicitness was doubtless part of their enormous appeal, yet few critics have commented on the paradox of how little Keble's own verses depend on the reserve, tension and irony so central to his poetic theory.

Similar, almost crass, explicitness often mars Newman's occasional verse. In 'On Nature and Art' (1826) we know that art is never going to stand much chance:

Art's labour'd toys of highest name
Are nerveless, cold, and dumb;
And man is fitted but to frame

> A coffin or a tomb;
> Well suit when sense is pass'd away,
> Such lifeless works the lifeless clay.
>
> (ll. 19–24)

More ironic bite, if no more artistic merit, informs the misogyny of his 1834 paraphrase of St Gregory Nazianzen's *The Married and the Single*:

> Ye countless multitudes, content to bow
> To the soft thraldom of the marriage vow!
> I mark your haughty step, your froward gaze,
> Gems deck your hair, and silk your limbs arrays;
> Come, tell the gain which wedlock has conferr'd
> On man; and then the single shall be heard.
>
> (ll. 27–32)

By contrast, 'Lead Kindly Light' is wrapped in metaphorical obscurity:

> Lead, kindly Light, amid the encircling gloom,
>   Lead thou me on;
> The night is dark, and I am far from home,
>   Lead thou me on.
> Keep thou my feet; I do not ask to see
> The distant scene; one step enough for me.

Written in 1833 on board ship off Sardinia, this poem does indeed meet all Keble's poetic criteria. Newman's recent illness, his subsequent depression over the passing of the 1833 Reform Bill, the overthrow of the Bourbons in France, and the liberalization of the English church – events that many of his admirers would have welcomed – are never mentioned. What we are offered instead are two linked images: life as a journey, and movement from darkness towards light. Both tropes are, of course, Biblical, but Newman's appropriation is at once strongly nineteenth-century and deeply idiosyncratic. For religious writers, post-Bunyan, metaphors of travel implied progress. Yet this spiritual journey is towards neither wisdom nor enlightenment – or, rather, any such 'enlightenment' and wisdom only point to a greater childlikeness. As for the great German theologian Friedrich Schleiermacher, whom Newman claimed never to have read, the essence of this religion is absolute dependence; like Yeats after him, the thirty-something Newman has already assumed the persona of an old sage, surveying the follies of life and death with a cold eye:

> I was not ever thus, nor prayed that thou
>   Should'st lead me on;
> I loved to choose and see my path; but now
>   Lead thou me on.
> I loved the garish day, and, spite of fears,
> Pride ruled my will: remember not past years.

The poem's archetypal imagery and sharply personal intelligence lift it from the banal to fulfil Keble's criteria, but (as often with Newman) belie the submissive meekness that it proclaims.

Yet Newman's is still an explicitly metaphorical journey. In 'Uphill' (1861) another Tractarian poet, Christina Rossetti, tells a similar story in a quite different idiom:

> Does the road wind uphill all the way?
>   Yes, to the very end.
> Will the day's journey take the whole long day?
>   From morn to night, my friend.
>
> But is there for the night a resting place?
>   A roof for when the slow dark hours begin.
> May not the darkness hide it from my face?
>   You cannot miss that inn.
>
> Shall I meet other wayfarers at night?
>   Those who have gone before.
> Then must I knock, or call when just in sight?
>   They will not keep you standing at that door.
>
> Shall I find comfort, travel-sore and weak?
>   Of labour you shall find the sum.
> Will there be beds for me and all who seek?
>   Yea, beds for all who come.

This is certainly one of the most extraordinary poems in English, in that it supplies a single coherent dialogue, with none of the shifts of metaphor that might suggest hidden allegory, even while alerting almost every reader to its presence. Yet, as Owen Barfield has observed, simply categorizing it as allegory oversimplifies (1962: 53). 'Is it fair', he asks, 'to say that Christina Rossetti says B but that she *really means* A? I do not think that this is a question which can be answered with a simple "yes" or "no". In fact the difficult and elusive relation between A and B is the heart of the matter.' The metonymy of life as a journey and death as an inn is surely not a simple case of replacing one (explicit) term by another that is implied, but never articulated. 'Life' and 'death' are alike abstractions. We cannot envision either without *some* kind of metonymy or symbol. The test is simply to invite readers to paraphrase the poem, replacing each symbol B by the corresponding literal statement A.

It is the very absence of explanation of A in the text of B that is so effective. G. K. Chesterton's 'the decent inn of death' is clearly an echo of Rossetti's 'You cannot miss that inn', but one that seems contrived by comparison, completely missing the point of Rossetti's line. To make the metaphor explicit diminishes its force. Barfield again:

We feel that B, which is actually said, ought to be necessary, even inevitable in some way. It ought to be in some sense the best, if not the only way of expressing A satisfactorily. The mind should dwell on it as well as on A and thus the two should be somehow inevitably fused together into one simple meaning. But if A is too obvious and could be equally or

almost as well expressed by other and more direct means, then the mind jumps straight to
A, remains focused on it, and loses interest in B, which shrinks to a kind of dry and hollow
husk. (1962: 54)

Unlike Barfield, however, I think that in Rossetti's poem the two layers *do* fuse. The surface
narrative is transparent enough to reveal the underlying meaning, while being opaque
enough to give a new perspective. If the metaphor of life as a journey reaches back to the
Old Testament, the image of death as an inn neatly inverts the New. Christ's birth in a
stable, because there was no room at the inn, now means room for all in *this* inn.

If all this seems familiar, it should be. The idea that the visible and mundane is charged
with underlying meaning, invisible to the eye but plain for all to see, is, in effect, Richard
Hurrell Froude's 'doctrine of reserve'. A principle of religious devotion, elevated by Keble
into aesthetic theory, becomes living art through the studied understatement of Christina
Rossetti.

Yet the real poetic climax of this doctrine comes not with Rossetti, but with another
poet too young to have been a Tractarian. Gerard Manley Hopkins was to transform
not A, the underlying Christian vision, but B – what Barfield feared in Rossetti threatened to become merely the 'husk' of meaning. If poems like 'Pied Beauty' and 'The Windhover' seem to be affirming nature only as the visible form of an underlying spiritual
reality, that sacramentalism created unexpected repercussions in the whole concept of
nature.

While the so-called Victorian 'crisis of faith' over Darwinism was still thirty years away,
elements that were to come together in 1859 were already present in *The Christian Year*
in 1827. Though, as Gillian Beer (1983) reminds us, Darwinism was a myth of origins
as potent as anything presented in Genesis, we recall that the roots of Darwinism lay not
in prose narrative, but in poetry – in particular that of Darwin's eccentric and poetic
grandfather Erasmus Darwin. *The Loves of the Plants* (1789), despite neoclassical heroic
couplets, had scandalized many by its frank sexuality; while his later work, *Zoonomia*
(1794–6), contained the first description of evolution.

But the fifty years between Charles Darwin and his grandfather had seen not merely
the huge geological paradigm-change concerning the age of the earth, but an aesthetic
shift of almost equal importance. As Peacock observed in the *Four Ages of Poetry* (1819),
the main stream of creative writing in English had gone over from verse to prose. Despite
the quality of much early nineteenth-century prose, or later Victorian poetry, when one
thinks of the Romantics, one thinks primarily of poets; of the Victorians, one thinks primarily of their prose.

Though there is no question of Erasmus Darwin's eccentricity in publishing his botanical theories in verse, in the 1790s it was still possible. When his grandson reluctantly
came to formulate his ideas on natural selection in 1859, there was equally no question
that it must be in prose. Beer's concentration on the prose developments of Darwinism
illustrates the aesthetic paradigm-shift that had already occurred. New concepts of biology
were not matter for poetry. Where such references do occur, as in *In Memoriam* , almost a
decade before the *Origin of Species*, they are not expositions, but (horrified) reactions:

Are God and Nature then at strife,
   That Nature lends such evil dreams?
   So careful of the type she seems,
So careless of the single life.
               (*In Memoriam*, LIV)

Tennyson's alarm is the more poignant in that it concerns the relatively benign Lamarckian evolution, where it was believed that acquired characteristics could be inherited, and not the more brutal mechanisms envisaged by Darwin.

In Memoriam was thus a marginalized work in no fewer than three different senses. Published the same year as Wordsworth's posthumous *Prelude*, it has nothing of the intellectual confidence of Wordsworth and the first-generation Romantics; it is no longer at the cutting edge of human experience. The days when poets were expected to understand all fields of knowledge, let alone participate in them, were long gone. Second, even the medium, that of poetry itself, has passed from being the central aesthetic form of the culture to a marginal status. Though a great comfort to Queen Victoria on the death of her husband, it was not where the major intellectual and metaphysical debates of the day were expected to take place. All poetry could do was register disturbance and fears at the way science seemed to be leading. Finally, not merely is the science it fears most already outdated, but so is the religion over whose truth or falsehood Tennyson so painstakingly agonizes.

The opening poem of *In Memoriam*, written last, in 1849, just before the publication of the whole twenty-year sequence, contains one of the most startling and revealing theological statements of the whole Victorian age:

Strong Son of God, immortal Love,
   Whom we, that have not seen thy face,
   By faith, and faith alone, embrace,
Believing where we cannot prove.

What in retrospect is so astounding about this opening definition of 'faith' is that it was evidently so common to its age that it passed almost without comment from its multitude of early readers. Yet the idea of a 'faith' that consisted merely of being able to believe where proof was lacking would have seemed extraordinary to an earlier generation of religious poets, such as Donne, Herbert and Vaughan – not to mention Dante, Augustine or St Paul. Tennyson's God-of-the-gap theology is already such a weak and attenuated thing that it was unlikely to survive very long even without the impact of Darwin. In other words, whatever its very considerable poetic merits, so far from being the classic restatement of Victorian religion that is sometimes assumed, *In Memoriam* was not merely a scientific but a theological cul-de-sac.

It is in this sense that Keble's *Christian Year*, and, indeed, the entire poetic output of the Oxford Movement, must be seen as both the fulfilment of the Romantic movement and, at the same time, a dead end, theologically and aesthetically alike. The very unified poetic sensibility of a Keble, a Froude or a Newman was deeply at odds with the increasing fragmentation of their world. Their common suspicion of private judgement was an anachronism. The task of the major poets, Tennyson, Browning or Swinburne, seemed increasingly to be to reflect their world of doubt, institutional religious decay, and plurality of values. Ridiculed by Dickens, sympathetically analysed by George Eliot, doubted by Hardy, the one thing that Tractarianism could not lead to, it seemed, was a new kind of poetry – and certainly not a new nature poetry.

All of which makes the emergence of precisely that in the 1880s seem, to say the least, improbable; for a cultural determinist, impossible. If one adds that the philosophic inspiration was not merely inspired by the Tractarians, but also by a little-known Scottish medieval monk, Duns Scotus, even the most openminded literary historian might be forgiven for being sceptical. Yet Hopkins, though too young ever to have been a Tractarian, was a convert of Newman, and very much the natural heir of the Tractarian aesthetic. Though he was not to be published until 1918, Hopkins was at work throughout the 1880s creating a poetry and a natural theology that were at once deeply traditional and very much a part of the contemporary sensibility. Consider, for instance, this example:

> As kingfishers catch fire, dragonflies draw flame;
> As tumbled over rim in roundy wells
>   Stones ring; like each tucked string tells, each hung bell's
> Bow swung finds tongue to fling out broad its name;
> Each mortal thing does one thing and the same:
>   Deals out that being indoors each one dwells;
>   Selves – goes itself; *myself* it speaks and spells,
> Crying *what I do is me: for that I came.*
>
> Í say more: the just man justices;
> Keeps gráce: that keeps all his goings graces;
> Acts in God's eye what in God's eye he is –
>   Chríst. For Christ plays in ten thousand places,
> Lovely in limbs, and lovely in eyes not his
>   To the Father through the features of men's faces.

Despite its unconventional appearance, this is of course a perfectly regular sonnet consisting of an octet of eight lines, divided into two four-line rhyming quatrains (*abba abba*), and a six-line sestet. The unfamiliarity comes from a certain neologism and unfamiliarity of diction ('selves' and 'justices' as verbs, for instance) and the irregularity of line-length engendered by Hopkins's famous 'sprung rhythm'.

Scarcely less traditional is the basic theology of the poem, which is sharply at odds with the modernity of its treatment. The innate hierarchy of nature is familiar to us as the Great Chain of Being, which connects humanity both downwards through animal and vegetable life to the simplest mineral and stone, and upwards towards God. Man is at once the apex of the material world and the lowliest of spiritual beings.

But at this point the medieval synthesis is given a sharply nineteenth-century twist. God and nature are not so much at strife as internalized. The essential quality of each thing, be it the vivid beauty of kingfishers or dragonflies in sunlight or the noise of a falling stone in a well, is experienced *existentially*. What each thing 'does' reveals its particular 'being indoors'. We know it not by its essence, but by the way it *presents* itself. In Barfield's terms, B reveals to us A. But so far from being the 'husk of meaning' that both frightened and delighted T. S. Eliot, the world of nature shapes and expresses meaning. Individuation is defined here in terms of communication. Thus music reveals its instrument: 'each tucked string tells, each hung bell's / Bow swung finds tongue'. The key word is 'Selves' – a Hopkins coinage from an Anglo-Saxon root meaning roughly the same as the Latinate verb 'to individuate'. The Aristotelian process by which each thing strives to become more and more fully itself is now seen (in a most un-Aristotelian way) in terms of its power to interact with its environment. The medieval world-picture has, as it were, been turned inside out. The normative intelligence of the age is not Aristotle but Schleiermacher. As so often, we are reminded of the importance of individuation to the Victorians. Just as the *Bildungsroman* came to dominate the novelistic forms of Dickens, Gaskell, Eliot or Thackeray, so even words themselves were being progressively differentiated – or, to use Coleridge's term, 'desynonymized'. Part of the intense vigour and freshness of Hopkins's nature poetry is due simply to the fact that it was not until the nineteenth century that the fundamental separation of humanity and nature can be said to be complete. It was, in this sense, speaking and spelling 'myself' almost for the first time to Hopkins's generation.

Hopkins's emphatic 'I say more' is, in this sense, an assertion of modernity in the face of Catholic tradition. But, as we have seen, the downside of this very sense of personal individuality was a corresponding loss of the older sense of religious communality. 'Faith', as for Tennyson, was less a way of life than an act of willed credulity. For Hopkins, however, the individuation of religious experience was not so much loss as an opening to far greater gain.

What now distinguishes humanity from rocks or kingfishers is inwardness – not merely a sense of self, but a *self-conscious* sense of self. Its focus is to be found in a pun that encapsulates the entire action of the poem: 'Christ plays in ten thousand places'. To 'play' is the activity of a supremely self-conscious creature, and in thus celebrating the new sense of endless self-creation, humanity only follows Christ himself. Thus if Christ 'plays' in man as a musician, it is to take up the theme of musical harmony in creation with which the octet of Hopkins's poem is overtly charged. If Christ's 'playing' is as an actor, it is to 'act' the just man's part, 'that keeps all his goings graces'. If Christ 'plays' as a child might play a game, it is to express the joy of creation as the Great Dance in which dragonfly and kingfisher play their parts – and '[deal] out [their] being' as a card-player 'deals' from a deck of cards: which, seen from the back, are identical, but turned face up, are distinct, individuated and utterly unique. If Christ 'plays' as a fountain of water, we are reminded of the well wherein 'stones ring', not to mention older echoes of the fountain in the midst of the garden, and the river of life, and even Marlowe's Faustian vision of 'where Christ's blood streams in the universe'. If Christ 'plays' across the face of all nature like the subtle play of light and shade, he is the Light of the World that glances off kingfisher and dragonfly alike to reveal their utterly distinctive inscape. If Christ is to be found in the free 'play' of the mind of its subject, we are brought back reflexively to the poem itself as creative artefact. If Christ is thus held to be at 'play' within the very pattern of words in language, and in the 'wordplay' of puns themselves, including this one, it is only a minute example of the involuted complexity of the ten thousand places where he is to be glimpsed, fleetingly as the flash of sunlight on a bird's wing, in the creation of new meaning.

What Christ is *not*, however, is a hidden theological abstraction. Between Christina Rossetti and Hopkins there has been a complete inversion of the relationship between surface and depth, B and A. Allegory has totally disappeared in favour of something that should, in theological terms, be more like sacramentalism, but in literary and aesthetic terms actually appears in a quality more like irony. Here, certainly, is an essentially Tractarian myth of origins, deeply Christian, deeply traditional in material, yet, in its poetic expression of the doctrine of reserve, radically self-conscious, post-Feuerbachian and post-Darwinian – moreover, utterly unpredictable in the nineteenth-century context.

See also: HYMN; POETRY AND RELIGION.

REFERENCES AND FURTHER READING

Abrams, M. H. (1953) *The Mirror and the Lamp*. New York: Oxford University Press.

Barfield, Owen (1962) 'Poetic Diction and Legal Fiction'. In Max Black (ed.). *The Importance of Language* (pp. 51–71). Englewood Cliffs, N. J.: Prentice-Hall.

Battiscombe, Georgina (1963) *John Keble: A Study in Limitations*. London: Constable.

Beer, Gillian (1983) *Darwin's Plots*. London: Routledge.

Bradley, Ian (1997) *Abide with Me: The World of Victorian Hymns*. London: SCM Press.

Carpenter, S. C. (1933) *Church and People 1789–1889*. London: SPCK.

Coleridge, J. T. (1869) *Memoir of the Rev. John Keble*. Oxford: Parker.

Faber, Geoffrey (1933) *Oxford Apostles*. London: Faber.

Griffiths, Eric (1989) *The Printed Voice of Victorian Poetry*. Oxford: Clarendon Press.

Harrison, Peter (1990) *'Religion' and Religions in the English Enlightenment*. Cambridge: Cambridge University Press.

Johnson, Margaret (1997) *Gerard Manley Hopkins and Tractarian Poetry*. London: Ashgate.

Keble, John (1877) *Occasional Papers and Reviews*. Ed. E. B. Pusey. Oxford: J. Parker.

Keble, John (1912) *Lectures on Poetry*. Trans. E. K.

Francis. 2 vols. Oxford: Oxford University Press.

Keble, John (1914) *The Christian Year*. First published 1827. London: Dent.

Moorman, Mary (1965) *William Wordsworth: The Later Years*. Oxford: Oxford University Press.

Mozley, Thomas (1992) *Reminiscences, Chiefly of Oriel College and the Oxford Movement*. 2 vols. London: Longman.

Newman, J. H. (1867) *Verses on Various Occasions*. London: Burns Oates.

Newman, J. H. (1967) *Apologia Pro Vita Sua*. Ed. M. J. Svaglic. Oxford: Oxford University Press.

Prickett, Stephen (1976) *Romanticism and Religion: The Tradition of Coleridge and Wordsworth in the Victorian Church*. Cambridge: Cambridge University Press.

Rowell, Geoffrey (ed.) (1992) *The English Religious Tradition and the Genius of Anglicanism*. Wantage: Ikon Press.

Strachey, Lytton (1918) *Eminent Victorians*. London: Chatto.

Tennyson, G. B. (1981) *Victorian Devotional Poetry: The Tractarian Mode*. Cambridge, Mass.: Harvard University Press.

Ward, Wilfred (1912) *The Life of John Henry Cardinal Newman*. London: Longman.

16

The Spasmodics

Richard Cronin

The Spasmodic School was christened by its detractors. The term was coined by W. E. Aytoun in his review in *Blackwood's* of Alexander Smith's *Poems* of 1853 (75 [March 1854]: 358), and, to quote Smith himself, it 'had a nickname's best prosperity – it stuck' (Smith 1868: 171). Aytoun continued his assault by reviewing *Firmilian: A Spasmodic Tragedy* by T. Percy Jones (75 [May 1854]: 533–51). Both the poem and its author were Aytoun's inventions. Aytoun thought so well of his spoof that he completed Jones's tragedy and published it as an independent volume. It quickly had the desired effect. The work of a group of young poets was laughed out of fashion. Smith's *A Life-Drama*, the major poem in his 1853 volume, and Sydney Dobell's *Balder* (1854) are the chief targets of Aytoun's parody. The third is George Gilfillan, the Dundee minister and man of letters who had championed Smith's and Dobell's work in the *Critic* and the *Eclectic Review*. These then are the central figures of the Spasmodic School, but other poets, many of them also praised by Gilfillan, associated with it, amongst them J. Westland Marston, particularly for his *Gerald: A Dramatic Poem* (1842), Gerald Massey, John Stanyan Bigg and Ebenezer Jones. But the founder of the School was generally identified as Philip Bailey, whose *Festus*, first published in 1839, was recognized rather widely, not just by Gilfillan, as the great poem of the age (Bailey continued to expand *Festus* throughout his life, in part by subsuming into it almost all his later poems. Throughout, I quote from the edition of 1848, the version of the poem most easily available to the other Spasmodic poets.)

The Spasmodic poets are no longer read. Nevertheless, their work is still of interest to students of Victorian poetry. First, it is important as an index of Victorian taste. The popularity of *Festus*, for example, outlived Aytoun's attack. In 1877 it reached its tenth English edition, and its British popularity was outdone in the United States, where it reached its thirtieth edition before the end of the century. Smith's *A Life-Drama* from his *Poems* of 1853 made an immediate impact unmatched by any other debut volume in the period. He was the first poet since Byron of whom it might reasonably be claimed that he awoke and found himself famous (Gilfillan 1854: 160). Second, Spasmodic poetry, in its extreme subjectivity, illustrates more clearly than poetry of any other kind one important aspect of Victorian poetics. Third, it illuminates some of the major work of poets who were then and are now recognized as amongst the most important of the century. Bailey denied that he had borrowed the name of his central character from Robert Browning's *Paracelsus* (Weinstein 1968: 77) – Festus is the name of Paracelsus' oldest friend – but, nevertheless, Browning has good claims to have instigated Spasmodic poetry, not just in *Paracelsus*, but in *Pauline* before it and *Sordello* after. It seems likely that Browning himself recognized as much. In 'Popularity' (1855), Browning lampoons a group of poets, 'Hobbs, Nobbs, Stokes and Nokes', who have achieved their success by imitating the work of more original writers. It has long been suspected that the Spasmodics were the poets that Browning had in mind (Thrale 1955; Harrison 1990: 56–8), but the final line of the poem, 'What porridge had John Keats?', is sharpened if we accept that Browning found the Spasmodics' commercial success particularly galling because he thought of them as imitators not just of Keats but of himself. His own poems, after all, ever since his fateful publication of *Sordello*, had proved almost completely unsaleable. Neither Tennyson's *Maud* (1855) nor Elizabeth Barrett Browning's *Aurora Leigh* (1856, dated 1857), as their reviewers were quick to note, would have taken quite the form that they did had it not been for the example of Spasmodic poets. The negative influence of Spasmodic poetry was as important as the positive. It is clear from Arnold's preface to his *Poems* of 1853 that he felt impelled to formulate his own aesthetic in reaction to the startling success of *A Life-Drama*, and that he made his decision to exclude *Empedocles on Etna* from that volume in part because he had come to recognize that it might itself be identified as a Spasmodic poem.

Spasmodic poetry is distinctive in its form, in its manner and content, and in its style. Bailey's *Festus*, Marston's *Gerald*, Dobell's *The Roman* and *Balder*, Smith's *A Life-Drama* and Bigg's *Night and the Soul* are all of them verse dramas, but they are emphatically unactable dramas. Robert Browning, in his manuscript preface to *Paracelsus*, speaks for them all:

> I do not very well understand what is called a Dramatic Poem, wherein all those restrictions only submitted to on account of some compensating good in the original scheme, are scrupulously retained as tho' for some special fitness in themselves, – & all new faculties placed at an author's disposal by the vehicle he selects, as pertinaciously rejected.

So, in the dramatic poem as practised by the Spasmodics, speeches are untheatrically long, dialogue is subordinated to soliloquy, action to reflection, and scenes, though they may be located in a social space, are just as likely to be set in an entirely abstract, allegorical location ('Scene – A Garden and Pleasure House', 'Scene – Everywhere' [*Festus*, 165, 279]). But the Spasmodics are not adequately defined by the poetic form that they preferred. The dramatic poem, the drama not intended for stage production, is a neglected but important Victorian form, not least because it became a pivot in a central Victorian aesthetic dispute. Henry Taylor, as I shall indicate, was the antithesis of a Spasmodic poet, and his major work, *Philip van Artevelde*, itself took the form of an unactable dramatic poem.

The Spasmodics are more exactly defined by their manner. First, and oddly given their preference for the dramatic form, Spasmodic poems are remarkable for their extreme subjectivity. Spasmodic poems trace, as Browning claimed of his own *Sordello*, 'the incidents in the development of a soul' (the Dedication of the 1863 edition). They share the ambition of Bailey's Festus, which is to offer:

> the most truthful likeness of a mind,
> Which hath as yet been limned; the mind of youth
> In strength and failings, in its overcomings,
> And in its shortcomings.
>
> (1848: 257)

Crucially, they are written on the premise that the mind is best revealed not in its dealings with others but in its self-communings. The Spasmodics are contemptuous of poets whose interest strays from the inner world of mind to the external circumstances of life. As Marston puts it in *Gerald*, if your interest is in:

> The stature of a man, his gait, his dress,
> The colour of his hair, what meat he loved,
> Where he abode, what haunts he frequented,
> His place and time of birth, his age at death,
> And how much crape and cambric marked his end –
> Write a biography!
>
> (1842: 47)

The dramatic form seems preferred by the Spasmodics because it allows them to write in strictly literal obedience to John Stuart Mill's notion that poetry is a kind of 'soliloquy'. The 'highest aim' of the Spasmodic poet, as Bigg puts it in *Night and the Soul*, is 'self-revealment' (1854: 53). This is poetry, then, at an extreme remove from the kind recommended by Taylor in his preface to *Philip van Artevelde*, an objective poetry founded on careful observation of mankind 'in all its classes and under all its circumstances'.

It is almost inevitable that a poetry so committed to a subjectivist aesthetic should strike the unsympathetic reader as remarkable for its egotism. In the central scene of *Night and the Soul*, Alexis sits alone in a room 'looking upon a Public Street', and soliloquizes for fourteen pages on the theme that 'the soul seeth nothing but the soul' and '*self* is the beginning and the end, / The Alpha and the Omega, and the *all*' (1854: 53). Any Spasmodic poem might prompt the response that Mill made to Browning's *Pauline*: 'this writer seems to me possessed with a more intense and morbid self-consciousness than I ever knew in any sane human being'. It is, it is true, an egotism that is ascribed to the Spasmodic hero, not to the Spasmodic poet himself. Egotism is the spiritual disease from which the representative Spasmodic hero suffers, but it is also the condition of Spasmodic poetry, so that the hero's recovery necessarily concludes the poem.

In the preface to the second edition of *Balder*, Dobell complains of the 'indecorous haste and uncharitable dogmatism with which, as I have seen and am informed, [readers] have taken for granted that I must admire the character I think fit to delineate, and that I present as a model what, in truth, I expose as a warning'. Since Balder murders his own child, and is about, as the poem closes, to smother his wife, Dobell's touchiness seems understandable, but, in fact, Spasmodic poets, like Browning in *Pauline*, characteristically tease the reader by hinting at the identity of the poet and his character. Even in his preface Dobell admits that he is himself 'not altogether free' from 'Balderism', and in the poem itself he allows Balder to meditate eloquently on the impossibility of distinguishing the poet from the poem. Balder's poems are:

> my autograph, wherein
> The hand that writes is part of what is writ,
> And I, like the steeped roses of the east,
> Become the necessary element
> Of that which doth preserve me.
>
>   (1875: 25)

In *A Life-Drama*, Alexander Smith plays still more teasingly with the relationship between himself and his hero. On the face of it, the two could not be more widely distinguished. When he published *A Life Drama*, Smith, who had left school at the age of 10, was still employed as a designer in a Glasgow textile factory. His hero, Walter, has an estate in Kent, and is confident enough of his social position to refer to a tenant as 'one of my peasants' (1853: 86). And yet, within the poem, Walter admits that one of his tales is his own life story 'tricked out in a quaint disguise' (1853: 102), and intermittently throughout the poem the disguise slips, and Walter is revealed as a quite different person, someone indistinguishable from Smith himself: 'Within a city One was born to toil / Whose heart could not mate with the common doom' (1853: 131). There is a sense in which all Spasmodic heroes are the Spasmodic poets themselves, tricked out in 'a quaint disguise', and their poems fictions to which the reader is invited to respond as Violet does to Walter's tales:

> you shine through each disguise;
> You are a masker in a mask of glass,
> You've such transparent sides, each casual eye
> May see the heaving heart.
>
>   (1853: 145)

One reason that Spasmodic poet and Spasmodic hero must merge is that the poets are anxious to insist on the representative function of their characters. Dobell has to admit that he is not free from 'Balderism', because '"Balderism" in one form or another is a predominant intellectual misfortune of our day'. These are poets committed to the view that outraged Arnold: 'A true allegory of the state of one's own mind in a representative history is perhaps the highest thing that one can attempt in the way of poetry' ('Theories of Poetry and a New Poet', *North British Review*, 19 [August, 1853]: 338, as quoted in Arnold's 1853 Preface – the new poet was Alexander Smith). They write life dramas, which attempt to incorporate in the history of the single soul the history of the age. George Gilfillan, their champion, was engaged throughout his critical career in a single-minded quest to find the poet of the age. His critical essays are best thought of as a series of advertisements: 'Wanted, a tutor to the rising age; he must be a creedless Christian – full of faith, but full of charity – wise in head and large in heart – a poet and a priest – an "eternal child", as well as a thoroughly furnished man' (Gilfillan 1850: 393). One after another he nominated candidates for the position – Bailey, Dobell, Smith, Bigg – and their poems are best thought of as applications for the post.

Gilfillan is naively enthusiastic in his expression, but it was a want that was rather widely felt in the mid-Victorian period. It had been most powerfully expressed by Thomas Carlyle. In 'The Hero as Man of Letters' (1840) Carlyle at once establishes the poet as the truly heroic figure of the present age, and mourns the absence of any figure in modern Britain who had shown himself, like Goethe in Germany, fully adequate to the role. To Gilfillan, Philip Bailey seemed the obvious candidate. So, Gilfillan praised *Festus* as 'the poem of the age's hope, even as *Sartor Resartus* is the prose record of the age's experience' (Gilfillan 1850: 393). Spasmodic poetry might reasonably be defined as the poetic expression of Carlylism, a point that Aytoun makes when he introduces into *Firmilian* a character called Teufelsdröckh who rails against 'Terrestrial Law-words, Lords, and Law-bringers' in such 'hideous jargon' that he is quite incomprehensible (1854: 108–9).

Like Carlyle, the Spasmodic poets claim to speak for their age, but, also like Carlyle, they address the age from a distance, a distance at once social and geographic. Gilfillan lived throughout his career in Dundee, where he was a minister of the Church of Scotland, rarely visiting London, and never moving to Edinburgh. Of the Spasmodic poets, only Marston moved in metropolitan literary circles. Bailey lived all his life in Nottingham, Dobell in Gloucestershire, and Bigg in Warwickshire. Glasgow, where Smith lived and worked and Gilfillan and Bailey attended university, is the city with which Spasmodic poetry is most closely associated, and Glasgow defined itself by its distance from Edinburgh, Scotland's cultural capital. This is significant for two reasons. First, it helps to explain the animosity that the success of the Spasmodic poets so quickly provoked. Aytoun led the *Blackwood's* reviewers in a concerted attack on their work that was self-consciously modelled on the attacks orchestrated by an earlier generation of *Blackwood's* reviewers, led by J. G. Lockhart, on the Cockney School of Poetry, and Aytoun's attack, like the earlier assault, was motivated by the belief that Gilfillan, Smith and Dobell were ill-educated and presumptuous interlopers into cultural precincts that ought to be reserved to their social superiors. Alexander Smith, a factory worker who was largely self-educated, was particularly vulnerable to this kind of assault. In *Firmilian*, he appears as Sancho, a costermonger, who is hailed by the critic Apollodorus (one of Gilfillan's pen names) as a 'genuine bard' when Apollodorus overhears him singing. But it is important, too, because it explains the aggression with which the Spasmodic poets address the age for which they claim to speak. The Spasmodic poet has heady ambitions. He is determined to 'hew his name out upon time / As on a rock' (Smith 1853: 3), but remains haunted by the fear that the world will prove unresponsive, and the poems remain 'shouts to gain the notice of the Sphynx, / Staring right on with calm eternal eyes' (1853: 6). The Spasmodic response was to shout louder.

The poems attempt to force themselves on the public attention most obviously by challenging conventional orthodoxies; ethical, religious, sexual and political. As Aytoun points out in the preface to *Firmilian*, the Spasmodic hero is marked by his 'moral obliquity'. Balder is the extreme example. He believes that he can fulfil his poetic ambitions only if he experiences death, his problem being that were he himself to die he would be unable to record the experience in verse. He dreams of becoming a creature 'whereof the half could die / And the remainder watch it' (Dobell 1875: 74), but recognizes that this is impracticable. The question remains:

> Who is to die? It is not credible
> That this I have begun should come to end
> For lack of human lives.
>
> (1875: 72)

He takes the perversely logical decision to kill the person whose death he will experience as most like his own death, his own infant child. His wife, Amy, goes mad in her grief, and the play ends with Balder about to kill her too. Dobell seems anxious to test the notion that the poet is freed from the ordinary duty of obedience to the moral law. Aytoun deftly parodies the idea by giving Firmilian the ambition to 'paint the mental spasms that tortured Cain!', an attempt in which he has failed, he believes, because 'What we write / Must be the reflex of the thing we know' (1854: 6). He sets about acquiring the knowledge of guilt by poisoning three of his friends during a drunken roister, and, when he finds that this does not leave him racked with guilt, he blows up a church and kills its whole congregation. This, too, does not avail, and so he murders his friend and fellow poet, Haverillo, the brother of his intended bride, by throwing him from a high tower. Haverillo lands on the head of the critic Apollodorus (Gilfillan), killing both, but again Firmilian fails to feel any guilt. Frustrated, he abandons his poem. The crimes of Smith's hero, Walter, are less lurid than Balder's, but the climax of his story is his rape of the woman that he will later marry. By comparison, Marston's Gerald and Bigg's Alexis seem scarcely culpable: they are guilty only of abandoning the women who love them in order to devote themselves to poetry. But there seems a determined attempt to offer, through the behaviour of the hero, calculated affronts to a bourgeois code of proprieties.

Spasmodic heroes seem all to have inherited something of the enthusiastic antinomianism that Bailey credits to Festus, who holds that that 'evil' is only 'Good in another way we are not skilled in', and that 'no soul / Though buried in the centre of all sin / Is lost to God' (1848: 162). Dobell's and Smith's heroes, by contrast, are afflicted by religious doubts. Dobell records that *Balder* was intended as the first in a trilogy of poems designed to show 'the Progress of a Human Being from Doubt to Faith', and Smith's Walter, too, loses his faith. Gilfillan, a clergyman, might seem an odd champion of such verse, but Gilfillan was an unusual minister, who wrote enthusiastic appreciations of Godwin, Shelley and Carlyle, and who believed that the poet of the age must be a Christian but a 'creedless Christian'.

Festus is freed by his comfortably antinomian doctrine to give full bent to his sexual rapacity. A succession of women succumb to his advances until he achieves his supreme triumph by successfully seducing the mistress of Lucifer himself. After Bailey the Spasmodics continued to practise a kind of erotic brinkmanship, flirting with the limits of the acceptable. In *Festus*, the technique can be comically naïve, as when Festus declares that to young men such as him 'woman is / All bosom' (Bailey 1848: 100). Throughout the poem breasts make repeated and heated appearances as Festus lays his 'famished lips' on the 'dazzling bosom' of a succession of women (1848: 231; this one is called Helen). But far more often the eroticism of Spasmodic verse is metaphorical. For Smith the ocean lapping on the sand is the image to which he repeatedly returns to figure his utmost dreams of delicious erotic refinement (Smith 1853: 38, 43, 111, 127), and the same image serves him when Walter's erotic yearnings collapse, after his rape of Violet, into self-disgust:

> Like a wild lover, who has found his love
> Worthless and foul, our friend, the sea, has left
> His paramour the shore; naked she lies,
> Ugly and black and bare. Hark how he moans!
> The pain is in his heart. Inconstant fool!
> He will be up upon her breast tomorrow
> As eager as today.
>
> (Smith 1853: 120)

The attempt is clearly to revive the insistent figurative eroticism of Keats and Shelley, but it is inflected by a heady consciousness of the daring with which this material challenges Victorian proprieties.

Spasmodic verse, then, lays itself open to the charges that Aytoun and other brought against it; that it is immoral, impious and licentious; but, as in Lockhart's attacks on the Cockneys, moral outrage is a front for political hostility. The Spasmodics are a poetic school to which 'none but liberals and progressionists need apply' (*Blackwood's*, 75 [March, 1854]: 349). Gilfillan was Aytoun's prime target not only because of the poets he championed, but because Gilfillan was one of the most active radical campaigners in mid-century Scotland. Aytoun's political animus is evident enough in the most unpleasant episode of *Firmilian*. Firmilian is involved with three women, Mariana, whose attractions are magnified by her large dowry, Lilian and Indiana (the names Mariana and Lilian offer interesting evidence that even before *Maud* Tennyson might be, however loosely, associated with the Spasmodics). Unwilling to give up any of them, Firmilian tries to persuade them to share his affections. Mariana and Lilian seem at first to respond sympathetically to the proposal, but then they learn that Indiana is black. Mariana is horrified, 'A filthy negress!', and Lilian is appalled, 'what blubber lips she has!' (Aytoun 1854: 144). In *A Life-Drama* the poet Walter confesses his love by telling the young woman a story of an Indian page, a 'dusk Hyperion', who declares his love for a white princess. She responds by mocking his pretension, and dismissing him (Smith 1853: 75). It is a story through which Smith expresses his own anxiety that the attempt of a self-educated Glasgow factory worker to win a place among the English poets will meet with a similar contemptuous rebuff. But the episode from Smith's poem scarcely accounts for Aytoun's virulence. That can only be explained by Aytoun's recognition that the anti-slavery movement, into which Gilfillan 'threw himself with his whole heart', had become a central focus for radical energies. In March 1846, Gilfillan invited Frederick Douglass to give a lecture at his church in Dundee, at which 'Douglass outdid himself in the boldness of his charges against those whom he held faithless to the cause of liberty', and in 1853 he responded to Harriet Beecher Stowe's visit to his city with 'a thrill of sublime emotion' (Watson and Watson 1892: 79, 165). But the link that Aytoun detected between Gilfillan's two areas of activity was not imaginary.

Paracelsus might be said to have inaugurated Spasmodic poetry, and Browning was nervously aware of the poem's political bent. He wrote to W. J. Fox, editor of the radical *Monthly Repository*: 'there are precious bold bits here & there, & the drift & scope are awfully radical' (16 April 1835). The 'drift & scope' of *Festus* are still clearer. The poem is dedicated to an ideal of 'full and holy equalness' (Bailey 1848: 215), and aspires to a state in which 'all ranks, all classes . . . May mingle into one' (1848: 46). Dobell's first major work, *The Roman*, celebrates another great radical cause, the Roman revolution of 1848. In *Balder* and in Smith's *A Life-Drama* political energies are almost as evident, but their character has changed. Radical political enthusiasms are consistently displaced, into amatory adventures, for example:

> O untouched lips!
> I see them as a glorious rebel sees
> A crown within his reach.
> (Smith 1853: 79)

Still more commonly, they are diverted from an assault on the bastions of economic and political privilege to an assault on the summits of literary success:

> Dungeoned in poverty, he saw afar
> The shining peaks of fame that wore the sun
> Most heavenly bright, they mocked him through the bars.
> (1853: 135)

Smith had witnessed and perhaps participated in the Glasgow riots of 1848, the most serious riots in Britain in the year of revolutions, but, after the suppression of the riots and the collapse of Chartism in the city, Smith was left with no outlet for his political energies (Cronin 1990: 134–6). Spasmodic poetry might be described as the characteristic radical poetry of the mid-century, the radical poetry written by those who found themselves, after the failure of the 1848 revolutions, without a cause, and hence without a theme, or at least without any theme other than the poem itself. So it is that Spasmodic poems, poems written by young poets in an attempt to win fame, should so consistently take as their subject a young poet's struggle to write the poem that will make him famous.

For contemporary readers, the defining mark of the Spasmodic poem was that it should be a poem about a poet. In a crucial scene in *Festus* an aspiring poet comes to Festus looking for instruction. Festus tells him of a poet friend, who 'wrote amid the ruins' of his heart: 'They were his throne and theme' (Bailey 1848: 235). He recommends that the student study his poem, which is Spasmodic in the vastness of its theme, in the looseness of its construction ('It has a plan, but no plot. Life hath none' [1848: 245]), and in its style. It is unsurprising that Festus confesses at last (1848: 266) that he is himself that poet, and it is equally unsurprising that the poem that he recommends to the student is indistinguishable from *Festus* itself. Balder is given to quoting from his own poems at tedious length, chief amongst them his 'early planned, / Long meditate, and slowly written epic!' (Dobell 1875: 24), a work that seems very similar to *Balder*. Marston's Gerald is also a poet. He is embittered by his neglect, and only saved from suicide by a visit from Lord Roxmore, who wishes on behalf of himself and his wife to thank the author of the poem that has transformed their lives. Gerald dies young, but not before the appearance of newspaper articles belatedly recognizing his greatness. Bigg's *Night and the Soul* ends with Alexis reading one of his poems to his friends. They are unlikely to be surprised when he explains, 'The Poet's mighty mission is its theme' (1854: 183). At the end of *A Life-Drama* Walter embarks on a life of domestic contentment with the woman that he has raped and abandoned, but not before he has recorded his agonies of remorse in a poem. 'That was a hit!', one of his friends assures us: 'The world is murmuring like a hive of bees; / He is its theme' (Smith 1853: 182). Again it seems a poem indistinguishable from *A Life-Drama*.

In poems about poets, style becomes an aspect of a poem's content as much as of its form, and hence it is unsurprising that Spasmodic poems should cultivate extreme stylistic idiosyncrasies, as in this remarkable passage from *Balder*:

> Ah! ah! ah!
> Ah! ah! ah! ah! ah! ah! ah! ah! ah! ah!
> (Dobell 1875: 260)

Spasmodic poetry aspires to a single pitch of stylistic intensity from which, inevitably, it often tumbles into bathos, with the odd result that the Spasmodic poets often seem to parody themselves more deftly than Aytoun parodies them. Firmilian threatens to throw Haverillo from a tower as Dobell's Balder had threatened his wife's doctor. Firmilian directs Haverillo's attention to a 'melon-vendor's stall down i' the square':

> Methinks the fruit that, close, beside the eye,
> Would show as largely as a giant's head,
> Is dwindled to a heap of gooseberries!
> (Aytoun 1854: 93)

But this is only mildly amusing in comparison with the original:

My Dog,
Whose stature thou didst praise, seen hence appears
Notably less.

(Dobell 1875: 218)

Spasmodic verse characteristically trembles on the edge of self-parody.

Its most obvious characteristic is its extreme metaphorical vitality. Bailey's Festus tells us that the 'world is full of glorious likenesses. / The poet's duty is to sort these out' (1848: 239). In *A Life-Drama*, Walter, recalling his youthful friendship with another poet, says that:

our chief joy
Was to draw images from everything;
And images lay thick upon our talk,
As shells on ocean sands.

(Smith 1853: 151)

For unsympathetic readers, such as the *Blackwood's* reviewer, the Spasmodic poets subject the reader to 'a shower of similes, pelting upon us like the *bonbons* of a carnival' (79 [February 1856]: 135). But it is the character of the similitudes, not just their profusion, that characterizes Spasmodic verse. Its energy is manufactured by establishing a strained gap between the two parts of a comparison. Dobell's Balder, for example, invites his wife to climb with him to the top of a hill:

The bare hill-top
Shines near above us; I feel like a child
Nursed on his grandsire's knee that longs to stroke
The bald bright forehead; shall we climb?

(1875: 147)

It is the undue prominence of the similitude that marks it as Spasmodic. The manner is always potentially comical, and the potential is recognized by the Spasmodics themselves. In *A Life-Drama*, for example, a recollection of a young poet who, stung by a rebuff, 'foamed at God and died', prompts an invitation to 'rain similes upon his corse like tears'. He is a frail, March flower, a 'Lapland fool' who runs mad because his own poor hut cannot match in grandeur the aurora borealis, and then a less reverent speaker interrupts to compare him to a 'ginger-beer bottle burst' (Smith 1853: 139–40). A character in *Festus* notes how proud Lucifer is of being always on time: 'With not / More pride an Indian shows his foeman's scalp / Than he his watch for punctuality' (Bailey 1848: 230).

In its style as in its manner, it is a verse that defines itself in opposition to the ideal that Henry Taylor had promoted in *Philip van Artevelde*, in which he cultivates a style at once chaste and chastened, sparing of metaphor and simile, always preferring to risk prosaicism than to seem bombastic. In *A New Spirit of the Age* (1844) R. H. Horne already recognizes that Taylor's and Bailey's are the two styles that divide modern poetry. His own preference is for Bailey: 'if the absence of a power to call up imagery, or the levelling down of imagery to a barren regularity, be now considered as the true principle and style for the greatest poetry, then all our great poets of by-gone ages have written in error, and must no longer be accounted great' (II, 284). Poets such as Taylor aim at 'stunting the growth of the imagination by never suffering it to rise beyond the calm level of reason and common sense' (II, 289). Reason, Horne suggests, is celebrated by Taylor as a disciplinary agent that functions to repress the insubordinate ambition to rise beyond one's proper station that so many Spasmodic poems articulate.

Tennyson's *Maud* was identified as soon as it was published as a Spasmodic poem, and in particular as a poem in which Tennyson, the poet laureate, had indecorously yielded to the influence of a 23-year-old Glasgow factory worker. Strong similarities of plot link *Maud* and *A Life-Drama*. Walter's first love dies of grief after she has been forced by her family to marry for money, the fate that threatens Maud. Both Walter and Tennyson's speaker commit a crime – Walter rapes Violet, and Tennyson's speaker kills Maud's brother in a duel. In both cases remorse leads to madness, but both recover their sanity at the last. Walter is even infected with the war fever of Tennyson's speaker:

> Oh, for mad War!
> I'd give my next twelve years to head but once
> Ten thousand horse in a victorious charge.
> (Smith 1853: 185)

Other similarities are more significant. Throughout *A Life-Drama*, Smith's own sense of embittered resentment that his lowly social station threatens to stifle his poetic ambitions is allowed incongruously to infiltrate the meditations of his privileged hero, Walter. Tennyson's speaker, whose father has been cheated of his inheritance by his brother, is infected by a similar rancour. Walter is a 'quaint disguise' for Smith himself, a mask that is always in danger of becoming a 'mask of glass' which fully exposes Smith's 'heaving heart'. Tennyson is cagier, but his poem, like Smith's, flirts with autobiography; his father's disinheritance in favour of his younger brother, the rejection of his proposal to Rosa Baring on the ground of his poverty. Most importantly Spasmodic poetry left its mark on both the form and the style of Tennyson's poem. The form, which Tennyson thought of as 'a new form of dramatic composition' and which he was later to describe as a 'monodrama', a narrative presented dramatically in a series of lyrics expressing the successive moods of the speaker, is the form towards which all Spasmodic poems tend. Marston's description of his own *Gerald* could serve for *Maud*: 'The Reader will bear in mind that all I have contemplated in the illumination of *certain points* in Gerald's mental history is to show the *crises* of his development, not their *progress*' (1842: preface to the poem). Finally, particularly in its opening sections, the energy of Tennyson's verse is produced Spasmodically, by forcing apart the tenor and the vehicle of the metaphor, and by rendering all perceptions with a monotonous and often incongruous intensity. There remains, of course, a crucial distinction. In Tennyson's hands, the style becomes diagnostic: it expresses his speaker's madness. There were, as even Gilfillan recognized, three schools of Victorian poetry, 'the objective, the subjective, and the combination of the two' (1854: 163). Tennyson, like Robert Browning, was a member of the third, a practitioner of the art of compromise. Tennyson was on cordial terms with both Henry Taylor and Sydney Dobell. He admired *Festus*, and was impressed by *A Life-Drama*, but he was equally prepared to admire *Philip van Artevelde*. *Maud* is a characteristic product of his art, because, strictly speaking, *Maud* leaves it uncertain whether Tennyson is a proponent of a subjective, expressionist aesthetics or of the objectivity insisted on by Henry Taylor, uncertain whether Tennyson reveals himself in *Maud* as an exponent of Spasmodic poetry, or as its most subtle satirist.

Elizabeth Barrett Browning, unlike Tennyson, and much more clearly than her husband, remained throughout her life committed to the radical aesthetic that Horne promoted in *A New Spirit of the Age*. *Blackwood's* was thankful that in one respect Tennyson had preserved his distinction from the Spasmodics: his speaker 'is not – let us be grateful – a poet'. But in *Aurora Leigh*, Elizabeth Barrett Browning, by refusing the laureate's sensible view that 'a poet's hero ought not to be a poet', fully enrolled herself in the Spasmodic school:

> There is but one sister in the melodious household, and she is quite what the one sister generally is in such a family – not untouched even by the schoolboy pranks of the surrounding brothers – falling into their ways of speaking – moved by their commotions – very feminine, yet more acquainted with masculine fancies than with the common ways of women. (79 [February 1856]: 137)

For contemporary readers *Aurora Leigh* was evidently a Spasmodic poem. In *Festus*, *Gerald*, *A Life-Drama* and *Balder*, the poem's central figure, like Aurora Leigh, is represented as engaged in the composition of a poem that is insecurely distinguished from the poems in which they are characters. The links between *Aurora Leigh* and the poems by Marston and Smith are particularly strong. Like Gerald and Smith's Walter, Aurora writes a poem that makes her famous, and like them she finds that her fame is no compensation for her failure to find domestic contentment. The parallels with *Gerald* are even closer than those with *A Life-Drama*, and there is presumptive evidence that it was a poem that Barrett Browning knew well. In *A New Spirit of the Age*, Horne couples Marston with Robert Browning (1844: II, 155–86). Like Gerald, Aurora goes to London in an attempt to secure a reputation as a poet, like him she suffers from poverty (though his suffering is more melodramatically extreme), like him she eventually wins recognition (though his is more delayed), and like him she concludes that literary fame is an inadequate substitute for marital happiness (though he dies before he can act on his new belief).

There remain significant differences. Spasmodic verse is remarkable for its exclusive interest in the masculine. The representative Spasmodic woman is, as Mill remarked of Robert Browning's *Pauline*, 'a mere phantom'. Her role is to be seduced, raped, abandoned, or driven mad by grief, and in doing so to provide the Spasmodic hero with food for reflection. Barrett Browning's most radical innovation is to transform the Spasmodic hero into a woman. The consequences of that simple decision are too complex to explore, but it is worth making just one point. In *Aurora Leigh*, Barrett Browning's verse is more densely and daringly figurative than in her earlier work. She has borrowed, it might seem, the metaphorical habits of the Spasmodics, but they are habits that allow her to devise 'woman's figures'. Like the Spasmodics, Barrett Browning attempts to write a poem that will give a voice to the age, but hers is emphatically a 'double-breasted age' (*Aurora Leigh*, V, 216). Like the Spasmodics she generates the energy of her verse by forcing apart the tenor and vehicle of her metaphors, but whereas in them it is a figurative habit through which they express their sense of the social chasm that separates them from Britain's centres of cultural authority, in *Aurora Leigh* it signifies the divide that the poem threatens, which separates a woman poet from full participation in a poetic tradition that has defined itself as male.

A third great Victorian poet was decisively influenced by the Spasmodics. In *Festus* Bailey had claimed for his poem the authority of Goethe. Both in its title and in its subject matter he offered the poem to his reader as an English *Faust*. Arnold, like Bailey, recognized Goethe as 'the greatest poet of modern times', but Arnold's Goethe is a classicist, a poet who saw it as his duty to represent the objective world. *Faust*, 'judged as a whole, and judged strictly as a poetical work, is defective'. The judgement was forced on Arnold by his outrage that a 'true allegory of the state of one's own mind in a representative history' (preface to *Poems*, 1853) might be thought 'the highest thing that one can attempt in the way of poetry', a proposition that Arnold found so uncomfortable that it persuaded him not simply to dismiss *Faust* from its central place in Goethe's oeuvre, but also to exclude from his new edition of his poems his own *Empedocles on Etna*. It is as if he had already conceded the justice of the rebuke that Aytoun was lightly to deliver when his *Firmilian*, just before his death, compares himself to 'rash Empedocles' (1854: 147). Arnold came to see how his own poem could be thought of as representing in a quaint and transparent disguise a representation of the state of his own mind, itself offered as representative of the modern mind. He came to see, in other words, that *Empedocles on Etna* might be a Spasmodic poem.

In the preface to the 1853 volume, Arnold breaks decisively with the subjective school of Victorian poetry, and in doing so he broke with his closest poetic associate, Arthur Hugh Clough. When Clough came to review the *Poems*, he did so by comparing them unfavourably with Smith's *A Life-Drama* (Clough 1888: 355–78). Several explanations have been offered for Clough's action, but it may be worth advancing one more. As Clough read *A Life-Drama* and Arnold's preface, he did so in the knowledge that he had himself already written, in 1852, the first draft of *Dipsychus*, a poem, like Bailey's *Festus*, closely modelled on *Faust*, and a poem in which Clough offers an allegory of the state of his own mind, which is also offered as a representative mind of the mid-century, trapped in an unending dialogue with itself, unable to find any outlet in action. Arnold, he may have come to feel, in attacking the Spasmodic school, was launching an attack on Clough himself.

See also: EPIC; VERSE DRAMA.

REFERENCES AND FURTHER READING

Aytoun, William Edmonstoune, writing as T. Percy Jones (1854) *Firmilian; or The Student of Badajoz. A Spasmodic Tragedy.* Edinburgh and London: William Blackwood.

Bailey, Philip (1848) *Festus.* First published 1839. London: William Pickering.

Bigg, John Stanyan (1854) *Night and the Soul.* London: Groombridge.

Buckley, Jerome Hamilton (1952) *The Victorian Temper: A Study in Literary Culture.* London: George Allen and Unwin.

Clough, Arthur Hugh (1888) *Prose Remains of Arthur Hugh Clough.* Ed. Blanche Clough. London: Macmillan.

Cronin, Richard (1990) 'Alexander Smith and the Poetry of Displacement.' *Victorian Poetry*, 28, 129–45.

Dobell, Sydney (1875) *The Poetical Works.* 2 vols. Ed. John Nichol. London: Smith, Elder.

Gilfillan, George (1845) *A Gallery of Literary Portraits.* Edinburgh: William Tait.

Gilfillan, George (1850) *A Second Gallery of Literary Portraits.* Edinburgh: James Hogg.

Gilfillan, George (1854) *A Third Gallery of Portraits.* Edinburgh: James Hogg.

Harrison, Anthony H. (1990) *Victorian Poets and Romantic Poems.* Charlottesville: University Press of Virginia.

Horne, Richard Hengist (1844) *A New Spirit of the Age.* London: Smith, Elder.

Marston, John Westland (1842) *Gerald: A Dramatic Poem, and Other Poems.* London: C. Mitchell.

Smith, Alexander (1853) *Poems.* London: David Bogue.

Smith, Alexander (1868) *Last Leaves: Sketches and Criticisms.* Ed. Patrick Proctor Alexander. Edinburgh: William P. Nimmo.

Taylor, Henry (1834) *Philip van Artevelde: A Dramatic Romance.* 2 vols. London: Edward Moxon.

Thrale, Jeremy (1955) 'Browning's "Popularity" and the Spasmodic Poets.' *Journal of English and Germanic Philology*, 54, 353–4.

Watson, Robert A. and Elizabeth S. Watson (1892) *George Gilfillan: Letters and Journals, with Memoir.* London: Hodder and Stoughton.

Weinstein, Mark A. (1968) *William Edmonstoune Aytoun and the Spasmodic Controversy.* New Haven and London: Yale University Press.

17

The Pre-Raphaelite School

David Riede

The word 'Pre-Raphaelite' emerged in Victorian culture to designate not writers but a group of very young painters in rebellion against the reigning artistic establishment, the Royal Academy. Since the eighteenth century the Royal Academy had taught and enforced certain formal rules of painting deduced from the practices of Raphael, but in 1848 three students in the schools of the Royal Academy, Dante Gabriel Rossetti, William Holman Hunt and John Everett Millais, saw this rule-bound condition of art as 'offensive, contemptible, and even scandalous' (*Germ*, 6), and decided to eschew Raphaelite rules and to promote principles of art that they saw as prevailing before Raphael and the subsequent Raphaelitism of the academies. They would be 'Pre-Raphaelite', and in September of 1848 these three joined with four friends to celebrate their comradeship and common purposes by founding themselves as what they called the 'Pre-Raphaelite Brotherhood'.

Despite its very clear origin, the term 'Pre-Raphaelite' remains difficult to define, partly because the Brethren did not entirely agree about what it should mean, and even more because the term, originally intended to describe a school of painting, came eventually to be associated with literature and other arts as the original brethren and their later associates developed and broadened their aesthetic interests. As a literary term 'Pre-Raphaelite' came to suggest the characteristic styles of the most literary of the brethren, Rossetti, and his various associates, especially his sister Christina, William Morris and Algernon Swinburne, and to a lesser extent George Meredith and a host of minor artists and versifiers in Rossetti's wake. Even though the term came to be used for a variety of arts, however, it never entirely lost its original associations with painting, but later in the century the principal original Brethren disagreed on what these associations were, on what their common purpose had been, on who had most inspired the movement, and who had been most true to it. Even from the very beginning, the paintings they exhibited in 1849, mysteriously inscribed with the letters 'PRB', do not very clearly show any common purpose beyond the desire to flout the academic rules, but a few aspirations can nevertheless be isolated. The brethren clearly were eager to follow the precepts of John Ruskin to 'go to nature in all singleness of heart, and walk with her laboriously and trustingly, having no other thought but how best to penetrate her meaning; rejecting nothing, selecting nothing, and scorning nothing' (1903–12: III, 624). As the young painters understood the advice, they were to paint everything they saw exactly as they saw it in every detail, and they trusted Ruskin's assertion that accurate, honest visual representation would be sufficient to penetrate nature's 'meaning', evidently on the grounds later offered by Browning's 'Fra Lippo Lippi', a monologue spoken by an early Italian painter who was by definition Pre-Raphaelite:

> The beauty and the wonder and the power,
> The shapes of things, their colours, lights and shades,
> Changes, surprises – and God made it all
>   . . . paint these
> Just as they are, careless what comes of it[.]
> God's works – paint any one, and count it crime
> To let a truth slip.
>
>   (ll. 283–5, 293–6)

For Ruskin and the latter-day Pre-Raphaelites as well as for Lippi, nature was apparently charged with the grandeur of God, so that, in Rossetti's phrase, all natural things could be, like Biblical types, 'symbols also in some deeper way' ('St Luke the Painter', l. 7). Minute fidelity to nature characterized Millais's and Hunt's pictures of this period, and Hunt, especially, remained arduously Pre-Raphaelite in this Ruskinian way. Especially after Ruskin himself polemically praised Pre-Raphaelite 'truth to nature' in a series of letters to *The Times*, contemporaries regarded truth to nature as the hallmark of Pre-Raphaelite art.

Contemporaries also, however, were aware of archaism in a style that manifestly recalled the early Italian devotional art prior to Raphael, and indeed this archaic tendency was an important element especially in the art of Rossetti. In looking back for inspiration to early Italian religious art the Brethren were, again, following the lead of Ruskin, but they were also influenced by the recent artistic movement of the German Nazarenes, whose early Italian style had been brought back to England by such painters as William Dyce and Rossetti's teacher, Ford Madox Brown. The perception of early Italian religious art of this time is perhaps best seen in Lord Lindsay's *History of Christian Art*, published in 1847, which described 'a holy purity, an innocent naiveté, a childlike grace and simplicity, a freshness, a fearlessness, an utter freedom from affectation, a yearning after all things truthful, lovely, and of good report' (quoted in Grieve 1973: 9). The archaic and early Italian religious influence was associated with Catholicism and with the Anglo-Catholic Oxford Movement by vigorously Protestant contemporaries, and the Pre-Raphaelites consequently disavowed it, but it was in fact the dominant characteristic in the works of D. G. Rossetti, the most literary of the Brethren. Most scholars agree that Rossetti had little or no sincere Christian faith, but he had been raised by a father who was steeped in Dante scholarship, and by a devoutly Anglo-Catholic mother. He had called himself an 'Art-Catholic' prior to adopting the label 'Pre-Raphaelite', and his artistic practice corresponded closely with the Anglo-Catholic belief that visible reality simultaneously veils and suggests a deep indwelling significance in things. For true believers like the Oxford priest-poets John Henry Newman and John Keble as well as Christina Rossetti, the indwelling presence was God, but for the sceptical Rossetti it seems to have been sufficient simply to suggest any meaning or mystery beyond the apparent surfaces of things. Rossetti's 'Art-Catholicism' can hardly be called the dominant characteristic of the PRB, but it may be seen as the germ of Pre-Raphaelitism as a literary movement.

The first undeniably Pre-Raphaelite poems to be published are perhaps the sonnets that Rossetti wrote to accompany his 1849 painting, *The Girlhood of Mary Virgin*. The first of these sonnets expresses the 'Mariolatry' typical of Rossetti's Art-Catholicism, but it also expresses the chaste reverence for women and 'mystery' that came to characterize early Pre-Raphaelite poetry:

> This is that blessed Mary, pre-elect
> God's Virgin. Gone is a great while, and she
> Was young in Nazareth of Galilee.
> Her kin she cherished with devout respect:
> Her gifts were simpleness of intellect
> And supreme patience. From her mother's-knee
> Fruitful and hopeful; wise in charity;
> Strong in grave peace; in duty circumspect.
>
> So held she through her girlhood; as it were
> An angel-watered lily, that near God
> Grows, and is quiet. Till one dawn, at home,
> She woke in her white bed, and had no fear
> At all, – but wept till sunshine, and felt awed;
> Because the fullness of the time was come.

Quite evidently this sonnet is concerned not with the Ruskinian truth to nature that characterized Hunt's Pre-Raphaelitism, but with the tone of hushed awe, religious wonder and even paradoxically chaste eroticism of the Art-Catholicism that Rossetti had derived from his love of the poetry of Dante and his contemporaries. The moral tone of the sonnet and of Rossetti's other Art-Catholic work is imitative of that perceived by Lord Lindsay in early Italian art. Some contemporaries, nevertheless, thought the Anglo-Catholicism of the work rather too close to the Mariolatry of Roman Catholicism, which was stigmatized as too sensual for Protestant England.

D. M. R. Bentley (1977) has demonstrated in detail how faithfully Rossetti's early art represents contemporary Anglo-Catholic beliefs and practices, but Jerome McGann has argued that Rossetti's art is readily distinguishable from the Christian faith it mimics. In a brilliant recent study, McGann has argued that Rossetti's imitations of early Italian aesthetic forms attempt to recapture not the archaic beliefs informing the works, but rather the aesthetic methods employed: 'For an agnostic like Rossetti, the critical presentation of Christian materials allows him to construct his contemporary artistic manifesto. The manifesto is performative, coming as the image of a pastiche of an antique set of signs'

(McGann 2000: 30). For Rossetti, Dante's Beatrice was not to be allegorized in Christian mysticism, but revered as a flesh-and-blood woman, and his own version of the Virgin is similarly set forth in a somewhat secular, fully humanized representation of 'girlhood'. As Rossetti put it, 'that picture of mine was a symbol of female excellence. The Virgin being taken as its highest type. It was not her *Childhood* but *Girlhood*' (cited in Grieve 1973: 8). Still, the images of the lily and the apocalyptically gravid phrase 'the fullness of the time' suggest a desire to imply a meaning beyond the powers of painting to represent. For Rossetti, however, painting was to be charged with as much meaning as possible, and the second of his two sonnets on the Girlhood of Mary Virgin explains the religious symbolism included in the painting: 'These are the symbols', it begins, and goes on to explicate their meaning. The books symbolize the writers, the lilies' innocence, and so forth.

For Rossetti, as for most of his later Pre-Raphaelite followers, Art was far more important than Christianity. In fact, a crucial feature of emergent Pre-Raphaelitism was the supplementing or supplanting of Christian faith with a faith in the power of art. For a variety of reasons, no doubt including Rossetti's desire to link painting with poetry and the Brotherhood's desire to publicize their cause, in 1850 the PRB launched its own periodical, *The Germ: Thoughts Towards Nature In Poetry, Literature, and Art*, a journal of historical importance as the first of many subsequent self-consciously avant-garde organs of artistic coteries. The *Germ* was certainly intended to advance the cause of Pre-Raphaelitism, and under the editorship of Rossetti's brother, William Michael, it was to publish the writings and occasional etchings of the Brotherhood and other like-minded contributors. Inevitably, the *Germ* failed as a commercial enterprise, folding after just four numbers, but it was a success not only as the prototype for later avant-garde journals, but also as the origin of Pre-Raphaelite literature. Some of the writing in the *Germ* was programmatic about Pre-Raphaelite doctrine – William Rossetti's rather obscure sonnet on the title page, for example, was meant to affirm, in his more lucid paraphrase, that 'a writer ought to think out his subject honestly and personally, and not imitatively, and ought to express it with directness and precision; if he does this, we should respect his performance as truthful, even though it may not be important. This indicated, for writers, much the same principle which the PRB professed for painters' (*Germ*, 16). Unfortunately, William Rossetti's sonnet, as well as various other poems and essays about Pre-Raphaelite principles, only made clear that the Brotherhood did not have anything very remarkable to say about art. What were genuinely valuable in the *Germ* were the poetic contributions of D. G. and Christina Rossetti, poetry that made the *Germ* influential beyond its own brief lifetime.

Dante Rossetti's emphatically Art-Catholic contributions included early versions of two of his most celebrated works, 'My Sister's Sleep' and 'The Blessed Damozel', poems which, along with the sonnets for Mary's girlhood, represent the origins of Pre-Raphaelite poetry, though this poetry was to develop in a variety of directions under Rossetti's various 'disciples'. By far the best known of his Art-Catholic poems, 'The Blessed Damozel' established the grounds for Rossetti's reputation as a precocious genius. The poem describes a recently deceased woman, gazing longingly from the ramparts of heaven upon her earthly lover, and its vaguely mystical imagery is akin to the 'symbols' of the painting of 'The Girlhood of Mary Virgin':

> The blessed damozel leaned out
> > From the gold bar of Heaven;
> Her blue grave eyes were deeper much
> > Than deep water, even.
> She had three lilies in her hands,
> > And the stars in her hair were seven.

Within these 'Dantesque heavens', as Leigh Hunt called them, the lilies and the mystic numbers three and seven assimilate the Damozel to the Virgin, 'our Lady of the seven sorrows', but the more significant mystery, suggested in the depths of 'blue grave eyes', seems to be the mystery simultaneously revealed and concealed in female beauty and in death. In addition the poem's specificity as to the number of stars and lilies and the colours of the bar of heaven and the woman's eyes and hair give the poem pictorial qualities that suggest the close kinship of poetry and painting in Pre-Raphaelite aesthetics, as well as demonstrating Rossetti's interest in juxtaposing obviously 'mystic' symbols with natural images that also 'are symbols in some deeper way'. The Christian symbolism does not reveal occult meaning, but suggests that the aesthetic surface may be charged with such meaning. Ultimately the effect is to secularize the Christian imagery, so that the three lilies have no more and no less meaning than the Damozel's hair, 'yellow like ripe corn', and the deepest meaning of the poem is in the depth of the Damozel's 'blue grave eyes'. The obvious evidence that this is not Dante's heaven, or any orthodox heaven, is that the Damozel is unhappy, weeping to be reunited with her lover: 'Alas for lonely heaven! Alas / For life wrung out alone.' The most famous lines of the poem emphasize both that the 'gold bar of heaven' is an imprisoning barrier, and that the poet's emphasis is not on the soul of the Damozel, but on her still warm and sensual flesh: 'her bosom's pressure must have made / The bar she leaned on warm.' Despite the warmth of the Damozel's bosom, the simple archaic diction and the setting in heaven retain the air of 'a holy purity, an innocent naiveté, a child-like grace and simplicity', but the poem shows a stage in the Pre-Raphaelite transition from Christian faith to a secularized awe inspired by the beauty of both women and artistic representation.

   'My Sister's Sleep' also appears on the surface to be a poem of Christian devotion as it describes the hushed reverence of a family's deathbed vigil on Christmas Eve, and the consolation to be drawn from faith. At the moment of his sister's death, the poem's speaker is calmly accepting:

> Silence was speaking at my side
> > With an exceedingly clear voice:
> > I knew the calm as of a choice
> Made in God for me, to abide.

This poem is much closer than 'The Blessed Damozel' to Victorian ideals of 'holy purity', if only because its focus is on domestic familial love rather than erotic love, but in 'My Sister's Sleep', also, the ultimate meaning, as McGann (1969) has shown, is not that

Christian faith conquers death, but that when death separates loved ones, a grasping for meaning produces a hushed awe that oddly awakens sensual perceptions. The poem describes a heightened aesthetic state, in which the slightest details are endowed with importance, seemingly pregnant with occult meaning: everything is important enough to be recorded, from the sound of chairs being moved upstairs to the clicking sounds of the mother's knitting needles to the faint rustling of her silk dress. For Rossetti, Pre-Raphaelite attention to detail meant not only the physical appearance of details, but also the depths of vague symbolic meaning in every detail of the material world.

Possibly Rossetti's most important contribution to the *Germ* was a prose tale, 'Hand and Soul', an indirect manifesto for his artistic principles and ambitions of this period. 'Hand and Soul' most obviously aligns itself with Pre-Raphaelite art by taking as its subject an early Italian painter, the fictional Chiaro dell'Erma, who struggles to find the best possible goals for his art and is finally enlightened by a vision of a beautiful woman, who claims to be an image of his own soul and advises him, 'Chiaro, servant of God, take now this Art unto thee, and paint me thus, as I am, to know me: . . . Do this; so shall thy soul stand before thee always, and perplex thee no more' (*Germ*, 33). The point is obvious: contrary to the Ruskinian project of painting external nature with scrupulous attention to detail, the artist should be concerned to express his own inner self, his soul or genius. This ideal of self-expression, however, is made unnaturally easy for Chiaro because his soul has supernaturally taken material form and come to sit for its portrait. As an aesthetic manifesto, the tale offers no practical course of action except to paint beautiful women in order to express the inner mystery of artistic aspiration and creativity. As Rossetti's career proceeded, this is exactly what he did, painting beautiful women as both the ideal of aesthetic beauty and the symbolic portrait of his own otherwise undefined poetic longing, what in another prose tale, 'Saint Agnes of Intercession', he called the mystery hidden in the artist's tabernacle.

The development of Rossetti's Art-Catholic Pre-Raphaelitism into a cult of artistically rendered female beauty becomes even clearer in his other major contribution to the *Germ*, a series of sonnets inspired by paintings featuring different manifestations of female beauty, from a Virgin by Hans Memling to nymphs by Andrea Mantegna, a nude Angelica by Ingres and a naked picnicker by Giorgione. Two of the sonnets begin with the word 'Mystery' and all of them suggest that the aesthetic representation contains an occult meaning unavailable to rational analysis; in each painting

> Its meaning filleth it,
> A portion of most secret life: to wit: –
> Each human pulse shall keep the sense it had
> With all, though the mind's labour run to naught.
>
> (*Germ*, 181)

From his earliest 'Art-Catholic' poems and PRB paintings to his later love poetry and paintings of beautiful women, Rossetti's characteristic art expressed the conviction that beauty, in women or in art, was freighted with inexpressible but quite extraordinary depths of meaning, of 'solemn poetry' (*Germ*, 181). For contemporaries, Rossetti's association of aesthetic beauty with beautiful women seemed dangerously sensual, but for modern readers the association is disturbing because, as Griselda Pollock (1988), Kathy Psomiades (1997; Psomiades and Schaffer 1999) and others have argued, the effect is to reduce women to aesthetic objects. Rossetti used the phrase 'solemn poetry' to heighten the sense of awe solemnized already in Giorgione's painting, but he later came to think that '"Solemn poetry" belongs to a class of phrases absolutely forbidden . . . in poetry. It is intellectually incestuous, – poetry seeking to beget its emotional offspring on its own identity' (Rossetti 1965–7: II, 726–7). If it can be separated from its moral connotations, however, the phrase 'intellectual incest' does seem accurately to describe the leading tendency in Rossetti's poetry, and perhaps in Pre-Raphaelite poetry generally. Characteristically, it is poetry about poetry, or about the incarnation of poetic 'mystery' in aesthetic beauty.

The other great poet who contributed to the *Germ*, Christina Rossetti, was barred by her gender from being a Pre-Raphaelite brother, but she was an honorary sister, as the biological sister to two of the Brethren. Her exclusion from the Brotherhood was inevitable not only because of the term 'Brotherhood', but because of the gender ideology that made the term seem unobjectionable, and that was so clearly reflected in Dante Rossetti's work and his depiction of women as the embodiments of beauty, not producers of it.

Christina Rossetti could be called, like her brother, an Art-Catholic: like his, her poetry and artistic sensibility were shaped in part by the family preoccupation with Dante and the early Italians and, more strongly in her case, by the contemporary Anglo-Catholic movement that was spreading from Oxford through the Anglican church. Like the great leaders of the Oxford movement, and important contemporary poets Newman and Keble, Rossetti wrote poetry that was frequently devotional and expressed the sacramental symbolism mimicked by her brother's painting and poetry. In her case, however, the label 'Art-Catholic' is radically misleading unless the emphasis is put so heavily on the Christian term as to swamp the aesthetic one: for her the great mystery of human life, and its entire meaning, were to be found in Christianity, not art. The genuine piety of her poetry in the *Germ*, however, bears more than a passing resemblance to the dubious 'holy purity' of her brother's. All seven of her poems in the *Germ* share her brother's thematic interest in the barrier separating the dead from life, though they make the more didactic point that life is only preparation for the 'perfect peace' ('Dream Land', *Germ*, 20) of Christian death.

Like her brother's poems, Rossetti's carefully crafted verses share in the age's Keatsian, Tennysonian project of transforming melancholy brooding into the beauty of art. Like 'The Blessed Damozel', for example, her 'Repining' draws on the mood of Keats's 'Ode: On Melancholy' and the theme of Tennyson's 'Mariana' to depict the 'wakeful anguish' of the soul of a woman mournfully waiting for her lover:

> She sat alway thro' the long day
> Spinning the weary thread away;
>   And ever said in undertone:
> 'Come, that I be no more alone.'

Unlike the Damozel's or Mariana's, however, this speaker's prayers are answered, but by a being who shows her only that all life is vanity. Still, Rossetti's poem uses a situation and imagery like her brother's, and is 'Pre-Raphaelite' in its vivid pictorial imagery and especially in its evocation of portentous meaning beyond the surface truths of mere mortal life. As in her brother's Marian poems, 'Repining' emphasizes sensory perception by a heightened aesthetic awareness, as the damsel listens intently to the wind and the 'throbbing music' of the nightingale 'when the moonlight / Turned all the trees to silver white', but full meaning is not gleaned until the fullness of the time brings unearthly revelation, a 'whispered word': ' "Dearest, rise up; be not afraid; / For I am come at last," it said.'

Perhaps the most characteristic of Christina Rossetti's contributions to the *Germ*, 'Sweet Death', is also her most Pre-Raphaelite. 'Sweet Death' teaches the simple lesson that earthly life is vanity, that the 'God of truth' is 'Better than beauty and than youth', but it also acknowledges the attraction of earthly beauty, recording both the heightened sensual perception of melancholy reverie and the attention to latent meaningfulness that renders the details of perception symbolic:

> The sweetest blossoms die
> And so it was that, going day by day
>   Unto the church to praise and pray,
> And crossing the green church-yard thoughtfully,
>   I saw how on the graves the flowers
>   Shed their fresh leaves in showers;
> And how their perfume rose up to the sky
>   Before it passed away.

The melancholy, the sensual detail, the latent symbolic meaning, and especially the intricate, polished craftsmanship of the stanza combine to make this a poem not only of Christian 'holy purity' but also of Pre-Raphaelite pictorialism, symbolic detail and aestheticism.

Christina Rossetti's seven poems in the *Germ* display all the qualities that made her one of the greatest, most respected poets of the Victorian age. Her piety, of course, fitted the prevailing belief of the age and made her rather less 'counter-cultural' or avant-garde than her brother and other Pre-Raphaelite poets, but she was nevertheless clearly perceived by contemporaries as sharing the Pre-Raphaelite tone and aesthetic values. In fact, her first volume of poetry, *Goblin Market and Other Poems*, published in 1862, established her as a major Pre-Raphaelite poet long before her brother's first volume of poetry appeared in 1870. The poems in *Goblin Market* as well as those in her subsequent collection, *The Prince's Progress and Other Poems*, are characterized not only by the 'holy purity', Christian awe, symbolic detail and melancholy of early Pre-Raphaelitism, and in *Goblin Market*, especially, the lush sensuality and eroticism of later Pre-Raphaelitism; in *The Prince's Progress* her medievalism, like that of other Pre-Raphaelites, shifts from Dantean Christianity to chivalric romance. In addition, these volumes, partially shepherded into print by D. G. Rossetti, were further associated with Pre-Raphaelitism, and increased the cultural visibility of the Pre-Raphaelites, because they were illustrated by D. G. Rossetti's

woodcuts. The critical tradition, not surprisingly, has given much of t
Christina Rossetti's achievement to the guidance and encouragement of her
in recent years critics have recognized that more often than not she resist
fussy interference. Quite possibly her poetry had more to do with putting his
before the public than his influence had in establishing her reputation.

During the 1850s and early 1860s, while his sister was establishing herself as a major
poet, Dante Rossetti was writing very little poetry but was developing a reputation and
a following as a painter, first with watercolours of themes from chivalric romance, and
subsequently with stylized oil paintings of exotic female beauty. D. G. Rossetti was also
at the core of a second wave of Pre-Raphaelitism. In the early 1850s, Edward Jones (later
Burne-Jones) and William Morris met at Oxford, discovered that they had similar longings for a kind of beauty and significance more medieval than modern, and discovered in
Rossetti a shared sensibility and precursor. Burne-Jones and Morris formed the Oxford
Brotherhood, modelled on the PRB, and even launched an avant-garde magazine modelled on the *Germ*, the *Oxford and Cambridge Magazine*.

In 1857 Rossetti, Morris, Burne-Jones and others undertook the project of painting fres-
coes to decorate the Oxford Union, where they attracted the attention of the brilliant young
poet Algernon Swinburne. This second Pre-Raphaelite group, which soon came to include
also the poet and novelist George Meredith, shared the Pre-Raphaelite Brotherhood's moral
earnestness about art and aesthetic iconoclasm, but its real claim to the name 'Pre-
Raphaelite' was its association with D. G. Rossetti as its undisputed leader – 'our Master,
of all of us', according to Meredith (1920: I, 418). Quite simply, where Rossetti went, the
tag 'Pre-Raphaelite' followed, so that it is appropriate up to a point to see the word 'Pre-
Raphaelite' as a synonym for 'Rossettian' – especially if Christina Rossetti is also included
in the term. But it is only appropriate up to a point, since the other artists and writers came
to carry the label also, and carried it well beyond Rossetti's particular aim and achievements. Burne-Jones, for example, the only non-poet in the group, began painting in self-
conscious discipleship and imitation of Rossetti, but he ultimately developed a style of his
own that led to the art nouveau of the *fin de siècle*. Similarly, Morris began his artistic career
attempting to become a Rossettian painter and writing poetry influenced by Rossetti's
medievalism and sensualism, but Morris's social concerns soon led him to become the
crucial link between the Pre-Raphaelites and the important Arts and Crafts movement that
aspired to bring aesthetic beauty into daily life. Morris invested his considerable inheritance, and still more considerable energy, in founding a company that made the designs of
artists, including Burne-Jones, Ford Madox Brown and Rossetti into stained glass, wall-
paper, carpets, furniture and other decorative items. Morris's high standards of production
and refusal to use men as machines in mere production made his products too expensive for
all but the very wealthy, but his firm and his idealism nevertheless helped to set high
standards for the Victorian art of design. Through Morris, more than anyone else, Pre-
Raphaelitism became more than the concern of an elite artistic class, as it was diffused
through Victorian culture by the firm of Morris, Marshall, Faulkner & Co.

The distinction between the Pre-Raphaelitism of the Pre-Raphaelite Brotherhood and
that of this second, more influential Pre-Raphaelite group parallels the changing mean-

ings of 'Rossettian' between the earlier and later groups. By the middle 1850s Rossetti's paintings had shifted from Christian and Dantean religious themes to erotic chivalric romance, and his moral tone had shifted from a semblance of 'holy purity' to an eroticism openly defiant of Victorian morality. His painting generally left Art-Catholicism behind as he devoted himself first to brilliantly coloured watercolours of medieval lovers, and then to sensually coloured oil paintings celebrating erotic female beauty. In addition, the relatively few poems he wrote during this period explicitly disavow the truth of Christian teaching: 'The Burden of Nineveh' set the tone for other Pre-Raphaelite poems by treating Christianity as merely a passing historical phase. 'The Song of the Bower', written in 1860, is an erotic reverie, openly defying the sexual morality of the age:

> What were my prize, could I enter thy bower
>   This day, to-morrow, at eve or at morn?
> Large lovely arms and a neck like a tower,
>   Bosom then heaving that now lies forlorn,
> Kindled with love-breath, (the sun's kiss is colder!)
>   Thy sweetness all near me, so distant to-day;
> My hand round thy neck and thy hand on my shoulder,
>   My mouth to thy mouth as the world melts away.

Rossetti's erotic poetry culminated in the *Poems* of 1870, at a time when he was considering an Arthurian poem to be called 'God's Grail', 'wherein God and Guinevere will be weighed against each other by another table of weights and measures' (1965–7: II, 779) than those used by the morally orthodox Tennyson of *Idylls of the King*. Unlike Tennyson's, Rossetti's medievalism would emphasize the moral superiority of Guinevere's passion and beauty over Arthur's Christianity.

Perhaps the reason Rossetti never wrote 'God's Grail' was that he had been long preempted by William Morris's 'The Defence of Guenevere', the title poem of his first volume of poetry in 1858. Based on two episodes in Malory, Morris's 'The Defence of Guenevere' is primarily a dramatic monologue spoken by Guenevere under sentence of death by fire for adultery with Sir Lancelot. Guenevere's 'defence', however, consists of little more than her unsupported assertion that her accuser is lying. If he is, though, it must only be about minor details, since Guenevere admits to the adultery. More accurately, she brags about it, contrasting the beauty and passion of her love with Lancelot to her paltry marriage vows, made when she 'was bought / By Arthur's great name and his little love' (ll. 82–3). Though Guenevere is plainly guilty, her defence is akin to the modern defence of jury nullification: she has broken the letter of the law, but it is a bad law and should be set aside in deference to the higher law of beauty and passion. Her monologue is an effort to seduce the accusers with her beauty and it represents Morris's attempt to seduce his Victorian audience by having Guenevere paint a (Pre-Raphaelite) picture of her beauty:

> 'See my breast rise,
> Like waves of purple sea, as here I stand;
> And how my arms are moved in wonderful wise,

'Yes, also at my full heart's strong command,
See through my long throat how the words go up
In ripples to my mouth; how in my hand

'The shadow lies like wine within a cup
Of marvellously colour'd gold; yea now
This little wind is rising, look you up,

'And wonder how the light is falling so
Within my moving tresses.

(ll. 226–36)

Guenevere's defence is notable for its pictorial quality and its Pre-Raphaelite attention to detail. The poem is also Pre-Raphaelite as a direct descendent of Rossetti's 'The Blessed Damozel'. The Damozel is separated from her lover by the 'gold bar of heaven', and Guenevere is separated from Lancelot by Christian edict, metaphorically the gold bar of heaven.

As 'The Blessed Damozel' may be regarded as the first Pre-Raphaelite poem, so may 'The Defence of Guenevere' be seen as the first poem of the 'aesthetic school'. Arguing that beauty is its own defence is much the same as the aestheticist claim that art exists for its own sake, for the sake of beauty without regard to moral concerns. But more pointedly, when Walter Pater coined the term 'the aesthetic poetry', it was in a review essay on Morris that specifically cited 'The Defence of Guenevere' as 'the first typical specimen of aesthetic poetry':

> The poem which gives its name to the volume is a thing tormented and awry with passion, like the body of Guenevere defending herself from the charge of adultery, and the accent falls in strange, unwonted places with the effect of a great cry. In truth these Arthurian legends, in their origin, prior to Christianity, yield all their sweetness only in a Christian atmosphere. What is characteristic in them is the strange suggestion of a deliberate choice between Christ and a rival lover. (1974: 191)

Morris provides the clear links between Pre-Raphaelitism and the Arts and Crafts movement, between Pre-Raphaelites and aestheticists, and even between Pre-Raphaelites and symbolism. Most of the poems in *The Defence of Guenevere and Other Poems* are based on medieval sources, usually either Malory's *Morte d'Arthur* or Jean Froissart's chronicle history of medieval France, but the most indisputably 'Pre-Raphaelite' and most experimental were ekphrastic poems based on Rossetti's medievalist watercolours – strange, brightly coloured, elaborately patterned pictures full of portentous symbols that seemed to have no reference beyond themselves, but suggested a heavily eroticized aura of mystery that hinted at some occult meaning beyond the painted surface. Morris's 'King Arthur's Tomb', 'The Tune of Seven Towers' and especially 'The Blue Closet' all translated Rossetti's painted surfaces into poetry and, in the process, anticipated late-century symbolist poetry. 'The Blue Closet' creates an eerie symbolic context for the mysterious maidens in Rossetti's painting. The story behind the painting and poem is obscure, but the four women are represented as singing in a dream as the Lady Alice, Mariana-like, waits languidly for her lover to return from the land of the dead. Fittingly, the most dramatic event in the poem is the eruption of a dream-like erotic symbol as the maidens sing:

> Through the floor shot up a lily red,
> With a patch of earth from the land of the dead,
> For he was strong in the land of the dead.
>
> (ll. 60–2)

The white lilies of Rossetti's Christian symbolism have undergone a strange transformation, dyed red in the eroticism of second generation Pre-Raphaelitism, but appropriately for a proto-symbolist poem, the symbol has no very precise meaning, only a dream-like suggestiveness.

The Defence of Guenevere and Other Poems, published by Morris at his own expense, made little impression on the public, though Morris eventually became well known for a series of long narrative poems, particularly *The Earthly Paradise* (1868–70), a collection of tales gathered within a narrative frame akin to that of *The Canterbury Tales*. Lacking the intensity and vitality of his first volume, however, these later poems have been viewed as diluted Pre-Raphaelitism. In his comic 'recipe book' for writing Victorian poems, W. H. Mallock suggested that in order to make 'a Narrative Poem like Mr. Morris's', one shall:

> Take about sixty pages-full of the same word-mixture [as that used to make 'a modern Pre-Raphaelite poem' and dilute it with a double quantity of mild modern Anglo-Saxon. Pour this composition into two vessels of equal size, and into one of them empty a small mythological story. If this does not put your readers to sleep soon enough, add to it the rest of the language in the remaining vessel. (Mallock 1877: 24)

Unfortunately, most readers would agree with Mallock about the soporific effects of Morris's tales, but many of these do pursue the same themes as the earlier volume. Most strikingly, 'The Hill of Venus' returns to the 'deliberate choice between Christ and a rival lover', retelling the tale of the knight Tannhauser's seduction by the fallen goddess, Venus, and his deliberate choice of pagan eroticism over Christianity.

Though Pater did not mention him in his account of 'the aesthetic poetry', Algernon Swinburne even more emphatically than Rossetti or Morris makes the choice of the rival lover over Christ. One of his earliest poems, 'Laus Veneris', also tells the tale of Tannhauser's choice of Venus, but it is more deliberately shocking than Morris's version in Tannhauser's explicitly blasphemous assertion that Venus was 'more beautiful than God' (ll. 386–7). In addition, like Rossetti's 'The Burden of Nineveh', Swinburne's 'Hymn to Proserpine' treated Christianity as a mere passing phase in history, and a drab one at that, though momentarily triumphant: 'Thou hast conquered, O pale Galilean; the world has grown grey from thy breath' (l. 35). In a reversal of Rossetti's earlier Art-Catholicism, Swinburne explicitly contrasted the glory and colour of Venus with the baseness and greyness of the Virgin, 'A slave among slaves, and rejected' (l. 85). More shockingly still, in a parody of prayers to the Virgin, 'our lady of the seven sorrows', Swinburne sang of the erotic, sadomasochistic 'Dolores' as 'Our Lady of Pain'. Published in 1866, Swinburne's

Poems and Ballads shocked Victorian propriety by carrying the aestheticism of Rossetti and Morris to an extreme, insisting repeatedly on the erotic attractions of the rival lover. Because of their thematic content, Swinburne's poems are more easily assimilated to the works of Dante Rossetti and Morris than to the work of Christina Rossetti but, as Kathy Psomiades has recently shown, Christina Rossetti and Swinburne complemented and probably influenced one another particularly in their exploration of 'the gendered and sexualized terrain of the aesthetic' and in making 'the sensational experience of a feminine body the central aesthetic moment' (Psomiades and Schaffer 1999: 109). Rossetti's influence on Swinburne is also evident in Swinburne's poetry about the peacefulness of death after the mortal struggles of life, and more significantly, in his characteristic metres and style. Despite mutual admiration and influence on one another in technique and tone, however, Swinburne's eroticism was poles apart from Christina Rossetti's piety, and she was able to enjoy his poetry only by deleting the most offensive verses.

Poems and Ballads shocked the Victorian public, in Thomas Hardy's phrase, like 'a garland of red roses . . . fallen about the hood of some smug nun' ('A Singer Asleep', ll. 6–7), and some critics attempted to disparage it as merely a dirty book, unclean 'for the mere sake of uncleanness'. If Swinburne had been a lesser poet, no doubt his dirty book would have been simply dismissed, in the terms of hostile critics, as 'the spurious passion of a putrescent imagination' (Hyder 1970: 24) and quickly forgotten after its momentary shock value, but Swinburne's erudition and undeniable poetic virtuosity made his work difficult to discount. Further, his challenge to Victorian values had already been presented a year earlier, in *Atalanta in Calydon*, an astonishing revival of the Greek tragic drama everywhere accepted in Victorian culture as the ultimate aesthetic accomplishment. The chorus in *Atalanta in Calydon* attacks what it calls 'the supreme evil, God' (l. 1151), but most readers had rightly taken this as the dramatic representation of ancient Greeks speaking of the pagan gods. Moreover, the celebration of pagan love in *Atalanta* only put Swinburne on the same side as writers from Matthew Arnold to Friedrich Nietzsche, who saw Hellenic culture as the supreme expression of aesthetic beauty, and Christianity, for good or ill, as the dialectically opposed expression of moral regulation. Though Swinburne had undoubtedly intended *Poems and Ballads* to be shocking for the sake of being shocking, taken together with *Atalanta in Calydon*, the challenge they quite seriously posed for Victorian society was to illustrate that the high cultural ideal of Hellenism was incompatible with British culture's official religion and morality. As Swinburne made clear, the rival lover to Christianity was beauty, was art itself. Not surprisingly, his long critical essay on William Blake, published the year after *Poems and Ballads*, vigorously argued that art should be unconstrained by any moral limitations, that beauty is a higher ideal than morality, and that, art, like Guenevere, is justified by its own beauty. The essay on Blake is the first great English proclamation of the aesthetic doctrine of 'art for art's sake'.

Swinburne was arguably the greatest poet among the Pre-Raphaelites and would probably have developed in much the same way without the influences of the Rossettis or Morris, but his fortuitous association with the Rossetti circle helped bring Pre-Raphaelitism dramatically into conflict with official culture, to establish the modern condition in which the artist is characteristically seen rebelling against and challenging social conventions. Swinburne went on to write brilliant nature poetry and political poetry that have nothing to do with Pre-Raphaelitism, but for my present purposes it is sufficient to note that his work in the late 1860s made explicit the challenge that the Pre-Raphaelites had been long developing to Victorian society.

Swinburne himself positively revelled in the charges levelled against his poetry by outraged morality, but as it turned out, the controversy came at a very bad time for Rossetti. Rossetti had married the beautiful Elizabeth Siddal in 1861, and when she died shortly afterwards, he had buried his poems with her in a grand romantic gesture of remorse. Throughout the 1860s, he had written very little poetry though he was seen as the leader of a school of poets, including his sister, Christina, Morris, Swinburne and George Meredith, whose *Modern Love and Poems of the English Roadside* had been published in 1862. Perhaps inspired by the successes of poets seen as his disciples, or perhaps inspired by his passionate love for Morris's wife, Jane, Rossetti's poetic ambitions were rekindled in the late 1860s, and he began writing a great deal of love poetry. Finding himself still without enough poems to fill a volume, in 1869 he arranged to have his buried poems exhumed, so that in 1870 he was finally able to publish his first volume of poems.

Rossetti carefully orchestrated the response to *Poems*, arranging to have so many friendly reviews published that George Meredith wrote to Rossetti saying that he would have liked to join in the chorus of praise but had been unable to find a journal that had not already accepted a review from someone else. He remarked that Swinburne 'threw flowers on you in the *Fortnightly*: not one was undeserved. After finishing this book my voice would have been as unrestrained, less eloquent' (Rossetti 1965–7: II, 418).

In fact, Swinburne's review was wildly excessive, praising Rossetti as the greatest poet of the age and comparing him favourably with Shakespeare and Dante, but it convincingly pointed out the crucial, defining element in Rossetti's work, the attempt to arrive at spiritual truth through material forms. By far the most ambitious work in Rossetti's *Poems* was *The House of Life*, a series of sonnets mostly in the courtly love tradition that Rossetti had learned from his experience of translating Dante and the early Italian poets. Swinburne praised it accordingly:

> In all the glorious poem built up of all these poems, there is no great quality more notable than the sweet and sovereign unity of perfect spirit and sense, of fleshly form and intellectual fire. This Muse is as the woman praised in the divine words of the poet himself, 'Whose speech Truth knows not from her thought / Nor Love her body from her soul.' (1870: 18)

Rossetti's *Poems*, consisting of works written from his early Art-Catholicism to his recent love sonnets, draw together all of the Rossettian contributions to Pre-Raphaelitism and show clearly that from start to finish it had consisted of a secularized Dantean vision in which material form, whether a beautiful woman or a beautiful sonnet, symbolized a transcendent spiritual value. Whereas in Dante, transcendent value was found in the Christian God, in Rossetti it was found in erotic love, the beauty of women, or art, or simply mystery. The end result was the view most clearly expressed by Swinburne, that the highest human values were to be found in art, the repository of spiritual truth. The most important effect of Pre-Raphaelitism in literature was the establishment of British aestheticism, the belief in art for art's sake that asserted the independence of art from society.

The climax of Pre-Raphaelitism in Rossetti's *Poems*, however, was not to be without controversy. The reception of Swinburne's *Poems and Ballads* had already shown that any displacement of Christian morality by art would meet with considerable resistance. Apparently goaded by the excessive praise granted to Rossetti's work and by the furthering of the 'naughtiness' he had already chastised in Swinburne's work, Robert Buchanan, a minor poet, contributed to the notoriety of Pre-Raphaelitism by rechristening Rossetti and his circle the 'fleshly school of poetry' in 1871. Buchanan's attack was silly in its priggishness, though he did accurately point out that Rossetti's overt eroticism claimed for art the right to speak of matters generally under taboo in Victorian society. Unfortunately Buchanan's essay, when expanded into a pamphlet, contributed to Rossetti's major nervous breakdown and general decline in the 1870s, but it also clearly established the terms by which Pre-Raphaelite aestheticism challenged Victorian beliefs. Accusing Rossetti, Morris and Swinburne of 'fleshliness', Buchanan was also accusing them of aestheticism as artistic revolution:

> The fleshly gentlemen had bound themselves by solemn league and covenant to extol fleshliness as the distinct and supreme end of poetic and pictorial art; to aver that poetic expression is greater than poetic thought, and by inference that the body is greater than the soul; and soul superior to sense; and that the poet, properly to develop his poetic faculty, must be an intellectual hermaphrodite, to whom the very facts of day and night are lost in a whirl of aesthetic terminology. (1871: 25)

Buchanan's priggish excess opened a huge gap between artistic freedom and acceptable propriety, but he accidentally made propriety look ridiculous in the process. As a result, most Victorians ultimately sided with the poets, as they had presumably sided with Guenevere against her paltry accusers, and Buchanan was obliged to retreat and retract. Despite Buchanan's evident intentions, the 'Fleshly School' controversy ended in a victory for aestheticism and in the most important legacy of Pre-Raphaelitism, a widespread acceptance of artistic freedom as a counter-cultural challenge to cultural orthodoxy.

See also: ARTHURIAN POETRY AND MEDIEVALISM; POETRY IN TRANSLATION; POETRY AND ILLUSTRATION.

REFERENCES AND FURTHER READING

Bentley, D. M. R. (1977) 'Rossetti's "Ave" and Related Pictures.' *Victorian Poetry*, 15, 21–35.

Buchanan, Robert (1871) 'The Fleshly School of Poetry: Mr. D. G. Rossetti.' Reprinted in David G. Riede (ed.) (1992a) *Critical Essays on Dante Gabriel Rossetti* (pp. 24–39). New York: G. K. Hall.

Grieve, A. I. (1973) *The Art of Dante Gabriel Rossetti: The Pre-Raphaelite Period, 1848–50.* Hingham: Real World Publications.

Harrison, Antony (1984) *Christina Rossetti in Context.* Chapel Hill: University of North Carolina Press.

Hilton, Timothy (1970) *The Pre-Raphaelites.* New York: Oxford University Press.

Hunt, John Dixon (1968) *The Pre-Raphaelite Imagination, 1848–1900*. London: Routledge and Kegan Paul.

Hunt, William Holman (1905–6) *Pre-Raphaelitism and the Pre-Raphaelite Brotherhood*. New York: Macmillan.

Hyder, Clyde K. (1970) *Swinburne: The Critical Heritage*. New York: Barnes and Noble.

Kent, David A. (ed.) (1987) *The Achievement of Christina Rossetti*. Ithaca, N. Y.: Cornell University Press.

Lang, Cecil Y. (1975) *The Pre-Raphaelites and their Circle*. Second edition. Chicago: University of Chicago Press.

Louis, Margot (1990) *Swinburne and his Gods: The Roots and Growth of an Agnostic Poetry*. Buffalo: McGill-Queens Press.

Mallock, W. H. (1877) *Every Man His Own Poet; or The Inspired Singer's Recipe Book*. London: Simpkin, Marshall.

McGann, Jerome (1969) 'Rossetti's Significant Details.' *Victorian Poetry*, 7, 41–54. Reprinted in David G. Riede (ed.) (1992a) *Critical Essays on Dante Gabriel Rossetti* (pp. 76–88). New York: G. K. Hall.

McGann, Jerome (1971) *Swinburne: An Experiment in Criticism*. Chicago: University of Chicago Press.

McGann, Jerome (2000) *Dante Gabriel Rossetti and the Game that Must Be Lost*. New Haven: Yale University Press.

Meredith, George (1920) *The Collected Letters of George Meredith*. Ed. C. L. Cline. London: Oxford University Press.

Pater, Walter (1974) 'Aesthetic Poetry.' In Harold Bloom (ed.). *Selected Writings of Walter Pater* (pp. 190–8). New York: New American Library.

Pollock, Griselda (1988) *Vision and Difference: Femininity, Feminism, and Histories of Art*. New York: Routledge.

Psomiades, Kathy (1997) *Beauty's Body: Femininity and Representation in British Aestheticism*. Stanford: Stanford University Press.

Psomiades, Kathy and Talia Schaffer (eds) (1999) *Women and British Aestheticism*. Charlottesville: University Press of Virginia.

Riede, David (1983) *Dante Gabriel Rossetti and the Limits of Victorian Vision*. Ithaca, N. Y.: Cornell University Press.

Riede, David G. (ed.) (1992a) *Critical Essays on Dante Gabriel Rossetti*. New York: G. K. Hall.

Riede, David (1992b) *Dante Gabriel Rossetti Revisited*. New York: Twayne Publishers.

Rossetti, Dante Gabriel (1965–7) *The Letters of Dante Gabriel Rossetti*. 4 vols. Ed. Oswald Doughty and John Robert Wahl. Oxford: Clarendon Press.

Rossetti, William Michael (ed.) (1850, 1965) *The Germ: Thoughts towards Nature in Poetry, Literature, and Art*. New York: AMS Press.

Ruskin, John (1903–12) *The Works of John Ruskin*. Eds E. T. Cook and Alexander Wedderburn. 39 vols. London: George Allen.

Swinburne, Algernon (1870) 'The Poetry of Dante Gabriel Rossetti.' Reprinted in David G. Riede (ed.) (1992a) *Critical Essays on Dante Gabriel Rossetti* (pp. 15–23). New York: G. K. Hall.

18

The Poetry of the 1890s

Chris Snodgrass

Demythologizing Traditional Misconceptions

The 1890s is probably the most misunderstood decade of the entire Victorian Age. The myths and legends that have persistently clung to this ten-year period often still over-shadow its art. Identifying the *fin de siècle* with the autumnal dregs of a seasonal cycle, the popular imagination has traditionally represented the nineties as the Victorian period's effete 'decline' or 'decadence', which was presumably followed by the 'stronger', regenera-tive 'modern movements' of the early twentieth century. It is a view derived in part from propaganda by T. S. Eliot, Ezra Pound, Roger Fry and others, who postulated an autonomous poetic revolution emerging phoenix-like from the ashes of the nineteenth century. Nineties poet William Watson thought it self-evident that his age was in decay, complaining in 'Wordsworth's Grave' that poetry is 'powerless now' and 'deadens with ignoble sloth / Or deafens with shrill tumult, loudly weak'. But, in fact, popular myth-ology notwithstanding, the 1890s was a time of enormous energy rather than deadening enervation, and its poetry proved to be neither 'weak' nor 'ignoble'.

Frank Kermode has reminded us that the idea of decadence, usually paired with cor-responding regeneration, has been a fixture of the age-old 'apocalyptic paradigm', not least at the end of the nineteenth century (1966: 9–12). The specific belief in a Victorian 'deca-dence' gained impetus from Max Nordau's notorious *Degeneration* (1895) and William Butler Yeats's legend-making *Autobiography* (1916), which argued that 1890s art was epitomized by talented but self-indulgent and scandal-ridden 'heroic failures', a group Yeats dubbed the 'Tragic Generation'. This idea of a 'decadent' or 'yellow' nineties – surely one of the most tenacious in literary history – continues to transfix the historical imagi-nation, in part because many of the most famous nineties poets happened to die young, usually from diseases (tuberculosis, cerebral haemorrhage, alcoholism) traditionally linked to a decadent lifestyle, and in part, of course, because racy tales of the fated convergence of wilful iconoclasm, sexual scandal and personal tragedy are difficult narratives to let go of. In any case, critical commentary on the period has frequently allied itself with one or more of three highly dubious myths: (1) that the decade represents the creatively stale dead end of the Victorian Age, which immediately preceded the creatively resurgent

Modern Period; (2) that this 'dead end' was typified by the world-weary and dysfunctional decadents of Yeats's 'Tragic Generation'; and (3) that those decadent poets, dedicated to 'art for art's sake', sought to divorce art from morality and extol, instead, the pursuit of immoral sensations.

While modern critics have sometimes acknowledged the problematical nature of these judgements, much commentary still seems trapped within a set of supremely confident but highly flawed pontifications about the decade, issued in the middle half of the twentieth century. B. Ifor Evans more or less set the script in 1933, when he declared in his classic *English Poetry in the Later Nineteenth Century* that the nineties exhibited 'an increased emphasis on its detachment from morals' (1933: xxii). Some twenty years later Jerome Hamilton Buckley continued the litany at the end of his highly influential *The Victorian Temper*, where he proclaimed that because nineties writers 'lost the vision of an integrated pattern, the meaningful experience of a "transfigured life"', they fell victim to 'the ineffable weariness of strayed revelers lost in a palace of fading illusion' (1951: 225, 228–9). 'The gallantry of Decadent art', Buckley decreed, was 'effeminate, effete. At odds forever with Victorian "manliness", the Decadent hero . . . could never, on principle, face the social realities of his time' (1951: 230). In the 1960s critics like Russell M. Goldfarb underscored this formulation, affirming that an 'indulgence in a life of sensations' led to 'decadent literature [being] animated by the exploration of immoral and evil experiences; never does it preach morality, nor does it strongly insist upon ethical responsibilities' (1962: 373). So secure was this moralistic mythology that Derek Stanford could even feel comfortable claiming, 'the quality singularly lacking in both the lives and work of these men was a strain of toughness, of coarseness even' (1965: 30).

But, in fact, the actual poetry of the 1890s justifies none of these moralistic misconceptions. Far from reflecting waning decay, world-weary enervation or solipsistic insularity, the 1890s was an exceptionally vivacious and diverse age of experimental innovation and artistic adventure. Richard Le Gallienne, a nineties poet and critic who was no champion of decadence, judged that 'those last ten years of the nineteenth century properly belong to the twentieth century, and, far from being decadent, except in certain limited manifestations, they were years of an immense and multifarious renaissance' (1926: 136). Holbrook Jackson's definitive and incisive tribute is even more categorical; the 1890s, he declares, was characterized by:

> a quickening of the imagination, combined with pride of material prosperity, conquest and imperial expansion, as well as the desire for social service and a fuller communal and personal life . . . even [its] decadence was often decadence only in name, for much of the genius denounced by Max Nordau as degeneration was a sane and healthy expression of a vitality which, as it is not difficult to show, would have been better named regeneration. (1913: 18–19)

Several scholars, not least Morse Peckham (1967), have refuted the cultural-dead-end myth, pointing out that the heralded 'Modern poets', in fact, addressed the same basic problems as the 'Aesthetes and Decadents' and often appropriated dazzling technical effects developed by those same nineties poets. Indeed, many nineties writers became even more famous in the twentieth century, even though they did not significantly alter the supposedly 'jejune' themes and styles they had used in the nineties. David Perkins (1976) confirms that the 'new' and 'intellectual' poetry promoted by T. S. Eliot and others, as well as such 'modernist' tendencies as Symbolism, Imagism and urban realism, were already being practised well before the twentieth century.

Furthermore, any representative sampling of nineties verse reveals that even though the poets of Yeats's 'Tragic Generation' were clearly very important, their work did not constitute the whole, or even a majority, of the decade's poetry. Far from being mono-chromatically narrow and perverse, the 1890s was, in fact, one of the most heterogeneous and highly individualistic periods in English literature. Holbrook Jackson characterizes it in his landmark *The Eighteen Nineties* (still the best overview of the period) as 'the decade of a thousand "movements"', reflecting less a fear of decadence than the thrill of moder-nity (1913: 31). Even among the more than 100 nineties poets who were *not* so-called 'Decadents', there was an enormous range and variety of thematic and ideological interests – from the chauvinistic Rudyard Kipling to the iconoclastic John Davidson, from the pro-imperialist Henry Newbolt to the anti-imperialist Wilfrid Blunt, from the devout Alice Meynell to the atheist Mathilde Blind, from the stoical A. E. Housman to the flam-boyant Roden Noel, from the 'oriental' experimentalist and social gadfly 'Violet Fane' to the dispassionate Parnassian Austin Dobson.

Nor did the poets of any particular sensibility show themselves to be at all monolithic in their tastes. Poets as radically different as Davidson, Kipling and Arthur Symons all drew metrical inspiration from the music hall (and music-hall ballads). Norman Gale's Roman-tic nature poetry was said to constitute 'the denial of the Beardsley mode' (Evans 1933: 328), yet Ernest Dowson, Richard Le Gallienne and Victor Plarr all gave it glowing reviews. The so-called 'Decadents' made it part of their mission to break away from the 'old bondage of rhetoric' (Symons 1899: 8), yet it was probably their fiercely non-'Decadent' adversaries – such as Kipling, W. E. Henley or Thomas Hardy – who did the most to create colloquial idioms approximating spoken language. For that matter, poets of the 'Decadent' circle sometimes recoiled from what were supposedly essential 'Decadent' qualities. Herbert Horne felt his austere, architectonic tastes were antipathetic to both nineties-style Pre-Raphaelitism and art nouveau, which he ridiculed as the 'swirl and blob' style. The exotic, 'pagan' aesthetes 'Michael Field' (Katherine Bradley and Edith Cooper), who were good friends with Symons, John Gray, Lionel Johnson and other so-called 'Decadents', were none the less so repelled by Beardsleyan provocations in the highly successful *Yellow Book* periodical that they withdrew one of their poems from it in protest.

Indeed, what may have most characterized the 1890s was the large number of loose but highly visible coteries, composed of individuals who, in fact, held strikingly diverse views. Despite the mythic reputation of the famous Rhymers' Club as 'the distillery of nineties poetry' (Stanford 1965: 25), its members had no discernible common philosophy – except, perhaps, an intense opposition to Victorian bourgeois values and stale literary forms. The Club included figures as wildly different as Dowson, Davidson, Symons, Horne and even Sir William Watson, considered by many to be the most traditional poet of the age. While Watson certainly held the 'Decadents' to be an anathema – he even insisted that Aubrey Beardsley be fired as art editor of the *Yellow Book* – he, too, like most of the 'Tragic Generation', was so obsessed with technique that he would reportedly spend an entire day revising a single line. The *Yellow Book* itself was famous for being able to persuade enormously disparate figures to appear together within its covers – at one extreme, Will Wratislaw, Beardsley, Olive Custance, Rosamund Marriott Watson and Baron Corvo; and, at the other, Watson, Sir Frederic Leighton, George Saintsbury, Richard Garnett and Henry James.

Another of the more dogged misconceptions undergirding the myth of a 'weak' and 'debilitated' nineties is the assumption that the British 'Decadents' went to the French *décadents* for much of their poetic philosophy, as well as some of their provocative subject matter. Although British writers were frequently influenced by the French, the 'Decadence' in late Victorian Britain, contrary to popular belief, was profoundly different from the '*décadence*' in France and was not devoted to 'art for art's sake' in the traditional French conception of that creed. Any allegiance 1890s British poets may have claimed to 'art for art's sake' (and to a total separation of art from morally principled conduct) was, for the most part, a calculated rhetorical stance (as in the case of Oscar Wilde) or based on a distinctly British redefinition of the French doctrine (as in the case of the British Parnassians).

French Parnassianism, the movement with which *l'art pour l'art* was most closely associated, first emerged in the 1830s, led by Théophile Gautier, and gained momentum in Britain in the 1870s under the influence of Théodore de Banville, who urged among other things a return to older French fixed forms such as the ballade, the villanelle and the rondeau. The Parnassians believed that the poet's chief focus had to be the 'hard', sharply delineated, 'lapidarian' image – invoking gems, porcelains, marble tombs and exquisitely painted miniatures – without concern for the social utility or moral conventions of the age; the poet was thus committed to exquisite artifice for its own sake. Two elements of the art-for-art's-sake creed appealed powerfully to British 'Decadent' poets: its commitment to stylistically impeccable technique and execution; and its insistence that art not be a mere tool of, and smothered by, ruling-class morality, what Symons called 'bourgeois solemnity'. However, what the British 'Decadents' did *not* embrace about 'art for art's sake' was the suggestion that aesthetic integrity necessitated denying (or ignoring) art's moral function. Francis Thompson's exotic language and ritualistic aphorisms, after all, were explicitly designed to make him, in his words, 'the poet of the return of God'. Although Lionel Johnson's baroque aestheticism and personal eccentricities (transposing his days and nights, for example) stigmatized him as a leading 'Decadent', he nevertheless publicly rejected dilettantism in art and regarded the doctrine of *l'art pour l'art* as absurd ('The Cultured Faun', *Anti-Jacobin* [1891]). Indeed, it is one of the telling incongruities of 'yellow nineties' mythology that the poets who were probably most devoted to 'art for art's sake' were not the so-called 'Decadents' but the 'Counter-Decadents'. William Ernest Henley, who had spearheaded the 'Counter-Decadence', was one of the first late-Victorian poets to emphasize the value a work has on its own terms, rather than as a vehicle for religious or political indoctrination. Furthermore, in nineteenth-century Britain the poetry most routinely cited as the purest incarnation of 'art for art's sake' was the work not of Dowson or Wilde or Lee-Hamilton, but the phobically anti-'Decadent' Austin Dobson.

Despite what popular myths would have us expect, it is ludicrous to classify as 'art for art's sake' such forcefully didactic poems as Wilde's 'Harlot House' and *The Ballad of Reading Gaol* (not to mention his fairy tales and *The Picture of Dorian Gray*) or any of Symons's many moralistic poems, not least 'Emmy', in which the speaker surmises (addressing Emmy) that the soul of the man 'who wronged you first . . . / Shall answer for yours in hell'. Nor did Symons want to divorce art from its moral dimensions when he criticized Stephen Phillips's poetry for its lack of principled commitment: 'What Mr. Phillips lacks is sincerity; and without sincerity there can be no art' (Symons 1904: 255). While the 'Decadents' embraced Walter Pater's apotheosis of intensely experienced aesthetic moments, they almost invariably believed, also like Pater, that those moments would implicitly define a higher morality. In his landmark *The Symbolist Movement in Literature* Symons states that art 'is all an attempt to spiritualise literature', to 'disengage the ultimate essence, the soul', and thus 'becomes itself a kind of religion, with all the duties and responsibilities of the sacred ritual' (1899: 8–9). Yeats had intoned the virtually identical message in his essay 'The Autumn of the Body' (1898), which prophesies that the arts were about 'to take upon their shoulders the burdens that have fallen from the shoulders of the priests, and to lead us back upon our journey' (1961: 193). Refuting the prevalent view that carnal sin ruled the 'yellow nineties', Holbrook Jackson pointed out that, in fact, 'Every physical excess of the time went hard in hand with spiritual desire' (1913: 132).

As countless poems from the decade prove, 'the renaissance of the Nineties was far more concerned with art for the sake of life than with art for the sake of art' (Jackson 1913: 33). However much they may have followed the French in matters of style, especially with respect to meticulous poetic craftsmanship, poets of the 1890s ('Decadents' as well as 'Counter-Decadents') did *not* find the French art-for-art's-sake disregard for morality to be compatible with their temperaments. At some basic level almost all British nineties poets, like those in earlier decades, accepted John Ruskin's assumption that great art can only come from moral sources, and so they tended to dismiss as shallow and insufficient any aesthetic doctrine that disclaimed the artist's moral responsibility. Despite all the provocativeness in their verse, even the so-called 'Decadents' were, as Jackson proclaims, 'not decadent at all' in the sense that 'their central characteristic' was 'a widespread concern for the *correct* – that is, the most effective, the most powerful, the most *righteous* – mode of living' (1913: 64, 14, italics added).

If the characterization 'decadent' had any validity at all, it was not as a description of the moral character of nihilistic malcontents but as a crusading rhetoric intended to highlight the stultifying perversions some nineties poets saw in *mainstream* Victorian culture, and to signal those poets' recognition of the decay of beauty and human value that resulted from those perversions. As Karl Beckson has put it, 'The Decadents' ennui and disillusionment were, after all, a mask donned by the artist to proclaim his sensitivity to a decadent society, for clearly the pose was his defense against an incomprehensible, hostile world' (1981: vi). If poets like Symons and Wilde accepted the label 'Decadent' and welcomed the ridicule heaped upon them by satirists like George du Maurier in *Punch*, it was because such characterizations only confirmed their deviation from what they took to be the crude mediocrity of the bourgeois norm, thus revealing the superiority of a sensibility that abhorred the vulgar and commonplace and stood as an 'authentic' rebuke to bourgeois smugness and self-righteousness. What the 'Decadents' really longed for was ennobling refinement, the cultural beauty that Symons called '*la vérité vraie*, the very essence of truth' (Symons 1893: 859).

In a sense, the so-called 'Decadents' and their circle *were* the figures who most shaped and defined the character of the 1890s, either directly or because of the strong counter-reactions they provoked. But to the degree that is true, it was surely not because the 'Decadents' typified the weary stagnation or degenerate decline of the Victorian age, but because their themes and preoccupations were shared by most other artists in the decade – an unusual curiosity, a 'crusading' mentality, a desire for authenticity, a commitment to fine craftsmanship, and a need for spiritual validation.

Some General Themes and Characteristics

A great deal of 1890s poetry (such as the work of Kipling, Newbolt, Henley or Meynell) celebrated the health and vibrancy of Victorian culture – the evangelicalism of Victoria's Christian empire, the unique excellence of the English national character, the comfort of traditional faith and family. However, the emergence in the nineties of 'a thousand' cultural splinter groups also signalled great unrest and dissatisfaction. While British art has always had its share of rebels, the unusual hegemony of the Victorian middle class and its institutions, built up over sixty years of Victoria's reign, made the avant garde especially compelling in the 1890s and gave rise to the famous admonition that the true poet had to choose whether to be bourgeois society's servant or its outcast. Instead of embracing the traditional British puritanical principles of emotional discipline and frugal economy, most nineties poets exalted, to one degree or another, some form of intensifying 'excess' – luxuriant aestheticism, impassioned patriotism, radical social change, perfectionistic craftsmanship. Implicitly, if not explicitly, they challenged the foundations of the Victorian capitalist ethos, which privileged thrift and a buffering reserve in emotional matters as well as material ones. The so-called 'Decadents', in particular, represented an attempt to neutralize conventional bourgeois Victorian reticence, repression, decorum, and faith in unthinking materiality by substituting unconventional passion, confessional liberation, transvaluing 'perversity', and an honouring of intellectual spirituality. In so doing they were often turned into near martyrs at the hands of ruling-class critics.

To the degree that nineties poetry was 'revolutionary', its revolutions were rather paradoxical, integrating a nostalgic search for 'primary' truths with an intense desire for modern originality. Frank Kermode has explained that people who feel themselves to be in a period of 'transition' increasingly interpret their time as a period of 'transience', that is, a time whose only meaning is the certainty that it will soon be superseded (1966: 25). Harold Rosenberg (1959) has argued that as all ages become, in effect, ages of perpetual transition, the only criterion for meaning becomes novelty, modernity. As many avant-garde nineties poets believed, the key to being authentic was to be 'New', innovative, 'modern' in poetic form and subject matter. In this worldview the truly aesthetic spirit must reject any pedestrian technique, make no concession to conventional morality, and commit constantly to the ever-renewing properties of artifice, even the dandiacal novelty of artistic eccentricity. Paradoxically, one recaptures 'the very essence' of primal truths by a 'modern' transvaluation of old formulae.

For so many nineties poets the essence of authentic truth lay, in its most distilled form, in art, that most splendid transformer of vulgar reality. It was hardly accidental that Symons and Yeats described the artist as a priest in charge of a 'sacred ritual', or that figures as different as Johnson, Henley, Meynell, Kipling, Davidson, Housman and Charlotte Mew all emphasized the importance of technical mastery. Logically, fine crafts- manship – the incarnating medium for art's divine order – had to be the centre of any restorative cultural renaissance. In no small sense, elitist precision, even 'preciousness', became a vital counterweight to capitalist mass reproduction and the levelling democra- tization of human value. Yeats commented acidly that in the Victorian era the most famous poetry was often a long – sometimes very long – passage 'full of thoughts that might have been expressed in prose', and that the 'modern' poet's mission was, on the contrary, 'to express life at its intense moments, those moments that are brief because of their intensity' (1961: 494).

Nineties poets glorified intense moments not only because such moments were, in a sense, the distilled emotional equivalent of precision craftsmanship, but also because they were felt to be the conduit for true spiritual development. An almost invariable theme in 1890s poetry is the personal yearning for enhanced spiritual understanding, the search to find the answer to what Holbrook Jackson called the decade's ubiquitous question: 'How to Live?' (1913: 29–30). Admittedly, nineties poetry tends to define spirituality (and reli- gion generally) in more diverse and unorthodox ways than most previous decades had done, often advancing specifically agnostic or atheist themes (as in 'Trinity' by Michael Field or 'Madeleine in Church' by Charlotte Mew). Even ostensibly conventional religious relationships often border on the blasphemous, as seen in Gray's 'The Two Sinners' or Johnson's 'The Dark Angel'. Part of what made Roman Catholicism the spiritual 'home' for so many nineties figures was that the authoritarian, as well as ornately decorative, atmosphere of its rituals provided a secure refuge for the fragile aesthetic imagination, and yet, comfortingly, Catholicism was not a part of the British establishment, having traditionally been associated with the poor, the Irish, and European foreigners.

But whatever the spiritual variations, self-development in the nineties became almost inseparable from an obsessive search for some 'unity of being'. Whether it was the dandy's attempt to unite the arts in his own person, the patriot's effort to unify national purpose, the reformer's attempt to discern unity in disparate social problems, or the poet's mar- shalling myriad technical skills to produce a single effect, the poetry of the 1890s testi- fies repeatedly to a straining need for wholeness, for some ontological unity in what threatened to be a spiritually fragmented and impoverished world. Art was such a pow- erful weapon for the avant garde, as well as for more traditional ideologies, because it could satisfy the emotional need to protest forcefully against bourgeois Victorian inauthenticity, while simultaneously holding out hope for healing the nation's stultified soul. Most of the decade's avant-garde poetry protested against middle-class inauthenticity by implicitly demonstrating that adroit technical precision and 'modern' (albeit eccentric and idiosyncratic) treatment of subject matter created sounder and more personally truthful insights than those of more supposedly 'normal' people.

The setting which in the 1890s most incarnated 'transition' and 'modernity', and provided the most diverse opportunities for experiencing 'intense' moments and spiritual self-development, was, of course, the modern urban city. Over at least the previous century, with occasional exceptions, the city had been marginalized as a serious subject of poetry; but in the 1890s – particularly among the so-called 'Decadents', in poems like Le Gallienne's 'A Ballad of London' or Symons's 'City Nights' – urban streets, music halls and theatres exemplified the power of transfiguring artifice. The city was the site of the nineties' general fascination with theatre culture, fleeting moods, the transience of life, gypsies and other marginalized figures, the exotic and foreign (particularly things French), and, not least, the bizarre and the grotesque. The swirling 'irrationality' of the city was set against the staunch, presumably rational order of those key institutions of the British establishment – the country estate, the church, the military, the police. In much nineties verse the city looms as the very incarnation of change, diversity and intensity – and thus the fitting locus for constant recreations by a suffocated soul. Conversely, the city was also used to crystallize modern instability and danger – its fragmentation, its strangeness, its alienation. In the existential shift from sequestered home to vulnerable streets Coventry Patmore's iconic 'Angel in the House' frequently gives way to the destructively beautiful and alluring *femme fatale*, whose spell portends death. Nineties poetry treats sexuality more explicitly, emphasizing the carnal, than had generally been done before – whether as an agent of destruction, a tangible foundation for expanding understanding, or an aesthetic-erotic thing in itself.

There was much fine poetry written by women in the 1890s – though, with some exceptions, it has usually been significantly undervalued, when not ignored altogether. Whether these women poets were of the avant garde or more traditionalist in their sympathies, their work added new dimensions to the familiar nineties themes of cultural alienation and unstable identity. A. Mary F. Robinson, for example, often employs Italian peasant songs as an ironic frame to critique the ruling-class's marginalization of social and sexual 'Others'. In a Victorian age that had held up woman as the emblem of domesticity, chastity, stability and religious faith, women poets of the nineties wrote frequently about homelessness, sexual desire, a woman's secret self, and belligerent unbelief. As Angela Leighton has noted, these writers often make 'home' – traditionally both an ontological haven and a domicile – into a prison, 'playing on the tricky threshold between being in and out, between safety and the world'; moreover, the visual self-image of the speaker herself frequently appears as strange, even horrifying, suggesting 'a deep-rooted split in the very nature of the female self, as the poem tries to put together what the age has ideologically simplified or fragmented' (Leighton and Reynolds 1995: xxxvi–xxxvii).

Just as men had traditionally bonded through school ties, patriotic duty and capitalistic national progress, so women's friendships were represented as growing out of the common trials of marriage and motherhood. But here, too, as elsewhere, the nineties cast these social and cultural ties in a disturbing new light. Michael Field and Charlotte Mew, for example, write love poems in which mothers and lovers are ambiguously confused and sister relationships turn into mother–daughter relationships. Sometimes motherhood even becomes the site of horrific crime, as in several poems by 'Graham R. Tomson' (Rosamund Marriott Watson). The poems of Alice Meynell, Edith Nesbit and Dora Sigerson (Shorter) rarely separate the joys of motherhood from its haunting grief (Leighton and Reynolds 1995: xxxviii).

General Groupings and Key Figures

The numerous coteries of the 1890s were amorphous and not mutually exclusive, any more than were the diverse themes and sensibilities of the poets in them (who were frequently also accomplished fiction writers, playwrights and essayists); so any attempt to circumscribe the decade's poets into neat, self-contained categories will inevitably be inaccurate and misleading. But since at least some categorization, even if highly problematical, may be useful, I have tried to classify and briefly describe the most noteworthy 1890s poets under five very broad (and admittedly artificial) groupings: (1) so-called 'Decadents'; (2) traditionalists, imperialists and so-called 'Counter-Decadents'; (3) poets of the Celtic Revival; (4) poets of social reform; and (5) 'Others'.

So-called 'Decadents'

The poets who have traditionally been lumped together as 'the Decadents' were, in fact, a highly diverse group with widely varying, even contradictory, poetic styles and themes. The exotic, guilt-tinged poems of Arthur Symons (pronounced SIMM-ons) (1865–1945), who disdained politics, were thought to be the epitome of sex-crazed, hothouse decadence, while those of fellow Rhymer and *flâneur* Victor Plarr carry barely a hint of sexuality (let alone provocative sexuality) and often take up overtly political (particularly, French republican) themes. Both Lionel Johnson (1867–1902) and John Gray (1866–1934) were highly intellectual aesthetes who sought to resolve their internal spiritual conflicts through a disciplined, austere aestheticism – the paradoxical imposition of sculpted control on florid language – but the emotional effect conveyed in their respective poetry was strikingly different. The tension between Johnson's passionate love of beauty and the ascetic obedience he felt he owed to God manifests itself in relentless spiritual anguish, fatalistic melancholy and corrosive guilt. On the other hand, Gray (who eventually became a Catholic priest) expresses his equally vexing devotional struggles and passionate longings through a rather matter-of-fact rhetoric that implies, 'This is how things are, and they cannot be otherwise' (cf. Fletcher 1988: 19).

For all the myriad differences among the so-called 'Decadents', they did share several common themes, among them a deep commitment to precise technique, a privileging of refined art over unrefined nature (and cerebral reflection over raw materiality), a Romantic attraction to intensity and 'strangeness', a sensitivity to cosmic misery, and a quest for (and torment over) love, or spiritual truth, or both. Also uniting them was the implicit suggestion that tragedy inevitably awaited the idealistic effort to make life approximate art. It was an intimation – summed up often in the poems of Olive Custance (pseudonym 'Opals') (1874–1944) – that the quest for transcendentally exquisite sensations and divinely exotic beauty only reminds us that art is ultimately indifferent to and heedless of the needs of mortal human life and love, and that in the end the human can never fully embrace the divine, except in death.

Ernest Dowson (1867–1900), perhaps the most legendary member of the 'Tragic Generation', was among the most technically skilled and emotionally haunting poets of the *fin de siècle*. Time and again in Dowson's poetry – most of which was collected in *Verses* (1896) and *Decorations* (1899) – the figure of a little girl (or other sanctifying incarnation of innocence) is sequestered in a suspended 'lily time' 'beyond the reach of time and chance and change', beyond 'broken vows, / That sadden and estrange' ('Cease Smiling, Dear! A Little While Be Sad'). In Dowson's most famous poem *'Non Sum Qualis Eram Bonae Sub Regno Cynarae'* ('I Am Not What I Was Under Kind Cynara's Reign'), the title taken from the first poem in book IV of Horace's *Odes*, the poet-lover discovers that no matter how much he cries 'for madder music and for stronger wine', between him and those experiences – 'betwixt her lips and mine' – falls always the shadow of Cynara, his haunting ideal, an 'old passion' which blights any potential satisfaction in the earthly world and leaves the poet-lover 'desolate and sick', 'hungry for the lips of my desire'.

Heavily influenced by Schopenhauer, Dowson implicitly associates decay with 'wantonness' and 'surpassing vanity', suggesting a world where the 'fall' is irreversible and time is but an agent of cosmic retribution, a constant reminder of fundamental metaphysical alienation, the 'drear oblivion of lost things' that is 'the end of all the songs man sings' ('Dregs'). In a strategy that Symons called an 'ethics of renunciation', Dowson routinely seeks to rebuke the Schopenhauerean Will-to-Live by transforming his threatened innocents into the human equivalents of changeless and untainted works of art 'remaining *in perpetuo* without desire' – either virtual children (as in *'Ad Domnulam Suam'* ['To His Dear Little Mistress']) whom he protects in aestheticized gardens; or insulated saints (like the nuns of 'Nuns of the Perpetual Adoration' and 'Benedictio Domini') who turn their own lives into 'rosaries' of mystical devotion; or finally, entranced madmen (like the prisoner in 'To One in Bedlam') who, having lost touch with human reality, no longer suffer from its limitations. Frequently, however, Dowson's worshipful speakers only discover that the human condition itself, including even their aesthetic sensibility, inevitably contaminates – and stains with 'death, the host of all our golden dreams' – the very ideal they long to possess.

Dowson's verbal suggestiveness, technical precision, and mastery in melding form to meaning often turn his poems into near incantations. Routinely, even as his speakers seek to put emotions, memories and cherished beloveds outside the ravages of desire and decay, Dowson's diction and syntax, including the use of conditional modals such as 'would' and 'might', only call our attention to the very temporal process his protagonists seek to escape.

Repetition and parallelism accentuate the feeling of a 'closed' universe, installing a sense of paralysis and purposelessness, which the poet-lover's longing only intensifies. In addition, Dowson frequently underscores his themes of transience and melancholic resignation with line-ending feminine rhymes (ending with an unstressed syllable), which create a pronounced 'falling' effect, especially when alternating with powerful masculine rhymes, as in '*Vitae Summa Brevis Spem Nos Vetat Incohare Longam*' ('Life's Brief Span Forbids Long Enduring Hope'): 'They are not long, the weeping and the laughter, / Love and desire and hate: / I think they have no portion in us after / We pass the gate.'

'Michael Field' was the pseudonym of Katherine Bradley (1846–1914), who in public and private answered to 'Michael', and her niece Edith Cooper (1862–1913), who answered to 'Henry' or 'Field'. United inseparably by an intense emotional bond and a completely interdependent collaboration in both thought and style, the Michael Fields announced themselves 'pagan, pantheist', standing 'against the world to be / Poets and lovers evermore' (*Underneath the Bough*, 50). Their nineties poetry, collected in such volumes as *Sight and Song* (1892) and *Underneath the Bough* (1893), was lavishly praised for its Keats-like tonality, vitality and spontaneity. At a time when most of their contemporaries were still tied to conventional metrical stanzas, Michael Field's 'modernist' experiments with improvised metres, open-ended forms and unexpected rhymes offered a striking new style.

Running through Michael Field's work is an exhilarating streak of baroque unorthodoxy and exotic Orientalism, which crosses many moral and ideological borders, tacitly deconstructs Christian conventionality, and widens the parameters of romantic love. Their women are rarely depicted as melancholy victims. In '*La Giaconda*' a cruel Paterian Mona Lisa, who shows 'A breast / Where twilight touches ripeness amorously', proves to be supremely independent of 'those vicissitudes by which men die'. In 'A Dying Viper' the cursed snake of the Garden of Eden is female and 'like a star, hath central gravity / That draws and fascinates the soul to death'. Even when women die in a Field poem, often by a 'curse' from God, their self-affirming passion is defiant and undeterred, as in 'A Dance of Death', where the motion of Salome's head, though severed, is only 'subjugate / To its own law'.

Although largely ignored over the last century, 'Graham R. Tomson' (Rosamund Ball; later Rosamund Marriott Watson) (1860–1911) flourished in the early and mid-nineties as a well-connected critic and journalist, as well as a critically praised poet of 'aestheticized' ballads that exhibit supple, musical delicacy, vivid imagery and unnerving ghostly power. She commonly wrote about the bleak and eerie intensity of life and the attempt to cling to evanescent youth in the face of inevitable death. Tomson stated that the artist's 'first duty' is 'to create an atmosphere, to make an illusion' (*Academy*, 26 November 1892), and she does that to great effect in her most important works, *The Bird-Bride: A Volume of Ballads and Sonnets* (1889), *A Summer Night, and other Poems* (1891) and *Vespertilia and Other Verses* (1895), the last volume published under the name Rosamund Marriott Watson.

Some of her finest poems (several in dialect) use the form of the supernatural fairy tale cunningly to tell morally enigmatic stories of chilling domestic violence and brutal betrayal. In these narratives marriages are doomed by unforgiving destructive forces within woman, which link her to animal freedom and merciless savagery. A farmer's wife transmogrifies into a ruthless beast in the eerie and violent 'A Ballad of the Were Wolf'. In 'Ballad of the Bird-Bride' the alien bride evocatively fuses human and bird qualities. Almost always the result in such tales is permanent loss: 'Waste and wide is the wild gull's way, / And she comes never again' ('Ballad of the Bird-Bride').

So many of Marriott Watson's poems seem to argue that desire and fulfilment never ultimately intersect in that imprisoning 'medley of ironic things / We break our hearts upon from age to age' ('The Cage'). In the ghastly supernatural title poem of *Vespertilia* (1895) a young man encounters a hauntingly beautiful woman in ghostly Roman clothing; he refuses her offer of love, because he wants to remain true to the memory of a dead Englishwoman, only to remain forever restless when Vespertilia disappears. 'Children of the Mist', which may be a haunting reference to the fact that Tomson/Marriott Watson's sexual recklessness twice lost her custody of her own children, dramatizes the broken relationship between parents and children, in which the children have become 'voiceless and visionless' spectral wanderers, 'Waifs of the night that wander by, / . . . Ghosts of the years that never were, / The years that could not be'.

Other poets who were thought to have 'exotic' tendencies and were similarly concerned with 'aestheticized' technical precision include Francis Thompson (1859–1907), whose powerful sacramental imagery and quirky liturgical language sought to incarnate the spiritual world within 'Titanic glooms of chasmèd fears'; Theodore Wratislaw (1871–1933), whose meticulous metres and allusive metaphors epitomize the standard 'hothouse' image of the nineties as a 'temple of coloured sorrows and perfumed sins'; the half-brother of 'Vernon Lee' (Violet Paget), Eugene Lee-Hamilton (1845–1907), whose Parnassian *Sonnets of the Wingless Hours* (1894) Edith Wharton thought contained poems 'of exceptional beauty', which 'rank not far after the greatest in the language'; A. Mary F. Robinson (later Mme James Darmesterer; still later Mme Emile Duclaux) (1857–1949), whose cool, wryly meditative poems 'watch the world's disaster with a smile' and reveal the profundity of an 'ordinary' life not usually appreciated by the ruling culture; Victor Plarr (1863–1929), whose anxiety about the modern city and nostalgic fondness for beggars, gypsies, labouring men and exotic legends is almost invariably expressed in highly formal, controlled stanzas; the ardent and uncompromising socialist John Barlas (pseudonym 'Evelyn Douglas') (1860–1914), whom some touted as one of the finest poets of the period and whose verse reflects passionate empathy with all things imperilled by stupidity and ugliness; Oscar Wilde (1854–1900), whose only two noteworthy nineties poems were significant indeed – the 'decadent' *The Sphinx* (1894) and the very undecadent, reformist *Ballad of Reading Gaol* (1898); Richard Le Gallienne (1866–1947), a trendy personality whose poetry reflects key *fin-de-siècle* themes of the 'modern' city; Alfred Douglas (1870–1945), lightning rod of the scandalous Wilde trials, who made precise and skilful use of the ballad, verse satire (including nonsense verse) and, most particularly, the Italian sonnet; and Herbert Horne (1864–1916), whose usual themes are loss of love or faith and whose formal precision and musicality won accolades from Roger Fry.

Traditionalists, imperialists and so-called 'Counter-Decadents'

Some of the writers in this group were occasionally called 'the Hearties', presumably to distinguish them from the so-called 'Decadents'. For the most part, these 'Counter-Decadent' traditionalists proclaimed the virtues of an active life, were devotional in their spiritual verse, accepted with enthusiasm the technological advances of the modern age, and shared a belief in the civilizing mission of British imperial power and responsibilities.

A critic, dramatist and journalist, as well as a poet, W. E. Henley (1849–1903) was one of the most influential figures in British literary circles during the 1880s and 1890s, partly because of his role as editor of two significant journals – the *Scots Observer* (later, the *National Observer*) and the *New Review*. A staunchly conservative yet fiercely independent thinker, Henley was militantly pro-imperialist and unswervingly committed to rugged self-reliance and the active pursuit of excellence in all human endeavour – values he championed vigorously in the six volumes of poetry he produced in the nineties. Henley's own sometimes truculent self-reliance – reflected in his famous lines 'I am the master of my fate: / I am the captain of my soul' ('Invictus') – was perhaps influenced by his experience of, first, having his left foot amputated as a child (due to tubercular arthritis) and, then, in his twenties saving his other foot only by independently travelling to Edinburgh against medical advice to seek out treatment from Joseph Lister, whose new antiseptic techniques saved his leg and his life.

The Song of the Sword and Other Verses (1892), whose title poem was dedicated to Kipling, is an exultant celebration of warfare and expansionist fervour in the service of British imperial conquest. Henley's patriotic verses generally express his pride in England's willingness to shoulder the responsibility for crafting world order. For him, a vigorous British Empire was only a larger manifestation of the same spiritual health that produced clear critical discernment, powerful poetry, well-crafted prose, social conscience, admiration for heroism, and a passion to experience 'all for which life lives to long, / Wanton and wondrous and for ever well' ('London Voluntaries'). In the best of his verse Henley succeeds in identifying his own passion for life with a larger vital force that embraces the endless cycle of the seasons and the immediate urban realities of the crowded city.

Under the Parnassian banner, Henley routinely employed French fixed forms and other metrically regular poetry, but he also experimented robustly with 'modernist' ways of bringing rhythmic order to freer verse forms – occasionally using colloquial speech to brilliant effect – as he does with typical rhetorical flourish in describing sunken ships: 'Deep cellared in primeval ooze, / Ruined, dishonoured, spoiled, / They lie where the lean water-worm / Crawls free of their secrets' ('Song of the Sword').

Rudyard Kipling (1865–1936) was probably the most prolific and commercially popular writer of the 1890s, publishing over 200 works of poetry and prose during the decade. Kipling was uncompromisingly dedicated to the 'popular' taste and endorsed values that other writers questioned – conventional morality, strict conjugal fidelity, aggressively militaristic patriotism, and a predominantly hopeful attitude to life. Like an old-fashioned moralist, he preached an allegiance to 'duty', the duty 'to live stoically, to live cleanly, to live cheerfully'. Part of Kipling's appeal after the Wilde trials was precisely his unequivocally conventional vision of English manhood; characteristically, the speaker of 'In Partibus' sneers at 'long-haired things / In velvet collar-rolls, / Who talk about the Aims of Art' and finds it a joy 'to meet an Army man / Set up, and trimmed and taut'.

In volumes like *Barrack-Room Ballads* (1890, 1892), *The Seven Seas* (1896) and *Recessional and Other Poems* (1899), Kipling extolled the 'four-hundred-year adventure' of European colonial expansion and the duties he believed that 'the imperial races' had to 'the lesser breeds' ('The White Man's Burden'). Although he usually seemed to glorify the British Empire unselfconsciously, Kipling also problematized those imperialist sensibilities with wry irony and scepticism, viewing all human endeavour as ultimately transitory. His famous hymn 'Recessional', which decries the hubris of the Diamond Jubilee, is a haunting elegy recognizing the fragility of Britain's nineteenth-century achievements: 'Far-called, our navies melt away – / On dune and headland sinks the fire – / Lo, all our pomp of yesterday / Is one with Nineveh and Tyre!' In investigating the lower depths of Indian life, Kipling showcased the common working-class soldier, whose fresh perspective – expressed in the accent of the London cockney – proved to be an effective and highly popular way to portray modern social experience and on occasion exposed imperial racist attitudes (e.g. 'The Ladies').

Kipling's vast audience was captivated by the freshness of his subjects, the boldness and accessibility of his declamatory style, and his mastery of vernacular speech patterns, derived in part from the somewhat antithetical influences of Protestant hymns and music-hall songs. Having schooled himself on Browning's dramatic monologues, Kipling developed a keen ear for the forceful orality of language. Although he was no fan of the Aesthetes or the Parnassians, he shared their reverence for technical control, discipline in workmanship, and mastery of one's craft. In some respects, it is as logical as it is astonishing that Henry James called Kipling 'the most complete man of genius (as distinct from fine intelligence) that I have ever known' (Cunningham 2000: 1034).

Other poets considered generally (sometimes very generally) as 'traditionalists' include Alice Meynell (pronounced MEN-nell) (1847–1922), regarded by contemporaries as one of the finest poets of her generation, whose lyric poetry, marked by strikingly economic precision and impassioned observation, wistfully emphasizes lost love, change, rectitude (grounded in the church), renunciation and, not least, children and family; Austin Dobson (1840–1921), whose urbane, beautifully clear and seemingly effortless poems, written mostly in exacting 'Old French' fixed forms, reflect the bourgeois desire to remain free of the uncontrollable pressures of social, ethical or intellectual conflict; Henry Newbolt (1862–1938), whose upbeat, emotional songs about the sea celebrate male bravery, the cult of male duty, unflinching imperial service, 'muscular Christianity', and staunch allegiance to a greater community; William Watson (1858–1935), a very popular and highly respected personification of Victorian earnestness, who was none the less undeniably agnostic and willing to champion very unpopular causes; Stephen Phillips (1864–1915), who applied an opulent, highly rhetorical style to either blank verse on classical and Biblical themes or starkly melodramatic rhymed verse depicting the sordidness of modern urban life; 'Violet Fane', the pen name of the witty socialite Mary Montgomerie Lamb

(1843–1905), whose innovative, highly stylized lyric poetry is usually set in a wealthy upper-class environment and frequently casts a sharply critical eye on sexual orthodoxies; Robert Bridges (1844–1930), whose lyrical poems explore love and nature, and advocate classical artistic control and reflective emotional decorum; Robert Louis Stevenson (1850–94), whose poetry espouses courage, ambition, instinctive morality, friendship with nature and conscious optimism; Alfred Austin (1835–1913), who was appointed poet laureate, to the surprise of many, in 1896; Edmund Gosse (1849–1928), ubiquitous man of letters, who befriended poets from widely disparate literary 'camps'; Andrew Lang (1844–1912), whose poems were described by Graham R. Tomson as evoking 'the sentiment of old romance, of dim memories, all the more beautiful for their vagueness'; R. W. Dixon (1833–1900), a steadfast friend and sympathetic correspondent of Gerard Manley Hopkins; and Norman Gale (1862–1942), whom Le Gallienne praised as a 'six-foot-three nightingale' whose poetry is the 'union of warmth and chasteness'.

Poets of the Celtic Revival

Building in the 1890s towards its zenith, the Celtic Revival, known also as the Irish Literary Renaissance, championed a recovery of the Irish past, its chief institutional organs being the (Irish) National Literary Society and the Irish Literary Theatre. Although in many respects it was not a well-defined 'movement' at all, the Celtic Revival deeply influenced British social and artistic activity and played a key role in late-Victorian attempts to escape three overly 'rational' and 'scientific' explanations of the human spirit – rationalism, materialism and scientific positivism. The Revival made innovative use of 'irrational' myth and folklore, most obviously Irish mythology, in order to provide an alternative to hegemonic English national legend and to create another useful screen through which to mimic provocatively (and mock) the values of the contemporary bourgeois world. It espoused the view that country people are the living embodiment of the Celtic imagination, including its often mystical and supernatural 'cult of beauty'.

The movement's dominant figure was Yeats (1865–1939), whose nineties poetry evolved from evocative quasi-Pre-Raphaelite aestheticism to a much simpler style, patterned on the speech of Irish peasants. Other important figures include Dora Sigerson (later Shorter) (1866–1918), a fervent Irish Republican whose nostalgic and passionate ballad narratives are permeated by Gothic melancholy, ghostly melodrama and, in her domestic poems, the claustrophobic unhappiness of family life; William Sharp (1855–1905), a Scot who wrote secretly under the guise of 'Fiona Macleod' and whose poignantly nostalgic poetry deals with 'ancestral memories' of the Highlands, folklorish themes of the supernatural, and wistfully ecstatic inner visions of transcendental beauty; Ernest Rhys (1859–1946), a Welsh co-founder of the Rhymers' Club; Katherine Tynan (later Hinkson) (1861–1931), whose poetry reflects her passionate Irish nationalist concerns, as well as a distinctively Irish blend of devout Catholic mysticism and rural sentiment; George Russell ('A. E.') (1867–1935), whose mystic poetry reflects his interest in theosophy and focuses on moments of rapture prefiguring a destined absorption into 'Universal Being'; George Arthur Greene (1853–1921), the honorary secretary of the

Rhymers' Club, whose poetry (most often in Petrarchan sonnets) soberly and sometimes bitterly contemplates contemporary loss of faith; Emily Hickey (1845–1924), co-founder of the Browning Society and member of the Irish Literary Society, best known for her pensive and introspective poetry; Nora Hopper (1871–1906), whose poetry reflects an unusually keen knowledge of Irish folklore and Celtic culture; T. W. Rolleston (1857–1940), the strikingly handsome co-founder of the Rhymers' Club, who helped introduce Turgenev to the English-speaking world; John Todhunter (1839–1916), much of whose poetry celebrates the simple life, the wonders of nature and the fragility of beauty; Samuel Crockett (1859–1914), whose nostalgic, sentimental and very commercial work as a part of the 'Kailyard School' argues for Scottish nationalism and a separate national character; and Douglas Hyde (1860–1949), scholar of Irish folklore and champion of preserving the Irish language, whose work furnished countless Irish writers with native themes and idioms.

Poets of social reform

Poetry in the 1890s made assaults on social injustice of all sorts, including urban poverty, child labour, prostitution, animal vivisection and treatment of the insane. John Barlas and John Davidson were particularly forceful in addressing the economic and social indignities plaguing the urban poor and struggling lower classes. But there were other effective voices of reform, such as Wilfred Scawen Blunt (1840–1922), who attacked immoral British colonial practices in Africa and India, which he felt were heralding the end of the British Empire; May Kendall (1861–1943), whose exceptionally witty satires sceptically probed the scientific debates of the day, particularly Darwinism; L. S. Bevington (later Guggenberger) (1845–95), whose radical, if gentle, critiques skewered the conservative, Christian, imperialist core of British life; and Dollie Radford (1858–1920) and Ernest Radford (1857–1919), whose socialist agitations impugned bourgeois faith in religious orthodoxy and capitalist materialism. The innovative techniques employed in 'reform' poetry were at least as thoroughgoing as those developed in the 'Decadent' and 'traditionalist' poems of the period.

Scotsman John Davidson (1857–1909) was a highly prolific London novelist, playwright, essayist and poet – producing six volumes of poetry during the nineties – who had a complex and oblique, even standoffish, relationship with the principal literary movements and personalities of his time. He was deeply sceptical of traditional dogma and sought relentlessly to find a workable replacement for it. A militant atheist and fierce Nietzschean iconoclast, Davidson nevertheless lived a very 'respectable' life, expressing distaste for and wittily satirizing what he took to be the aesthetic perversities and bohemian ways of his younger colleagues in the Rhymers' Club. His tongue-in-cheek 'Ballad of a Nun', for example, tells the tale of a reclusive nun who is saved rather than damned by surrendering to 'all her passion's hoard'.

Obsessed as he was with questions of social justice, the difficulties of religious belief and the torments of the artist, Davidson's poetry, while rarely optimistic, reveals a strong, vital belief in the need to affirm life and its authentic values. In 'A Ballad of a Coward', he argues categorically that a retreat into 'love' or 'art' is no answer to the challenge of life; and in 'A Ballad of an Artist's Wife' he contends that great art is produced only by great suffering. The most striking of his London poems appeared in two series of *Fleet Street Eclogues* (1893, 1895), the title suggesting the ironic combination of Virgilian pastoral form with modern urban settings and characters. Organized around various religious holidays (e.g. Michaelmas, All-Hallows Eve) and told from an astonishing variety of viewpoints, each eclogue features an often colloquial discussion among 'shepherd-journalists' on the various vulgarities and social inequities of modern London. In general, the poems argue that the enjoyment of nature in earlier times has been marred by increasing societal injustice. In 'St George's Day' the speaker laments, 'I cannot see the stars and flowers, / Nor hear the lark's soprano ring', because 'I hear the rotting match-girl whine; . . . / I hear the explosion in the mine; . . . / I hear the tired quick tripping feet / Of sad, gay girls who ply for hire'. Rebelling against Victorian sentimentality and the soft diction and prosody that often accompanied it, Davidson sought to create an entirely new, free and flexible idiom, derived from the tight narratives of the ballad, marked by fresh imagery, innovative metres and often colloquial diction – an emphasis on 'verse as speech' which impressed T. S. Eliot, among others.

Although better known for her considerable success as a writer of children's fiction, Edith Nesbit (1858–1924), who co-founded the Fabian Society in 1884, claimed that 'Only my socialist poems are *real me*.' Verses like 'A Great Industrial Centre' testify to her deep awareness of the plight of the poor and her efforts to alleviate it. Upon seeing 'Squalid street after squalid street, / Endless rows of them, each the same, / Black dust under your weary feet, / . . . Dust in the place of dreams', the speaker asks the privileged if God will question them on why they have done nothing to ease the suffering of the workers who have subsidized their 'glad lives in the sun'.

But, in fact, the tone, style and subject matter of Nesbit's poems, which range widely from short, sensual lyrics to patriotic verses, are as varied as her own paradoxical sensibilities. (Although she was extremely bohemian and was friends with such emancipated women as Eleanor Marx and Annie Besant, she never had much sympathy for the suffrage movement and converted to Roman Catholicism.) Nesbit's best poems – contrary to her own beliefs – are probably those that catch the flavour of her ambiguous and tension-filled emotional life with the volatile Hubert Bland, whose two illegitimate children by their housekeeper Nesbit raised as her own (along with Nesbit's four children by Bland). Many of her poems hint at the vexing complexities of a 'free' marriage – she had several extramarital affairs herself – and often, not surprisingly, express wry ambivalence about romantic love. In 'Love's Guerdon', from *A Pomander of Verse* (1895), the female speaker addresses her dead husband, observing at his graveside that now (in implicit contrast to his living years) 'No one's heart but mine has beat and bled for you, / No one else's flowers push mine away'. Like Alice Meynell's, Nesbit's emotional allegiance was ultimately to children. In 'The Dead to the Living', she movingly turns private, domestic grief over a dead child into political hope for future generations, shifting from a loss that 'set its teeth in this heart of mine, / And fastened its claws in my brain' to the dream 'of a coming day / When life shall not envy death . . . / And those who come after will find life fair, / And their lives worth living'.

Mathilde Blind (also 'Claude Lake') (1841–96), whose collected poems Arthur Symons edited in 1900, was one of her era's most impressive crusading intellectuals. An independent feminist, socialist and religious sceptic, one of whose closest friends and allies was noted novelist and social critic Mona Caird, Blind advocated women's suffrage, the radical improvement of women's education (she bequeathed the greater part of her estate to Newnham College, Cambridge), and the opening of almost all professions to women. She was strongly committed to late-nineteenth-century positivism, and the impact of evolutionary thinking is evident in much of her poetry. Her celebratory epic poem *The Ascent of Man* (1889) was the first poem in English to provide a comprehensive account of Darwinian theory. Her lyric poems often deal with a woman's despair, frustration and sense of failure; her most fascinating work is probably contained in *Dramas in Miniature* (1891), which implicitly addresses inequality between the sexes.

Many of Blind's poems represent romantic love as a destructive power struggle operating often on the edge of madness. The mesmerizing 'A Carnival Episode', which never makes entirely clear whether it relates actual events or a frenzied delusion, is a tale of illicit love, in which a 'fatally fair' woman with 'opulent hair, / That uncoiled the brown snakes of its tresses', makes the narrator 'wild with passion', then dismisses him as 'but a Carnival joke'. 'The Russian Student's Tale' is another story of doomed love, set in a city landscape that seems like 'bodies without heart or will'. In the poem a girl with the face of 'innocent sweetness undefiled' loves a Russian Student, who loves her passionately in return but refuses to marry her, because as an impoverished, 'unprotected' child she was 'beguiled' by 'all sorts of tempters' until forced into 'The odious barter of her youth, / . . . for the sake of gold', a fall the Russian Student cannot bring himself to forgive.

Some other poets whose work, explicitly or implicitly, carries a reformist agenda include Roden Noel (1834–94), a happily bisexual socialist, many of whose poems celebrate male beauty; Laurence Housman (1865–1959), a left-leaning progressive humanist, supportive of women's suffrage, whose poetry carries many 'Decadent' resonances; and George Sims (1847–1922), whose sentimental ballads indict social injustice and celebrate the capacity of faith, love and childlike innocence.

'Others'

The following four poets do not fit comfortably into any of the previous categories but were nevertheless key figures addressing the social and spiritual uncertainties of the *fin de siècle*. They all see their world as alien – thus marking themselves as fundamentally 'Other'. It is a world that manifests cosmic indifference and fatalism, a haunting sense of almost inevitable betrayal and loss, or some other eerie threat to human security and identity. All these poets also created new styles and idioms which later decades considered characteristically 'modern', remote from the ornament and rhetoric of the Victorian 'grand style'.

The linguistic sobriety, resigned stoicism and wryly humorous irony in the episodic ballads of A. E. Housman (1859–1936) often mask a surprisingly grim and fatalistic world, as well as the psychological subtlety of his speakers, who poignantly confront heart-rending predicaments. The poetry of Thomas Hardy (1840–1928), first collected in 1898 as *Wessex Poems*, presents vexing conflict between ancient rural traditions and modern urban advances. Exhibiting elemental ballad rhythms and idiosyncratic diction, his poems question with insistent irony the cosmic order of things – expressing the pain and near-despair of trying to assert the value of human life 'in the face of an indifferent universe'.

However, two less-well-recognized woman poets produced work that in key respects is equally interesting and innovative. Although Mary E. Coleridge (also 'Anodos') (1861–1907) was known by Victorians chiefly as the author of popular romantic (mostly historical) novels, in 1917 the *Cambridge History of English Literature* ranked her as the nineteenth century's 'most remarkable poetess, after Elizabeth Barrett Browning and Christina Rossetti'. In spite of being highly regarded by other poets, she drew very little attention until her poems, which were originally published as *Fancy's Following* (1896) and *Fancy's Guerdon* (1897), were collected by Henry Newbolt in 1907, shortly after her death. Her poems are remarkable for their striking imagery, eerie mystery and intense emotional power – the kind that surfaces when the speaker in 'The Other Side of the Mirror' discovers, in place of her usual 'glad and gay' reflection, 'The vision of a woman, wild / With more than womanly despair'. Many of Coleridge's poems, which often employ psychic and dream states, address the elusiveness of love, the fragility of identity, or the seminal need to protect the integrity of the private self from social intrusion and betrayal. The speaker of 'True to Myself Am I and False to All' concludes that to tell the truth and expose her yearnings would be to 'let terror slay me, ere I call / For aid of men', so she lies through her social mask.

Some poems ('Gone', 'Friends', 'Broken Friendship', 'Marriage') are about loyalty in friendship, especially female friendship, and not only assume a female perspective but seem to endorse a virtually separate, all-female world. As Angela Leighton has noted, poems like 'A Day-dream', 'The Witches' Wood' and 'The White Woman', which often set up a sexualized maiden landscape fraught with lesbian subtexts, are permeated by intense hidden passion, sexual power and dangerous secret knowledge (Leighton 1995: 612). Coleridge believed that gender is the essence of identity and that men and women are 'separate in soul' (1910: 233). Men are rarely a source of comfort or security in her poetry; in poems like 'He Knoweth Not That the Dead Are Thine' and 'Mortal Combat' they inflict pain by being oblivious or duplicitous. In 'Marriage' a formerly joyful maiden forsakes her circle of 'merry sisters' in order to marry, and discovers that having done so she is unable ever again to be 'Wantonly free' and 'wild with glee'.

Although none of her poetry was collected until 1916, Charlotte Mew (also 'Charles Catty') (1869–1928) has often been considered a Victorian poet, not least because her own temperament was ever torn between sexual longing and rigid self-denial. As Cora Kaplan has noted, there is a strong moral-religious axis in Mew's verse, which normally presents one of two kinds of tragic women – those, like 'Madeleine', who have bartered their souls for the comforts of sexual love; or those, like the speaker in 'Fame', whom experience has passed by and who see their lost dreams as 'A frail dead, new born lamb, ghostly and pitiful and white, / A blot upon the night, / The moon's dropped child!' (Kaplan 1975: 192). Often cast as innovative and psychologically intricate dramatic monologues, Mew's poetry returns again and again to the tormenting, strangely familiar world of the mad and focuses particularly on the themes of frustrated and obsessive sexual passion, female self-repression, extreme psychological isolation, and speech that cannot overcome fear or misunderstanding. The title poem of her collection *The Farmer's Bride* is a tragedy, told by a middle-aged farmer, about how his hastily 'woo'd and wed' teenage wife has 'turned afraid / Of love . . . and all things human'. The bride is represented as a frightened, imprisoned small animal: 'We chased her, flying like a hare / Before our lanterns . . . / We caught her, fetched her home at last / And turned the key upon her, fast.' Even Mew's erotic love poems, despite all their nineties extravagance, end by affirming cold and bleak lovelessness. In 'Pécheresse' illicit passion results in separation from God and subsequent damnation: 'His is the only face I know, / . . . / It shuts God out; it comes between.'

Showing great technical innovation, Mew's poems are generally written in rhyming free verse, which allows her to manipulate metre and line length, as well as rhyme, to match the yearning ebb and flow of the speaker's emotions. In 'Madeleine in Church' some lines contain as many as fourteen feet, as if Mew (who insisted that her publishers not break up these extraordinarily long lines) wanted to suggest that the speaker is skirting the boundaries of human sanity – until momentarily rescued, perhaps, by the surprise rhyme at the end. Shortly after her collected poems appeared in 1916, both Hardy and Virginia Woolf acclaimed her to be the best living woman poet.

See also: POETRY AND ILLUSTRATION; LANDSCAPE AND CITYSCAPE.

REFERENCES AND FURTHER READING

Alford, Norman (1994) *The Rhymers' Club: Poets of the Tragic Generation*. New York: St Martin's.

Beckson, Karl (1966) 'Introduction' to Holbrook Jackson. *The Eighteen Nineties* (pp. v–viii). New York: Capricorn.

Beckson, Karl (ed.) (1981) *Aesthetes and Decadents of the 1890's*. Chicago: Academy Chicago.

Bergonzi, Bernard (1970) 'Aspects of the *Fin de Siècle*.' In Arthur Pollard (ed.). *The Victorians* (pp. 463–81). New York: Peter Bedrick.

Bradbury, Malcolm and James McFarlane (eds) (1976) *Modernism 1890–1930*. Harmondsworth: Penguin.

Buckley, Jerome H. (1951) *The Victorian Temper*. Cambridge, Mass.: Harvard University Press.

Cevasco, G. A. (ed.) (1993) *The 1890s: An Encyclopedia of British Literature, Art, and Culture*. London and New York: Garland.

Coleridge, Mary E. (1910) *Gathered Leaves*. London: Constable.

Cunningham, Valerie (ed.) (2000) *The Victorians: An Anthology of Poetry and Poetics*. Oxford: Blackwell.

Evans, B. Ifor (1933) *English Poetry in the Later Nineteenth Century*. London: Methuen.

Fletcher, Ian (ed.) (1987a) *British Poetry and Prose 1870–1905*. Oxford and New York: Oxford University Press.

Fletcher, Ian (1987b) *W. B. Yeats and his Contemporaries*. New York: St Martins.

Fletcher, Ian (ed.) (1988) *The Poems of John Gray*. Greensboro, N. C.: ELT Press.

Goldfarb, Russell M. (1962) 'Late-Victorian Decadence.' *Journal of Art and Art Criticism*, 20, 369–73.

Gordon, Jan B. (1971) 'The Danse Macabre of Symons' *London Nights*.' *Victorian Poetry*, 9, 429–43.

Hughes, Linda K. (ed.) (1995) *Victorian Poetry* (Special issue on women poets), 33.1.

Jackson, Holbrook (1913) *The Eighteen Nineties*. London: Grant Richards.

Kaplan, Cora (1975) *Salt and Bitter and Good*. New York: Paddington.

Kermode, Frank (1966) *The Sense of an Ending*. Oxford: Oxford University Press.

Le Gallienne, Richard (1926) *The Romantic '90s.* Garden City, N. Y.: Doubleday.

Lester, John A., Jr (1968) *Journey through Despair, 1880–1914: Transformations in British Literary Culture.* Princeton, N. J.: Princeton University Press

Leighton, Angela (1992) *Victorian Women Poets: Writing Against the Heart.* Charlottesville: University Press of Virginia.

Leighton, Angela (1996) *Victorian Women Poets: A Critical Reader.* Oxford: Blackwell.

Leighton, Angela and Margaret Reynolds (eds) (1995) *Victorian Women Poets: An Anthology.* Oxford: Blackwell.

Munro, John M. (1968) *English Poetry in Transition 1880–1920.* New York: Pegasus.

O'Brien, Kevin (1978) 'Matthew Arnold and the Hellenists of the 1890s.' *Antigonish Review*, 35, 79–93.

Peckham, Morse (1967) 'Aestheticism to Modernism: Fulfillment or Revolution.' *Mundus Artium*, 1, 36–55.

Perkins, David (1976) *A History of Modern Poetry.* Cambridge, Mass: Harvard University Press.

Pittock, Murray G. H. (1993) *Spectrum of Decadence: Literature of the 1890s.* New York: Routledge.

Robinson, James K. (1953) 'A Neglected Phase of the Aesthetic Movement: English Parnassianism.' *PMLA*, 68, 733–54.

Rosenberg, Harold (1959) *The Tradition of the New.* New York: Horizon.

Snodgrass, Chris (1992) 'Aesthetic Memory's Cul-de-Sac: The Art of Ernest Dowson.' *ELT*, 35 (1), 26–53.

Stanford, Derek (1965) *Poets of the '90s: A Biographical Anthology.* London: Baker.

Stokes, John (1989) *In the Nineties.* Chicago: University of Chicago Press.

Symons, Arthur (1893) 'The Decadent Movement.' *Harper's New Monthly Magazine*, 26, 851–68.

Symons, Arthur (1899) *The Symbolist Movement in Literature.* London: Constable.

Symons, Arthur (1904) *Studies in Prose and Verse.* London: Dent.

Williams, Linda (1994) 'Victorian Poetry: 1830–1900.' In Jane Thomas (ed.). *Bloomsbury Guides to English Literature* (pp. 43–58). London: Bloomsbury.

Wilson, Jean (1971) 'The 'Nineties Movement in Poetry: Myth or Reality?' *Yearbook of English Studies*, 1, 160–74.

Yeats, William Butler (1961) *Essays and Introductions.* New York: Macmillan.

PART TWO
Production, Distribution and Reception

19

The Market

Lee Erickson

The industrialization of publishing that occurred in the early nineteenth century marginalized poetry in comparison with other literary genres. Consequently, almost all Victorian poets struggled to find an audience, were better known than read, and achieved popularity late in their careers. Although Tennyson eventually acquired fame, fortune and a title through writing poetry, he had few readers until the publication of *In Memoriam* and his being named poet laureate in 1850. The inventions of stereotyping, of the Fourdrinier paper-making machine and later of the power press enabled publishers to print more books more cheaply and so allowed more readers to read than before, but they also created more competition for poetry. Throughout the great Victorian expansion of publishing and reading, poetry suffered in comparison with other genres. Most new poetry books continued to be printed in editions of 500 copies, found fewer readers, and made no money. In addition, the invention of steel-engraving for pictorial reproduction led to the development of the literary Annuals, which competed with slim poetry volumes in the giftbook market. As the Annuals' vogue faded in the 1850s, they were supplanted by popular, lyric giftbook anthologies, most notably by Francis Palgrave's *Golden Treasury* (1861), and towards the century's end by Walter Scott's one-shilling poetry reprints and anthologies in the Canterbury Poets series. By 1900, contemporary poetry sometimes became associated with fine printing and private presses, which anachronistically employed pre-industrial paper-making and printing practices. Devotional, humorous and narrative poetry had steadily increasing sales during the nineteenth century, but only a few contemporary poets sold as many copies of their work as popular novelists such as Charles Dickens and George Eliot.

The Victorian poetry market effectively begins in 1825. The literary Annuals were then coming to monopolize the giftbook market, which individual volumes of poetry had previously dominated. The Annuals' popularity stemmed not from their poetry but from their steel-engraved pictures of famous paintings and fashionable people. Most of the Annuals' poetry merely described the engraved reproductions. The Annuals dominated the market for poetry from 1825 to 1835, and a few individual Annuals had sales that rivalled those of Scott's and Byron's earlier volumes. In 1825 *The Literary Souvenir* sold 6,000 copies and by 1829 was expected to sell between 8,000 and 9,000; and in its first issue *The Keepsake* of 1828 sold 15,000. The Annuals attracted the readers of new poetry and so significantly reduced the market for volumes of verse written by individual poets. An average poetry volume would sell 300 of its 500 copies at five shillings a copy, so in 1826 the sales of the *Forget Me Not* and *The Literary Souvenir*, which together totalled 16,000 copies costing twelve shillings each, amounted to the sales of 125 individual poetry volumes. The Annuals' editors quickly learned to focus on the pictures, because they had to arrange for engravings long in advance and had to pay large sums for them. For example, the publisher of *The Keepsake* for 1829 paid £11,000 for the volume's plates. This made the pictures much more important than the poetry and meant that editors sent pictures to poets to serve as the subjects for their poems instead of commissioning engravers to illustrate poems. Thackeray's *History of Pendennis* (1848–50) describes Bacon's spring Annual as 'daintily illustrated with pictures of reigning beauties, or other prints of a tender and voluptuous character; and, as these plates were prepared long beforehand, requiring much time in engraving, it was the eminent poets who had to write to the plates, and not the painters who illustrated the poems'. To earn her money as the editor of and sole contributor to *Fisher's Drawing-Room Scrap-Book*, Letitia Landon supplied poems for the pictures. Once the novelty of writing a poem to serve as a pendant to a picture had passed, no serious poet endured such indignity, unless, like Landon, desperate for money.

The shift from the Romantic to the Victorian poetry market stemmed directly from the literary Annuals and their popular demand that poetry conform to a pictorial aesthetic. For a short while the Annuals solicited the best-known and most highly regarded poets to contribute. *The Keepsake* of 1829 had Wordsworth, Coleridge, Southey, Scott and, posthumously, Shelley as contributors. Early in his career, Tennyson's poems appeared in *The Gem, The Tribute, Friendship's Offering* and *The Keepsake*. Replying in 1831 to William Henry Brookfield, who had requested a poem from him for the *Yorkshire Literary Annual*, Tennyson says, 'I have been so beGemmed and beAmuletted and be-forget-me-not-ted that I have given all these things up.' While Tennyson felt oppressed by being asked to write to order, the Annuals' editors soon discovered that requesting poetry from good poets cost more than it was worth, so the quality of the Annuals' poetry soon declined as their payments became paltry.

In the wake of the Annuals the market for new poetry volumes by less well-known poets vanished almost overnight, and left a struggling poet like John Clare unable to find a publisher. Thomas Hood, who did find publishers for his poetry in the 1830s, could not support his family and was forced to serve briefly as a mercenary soldier in Germany. Indeed, Benjamin Disraeli rightly declared in *Vivian Grey* (1826–7) that because of the 1825–6 banking crisis, the 'reign of poetry was over for half a century'. Only poets like Tennyson and Browning, who could afford to share any losses their publishers might incur from printing their poetry, could persist for long as poets. Middle-class authors like Matthew Arnold turned their hands to prose or found paying jobs or both.

Devotional and religious poetry flourished throughout the period. John Keble's *Christian Year* (1827) sold 305,500 copies from 1827 until the copyright expired in 1873 seven years after the author's death. The distribution of its sales by decades provides an index of the steadily increasing market for such poetry: from 1827 to 1837, 26,500 copies were sold; from 1838 to 1847, 39,000; from 1848 to 1857, 63,000; from 1858 to 1867, 119,500; and from 1868 to 1873, 57,500. In the two years following the copyright's expiration, the publishers printed 70,000 copies of a cheap edition. Robert Pollok's *Course of Time* (1827) sold 12,000 copies in eighteen months and 78,000 copies by 1869. Josiah Conder's 1836 supplement to Isaac Watts's *Psalms and Hymns* had sold 40,000 copies by 1839. And the versified pieties of Martin Tupper's *Proverbial Philosophy* (1838–42) sold 200,000 copies by 1866. First published in the *Month* in 1865, John Henry Newman's *Dream of Gerontius* went through thirty-one editions from 1866 to 1898. If poets courted the readership for devotional poetry but mixed too much thought with their religious feeling, they became frustrated. For instance, Robert Browning wrote *Christmas-Eve and Easter-Day* (1851) for these readers, and had moved to Dickens's publisher, Chapman and Hall, in hopes of profiting by appealing to the audience for religious Christmas giftbooks, but found that he did not understand what readers of pious verse wanted.

Humorous verse and narrative poetry were especially popular. Richard Barham's *Ingoldsby Legends* (1840–7) sold about 450,000 authorized copies by 1895. In 1881 a six-penny edition of Barham's work was printed in a run of 100,000 copies and over 60,000 were sold on the first day of publication. Thomas Macaulay's *Lays of Ancient Rome* (1842) sold 18,000 copies by 1852, 40,000 copies by 1862, and a total of over 100,000 by the middle of 1875. William E. Aytoun and Theodore Martin's 'Bon Gaultier's' *Book of Ballads* (1845) sold 32,000 copies from the fifth edition of 1857 to 1909; and Aytoun's *Lays of the Scottish Cavaliers* (1849) sold 60,000 copies by the Victorian period's end. After appearing in the magazine *Fun*, W. S. Gilbert's *Bab Ballads* (1869) were collected in a volume published by J. C. Hotten in an edition of over 2,000 copies. Gilbert then moved the volume to George Routledge and Sons, who brought out a shilling edition of 10,000 copies in 1870, and printed four more editions by 1900. Humorous poetry also found a new outlet in *Punch*, which began in 1843. Elizabeth Barrett Browning's most popular work was her verse novel *Aurora Leigh* (1857). Coventry Patmore's *The Angel in the House* (1854–62) sold between 200,000 and 250,000 copies by 1896. Perhaps the most popular single Victorian poem was Tennyson's *Enoch Arden* (1864), which had a first edition of 60,000 copies. And the later popularity of Rudyard Kipling's poetry, beginning with *Departmental Ditties* (1886) and *Barrack-Room Ballads* (1892), stemmed from his gift for versifying stories. The chief American contributions to the period's best-selling narrative poetry were Henry Longfellow's *Courtship of Miles Standish* (1858), which sold 10,000 copies on the first day of publication in England, and James Russell Lowell's *Biglow Papers* (1859), which sold 50,000 copies in England between publication and 1873.

Although we conventionally think of Victorian poetry as beginning with Tennyson's *Poems, Chiefly Lyrical* in 1830, the most popular contemporary poet of secular poetry was Sir Walter Scott, whose collected poetry sold over 41,000 copies between 1829 and 1849. In contrast, when Edward Moxon offered to publish Wordsworth's collected poetry in a six-volume edition in 1836, he planned to print only 3,000 copies, showed a loss on the edition in 1842, and only turned a profit after Wordsworth was named poet laureate in 1843. In the 1840s Macaulay ran a respectable second to Scott with *Lays of Ancient Rome*

(1842) and succeeded by adapting his classical material to the public's taste for Scott's poetic forms. The eclipse of Wordsworth by the new laureate Tennyson in 1850 marks the moment when the contemporary readership finally recognized the best Victorian poetry. This development was reflected by the first printings and initial reception of the *Prelude* and *In Memoriam* in 1850. The *Prelude* was published in a posthumous edition of 2,000 that took almost a year to sell, while *In Memoriam* appeared in an edition of 5,000 copies and went through five editions and probably 25,000 copies in a year and half. And since, like Wordsworth, Tennyson retained his copyrights, his great publishing success made him wealthy. Unlike Wordsworth, however, Tennyson could not have sold his copyrights at the beginning of his career even if he had wished.

Once publishers recognized that the market for new poetry had virtually disappeared, they usually required poets to publish on the basis of half profits. That is, in order to publish, poets had to take half of the publishing risks and assume half of any losses; and, in return, they would retain copyright and receive half of any profit, which, if the whole small edition sold, equalled 10 per cent of the sales. The break-even point was usually around 70 per cent of the number printed, although since poetry publication was often subsidized by the poet, small, uneconomical editions might well be published. This practice confined poetry publishing to a handful of publishers and guaranteed that almost every poet had to have independent means. John Clare, for instance, approached John Taylor in 1829, but found that Taylor was no longer willing to publish Clare's work on terms that he could afford, because Clare's *Shepherd's Calendar* (1827) had not sold more than 400 copies by 1829. For several years no other publisher would assume the risk either, until Whittaker and How paid Clare a small sum for *The Rural Muse* in 1835. Working-class poets found themselves generally unable to publish and were unlikely to have a solvent publisher when they could. Jeremiah How, who was Clare's last publisher, did take such risks, and also published Thomas Cooper's *Purgatory of Suicides* in 1845. But How paid personally for his financial imprudence and went bankrupt in 1846. In the 1830s and 1840s few contemporary poets reached an audience large enough to make a profit.

When the market for individual volumes of poetry collapsed in the late 1820s, publishers forced slow-selling poets like Wordsworth to assume more of the publishing risk. During this period Wordsworth had faith that his poetry would eventually find a popular readership, and so took on two-thirds of the risk. When Edward Moxon paid Wordsworth £1,000 in 1837 for publishing his poetic works, that surpassed what Wordsworth had made from all of his previous publications. But just when his poetry was providing substantial returns, Wordsworth realized that he would lose control in 1842 of the copyright for his most popular work, *The Excursion*. Wordsworth then campaigned for Sergeant Thomas Noon Talfourd's new copyright bill. The bill would have extended copyright from twenty-eight to sixty years for living authors. Since few literary properties were worth publishing after that much time, and since those few were almost all the works of great poets, the history of English copyright law from the House of Lords' decision in *Donaldson* v. *Beckett* of 1774 to the Copyright Bill of 1842 centred on copyrights for poetry. The legal decision in 1774 concerned the reprinting of James Thomson's *Seasons*.

Similarly, arguments for and against the extension of copyright during Sergeant Thomas Talfourd's parliamentary campaign from 1837 to 1841 focused on the poetry of Wordsworth and Coleridge. Further, few authors owned profitable copyrights as Wordsworth did, since almost all authors happily sold their copyrights to publishers who assumed the financial risk. The major publishers, who owned almost all existing copyrights, privately supported .Talfourd's bill, but the bill encountered resistance led by Thomas Tegg from the cheap reprint trade, which would lose from the lack of expiring copyrights. However, in the depth of the 1842 depression, after consulting the large publishing houses, the government passed a new law that extended copyright from twenty-eight to forty-two years during an author's life, and, as a sop to the reprinters, shortened posthumous copyrights from fourteen to seven years. Popular novelists like Charles Dickens were soon buying their copyrights back from their publishers, while the few popular poets who held their copyrights found themselves unexpectedly having made a fortune, and were unaffected when their publishers went bankrupt.

Because Victorian poets retained their copyrights, they could revise and add to their previously published work in print rather than in manuscript even more than previous poets had. Tennyson revised many of his *Poems* of 1833 for the 1842 edition. He also slowly added to *Idylls of the King*, first publishing 'Morte d'Arthur' in 1842, and not finishing his epic until 1885. And despite deploring Tennyson's revision of published poems to suit the critics, Robert Browning overhauled *Sordello* (1840) in his *Poems* of 1863 and supplied running titles to summarize each page's action for his bewildered readers. Whitman's *Leaves of Grass* (1855) offers an American parallel. Since they retained their copyrights, poets controlled their texts in a way that earlier poets did not and so published revised work that has necessitated the modern variorum editions.

Accurate figures for publishers' printing runs and sales of poetry are especially rare in the period, and are generally drawn from the surviving correspondence of famous and well-known poets. However, the microfilmed archives of several major nineteenth-century English literary publishers await the patience and perseverance of future publishing historians. Edition size varied greatly according to the publisher's judgement about a poet's probable sale. Tennyson's *Enoch Arden* (1864), his most popular poem, was first published in an edition of 60,000 and sold quickly. In contrast, Browning's two-volume *Ring and the Book* (1868–9) had a first edition of 3,000, which was not exhausted until the height of Browning's popularity in 1882. This contrast shows that the number of editions which any poetry volume went through cannot be used to estimate reliably the number of readers that a poet had. None the less, since poets generally made their reputations slowly, poetry publishers were cautious about printing many copies of volumes by poets who were early in their careers, and usually published a poet's first few volumes in editions of about 500 copies. This caution was applied universally, as the case of Thomas Hardy illustrates. Three months after its publication in 1895, 20,000 copies of *Jude the Obscure* had been sold. But when Hardy approached Harper and Brothers about his first poetry volume, *Wessex Poems*, he knew enough to offer to cover the book's publication costs. The firm was willing to assume the risk, but printed only 500 copies of it in 1898. Later, when his second volume, *Poems of Past and Present*, was printed in 1901, the first edition again had only 500 copies.

His publisher did not expect that the readers of Hardy's novels would read his poetry or purchase either volume, and realized that Hardy would have to establish a separate reputation as a poet, even though his career as a novelist would guarantee prominent reviews of his poetry. However, if an individual work went to a second edition, both the publisher and the poet probably profited. Further, since reprinting fewer than 250 copies of a book could not make money, a poetic work that went to a third edition can be expected to have had at least 1,000 copies printed. Piratical publishers of poetry both in England and in America operated similarly, printing small editions that they hoped to sell quickly. Most poetry volumes sold in the way that other books did, and so would achieve almost all of their sale in the first six months after publication. A sudden vogue for a volume or an author thus required a publisher to judge the evanescent demand correctly in reprinting.

Even if an edition of 500 copies costing five shillings sold out, the poet would usually earn as the half-profits share only £12. 10*s*. Of course, economies of scale were available if a volume went to a second edition, or if a volume was first printed in a larger edition and could be sold quickly. The collected poetry of well-established poets usually had initial printings of between 2,000 and 3,000 copies. Largely because of the sales of her collected poems, Jean Ingelow made over £1,300 between 1863 and 1875, which was a remarkable sum, even if it did not equal the £2,000 that Scott had received as an advance on *Rokeby*'s sales in 1812 or the £3,000 that Thomas Moore was paid for the copyright of *Lalla Rookh* in 1817. The market and readership for Victorian poetry were also far different from and much smaller than those for novels and periodicals. Throughout the nineteenth century most of a novel's first printing was sold to circulating libraries, and so, despite the deep discounts given to libraries such as Mudie's, a publisher could sell at least several hundred copies of any novel and thus make money whether or not any reader bought a single copy. No such cushion existed for poetry publishers, because poetry readers usually purchased rather than borrowed books, and because the circulating libraries stocked only popular and well-established poets like Tennyson. A poetry publisher thus ran a much greater risk of a poetry volume becoming a complete loss.

Estimates of the size of poetry readership around 1850 have suggested that poetry's audience was limited to 27,000 families, which had incomes in the top 3 per cent. Those estimates seem mistaken, because the poetry market was primarily a giftbook market centred on Christmas, so that a poetry book's price of five shillings mattered less than the reading interests of those giving and receiving the books. Still, books were relatively much more expensive in the mid-nineteenth century than they are at the beginning of the twenty-first century. If one considers the new poet laureate's *In Memoriam* as the mid-century's poetic bestseller, since it sold 25,000 copies in a year and a half, and if one assumes the volume achieved the average bestseller's market penetration of 10 per cent of poetry's audience, one would more reasonably estimate that in 1851 there were about 250,000 readers in Britain who might buy a poetry book. Later, in 1900, there would appear to be about 1,000,000 of them. The focus of and interest in Victorian poetry became more associated with intellectual and religious seriousness than with entertaining diversion, even though those poets who possessed a turn for humorous versification and narrative found an eager readership. As opposed to the fashionable wealthy who had eagerly bought Scott's and Byron's poetry in the 1810s, these readers were much more likely to be part of the intellectual elite.

Except for the most popular poets and poetry books, the general public's awareness of poets was formed through periodical reviews, since a reader was more likely to read a contemporary poet in a reviewer's extract than to read a given poetry volume. But even good reviews did not guarantee an audience, since the enthusiastic ones of Tennyson's 1842 *Poems* written by his friends did not appreciably affect the volume's sales. What really mattered were not favourable reviews, but whether a poet was reviewed at all and so taken seriously. Except for the *Athenaeum*, no Victorian periodical could be counted on to notice any given poetry book. Poets needed to be persistent to gain the Victorian public's attention and could not expect that their publisher could help, even if the publisher had a convenient journal that could provide a favourable notice. Anyone who could not afford to keep publishing without public attention or approval was likely to abandon writing poetry quickly.

Because of the financial risks involved, a small number of publishing firms account for the Victorian period's most important and best-known poetry. The two most notable were Edward Moxon from 1830 to 1869 and Alexander Macmillan from 1857 to the period's end; however, Longmans, Elkin Mathews, John Lane, Strahan, H. S. King, C. Kegan Paul, T. Fisher Unwin, F. S. Ellis and his various partners, Bell and Daldy, Chatto and Windus, George Bell, the Daniel Press, Leonard Smithers, and Smith, Elder all published significant poetry during the Victorian period. Moxon focused on publishing poetry from the beginning of his firm. Samuel Rogers loaned Moxon the money to establish his business and underwrote the £7,000 cost of the 1830 edition of Rogers's *Italy*, which was illustrated by J. M. W. Turner among others. As other publishers stopped accepting poetry manuscripts, Moxon accepted only those from authors who were willing to cover half of any publishing losses. He took over publishing Wordsworth's poetry from Longman after 1835, brought out Shelley's posthumous *Masque of Anarchy* of 1832 and his *Works* of 1839–40, began to issue Leigh Hunt's poetry with his *Poetical Works* of 1832, and printed Tennyson's poetry from the *Poems* of 1833 until 1868. His firm published Browning's *Sordello* and *Bells and Pomegranates* in the 1840s, Elizabeth Barrett's *Poems* of 1844, Coventry Patmore's *Poems* of 1844, Milnes's edition of Keats's *Life, Letters, and Literary Remains* in 1848, Derwent Coleridge's edition of W. M. Praed's *Poems* in 1864, Swinburne's *Atalanta in Calydon* in 1865 and *Poems and Ballads* in 1866, and the works of many minor poets. Even though Moxon's list displays his fine taste in contemporary poetry, he printed the manuscripts of everyone who could pay for publication, and he judged correctly that limiting an edition's size was better than presenting a poet with a large bill, since he knew that most poets imagined that more readers wanted their verse than actually did. He was extremely cautious and advertised very little.

Alexander Macmillan had begun as an academic and scientific publisher in Cambridge, and then expanded his firm's list in the late 1850s beyond scientific publication, and so assembled a remarkable list of Victorian poets. One of his first poetry publications was Alexander Smith's *City Poems* (1857). However, the publication that brought the firm to the poets' notice was the age's most famous poetry anthology, Francis Palgrave's *Golden*

Treasury (1861). This volume's success encouraged Macmillan to publish more contemporary poets and also fostered the submission of fine poetry manuscripts. In 1862 Macmillan published Christina Rossetti's *Goblin Market*, in 1866 her second volume *Prince's Progress*, and in 1896 her posthumous *New Poems*. In 1862 the firm published Coventry Patmore's *Victories of Love* and his popular *Children's Garland*, a poetry anthology for children in Macmillan's new Golden Treasury series. In the same year A. H. Clough's *Poems* came out and were followed in 1868 by his *Poems and Prose Remains*. In 1863 W. M. Rossetti's edition of Alexander Gilchrist's *Life of William Blake* appeared in two volumes, which, by publishing for the first time a selection of Blake's poetry, rescued Blake from the art collectors who owned the very few engraved prints, and so brought his work to the attention of poetry readers. Matthew Arnold's poetry appeared under Macmillan's imprint beginning with *New Poems* in 1867. Most important, after Tennyson left Kegan Paul, Alexander Macmillan published Tennyson's work from *The Cup and the Falcon* in 1884 through to the end of his career. Once the firm added Tennyson to its list, Macmillan guaranteed its pre-eminence in poetry publishing for the next thirty years. Macmillan published William Barnes's *Poems of Rural Life in Common English* (1868), George Meredith's poetry beginning with *Poems and Lyrics of the Joy of Earth* (1883), W. B. Yeats's work beginning with *In the Seven Woods* (1903), Thomas Hardy's poetry beginning with a reprint of his *Wessex Poems* in 1903, and Rudyard Kipling's poetry first in America in the 1890s and then in England after the turn of the century. The firm published the favourites of high-church Anglican readers such as William Watson, Richard Trench and Alfred Austin. And, of course, it published Lewis Carroll's *Phantasmagoria, and Other Poems* (1869) and *The Hunting of the Snark* (1876). A number of neglected minor Victorian poets were also printed by Macmillan: Charles Tennyson-Turner, Sebastian Evans, Augusta Webster, T. E. Brown, J. K. Stephen and Lord de Tabley, to name those most familiar to readers of Victorian poetry anthologies.

In the last half of the nineteenth century Longmans had a reputation for publishing women's poetry, especially because they had long published Joanna Baillie and had brought out her *Dramatic and Poetical Works* in 1851. The firm published Jean Ingelow's *Rhyming Chronicles of Incidents and Feelings* in 1850 and her very popular *Poems* of 1863, which included her best-known narrative poem, 'The High Tide on the Coast of Lincolnshire, 1571'. Longmans also had published Macaulay's *Lays of Ancient Rome* and Matthew Arnold's *Poems* of 1853 and were to publish Robert Louis Stevenson's *A Child's Garden of Verses* (1885), but the works of Baillie and Ingelow continued to attract poetry manuscripts from women. Violet Fane published her first volume, *From Dawn to Noon*, in 1872 with Longmans; May Kendall's *Dreams to Sell* appeared in 1887 and her *Songs from Dreamland* in 1894; Rosamund Marriot's second volume of poetry, *Bird-Bride*, was printed in 1889; and Edith Nesbit brought out *Lays and Legends* in 1886, *Leaves of Life* in 1888, and *Lays and Legends, Second Series* in 1892. Longmans also published Nesbit's last poetry book, *The Rainbow and the Rose* (1905), but found that her successful juvenile fiction did not attract more readers to her poetry.

In the 1890s Elkin Mathews and John Lane, separately and in partnership, published many women poets and helped to develop many other young poets who later became famous. They published Dollie Radford's *A Light Load* (1891), *Songs and Other Verses* (1895) and *Poems* (1910). Katherine Bradley and Edith Cooper, appearing together under the pen name of Michael Field, published with Mathews and Lane their second volume of poetry, *Sight and Song* (1892). The partnership also printed Alice Meynell's *Poems* of 1892, which went to seven editions by 1900. In 1895 Edith Nesbit's fourth poetry book, *Pomander of Verse*, appeared under Lane's imprint, as did Rosamund Marriott's third volume, *Vespertilia*. In 1897 Mathews printed Mary Coleridge's *Fancy's Guerdon*, which appeared in his Shilling Garland series. Together Mathews and Lane published the *Yellow Book* from 1894 to 1897, which included some poetry. Mathews had also brought out in 1892 and 1894 the two *Books of the Rhymers' Club*, which had contributions from W. B. Yeats, Lionel Johnson and Arthur Symons among others. Mathews later published Lionel Johnson's *Poems* of 1895 and his *Ireland* (1897); and he also issued a volume of Yeats's verse, *The Wind Among the Reeds* (1899). Oscar Wilde's *Sphinx* with Charles Ricketts's illustrations was printed by the Ballantyne Press for the firm in 1894, and in the same year Mathews published Francis Thompson's *Poems*. Mathews issued the first and second series of Laurence Binyon's *London Visions* as numbers 1 and 10 of the Shilling Garland series in 1896 and 1899, and Robert Bridges's *Ode for the Bicentenary Commemoration of Henry Purcell with Other Poems* in 1896 as number 2 of the series. And Mathews later published James Joyce's first volume of poetry, *Chamber Music* (1907), and Ezra Pound's poetry from *Personae* in 1909 to *Umbra* in 1920.

As the careers of Joyce and of Edith Nesbit should remind one, aspiring poets often achieved their success in other literary genres that their poetry publishers did not profit from. Longmans, for example, was unfortunate with Nesbit. If the firm had accepted her fourth volume for publication in 1895, they might have published the popular Bastable family fictions that were first serialized in 1897 with Macmillan. Further, successful essayists and fiction writers became restless with their publishers because they imagined that their verse sales should be greater. For instance, Jane Barlow had published with Hodder and Stoughton a volume of Irish short stories, *Irish Idylls* (1892), which went through eight editions. That same year T. F. Unwin brought out her verse tales, *Bog-Land Studies*. The success of her short stories contributed to her poetry sales, but she was evidently dissatisfied with Unwin and brought out a second, revised and enlarged edition of her poetry with Hodder and Stoughton in 1893. She never repeated her first success either as a short-story writer or as a narrative poet, but she changed the publishers of her poetry more often: Macmillan printed *The End of Elfintown* with illustrations by Lawrence Housman in 1894; Smith, Elder issued her *Ghost-Bereft* in 1901; and George Allen published *The Mockers* in 1908. Like many other authors of fiction who enjoyed the profits from their stories, she was never contented with the much smaller audience for her poetry. Further, like Barlow, many other poets of the late Victorian period moved from publisher to publisher, often because their previous volume had sold poorly and their publisher was unwilling to print a second volume, but also, since the poets were almost always assuming some of the publication risk, because they felt that another publisher would offer a better chance of success.

Most poets who could get into print and who developed a readership changed their publishers less frequently. Robert Browning, who had been published by Edward Moxon throughout the 1840s, became unhappy with the sale and promotion of his *Poems* of 1849, and moved both his and his wife's poetry to Chapman and Hall. Although his individual volumes of verse published by the firm – *Christmas-Eve and Easter-Day* (1851), *Men and Women* (1855) and *Dramatis Personae* (1864) – did not go to second editions, his collected *Poetic Works* of 1863 went to a fourth edition in 1865. Elizabeth Barrett Browning's poetry benefited even more than his from better advertising and marketing. As they were gradually added to, her *Poems* went with Chapman and Hall from their second edition in 1850 to a seventh edition in 1866. Further, her *Aurora Leigh* (1857) went to its sixth edition in 1864. Several years after his wife died, Browning became convinced by George Smith that both his forthcoming *Ring and the Book* and his wife's work would receive better treatment at Smith, Elder. The firm flatteringly printed the two volumes of his epic in an edition of 3,000 copies beginning in 1868; and in 1869 it reprinted another seventh edition of her *Poetical Works*. Smith had clearly calculated that however slowly Robert's poetry sold, the profits on Elizabeth's poetry would offset any risk in publishing her husband's. When Robert died in 1889, a fourteenth edition of her *Poetical Works* had recently been published, in 1886, and another was coming out. This should remind readers of Victorian poetry that as fascinating as the sales of individual poetry books might be in reflecting the popular taste of the moment, the real money in publishing poetry came from collected and selected editions, which began to appear in the middle of a successful poet's career and were issued in various sizes and formats to suit the readers' pockets.

Tennyson's movements from publisher to publisher late in his career attracted other poets to those publishers. After leaving Moxon, Tennyson went to Strahan between 1869 and 1872. When Strahan retired in 1873 and turned his authors over to H. S. King, Tennyson followed and published with King from 1874 to 1877. When King's firm was amalgamated into Kegan Paul, Tennyson then appeared under that imprint from 1878 to 1882 before ending his career with Macmillan. Only a few other poets were published by Strahan during this period: Robert Buchanan, Dora Greenwell and Roden Noel, for example. While Tennyson was with King, the publisher brought out Austin Dobson's *Vignettes in Rhyme* (1873) and *Proverbs in Porcelain* (1877), Alice Meynell's *Preludes* (1875), Frederick Locker-Lampson's *London Lyrics* (1876) and Aubrey DeVere's *Antar and Zara* (1877). In addition to Tennyson, Kegan Paul's list in the 1870s, 1880s and 1890s included H. C. Beeching, Louisa Bevington, W. S. Blunt, Austin Dobson, Edmund Gosse, A. E. Housman, Andrew Lang, Emily Pfeiffer, Stephen Philips and W. B. Yeats. The most popular of these poets was Austin Dobson, whose *Old World Idylls* (1883) reached its eleventh edition in 1892 and almost single-handedly sparked the Queen Anne revival of the century's last two decades, which celebrated early eighteenth-century culture and literary style.

Other publishers had fewer significant poets on their lists. D. G. Rossetti, William Morris and A. C. Swinburne published poetry with F. S. Ellis and his various partners; Swinburne primarily appeared with Chatto and Windus after Moxon's old firm went bankrupt; William Morris, C. S. Calverley and Dora Greenwell originally appeared under the imprint of Bell and Daldy; Coventry Patmore, Michael Field and Robert Bridges were printed by George Bell; Ernest Dowson and Oscar Wilde had their late work undertaken by Leonard Smithers; Amy Levy, Michael Field, Mathilde Blind and W. B. Yeats all had T. Fisher Unwin as their publisher; and in addition to the Brownings, the Brontë sisters, Violet Fane and Robert Bridges all appeared under the imprint of Smith, Elder. Most major Victorian publishers felt that their lists required a poet or two for intellectual and literary tone, but they knew that few contemporary poets sold well and so concentrated on publishing other books that would sell better.

The technological improvements in printing made publishing Victorian poetry cheaper and so available to many more readers, but publishers found that most poetry sold to a smaller proportion of the reading public than it had earlier and so kept its price high. The cost of poetry books remained stable throughout the period. In 1831 Edward Moxon brought out *Selections from the Poems of William Wordsworth* at five shillings. In 1849 B. Fellowes asked four shillings and sixpence for Matthew Arnold's *Strayed Reveller and Other Poems*. Later in 1914, Macmillan sold Thomas Hardy's *Satires of Circumstance* at the same price. In the early 1840s poetry publishers lowered their prices to appeal to working-class readers, but quickly retreated. Edward Moxon sold Robert Browning's *Pippa Passes*, the first pamphlet number of *Bells and Pomegranates*, for sixpence in 1841, but raised the price to two shillings and sixpence by the final number in 1846. Browning's *Dramatic Lyrics* in pamphlet form cost only a shilling, but could not find 500 readers in 1842. As a publicity stunt Henry Hengist Horne's *Orion* was sold in 1843 for a farthing in its first edition, and when this quickly sold out, his publisher J. Miller gradually raised the price of subsequent editions and was selling the epic poem's fifth edition for two shillings and sixpence. Only later, in the 1880s and 1890s, were cheap reprints and anthologies sold again for a shilling. In sharp contrast, seeking to capitalize upon the new poet laureate's popularity, Edward Moxon asked one and a half guineas for the 1857 reprint in quarto of Tennyson's *Poems* of 1842. The 1857 *Poems* thus resembled Moxon's 1830 illustrated edition of Rogers's *Italy*, in that Tennyson's quarto was also published in an edition of 10,000 copies and had illustrations by J. E. Millais, D. G. Rossetti and W. H. Hunt among others. This made the volume into an expensive art book. However, it did not sell and was remaindered, further proving that the wealthy, fashion-conscious readers, who created the poetry boom of the 1810s and who had eagerly purchased Scott's poetry in quarto for two guineas a volume, had long ago faded into publishing legend.

Publishers did try to market popular verse to lower middle-class and upper working-class audiences, but found few buyers. For example, Longmans' most popular volume of devotional verse during the mid-Victorian era was Catherine Winkworth's *Lyra Germanica* (1855), an anthology of translations of German religious verse that went through fourteen editions. From 1855 to 1873 over 23,000 copies were sold at five shillings each. Another volume of *Lyra Germanica: Second Series* appeared in 1858 at the same price; and in 1859 an inexpensive selection from both volumes costing just one shilling was made by the bishop of Argyll 'for use among the poorer classes and for distribution in districts and schools'. Because the firm had already sold over 10,000 copies of the first series by 1859, Longmans printed 5,000 copies of the cheaper selection that year, but by 1873 had only sold 3,982 copies of the printing. By all accounts working-class readers had little appetite for pious verse and even less for literary poetry. Aimed squarely at an educated middle-class audience, the cheap shilling pocket-books of Walter Scott's Canterbury Poets series, which provided reprints of famous nineteenth-century poets out of copyright and also offered anthologies of generic and national poetry, met with great success from 1884 to 1900. William Sharp's *Sonnets of this Century* (1886), perhaps the series' best-known volume, sold 30,000 copies in ten years. However, as Elkin Mathews' Shilling Garland series showed in the 1890s, original contemporary poetry in a shilling format did not sell.

More difficult to describe, except for Scotland, are the markets for regional and dialect volumes of verse, much of which was inspired by the enduring success of Robert Burns's Scots poetry. The best-known Victorian work of this kind was William Barnes's *Poems of Rural Life in the Dorset Dialect* (1844–62), but one might also cite Joseph Philip Robson's large collection of local newspaper poetry largely in the Geordie dialect, *Songs of the Bards of the Tyne* (1849), which was published in Newcastle-upon-Tyne by T. France, as better representing an appeal to a regional poetry market. This should remind one that the audience for many poets was highly localized. Indeed, many poets found it troublesome to correspond with London publishers and so took their work to local printers. For instance, Robert Stephen Hawker, who was the vicar of Morwenstow in Cornwall, had the second edition of his *Records from the Western Shore* (1836) published locally in Stratton. This volume reflected a disappointed poet, since it contained his new poems, called the second series of *Records from the Western Shore*, a copy of the first edition of 1832 (now called the first series) bound in with the Oxford title page cancelled, and a copy of his Oxford prize poem *Pompeii* (1827), which retained the Oxford printer's colophon. Hawker had evidently taken the unsold stock, got his Stratton printer to add his new poems and a new title page, and had them bound together with the copies that he had of his previous works. This conglomerate volume has confused more than one subsequent bibliographer, although Hawker was just trying to present his work in a book for others to read. Later, in 1864, he had *The Quest of the Sangraal* printed for him in Exeter; and, similarly in 1873 he had twenty-five copies of *Aurora* privately printed in Bude. Hawker had long gone unnoticed, had learned that seeking a wide distribution for his work cost him more than it was worth, and had finally expected to be read only by those that knew him. His dreams of fame and fortune had disappeared in the face of general public indifference. Because so few copies of his individual volumes have survived, studying his work is hard for the bibliographer and harder still for scholars and critics.

A more general bibliographical difficulty has arisen from the Victorian publishing practice in dating poetry, especially with respect to Tennyson. Since volumes of poetry were primarily bought as giftbooks throughout the nineteenth century, publishers usually brought them out in November and December for Christmas, but dated the title pages with the following year so that their shelf life would not be shortened by their having been published at the end of the year. In 1832, which was a particularly poor year for the sale of literature because public attention was riveted by the Reform Bill, Edward Moxon published Tennyson's *Poems* of 1833 and postdated the volume by more than the usual month or two. However, the misplaced enthusiasm for bibliographical exactitude now conventional in Tennyson studies courts historical confusion, by considering, for example, the first edition dated 1870 that Strahan issued of Tennyson's *The Holy Grail and Other*

Poems, and declaring it to have been published in 1869. On the other hand, editors of the period's correspondence need to be cautious about dating letters written in November and December solely on the basis of poetry-book publication dates.

Publishing and literary historians have generally neglected the poetry from 1870 until the advent of Rudyard Kipling, W. B. Yeats and Thomas Hardy at the end of the century. Little of the period's poetry has been reprinted, even in anthologies, something which should remind us that poetry usually does poorly in a financial depression such as the one that lasted from 1875 to 1895. Even Tennyson experienced a gradual lessening of enthusiasm for his poetry then. *The Holy Grail* (1870) from *Idylls of the King* had a pre-publication order of 40,000 copies. However, *Harold* (1876) sold only 15,000 copies in its first two months; *Tiresias and Other Poems* (1885) sold only 15,771 copies in the first year; *Locksley Hall, Sixty Years After* (1886) only 14,293 in the first year; but *Demeter and Other Poems* (1889) had a much better sale of 20,000 copies in the first two weeks. However, Tennyson was competing against himself with the sale of editions of his collected works, which were averaging about 15,000 copies yearly in the late 1880s and 19,000 copies yearly in the early 1890s before his death. More typical are the sales of the two *Books of the Rhymers' Club* published in 1892 and 1894, which respectively sold 350 and 400 copies. The great chasm between the late laureate's sales and their own no doubt intensified the young poets' sense of being isolated from late Victorian poetry readers.

Even as they were overshadowed by Tennyson and later by Browning, some poets of the late nineteenth century sought to make their publications bibliographically valuable objects, even if that resulted in a limited audience. Poets often underwrote their work's publication by private printers, who either issued the poets' work through other publishers or distributed the poetry in small, limited editions that were often individually numbered. The poet most associated with this practice is William Morris, who founded the Kelmscott Press in the 1890s. Morris's *Life and Death of Jason* (1867) had been printed in a run of 500 copies by the Chiswick Press for Bell and Daldy. Later, in 1888, when Morris established his own press, he turned to printers from Chiswick Press. However, his Kelmscott Press concentrated on creating finely printed works of poets already in the English literary pantheon and rarely published a living author's poetry. The most notable exception was W. S. Blunt's *Love Lyrics and Songs of Proteus* in 1892, which was published with a substantial subvention from Blunt in an edition of 300 copies. Besides Morris, a few other poets cared enough about the appearance of their books, or had publishers that did, to have them printed at the Chiswick Press: A. H. Clough with *The Bothie of Toper-na-fuosich* (1848), Coventry Patmore with *Tamerton Church-Tower* (1853), Frederick Locker-Lampson with *London Lyrics* (1857) and *London Rhymes* (1881), Robert Bridges with *Poems* (1873) and his revised translation of *Eros and Psyche* (1894), Andrew Lang with *XXXII Ballades in Blue China* (1881), Austin Dobson with *Old World Idylls* (1883), Edmund Gosse with *On Viol and Flute* (1890), Lionel Johnson with *Poems* (1895), and Ernest Dowson with *Verses* (1896) and *Decorations* (1899). The association of poetry publishing with finely printed and expensive books, especially in the case of the Kelmscott Press, led Thorstein Veblen, for one, to link their appearance with their wealthy audience's 'conspicuous consumption' in his *Theory of the Leisure Class* in 1899.

Robert Bridges was the poet most enamoured of having his work privately printed in small print runs on handmade paper, and found the Daniel Press, run by the Reverend C. Henry Daniel in Oxford, to be particularly attractive. He had contributed first to *The Garland of Rachel* in 1881, a poetry volume which Daniel used to announce his press and which contains contributed poems from his friends, who, besides Bridges, included Lewis Carroll, Austin Dobson, Edmund Gosse, Andrew Lang, J. A. Symonds and Margaret L. Woods. Between 1881 and 1903 Bridges published ten books with the Daniel Press, the smallest edition having twenty-two copies and the largest 300. His volumes of poetry included *Poems* (1884), an augmented edition of *Growth of Love* (1889), and most notably his *Shorter Poems* (1893–4). This edition of his *Shorter Poems* added a fifth book of new, unpublished poems to the 1890 edition, which had been published with George Bell in both a regular edition and a limited one of 110 copies on handmade paper. Bridges then emerged as a public poet with his *Poetical Works*, which appeared in six volumes from 1898 to 1905 and were published by Smith, Elder in an edition of 1,500 copies. Many other noteworthy minor poets published volumes with the Daniel Press, including Laurence Binyon, Mary Coleridge, Richard Watson Dixon and Margaret L. Woods. In a similar fashion, W. B. Yeats later had much of his poetry published by the Cuala Press that had been established in 1902 by his sisters, Elizabeth and Lily Yeats.

Appealing to collectors, who were interested in poetry books as examples of the printing arts and who often preserved their copies with the pages uncut, might not seem likely to have developed a poet's reputation, but the association of poets and their poetry with the visual arts was integral to late Victorian and early modernist aesthetics. The issuing of poetry in such extremely small editions often acquired an academic air and limited a poet's readership to a select few, but it also allowed poets to work out their poetic ideas in print and to acquire a reputation for aesthetic taste because of their association with a private press's imprint. The attractiveness of limited editions among collectors also encouraged poetry publishers in the 1890s to advertise their usual practice of publishing poetry in small editions. For instance, many volumes published by Elkin Mathews in the 1890s carry the notice, 'this edition limited to 550 copies'. In so doing publishers made a marketing virtue out of a practical reality: only a few poets sold well enough to justify the publication of larger first editions. Such small and finely printed editions have, however, encouraged librarians to place these poetry volumes in rare book rooms; consequently, access to them is now limited to their curators, careful bibliographers, industrious editors and committed scholars.

Primarily interested in the great publishing expansion of the age, Victorian publishing historians have concentrated on the novel and have little help to offer to readers and scholars of Victorian poetry. The history of Victorian poetry publishing remains to be written. The complex relationship between Victorian readers and the contemporary critical reception of Victorian poetry has been explored carefully only for the major poets. In his 'Milton', which first appeared in the *Edinburgh Review* of 1825, Macaulay gave voice to the Whiggish view that 'as civilization advances, poetry almost necessarily declines'; and a few years later in his review of Robert Montgomery's poetry, he observed of the Victorian publishing market that 'it is no small evil that the avenues to fame should be blocked up by a swarm of noisy pushing, elbowing pretenders' and that few 'have suffi-cient confidence in their own powers and sufficient elevation of mind, to wait with secure and contemptuous patience, while dunce after dunce presses before them'. For Victorian poets like Tennyson and Browning this meant that between twenty and thirty years had to pass before they were recognized by the general Victorian reading public as significant poets. The same held true for Bridges and Yeats at the age's end, and even for Hardy, who already had an established reputation as a novelist.

Few readers have ever been able to recognize the most significant poets among their contemporaries immediately, so that, once periodicals became the centre of intellectual culture in the early nineteenth century, even fewer insightful readers were well placed to announce the advent of important new poetic voices. The Victorian poets were the first to experience the publishing-market consequences of poetry's having been culturally mar-ginalized and to find few publishers willing to publish their work and almost none to buy their copyrights. Because most poets were forced to retain their copyrights and because a few of these remained valuable far beyond the three-months' vogue that most literary works experienced, poets usually made money only from editions of their collected works close to the end of their careers. By the end of the Victorian period, poets were beginning to adopt avant-garde strategies that gained publicity because of their aesthetic exclusive-ness, but were unable to change the readership's neglect of contemporary poetry. One should remember that Victorian readers liked poetry that made a religious statement, told an interesting story, or fashioned an amusing point. Further, the intellectual elite gener-ally preferred prose to poetry and rarely felt that a contemporary poet deserved their atten-tion. Once satisfied with Tennyson, they elevated him to an official cultural status above all other contemporary poets in the publishing market, and so for a generation paid little attention to those other poets.

Above all, given the power of reading fashions to shape the poetry market from the beginning of the Victorian era, when the literary Annuals predominated, one should be cautious about conferring much significance upon poetic popularity, about supposing that the popularity of a poet's works was connected to anything intrinsically poetic, and about believing that contemporary popularity reflects a poem's or a poet's literary merit or value. Indeed, all would-be sociologists of the Victorian age's poetic taste need to read through the age's popular devotional poetry first before accounting for the vogue of any poem or any poet in other than religious terms. In addition, both the Victorian poets and subse-quent literary historians have overemphasized the power of positive or negative reviews, since what really mattered was being reviewed at all. Intellectual or poetic snobbery had little effect upon the Victorian readership's taste in poetry. Wordsworth, for instance, was made poet laureate in 1843 and was beloved by Matthew Arnold, but the Victorians could not be made to read the *Prelude*. Robert Browning achieved a similar currency among the intellectual elite in the 1880s with the advent of the Browning societies, but his poetry was never clear enough for most Victorian readers and so he never became as popular as his wife, even if he was enshrined in the poetic canon by professors of English literature in the early twentieth century. Taking pleasure in poetry in the Victorian age was still very much a relatively expensive indulgence of the personal taste of readers who wished to read 'what oft was thought but ne'er so well expressed'. Those Victorian poets who had new thoughts to express in new forms had to wait a long time to find an audience, if they ever found one at all.

See also: REVIEWING; ANTHOLOGIES AND THE MAKING OF THE POETIC CANON.

REFERENCES AND FURTHER READING

Altick, Richard D. (1957) *The English Common Reader: A Social History of the Mass Reading Public, 1800–1900*. Chicago: University of Chicago Press.

Altick, Richard D. (1962) 'The Sociology of Authorship: The Social Origins, Education and Occupations of 1,100 British Writers, 1800–1935.' *Bulletin of the New York Public Library*, 66, 389–404.

Altick, Richard D. (1969) 'Nineteenth-Century Best-Sellers: A Further List.' *Studies in Bibliography*, 22, 197–206.

Altick, Richard D. (1986) 'Nineteenth-Century Best-Sellers: A Third List.' *Studies in Bibliography*, 39, 235–41.

Altick, Richard D. (1999) 'Publishing.' In Herbert F. Tucker (ed.). *A Companion to Victorian Literature and Culture* (pp. 289–304). Oxford: Blackwell.

Barnes, J. J. (1974) *Authors, Publishers, and Politicians: The Quest for an Anglo-American Copyright Agreement, 1815–1854*. Columbus: Ohio State University Press.

Boyle, Andrew (1967) *An Index to the Annuals, 1820–1850*. Worcester: Andrew Boyle.

British Publishers' Archives on Microfilm (1973–82) Cambridge: Chadwyck-Healey.

Broughton, Leslie Nathan, Clark Sutherland Northrop and Robert Pearsall (eds) (1953) *Robert Browning: A Bibliography*. Cornell Studies in English, 39. Ithaca, N. Y.: Cornell University Press.

Cave, Roderick (1971) *The Private Press*. London: Faber and Faber.

Erickson, Lee (1996) *The Economy of Literary Form: English Literature and the Industrialization of Publishing, 1800–1850*. Baltimore: Johns Hopkins University Press.

Feather, John (1989) 'Publishers and Politicians: The Remaking of the Law of Copyright in Britain, 1775–1842. Part II: The Rights of Authors.' *Publishing History*, 25, 45–72.

Franklin, Colin (1988) *Poets of the Daniel Press*. Cambridge: Rampant Lions Press.

Gettmann, Royal A. (1960) *A Victorian Publisher: A Study of the Bentley Papers*. Cambridge: Cambridge University Press.

Haas, Sabine (1985) 'Victorian Poetry Anthologies: Their Role and Success in the Nineteenth Century Book Market.' *Publishing History*, 17, 51–64.

Hagen, June Steffensen (1979) *Tennyson and his Publishers*. University Park: Pennsylvania State University Press.

May, J. Lewis (1936) *John Lane and the Nineties*. London: John Lane.

McKay, George L. (1933) *A Bibliography of Robert Bridges*. New York: Columbia University Press.

Nelson, James G. (1989) *Elkin Mathews: Publisher to Yeats, Pound, and Joyce*. Madison: University of Wisconsin Press.

Plant, Marjorie (1974) *The English Book Trade: An Economic History of the Making and Sale of Books*. Third edition. London: George Allen and Unwin.

Purdy, Richard Little (1954) *Thomas Hardy: A Bibliographical Study*. London: Oxford University Press.

Renier, Anne (1964) *Friendship's Offering: An Essay on the Annuals and Gift Books of the 19th Century*. London: Private Libraries Association.

Saunders, J. W. (1964) *The Profession of English Letters*. London: Routledge and Kegan Paul.

Scott, Rosemary (1993) 'Pious Verse in the Mid-Victorian Market Place: Facts and Figures.' *Publishing History*, 33, 37–58.

Wade, Allan (1968) *Bibliography of the Writings of W. B. Yeats*. Third edition. Ed. Russell K. Alspach. London: Hart-Davis.

20

Anthologies and the Making of the Poetic Canon

Natalie M. Houston

In recent years, many critical debates about the teaching and study of literature have focused on the development, maintenance or revision of the literary canon. Our contemporary debates, which have occurred both within specialized academic sub-fields and in the larger realm of public discussion about literature and culture, are one mark of our continued connection to Victorian debates about the function of literature in modern industrial society. During the Victorian period, increasing public literacy, new publishing technologies and changes in the educational system focused public attention on the value of literature and the formation of a canon of important works. Literary anthologies, whether designed for use as textbooks or for the general reader, are an especially important mechanism of canon formation, as they present a selection of literary texts to a wide audience and thereby contribute to those readers' understanding of literary history. Nineteenth-century poetry anthologies offer extensive information that we can use to investigate the history of literary taste, the cultural functions of poetry, and the histories of reading throughout the Victorian period. In this chapter, I first discuss the history of canon formation and Victorian reading practices and their relationship to literary anthologies. I then survey the important types of anthologies published throughout the period and suggest some methodological issues in analysing their contributions to shaping the Victorian canon.

Defining the Canon

The word 'canon' was originally used to designate rule, measure or authority, and many subsequent uses of the term similarly invoke notions of restrictive authority, as when literary critics speak of the need to 'teach the canon' or to 'expand the canon' or to 'dispense with the canon'. In actuality, there is not (and there has never been) only one literary canon. Simply put, a canon is a list or group of texts that describes certain boundaries to literary knowledge or expression. Alastair Fowler describes six major kinds of canons: the *potential* canon would theoretically contain all works of written and oral literature; the *accessible* canon, in contrast, would consist of those works readers would actually come into contact with. Different criteria further narrow the accessible canon to produce *selective* canons. Some of these include the *official* canons produced by mechanisms of patronage, education or censorship; the *critical* canons evidenced in trends in literary scholarship; and the *personal* canon of any individual reader's tastes and knowledge (1979: 98). Wendell Harris further categorizes some additional selective canons, including the *pedagogical* canon of specific works that are frequently taught and a *diachronic* canon, which consists of works that remain in critical or teaching canons over long periods of time (1991: 112–13). Such categories are useful in describing the many different canons that may be circulating within a specific culture during a particular historical period. Readers of different social and economic positions will have different means of accessing literary works, and different educational and social experiences will undoubtedly affect the value and interpretation an individual reader attaches to a particular work.

Recent theorists of canon formation have begun to investigate how historical changes in literary taste intersect with larger structures of social and economic power. Pierre Bourdieu (1984) offers the concept of 'cultural capital' to describe how, within a given socio-economic setting, the knowledge of certain literary texts (or art, music and so forth) is necessary in order to achieve a certain level of social power. Just as the structures and movement of economic capital can be used to describe social competition and stratification, Bourdieu suggests that certain kinds of cultural knowledge also participate in (and construct) similar hierarchies. Bourdieu's elaborate study of twentieth-century French society in *Distinction: A Social Critique of the Judgement of Taste* points to some of the ways that cultural knowledge is obtained and enhanced: through direct experience (reading a poem), through education (learning how to read the poem; learning which poems are valued by scholars), through popular culture (hearing references to a poem), and through secondary or tertiary contacts (reading a book review, study guide or other text about the poem). The work of Bourdieu and other scholars on nineteenth-century texts suggests that similar mechanisms were at work within Victorian culture, although of course these must be carefully specified and analysed in relation to that historical period.

John Guillory, in *Cultural Capital: The Problem of Literary Canon Formation*, draws on Bourdieu's notion of cultural capital in order to investigate the mechanisms by which cultural value is attached to literary works: 'Canonicity is not a property of the work itself but of its transmission, its relation to other works in a collocation of works' (1993: 55). To understand how our current Victorian canon was constituted, we have to examine the various mechanisms that have constructed our notion of 'Victorian literature'. Guillory emphasizes that the institution of the school and its syllabuses, course plans and curricula are the primary means by which cultural value is produced, and suggests that understanding 'what historical forms of cultural capital are embodied in *literary* texts . . . will of course entail recognizing the historicity of the category of literature itself, the recognition that its history cannot be dissociated from the history of the school' (1993: 60). However, in order to excavate how Victorian writers and readers might have constituted a canon of literary works, we must also examine other nineteenth-century mechanisms that were equally important in constructing readers' understanding of what constituted 'literature', what defined 'good literature', and why and how these texts should be preserved, studied, enjoyed and valued.

A key figure for Victorian and contemporary debates about the value of literature is Matthew Arnold, whose work in educational reform promoted the adoption of literary anthologies in schools and whose critical essays, like 'The Study of Poetry', proposed that literature did have something to offer readers in the modern age: 'we have to turn to poetry to interpret life for us, to console us, to sustain us' (1973: 161). Arnold takes up the question of how readers should value particular poems: 'A poet or a poem may count to us historically, they may count to us on grounds personal to ourselves, and they may count to us really' (1973: 163). Famously, Arnold suggested that one should 'have always in one's mind lines and expressions of the great masters, and . . . apply them as a touchstone to other poetry' (1973: 168). Although this passage is often seen as the epitome of Victorian criticism, Arnold first published this essay as the general introduction to T. H. Ward's anthology *The English Poets* (1880), the first late Victorian anthology to offer readers an historical framework for understanding nineteenth-century poetry. Jonah Siegel (1999) suggests that Arnold's claims about the value of literature and the need for ever-greater selectivity act as a kind of defence against the broad scope of the very anthology his essay introduces.

Discussion about the value of literature became an integral part of the Victorian cultural climate because the rapid growth of the publishing industry during the first half of the century radically altered the Victorian intellectual and literary landscape. Many journals and newspapers included ample reviews and debates about literary topics. Less explicit debates about literary canons can also be found in the material history of the Victorian period, in the publishing practices which shaped many readers' encounters with poetry – the contents, organization, design and intent of the numerous poetry anthologies published throughout the period.

Victorian Reading Practices

During the Napoleonic wars, the importing of rags from France to make paper was curtailed, which combined with increased demand to cause a steep rise in the cost of paper. Lee Erickson suggests that the rise in the cost of books 'generally encouraged poetry at the expense of prose' during the first two decades of the nineteenth century because of its condensed expression (1996: 20). However, technological advancements soon paved the way for the dominance of the novel in the Victorian literary marketplace. The Fourdrinier continuous paper-making machine began to be used by 1807, which reduced the cost of paper-making considerably. Because machine-made paper was of more consistent quality, it reduced printing costs and waste as well, and by the mid-1820s was widely used in England. Printing technology, which had remained fairly stable since Gutenberg's introduction of movable pieces of type, changed in the early nineteenth century with the development of stereotype printing, in which a plaster cast would be made of an entire page of set type, and then used to produce metal plates that would be used in the printing press. Stereotype technology meant that multiple exact copies of a text could be printed at the same time on different presses, and also reduced the costs of maintaining multiple sets of type. These and other technological developments dramatically decreased the cost of publishing periodicals and books of all kinds after 1820.

One of the most visible effects of this decrease was the growth of periodicals and newspapers between 1820 and 1840 (Altick 1957: 318–47). These journals transformed Victorian reading and publishing in several different ways. Although the journals were largely divided along class lines, they opened new possibilities for communication and participation in the public sphere for the middle class and, with the growth of penny papers, for the working classes. Newspapers and journals created a large market for topical essays and reviews, which brought contemporary issues and debates to a wide audience and also, in the case of literary reviewing, created interest in and knowledge of new poems and novels.

The growth and diversification of the reading public throughout the Victorian period was met by a matching growth and specialization in literary publishing. Although general interest anthologies were popular, numerous poetry collections were tailored to specific types of readers and designed to appeal to certain interests or tastes. Trends in nineteenth-century anthology publishing can provide information about how publishers and editors viewed the reading public, as well as their expectations about how poetry was valued by its readers. Statistics regarding the readership of any particular anthology are difficult to obtain, in part because poetry collections were often shared among members of a household, so that for each copy purchased, anywhere from one to twenty persons might have access to it. Although many Victorian anthologies were published in numerous editions, ascertaining the exact size of each can also be difficult. Publishers would frequently print a small first edition in order to see how well the collection sold. Given the generally poor market in publishing poetry, an anthology which sold out more than two editions, even if each consisted of only 2,000 copies, could be considered fairly successful. Without a doubt, Francis Turner Palgrave's *The Golden Treasury* (1861) was one of the most successful Victorian anthologies, selling 9,000 copies in the first five months of publication and over 50,000 more in subsequent years. Other popular anthologies included Charles Mackay's *A Thousand and One Gems of English Poetry* (1867), Palgrave's *A Children's Treasury* (1875) and Coventry Patmore's *The Children's Garland* (1862).

Historians of reading in the West locate an important shift in reading practice during the late eighteenth century: Rolf Engelsing's formulation suggests that, whereas German readers in earlier centuries read a small number of books *intensively*, reviewing them numerous times and often committing them to memory, readers after 1750 tended to read *extensively*, reading a wide variety of different texts, and often skimming or skipping sections. David Hall's research on reading in colonial New England suggests a similar shift in reading practices around 1800 (Darnton 1990: 165–7; Chartier 1994: 1–23). Certainly, the new abundance of published materials led many Victorian critics and anthology editors to write about the need for readers to make careful choices among the many texts being published: 'The root of the wrong appears to be, that people, unless profession or scientific interest influences them, go to books for something almost similar to what they find in social conversation. Reading tends to become only another kind of gossip. Everything is to be read, and everything only once' (Palgrave 1860: 453). Leah Price suggests that rather than 'replicating the move away from intensive reading that its editors registered in the culture at large, the history of the anthology inverts it', by focusing readers' attention on a selection from the bulk of available material (2000: 4). Thus, even though readers might skim through the pages of a given anthology, its editors had already remarkably narrowed the field of reading possibilities. Finally, any hypotheses about the history of reading must take into account the wide range of possible individual responses to a given text. Michel de Certeau reminds us that readers do not necessarily follow the rules laid down for them by editors, teachers or authors, preferring instead to create their own meanings: 'Far from being writers – founders of their own place . . . readers are travellers; they move across lands belonging to someone else, like nomads poaching their way across fields they did not write, despoiling the wealth of Egypt to enjoy it themselves' (1984: 174).

Poetry Anthologies and the Canon

Poetry anthologies are instrumental in shaping readers' understanding of literary history and poetic value, or, as Pierre Bourdieu suggests in 'The Field of Cultural Production', in producing 'consumers capable of knowing and recognizing the work of art as such' (1993: 37). Any anthology, whether designed for the general reader or for the student, attaches cultural value to certain texts, teaching its readers about its particular definition of 'art' or 'poetry'. Literary anthologies function within larger institutions of cultural production, such as the school and the mechanisms of literary reviewing, but they are also important institutions themselves in what Bourdieu calls 'the symbolic production of the work, i.e. the production of the value of the work or, which amounts to the same thing, of belief in the value of the work' (1993: 37). Depending on the kind of anthology, the value of the work might be expressed in aesthetic, moral or affective terms. During the Victorian period, the cultural value of poetry was frequently expressed in metaphors of accumulation and wealth, such as 'treasury', 'casket' and 'gem'. Bourdieu and Guillory suggest that institutions like the school and other mechanisms that produce the cultural values of literature, like anthologies, do so in part through the narratives of literary history that they (re)produce. Anthologies always both reflect and create literary histories, both explicitly, in their titles, prefaces and notes, and implicitly, in their content and organization.

Our contemporary debates about literary canons have led several scholars to scrutinize the Victorian canon as it was produced by the Victorians themselves and as it has been transformed throughout the twentieth century (Golding 1984; Harris 1991; Hemphill 1984; Peterson 1999). The history of anthologies reveals poets who were once considered important or valuable and who have since disappeared; the different kinds of criteria for inclusion applied during different historical periods; and the relation between academic trends and changing classroom practices. However, most discussions of Victorian anthologies and their relation to literary canon formation have not questioned the models of literary history that anthologies tend to produce, which, contested though they might be in their specific details, tend, in Guillory's terms, to create 'an ideology of tradition, that . . . collapses the history of canon formation into an autonomous history of literature, which is always a history of writers and not of *writing*' (1993: 63). Guillory argues that we need to think beyond the simple binary of inclusion/exclusion when we analyse the complex mechanisms of canon formation and their effects on the history of reading. Historically and methodologically prior to the question of *who* counts as a poet is the question of *what* counts as literature. Yet our methodological tools for considering the questions of literary history and canons of taste tend invariably to rely upon lists of writers – a mark, in large part, of our Victorian inheritance.

Such investigations into the history of poetry anthologies – the history, in other words, of one institution of canon formation – need to take into account the material history of the anthologies to a greater extent than they have hitherto done. Anthologies produce literary history and aesthetic conditioning not simply through their contents, which have generally been the focus of academic study, but also in their material design, which determines how readers relate contextual information to literary texts. Gérard Genette (1991) offers the term *paratext* to describe the many features of a published work that present it to its reader, such as the cover, title page and preface, as well as the arrangement of particular information within those elements. All of these paratextual elements shape and reflect the work's interactions with the world. In the case of literary anthologies, these transactions of meaning enacted within and by the paratext are particularly complex, involving not simply the notional author and reader but also the editor of the anthology, and the cultural institutions in which the anthology takes part. Examining what information is given on the page with the poem, how it is presented and how the anthology as a whole is organized, along with the editor's introductory remarks and other paratextual elements, can reveal changing conceptions of the role of the reader, the editors and the anthology itself.

To understand the work that anthologies do in forming individual and institutional tastes, values and canons, we have to begin with the material design of the anthology and what it can tell us about the collection's intended audience and mode of use. Examining the material forms of Victorian poetry anthologies reveals how Victorian critical debates and publishing practices gradually shifted the terms of literary value away from formal or aesthetic criteria applied to *texts*, to particular *poets* as repositories of cultural meaning, making the ideal of the poet as moral exemplar or rebellious individual central to the shape of literary history. If the study of anthologies and canons is expanded beyond simply tabulating their contents, we gain the capacity to understand anew how the Victorians wrote literary history – and our own literary-historical narratives. In the sections that follow, I first survey the chronological development of different types of Victorian anthologies and analyse the key functions each type played in Victorian culture. I then discuss some of the methodological issues in describing and analysing a Victorian literary canon.

The History of Victorian Anthologies

As suggested above, anthologies play an important function in proposing and transmitting selective literary canons: any anthology necessarily presents a limited group of texts, chosen according to explicit or implicit principles. Tracing the history of those selective principles throughout the nineteenth century reveals shifts in Victorian ideas about the function of literature in the larger culture (Golding 1984). In addition to examining the editor's commentary and selections, examining the publishing history and intended audience of a given volume helps us to understand the functions of particular collections (Haass 1985). Anthologies also reflect and participate in larger trends in Victorian publishing (Altick 1957; Erickson 1996). Anthologies make visible the multiple processes of mediation that always occur in the communication process between poet and reader (what Darnton 1990 calls the 'communication network' and McGann 1991 terms the 'textual condition'), because the reader's encounter with the poems occurs through the material form of the anthology. Numerous persons (editors, publishers, printers) and material choices (paper, typeface, book design) all contribute to the meaning of any text. Here I focus on the simplified communication triangle of editor, reader and book as the most significant for understanding Victorian anthologies and their role in canon formation.

The root meaning of the word *anthology* is a garland of flowers, or bouquet, and many of the earliest modern anthologies were constructed around metaphors of plenitude, such as the cornucopia, the feast and the bouquet (Benedict 1996: 9–12). Such *productive* anthologies proliferate meaning and emphasize their variety of texts as a range of choices available to the reader. *Selective* anthologies, in contrast, emphasize the editor's knowledge, experience or taste in choosing particular texts and thereby limiting the reader's experience. *Comprehensive* anthologies, those which aim to present all examples of a particular type of poem, or to survey a period of history exhaustively, emphasize the importance of the anthology itself in the communication process, suggesting in their size and scope their cultural or scholarly value. Although a particular anthology may fulfil more than one of these functions, these terms are useful in examining not simply the contents but also the organization and material design of the anthologies.

In the 1820s, the growth of affordable publishing gave rise to a new kind of poetry anthology, the annual or 'giftbook'. The first was the *Forget-Me-Not*, published in 1823, followed shortly by *Friendship's Offering, The Literary Souvenir, The Amulet; or Christian and Literary Remembrance, The Keepsake* and many others. These collections were lavishly bound and illustrated, generally published near the Christmas season, and expressly intended to be given as gifts to friends and family members. They contained new poems written by both famous and unknown poets, who were sometimes assigned by the publishers to write a poem to accompany a particular engraving. Although an author's reputation might well enhance the sales of a particular giftbook, thematic coherence and affective values generally governed the arrangement and marketing of these volumes. The most successful annuals were issued each year, and competition between them could be fierce (Faxon 1973).

The annuals mark the increasing commodification of literature in the Victorian period in their treatment of poems as items to be marketed and sold to a variety of consumers. The annuals often reprinted poems from other periodicals, recirculating those texts to a different audience, and sometimes the entire contents of an annual were reissued by a later publisher under a new name. These books were intended for casual reading and were frequently the centrepiece of drawing-room conversation, as George Eliot describes in *Middlemarch* (1871–2) when one of Rosamond Vincy's suitors arrives with a copy of the latest *Keepsake*:

> He had brought the last *Keepsake*, the gorgeous watered-silk publication which marked modern progress at that time; and he considered himself very fortunate that he could be the first to look it over with her, dwelling on the ladies and gentlemen with shiny copper-plate cheeks and copper-plate smiles, and pointing to comic verses as capital and sentimental stories as interesting. (Eliot 1965: 302)

By the 1850s, the annuals had all but disappeared in England, and Eliot's retrospective historical irony reveals how dated this form of publication seemed to later Victorians. Some poets and critics feared that the annuals detracted from the reading public's ability to appreciate poetry seriously, because the illustrations would be distracting or would overshadow the readers' ability to interpret the poem on their own. Others recognized that participating in the newly evolving visual commodity culture would help them to reach new readers.

The success of the annuals in the 1820s and 1830s set the stage for the success of more expensive illustrated anthologies of poetry, like Henry Vizetelly's *Christmas with the Poets* (1851; six editions by 1872) and Robert Willmott's *Poets of the Nineteenth Century* (1856; six editions by 1885). With the advent of photography and new lithographic and engraving processes, Victorian culture was increasingly visual, and popular anthologies met that demand for associated images and texts. Pressures on the poetry market from the annuals also made other poetry collections designed for particular readers (e.g. young ladies) or with particular themes (seashore poems) more marketable than many single-author volumes.

In the 1860s, three important anthologies were published that made substantially different claims about the value of their contents and aimed to reach a general audience: William Allingham's *Nightingale Valley: A Collection, Including a Great Number of the Choicest Lyrics and Short Poems in the English Language* (1860), Francis Turner Palgrave's *The Golden Treasury of the Best Songs and Lyrical Poems in the English Language* (1861) and Richard Chenevix Trench's *A Household Book of English Poetry* (1868). Each of these volumes claimed to select only a few 'excellent' poems for their reader's enjoyment and illumination, and presented their contents in thematic or idiosyncratic ways. The very titles of Allingham's and Palgrave's collections reveal their selective goals, as compared to earlier anthologies of 'works' or 'specimens', or to the wide range of texts and images included in the annuals. In his preface, William Allingham distinguished his project in *Nightingale Valley* from both of these earlier types of collections:

> The intention of this book simply is to delight the lover of poetry. Specimens critical and chronological have their own worth; we desire to present a jewel, aptly arranged of many stones, various in colour and value, but all precious. Nothing personal or circumstantial, nothing below a pure and loving loyalty to the Muse, has been wittingly suffered to interfere betwixt the idea and its realization. (1860: v)

The selective anthologists of the 1860s declared their principles of selection to be both narrower than those of the historical anthologies at the turn of the century, and less influenced by fame and commercial success than those of the annuals, which were frequently associated with particular social or artistic coteries. In thus claiming for his anthology an aesthetic or literary purity, Allingham borrows the metaphors of the precious gem frequent throughout nineteenth-century poetic criticism.

These same metaphors of precious worth were extended in Palgrave's ambitious project in *The Golden Treasury* not simply to select *some* of the best poems, but 'all the best original Lyrical pieces and Songs in our language, by writers not living, – and none beside the best' (1861: ix). Palgrave's decision to exclude the work of living writers freed him from issues around copyright ownership, as well as potential personal conflicts with the poets he knew. This practice, which was followed by many other editors, meant that very few Victorian poems were included in some of the more popular Victorian anthologies. Palgrave's anthology, which I discuss in more detail in the following section, was hugely successful: twenty impressions were made of the 1861 version, and the revised editions of 1884 and 1890 were issued several times. After 1900 Macmillan issued the separate books of *The Golden Treasury* as school texts, and when the anthology went out of copyright other publishers issued their own versions. *The Golden Treasury* has been updated several times by subsequent editors and remains in print to this day, its design still remarkably similar to its original one. The success of Palgrave's anthology had many effects on the Victorian anthology market, particularly in its focus on shorter lyrics.

In the preface to his *Household Book of English Poetry*, Richard Trench justifies the need for his anthology by emphasizing the editor's 'direct and immediate investigation . . . into the treasures of our English Poetry'. He criticizes other anthologies, commenting that 'it is difficult to think that any one who had himself wandered in this garden of riches would not have carried off some flowers and fruits of his own gathering; instead of offering to us again, as most do, though it may be in somewhat different combinations, what already has been offered by others' (1868: vi). The work of the anthologist was explicitly conceived in the 1860s as that of selection, of carefully culling from the vast resources of English poetry those poems which would bring the greatest wisdom, delight or edification to the reader. This canon was, in these anthologies, not explicitly organized by author. Although Palgrave's and Trench's are each divided into four sections, one for each century, the arrangement of individual poems in all three of these anthologies is primarily by theme or mood, or in Palgrave's terms, 'gradations of feeling or subject' (1861: xi). In each of these three anthologies, the poems of any particular poet are interspersed with those of other poets, frustrating any author-centred reading practice. The underlying goal of these collections was not simply the reader's casual enjoyment, but instead the 'Wisdom which comes through Pleasure' in accidentally encountering 'great' works by diverse poets (Palgrave 1861: xi).

In each of these selective anthologies, the work of choosing favourite poems has, in a sense, already been performed by the editor. The reader is meant to accept those choices and the arrangement by mood or theme, which are necessarily subjective components of poetry. The reading protocol encouraged by this arrangement and the lack of biographical information minimizes attention to particular poets, conflating all of them into the voice of the anthology. In the case of the *Golden Treasury*, the emphasis on short lyrics (which Palgrave frequently condensed or altered to suit his personal aesthetic) works even more strongly to create the sense of a corporate lyric speaker or the 'voice' of English poetry (Nelson 1985). In general, the design and organization of these three anthologies highlight the selectivity and authority of their editors, rather than the weight of literary history and tradition.

This selectivity was presented as simultaneously convenient and valuable for the reader. Palgrave worked with Macmillan to ensure that his *Golden Treasury* would be small and portable, and Trench hoped that his book could be found in the emigrant's trunk and the traveller's knapsack (1868: viii). These editors responded to the pressures of urban modernity by insisting that poetry need no longer be limited to the genteel drawing room, and could instead provide solace and delight of the highest quality in any location to any reader. In an essay published in 1860, Palgrave advised:

> let a man, or a woman who wishes to claim her natural mental rights and position, read mainly the best books, and begin again when the series is ended. Life is not long; but the available list is briefer still. Putting aside the books which give special information or discuss points of theory, a few shelves would hold all the modern master-works – how few the ancient! (Palgrave 1860: 454)

The *Treasury* Palgrave would publish the following year was intended as a storehouse of these few great texts. These selective reading anthologies were no less commercial than the annuals and illustrated giftbooks – and Palgrave's was certainly far more commercially successful – yet the rhetoric of cultural value in these volumes asserted the importance of poetry in entirely different terms.

Other kinds of selective anthologies were also important during the mid-Victorian period, as editors and publishers responded to the increasing specialization of the reading public, of the publishing industry and of literary criticism. Anthologies of religious poetry included B. W. Savile's *Lyra Sacra: Being a Collection of Hymns Ancient and Modern, Odes and Fragments of Sacred Poetry* (1861) and Orby Shipley's *Lyra Eucharistica* (1863) and *Lyra Mystica* (1864). Anthologies focused on particular forms included Edmund Gosse and J. A. Blaikie's *Madrigals, Songs, and Sonnets* (1870) and the many collections devoted solely to the sonnet, such as Leigh Hunt's *The Book of the Sonnet* (1867), John Dennis's *English Sonnets: A Selection* (1873) and David Main's *A Treasury of English Sonnets* (1880).

One of the most significant developments around mid-century was the articulation of a separate history of women's poetry. Twenty years after Alexander Dyce's *Specimens of British Poetesses* (1825), a number of very successful anthologies were published in England and in the United States that focused solely on women writers, including George Bethune's *The British Female Poets* (1848), Frederic Rowton's *The Female Poets of Great Britain* (1848), Caroline May's *The American Female Poets* (1850) and Rufus Griswold's *The Female Poets of America* (1849). Linda Peterson (1999) suggests that because women's poetry began to be seen as having its own lineage, women poets were increasingly excluded from general poetry anthologies at mid-century. Certainly, the separation of women's poetry reflected the Victorian ideology of separate spheres, as Rowton's preface makes clear:

> while Man's intellect is meant to make the world stronger and wiser, Woman's is intended to make it purer and better . . . It is not, however, to promote a rivalry between the sexes that these pages are written. They aim, not at separating the two half minds of the world, but at making them act in concert and unison. Single, they are incomplete; but together they are powerful for every kind of good. (1981: xxxix)

Rowton argues that his anthology should be the companion to the existing collections of male poets just as Victorian women were expected to be the moral guide and support of men. The increasing interest throughout the Victorian period in the biography of the poet, rather than in generic or formal distinctions among texts, also fostered interest in the lives of women poets as a separate group.

Children's literature too developed as a distinct publishing category. Coventry Patmore's *The Children's Garland from the Best Poets* (1862) and Francis Turner Palgrave's *The Children's Treasury* (1875) were both quite successful up to the end of the century, and were adopted for use in some primary schools during the later 1880s. Other important anthologies of poetry for children at the end of the Victorian period included Andrew Lang's *Blue Poetry Book* (1891) and W. E. Henley's *Lyra Heroica: A Book of Verse for Boys* (1892).

As the nineteenth century drew to a close, several comprehensive anthologies offered extensive selections from large numbers of poets, creating multi-volume histories of English poetry that were updated and expanded through the early twentieth century. Thomas Humphry Ward's *The English Poets*, first published in four volumes in 1880, is organized chronologically and includes a critical essay prefacing the selections from each of the poets. Ward excluded living poets from his collection, which he updated in later editions by adding texts from poets who died after 1880, first in an appendix to volume IV, and then finally in a separate fifth volume, rather than changing any of his original selections. Ward's preface to the first volume explains that he is attempting to do what Thomas Campbell had done for a previous generation: 'represent the vast and varied field of English Poetry . . . to cover the whole ground and to select on a large scale . . . to collect as many of the best and most characteristic of their writings as should fully represent the great poets, and at the same time to omit no one who is poetically considerable' (1921: I, v–vi). Granting that 'It is indeed impossible that a selection of the kind should be really well done, should be done with an approach to finality, if it is the work of one critic alone', his collection draws on many different scholars to select the texts and write the introductions for each poet (I, v). The table of contents lists the author's full name and dates, as well as the name of the writer of the critical introduction and the specific titles included in the anthology. In both the table of contents and the bulk of the anthology's many volumes, the individual careers of numerous poets are shown to be the basis of English literature, and worthy of specialized attention. The authority of Ward's anthology – both in its selections and in its team of editors – is thus simultaneously collective and specialized.

Alfred Miles's *The Poets and the Poetry of the Century* (1892–7), updated and reissued in ten volumes in 1905, follows a very similar plan, except that Miles does include the work of living poets. The first six volumes are organized chronologically; later volumes present the work of women poets and religious poets separately. Like Ward's, Miles's anthology relies on the work of numerous critics to write the introductory essays, and they are indicated in the table of contents just as in Ward's. Miles's preface focuses on the history of nineteenth-century poetry as a history of poets, and on the difficulty of allotting appropriate representation to major and minor figures. Because Miles includes the work of living poets (whom he consulted in selecting their works) he is sensitive to the work of canon formation that his collection would necessarily perform. Unlike Palgrave or Allingham's selective anthologies of the 1860s, which were organized according to aesthetic or affective responses, both Ward and Miles construct documented histories of English poetry, including copious biographical notes as well as critical commentaries. Miles, for instance, explicitly links the two forms of criticism in his introductory preface: 'This work aims to be an Encyclopaedia of Modern Poetry . . . Its plan is to represent each poet in the variety of his work, giving such biographical data and such criticism as may serve to illustrate it' (1891–7: I, iii).

The American critic Edmund Clarence Stedman, who in 1875 had published a very successful critical account of Victorian poetry (*Victorian Poets,* published in England in 1876, updated in 1887), published *A Victorian Anthology 1837–1895* in 1895 as a companion volume. Both were reissued many times and helped, along with Ward and Miles, to define Victorian poetry for later generations. Stedman explicitly presents the goal of his anthology as critical; rather than following Palgrave's selective model, he intends to display the:

> poetry of the English people . . . at this stage of their manifold development . . . not to offer a collection of absolutely flawless poems, long since become classic and accepted as models; but in fact to make a truthful exhibit of the course of song during the last sixty years, as shown by the poets of Great Britain in the best of their shorter productions. (1895: ix)

To assist the reader in understanding the development of English poetry, Stedman divides his anthology into three chronological divisions ('Early Years of the Reign', 'The Victorian Epoch' and 'Close of the Era') which are further subdivided into groups or schools of poets, such as the 'Composite Idyllic School', 'Meditative Poets', 'Balladists and Lyrists' and 'Elegantiae'. These groupings reflect both generic distinctions and thematic preoccupations.

Of course, anthologists' prefatory remarks follow certain conventions which require them both to acknowledge the work of previous editors, particularly Palgrave, and yet also to stake claim to some new territory or a new method of selection that would make a new anthology worthwhile. Yet it is clear that the goals of these comprehensive anthologies were very different from those of the 1860s. All three of these comprehensive anthologies extensively document their contents and integrate chronological and critical terms either in the critical commentaries or in the organization of the volume itself. Elements of the poets' biography are presented as necessary information to assist the reader in understanding the poem. These anthologies began to name and codify certain traditions of English poetry, and certain ways of writing literary history, that would for many decades constitute the Victorian canon. Relying on the authority of several poets and literary critics, these anthologies also reflect the increasing specialization of knowledge in the literary field during the Victorian period, granting authority to the book as a collection of learned opinion and commentary. The weighted point of the communication triangle for these anthologies is the book itself, which metonymically represents the field of literary knowledge.

Analysing the Victorian Canon

As suggested in the brief survey above, each of the different types of Victorian anthology fulfilled a different cultural function, whether it aimed to produce new texts and readers, to select only a few poems according to certain criteria, or to document comprehensively the range and history of nineteenth-century poetry. Each of these functions contributes different texts and prescriptions for reading to the larger cultural discourse about literature, as well as to a generalized literary canon.

Some necessary first steps, in describing and analysing a Victorian canon as seen in nineteenth-century anthologies, would include specifying which kind of canon one is investigating (the educational canon; the popular canon; the critical canon) and then choosing which kinds of anthologies to use to document it. The method one chooses to use to analyse the selected anthology will produce rather different definitions of the literary canon. The simplest method is to examine which writers are included in which anthologies, and to determine which writers appear most frequently. Wendell Harris's analysis of anthologies of Victorian poetry throughout the twentieth century, for instance, reveals a significant reduction in the number of poets included, particularly in collections designed for classroom use, reflecting the codification of the teaching canon (Harris 1991: 114). Alan Golding (1984) ties his analysis of the authors included in nineteenth-century American poetry anthologies to larger cultural and historical shifts that are similar to those I have described in British anthologies. Examining the contents of Victorian anthologies can also reveal important differences between our contemporary canons and those of the nineteenth century. Surveying the contents of Ward, Miles and Stedman's anthologies, for instance, reveals a number of poets who are rarely anthologized today: William Caldwell Roscoe, Cosmo Monkhouse, Philip Bourke Marston, Emily Pfeiffer, Lord de Tabley (John Leicester Warren), Dora Greenwell and Aubrey de Vere, among others. Much recent critical work in Victorian studies has been fuelled by feminist and historicist scholarship interested in recovering such 'lost' writers, and in determining when and why they disappeared from the critical and pedagogical canons.

Although this kind of tabulation provides a general picture of the history of literary taste and canon formation, it does not reflect the relative importance assigned to particular writers within an anthology. Anita Hemphill (1984) attempts to establish this in her description of the Victorian canon by estimating the number of pages devoted to each author in an anthology, and assuming that those with more pages were considered more important. Yet even setting aside differences in typeface, margins and page design, this kind of analysis still does not account for the myriad complexities of nineteenth-century anthology publishing: poems are frequently printed in columns and over one or more pages; some writers are represented by one long poem and others by several shorter poems; some works are extracted and some are given in their entirety. To estimate a canonical hierarchy accurately requires more specific analysis of the texts included in a given anthology and their relation to aesthetic and generic preferences.

The selections from Elizabeth Barrett Browning's poetry in Ward, Miles and Stedman's anthologies, for example, raise a number of questions for further research. One of the pre-eminent Victorian poets during her lifetime, Barrett Browning's status in the critical and teaching canon declined during the twentieth century, until feminist scholarship revived interest in her verse novel *Aurora Leigh* and drew attention to the reception history of her poetry. The critical introductions in Ward and Miles both include biographical details, such as her ill health and domineering father, but also emphasize the breadth of her learning and the linguistic variety of her writing. Each editor selects rather different poems, with only 'A Musical Instrument' and some brief selections from 'Sonnets from the Portuguese' and from *Aurora Leigh* being included in all three anthologies. The extracts from *Aurora Leigh* in no way attempt to represent the work as a whole, and function instead to highlight moments of intensity. Stedman's and Ward's anthologies add titles to their extracts from *Aurora Leigh*, such as 'The Beauty of England' and 'Marian's Child', in essence creating short lyrics from the original narrative poem.

Estimating Barrett Browning's relative importance within any one of these anthologies is difficult because her sonnets and shorter lyrics are given pre-eminence in the critical accounts for their compelling language. Miles's selections are the most extensive, but the size and scope of his anthology are much greater than those of the other anthologists, and sheer length of selections does not account for the way Victorian critical principles were applied and manifested in anthology selections. A comparative assessment among the different anthologies would also need to take into account the significance of Barrett Browning's placement. In Stedman's anthology she is grouped under the heading 'Poets of the New Day: Humanity – Free Thought – Political, Social and Artistic Reform', which perhaps explains why 'The Cry of the Children' is the first poem he prints. Miles presents the work of women poets in two volumes separate from his main chronology of nineteenth-century poetry, reflecting the Victorian critical tendency towards biographical interpretation. In Ward's anthology, Barrett Browning is presented as part of the main chronological narrative of English poetry, between Thomas Lovell Beddoes and Emily Brontë. Analysis too extensive to perform here would be required to uncover the significance of these different arrangements and selections in determining the late Victorian assessment of Barrett Browning as reflected in and created by these anthologies.

Victorian anthologies can contribute a great deal to our understanding of the reception history of particular writers. However, to focus discussions of the Victorian canon only on particular poets actually reveals more about our reading perceptions and assumptions than about those of Victorian readers. If our analysis of the anthologies stays focused on the inclusion/exclusion binary – counting who gets 'in' to 'the' canon, or even, at the more particular level, who gets included in which anthologies and why – we stay within an author-based mode of writing literary history. Such a paradigm necessarily retains assumptions from our own version of the Victorian canon, which colours our understanding of the lists of names generated from the anthologies: we cannot look at these lists without recognizing some, and not recognizing others. Our reactions differ depending on our ideological assumptions, but it is important to recognize that valorizing either the known, canonical figure (Wordsworth, the Rossettis) or the unknown (Pfeiffer, Marston) results in the same thing: an author-based narrative of literary change and periodization that obscures other aspects of the social meaning of writing, as John Guillory suggests:

> histories of canon formation, when they consist primarily of a narrative of *reputations*, of the names which pass in and out of literary anthologies, explain nothing. Such narrative histories fail to recognize generic or linguistic shifts which underlie the fortunes of individual authors by establishing what counts as literature at a given historical moment. (1993: 64)

Victorian anthologies offer a variety of other kinds of information that we can use to complicate our understanding of what counted as literature for Victorian readers and editors, and why and how it was read. Our focus on an author-centred model of the literary canon stems from the ways we tend to write literary history, which developed out of Victorian criticism and publishing practices. The pages of Victorian anthologies offer us discrete examples of the literary text's communication process, which we can describe by examining the kinds of information on the page with the text of the poem.

The selective anthologies edited by Allingham, Palgrave and Trench deliberately minimize the presence of the poet on the printed page by placing the poet's name after the poem, in very small type. A reader's first engagement with the poem thus occurs *without* the name of the poet, reinforcing the collection's claim to aesthetic selectivity. Such collections were designed to discipline the taste of the increasingly literate Victorian consumers. Visually, the pages of these collections focus on the text of the poems – the largest type presents the poem's title, rather than the poet's name, and the running heads on each page reinforce the name of the collection. *Nightingale Valley* or *The Golden Treasury* or the *Household Book* thus become significant entities unto themselves as they are repeatedly invoked on each page. These cultural treasuries offer the condensation of lyric through pages uncluttered by historical information, just as their overall organization rejects chronology in favour of mood or tone.

As the purpose and range of the later comprehensive anthologies edited by Ward, Miles and Stedman differed from those of the 1860s, so too does the page design in these volumes. Not only is biographical information considered an integral part of the critical account that precedes each entry, but it also helps to organize the reader's orientation to the page. In each of these anthologies, the poet's name is placed in one of the running heads, so that at any opening of the collection, one knows instantly which poet's work one is seeing. Biographical information, in the form of names and dates or in lengthy notes, is one mechanism by which the field of literary value is produced. In these anthologies the literary labour of both the poet and the critic is individualized and specialized, made explicit on the page where it was only implied in the mid-century volumes.

Taking these differences in page design and implied reading protocol into account reveals how our very ideas of who can be a poet, what a poet's role is, and what counts as significant poetry are rooted in collections like these Victorian anthologies. The differences in content among the anthologies in terms of poetic texts, or numbers of poets, can be tabulated easily enough. The different representations of particular poets in the biographical notes are also easily enough compared in order to reveal the ideological constraints of particular critics or anthologies. But in theorizing the cultural effects of any anthology, especially in relation to questions of canon formation, the material elements matter. To begin to examine the material construction of these ideas might be the first step in rewriting Victorian literary history, and our accounts of its canons, as a history of *writing* and not simply a history of writers.

See also: THE MARKET; LYRIC; SONNET AND SONNET SEQUENCE.

REFERENCES AND FURTHER READING

[Allingham, William] 'Giraldus' (ed.) (1860) *Nightingale Valley: A Collection, Including a Great Number of the Choicest Lyrics and Short Poems in the English Language*. London: Bell and Daldy.

Altick, Richard D. (1957) *The English Common Reader: A Social History of the Mass Reading Public 1800–1900*. Chicago: University of Chicago Press.

Arnold, Matthew (1973) 'The Study of Poetry.' In *The Complete Prose Works of Matthew Arnold* (IX, 161–88). Ann Arbor: University of Michigan Press.

Benedict, Barbara M. (1996) *Making the Modern Reader: Cultural Mediation in Early Modern Literary Anthologies*. Princeton, N. J.: Princeton University Press.

Bourdieu, Pierre (1984) *Distinction: A Social Critique of the Judgement of Taste*. Cambridge, Mass.: Harvard University Press.

Bourdieu, Pierre (1993) 'The Field of Cultural Production, or: The Economic World Reversed.' In R. Johnson (ed.). *The Field of Cultural Production: Essays on Art and Literature* (pp. 29–73). New York: Columbia University Press.

Certeau, Michel de (1984) *The Practice of Everyday Life*. Berkeley: University of California Press.

Chartier, Roger (1994) *The Order of Books: Readers,*

Authors, and Libraries in Europe Between the Fourteenth and Eighteenth Centuries. Stanford: Stanford University Press.

Darnton, Robert (1990) *The Kiss of Lamourette: Reflections in Cultural History*. New York: Norton.

Eliot, George (1965) *Middlemarch*. London: Penguin.

Erickson, Lee (1996) *The Economy of Literary Form: English Literature and the Industrialization of Publishing, 1800–1850*. Baltimore, London: Johns Hopkins University Press.

Faxon, Frederick W. (1973) *Literary Annuals and Gift Books: A Bibliography 1823–1903*. Pinner: Private Libraries Association.

Fowler, Alastair (1979) 'Genre and the Literary Canon.' *New Literary History*, 11, 97–119.

Genette, Gérard (1991) 'Introduction to the Paratext.' *New Literary History*, 22, 261–72.

Golding, Alan C. (1984) 'A History of American Poetry Anthologies.' In R. von Hallberg (ed.). *Canons* (pp. 279–307). Chicago, London: University of Chicago Press.

Guillory, John (1993) *Cultural Capital: The Problem of Literary Canon Formation*. Chicago, London: University of Chicago Press.

Haass, Sabine (1985) 'Victorian Poetry Anthologies: Their Role and Success in the Nineteenth-Century Book Market.' *Publishing History*, 17, 51–64.

Harris, Wendell (1991) 'Canonicity' *PMLA*, 106, 110–21.

Hemphill, Anita (1984) 'Victorian and Edwardian Poetry Anthologies, 1861–1914.' Ph.D. diss., UCLA.

Houston, Natalie M. (1999) 'Valuable by Design: Material Features and Cultural Value in Nineteenth-Century Sonnet Anthologies.' *Victorian Poetry*, 37, 243–72.

McGann, Jerome J. (1991) *The Textual Condition*. Princeton, N. J.: Princeton University Press.

Miles, Alfred (1892–7) *The Poets and the Poetry of the Century*. 10 vols. London: Hutchinson.

Nelson, Megan Jane (1985) 'Francis Turner Palgrave and *The Golden Treasury*.' Ph.D. diss., University of British Columbia.

Palgrave, Francis Turner (1860) 'On Readers in 1760 and 1860.' *Macmillan's*, 1. Reprinted in Francis Turner Palgrave (1991) *The Golden Treasury* (pp. 451–4). Ed. Christopher Ricks. London: Penguin.

Palgrave, Francis Turner (ed.) (1861) *The Golden Treasury of the Best Songs and Lyrical Poems in the English Language*. Cambridge: Macmillan.

Peterson, Linda H. (1999) 'Anthologizing Women: Women Poets in Early Victorian Collections of Lyric.' *Victorian Poetry*, 37, 193–209.

Price, Leah (2000) *The Anthology and the Rise of the Novel*. Cambridge: Cambridge University Press.

Rowton, Frederic (1981) *The Female Poets of Great Britain*. Ed. M. Williamson. Detroit: Wayne State University Press.

Siegel, Jonah (1999) 'Among the English Poets: Keats, Arnold, and the Placement of Fragments.' *Victorian Poetry*, 37, 215–31.

Stedman, Edmund Clarence (1895) *A Victorian Anthology 1837–1895*. Boston, New York: Houghton Mifflin.

Trench, Richard Chenevix (1868) *A Household Book of English Poetry*. London: Macmillan.

Ward, Thomas Humphry (ed.) (1921) *The English Poets. Selections With Critical Introductions by Various Writers and a General Introduction by Matthew Arnold*. New York: Macmillan.

21
Reviewing
Joanne Shattock

When poetry was noisy, criticism was loud; now poetry is a still small voice, and criticism must be smaller and stiller.

Walter Bagehot, 'Wordsworth, Tennyson and Browning'

I should like now to go abroad – to see no English, and to hear nothing more about my Poems. It does me no good hearing the discussion of them – and yet of course I cannot help being occupied by it.

Matthew Arnold to Mrs Forster, 1853

I never wanted a real set of good hearty praisers – and no bad reviewers – I am quite content with my share. No – what I laughed at in my 'gentle audience' is a sad trick the real admirers have of admiring at the wrong place – enough to make an apostle swear.

Robert Browning to Elizabeth Barrett, 1845

The period from the 1830s to the 1870s, 'the prolific years of high Victorian poetry' as they have been described (Armstrong 1972: 1), was also a period of intense and self-conscious scrutiny of that poetry. Looking back on the earlier generation of Romantic poets in his essay on 'Wordsworth, Tennyson and Browning; or, Pure, Ornate and Grotesque Art in Poetry' (1864), Walter Bagehot suggested that in contrast to the excitement and sensation produced by those poets, the present age struggled unsuccessfully to find a faith in poetry, and that this had implications for the state of criticism: 'Years ago, when criticism only tried to show how poetry could be made a good amusement, it was not impossible that criticism itself should be amusing. But now it must at least be serious, for we believe that poetry is a serious and a deep thing' (1864: 341). Few practitioners, whether poets or critics, would have disagreed. The criticism of Victorian poetry was articulate, deeply serious, especially in its anxiety about the place of poetry in an unpropitious age, and determined to reinforce its position against the competing discourses of the novel and of science. The impact of that criticism, both on individual poets and on the wider debates which constituted Victorian poetics, was profound.

The reviewing culture in the middle decades of the nineteenth century was buoyant. The periodical press was the outlet for some of the best critical energies of the time. As

Christopher Kent (1969) has demonstrated, the role of journalist had acquired a new professionalism and respectability as university men sought alternative careers in the press to those in politics or the law, or often combined the two. The expansion of the periodical press in the post-Romantic period, in tandem with the growth of the reading public, produced more and varied outlets for reviewing. The quarterlies, beginning with the 'great triumvirate' of the *Edinburgh*, the *Quarterly* and the *Westminster*, had always regarded poetry as a major subject for review, in contrast to the novel, which took much longer to establish itself. These three were joined in the 1840s by a number of new publications with sectarian affiliations – the *North British* (Free Church of Scotland), the *British Quarterly* (Congregationalist), the *Prospective* (Unitarian), the *Christian Remembrancer* (high church), the *British Critic* (Anglo-Catholic) – and later still by the *National Review*, the successor to the *Prospective*, another Unitarian organ. Matthew Arnold, in his essay 'The Function of Criticism in the Present Time' (1864), was to deplore the political and religious allegiances of these reviews for preventing, as he saw it, an essential 'disinterestedness' in their reviewing. In practice these periodicals attracted able and sympathetic reviewers of poetry whose criticism was rarely tainted by sectarian views.

The weekly reviews, from the long-established *Athenaeum* and *Spectator* to the more recent and iconoclastic *Saturday Review*, founded in 1855, had developed a reputation for hard-hitting and astute reviews of both poetry and fiction. Of the monthlies, the Unitarian *Monthly Repository* had from the late 1820s carved out a special niche for itself as a discerning critical organ, particularly as regards poetry. In the 1830s *Blackwood's Magazine* was a comparatively sedate publication, having put aside its reputation for near-scurrilous and politically motivated attacks on poets of liberal persuasion. 'Christopher North', or John Wilson, re-emerged as a crotchety remnant of the previous generation when he linked Tennyson's *Poems, Chiefly Lyrical* (1830) with the 'Cockney School' of poets (*Blackwood's Magazine*, May 1832) but otherwise *Maga's* teeth were drawn. By the late 1850s the weeklies and monthlies had supplanted the quarterlies as the most powerful journals in the reviewing of poetry. The monthly magazines and reviews founded in the 1860s, among them *Macmillan's*, the *Cornhill* and the *Fortnightly* (which became a monthly in 1866), were geared to the new middle-class reading public and published original poems by new and established poets as well as reviews of poetry. Three new reviews which were to become particularly influential in the reviewing of poetry emerged from the late sixties onwards: the *Contemporary Review*, founded by the publishing firm of Alexander Strahan in 1866; the *Academy*, a fortnightly and later a monthly review begun in 1870; and the *Nineteenth Century* (1877–1900), owned and edited by the architect and critic James Knowles.

Reviewers of poetry were non-specialists. Some were high-profile critics who wrote across a spectrum of subjects. Bagehot, G. H. Lewes, John Stuart Mill, John Morley, Carlyle and Ruskin made significant contributions to the debates about the function of poetry and the role of the poet, much of it enclosed within reviews of individual poets or volumes of poetry. Tennyson's reviewers included Gladstone, the French historian H. A. Taine, the historian and politician Goldwin Smith, the Roman Catholic theologian

Richard Simpson, and Henry Alford, dean of Canterbury, illustrating the attractions of poetry to a broad cross-section of professional men.

But it is also the case that poets regularly reviewed one another. This is not surprising given, as David Latané has pointed out, that some of the best practical criticism of Victorian poetry was contained in poets' letters to one another (Latané 1999: 390). He instances the Brownings' letters and those from Gerard Manley Hopkins to Robert Bridges. Leigh Hunt, Charles Kingsley, Arnold, Hopkins, Algernon Swinburne, Walt Whitman and W. E. Henley all reviewed Tennyson at least once during his lengthy career. A. H. Clough famously reviewed Arnold's *The Strayed Reveller* and *Empedocles on Etna* in the *North American Review* (July 1853), criticizing his friend's poetry for qualities he found too prominent in his own. Swinburne reviewed Arnold's 1867 volume favourably in the *Fortnightly*, an important intervention in the consolidation of Arnold's reputation as a poet. Coventry Patmore reviewed both Tennyson's *The Princess* and Arnold's 1853 volume, describing Arnold in the *North British Review* as 'a kindred spirit'. As a principal poetry reviewer in both the *Edinburgh* and the *North British* reviews in the 1840s and 1850s, Patmore reviewed many of his contemporaries, including William Allingham, Adelaide Procter, William Barnes, 'Owen Meredith', P. J. Bailey and Sydney Dobell. Charles Kingsley was one of the first to review contemporary working-class poets ('Burns and his School', *North British Review*, November 1851). William Morris wrote a laudatory review of Dante Gabriel Rossetti's 1870 volume in the *Academy* (14 May 1870), as if instinctively sensing the harsher criticism which was to follow (discussed below).

The days of 'puffing', of deliberately orchestrating favourable notices in the press, were over, but in this gentlemanly world it was not unusual for a poet's friends to generate appropriate enthusiasm for a new volume. Arthur Hallam's review of Tennyson's *Poems, Chiefly Lyrical* (1830) in the *Englishman's Magazine* (August 1831) was acknowledged to have been crucial in establishing Tennyson's reputation and also to have set the agenda for the discussion of his poetry in the years to come. Browning was particularly well served by his friends. He dubbed W. J. Fox of the *Monthly Repository* his 'literary god-father' as the result of his review of *Pauline*. The Pre-Raphaelite circle were vociferous proselytisers on his behalf from the 1840s onwards. Both William Michael and Dante Gabriel Rossetti, as well as William Morris, wrote supportively at strategic points. R. H. Horne, Leigh Hunt, H. F. Chorley and Joseph Arnould were among other members of Browning's circle who wrote reviews (see Litzinger and Smalley 1970).

Arnold was embarrassed by an overly enthusiastic review in the *Christian Remembrancer* by his friend J. D. Coleridge, writing to a mutual friend: 'My love to J. D. C., and tell him that the limited circulation of the *Christian Remembrancer* makes the unquestionable viciousness of his article of little importance' (Dawson 1973: 96). A review in the *North British* by fellow poet and friend J. C. Shairp, in contrast, was described by a third party as 'a case of physic from a loving hand'. Swinburne's friends were both protective and assertive in the periods when his work was under attack: W. M. Rossetti and Henry Morley wrote positive reviews at crucial moments, and Swinburne's friend and companion Theodore Watts-Dunton regularly reviewed his work in the *Athenaeum* between 1877 and 1899.

Despite the seeming cosiness of this world, it was also an exclusive one. Women were conspicuous by their absence, both as subjects and as reviewers, at a time when the number of practising women poets was increasing. Whereas women regularly reviewed fiction, biography, art, history and even political economy, until the 1870s very few wrote reviews of poetry. In her discussion of what she terms the 'gendered space' of Victorian periodicals, Laurel Brake identifies poetry, along with politics, science, psychology, philosophy and the classics, as subjects associated with men and, by extension, masculine reviewers. It was novels, popularly associated with women readers and authors, that were regularly assigned to female reviewers (1994: 30). Conversely, Marysa Demoor has noted the boost given to women's poetry in the *Athenaeum* of the 1870s by the addition to the reviewing staff of poets Mathilde Blind, Edith Nesbit, Mary Robinson and Rosamund Marriott Watson (2000: 103–27). The women reviewed poetry by men as well as by women, but there was a perceptible sharpening of the focus on women's poetry once their presence made itself felt. Virginia Blain (2001) similarly notes the impact of Augusta Webster and Alice Meynell in improving the treatment of women poets in the *Athenaeum* at a later stage. Blain credits the reviewing scene at the end of the nineteenth century with facilitating the networking of women poets, creating occasions when these women could have informal public 'conversations' with one another through their reviewing.

There was an inherent risk in the engagement of women reviewers for poetry, as Demoor points out. Once the subject came to be recognized as the preserve of women it was likely to be regarded as 'feminized', and therefore 'secondary' as a subject for review. As Joseph Bristow has observed, the more poetry was identified with women, the less influential it became to the Victorians. Alfred Austin's pointed association of Tennyson with the 'feminine, narrow, domesticated, timorous Poetry of the Period' in 1870 was a signal for the gradual decline in Tennyson's reputation (Bristow 1987: 124).

One of the most striking features of Victorian reviews was their expansiveness. Forty or fifty pages was a not uncommon length for articles in the quarterlies. Those in the monthlies were slightly shorter, and the weeklies confined their reviewers to five or six full-page columns. Bagehot coined the phrase 'the review-like essay' and 'the essay-like review' to describe the review article as it evolved from the early years of the quarterlies to become the standard format for Victorian reviewing. The extensive quotations which characterized the reviews of poetry were an essential part of the critical process, and not, as the modern reader is tempted to think, an example of desperate or irresponsible padding. Bagehot speculated on the shift in popular taste from the 'pure' poetry of Wordsworth to the 'ornate' or Romantic sensibility of Tennyson's *Enoch Arden* volume, and the startling contrasts and incongruities inherent in Browning's 'grotesque' *Dramatis Personae*. In the course of his 1864 article, which ran to over fifty pages, Bagehot quoted five sonnets by Hartley Coleridge, forty-one lines from *Empedocles on Etna*, sixty lines from *Paradise Lost*, forty from *Enoch Arden*, forty-four lines from Browning's 'Caliban upon Setebos', and thirteen stanzas from 'Holy-Cross Day' – all essential to his project of demonstrating the emergence of alternative strands of sensibility in modern poetry.

The impact of these quotations on nineteenth-century readers should not be underestimated. In her richly informative introduction to *Victorian Scrutinies: Reviews of Poetry*

1830–1870, Isobel Armstrong argues that critical assumptions and evaluations emerge in the kind of tone a writer adopts, and in the way he or she presents the theme, form and language of a poem, as much as in the explicit statements he or she makes (1972: 2). As Armstrong points out, modern reprints of Victorian reviews which routinely omit the quotations for reasons of space lose an essential element of the texture and the argument of the reviews.

Modern readers of Victorian reviews of poetry frequently comment on the absence of technical language and the reluctance on the part of reviewers to engage in close reading or practical criticism. John D. Jump in his introduction to *Tennyson: The Critical Heritage* highlighted the 'leisurely comparisons and confident generalizations' which characterized so much of Victorian reviewing. In this he was right, but he was also astute in his observation that the modern reader should not underestimate the closeness of the reading that underlies these 'general formulations' or 'the delicacy of the analysis which can be conducted in these general terms' (1967: 17).

Isobel Armstrong links the absence of technical or specialized critical vocabulary in the reviews to a 'grand disregard of the purely aesthetic' and an 'imperial refusal in Victorian criticism to regard the poem as a self-contained, sealed-off entity on which moral and social questions external to it do not impinge'. Exclusively 'literary' criticism did not exist, she points out, and the Victorian critic would 'cross boundaries established by the restrictions and delimitations of literary criticism today without even knowing that they were there' (1972: 4–5). Poetry was seen in its broad cultural contexts and reviewers were concerned with the effect of poetry on the reader, with the needs of the reader, and with poetry's all-important appeal to the sympathies. The proper materials for poetry, the role of the poet in the modern age, the attractions and the dangers of 'subjective' poetry, the anxiety that the present age was inimical to poetry – all of which were questions at the heart of Victorian poetics – were canvassed in the reviews of individual poets and volumes of poetry. The use of a specialist or technical critical vocabulary would have been inappropriate for a discussion of such wide-ranging issues and general concerns.

The debates which constituted Victorian poetics and which are discussed by Carol T. Christ in the introduction to this *Companion* had a number of key texts in the form of separately published treatises, essays and prefaces. Works like J. H. Newman's *Poetry, with Reference to Aristotle's Poetics* (1829), John Keble's Oxford *Lectures on Poetry* (1832–41), John Stuart Mill's essays 'What is Poetry' and 'Two Kinds of Poetry', published in the *Monthly Repository* for 1833, E. S. Dallas's *Poetics: An Essay on Poetry* (1852), G. H. Lewes's *The Principles of Success in Literature* (1885), reprinted from articles in the *Fortnightly* in 1865, as well as Arnold's preface to his *Poems* (1853) and his 'The Study of Poetry' (1880), were the nearest Victorian equivalents to the great Romantic manifestos. But much of the serious debate which constituted Victorian poetics took place in the reviews of individual poets and volumes of poetry, so that it is less easy to identify and to isolate a discrete body of materials. In terms of substance, the two modes of discourse – the so-called 'treatises' and the reviews – have much in common, but, as Armstrong (1972) points out, there are essential differences. The treatises are distinguished by the abstract nature of their concerns. The reviews of individual poets and volumes of poetry share these concerns, but give them specificity, focus, and an attractive sense of urgency.

The close connections and interaction of the two modes of criticism are illustrated by the reverberations of an article on 'Theories of Poetry and a New Poet' by David Masson in the *North British Review* for August 1853. Masson was reviewing Alexander Smith's *A Life Drama* together with Dallas's *Poetics*. It was in fact a wide-ranging article on poetic theory, influenced by the publication in 1848 of R. M. Milnes's *Life, Letters and Literary Remains of John Keats*. Matthew Arnold seized on Masson's assertion, in his discussion of Smith, that 'a true allegory of the state of one's own mind in a representative history, whether narrative or dramatic in form, is perhaps the highest thing that one attempts in the way of fictitious art', and presented it as typical of the point of view to which his 1853 preface was a determined reaction. Arnold argued that 'the dialogue of the mind with itself' was precisely what contemporary poetry should avoid. The fact that a review of a contemporary poet (Smith) in a sectarian quarterly review (the *North British Review*) prompted a major statement of Victorian poetic theory (Arnold's 1853 preface) is a further endorsement of the richness and extent of debate produced by Victorian reviews of poetry and of their vital role in the articulation of Victorian poetics.

A significant proportion of the articles on poetry during the period focused not on contemporary poets but on new editions of poets from Chaucer through to the Romantics. The latter cast a long shadow, and reviewers of current poets instinctively looked over their shoulders, comparing present achievements with those of the recent past. A number of publications triggered retrospection, among them Francis Jeffrey's collected *Contributions to the Edinburgh Review* (1844), which revived memories of an earlier generation of reviewers and the fate of Wordsworth in particular at their hands. The ubiquity of Wordsworth in reviews of Victorian poetry, and his position as a universally accepted touchstone of poetic achievement, are confirmed by Stephen Gill's extensive study *Wordsworth and the Victorians* (1998). Wordsworth was routinely invoked by reviewers as *the* poet of the century, to whom all successful contemporary poets were to be compared. By the same token Tennyson became the standard against whom the present generation was measured. As early as 1844 R. H. Horne's *A New Spirit of the Age* claimed for him 'solely on account of what he has already accomplished – the title of a true poet of the highest class of genius', and later in the same essay he was declared 'one of the most original poets that ever lived'. Poets were labelled 'Tennysonian' or 'sub-Tennysonian', or compared with him in other ways with a frequency which was never equalled by Browning, Arnold or later poets. His seniority was further endorsed by the fact that he was the one nineteenth-century poet who had books written about him during his lifetime.

As an epoch in the history of criticism, the period between 1830 and 1870 was distinguished from the more rumbustious 1820s and the Aesthetic movement which followed. The period was also not without internal development in terms of criticism. John Woolford (1982) has identified the years between the publication of Browning's *Men and Women* in 1855 and his *Dramatis Personae* in 1864 as the point at which literary criticism moved from what he terms 'adjectival' criticism, characterized by self-display and superiority on the part of the critic, to more analytical criticism, in which the critic positioned himself in the role of advocate and interpreter rather than judge of his subject. Woolford sees this transition as the final rejection of the methods of Romantic reviewers like Lord Jeffrey, and also as a complex response to the writing of Arnold. The impact of this shift was felt most immediately by Browning. The enthusiastic reception of *Dramatis Personae* in contrast to the muted and even hostile response to *Men and Women* marked a decisive change in his reputation. But Woolford argues that a major reorientation of the idea of criticism itself had taken place. One of the changes he notes is that critics began to engage in something like modern 'practical criticism'.

'Minute criticism', as it was called, detailed comment directed towards individual poems and passages, was notable by its absence from most reviews of poetry until the 1860s. The Victorian critic offered a more general account of the 'nature' and success of the poems with which he was concerned. Reviewers did offer judgements – on a poet's achievement, on his or her potential, on any new direction the poet was perceived as having taken since his or her last volume. And their views mattered. In response to Elizabeth Barrett's enquiry in 1845 about his 'sensitiveness to criticism' Browning affected to be unperturbed by his reviewers, insisting that 'they are so well-behaved in ordinary, these critics; and for Keats and Tennyson "to go softly all their days" for a gruff word or two is quite inexplicable to me, and always has been'. 'Tennyson', he continued, 'reads the Quarterly and does as they bid him, with the most solemn face in the world – out goes this, in goes that, all is changed and ranged. Oh me!' (Browning 1900: I, 19–20). Despite the professed nonchalance Browning is known to have paid obsessive attention to his critics.

The popular view that Tennyson's so called 'Ten Years' Silence' between the publication of the 1832 and 1842 volumes was the result of severe wounding at the hands of his early critics has been disproved by modern biographers. Both Christopher Ricks (1972) and R. B. Martin (1980) emphasize the incessant writing that occupied that decade, not the response of a man who was numbed to silence by his critics. His revisions to the *Poems* of 1842, however, often followed the lines indicated by his critics. And his close friend James Knowles revealed his sensitivity to adverse criticism shortly after his death:

> All the mass of eulogy he took comparatively little notice of, but he never could forget an unfriendly word, even from the most obscure and insignificant and unknown quarter. He was hurt by it as a sensitive child might be hurt by the cross look of a passing stranger; or, rather as a supersensitive skin is hurt by the sting of an invisible midge. He knew it was a weakness in him, and could be laughed out of it for a time, but it soon returned upon him, and had given him from his early youth exaggerated vexation. (1893: 173–4)

Arnold too was known to pay close and consistent attention to what his critics said, despite his protestations of indifference. He withdrew both the *Strayed Reveller* and *Empedocles* volumes from circulation shortly after they were published, probably because he was dissatisfied with them. But in the view of Carl Dawson, it is also likely that he was influenced by their unfavourable reception at the hands of his critics: 'Not to have published the volumes in the first place would have indicated doubt about their quality; to withdraw them after publication suggested concern about reputation' (1973: 4).

The excitement generated by the reviews of Tennyson's *Poems, Chiefly Lyrical* (1830) and *Poems* (1832) and that which followed Arnold's *Poems* (1853) are identified by Isobel Armstrong as two occasions on which critical debate was 'particularly lively and urgent' (1972: 1). There were other celebrated occasions when the critical temperature rose, but the resulting discussion was less productive. The attack by the poet and critic W. E. Aytoun on what he termed the 'Spasmodic School' of poets – the work of P. J. Bailey, J. W. Marston, Sydney Dobell and Alexander Smith among others – was one occasion when the reviewing of Victorian poetry reverted to the squibs and satire of the 1820s. Aytoun parodied the intensely psychological and subjective poetry of these modern poets in a spoof review in *Blackwood's* (May 1854) of a non-existent verse-drama, *Firmilian* by 'T. Percy Jones'. The fallout from this review and a follow-up volume was extensive and the 'Spasmodics' became the butt of critical jokes in the mid-1850s, as in Patmore's soubriquet 'Balder-dash' for Sydney Dobell's best-known work. In his attack on the subjective nature of contemporary poetry Aytoun adopted the same position towards the popular poets of the day as Arnold had done. But as Mark Weinstein points out in his study of the Spasmodic controversy, whereas few readers today know *Firmilian*, Arnold's preface 'stands secure as a classic' (1968: 106).

Another occasion when the line between critical excitement and notoriety was blurred was the publication of Swinburne's *Poems and Ballads* (1866). The ramifications of this affair extended to the publication of D. G. Rossetti's *Poems* (1870) and beyond. John Morley's review of *Poems and Ballads* in the *Saturday Review* for 4 August 1866 in which he referred to Swinburne as 'the libidinous laureate of a pack of satyrs' (Hyder 1970: 29) has become one of the legends of Victorian literary criticism. In fact his was only one of a chorus of reviews to attack the work variously for sensuality, paganism and blasphemy. The furore was notable for the intemperate language of the reviewers, and for Swinburne's vigorous response to his critics. The extent and the nature of the critical attacks linked him in the minds of his contemporaries with Byron, as did the pugnacity of his replies. His 'Notes on Poems and Reviews' (1866), he insisted, was intended neither as an apology nor as an answer to his critics, but 'rather a casual set of notes on my poems such as Coleridge and Byron (under other circumstances) did on theirs'. *Punch's* reaction, 'having read Mr. Swinburne's defence of his prurient poetics' was to give him licence to change his name to 'Swine-born' (Hyder 1970: xxi–ii). It might have seemed yet another return to the rough-and-tumble of the 1820s, but there was a very serious edge to the discussion. A generation of readers was at war with the poet.

One of the original reviewers of *Poems and Ballads*, whose review in the *Athenaeum* was published on the same day as Morley's, was the poet Robert Buchanan. Buchanan persisted in a series of attacks on Swinburne, and then in the *Contemporary Review* for October 1871, under the pseudonym 'Thomas Maitland', he published a review of the fifth edition of Rossetti's 1870 volume, with the title 'The Fleshly School of Poetry: Mr. D. G. Rossetti'. This triggered a further war of words, the nature of which was unprecedented in Victorian reviewing of poetry.

Buchanan linked Swinburne with Rossetti as members of the sub-Tennysonian 'Fleshly School' of poetry. For once a Victorian reviewer engaged in a version of 'minute criticism'. Buchanan quoted lines and segments from various of Rossetti's *House of Life* sonnets as illustrations of their erotic content, in a manner which suggested, as W. E. Houghton and G. Robert Stange observe, that he was rather enjoying some of the 'fleshly' aspects which he was condemning. The tone of the review was curious:

> Passages like these are the common stock of the walking gentlemen of the fleshly school. We cannot forbear expressing our wonder, by the way, at the kind of women whom it seems the unhappy lot of these gentlemen to encounter. We have lived as long in the world as they have, but never yet came across persons of the other sex who conduct themselves in the manner described. Females who bite, scratch, scream, bubble, munch, sweat, writhe, twist, wriggle, foam, and in a general way slaver over their lovers, must surely possess some extraordinary qualities to counteract their otherwise most offensive mode of conducting themselves. It appears, however, on examination, that their poet-lovers conduct themselves in a similar manner. They, too, bite, scratch, scream, bubble, munch, sweat, writhe, twist, wriggle, foam and slaver, in a style frightful to hear of . . . We get very weary of this protracted hankering after a person of the other sex; it seems meat, drink, thought, sinew, religion for the fleshly school. There is no limit to the fleshliness, and Mr. Rossetti finds in it its own religious justification. (Houghton and Stange 1968: 893)

Rossetti's response in the *Athenaeum* (16 December 1871), entitled 'The Stealthy School of Criticism', was also an exercise in 'minute criticism' of a kind, taking on Buchanan line by line, passage by passage, refuting the charge of eroticism. But his most telling point was Buchanan's pseudonymity, writing as he did from 'behind his mask'. The article concluded: 'And thus the sheath of deceit which this pseudonymous undertaking presents at the outset insures in fact what will be found to be its real character to the core.' Rossetti's counter-attack bore his signature.

The use of a pseudonym, as Rossetti implied, was a sign of cowardice all the more shaming in the 1870s, when signature was the norm. The move from anonymity had taken place gradually from the late 1850s, with profuse and impassioned arguments on both sides. Whether reviews gained in authority or sincerity as a result remains the subject of debate now, as it did then. Most of the poets reviewed between 1830 and 1870 had experienced both conventions, although in the intimate world of poetry reviewing no reviewer's anonymity remained intact for long.

The reviewers of poetry took fewer risks than reviewers of fiction. There was less of an urge to seek out new talent, to review a single volume of poetry by a new poet. Whereas 'New Novels' and 'Recent Fiction' were frequently used as headings for collective reviews of a range of work by new novelists, poetry reviewers played safe, focusing on individual and usually known poets, thus building into their reviewing a process of canon formation and reinforcement. Occasionally reviewers took a larger snapshot, but these were almost always of poets on the margins. It is significant that two well-known instances of survey-reviews were directed towards working-class and women poets.

In his introduction to *The Victorian Poet: Poetics and Persona* (1987), a collection of contemporary reviews of poetry, Joseph Bristow notes apologetically that he could find no reviews of women poets substantial enough to warrant reprinting. H. N. Coleridge's essay 'Modern English Poetesses' in the *Quarterly Review* for 1840 is helpful in explaining this failure. Coleridge's review, which encompassed volumes by Caroline Norton, Elizabeth Barrett, Caroline Clive, Caroline Bowles Southey and his wife Sara Coleridge, was a model of masculine condescension. His critical faculties deserted him, and his eyes misted over, he began, when he saw the engraving of the 'poetess' on the frontispiece of each volume. To his credit his 'nine Muses' were astutely selected, and he acknowledged the absence of 'emeritae' like Felicia Hemans, Letitia Landon and Joanna Baillie. And the impact of the extensive quotations from each of the nine, as Armstrong suggests, should not be underestimated. Four years later, R. H. Horne termed Coleridge's article not merely a 'tribute of admiration' but 'a tribute of justice' (1844: II, 131).

More impressive in its critical judgements as well as in its perspicacity is Charles Kingsley's lengthy review-article 'Burns and his School' (1851). That the author of *Yeast* and *Alton Locke* should be interested in working men's poetry is perhaps not surprising. Kingsley traced the influence of Burns on fellow Scots Robert Nicoll, John and Alexander Bethune, William Thom and Alexander Whitelaw. He was critical of the tone of 'deliberate savageness' in the work of Ebenezer Elliott, the so-called 'Corn-Law Rhymer', the one discordant voice in his working-class tradition. The work of individual poets is celebrated without condescension, and popular poetry is saluted as 'an agent of incalculable power in moulding the minds of nations'.

The move towards a more recognizably 'modern' style of reviewing can be seen in the poetry reviews in the *Athenaeum* in the 1880s and 1890s. Rosemary Scott (1996), in a comparative snapshot of poetry reviewing in the weekly in 1851 and 1881, identifies the change with Theodore Watts-Dunton's tenure as chief poetry reviewer from 1876. It was Watts-Dunton who secured the services of a number of women poets, and it was at this time too that the appearance of the weekly changed, with larger type fonts for both text and quotations. As Marysa Demoor (2000) points out, the suggestion that technical language and practical criticism played little part in Victorian reviewing of poetry is countered by the *Athenaeum*'s sustained attention to the formal properties of poetry in this period, and its emphasis, too, on close quotation. The latter was not the expansive 'sampling' favoured by mid-Victorian reviews, but carefully focused quotations which were illustrative of the reviewers' points.

In his obituary of Augusta Webster, Watts-Dunton (1894) claimed that 'as a conscientious and painstaking critic . . . she had no superior, scarcely an equal'. Her reviews of poetry, more than 200 in total in the late 1880s and early 1890s, outnumber those of Watts-Dunton himself (Demoor 2000: 114.) The anonymous reviews were those of a practitioner, a successful and confident poet in her own right. She was tough, knowledgeable and at times crisply dismissive, as with William Allingham's *Flower Pieces and Other Poems* (Webster 1889b): 'We ask for something better from a man of Mr. Allingham's repute and ability.' She considered Robert Bridges's *Eros and Psyche* not a patch on William

Morris's treatment of the story in *The Earthly Paradise*: 'If Mr. Bridges had known it he would scarcely have spent his poet's pains on retelling the tale Mr. William Morris has told' (Webster 1886). George Barlow's *The Pageant of Life: An Epic Poem in Five Books* she considered mistitled: 'Treating it as a collection of verse, we can say that the language and versification are well up to the average, and that there are poems and portions of poems which are acceptable reading – although with few or none of those touches of pathos or unstrained force which denote the true poet' (1889a). She wrote scathingly of Wilfrid Scawen Blunt's preface to *A New Pilgrimage and other Poems*: 'He has taken it into his head to set forth in what his sort of sonnet excels the Petrarchan sort, and to teach all English poets present or future how the sonnet should be written . . . On the whole Mr. Wilfrid Blunt would be wise to desist from reforming English poetry and content himself with trying to write his best' (1890a). Webster knew a thing or two about sonnets, as a subsequent review of Samuel Waddington's *A Century of Sonnets* (1890b) makes clear: 'The more perfect the sonnet the more the art that went to its making is concealed, but, whatever its inspiration, the sonnet derives more from art than does any other of the serious forms of poetic expression, and it can never throw off a slight artificial constraint which is one of its beauties.' In contrast to the irritable tone which pervaded the reviews of some of her male contemporaries, her praise of *Underneath the Bough* by 'Michael Field' (Katherine Bradley and Edith Cooper) was a cause for celebration by the two women poets:

> The intellectual strength and originality – the acquired mannerism – the rich condensed expression – the fine intensity, planned and dominatingly present, yet skilfully kept half concealed – the splendid control of metre . . . – are, while always recognizable in any of Michael Field's songs and brief separate lyrics, brought into still stronger prominence as essential characteristics by the close kindred resemblance apparent when these poems are grouped together.(Webster 1893)

Field's journal entry for the following day recorded: 'the *Athenaeum* review of *Underneath the Bough* is taken up to a high knoll top, encircled with bushes of oak. We read, rejoice, dance madly, pluck the oak apples' (quoted in Demoor 2000: 117).

The history of Victorian reviewing of poetry is the history of innumerable reputations. One persuasive testimony to the impact of reviews and of critics on the professional lives of poets is contained in the introductory essays in A. H. Miles's monumental ten-volume anthology *The Poets and the Poetry of the Century* (1891–7). The essays were the work of late nineteenth-century critics who offered retrospective assessments of their subjects – assessments which were shot through with the words of their Victorian reviewers. 'It is unnecessary to linger among these "cobwebs of criticism"', Samuel Waddington inserts apologetically, bringing himself up short after a detailed account of Arnold's treatment at the hands of his critics (V, 92). But this is precisely what most of the introductory sections provide – a digest of contemporary critical assessments. Old arguments are revisited, telling phrases repeated, critical foresight and blindness related in a series of quotations that, while truncated, still convey some of the texture of the original reviews. Miles and his colleagues offer a history of the reviewing of Victorian poetry in ten volumes.

Oscar Wilde's cynical remark in 'The Soul of Man under Socialism' (1890) was, as Joseph Bristow (1987: 23) has observed, historically accurate:

> In England, the arts that have escaped best are the arts in which the public take no interest. Poetry is an instance of what I mean. We have been able to have fine poetry in England because the public do not read it, and consequently do not influence it. The public like to insult poets because they are individual, but once they have insulted them, they leave them alone.

By the 1890s poetry had been moved to the margins. Yet paradoxically the crowds who thronged the streets of London to witness Tennyson's funeral two years later, as Edmund Gosse pointed out, were in marked contrast to the handful who had attended Wordsworth's funeral in 1850. An editorial in the *National Observer* ('The Cheapening of Poetry' 1892) was quick to quash any suggestion that there had been a change of heart as regards popular perceptions of poetry: 'For the noisy demonstrations of the street and of the press are all unconcerned with literature and honour was paid to Alfred Tennyson by the Mob, not because the Many-Headed Monster reads or understands his poetry, but because it saw in his funeral the chance of a pageant and a bustle.' Referring to an article by Edmund Gosse in the *New Review*, the editorial insisted that it was up to the critics of poetry to reinforce the point that literary merit was not commensurate with popularity:

> The critic who is worthy his name and office will still insist that books and poems are not to be esteemed, like loaves of bread or pots of ale, by the number of their purchasers; that popularity, save in such rare instances as Tennyson's, is the most fallible of tests; that literature exists of itself and for itself; that the wail of grief which was put up at Tennyson's death can affect English poetry neither for evil nor for good. For poetry dwells apart from the People, and needs no influence for its production save the genius of the Poet.

Poetry may have been moved to the margins, but the role of the poet, and of the critic too, appears not to have been diminished. The reviewing culture which had scrutinized the poets and their work with such earnestness and had produced such intense debate, about the role of the poet, the function of poetry and the proper subject for poetry, was about to move, with the end of the Victorian era, into a new phase.

See also: THE MARKET.

REFERENCES AND FURTHER READING

Armstrong, Isobel (ed.) (1972) *Victorian Scrutinies: Reviews of Poetry 1830–1870*. London: Athlone Press.

Arnold, Matthew (1864) 'The Function of Criticism at the Present Time', *National Review*, 19, 320–51. Reprinted in Matthew Arnold (1865). *Essays in Criticism First Series*. London: Macmillan.

Arnold, Matthew (1923) *The Unpublished Letters of Matthew Arnold*. Ed. A. Whitridge. New Haven: Yale University Press.

Aytoun, W. E. (1854) '*Firmilian: A Tragedy.*' *Blackwood's Magazine*, 75, 533–51.

Bagehot, Walter (1864) 'Wordsworth, Tennyson and Browning; or, Pure, Ornate and Grotesque Art in English Poetry.' Reprinted in Walter

Bagehot (1884). *Literary Studies* (II, 338–90). London: Longmans, Green.

Blain, Virginia (2001) 'Women Poets and the Challenge of Genre.' In Joanne Shattock (ed.). *Women and Literature in Britain 1800–1900* (pp. 164–90). Cambridge: Cambridge University Press.

Brake, Laurel (1994) *Subjugated Knowledges: Journalism, Gender and Literature in the Nineteenth Century*. London: Macmillan.

Bristow, Joseph (ed.) (1987) *The Victorian Poet: Poetics and Persona*. London: Croom Helm.

Browning, Robert (1900) *The Letters of Robert Browning and Elizabeth Barrett Barrett 1845–46*. 2 vols. London: Smith, Elder.

Buchanan, Robert (1871) 'The Fleshly School of Poetry: Mr. D. G. Rossetti.' In W. E. Houghton and G. Robert Stange (eds) (1968). *Victorian Poetry and Poetics*. Second edition (pp. 888–98). Boston: Houghton, Mifflin.

'The Cheapening of Poetry' (1892) *National Observer*, 5 November, 624–5.

[Coleridge, H. N.] (1840) 'Modern English Poetesses.' *Quarterly Review*, 66, 374–418.

Collins, Thomas J. and Vivienne J. Rundle (eds) (2000) *The Broadview Anthology of Victorian Poetry and Poetic Theory*. Peterborough, Ont.: Broadview Press.

Coulling, Sidney (1974) *Matthew Arnold and his Critics: A Study of Arnold's Controversies*. Athens, Ohio: Ohio University Press.

Dawson, Carl (ed.) (1973) *Matthew Arnold: The Critical Heritage*. London: Routledge and Kegan Paul.

Demoor, Marysa (2000) *Their Fair Share: Women, Power and Criticism in the Athenaeum, from Millicent Garrett Fawcett to Katherine Mansfield, 1870–1920*. Aldershot: Ashgate.

Gill, Stephen (1998) *Wordsworth and the Victorians*. Oxford: Clarendon Press.

Horne, R. H. (1844) *A New Spirit of the Age*. London: Smith, Elder. Reprinted (1971) Farnborough: Gregg.

Houghton, W. E., and Robert Stange (eds) (1968) *Victorian Poetry and Poetics*. Second edition. Boston: Houghton Mifflin.

Hyder, Clyde K. (ed.) (1970) *Swinburne: The Critical Heritage*. London: Routledge and Kegan Paul.

Jump, John D. (ed.) (1967) *Tennyson: The Critical Heritage*. London: Routledge and Kegan Paul.

Kent, Christopher (1969) 'Higher Journalism and the Mid-Victorian Clerisy.' *Victorian Studies*, 13, 181–98.

[Kingsley, Charles] (1851) 'Burns and his School.' Reprinted in Charles Kingsley (1890). *Literary and General Lectures and Essays* (pp. 127–84). London: Macmillan.

Knowles, James (1893) 'Aspects of Tennyson II.' *Nineteenth Century*, January 1893, 164–88.

Latané, David E., Jr (1999) 'Literary Criticism.' In Herbert F. Tucker (ed.). *A Companion to Victorian Literature and Culture* (pp. 388–404). Oxford: Blackwell.

Litzinger, Boyd, and Donald Smalley (eds) (1970) *Browning: The Critical Heritage*. London: Routledge and Kegan Paul.

Martin, R. B. (1980) *Tennyson: The Unquiet Heart*. Oxford: Clarendon Press.

Masson, David (1853) 'Theories of Poetry and a New Poet.' *North British Review*, 19, 297–344.

Miles, A. H. (ed.) (1891–7) *The Poets and the Poetry of the Century*. 10 vols. London: Hutchinson.

Parrinder, Patrick (1977) *Authors and Authority: A Study of English Literary Criticism and its Relation to Culture*. London: Routledge.

Ricks, Christopher (1972) *Tennyson*. London: Macmillan.

Rossetti, D. G. (1871) 'The Stealthy School of Criticism.' *Athenaeum*, 16 December, 792–4.

Scott, Rosemary (1996) 'Poetry in the Athenaeum: 1851 and 1881.' *Victorian Periodicals Review*, 29. 1, 19–32.

Shannon, Edgar Finley, Jr (1952) *Tennyson and the Reviewers*. Cambridge, Mass.: Harvard University Press.

Watts-Dunton, Theodore (1894) 'Mrs Augusta Webster.' *Athenaeum*, 15 September, 355.

[Webster, Augusta] (1886) 'Eros and Psyche.' *Athenaeum*, 3 April, 450–5.

[Webster, Augusta] (1889a) 'Recent Verse.' *Athenaeum*, 13 April, 470–1.

[Webster, Augusta] (1889b) 'Flower Pieces, and Other Poems.' *Athenaeum*, 18 May, 623–4.

[Webster, Augusta] (1890a) 'A New Pilgrimage and Other Poems.' *Athenaeum*, 1 March, 271–2.

[Webster, Augusta] (1890b) 'A Century of Sonnets.' *Athenaeum*, 5 April, 428–9.

[Webster, Augusta] (1893) 'Underneath the Bough.' *Athenaeum*, 9 September, 345–6.

Weinstein, Mark A. (1968) *W. E. Aytoun and the 'Spasmodic' Controversy*. New Haven: Yale University Press.

Woolford, John (1982) 'Periodicals and the Practice of Literary Criticism.' In Joanne Shattock and Michael Wolff (eds). *The Victorian Periodical Press: Samplings and Soundings* (pp. 109–42). Leicester: Leicester University Press.

22

Poetry and Illustration

Lorraine Janzen Kooistra

As the book trade in the Victorian period changed from cottage industry to international big business, publishers became increasingly adept at identifying and expanding target markets of consumers. Nowhere was this entrepreneurial spirit more evident than in the production of books of verses, for then as now the publication of poetry was the area of the trade least likely to turn a profit. As Alexander Macmillan told an aspiring poet at mid-century, it was the publisher's business 'to calculate what will commercially pay. Unless it will there is no reason why it should be printed.' Macmillan expressed two insights into the profitable publication of poetry that seem to have been generally shared by his fellow publishers, as they clearly underpinned the industry's marketing strategy throughout the century. The first was that 'People who want to read poetry generally buy it.' While Mudie's Circulating Library might exert extraordinary control over the production and reception of contemporary fiction and prose non-fiction, there remained a niche market open to the enterprising publisher who knew how to package poetry. This is where Macmillan's second insight comes into play. 'You don't know the influence of prettiness on even sensible people', he explained to his brother Daniel when they launched their joint publishing business (see Graves 1910: 196, 67). Victorian publishers like Routledge and Moxon at mid-century, and John Lane at the *fin de siècle*, capitalized on the fact that a book's 'prettiness' could be used to attract consumers for whom an illustrated volume of poetry, displayed in a lady's drawing room or an aesthete's private library, provided a visible sign of the owner's cultivation and refinement. Over the course of the century, publishers learned that pictures and poetry were a winning combination in the giftbook market that dominated each year's increasingly large Christmas season.

Technological developments and social changes accompanied the production and reception of illustrated poetry in its various forms through three broadly defined phases: the annuals of the 1830s and 1840s; the giftbooks of the 1860s; and the *belles lettres* of the *fin de siècle*. At the beginning of Victoria's reign books were luxury items even in middle-class homes. By the end of the century decreasing costs and the economies of scale made books of all kinds affordable to a new mass reading public. Simultaneous advances in pictorial reproduction made illustrations the norm even in books for adults. From the 1840s stereotyping – and, later, electrotyping – permitted publishers to reissue proven good sellers profitably (Altick 1967: chs 12 and 13; Wakeman 1973).

With the development of the wood-engraving industry in the following decade publishers were quick to see that reprint sales could be enhanced, and perhaps directed at a wider market, by the addition of pictures specially commissioned to accompany well-known verses that had already demonstrated their saleability. This new departure in the publication of illustrated poetry built on the market established earlier by the annuals, but took it in new directions. In the thirties and forties, the main selling feature of the popular annuals was the steel-engraved reproductions of contemporary art works. In a reversal of what later became standard illustrative practice, it was the letterpress that was commissioned to go with the pictures. The steel plates adapted in the 1820s had much greater durability than the copper plates used early in the century, enabling the production of the illustrated annuals in print runs as high as 10,000 or 15,000. The shift from steel to wood as the preferred method of pictorial reproduction at mid-century meant that even larger print runs could be produced, and with greater speed and decreased cost. Moreover, wood engraving permitted pictures to be printed with the letterpress, allowing for the introduction of vignettes, head- and tail-pieces around the verses, and a potentially much closer relationship between image and text. Another important technical innovation was the development of photography. The ability to photograph the artists' drawings onto the surface of the wood block as a guide to the engraver came as early as the 1860s. However, the full potential of photography as a means of pictorial reproduction was not realized until the 1880s, when the adaptation of process blocks inaugurated a completely new era in illustrated books (Wakeman 1973: 76–9, 104; McLean 1972).

Along with these technological developments in printing and mass reproduction, social, economic and aesthetic changes affected the production, distribution and reception of illustrated books in the period. The expansion of the railway brought with it an enhanced distribution system, the development of provincial publishing houses, and the cultivation of reading as a regular practice. Moreover, the shift in population to urban centres provided a concentrated market, while the increase in literacy, leisure and disposable income contributed the necessary conditions for the development of a society of book buyers (Altick 1967: 306). At the same time, publishers were increasingly aware of the power of pictures to sell books to newly literate, or newly leisured, readers. Joseph Cundall, for example, established at mid-century a series of 'Illustrated Present Books' – small booklets of poetry with wood engravings on each page – to be given as gifts, prizes or rewards to deserving children (McLean 1972: 145). Throughout the period, many publishers produced similar books for Christmas and birthday giving as well as for school prizes. The combination of uplifting poetry and beautiful pictures was intended to cultivate both moral sensibility and aesthetic taste in the recipient.

Giftbooks on a grander scale were the Christmas annuals of the early period and their immediate followers, the sumptuous quartos of the 1860s. Despite their high prices, these volumes of illustrated poetry sold very well. The illustrated anthologies of the sixties, for instance, often remained in print well into the eighties. Assuming that the largest readership was found in middle-class women and the young, publishers specifically targeted this sector of the consumer market, particularly in the months leading up to Christmas (Haass 1985: 57). Starting in the 1840s, the Christmas trade grew dramatically, until October to December regularly saw the largest concentration of annual sales (Eliot 1995). Illustrated collections and anthologies appealed to the middle-class consumer looking not only for a suitable gift for a wife or daughter, but also for an object whose display value would enhance his own status as a discerning person of cultivated taste. Given the intended destination of such books – the Victorian drawing-room – it is not surprising that the largest group of illustrated titles after children's books belonged to religious works and secular poetry books (Goldman 1994: 26–9).

With the establishment of the Pre-Raphaelite Brotherhood at mid-century the juxta-position, collaboration and even cannibalization of 'Art and Poetry' (the terms signifi-cantly conjoined on the titlepage of their short-lived organ, the *Germ*) received a new impetus that was to last to the end of the century and beyond. Fundamental to the Pre-Raphaelite innovation was a new concern with illustration. For the first time, artists of the first rank entered the field of literary illustration for commercial books without loss of status. And they brought with them a new approach to the genre, one which empha-sized illustration's function as the imaginative interpretation of a text by an artist who was the writer's equal partner in the production of meaning. The enormous growth in illustrated periodicals that took place at this time developed a receptive public eager for pictorial material of all kinds. Poets who wanted their work to sell, whether in magazine or in book form, frequently had to submit to having their verses visually interpreted.

Alfred Tennyson, who (after Longfellow) was the period's most illustrated poet, was a reluctant collaborator at best, and a subversive one at worst. A confirmed literalist when it came to visual representation, the laureate was convinced that 'an illustrator ought never to add anything to what he finds in the text', according to William Holman Hunt's tes-timony (Hunt 1913: I, 95). Unhappy with the results of the Moxon illustrated edition of his *Poems* in 1857, Tennyson tried to prevent the publication of *The Princess* in 1860 with illustrations by Daniel Maclise. Yet when *Enoch Arden* (1864) quickly sold out its first edition of 60,000, even the poet recognized that he could sell the book again to another market by putting out an illustrated edition. Arthur Hughes illustrated *Enoch Arden* in 1866 to rave reviews in the press and brisk sales in the shops. And for several years an expectant Christmas market looked forward to folio editions of *Idylls of the King* with illus-trations by Gustave Doré (1867–9). Tennyson may not have liked sharing the acclaim with another artist, or enduring what he viewed as visual misprisions of his work, but he could not ignore the commercial viability of reissuing his poetry in illustrated form.

Reviewers helped develop the market for illustrated poetry and define its parameters. The *Athenaeum*, for instance, regularly featured reviews of illustrated books under the head-ings 'Fine Arts' or 'Gift Books', suggesting that the books were targeted as much at the educated art lover as at the refined reader of poetry – and, perhaps, also at those who wished to be *seen* as cultivated and *au courant*. In keeping with the growing Christmas market, the amount of letterpress devoted to such reviews always expanded in November and December. The *Bookseller* produced lists 'of illustrated and other Books suitable for

Presents, School Prizes or Rewards with numerous specimens of the Illustrations' in their special Christmas number. Samuel Lucas, who wrote reviews of illustrated books in *The Times*, became the first editor of *Once a Week*, arguably the greatest of the mid-century illustrated magazines. His influence on illustration was therefore both theoretical and practical, and his view 'that the details of any illustration must be in harmony with the spirit of the work illustrated' (see Buckler 1952: 929) was widely shared by his contemporaries.

Illustrated poetry, then, was a significant part of Victorian visual and literary culture, and with its proliferation, a new discourse on illustration began to emerge, as well as a whole literature about books. Victorian illustrated poetry must be situated within this changing theoretical discourse about the proper relations between art and literature, as well as within the varying material contexts of its production. As recent studies in the history of the book have shown, the meaning of a literary work emerges from the intersection of linguistic and bibliographic codes within a cultural context always in process (McGann 1991). We do disservice to our understanding of the poetry of the Victorian period by failing to take into account all the variations of its material existence, including its appearance with illustrations. With that in mind, then, let us turn to an examination of the production and reception of particular books of illustrated poetry under the changing social, economic, technological and aesthetic circumstances in the nineteenth-century world of authors, artists, publishers and readers.

Early Victorian Annuals

In a sonnet written in 1846 William Wordsworth considered the pairing of pictures and poetry that characterized the best-selling annuals and parlour albums of the day to be a sign of social atrophy and intellectual degeneration. Like Tennyson in his *In Memoriam* sequence then in progress, Wordsworth couched his criticism in evolutionary discourse. Illustrated poetry was evidence of regression to a lower, more material, stage of life. The poet associates pictures with the childlike and primitive, which are in turn – in a surprising move for Wordsworth – associated not with innocence and spiritual elevation, but rather with a dangerous femininity undermining a noble masculine culture:

> Now prose and verse sunk into disrepute
> Must lacquey a dumb Art that best can suit
> The taste of this once-intellectual Land.
> A backward movement surely have we here,
> From manhood – back to childhood; for the age –
> Back towards caverned life's first rude career.
> Avaunt this vile abuse of pictured page!
> Must eyes be all in all, the tongue and ear
> Nothing? Heaven keep us from a lower stage!
> (*Poetical Works* 1966: 383)

Underlying Wordsworth's polemic is a fear of feminine subversion. Illustration theory in the nineteenth century assumed a hierarchical model for image/text relations based on a sexual paradigm. Critics identified the pictorial as a lesser art associated with such 'feminine' attributes as imitation, sympathy, charm, grace and beauty, and the verbal as a superior art associated with such 'masculine' attributes as intellect, power and mastery (see Kooistra 1995: 9–10). Wordsworth's hostility to the 'pictured page' thus reproduces not only contemporary concerns about image/text relations, but also prevailing cultural attitudes about relations between the sexes.

In the context of publishing history, Wordsworth's anxiety is not only theoretical but also practical and social, for the annuals were indeed a woman-centred genre, written and edited largely (though not exclusively) by women for women. Encased in elaborate bindings of watered silk, velvet and tooled leather, the typical annual consisted of a series of steel-engraved plates reproducing the art work of contemporary painters, usually drawn from three classes of painting: portraiture, landscape and genre. Women writers provided most of the verbal 'illustrations' accompanying the steel engravings. Often, the female editor herself would supply the illustrative letterpress. First L. E. L. (Letitia Elizabeth Landon) and then Caroline Norton provided all the verses for the thirty-six plates in *Fisher's Drawing-Room Scrap-Book*. Lady Blessington wrote much of the letterpress for *Heath's Book of Beauty* when she took over the editorship from L. E. L. and later for *The Keepsake* as well, while Mary Russell Mitford was responsible for much of the writing when she began to edit *Finden's Tableaux*.

Writing for (and editing) the annuals was, in fact, one of the most lucrative means of earning a livelihood for women in early Victorian England. When Lady Blessington took over the editorship of *The Keepsake* in 1840 (and continued to edit the *Book of Beauty*) she was probably the highest-paid woman in the country, earning between £2,000 and £3,000 a year (Adburgham 1972: 250). Women writers like Mary Shelley, Mary Mitford, Mary Howitt, Anna Barbauld and L. E. L. were able to gain steady employment and a liveable income from their contributions to the annuals (Renier 1964: 14). The combination of a sound economic base and irreproachable content made the annuals an ideal venue for women looking to improve their income or career without loss of status. As a result, the women editors of these annuals went out of their way to network with other women writers, encouraging and cajoling them to send in contributions. No wonder contemporary male writers looked askance at the annuals as a site of potentially subversive female power.

Elizabeth Barrett Browning's contributions to *Finden's Tableaux*, edited by Mary Russell Mitford, provide a good example of this woman's community at work. Barrett Browning met Mitford in the spring of 1836, when the poet was 30 and the well-known writer of prose idylls was 49. A year later, when Mitford took on the editorship of *Finden's Tableaux*, her first thought was to include her young friend in the publication. At this point in her career, Barrett Browning had not yet published her first book of original verse on the commercial market, and the invitation was taken as a great kindness. Yet Mitford was not asking Barrett Browning to send in any contribution she might have on hand. She was asking her specifically 'to write me a poem in illustration of a very charming group of

Plate 1   India. Steel engraving by H. Eagleton after a painting by J. Brown, reproduced opposite 'A Romance of the Ganges' by Elizabeth Barrett, in *Finden's Tableaux* (pub. Tilt, 1838), facing p. 29. By permission of the Victoria and Albert Picture Library.

Hindoo girls floating their lamps upon the Ganges'; to write it in stanzas 'long enough for two large pages'; and to provide 'it within a fortnight or three weeks if possible' – all for a payment of £5 (Raymond and Sullivan 1987: 10–11). Mitford clearly saw this as a chance to boost the profile and career of her protégée. Recognizing the friendly mentorship, Barrett Browning professed herself happy to provide letterpress for J. Brown's painting of the Indian scene. The result was 'A Romance of the Ganges', a ballad in twenty-three stanzas (plate 1).

Mitford was prepared to send Barrett Browning the proof of the engraving immediately, but the poet did not require it; she remembered seeing the painting at the Royal Academy and was willing to return to the exhibition to refresh her memory before undertaking the commission. Barrett Browning's familiarity with Brown's painting suggests how desirable the engravings in the annuals must have been for art lovers who did not have easy access to London's art shows; the engravings provided them with a portable gallery of some of the year's popular paintings to peruse at their leisure. The selected picture, too, seems particularly appropriate for the targeted audience. Like many of the engravings ornamenting these parlour albums, the subject matter focuses on a beautiful woman (or women) in a romantic situation – in this case, the exotic East. In her poem, Barrett Browning develops a dialogue between two of the Indian maids floating their lamps on the river as a traditional test of a lover's fidelity in order to explore male betrayal on a number of levels. In other words, she uses the exotic, romanticized, feminine 'other' of the painting as an opportunity to make a statement on behalf of women and their lot. In the ballad she provided for the following Christmas's issue of *Finden's*, 'The Romaunt of the Page', Barrett Browning similarly uses the engraving after a romantic painting by W. Perring as a pre-text for her attack on the presuppositions of chivalry and its patriarchal trappings.

Empowered by a publishing community of women readers, writers and editors, Barrett Browning clearly finds the annual's elevation of picture over word a liberating rather than limiting opportunity, enabling her to explore other areas in which the feminine might take precedence over the masculine. But she was also willing to have the aesthetic tables turned, and subject her original poetry to the visual interpretation of the artist. When the illustrated periodicals began to emerge at the end of the 1850s with the widespread adaptation of wood engraving as the predominant means of pictorial reproduction, Barrett Browning sent some of her poems to the *Cornhill Magazine*. Frederic Leighton illustrated 'The Great God Pan' for the July 1860 issue and 'Ariadne at Naxos' in December of the same year. Along with the *Cornhill Magazine*, other outstanding illustrated magazines such as *Once a Week* and *Good Words* brought pictorial work by the best contemporary draughtsmen to a larger audience, and on a more frequent basis, than ever before. Priced moderately at a shilling, and published on a weekly or monthly basis, these periodicals completely supplanted the now old-fashioned and expensive annuals of the thirties and forties, whose price at 12*s* put them beyond the means of all but the comfortably well-to-do. In place of the annuals rose a new kind of Christmas giftbook: the collection or anthology with original wood-engraved drawings reproduced as decorative and interpretative accompaniments for the poetry. These giftbooks characterize the 'golden age' in British book illustration known as 'the sixties', a period which actually occupied the decades stretching from 1855 to 1875.

Giftbooks of the Sixties

The year 1857 offers a convenient date for identifying a significant change in the history of illustrated poetry in Victorian England. This year saw the last *Keepsake* for the

Christmas market – taken by many critics to mark the dying gasp of the annuals – and the publication of two important giftbooks which ushered in the sixties, Edward Moxon's illustrated edition of Tennyson's *Poems* and the first of the 'Dalziels' Fine Art Gift Books' published under the Routledge imprint, Willmott's *The Poets of the Nineteenth Century*. Each of these in its own way represents the sea change in illustrated poetry that came about as a result of two important influences: the technological development of wood engraving; and the aesthetic innovation of the Pre-Raphaelite artists and their followers.

The Poets of the Nineteenth Century and the Moxon *Tennyson* are characteristic sixties books for a number of reasons. Both were initiated by a publisher with an eye to the market, and both were collaborative projects involving many producers. Willmott's anthology not only involved the editor and the poets he selected, many of whom – such as Robert Browning, Alfred Tennyson, Elizabeth Barrett Browning, Charles Kingsley, William Allingham, Charles Mackay, Alexander Smith and Mary Howitt, to name but a sampling – were living. *The Poets of the Nineteenth Century* also included eighteen different artists for the 100 engravings produced by various workers at the Dalziel Brothers' firm. Such multi-artist books, in which poems would be farmed out to various illustrators and engravers with little thought given to the effect such a variety of style and approach might have on the overall design, were characteristic of the period.

The book whose clash of incongruent styles has made it a by-word for the 'book-cobbling' and 'hodge-podge' design often associated with the sixties book is the Moxon *Tennyson*. Publisher Edward Moxon divided the work among established artists – T. Creswick, W. Mulready, D. Maclise, C. Stanfield, J. C. Horsley – and, for reasons not entirely clear, young artists of an entirely different school: John Millais, William Holman Hunt and Dante Gabriel Rossetti. Moxon also distributed the drawings to a variety of engravers, whose job it was to translate the artists' designs into reproducible woodcuts. The final collaborator in this mix is, of course, the poet himself, who by all accounts was a reluctant member of the team, despite the fact that he had the most to gain. When Moxon showed him an illustrated edition of Keats he had recently published, and assured him the market was such that he could be sure of at least £2,000 – badly needed just then for his new house at Farringford – Tennyson agreed to the proposal. But he did not take much subsequent interest in the drawings until they were cut on the wood. His initial attitude seems to have been that they were simply part of a marketing strategy – if his public wanted them, and would pay for them, they should have them, and there was an end of it (Hagen 1979: 100; Reid 1975: 43). After the fact, however, the poet's view of the matter changed, and he regretted agreeing to an illustrated edition.

In giving his financial assurances to Tennyson, Moxon was, of course, aiming for the Christmas market, when sales of illustrated books were most brisk. While most of the sixties giftbooks were destined for the October-to-December sales season, however, not all of them were able to meet this publishing objective. The nature of collaborative projects dictates that deadlines are not in the control of the publisher, but rather in the various hands of the publisher's partners in production, all of whom have their own schedules and

individual projects to consider. Whenever Dante Gabriel Rossetti was a member of a collaborative project, the book was sure to miss its destined Christmas season. Rossetti's
slowness in producing his drawings meant that all four books he illustrated – William
Allingham's *The Music Master* (1855), Tennyson's *Poems*, and Christina Rossetti's *Goblin
Market and Other Poems* (1862) and *The Prince's Progess and Other Poems* (1866) – came out
in spring rather than autumn, thus missing a large potential market. Moxon was unpre-
pared for the missed Christmas deadline. Anticipating a large demand for a book of illustrations ornamenting the work of the popular laureate, Moxon produced 10,000 copies.
But the illustrated *Poems*, coming out at the wrong season, and priced too highly at a
guinea and a half, was a commercial failure (Hagen 1979: 106–9). In contrast, *The Poets
of the Nineteenth Century* – priced at the usual guinea for an illustrated quarto, and nicely
timed to come out for Christmas gift buyers – sold out its first edition of 5,000 copies
and went into a second edition of 3,000 within the year, with further reissues in 1865,
1868, 1878 and 1885 (Haass 1985: 55).

Another characteristic of the sixties giftbook evident in both *The Poets of the Nineteenth
Century* and the illustrated edition of Tennyson's *Poems* is the close association between letterpress and picture, made possible by the switch from steel plates to wood engraving.
The new reproduction process meant that the pictures could be printed in relief with the
type, thereby permitting the introduction of illustrations into the letterpress. Thereafter
the half-page vignette, most often positioned above the title, became the standard form
for illustration in the period. The practice of introducing poems with headpieces meant
that the reader's reception of the poem would be influenced by the artist's selection and
presentation of the subject. Finally, Pre-Raphaelite pictures combining natural detail
(even their illustrations were produced from models) with symbolic motifs, in designs
unusually black and bold, demanded to be read themselves as visual 'texts' ancillary to
the poem but not necessarily subordinate to it.

Of all the Pre-Raphaelite illustrators, it was the one who produced only a handful of
illustrations who proved to have the most impact on the future direction of Victorian
illustrated poetry. Perhaps because he was himself a poet as well as a painter, Dante Gabriel
Rossetti had some idiosyncratic views on the relations between art and poetry. He had a
personal antipathy to the then popular 'illustrated editions', which he believed often had
the unpleasant effect of 'killing, for oneself and everyone, a distinct idea of the poet's'. He
himself, he claimed, only felt disposed to illustrate 'once a century', a view amply borne
out by his small output of ten illustrations – one for Allingham's *Music Master*, five for
the Moxon *Tennyson*, and four for his sister's first two volumes of poetry. His illustrative
work shows a predilection for narrative poetry consistent with the Pre-Raphaelite anec-
dotal tendency in painting. It also provides practical examples of his theory that the best
verses to illustrate were those narrative poems 'where one can allegorize on one's own hook
on the subject of the poem' without detracting from the poet's conception (Doughty and
Wahl 1965: I, 239, 385).

Understandably, critics of the day were not quite sure what to make of Rossetti's
innovative art. Such a bizarre form of illustration, seemingly 'without the slightest reference to any descriptive line in the poem it professes to illustrate', was 'beyond the pale

of criticism', one reviewer complained, unsure whether the artist were more deserving of 'ridicule' or 'pity'. The illustrations of Hunt and Millais for Tennyson's *Poems* fared only slightly better ('Review of *Poems*' 1857: 231). The poet himself seemed resigned to the illustrations of his friend John Millais, but suspicious of the unlicensed additions evident in the work of Hunt and Rossetti. Holman Hunt records the poet as protesting over his drawing of the Lady of Shalott, with her wildly tossing hair and her figure caught in the entwining web, and Dante Gabriel Rossetti admitted that the Laureate 'loathe[d]' his illustrations (Hunt 1913: 95–6; Doughty and Wahl 1965: I, 325).

The Moxon *Tennyson*, then, presents a contested site in the history of illustrated poetry. What the poet was really protesting against was the right of the reader to interpret and envision a train of associations sparked by the images and situations in his text. It is for this reason that illustrated poetry in the latter part of the nineteenth century becomes so important for understanding poetic (con)texts. Illustration offers the student of Victorian literature a material trace of contemporary readers' responses to a poem, not only in the pictures themselves, but also in the critical reviews assessing the pictures in relation to their poems.

When a single poem is illustrated by a number of different illustrators, it is possible to follow a particularized history of responses to an unchanging set of words whose 'meaning' none the less is always in the process of production by new sets of collaborators and co-producers (readers, illustrators, publishers, critics) in changing circumstances. Tennyson's 'The Lady of Shalott' is a particularly good example of a poem with multiple illustrators. Even in the Moxon edition it is framed by the visual interpretations of two artists: a headpiece by Holman Hunt (plate 2) and a tailpiece by D. G. Rossetti (plate 3); by the end of the Victorian period at least fifty works of art had been based on this ballad.

In their illustrations, Hunt and Rossetti followed good illustrative practice by seizing on significant moments in Tennyson's poem to visualize and interpret for the reader, who had, as a result, two texts to decipher: the poet's verbal one and the artists' visual ones. Hunt depicts the Lady when the 'curse' comes upon her after she defies the prohibition against looking out her window, and the mirror cracks and the web unravels in consequence. Rossetti focuses on the poem's ironic ending, when Lancelot, looking into the dead face of the mysterious Lady, is briefly attracted to her beauty, unaware that her story intersects in any way with his own. Each artist packs an enormous amount of detail into the confines of a small frame, introducing, in the process, personal interpretative symbols as they 'allegorize on their own hooks'.

In addition to the wildly tossing hair and encircling threads objected to by the poet as lacking direct textual referents, Hunt introduces an even more specific and significant symbol of his personal interpretation of the poem, curiously not recorded as being offensive to the laureate: the image of the crucified Christ in the roundel on the right (plate 2). The Christian symbolism has little to do with the immediate world of the poem. It does, however, embody Hunt's personal position as an artist who took art's task of moral elevation very seriously. He later claimed that Tennyson's poem was an allegory repre-

THE LADY OF SHALOTT.

PART I.

I.

On either side the river lie
Long fields of barley and of rye,
That clothe the wold and meet the sky;
And thro' the field the road runs by
  To many-tower'd Camelot;

Plate 2 'The Lady of Shalott.' Wood engraving by J. Thompson after a design by William Holman Hunt for Tennyson's *Poems* (pub. Moxon, 1857), p. 67. By permission of the Thomas Fisher Rare Book Library, University of Toronto.

senting the soul's failure to accept faithfully the high purpose of life. Some of the iconography, however, specifically evokes the images of the 'fallen woman' so ubiquitous in Victorian literature and painting, thus introducing a more secular hermeneutics (see Leng 1991: 323, 320). Hunt's illustration, positioned at the opening of Tennyson's

THE LADY OF SHALOTT.

Died the sound of royal cheer;
And they cross'd themselves for fear,
    All the knights at Camelot:
But Lancelot mused a little space;
He said, " She has a lovely face;
God in his mercy lend her grace,
    The Lady of Shalott."

Plate 3   'The Lady of Shalott.' Wood engraving by the Dalziel Brothers after a design by Dante Gabriel Rossetti for Tennyson's *Poems* (pub. Moxon, 1857), p. 75. By permission of the Thomas Fisher Rare Book Library, University of Toronto.

poem and functioning as a preface or abstract of the whole, invites the reader to consider 'The Lady of Shalott' allegorically. The reader is offered the option of receiving the poem as a general spiritual allegory showing the inevitable downfall of those who follow an earthly rather than a spiritual path in life; or as a specific social allegory expressing anxiety about unlicensed female sexuality. The two readings are not, of course, incompatible.

D. G. Rossetti's tailpiece for 'The Lady of Shalott' (plate 3) provides a summation or 'end note' to the verbal text. By focusing on Sir Lancelot and his response the artist provides an accessible subject position for the reader of the poem, removed from the action and yet subtly drawn into its charm. The knight is trying to 'read' the Lady's inscrutable face, needing to find meaning in her silence. Around him Camelot's active life teems and swells, but his placement in the picture plane separates him from the bustle. Looking down into the beautiful face of the dead woman, her face turned aside from his gaze, Lancelot remains supremely unaware that it was her looking upon him that brought her to this pass. Rossetti's illustration thus responds to the scopic and sexual themes of a text concerned with desire and its limits. His image makes the Lady herself – rather than Hunt's crucified Christ – the icon and spiritual centre of the poem. As visual 'readings' framing Tennyson's poem, Hunt's headpiece and Rossetti's tailpiece offer varied and complex interpretations to guide readers in their own understanding of the poem. It is no wonder that the laureate felt his control of meaning and 'intention' challenged by such a bold pictorial partnership.

Not all poets in the period, however, shared Tennyson's mistrust of illustration as a potentially subversive element undermining authorial control. William Allingham, William Morris and Christina Rossetti stand out as writers who actively sought out opportunities for visual/verbal collaboration. In some ways, Allingham may be seen as the poet who initiated the new approach to pairing pictures and poetry. Along with the Moxon *Tennyson*, it is Allingham's *Music Master* (1855), illustrated by Arthur Hughes, Millais and Rossetti, which critics identify most frequently as the book which launched the wood-engraving revival. It is indeed an important work, not only because it represents the Pre-Raphaelite artists' first foray into illustration, but also because the poet himself played such an active role in the book's production. Unlike the typical sixties book, *The Music Master* was conceived by the poet himself as an illustrated volume. Eager for a well-produced book with a high circulation, Allingham approached Routledge with a proposal to reprint his poems in illustrated form. Subsequently, he conducted a detailed correspondence with the illustrators he himself selected, participating in their choice of subject and commenting on their interpretations in progress. Sensitive to the contemporary market, Allingham was particularly concerned that *The Music Master* be 'a regular *illustrated* book', and not 'merely *a volume with woodcuts*', because he felt this would improve sales to art lovers as well as poetry readers (see Boyd 1995: 20, 21; Roberts 1997: 252–4).

Unlike Tennyson, Allingham was delighted when his illustrators became equal partners in the production of meaning. He persuaded an irate Rossetti, in despair over the Dalziels' cutting of his drawing for 'The Maids of Elfen-Mere', not to remove his illustration from the volume – an act which would have altered the history of Victorian art. Edward Burne-Jones later claimed it was this illustration that made him decide to become an artist. It was not to Rossetti, however, but to his principal illustrator, Arthur Hughes (who produced eight illustrations and four ornamental designs for the book), that Allingham gave special praise. Singling out his extraordinary visualization of 'The Fairies' (plate

Plate 4 'The Fairies.' Wood engraving by the Dalziel Brothers after a design by Arthur Hughes for William Allingham's *The Music Master* (pub. Routledge, 1855), facing p. 19. By permission of the Thomas Fisher Rare Book Library, University of Toronto.

4), Allingham wrote the artist that 'this is an inspiration, direct from Mab, and makes the poet half jealous of the painter as they walk arm in arm' (see Roberts 1997: 14).

Allingham's concern to have a close relationship between image and text and a collaborative ('arm in arm') relationship between artist and poet was shared by William Morris. Morris met Dante Gabriel Rossetti when Burne-Jones effected an introduction after seeing Rossetti's 'Elfen-Mere' illustration in *The Music Master* volume. Thereafter Morris became an important member of Pre-Raphaelitism's second phase, with his own special interest in the making and illustrating of books as both a poet and a designer. He and Burne-Jones initiated an abortive collaborative project in the sixties – an illustrated edition of Morris's *The Earthly Paradise* – but Morris did not publish an illustrated book until he began printing at his own Kelmscott Press at the *fin de siècle*. Thus it was left for Christina Rossetti to realize the Pre-Raphaelite collaborative aesthetic under the conditions of commercial publishing in the sixties.

Christina Rossetti's commitment to producing her poetry in illustrated form was such that she refused to go to print without Dante Gabriel's accompanying woodcuts in her first two volumes, *Goblin Market and Other Poems* (1862) and *The Prince's Progress and Other Poems* (1866), even though this meant losing the Christmas market. In the case of her third book of poetry, *Sing-Song: A Nursery Rhyme Book* (1872), it is evident that she conceived the work as a composite of image and text from the outset: her illustrated manuscript guided the hand of her professional illustrator, Arthur Hughes. The importance of Christina Rossetti's books to the history of illustrated poetry in England cannot be overemphasized. In the age of the illustrated reprint, her books are unique as illustrated first editions. In addition, all three publications went against the general trend of multi-artist books by being the product of a single artist working in conjunction with the poet. Such innovation antici-pates the illustrated poetry of the *fin de siècle* and provides the connecting link between the early Pre-Raphaelites and the later book artists (see Kooistra 1999).

While Dante Gabriel Rossetti was clearly a sensitive reader of his sister's work, he also felt free to 'allegorize on his own hook on the subject of the poem' in his usual way, hon-ouring 'the idea of the poet' but elaborating his own symbolic interpretation. The fron-tispiece illustration for *The Prince's Progress*, 'You Should Have Wept Her Yesterday' (plate 5), for example, supports one of Christina's central motifs by alluding to the parable of the virgins who must watch and pray all night, ready to light their lamps when the expected bridegroom arrives. In this illustration the praying virgins welcome the belated prince to a chamber of death rather than a marriage feast. Six of them are grouped in front of the raised and recessed tomb, while the seventh arrests the prince on the threshold. Dante Gabriel revises the scriptural reference by incorporating seven, rather than five, wise virgins, with seven lamps burning brightly – and uselessly – above the bier of the dead princess whose life of watching and waiting proved so futile.

The artist's intertexts also include a visual iconography specific to his own medium and message, which introduces a new range of allusion and reference not originally included in the poet's verbal text. The six kneeling maidens cite another illustrator's design (and therefore also the poem it accompanies), showing that the wood engravings of illustrated anthologies could influence even so independent and original an artist as Dante Gabriel Rossetti. The artist is clearly drawing on an earlier illustration by John Gilbert for Felicia Hemans's 'Evening Prayer at a Girls' School' (plate 6) in Willmott's *English Sacred Poetry* (1862). A preliminary study for Rossetti's frontispiece drawing includes the desk on either side of which the kneeling maidens, like those in Gilbert's composition, pray (see Surtees 1971: no. 272). The prayer desk has a logical place in Gilbert's design of the girls' school but not in Rossetti's of the princess's bedchamber, and so it was later deleted from the composition. Nevertheless, the visual allusion, with its evocation of Hemans's poem of loss, transience and woman's 'lot' of 'watching . . . / With a pale cheek' with little hope of earthly joy (Willmott 1862: 278), seems a particularly apt intertext for *The Prince's Progress*. Illustrated poetry always brings with it two levels of reference and historical tradition, which may or may not work in concert: the verbal intertexts cited by the poet, and the visual iconography alluded to by the artist. A strong collaborative partnership is one in which the two distinct mediums and their separate messages enhance, extend and enrich each other.

Plate 5 'You Should Have Wept Her Yesterday.' Wood engraving by W. J. Linton after a design by Dante Gabriel Rossetti for the frontispiece to Christina Rossetti's *The Prince's Progress and Other Poems* (pub. Macmillan, 1866). By permission of the Thomas Fisher Rare Book Library, University of Toronto.

EVENING PRAYER AT A GIRLS' SCHOOL.

Hush! 'tis a holy hour—the quiet room
　　Seems like a temple, while yon soft lamp sheds
A faint and starry radiance, through the gloom
　　And the sweet stillness, down on fair young heads,
With all their clust'ring locks, untouch'd by care,
And bow'd, as flowers are bow'd with night, in prayer.

Gaze on—'tis lovely! Childhood's lip and cheek,
　　Mantling beneath its earnest brow of thought—
Gaze—yet what seest thou in those fair and meek,
　　And fragile things, as but for sunshine wrought?—
Thou seest what grief must nurture for the sky,
What death must fashion for Eternity!

277

Plate 6　'Evening Prayer at a Girls' School.' Wood engraving by the Dalziel Brothers after a design
by John Gilbert for Felicia Hemans's poem in R. A. Willmott's *English Sacred Poetry* (pub. Routledge,
1862), p. 277. By permission of the Robertson Davies Library, Massey College, University of Toronto.

While Christina Rossetti's *Goblin Market* and *The Prince's Progress*, like Allingham's *The Music Master*, were intended for a general audience, many of the illustrated gift books of the sixties were directed, like their predecessors the annuals, at a principally female readership, or at least a family setting. Volumes like Willmott's *English Sacred Poetry* (1862), Charles Mackay's *The Home Affections Pourtrayed by the Poets* (1858), and the Dalziels's *Home Thoughts and Home Scenes* (1865), *A Round of Days* (1866) and *Golden Thoughts from Golden Fountains* (1867) were clearly calculated not to bring a blush to the cheek of any young person or lady by anything indiscreet in picture or word. The Dalziels's 'Fine Art Gift Book', *Home Thoughts and Home Scenes*, is a particularly interesting example of the 1860s' modulation of the annuals' practice of marketing writing by women for women. Composed entirely of poems written by women writers (such as Dora Greenwell, Jean Ingelow and the Honourable Mrs Norton, to name a few), and illustrated with pictures of domestic scenes by A. B. Houghton, this remarkable giftbook reproduces its audience in its content and form (plate 7). On publication, the *Daily News* reviewer declared it was 'A work which will be doated over by ladies and which will even be tenderly regarded by those of the male sex who have an amiable fondness for children' (cited in publisher's advertisements).

Such tender sentiment and delicate propriety, however, were abandoned with the new illustrated poetry of the *fin de siècle*. Far from targeting women and children, or even the family drawing room, with ornate quartos in large print runs, publishers in the last years of Victoria's reign discovered a new market in limited or small issues of first editions for an eager audience of aesthetic consumers and collectors. A little shocking or subversive subject matter in picture or print only enhanced the value of these books for the refined aesthete wishing to distinguish himself (and sometimes herself) from the middle-class respectability of Podsnaps and philistines.

Belles Lettres at the *Fin de Siècle*

The early Arts and Crafts movement converged with aestheticism in the 1880s to bring about a new interest in the book as an object of design. Design practitioners and theorists developed a whole new vocabulary for the book that borrowed its language from Gothic architecture. People now 'built' illustrated books and were concerned with the 'architecture' of what Burne-Jones aptly called (referring to the monumental Kelmscott Chaucer, which he had illustrated and Morris had printed) 'pocket cathedral[s]' (Houfe 1992: 39–40). Artists now 'pictured', 'decorated', 'designed', 'ornamented' and even 'embroidered'; they did not 'illustrate'. The relation of picture to type became as important a question as the relation of picture to poem. In short, the page was reconceived as a unit of two-dimensional design and the book as a three-dimensional art object that had the potential to be a thing of beauty as well as utility. The artist took control of the book as a whole in a way that sometimes left both publishers and authors puzzling over the results. In the 1890s the visual held sway over the verbal as never before.

14

Plate 7 'The Enemy on the Wall.' Wood engraving by the Dalziel Brothers after a design by Arthur Boyd Houghton for Dinah Mulock Craik's poem in *Home Thoughts and Home Scenes* (pub. Routledge, 1865), p. 13. By permission of the British Library. Shelfmark 1347 K 15.

The advent of photographic processes for the reproduction of pictures had the effect of eliminating the wood-engraving industry (the Dalziels' firm went bankrupt in 1893) and instigating a new approach to black-and-white illustration through the medium of pen and ink. No longer at the mercy of the engraver's translation of their drawings,

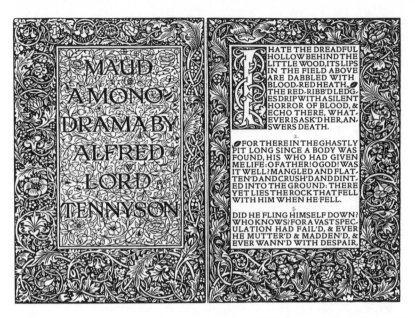

Plate 8   Wood-engraved border design and initial letter by William Morris for Tennyson's *Maud, a Monodrama* (pub. Kelmscott Press, 1893). By permission of the William Andrews Clark Memorial Library, University of California, Los Angeles.

artists were now assured that their lines would be reproduced exactly as they drew them. New art schools, magazines, competitions and exhibitions promoted the development of pen draughtsmanship and book illustration as never before, with the result that the *fin de siècle* produced an even greater number of prolific and talented book artists than had the sixties (Houfe 1992). The rediscovery of the sixties artists by the next generation ironically led to a revival of wood engraving as a craft for producing fine books just as the industry itself as a means of mass production disappeared. Charles Ricketts and William Morris, who founded the Vale Press and the Kelmscott Press respectively, both trained themselves in the art of wood engraving, and produced many decorated initials, borders and pictures for the books they printed (plate 8). Laurence Housman, one of the most remarkable of the period's book artists, had much of his work engraved by his sister, Clemence. Ricketts and Housman were also instrumental in bringing the ideas of fine book production to the commercial market, especially in their work for John Lane. Probably the most enterprising publisher of the decade, Lane, together with his partner Elkin Mathews, published books at the Bodley Head for a cultivated market of consumers who wanted literary objects that would convey their sophisticated taste and superior cultivation. To assist such self-conscious book buyers in purchasing the right books, Lane entitled his catalogue 'A List of Books in Belles Lettres' (Stetz and Lasner 1990: viii).

THE SPHINX

LIFT UP YOUR LARGE BLACK SATIN EYES WHICH ARE LIKE CUSHIONS
WHERE ONE SINKS!
FAWN AT MY FEET FANTASTIC SPHINX! AND SING ME ALL YOUR MEMORIES!

SING TO ME OF THE JEWISH MAID WHO WANDERED WITH THE HOLY CHILD,
AND HOW YOU LED THEM THROUGH THE WILD, AND HOW THEY SLEPT BENEATH
YOUR SHADE.

Plate 9 'The Moon-horned Io.' Process engraving after a design by Charles Ricketts for Oscar Wilde's *The Sphinx* (pub. Elkin Mathews and John Lane, 1894), n.p. By permission of the William Andrews Clark Memorial Library, University of California, Los Angeles.

Lane learned about the marketability of a beautiful book when Oscar Wilde brought him 220 unbound copies of his *Poems*, originally published a decade earlier with David Bogue, and arranged for Charles Ricketts to design a title page, endpapers and cover for a new edition. As an added inducement to the collector, Wilde signed every copy, thus making the limited edition 'immediately saleable'. Like Christina Rossetti, Wilde actively sought to bring out his poetry with the accompaniment of interpretative or decorative designs by a visual artist. Indeed, it was only when Ricketts agreed to illustrate *The Sphinx* that Wilde determined to bring it out as a single-poem publication. While the book's high price (two guineas for ordinary copies, five for the large paper) and Wilde's refusal to send it out for review ultimately resulted in its commercial failure, *The Sphinx* (1894) is, nevertheless, one of the decade's most luxurious and elegantly designed volumes of poetry (Stetz and Lasner 1990: 13–14).

One of the young book artists who, along with Laurence Housman, helped revive the Pre-Raphaelite approach to illustration in the nineties, Ricketts treats Wilde's text in the manner of Rossetti, as an opportunity to 'allegorize on his own hook'. A fascinating example of this independent symbolic development by the artist is the half-page design, 'The Moon-horned Io' (plate 9). Ricketts's illustration recalls Rossetti's famous design of

THE PALACE OF ART.

I BUILT my soul a lordly pleasure-house,
    Wherein at ease for aye to dwell.
I said, " O Soul, make merry and carouse,
    Dear soul, for all is well."

Plate 10 'St Cecilia.' Wood engraving by the Dalziel Brothers after a design by Dante Gabriel Rossetti for 'The Palace of Art' in Alfred Tennyson's *Poems* (pub. Moxon, 1857), p. 113. By permission of the Thomas Fisher Rare Book Library, University of Toronto.

St Cecilia for Tennyson's 'Palace of Art', in which the artist chose to select an incidentally described tapestry rather than a significant moment in the text as the subject for his illustration (plate 10). Like his admired predecessor, Ricketts also seizes on one of the poem's decorative images, a half-line that is simply a part of the speaker's questioning of the Sphinx: 'And did you talk with Thoth, and did you hear the moon-horned Io weep?' There is no textual referent for the design's three supporting women, but the fierce face of the Pre-Raphaelite female with her chin in Io's neck seems to suggest both sexual passion and vampirism. No wonder Wilde teased that his book 'would destroy domesticity in England' (Kooistra 1995: 94–9). Clearly, the collaborators and their publishers had a quite different audience in mind from the domestic family group targeted by the Victorian annuals and giftbooks. In both architecture and design the book embodies the poem's erotic, luxurious and perverse playfulness.

With a shape especially designed to accord with poetic line length and a typeface and distribution on the page responding to the rhythm and mood of the piece, *The Sphinx*'s meaning emerges from both its bibliographic and its linguistic codes. While such a materialist analysis may be applied to all books, it is especially important to an understanding of the illustrated poetry of the *fin de siècle*, when the printed text and illustrative scheme were conceived as a decorative whole by a single guiding hand. Laurence Housman, for example, specially designed a tall, slim, format for Christina Rossetti's *Goblin Market* (1893) to accord with that poem's brief lines, and a shorter, wider, format for the longer lines in Jane Barlow's *The End of Elfintown* (1894). Both of these books were for Macmillan, and both show the strong influence Dante Gabriel Rossetti exerted on his *fin-de-siècle* follower, a fact noted both by contemporary reviewers and by recent critics. The presence of *Goblin Market*'s first illustrator in Housman's designs for that poem is perhaps inevitable, but Rossetti's influence is omnipresent throughout Housman's work. One of his illustrations for *The End of Elfintown*, for example, clearly evokes Rossetti's 'St Cecilia' design for the Moxon *Tennyson* (plate 11; see plate 10).

Housman went on to design many first editions of poetry for John Lane, most limited to 750 copies or fewer and priced well within the grasp of a select book-buying public. Rather than the economies of scale, the enterprising publisher profited from the economy of the esoteric by putting relatively unknown poets into a marketable and attractive package. In 1893 Lane got Housman to design the cover, frontispiece and title page for Francis Thompson's *Poems* (plate 12). Pleased with this first commission, Lane put Housman in charge of book design for Katharine Tynan Hinkson's *Cuckoo Songs* (1894), Edith Nesbit's *A Pomander of Verse* (1895), Francis Thompson's *Sister-Songs* (1895), Charles Newton-Robinson's *The Viol of Love* (1895) and the artist's own *Green Arras* (1896). Typically, Housman used the frontispiece as an occasion to offer a visual statement about the whole of the book, encapsulating his personal, highly symbolic, reading of the work. Like most illustrators of poetry after mid-century, Housman saw his task as responding intellectually and emotionally to a poet's work rather than attempting to reproduce a poetic line in a graphic one.

Throughout the Victorian period illustrated poetry changed in bibliographic format, poetic style and artistic approach, in response to the technological and social developments

Plate 11   Process engraving after a design by Laurence Housman for Jane Barlow's *The End of Elfintown* (pub. Macmillan, 1894), p. 20. By permission of the Thomas Fisher Rare Book Library, University of Toronto.

that affected its market. One of the consequences of the pairing of picture and poem for an increasingly specialized market of gift buyers and collectors, however, was to associate verse with a commodity either feminine or effete. Hence the modernists' calls for manly, vigorous work, utterly unlike that of their Victorian predecessors, and designed in stark formats where the word, once again, assumed its proper mastery of the page. It is in consequence

Plate 12   Process engraving after a design by Laurence Housman for the frontispiece to Francis Thompson's *Poems* (pub. Elkin Mathews and John Lane, 1893). By permission of the Thomas Fisher Rare Book Library, University of Toronto.

of this modernist legacy that critics and students of Victorian poetry have long overlooked, ignored or downplayed the effect on meaning of its specific material format. It is time for a new, materialist analysis of Victorian poetry, precisely situated in the context of its publishing history and cognizant of the effects of its many illustrated forms.

See also: THE MARKET; THE POETRY OF THE 1890S; THE PRE-RAPHAELITE SCHOOL; ANTHOLOGIES AND THE MAKING OF THE POETIC CANON; VISION AND VISUALITY.

REFERENCES AND FURTHER READING

Adburgham, Alison (1972) *Women in Print: Writing Women and Women's Magazines from the Restoration to the Accession of Victoria*. London: George Allen and Unwin.

Allingham, William (1855) *The Music Master, A Love Story, and Two Series of Day and Night Songs*. London: Routledge.

Altick, Richard D. (1967) *The English Common Reader: A Social History of the Mass Reading Public, 1800–1900*. Chicago and London: University of Chicago Press.

Barlow, Jane (1894) *The End of Elfintown*. London: Macmillan.

Boyd, Timothy W. (1995) '"A Regular Illustrated Book": William Allingham and his Pre-Raphaelite Friends Make *The Music Master*, 1854–55.' *Publishing History*, 37, 17–49.

Buckler, William E. (1952) '*Once a Week* under Samuel Lucas 1859–65.' *PMLA*, 7.67, 924–41.

Casteras, Susan P. (ed.) (1991) *Pocket Cathedrals: Pre-Raphaelite Book Illustration*. New Haven: Yale Center for British Art.

Crane, Walter (1994) *The Decorative Illustration of Books*. Original work published 1896. London: Studio Editions.

Dalziel (ed.) (1865) *Home Thoughts and Home Scenes*. London: Routledge, Warne and Routledge.

Dalziel (1901) *The Brothers Dalziel: A Record of Fifty Years' Work in Conjunction with Many of the Most Distinguished Artists of the Period 1840–1890*. London: Methuen.

Doughty, Oswald, and John Robert Wahl (eds) (1965) *Letters of Dante Gabriel Rossetti*. Vol. I. Oxford: Clarendon Press.

Eliot, Simon (1995) 'Some Trends in British Book Production, 1800–1919.' In John O. Jordan and Robert L. Patten (eds). *Literature in the Marketplace: Nineteenth-Century British Publishing and Reading Practices* (pp. 19–43). Cambridge: Cambridge University Press.

Fredeman, W. E. (1965) *Pre-Raphaelitism: A Bibliocritical Study*. Cambridge, Mass.: Harvard University Press.

Goldman, Paul (1994) *Victorian Illustrated Books 1850–1870: The Heyday of Wood-Engraving*. London: British Museum Press.

Graves, Charles L. (1910) *Life and Letters of Alexander Macmillan*. London: Macmillan.

Haass, Sabine (1985) 'Victorian Poetry Anthologies: Their Role and Success in the Nineteenth-Century Book Market.' *Publishing History*, 17, 51–64.

Hagen, June Steffensen (1979) *Tennyson and his Publishers*. London: Macmillan.

Houfe, Simon (1992) *Fin de Siècle: The Illustrators of the Nineties*. London: Barrie and Jenkins.

Hunt, William Holman (1913) *Pre-Raphaelitism and the Pre-Raphaelite Brotherhood*. London: Chapman and Hall.

Layard, George Somes (1894) *Tennyson and his Pre-Raphaelite Illustrators: A Book about a Book*. London: Elliot Stock.

Kooistra, Lorraine Janzen (1995) *The Artist as Critic: Bitextuality in Fin-de-Siècle Illustrated Books*. Aldershot: Scolar Press.

Kooistra, Lorraine Janzen (1999) 'The Jael who Led the Hosts to Victory: Christina Rossetti and Pre-Raphaelite Book-Making.' *Journal of Pre-Raphaelite Studies*, n.s. 18, 50–68.

Leng, Andrew (1991) 'The Ideology of "Eternal Truth": William Holman Hunt and *The Lady of Shalott* 1850–1905.' *Word and Image*, 7. 4, 314–28.

McGann, Jerome J. (1991) *The Textual Condition*. Princeton, N. J.: Princeton University Press.

McLean, Ruari (1972) *Victorian Book Design and Colour Printing*. London: Faber and Faber.

Mitford, Mary Russell (ed.) (1838) *Finden's Tableaux*. London: Charles Tilt.

Muir, Percy (1971) *Victorian Illustrated Books*. London: Batsford.

Poulson, Christine (1996) 'Death and the Maiden: *The Lady of Shalott* and the Pre-Raphaelites.' In Ellen Harding (ed.). *Re-framing the Pre-Raphaelites: Historical and Theoretical Essays* (pp. 173–94). Aldershot: Scolar Press.

Raymond, Meredith B., and Mary Rose Sullivan (eds) (1987) *Women of Letters: Selected Letters of Elizabeth Barrett Browning and Mary Russell Mitford*. Boston: Twayne.

Reid, Forrest (1975) *Illustrators of the Eighteen Sixties: An Illustrated Survey of the Work of 58*

British Artists. Original work published 1928. New York: Dover.

Renier, Anne (1964) *Friendship's Offering: An Essay on the Annuals and Gift Books of the Nineteenth Century*. London: Private Libraries Association.

'Review of *Poems*. By Alfred Tennyson. Published by E. Moxon' (1857) *Art-Journal*, 19, 231.

Roberts, Leonard (1997) *Arthur Hughes: His Life and Works. A Catalogue Raisonné*. Woodbridge: Antique Collectors' Club.

Rossetti, Christina (1866) *The Prince's Progress and Other Poems*. London: Macmillan.

Stetz, Margaret D., and Mark Samuels Lasner (1990) *England in the 1890s: Literary Publishing at the Bodley Head*. Washington, D. C.: Georgetown University Press.

Surtees, Virginia (1971) *The Paintings and Drawings of Dante Gabriel Rossetti (1828–1882): A Catalogue Raisonné*. Oxford: Clarendon Press.

Taylor, John Russell (1966) *The Art Nouveau Book in Britain*. London: Methuen.

Tennyson, Alfred (1893) *Maud, a Monodrama*. London: Kelmscott.

Tennyson, Alfred (1857) *Poems*. London: E. Moxon.

Thompson, Francis (1893) *Poems*. London: Elkin Mathews and John Lane.

Vaughan, William (1988) 'Incongruous Disciples: The Pre-Raphaelites and the Moxon *Tennyson*.' In *Imagination on a Long Rein: English Literature Illustrated* Ed. Joachim Möller (pp. 148–60). Marburg: Jonas Verlag.

Wakeman, Geoffrey (1973) *Victorian Book Illustrations: The Technical Revolution*. Newton Abbot: David and Charles.

White, Gleeson (1970) *English Illustration: 'The Sixties': 1855–1870*. Original work published 1897. Bath: Kingsmead Reprints.

Wilde, Oscar (1894) *The Sphinx*. London: Elkin Mathews and John Lane.

Willmott, R. A. (ed.) (1862) *English Sacred Poetry*. London: Routledge.

Wordsworth, William (1966) 'Illustrated Books and Newspapers.' In *Poetical Works*. Ed. Thomas Hutchinson. New revised edition by Ernest de Selincourt (p. 383). London: Oxford University Press.

PART THREE
Victorian Poetry and Victorian Culture

23

Nationhood and Empire

Margaret Linley

At the end of the nineteenth century Alfred Tennyson's status as a cultural icon resulted in part from both the confidence in and the crisis of empire that many of his works had evoked as aspects of the Victorians' sense of nationhood. That Tennyson embraced his public responsibility as laureate became apparent soon after he assumed the post on 18 November 1850; his first publication, the seventh edition of his *Poems* (1851), was prefaced with a dedication to the queen. Although from the outset of his career Tennyson drew on national and imperial discourse as primary material for his poetry and had celebrated in verse (along with Elizabeth Barrett Browning, Letitia Landon and many others) Victoria's accession to the throne in 1837, the 1851 dedication deals explicitly with the status of poetry at a time when empire was pressuring definitions of the nation, and the laureateship was beginning to be considered culturally redundant. Addressing the monarch in terms that assert poetry's stake in the relations between nation and empire, the poem establishes a parallel between Victoria's succession to 'warrior kings of old' (l. 4) and Tennyson's succession to Wordsworth as poet laureate. Although Tennyson deferentially acknowledges that it is Victoria who grants this poetic succession, the structure of the poem implicitly argues that the endurance of political empire depends on the sovereign power of poetry.

A draft of 'To the Queen' makes this argument explicit. In lines excised from the published version, the queen heads the superior 'Saxo-Norman race' (l. 2) while poets 'likewise are a kind of kings, / Nor is their empire all a dream' (ll. 11–12). Tennyson draws a direct comparison between political empire and the imaginative empire of poets. On the one hand, poetry gives specific spatial definition to the imperial map; for poets' 'words fly over land and main / Their warblings make the distance glad' (ll. 13–14), thereby locating dispersed individuals and connecting them emotionally and imaginatively to a cultural community across the vast geographical spaces of empire. On the other hand, poets' words are no less significant for their temporal power: 'Their voices heard hereafter add / A glory to a glorious reign' (ll. 15–16). Unlike the queen's political empire, imaginative empire is not subject to the constraints of time, for poets' voices live 'hereafter' and are thus indispensable to the historical narrative of geographical empire (Graham 1998: 39–40). This prophetic capacity to write the future history of the nation's empire turns out, moreover, to be a property of poetic tradition:

> I would I were of those of old,
>   A mellow mouth of song to fill
>   Your music which might still
> Be music when my lips are cold.
>
> That after men might turn the page
>   And light on fancies true and sweet,
>   And kindle with a loyal heart
> To fair Victoria's golden age.
>
>   (ll. 29–36)

The laureate claims 'sovereignty over the sovereign' (Harrison 1998: 47), speaking to, through and for the queen. Poetry and monarchy represent an organic oral-folk antiquity that the poet preserves into the era of the printed 'page' by resurrecting the monarch's memory in sentiments that 'kindle' emotional bonds of obligation and affection. Through this process of projecting, and thereby inciting, nostalgic desire in the 'loyal heart', Tennyson ironically renders Victoria most substantial and permanent after she is long gone, when the memory of her 'golden age' is reconstituted in the future on 'the page' as an enduring fiction of the past.

Tennyson's decision to omit these stanzas from the published version of the poem may reveal a reluctance to assert publicly the authority of his newly assumed laureateship or may suggest uncertainty as to how to compose a properly subordinated voice with which to address the Queen. His revisions also indicate an astute ability to make poetry essential to national identity, while inscribing the importance of empire in the British imagination. Tennyson effectively converts content – all those direct assertions in the unpublished stanzas about the magisterial and magic power of poetry – into form. In so doing, he fashions a poetic authority as ineffably mysterious, pervasive and autonomous – that is, as imperial.

In the published version of 'To the Queen', the poet suggests that Victoria's 'greatness, and the care / that yokes with empire' (ll. 9–10) ensure a need for poetry in her life personally and in the life of the nation generally. Empire, as blessing ('greatness') and as burden ('care / that yokes'), is that which may 'yield' the Monarch 'time / to make demand of modern rhyme / If aught of ancient worth be there' (ll. 11–12). Thus the poet's 'poor book of song' (l. 17) is conceived both as supplying a demand for distraction from that imperial burden and as fulfilling a desire for affirmation of Britain's greatness as natural precisely in its historical continuity. The poet's 'sweeter music' (l. 13) defers to future blessings he actually composes in the voices of the 'children of our children' (l. 23), who will memorialize Victoria's goodness, purity, serenity, peace and repose, those attributes that make this 'Mother, Wife, and Queen' (l. 28) so very different from the 'warrior kings of old' (l. 4). In addition, the children of the future will commemorate Victoria's other modern qualities, including her wise choice of council, her celebration of industrial progress on such occasions as the Great Exhibition (1851), and her balance of democratic and monarchical rule that is 'Broad-based upon her people's will, / And compassed by the inviolate sea' (ll. 35–6). Poetry thus imagines a break with the nation's past ('the warrior kings of old') while simultaneously reconstituting that rupture as a form of progress, which in turn makes possible the poet's prophecy of the continuation of tradition in the future when modern times will not simply pass away but will be recuperated and redeemed as ancient. In short, by prophesying an afterlife for political empire, poetry extends but also exceeds the monarch's power (Harrison 1998: 47).

Rewriting the Victorian Nation

The language of 'To the Queen' conforms in complex ways to mid-Victorian nationalist discourse. According to Eric Hobsbawm, modern nations typically claim to be the opposite of new, preferring to situate their roots in the remotest antiquity. Likewise, they claim to be the opposite of constructed, so natural as to be beyond definition (Hobsbawm 1983: 14). In order to authorize such claims, nations necessarily invent traditions, often incorporating already existing rituals, customs and conventions, and reworking them so as to create continuity with the past. Poetry is not only among the richest cultural materials to be used in the invention of traditions originating in antiquity but can itself be refigured in the national narrative, as 'To the Queen' suggests, as a sacred site of ancient prestige in the modern, and increasingly secular, nation.

However, the work of writing the nation in 1850 was actually a task of rewriting. In the 130 years preceding Victoria's reign, a good deal of energy and a lot of blood had been devoted to forging the British nation (see Colley 1996). The modern nation that emerged by the early nineteenth century as 'an imagined political community' inherently limited and sovereign, in Benedict Anderson's definition (1991: 12), was from the outset politically, ethnically, religiously and linguistically diverse, including within its bounds Wales, Ireland and Scotland along with England. Although British identity coalesced, however tenuously, around a shared Protestant identity defined by the threat of recurrent war, particularly with Catholic France, and around the triumphs, profits and otherness represented by a massive overseas empire (Colley 1996: 6), by the mid-nineteenth century demands for expansion of British citizenship through extension of political and religious freedoms both at home and abroad meant that Protestantism and anti-French sentiment no longer had the same cohesive force that they possessed a century earlier. The fact of empire is thus a crucial determinant in the creation and development of Victorian nationalism.

'Empire' was, however, like the forged British nation, a shifting term. Until well into the 1860s, the term could refer exclusively to the United Kingdom of the British Isles and England, and is thus consistent with the idea of the British nation including both ties and tensions. At the same time, empire designated the relationship between Britain and the white settler colonies (particularly Canada, Australia and New Zealand), a relationship that was frequently strained after the 1837 rebellions in Canada and the ensuing move towards self-government. Laden with patriotic and sentimental attachment for 'home' that also invoked the responsibilities and obligations of the 'mother country', the colonial idea of empire defined Britishness at the margins of vast geographical distance. A third idea of empire, referred to as the worldwide empire or overseas empire, focused especially on British India or the Indian Empire, though it included territories

around the globe, and was based on commerce and backed by military might. A source
of much exotic and erotic Oriental poetry in English, this empire grew slowly from the
post-Napoleonic period until the 1870s; however, in the final decades of Victoria's reign,
expansion of the overseas empire accelerated, particularly with the territorial parcelling
of Africa (at the Congress of Berlin, 1885), and became the major cause of political tension
(Koebner and Schmidt 1965). Through the course of the nineteenth century, the connotations of the word 'empire' had unquestionably expanded to reflect Britain's domination
over international trade and its dominion over one-quarter of the world's population.

When Tennyson took up his laureateship at mid-century, the destabilizing effects of
empire were beginning to rattle the fragile construct of a British nation that would
become increasingly understood as 'English'. Although the word 'imperialism' was not
widely applied to Britain in public discourse until the late 1870s (Koebner and Schmidt
1965), Tennyson certainly understood the official function of the laureateship as a project
of representing the cultural negotiation between the imperial demand for a 'broad based'
empire and the sovereignty of the nation 'compassed by the inviolate sea' ('To the Queen',
ll. 35–6). What may have assisted Tennyson's poetic apprehension of the incongruities
issuing between nation and empire was the nineteenth-century cultural discourse that
invoked 'empire' to describe the national role of poetry, and which also invested high
political stakes in the teleology of decline.

The Decline of the Empire of Poetry

It was possible in 1829 to declare that the sun never sets on the British empire, but
nothing quite so certain could be said about the cultural empire of poetry. Victorian poetry
was born amid proclamations of the death of poetry and a crisis about what to do with
its remains. In the years immediately preceding Victoria's ascension to the throne, the
idea that poetry declines as civilization advances was articulated (with ironic intention)
by Thomas Love Peacock in the assertion that 'the day is not distant, when the degraded
state of every species of poetry will be . . . generally recognized' (1820: 131). Thomas
Babington Macaulay, who would soon become a distinguished historian of imperial
ambitions and advocate of English state-sponsored education in India, agreed. In his first
essay for the *Edinburgh Review*, he announced that 'language, the machine of the poet, is
best fitted for his purpose in its rudest state' and thus as enlightenment progresses 'science
gains and poetry loses', resulting in 'better theories and worse poems' (1825: 5).

Poetry's new-found relation to commerce was, of course, at the core of anxious
ruminations on its national status. But it is significant that those worries are expressed
in figures drawn from discourses on empire. During the 1820s culture became thoroughly
enmeshed with the new industrial economy from the level of production to dissemination and consumption, and authorship was thereby marked by commodification, mechanical reproduction and professionalization. These years represent an especially exemplary
moment in the emergence of the nation as uniquely 'Victorian' and set the tone, moreover, for an entire century of ruminations on the steady growth in literacy, industry,

commerce, communications and state bureaucracies. Carlyle's brilliant analysis in 'Signs of the Times' of the insidious and disciplinary reach of industrial modernity, from individual consciousness to the social body itself, incisively captures an emerging cultural anxiety in the aphorism that 'not the external and physical alone is managed by machinery but the internal and spiritual also' (1904: 60). Equally important is the fact that he refers to poetry in a prophetic pitch explicitly accented with allusions to cyclical theories of empire: 'we have theories of [poetry's] rise, height, decline and fall – which latter, it would seem is now near, among all people' (1904: 76). Anachronistically, and therefore precariously, existing within historical time, poetry's cultural reign is all too discomfitingly like that of geographical empire. Declining at the height of imperial expansion, poetry's position in the marketplace is indeed an ominous secular sign of fallenness: not only of the end of a cultural empire but, as a dark prophecy, of what might happen in the realm of Britain's international pre-eminence.

Domesticating Empire

Carlyle's judgement of poetry's doom transfers to poetic tradition all of the transience and none of the endurance inherent in Felicia Hemans's paradoxical poetics of mourning and domesticity. Her work was reasserting and revaluing the role of poetry in the relations between Victorian nationhood and empire. Hemans's poetry endured with Victorians, despite its Romantic origins, in part because it represented a successful attempt to make nationalist sense of the post-Napoleonic territorial remapping of the world. A seemingly interminable, fragmented and unknowable British empire was made familiar through a poetry of the affections, nostalgia and mourning.

Benedict Anderson has usefully characterized the devotional language of patriotism: 'what the eye is to the lover . . . language . . . is to the patriot. Through the language, encountered at the mother's knee and parted with only at the grave, pasts are restored, fellowships are imagined, futures are dreamed' (1991: 154). The ideological weight of Hemans's poetry derives precisely from its focus on bonds of affection and nostalgic reverence for home. Such attachment, rooted in the vernacular, in domestic love and in the commonplace, seems unquestionably pure and disinterested precisely because not chosen. Learned from mothers, the language of affection establishes home as both metaphor and metonym for patriotic devotion to the mother country, and necessarily entails separation and homesickness in the displacement and dispersal that is the condition of national subjects of empire. Repetition and recitation of domestic affections in unison with distant and anonymous, but none the less homesick, patriots is the essence of Hemans's poetry.

Writing from the margins in northern Wales, rather than the cosmopolitan centre in London, Hemans produced a poetry that offered ideological expression to British inclusiveness and homogeneity, encompassing diverse topics in a variety of genres and in a broad range of transhistorical and global settings. At the heart of Hemans's poetic architecture, the home, as idea and as institution, naturalizes a relation to Britishness as habitual and timeless. Whether home is at the core of the British Empire, as in 'The

Homes of England' (1827), or at its periphery in the Ottoman empire, as in 'The Suliote Mother' (1825), Hemans encouraged readers to generalize from domestic sites they knew to those they did not, from homes that existed to those that were gone. Through this process of associational and analogical reading, Hemans ennobled not only all the homes of England, but all the homes of the anglicized Christian globe with the 'ideal aura of English national character' (Tucker 1994: 538).

However, despite the pervasiveness of Hemans's domesticity, her homes are fundamentally absent, accessible only as ideal fictions. Hemans is especially representative of the way in which the modern culture of nationalism is characterized by public ceremonial reverence for monuments of the past, monuments that are 'saturated with ghostly *national* imaginings' (Anderson 1991: 9). Her domestic sentimentality not only memorializes the cenotaphs and tombs strewn throughout the nation's history, but renders home itself, with its intrinsic mutability and built-in obsolescence, a self-conscious fiction of nostalgic desire for a lost, irrecoverable past. It is perhaps not surprising then that Hemans similarly familiarized an essentially Romantic alienation in the graveyards of nation and empire as a ghostly emptiness, a site of mutability and loss, frequently welding explicit connections between home and grave (Lootens 1994: 248). In 'England's Dead' (1822) the deceased and dispersed bodies of empire are recuperated and memorialized in the act of domestic mourning, while 'The Deserted House' (1827) 'mourn[s] the broken household band'. If the home is simultaneously a symbol of unity and of loss, so too is the nation and the empire that it binds.

Hemans's poetry about monuments and memories is deliberately designed as practice and exercise. Acts of recuperation through memorization and historicization give substance to the nation's monuments at the moment of their dissolution (Rothstein 1999: 55). Britishness materializes in the word as deed that needs to be repeated and learned by heart. Such writing has been named 'a poetry of quotation' (McGann 1993: 230), a poetry that 'risks stereotype' (Goslee 1996: 237), a poetry that popularizes, familiarizes, generalizes, a poetry in short that is ideological. Its relation to empire is therefore instrumental and suggests the importance of poetry in the development of Victorian nationalism as domestic and increasingly anglicized, a significance which would be fully realized and institutionalized in the Education Act in 1870 as well as in the educational role for poetry articulated by Matthew Arnold at the end of the century.

Rise of Imperial Poetics of Nationhood

Questions surrounding whether or not the empire of poetry was in fact fallen and what that fall might mean would themselves generate a good deal of poetry and poetic theory for the remainder of the century. It would be the task of the 1830s and beyond to determine how poetry might retain an exalted archaic status while helping to construct the nation's relation to empire. Early Victorian debates over the status of poetry were part of the attempt to give historical depth and mythic resonance to nationality through reconstruction of the culture's ideal linguistic monuments. Hemans's monuments and memorials of home and empire contributed to changing the focus of cultural debate from whether poetry should figure the nation to what kind of poetry should do so.

The reception of Tennyson's early poetry indicates the extent to which the cultural scene was fully politicized. In an 1831 review of Tennyson's *Poems, Chiefly Lyrical* (1830) William Johnson Fox, editor of the dissenting and radical *Monthly Repository*, directly challenged the perception of 'these supposed unpoetical days on which we are fallen' (1831: 23). In terms both religious and political, he insists that the 'unbounded and everlasting materials of poetry' ensure that poetry is tied ultimately to progress, especially poetry that analyses particular states of mind. For Fox, this subjective turn, where poetry begins at home, in the heart and in knowledge of the self, opens 'a new world' for the poet, in strikingly imperialist fashion, 'to conquer' (1831: 25). The poet's function is thus explicitly political, and the private experience of reading is ineffably linked to effects in the public sphere, to social responsibility to the country and the world. Poets, he concludes:

> can influence the associations of unnumbered minds; they can command the sympathies of unnumbered hearts; they can disseminate principles; they can give those principles power over men's imaginations; they can excite in a good cause the sustained enthusiasm that is sure to conquer; they can blast the laurels of the tyrants, and hallow the memories of the martyrs of patriotism; they can act with a force, the extent of which it is difficult to estimate, upon national feelings and character, and consequently upon national happiness. (1831: 33)

Fox clearly wants to put the empire of poetry back in business, and he does so by conceptualizing it in thoroughly modern and masculine terms. Fox in fact anticipates something like the concept of modern simultaneity, which Anderson, borrowing from Benjamin, calls 'homogeneous, empty time' (1991: 24): 'unnumbered' minds and hearts, who will always remain anonymous to each other, can be connected intellectually, emotionally and imaginatively in the temporal coincidence of simultaneous acts of reading. While according to Anderson the novel and the newspaper are the forms which provided the nineteenth century with the technical means for imagining the nation, Fox insists that poetry even more powerfully functions as a technology of nationhood precisely because it has the capacity to inspire the very self-sacrificing devotion to one's country that Anderson argues is at the heart of the imagined community of the nation.

Moreover, Fox recognizes that the historical significance of poetry in British culture authorizes the language of imperial conquest as a legitimate style of patriotic expression. The rhetoric of poetry's 'unbounded and everlasting' power to 'command', 'influence', 'excite' and ultimately unite readers in the present around historical 'memories of the martyrs of patriotism' suggests an imperial means to a patriotic end of acting 'with a force, the extent of which is difficult to estimate, upon national feelings and character'. Poetry thus speaks to and for the voiceless millions, the unknown patriots, and joins them within an 'unbounded' geographical empire by rewarding them with a specifically British '*national* happiness' (italics added). Fox astutely mobilizes imperialist discourse and patriotic sentiment for the purpose of refashioning the nation in the image of radical democratic principles on the eve of political reform.

Whereas Fox desires a national-patriotic poetry, Arthur Hallam, in 'On Some of the Characteristics of Modern Poetry', aims to promote a national poet practising a 'detached' but none the less imperial poetics. Hallam refuses an explicitly political agenda for poetry, attempting in fact to extricate Tennyson from the radicalism imputed to him by Tory critics (Sinfield 1986: 12) by claiming that the poet 'comes before the public unconnected with any political party or peculiar system of opinions' (Hallam 1831: 42). This outright repudiation of partisan and sectarian interests, and perhaps more veiled rejection of patriotic language under the euphemism of 'peculiar systems of opinions', is itself, however, far from apolitical. While Hallam implicitly expresses the Anglican and Tory perspective that he and Tennyson share with their Cambridge 'Apostle' circle, his object is to promote the poet as above politics and therefore as a genuinely English voice.

Hallam constructs this Englishness as a modern 'check acting for conservation against a propulsion toward change' (1831: 41). Positioning himself as well as his close friend Tennyson at the far end of a long period of social degradation marked by a painful struggle to harmonize the current 'over-civilized condition of thought' with the 'fresh productive spirit' that once characterized poetry (1831: 40), Hallam articulates that peculiarly Victorian subjectivity of a divided consciousness profoundly attuned to the fragmentation and dispersions of the heterogeneous modern British nation. This is, in short, the precursor to Matthew Arnold's tremulous cadences on a modernity that has Victorians 'wandering between two worlds, one dead, / The other powerless to be born' ('Stanzas from the Grande Chartreuse', 1855). Whereas Fox celebrates poetry's power to imagine a continuous link between the past and the political life of the present, Hallam laments modern culture's dislocation from a no less imagined organic, pre-industrial, cultural unity of 'old times', when 'the poetic impulse went along with the general impulse of the nation' (1831: 41). So much is it out of sympathy with the current pulse of the nation that poetry 'in proportion to its depth and truth is likely to have little immediate authority over public opinion' (1831: 41). Caught between nostalgia for an organic, mythic past and the overcivilized industrial nation, the modern spirit of poetry can only be characterized by melancholy, isolation and 'idiosyncrasies rather than community of interest' (1831: 41).

Melancholy is precisely what makes the poet paradoxically both modern (and English) and ancient. Twenty years before Tennyson would declare, in the omitted stanzas of 'To the Queen', that mournful poets are kings, Hallam attributes to poetry a disinterest that is imperial in scope, having 'immediate sympathy with the external universe' (1831: 37). Although poetry appears to have little 'interest' in the present, its future authority knows no limits, its effects being 'so boundless and so bewildering' (1831: 38). Disinterest, in other words, provides the framework for long-term dominion over public opinion precisely because poetry is not *about* 'community of interest' but actually *is* community, the very embodiment of the nation's language and history. Poetry may narrate and exalt the nation's history as Fox would have it, but more importantly for Hallam it offers the very means for incorporating the otherness of England's mythic past within continuous progressive time. The poet, Hallam argues, has the ability to transfer the spirit of the past and make it 'a temporary form for his own spirit, and so effect, by idealizing power, a new and legitimate combination' (1831: 45). While this combinatory ability may only be 'temporary', its poetic progeny gain enduring legitimacy because combination is fundamentally a constitutive element of English, which is to the core 'necessarily a compound language' (1831: 49).

'Legitimate combination' was a highly charged phrase in 1831, redolent of a class politics dating from the turn of the century, when Combination Acts (1799, 1800) were imposed to inhibit political trade unionism and prevent regional and national organization of the working classes. In direct opposition to the politics of patriotic sentiment and party affiliation, Hallam rewrites the meaning of combination in temporal and linguistic terms. In this different model, combination gets translated into the philological hybridity which forms the basic structure of English, and becomes insidious and inevitable on an entirely different scale. The language itself is paradigmatically open to change and intrinsically able to incorporate difference into itself. Despite the familiarity of the concept today, 'hybrid', as Robert Young reminds us, 'is the nineteenth century's word'. Although the term was in use early in the century, prior to the 1840s hybridity was not widely applied to questions of racial mixing in humans; by the 1860s it began to appear in linguistic contexts to denote words derived from elements of different languages; by the 1890s the linguistic and racial are linked: 'The Aryan languages present such indications of hybridity as would correspond with . . . racial intermixture' (Young 1995: 6). While the search for the scientific and ideological truth of race around biological and linguistic hybridity would not reach a vexed pitch until the post-Darwinian years, the ethnographic undertone of Hallam's argument is nevertheless traceable, from the classifying, even botanically minded, 'some characteristics' of the title to the barely latent pun in the phrase 'first raciness' (1831: 40; see Doyle 1996) and the reference to the 'Saxon element' constituting 'our native tongue', as well as to the multiple origins of English in Germanic and Latin and its European derivatives (1831: 49).

In the 1830s hybridity is of scientific interest in classifying the biological differences of species. In parallel fashion, Hallam identifies a taxonomic 'poetry of sensation' (1831: 36), running through Shakespeare and Milton to Shelley, Keats and Tennyson, which locates the mixed or compound nature of English poetry in the body, absorbing as it does the poet's 'whole being into the energy of the sense' (1831: 37). By thus drawing on notions of philological and vaguely physiological hybridity, Hallam retrieves the mythic past of England from its place elsewhere and remaps it across the primal zone of the body as the new expressive territory of English. The poetry of sensation, written thus on the body, becomes a repository for the disruptive potential that may occur when myth is temporarily and anachronistically translated into the present of linear time, offering an active site of challenge and resistance against the hegemony of the modern nation. Yet this corporal physicality is, significantly, not neutral but rather a primordial and feminized space that is disorderly by definition, in excess of rational time and outside the measure of national progress. It remains racially and culturally bounded, though, to the extent that the language of its profuse feeling is, as Hallam characterizes Tennyson's writing, 'thorough and sterling English' (1831: 48). Disdaining interest in the political nation, poetry's fusions maximize the 'fertility of expression and variety of harmony' (1831: 49) that is fundamentally Saxon English enabling the language, and by implication empire itself, to 'flourish and increase' (1831: 49). Constructions of race and gender combine to manage a dissident poetics that fashions poetry as the critical, because sovereign, voice of the nation.

Poetry's Civilizing Mission

If Fox and Hallam are representative of the dominant strains of progressive and conservative thought that would interpenetrate and develop together throughout the century, establishing the terms in which literary culture would be discussed (Armstrong 1993: 28), their formulations of poetry at the nexus of nationhood and empire can be usefully read beside an anonymously published essay attributed to Letitia Landon, 'On the Ancient and Modern Influence of Poetry'. Landon combines radical and conservative ideals to theorize poetry's role in civilizing the modern nation. Like Hemans, Landon refuses to extricate creativity from the moral and political into a separate ethical sphere, and she evinces a similarly sharp awareness of the gendered bifurcation of public and private as necessary to the emergence of the modern nation. But rather than draw on feminine figurations to make poetry more private, as Hallam does, she invokes the concept of feminine influence and refinement to render values associated with privacy more public. Just as Hallam appropriates the feminine, enacting a hybridization of genders, as a marginal discourse for the disaffected male poet, and Fox suggests a desire to remasculinize poetry against the overwhelming success of domestic nationalism, Landon draws on the moral authority and feminine virtue that had accrued to the idea of 'influence' since the late eighteenth century in an attempt to overcome the political ineffectuality imposed on women and poetry by the separation of spheres.

The 'ancient and modern' terms of Landon's title announce that she too is concerned with the cultural debate that situates poetry in the dialectic between an exalted past and a degraded present: 'the decline and fall of that Roman empire of the mind seems now advanced as in historical fact . . . and perhaps we shall more accurately say what poetry is by referring to what it has been' (1832: 160). Turning thus to poetry's beginnings, Landon insists that cultural history is not universal but differs according to geographical location and is determined, moreover, by structures of domination. Searching the globe for examples of 'the work and wonder of the imagination' (1832: 161) in foundational cultural myths, Landon points to the plurality of nations and shows that empire creates a cultural field in which sovereign nationality is forced to confront the paradox of its coexistence and putative equality with other cultures. However, in Africa, the 'least civilized quarter of the globe' (1832: 161), Landon finds the exception, thereby seeming to attribute to that territory the anachronistic status that found paradigmatic philosophical articulation in 1822 by Hegel, who figured the continent as a zone of extreme temporal as well as geographical difference from Europe. Typically described as the Dark Continent, Africa represented for Victorians the absolute measure of scientific, moral and biological difference. Landon's rendition of this ideology argues that Africa suffers from 'a total want of imagination' not so much from its 'savage' as from its 'apathetic' state.

This state, however, is not a consequence of nature but rather of empire: the 'curse' of Africans, and the reason they cannot be 'poetical', is 'slavery' (1832: 162).

Abolitionism became one of the vital underpinnings of British supremacy, especially in comparison with America and France, offering apparently irrefutable proof that British power was founded on religion, freedom and moral fibre – not just military might and economic interest. The discourse of slavery entered Victorian poetry as a prominent subject and language of cultural critique. Landon herself, like the Brontës, frequently employs metaphors of slavery to explore the power dynamics of romantic love or devotion to creative inspiration and, with Caroline Norton and Elizabeth Barrett Browning, she extends those metaphors into a social critique of the factory system. Landon's poem 'The African' (1832), published in *Fisher's Drawing-Room Scrap-Book* the same year as 'On the Ancient and Modern Influence of Poetry' appeared in the liberal-leaning *New Monthly Magazine*, recounts the capture and enslavement of an African prince, who dies finally a Christian convert 'in hope, as only those / Who die in Christ depart' (ll. 74–5). At mid-century, Barrett Browning forcefully denounced Christianity in the service of exploitation of slaves in America in 'The Runaway Slave at Pilgrim's Point' (1850), whose heroine dies not with hope but rather in her 'broken heart's disdain' (l. 253). Robert Browning, who along with Barrett Browning revolted against his family history of involvement in the slave system in the West Indies, similarly criticizes actual slavery in 'Cleon' (1855) and the conjugal slavery of Pompilia in *The Ring and the Book* (1869).

Yet as Landon's 'On the Ancient and Modern Influence of Poetry' shows, abolitionist politics are frequently replete with imperialist ideology, since after the abolition of slavery in 1807 British missionary work in Africa would be characterized as generous and enlightening. Landon's argument in the essay is, in contrast to her poem 'The African', wholly secular: conversion to poetry rather than religion enables a society to join the ranks of the civilized. In addition, Landon's global observations are directed inexorably to domestic cultural politics, as she draws on the analogy between colonial slavery abroad and industrial mechanization at home in order to warn her British readers. She constructs a history of poetry as instrumental in bringing about the very transition from the ancient era of military might to that of modern feeling and reflection. Imagination thus exists in opposition to military violence as the very spirit of enlightenment, the first cause and evidence of human progress and development: 'the imagination, which is the source of poetry, has in every country been the beginning as well as the ornament of civilization. It civilizes because it refines' (1832: 161).

Landon captures the idea of civilization as both a historical process and as an achieved condition; without poetry there will be no civil nation and without civility there will be no poetry. She also grasps the ambiguity that resonated for Victorians in the term 'civilization', evident for example in Hallam's characterization of the age as overcivilized as well as in contemporary writings by John Stuart Mill, when later in the essay she argues that once poetry has brought a society to civilization, it must then act to prevent that civilization from becoming artificial, 'too cold and too selfish'. Poetry thus guides the modern nation into being and also preserves it from degeneration. Through such arguments, Landon attempts to theorize a feminized imagination as the missionary spirit guiding the nation's imperial destiny; such a civilizing, creative disposition cannot but appear to be an orderly, even managerial, product of culture rather than nature, and one that furthermore exposes the inherent artificiality of lost natural bowers and organic myths. Poetry creates proper subjects for the nation, enlightens and refines them in preparation for their global mission, while the poet's love of poetry defines her as the very model of the modern patriotic citizen. For if poetry's ancient role was to overcome 'barbarism', its modern role is against 'selfishness'; all aspects of enlightened culture are under the 'guardianship of the poet' (1832: 168), who must sacrifice herself to poetry's own great reward.

Landon endows the moral imperative of poetry with substance, fixity and permanence by defining it as an object or 'ornament' of culture, that ensemble of artefacts and aesthetic practices representing a developed civilization. Initiating social institutions, poetry is the product of a constructive process. But, as ornament, poetry is a material object that can obscure the labour and potential violence involved in the display of beauty. Landon in effect generates a 'poetics of the ornament' that at once criticizes and justifies poetry's status, both as symbolic object and as commodity for consumption by middle-class Victorians supportive of England's national hegemony. Given that her career depended on literary annuals of the kind that published 'The African' (1832) and dominated the poetry scene in the second quarter of the nineteenth century, Landon knew all too well the importance of the beautiful book as signifier of status and as decoration in the home, recognizing that domestic space was implicated not only in the ideological ties between nation and empire but also as a site for the consumption of imperial goods. Elaborating on Walter Benjamin's observation that archaic images are often used to identify what is historically innovative about commodities, Anne McClintock argues that images of archaic time 'were systematically invoked to identify what was historically new about industrial modernity' (1995: 40). Landon's addition of ornament to the archaic status already attributed to poetry implicates it, along with other imperial artefacts, in the fetishistic compulsion to collect and exhibit that shaped Victorian middle-class culture and made it complicit in the museum mentality that seeks to display evidence of the nation's cultural inheritance and its global power.

The idea of poetry as artefact and ornament also emerges in Christina Rossetti's 'Goblin Market' (1862), as female desire comes under the influence of the fascinating charms of exotic commodities sold by implicitly foreign goblin men. As a narrative of both reverse colonization and the dangers of women's participation in the public sphere, the poem reveals that empire produces a dangerous, servile longing that undermines independence, and it suggests that the nation's marketplace is thoroughly implicated in an imperial trade which traffics with the female consumer only as colonized object. However, Rossetti redeems the civilizing mission of imperialism as a domestic project, ultimately managing the relationship between nation and empire under the orderly discipline of home and the devoted bonds of a sovereign sisterhood. Unlike Landon, though, Rossetti does not, indeed cannot in 1862, represent the contact with the 'other' entailed in such a mission as anything but violent. Indeed, violence and benevolence become increasingly intertwined in representations of the relationship between nation and empire, especially after the 1870s, when the tension between benevolent governance and violent preservation of the British territories would define the political poles of public debate in England.

Empire and Myth

In a significant body of Victorian poetry and poetic theory, the domestic sites of home, the archaic organic hybridity of English, and the civilizing mission give political expression of mythic proportion to the nation's immemorial past and limitless future. However, British myths – chivalric, medieval and Arthurian legends in particular – provided an already existing cultural legacy for writing the nation's past as a way of understanding and shaping Victorian nationhood in the present. Tennyson was by far the most influential architect of Arthurian legend in the nineteenth century and was occupied by the topic for the bulk of his career, from the composition of 'Morte d'Arthur' in 1833, published as 'The Epic' nine years later (1842), to the end of his life, with 'Akbar's Dream' (1892), whose hero, 'an Oriental King Arthur' (Brantlinger 1988: 10), 'would do the right / That only conquers men to conquer peace' (ll. 14–15).

As Victor Kiernan has argued, the imperial dimension of the *Idylls of the King* (1885) has its counterpart in British imperialism (Kiernan 1989: 141). Three particularly significant developments in the second half of the century stand out: the increasing anglicization of British territories (including the United Kingdom), self-government in the Canadian settler colonies in 1867, and violent confrontations in the worldwide empire, first in the Indian Mutiny of 1857 and then in the Jamaican Insurrection of 1865. At the same time, the medieval and chivalric revival that Tennyson took up was already deeply ingrained in British culture, having emerged in part against the social values exemplified by the utilitarian and positivist champions of industrial progress (Girouard 1981; Simpson 1990).

Tennyson invokes the ideological structures of contemporary Britain even in Arthur's mythic origins, which represent the interaction of myth and history in the formation of nationhood, while his mysterious death suggests the importance of memory and monuments to the nostalgic desire, Hemans's homesickness, that perpetuates empire. Imperialism, 'from the great deep to the great deep' ('The Coming of Arthur', l. 410), is the constant flux out of which the nation is formed and into which it must pass. In between, stability is constantly and inevitably eroded by both internal and external threats.

Initially, Arthur establishes credence in his leadership by battling with 'many a petty king' ('Coming of Arthur', l. 5) and demonstrating his own 'main might' until he gradually wins the allegiance of faithful knights willing to vow themselves to him and 'wage [his] wars' (l. 506). Introducing political, social and cultural renewal, Arthur drives out Rome so that 'The old order changeth, yielding place to new' (l. 508); the end, however, is prefigured in the beginning:

> for a space
> Were all one will, and thro' that strength the King
> Drew in the petty princedoms under him,
> Fought, and in twelve great battles overcame
> The heathen hordes, and made a realm and reign'd.
>
> (ll. 514–18)

Tennyson imagines pre-Arthurian Britain in colonial terms, ineffectively governed by a fading Roman Empire and 'doubly devastated by the invasions of heathen hordes and by the wasting disputes of its own petty kings' (David 1995: 173). In addition, the secret of Arthur's birth is given historical depth precisely because it will not be revealed until 'after-years' in Merlin's 'great annal book' ('The Coming of Arthur', l. 158) set down for him by his master Bleys, 'who taught him magic' (l. 153). Finally, instead of giving any concrete geographical origin to Arthur, Tennyson situates his hero's birth mythically, and partly through his appearance. Arthur's purported sister, Bellicent, queen of Orkney, contrasts her own and her mother's blackness against 'this king [who] is fair / Beyond the race of Britons and of men' (ll. 329–30). Through the combination of his military valour, mythical birth and racial purity, Arthur creates a national narrative whereby he builds, for a space, a limited and sovereign nation on consensual grounds (Graham 1998).

The repetition of this narrative throughout the remainder of the idylls is a form of exercising control, as Colin Graham notes, which not only requires iteration but also depends on memorialization (1998: 52). In 'The Last Tournament', Tristram remembers with nostalgia Arthur's early days, when he first beheld:

> That victor of the Pagan throned in hall –
> His hair, a sun that ray'd from off a brow
> Like hillsnow high in heaven, the steel-blue eyes,
> The golden beard that clothed his lips in light –
> Moreover, that weird legend of his birth,
> With Merlin's mystic babble about his end
> Amazed me.
>
> (ll. 660–9)

The assertion of Arthur's whiteness in 'The Coming' had linked him to spiritual purity, analogous to 'our fair father Christ' ('Guinevere', l. 559), as well as to chivalric (that is class) propriety, as he is described as a 'stainless King' and 'stainless gentleman' ('Merlin and Vivien', ll. 54, 790). This fair king inspires faith in his ability to whiten or 'cleanse the world' ('Gareth and Lynette', l. 25) and ensure the 'fair death' of those whom he converts to fight his cause ('Geraint and Enid', l. 967). The imperative 'To cleanse this common sewer' of Arthur's realm ('The Marriage of Geraint', l. 39; 'Geraint and Enid', l. 894), so that 'all men's hearts become / Clean for a season' ('Holy Grail', ll. 90–1), sounds something like the 'soap saga', described by Anne McClintock, that captured 'the hidden affinity between domesticity and empire' at the end of the century (1995: 208). While Arthur was shining up his kingdom, Victorian 'doorknobs, lamp stands and banisters, tables and chairs, mirrors and clocks, knives and forks, kettles and pans, shoes and boots were polished until they shimmered', suggesting an affinity between the desire for imperial appearances among the jumble of bric-a-brac that entered the Victorian home and Camelot itself as 'shining', fetishized icon of empire. Arthur's reign is deeply implicated in imperial cleansing, as his coming fills the land 'full of signs / And wonders' ('Guinevere', ll. 229–30) and erases 'for a season' acknowledgement of the labour and violence that go into making a nation within empire.

In 'The Passing of Arthur', Bedivere remembers the Round Table, now irrevocably dissolved, as 'an image of the mighty world' (l. 403). The process of decline plays itself out in part through a conflict between Arthur's domestic influence on the nation, the nation's benevolent civilizing mission and the military enforcement of empire, as well as in the tensions inherent in a chivalric code that demands 'impossible vows' ('Lancelot and Elaine', l. 130) of homosocial bonding in the name of devotion to women. In the end, the poem itself is left to emulate the monumental gate of Camelot, upon which 'New things and old co-twisted, as if Time / Were nothing' ('Gareth and Lynette', ll. 222–3), fashioning itself as the source and ornament of civilization. The *Idylls* enshrines Arthur's sacrifice in the already archaic crypt of the ideal patriot in the era of empire. Lacking a nation, he disappears into the diaspora ('the great deep'), a nationalist without a country; and he signifies most substantially and permanently when, like Victoria, he has passed into the returning time of memory to be turned over again and again in the pages of poetry's empire. In short, it is the magic of Tennyson's nationalism to turn the chance of nationhood into the destiny of empire, and to do so in the most uncertain and ambiguous terms.

The Burden of Empire

Two poems composed nearly fifty years apart encapsulate the burden of empire that Tennyson subtly explores in the *Idylls of the King* and that is variously expressed in poetry throughout the nineteenth century: one by the Pre-Raphaelite Dante Gabriel Rossetti, whose art was quickly assimilated to the mainstream, and the other by the Anglo-Indian Rudyard Kipling, who never felt at home in England despite his widespread acceptance as the ideal representative of the English empire. Rossetti's 'Burden of Nineveh' was composed in response to seeing 'a winged beast' (l. 10), which had recently been excavated by Sir Austen Henry Layard from the ruins of Nineveh between 1845 and 1851, brought into the British Museum. Standing amidst the diversity of the museum's historically and territorially remote collections of empire, Rossetti's speaker contemplates the homogenizing effect that ultimately erases the difference between London and Nineveh, as one culture becomes indistinguishable from and exchangeable for the other. The distancing that occurs in Rossetti's critique of the global hegemony of British empire and the democratization of national culture comes from within. The poet imagines that at some future date the winged beast will be borne afar and collected, ironically viewed as 'a relic now / Of London, not of Nineveh' (ll. 179–80). The museum culture that seeks to possess and preserve other cultures, Rossetti suggests, writes the narrative of its own inevitable decline. Rossetti criticizes not only acquisition but also the official institutionalization of cultural memorials and their dissemination. The confrontation with cultural plurality that occurs as a result of the imperial process has as one of its effects the reduction of differences to endlessly exchangeable signs. Imperial culture will continue while nations collapse into relics deposited in national museums of the future.

Kipling's 'White Man's Burden' (1899) was written during Britain's own South Africa campaign and amidst national concerns about the rise of German power. The poem was published in *The Times* of London but addressed to the United States, which was itself winning a war against Spain over the Philippines and Cuba. Exhorting Americans to 'take up the white man's burden', in gendered language signifying expansionist imperialism as a fulfilment of manhood, the poem appears to celebrate the selfless humanity of the civilizing mission. Americans are called upon to 'have done with childish days' (l. 50) and 'search' their 'manhood' (l. 53) by taking up the self-sacrificing task of bringing the globe under Anglo-Saxon rule. Empire is now seen as an obligation to be shared amongst a community of nations (Canada, New Zealand, Australia, America and Great Britain) and requires the creation of properly disciplined subjects needed to carry on the mission. The people who will do the work are the 'best ye breed' (l. 2), anonymous 'sons' sent into 'exile' (l. 3). These people are called upon to fulfil a covenant: taking up the burden of civilization ostensibly on behalf of 'sullen peoples' (l. 7) who will not recognize the benevolence of their work. In fact, the only rewards to be reaped are 'The blame of those ye better, / The hate of those ye guard – / The cry of hosts ye humour' (ll. 35–7). The white man should prepare to be undermined from centre and margin alike. The best of the nation will be sent out to the margins, possibly to die, suggesting a weakening of the centre itself. As Kipling thus avows empire, he also argues for an expansionism that is inimical to the idea of the sovereign nation, and articulates furthermore a struggle for the very survival of Englishness itself against the global proliferation of Saxon. Empire here is no less a sign than in Rossetti's 'The Burden of Nineveh', and the strenuous affirmation of the poem's pounding rhythmic repetitions suggests that empire exists mostly in the sheer effort of the structure that expresses 'The White Man's Burden'.

See also: Poetry in the Four Nations.

References and Further Reading

Altick, Richard (1957) *The English Common Reader: A Social History of the Mass Reading Public 1800–1900*. Chicago: University of Chicago Press.

Anderson, Benedict (1991) *Imagined Communities: Reflections on the Origin and Spread of Nationalism*. London and New York: Verso.

Armstrong, Isobel (1993) *Victorian Poetry: Poetry, Poetics and Politics*. London, New York: Routledge.

Barczewski, Stephanie L. (2000) *Myth and National Identity in Nineteenth-Century Britain*. Oxford: Oxford University Press.

Bayly, C. A. (1989) *Imperial Meridian: The British Empire and the World 1780–1830*. London, New York: Longman.

Brantlinger, Patrick (1988) *Rule of Darkness: British Literature and Imperialism 1830–1914*. Ithaca, N. Y.: Cornell University Press.

Carlyle, Thomas (1904) 'Signs of the Times.' First

published 1829. In *The Works of Thomas Carlyle in Thirty Volumes* (XXVII, 56–82). New York: Scribner's.

Carlyle, Thomas (1966) 'The Hero as Poet.' First published 1840. In Thomas Carlyle. *On Heroes, Hero-Worship and the Heroic in History* (pp. 78–114). Ed. Carl Niemeyer. Lincoln, Nebr.: University of Nebraska Press.

Colley, Linda (1996) *Britons: Forging the Nation 1707–1837*. London: Vintage.

David, Deirdre (1995) *Rule Britannia: Women, Empire, and Victorian Writing*. Ithaca, N. Y.: Cornell University Press.

Doyle, Laura (1996) 'The Racial Sublime.' In Alan Richardson and Sonia Hofkosh (eds). *Romanticism, Race, and Imperial Culture, 1780–1834* (pp. 15–39). Bloomington, Indianapolis: Indiana University Press.

Fox, W. J. (1831) 'On *Poems, Chiefly Lyrical* (1830).' Reprinted in John D. Jump (ed.) (1967). *Tennyson: The Critical Heritage* (pp. 21–33). London: Routledge and Kegan Paul.

Girouard, Mark (1981) *The Return to Camelot: Chivalry and the English Gentleman*. New Haven: Yale University Press.

Goslee, Nancy Moore (1996) 'Hemans's "Red Indians": Reading Stereotypes.' In Alan Richardson and Sonia Hofkosh (eds). *Romanticism, Race, and Imperial Culture, 1780–1834* (pp. 237–61). Bloomington, Indianapolis: Indiana University Press.

Graham, Colin (1998) *Ideologies of Epic: Nation, Empire and Victorian Epic Poetry*. Manchester, New York: Manchester University Press.

Hallam, A. H. (1831) 'On *Poems, Chiefly Lyrical* (1830) [On Some of the Characteristics of Modern Poetry].' Reprinted in John D. Jump (ed.) (1967). *Tennyson: The Critical Heritage* (pp. 34–49). London: Routledge and Kegan Paul.

Harrison, Antony H. (1998) *Victorian Poets and the Politics of Culture: Discourse and Ideology*. Charlottesville, London: University Press of Virginia.

Hobsbawm, Eric (1983) 'Introduction: Inventing Traditions.' In Eric Hobsbawm and Terence Ranger (eds). *Invention of Tradition* (pp. 1–14). Cambridge: Cambridge University Press.

Houghton, Walter E. (1957) *The Victorian Frame of Mind, 1830–1870*. New Haven: Yale University Press.

Kiernan, V. G. (1989) *Poets, Politics and the People*. Ed. Harvey J. Kaye. London, New York: Verso.

Koebner, Richard, and Helmut Dan Schmidt (1965) *Imperialism: The Story and Significance of a Political World, 1840–1960*. Cambridge: Cambridge University Press.

Landon, Letitia Elizabeth (1832) 'On the Ancient and Modern Influence of Poetry.' In Jerome McGann and Daniel Riess (eds) (1997). *Selected Writings* (pp. 160–9). Peterborough, Ont.: Broadview Press.

Lootens, Tricia (1994) 'Hemans and Home: Victorianism, Feminine "Internal Enemies," and the Domestication of National Identity.' *PMLA*, 109, 238–53.

Macaulay, Thomas Babington (1871) 'Milton.' First published 1825. Reprinted in *The Works of Lord Macaulay in Eight Volumes* (V, 1–45). London: Longmans, Green.

McClintock, Anne (1995) *Imperial Leather: Race, Gender and Sexuality in the Colonial Contest*. New York, London: Routledge.

McGann, Jerome (1993) 'Literary History, Romanticism, and Felicia Hemans.' *Modern Language Quarterly*, 54, 215–35.

Peacock, Thomas Love (1820) 'The Four Ages of Poetry.' Reprinted in Howard Mills (ed.) (1970). *Memoirs of Shelley and Other Essays and Reviews* (pp. 117–32). New York: New York University Press.

Rothstein, David (1999) 'Forming the Chivalric Subject: Felicia Hemans and the Cultural Uses of History, Memory, and Nostalgia.' *Victorian Literature and Culture*, 27, 49–68.

Simpson, Roger (1990) *Camelot Regained: The Arthurian Revival and Tennyson, 1800–1849*. Cambridge: D. S. Brewer.

Sinfield, Alan (1986) *Alfred Tennyson*. Oxford: Blackwell.

Tucker, Herbert F. (1988) *Tennyson and the Doom of Romanticism*. Cambridge, Mass.: Harvard University Press.

Tucker, Herbert F. (1994) 'House Arrest: The Domestication of English Poetry in the 1820s.' *New Literary History*, 25, 521–48.

Young, Robert J. C. (1995) *Colonial Desire: Hybridity in Theory, Culture and Race*. London, New York: Routledge.

24

Poetry in the Four Nations

Matthew Campbell

Alfred Tennyson's *Idylls of the King* moves towards its conclusion with the Great Battle of the West, performed in a fog at the winter solstice. Its location is at the Atlantic seaboard of Arthur's kingdom, as far from Camelot as he can possibly go:

> Then rose the King and moved his host by night,
> And ever pushed Sir Modred, league by league,
> Back to the sunset bound of Lyonesse –
> A land of old upheaven from the abyss
> By fire, to sink into the abyss again;
> Where fragments of forgotten peoples dwelt,
> And the long mountains ended in a coast
> Of ever-shifting sand, and far away
> The phantom circle of a moaning sea.
>
> (*Idylls of the King*, 'The Passing of Arthur',
> ll. 79–87)

Idylls of the King is an epic based on medieval myths of Britain, King Arthur and the Round Table. It is also, among many other things, a poem about Victoria's Britain, or more precisely her United Kingdom, a kingdom of islands bounded by water. Here at its far westerly point, the geography of that kingdom, physical and human, is shown uncertain of boundary or population.

'Fragments of forgotten peoples' still dwell here, and Tennyson's gloss on them is that they were 'Perhaps old Celts'. These forgotten peoples of the west live in a transitory place, next to the 'sunset bound' of land and sea. It is not only the demography or geology of these boundaries that remain moveable: so does their history, their very etymology. In Tennyson's curious phrasing, the land has been 'upheaven' from the abyss. This is a synthetic archaism. 'Heave' is Anglo-Saxon, as is its long-obsolete passive, 'heaven'. But the *OED* gives no instances of the passive sense of the word 'upheaven' in its distinctly un-medieval geological definition (1 b) of the word 'up-heave', 'To toss or throw up with violence; *spec.* in *Geol.*' (the first scientific example given is from 1813, along with the text that haunts much of *In Memoriam*, Lyell's *Principles of Geology* of 1830, I, 231, 'Great upheavings of the coast'). The boundaries of land, language and verse seem to be still in process, as Tennyson invents a linguistic past for what has been 'forgotten' in a place where mountain falls into coast, sand is 'ever-shifting' and all is surrounded by the magnificent Tennysonian cadence of its ghostly margins: 'far away / The phantom circle of a moaning sea'.

In *Maud*, the guilty lover is driven away from England after the death of the heroine's brother, and lands on a Celtic Coast – 'Breton, not Briton' – and this becomes 'a coast / Of ancient fable and fear' (*Maud*, II, 78–80). It is as if the fable and fear are suggested by the very geography itself, just as the landscape of the Great Battle of the West seems almost to fall off the Atlantic edges of Europe. In his life and poetry, Tennyson was an avid visitor to these places, obsessed with ocean and waves as he was, yet his ostensible interest was not always that of a mere tourist. The coasts of Cornwall, Wales, Scotland and Ireland are also places at the edge of Tennyson's own state, the Celtic fringe of the United Kingdom. The kingdom was united after the long and often violent history of the Atlantic archipelago often referred to as the 'British Isles'. From the death of Queen Elizabeth I, the kingdoms of Scotland and England shared a monarch, and in 1707 they were brought together under an Act of Union. After over a century of political unrest – the defeat of King James at the Battle of the Boyne and the Treaty of Limerick in Ireland in 1690–1, the invasion of England and defeat of the Jacobite cause at Culloden in Scotland in 1745, the failed Irish rising and French invasion of 1798 – Great Britain and the elite which ruled Ireland decided that the best way of solving the long-running political and economic problems of that nation was to complete the Union of the British Isles. As a consequence, in 1801 the Union flag incorporated the flag of St Patrick and was adopted as the national flag of a newly expanded state, the United Kingdom of Great Britain and Ireland. Along with the principality of Wales, the kingdom was now a union of four nations. The Whig version of history and the state that the Victorians inherited from the Irish politician and philosopher Edmund Burke now asserted that the United Kingdom was simply a completion of the long historical process which appeared to have been the inevitable result of centuries of rule from London by a highly evolved English parliament and a liberal English monarchy.

Tennyson was the poet laureate of this relatively new state formed from the incorporation of geographically proximate peoples, and *Idylls of the King* is a poem of its aspirations and destruction. Yet its author was perpetually reminded of the supposedly forgotten peoples who lived unreconciled to the Union alongside coasts of fable and fear. In 1848, Tennyson visited Cornwall, as he thought about taking up again the Arthurian poem begun with 'Morte d'Arthur' in the 1830s. And in the same year, he stayed with the Irish poet Aubrey de Vere in Limerick. Ireland was in the midst of famine which, de Vere tells us, shocked Tennyson. But his visit had to include a trip to Valencia Island off the coast of Kerry, in order to see the waves. De Vere says that on the way he brought him up Knock Patrick and describes the view thus:

> The sunset was one of extraordinary but minatory beauty. It gave, I remember, a darksome
> glory to the vast and desolate expanse with all its creeks and inlets from the Shannon, lighted
> the green islands in the mouth of the Fergus, fired the ruined Castle of Shanid, a stronghold

of the Desmonds, one of a hundred which they were said to have possessed. The western clouds hung low, a mass of crimson and gold; while, from the ledge of a nearer one, down plunged a glittering flood empurpled like wine. The scene was a thoroughly Irish one; and gave a stormy welcome to the Sassenach bard. (Aubrey de Vere, quoted in Tennyson 1897: 242–3)

Returning by Killarney, Tennyson heard the bugle sounded over the lakes and composed 'The Bugle Song': 'The splendour falls on castle walls / And snowy summits old in story'. It is a lyric of history and the fading of memory, suited to a land of forgotten peoples, literally fading before his eyes and ears:

> O love, they die in yon rich sky,
>   They faint on hill or field or river:
> Our echoes roll from soul to soul,
>   And grow for ever and for ever.
> Blow, bugle, blow, set the wild echoes flying,
> And answer, echoes, answer, dying, dying, dying.
>   (*The Princess*, Book IV)

De Vere's Romantic prose and Tennyson's poetry borrow Celticism, an established mode of Romantic and post-Romantic writing. From James Macpherson's controversial invention of the warrior-poet Ossian as the newly discovered author of a long-lost Scottish epic, the Celtic revivals of Irish, Scottish and Welsh literatures passed through a Romantic and Victorian poetry written in English which officially welcomed their place in the culture of a United Kingdom striving for their peaceful incorporation. Thus the most influential literary critic of Victorian Britain, Matthew Arnold, in his lectures *On the Study of Celtic Literature*, informed his philistine English audience that in order to assist good government they would need to understand the riches of the culture and sentiment of the Celt, so that the desired fusion of the Union could take place without resort to coercion: '*Behold England's difficulty in governing Ireland!* . . . There is nothing like love and admiration for bringing people to a likeness with what they love and admire; but the Englishman seems never to dream of employing these influences upon a race he wants to fuse with himself' (1973a: 392). Given the violent history of the fusion of the four nations of the United Kingdom, in which the imposition of the English language was but one result of centuries of cultural assimilation and coercion, Victorian poetry often shows that the writing which attempts to commemorate such fusion carries with it conflicting formal traces of conflict and rebellion.

Tennyson's dying echoes at Killarney rebounded off castles and mountains old in the story of political as well as geological upheaval. His host Aubrey de Vere knew also that the picturesque ruins of the hundred castles of the Desmonds had formerly served as fortification against rebellion and invasion, and that in 1848 de Vere and his family were working hard in the relief efforts aimed at alleviating the suffering of a starving people. The following year, the potatoes failed again, and de Vere saw famine return to Ireland. He could not help admonishing both his friend Tennyson and his own sense of the Celtic picturesque in the 'Autumn' section of his Famine poem, 'The Year of Sorrow: Ireland, 1849':

> I join that voice. No joy have I
>   In all thy purple and thy gold;
> Nor in that nine-fold harmony
>   From forest on to forest rolled;
>
> Nor in that stormy western fire
>   Which burns on ocean's gloomy bed,
> And hurls, as from a funeral pyre,
>   A glare that strikes the mountain's head;
>
> And writes on low-hung clouds its lines
>   Of ciphered flame, with hurrying hand;
> And flings amid the topmost pines
>   That crown the cliff, a burning brand.

Tennyson had heard nine echoes of the bugle the year before, yet here the 'nine-fold harmony' brings no joy. The re-experienced sunset becomes thunderous and is now explicitly linked with fire, death, violence and the burning sword of the persisting curse of famine.

'The Year of Sorrow' shifts a perception of weather into one of violence and doom. In doing so, though, de Vere is still working within the generic expectations of much post-Romantic writing within the Celtic. The aesthetic interest of European Romanticism and British Victorian poetry in the cultural forms of the Celt was founded on the quality of the authentic, a quality which by its very nature could not be assimilated within the mainstream of European art. The authentic was to be discovered among forgotten peoples, in the marginal western strangeness of the Celtic sublime. Aesthetics bears much political freight in this regard, as the authentic always threatens the control of the viewer: de Vere's sublime Shannon sunset cannot avoid its mention of castles and war, and the martial threat of the clouds and light. The very 'Irish' character of the picturesque admonishes the English poet with its 'stormy welcome'. De Vere's hostile Irish weather echoes 'The Bugle Song' and its echoes of sunset, war, famine and immortality. But it also echoes conventional 'Celtic' effects of meteorological splendour, such as this passage in Macpherson's *Fingal*, where the bard Ossian uses the Highland weather for a simile for battle:

How can I relate the deaths when we close in the strife of our steel? . . . Thou hast seen the sun retire red and slow behind his cloud; night gathering round on the mountain, while the unfrequent blast roared in narrow vales. At length the rain beats hard; and thunder rolls in peals. Lightning glances on the rocks. Spirits ride on beams of fire. And the strength of the mountain-streams comes roaring down the hills. Such was the noise of battle, maid of the arms of snow. Why, daughter of the hill, that tear? The maids of Lochlin have cause to weep. The people of their country fell, for bloody was the blue steel of the race of my heroes. But I am sad, forlorn, and blind; and no more the companion of heroes. Give lovely maid, to me thy tears, for I have seen the tombs of all my friends. (*Fingal*, IV)

For all the furore over the inauthenticity of his work, Macpherson, in Arnold's memorable phrases, convinced European literature of the 'piercing regret and passion' of the 'Titanism' of Celtic poetry, and his *Ossian* 'carried in the last century this vein like a flood of lava through Europe' (Arnold 1973a: 367). It added the stormy west to the Romantic and Victorian vogue for sublime locations, no matter how the striving for the epic in the extraordinarily extended simile here courts bathos. Early in his career, the Scottish poet Hugh MacDiarmid made the case for representing a literary identity which was both nationalist and modernist by writing in what he termed 'synthetic Scots', a variety of English that no one actually spoke but which could be adapted for a renaissance in poetry from Scotland. Over a century before him, Macpherson created a no less synthetic Celtic form in his supposed translations of Scottish epic, bringing together the extended simile from classical epic, a highly rhythmic and self-consciously poeticized English prose, the harsh landscape of the Highlands and the figure of the estranged, self-conscious poet, always at an elegiac remove from the heroic events he retells.

The Victorians Tennyson and de Vere write the Irish scene which confronts them in this synthetic Celtic mode, emphasizing the sublimity of weather and the seeming hostility of a geography which retains a capacity to challenge those who are not of this place ('the Sassenach Bard'). But Tennyson also takes another motif from Macpherson, that of the pining, melancholy poet who, for all the virtuoso simile-making, is aware only of the passing of time, loneliness and faint hopes of immortality. The return to the sublime land of 'forgotten peoples', 'the coast / Of ancient fable and fear', the long historical and geological past of 'snowy summits old in story', is an invocation of an alternative pre-Norman Celtic past which is neither classical nor Saxon. Through its seeming authenticity this Celtic past challenges the origins and history of Victoria's United Kingdom.

Macpherson pines for the lost Highland culture which was destroyed after Culloden; a hundred years later, Tennyson and de Vere could view Ireland suffering its catastrophe under the Famine. In both instances, it seemed that the United Kingdom at best forgot or at worst removed those at its margins who would not be merged into its powerful culture. In the nineteenth century, the strength of the Celtic poetry of the United Kingdom is a testimony to those who used it to reinforce both Union and empire, moving the evidences of cultural form – poetry itself – into the completed union of the miscegenated 'Briton'. Yet, in its unwillingness to hold together the marriage forced on it, it is also a record of the break-up of that heterogeneous state. The civil war which destroys the Arthurian epoch occurs at the dangerous western fringes of the Isles.

Much English Victorian poetry and criticism borrows wholesale from the writing of the Celtic fringes of the UK. Ostensibly, of course, this is not a matter of cultural appropriation, since the writing supposedly comes from the same state. Nevertheless, even those English Victorian voices who shared an interest in things Celtic betrayed the cultural gap that existed between themselves and their fellow subjects to the north and west. One of the academic achievements of Matthew Arnold's tenure as Oxford Professor of Poetry (1857–67) was no longer to lecture in Latin, but to lecture on non-classical vernacular subjects in English. *On the Study of Celtic Literature* (Oxford lectures of 1865–6, published in 1867) breaks through further: it opens with an ambivalent account of the Eisteddfod (the Welsh Bardic Congress which was revived in 1860) but ends hoping that Oxford will found a chair of Celtic, 'to send, through the gentle ministration of science, a message of peace to Ireland' (1973a: 86). However, writing later, in an 1880 essay subsequently titled 'The Study of Poetry', Arnold returns to a more anglocentric version of literary culture. In it, he reiterates a claim from Aristotle that 'the superiority of poetry over history consists in its possessing a higher truth and a higher seriousness'. This is a matter of style and movement as much as substance and matter, shown in the 'special character' of 'the best poetry', 'accent' (1973b: 171). 'Accent' is an undefinable quality, which is both the individual artist's 'high seriousness' and the means by which we recognize it. Diction, style and manner all share in the accents of high seriousness, and those who fail in high seriousness fail also in this crucial test of accent. Thus Arnold makes his celebrated refusal to enlist Chaucer as one of the 'classics', since he lacks both high seriousness and a high style. But, closer to his own time, Arnold also criticizes the Scottish poet Robert Burns, when he fails both in matter and in a more recognizable conception of accent, one which is resolutely provincial:

> The real Burns is of course in his Scotch poems. Let us boldly say that of much of this poetry, a poetry dealing perpetually with Scotch drink, Scotch religion, and Scotch manners, a Scotchman's estimate is likely to be personal. A Scotchman is used to this world of Scotch drink, Scotch religion and Scotch manners; he has a tenderness for it; he meets its poet half way. In this tender mood he reads pieces like the *Holy Fair* or *Halloween*. But this world of Scotch drink, Scotch religion, and Scotch manners is against a poet, not for him, when it is not a partial countryman who reads him; for in itself it is not a beautiful world, and no one can deny that it is of advantage to a poet to deal with a beautiful world. Burns's world of Scotch drink, Scotch religion, and Scotch manners, is often a harsh, a sordid, a repulsive world. (Arnold 1973b: 182)

Arnold's intentions are humorous, aimed as the passage is at an English audience which is separate from Burns in accent yet attuned to the jokes still easily gleaned from stereotypes of the drunken, sectarian, uncouth Scot. Only the Scots-speaking 'partial countryman' can understand Burns and form a 'personal' estimate of the drinking songs, Presbyterian satire and fantasy of much of his poetry. For the non-Scots-speaking, Anglican Englishman there is only 'a harsh, a sordid, a repulsive world'.

This is not the entirety of Arnold's view of Burns, which can admit the achievement of *Tam O'Shanter* and that most un-Victorian of sequences, *The Holy Beggars* ('It has a breadth, truth and power . . . which are only matched by Shakespeare and Aristophanes', 1973b: 186). Arnold's conception of 'accent' is something heard across all European languages, and where there is linguistic difficulty, as in Chaucer and Burns, 'it is a difficulty to be unhesitatingly accepted and overcome'. Yet from this surface quality Arnold demonstrates prejudices founded on the centrality of a southern English accent for 'the best poetry' in the English language. That accent benefits from an education in the classical and Romance languages: Dante and the French Romances share the high seriousness to which the colonized Chaucer only intermittently aspires. When the accent deviates from a high European culture, it pleases only a 'partial', 'personal' and provincial audience, and does not achieve the urbane cultural form which, in the nineteenth century, is to all intents and purposes the modernizing power of English itself.

Arnoldian talk of high seriousness, sweetness and light, culture and anarchy, has proved fertile ground for contemporary criticism of Victorian poetry and culture, keen to distance itself from those consequences of such concepts that we can see above: racism, sectarianism and elitism to the point of snobbishness. However, Arnold's Oxford deafness is common not only among critical and creative Victorian voices but also among contemporary critics. This is a deafness to the Victorian poetry not written in the accents of those educated in the south-east of England. Rare among critics, John Lucas has weighed heavily on Arnold's dismissal of the 'provincial', a word that Lucas says owes its pejorative sense to Dr Johnson, in whose *Dictionary* the word means 'not of the mother country; rude, unpolished'. Lucas shows how the literature of the late eighteenth and nineteenth centuries begins to be written in the 'tone of the provincial [which] can now be measured against what is said to be the tone of the centre' (Lucas 1982: 18). His interest is more in the Disraelian 'Two Nations', of capital and labour, than in the four nations of the United Kingdom, so he hears that tone primarily in the literature of the new English towns and cities rising as a result of the rapid industrialization of the first half of the nineteenth century. Lucas traces the word 'provincial' back to its Latin root, in which a province is 'a principal division of a kingdom or an empire' (1982: 14). The principal divisions of the Victorian United Kingdom were England, Scotland, Wales and Ireland. The language of power, of administration, law and commerce was English, however, so Arnold can claim that the 'accent' which is the 'special character' of the 'best poetry' should also be an English one. When critics such as Arnold make such claims for the high seriousness – of subject and style – of poetry in English, it is often at the expense of the poetry of those other nations which made up the United Kingdom, those nations at the Celtic fringe of Britain and Europe.

If English and American critics and historians have in practice not questioned Arnold's conception of the unified British 'nation', critics in Wales, Scotland and Ireland have certainly done so. The Scottish critic Robert Crawford's *Devolving English Literature* is but one example of the riposte to England-centred accounts of the history of literature in English. Indeed, the late twentieth century saw the limited devolution of power from London to Cardiff, Edinburgh and Belfast. Preceding this, the work of historians like J. G. A. Pocock (1982), Michael Hechter (1975), Hugh Kearney (1989), Linda Colley (1992) and Norman Davies (1999) has served to point out that 'British' history is not synonymous with that of England, and the history of the four nations can come to be written in a large and popular synthetic history like Davies's *The Isles*. English literary criticism is beginning to follow.

For all of the centralizing force of the establishment of the high seriousness of English poetry in Victorian Britain, the poetry of the other nations of the kingdom often struggled for audience, subject matter and style. The history of Victorian poetry in the United Kingdom as a whole is often one of assimilation or, to adopt a metaphor from postcolonial theory, hybridity. The four nations are quite distinct linguistically. While in the 1860s, Arnold mourned the loss of the last speaker of Cornish, Ireland, Wales and Scotland still speak their own Celtic languages, and varieties of English continue to thrive across the Isles. Arnold was keen to trace the high seriousness of English poetry from the classics through the Renaissance into the same cultural position in the world that was held by the British Empire. English poetry continues in a central and European tradition, a powerful universalizing and modernizing force. Yet it has other, much more partial, marginal elements, those which come from the languages and literatures of the British regions, provinces and nations. From those supposed margins the new Romantic vogue in European literature for Celticism began, crucial for Romantic and Victorian poetry.

The cultural impetus within Victorian England was for fusion, assimilation and incorporation with this Celtic element. Arnold opens his *Study* by contemplating a revived Eisteddfod in Llandudno, rain-soaked and miserable as it was, and goes on to conclude that a combination of the supremacy of English, the historical defeat of Welsh, and modernity itself will accelerate the hybrid and diminish the separate cultural and linguistic identity of the marginal:

> The fusion of all the inhabitants of these islands into one homogeneous, English-speaking whole, the breaking down of barriers between us, the swallowing up of separate provincial nationalities, is a consummation to which the natural course of things irresistibly tends; it is a necessity of what is called modern civilisation, and modern civilisation is a real legitimate force; the change must come and its accomplishment is a mere affair of time. The sooner the Welsh language disappears as an instrument of the practical, political, social life of Wales, the better. (Arnold 1973a: 296–7)

Whether or not Arnold has been proven to be right (both the Eisteddfod and Welsh, as a widely-spoken vernacular language, continue to thrive), his project is directed at the union of 'these islands', a union beset then and now with great cultural and political differences.

A key source for Arnold was the work of the French critic Ernest Renan, who had attempted to perform the same task for France, which also has a history of semi-autonomous provinces, wars, civil wars and colonization. According to Renan, the French nation is evidence of a successful hybrid or, in a version of another common metaphor, a 'melting pot': 'The Frenchman . . . is that which has come out of the great caldron, where, under the governance of the King of France, the most various elements have fermented together' (Renan 1896b: 74). Even given the onward homogenizing power of modernity, the literary culture of the Celt, still settled precariously at the rim of that cauldron, remains as a reminder of cultural differences as well as supposed differences of race. In Renan, these differences are conspicuously gendered, a set of racial characteristics which together create the assimilated characteristics of the culture: in the case of Brittany, a defeated and hitherto marginalized province of the state has intermingled with the dominant culture of the greater French state.

Renan was Breton himself, and in his essay 'The Poetry of the Celtic Races' (1859), he states that the basis of Western European Christian culture is its fusion of the Romantic, feminized literature of Brittany, Wales and Ireland with the epic poetry of Greece and

Rome. In the Welsh tales of the *Mabinogion* (translated into English by Lady Charlotte Guest, 1838–49) and the British and Breton Arthurian Romances, Renan found the key Celtic note which provided the culture that the Teutonic and Saxon races plundered when they pursued their aggressive wars of colonization and annexation. According to Renan, the success in conquest of the (Teutonic) Normans was in intellectual as much as military coercion, since they were 'men so prompt to seize and assimilate the ideas of the foreigner' (1896a: 32). Dominant over France and Britain, they stole Celtic poetry and added it to their own warlike natures, thus creating the codes of chivalric love of European medieval Romance.

The new code is founded in racial distinctions between the victor and the victim, which lead on to distinctions which are stated explicitly in terms of male and female. They thus create the conditions for the cultural assimilation of Teuton and Celt in the modern European state as a kind of marriage:

> If it be permitted us to assign sex to nations as to individuals, we should have to say without hesitance that the Celtic race, especially with regard to its Cymric or Breton branch, is an essentially feminine race. No human family, I believe, has carried so much mystery into love. No other has conceived with more delicacy the ideal of woman, or been more dominated by it. It is a sort of intoxication, a madness, a vertigo. (Renan 1896a: 8)

For Renan, and later Matthew Arnold, modern-day France and the United Kingdom are the result of an intermarriage of the feminine Celt and the masculine Saxon. This is a happy miscegenation for the Breton Renan, and its result is the culturally complete and centralizing modern nation. The English Arnold, aware that Britain has yet fully to consummate its union, puts a less positive gloss on its Celtic partners. The rebelliousness which is a characteristic of the sentimental Celt, '*always ready to react against the despotism of fact*' (Arnold 1973a: 344; Arnold's emphasis, translating a phrase from Henri Martin's *Histoire de France*), is less chivalric than hysterical: 'no doubt the sensibility of the Celtic nature, its nervous exaltation, have something feminine in them, and the Celt is thus peculiarly disposed to feminine idiosyncrasy' (1973a: 347).

While the 'feminine' is centred within accounts of the identity of Celtic poetry, the centring occurs within a culture that is located in marginal and liminal spaces; that is, spaces which mark not only boundaries, but also passing points through into other spaces. These are not only at the edge of Europe, sharing geographical borders with mountain and sea, but also at the linguistic edges between French and Breton, English and Welsh, Scots and Gaelic. To these are added the generic borders of romance and epic, lyric and ballad, and they contribute to the great synthetic genres of the Romantic and Victorian recreation of all things Arthurian, in poetry, fiction and art, through John Keats, Walter Scott, Tennyson, Elizabeth Barrett and Robert Browning, the Pre-Raphaelites, Algernon Swinburne and William Morris. By the time that the British Empire was given a vision of itself in ruins, destroyed by civil war at the end of the poem which spans much of Victoria's reign, Tennyson's *Idylls of the King* (1842–89), the young W. B. Yeats's turn to Irish myth in the late 1880s can work in an already well-established tradition of poetry in English which wrote of the resurgence of the formerly dominated and defeated who lived in marginal or liminal spaces. Through over a century of Romantic and Victorian Celticism, from Macpherson's Ossian (1760–3) to Yeats's *Wanderings of Oisin* (1889), the warlike meets the passing away of a great civilization from history. Consequently, the metropolitan centre, British and French, has contrasting conceptions of the Celt as either wild or submissive, reacting against the despotism of fact or, in Renan's words respecting the Irish monks of the Dark Ages, 'Credulous as a child, timid, indolent, inclined to submit and obey' (1896a: 49).

It is a remarkable story, not only of Victorian poetry but of the history of the hundred and twenty years of the United Kingdom of Great Britain and Ireland, that submission and obedience were not to be the characteristics of the cultural nationalism that such ideas of gender and race were designed to obliterate. The young Yeats's achievement in *The Wanderings of Oisin* is in a recognizably Victorian mixed genre, part romance and part epic, with strong elements of lyric and dialogue throughout. Returned from an eternally youthful land to an Ireland converted and domesticated by St Patrick, the suddenly aged Fenian hero Oisin rages to Patrick against the change that confronts him, in an accentual verse which challenges the bounds of metre in English:

> Put the staff in my hands; I will go to the Fenians, thou cleric, and chant
> The war-songs that roused them of old; they will rise, making clouds with their breath
> Innumerable, singing, exultant – the clay underneath them shall pant,
> And demons, all broken in pieces, and trampled beneath them in death.
>
> . . .
>
> We will tear out the red flaming stones, be trampled and will batter the gateway of brass
> And enter, and none sayeth 'nay' when there enters the strongly armed guest;
> Make clean as a broom cleans, and march on as oxen move over young grass;
> Then feast, making converse of Eire, of wars and of old wounds and rest.
>> (*The Wanderings of Oisin,* 1889 version, III, 201–4, 209–12)

Yeats's youthful friendship with former members of the Irish Republican Brotherhood, otherwise known as the Fenians (named after the warriors who followed Fionn mac Cumhaill – Macpherson's Fingal – in the Ossianic cycle), was a dabbling with violent work against the United Kingdom. Such a heroic final confrontation, which results in the freedom that Oisin envisages in the passage here, would move beyond the rhythmic confines of a Victorian poem in to the unravelling of that kingdom only thirty years later.

The example of Ireland is paramount here, since the inability of the British government to solve its Irish problem throughout Victoria's reign was to coincide with a remarkable renaissance of Irish writing in English, a renaissance founded both on the nineteenth century's general interest in nationalism and on its specific interest in the Celtic. As I have said, one intention of the parliamentary Union of 1801 was to attempt to bring together the administration of the four nations in forms which were more than just coercive. The example of eighteenth-century Scotland was strong in this regard. After 1745, the literary and linguistic culture of the Highlands of Scotland declined irrevocably as emigration and the Clearances rapidly depopulated the land. For many contemporary readers this was an example of a colonial enterprise – or in Michael Hechter's memorable phrase, 'internal colonialism' – even though it was carried out by fellow subjects of the same king. It appeared in the nineteenth century that the languages of Ireland and Wales would follow and that administrative union would be assisted by the establishment of a new, homogenized, Unionist British culture.

Many poets and scholars who wrote within this new culture worked actively for the Union in Ireland, Wales and Scotland as well as in London. Two of the most prestigious Victorian literary periodicals, *Blackwood's Magazine* and the *Edinburgh Review*, were based in Scotland, and an influential magazine like *Fraser's* had a succession of Irish editors, including the poet William Allingham. Indeed Edwin Morgan has said that one of the difficulties of writing about nineteenth-century Scottish poetry is that much of it was written by a diaspora of poets, many of whom chose to live in England and write on British subjects (1988: 337). Although George MacDonald, J. M. Barrie and Robert Louis Stevenson wrote on Celtic subjects or in Scots, their success was in England. James Thomson's *The City of Dreadful Night* is a poem of London, and the dialect of John Davidson's 'Thirty Bob a Week' is Cockney. Irish poet-immigrants in London included Oscar Wilde and Yeats, whose Fenianism was tempered by spending most of the 1890s in London literary (and occult) society. Despite the powerful pull of the centre, the result was often the persistence of difference, no matter that it was often written in the English language. Through philology, antiquarianism, translation and eventual cultural renaissance, the new poetry written in English came with accents all its own.

Throughout the Victorian period, Irish poetry in English was developing in parallel with English poetry. This is not to say that cultural 'assimilation' or 'fusion' was not taking place. The consequences of the Famine included the pushing of the Irish language far to the west, the massive emigration which led to the spread of an Irish diaspora across the British Empire and the English-speaking world, and the consolidation of English as the language of government and literature. Much Irish nationalist thought viewed the loss of the long traditions of Gaelic music and poetry as a catastrophic consequence of the penal laws, Union and Famine, but its partial compensation was the invention of Irish poetry in English in new synthetic forms, based on translations, ballads and song.

The first poet to contribute to this compensation was Thomas Moore, who in his lifetime (he did not die until 1852) rivalled his friend Byron as the most popular of all the English-language Romantic poets. Moore's *Irish Melodies*, English lyrics composed to Irish airs, were sung in drawing rooms across Britain and Europe throughout the nineteenth century. Around the 'Young Ireland' newspaper *The Nation*, poets like Thomas Davis, James Clarence Mangan and Jane Elgee (writing as *Speranza*; she was later Jane Wilde, Oscar's mother) wrote nationalist poetry which was to be collected in the bestselling pamphlets *The Spirit of the Nation*. Mangan also wrote for the Unionist *Dublin University Magazine*, which showed an early willingness to publish translations and criticism of Irish-language poetry. Its most distinguished contributor in this respect was Samuel Ferguson, whose four-part 1834 review of James Hardiman's *Irish Minstrelsy* (1831) provided a model for much linguistic and poetic interest in translations and imitations of Irish poetry, as developed later in the nineteenth century by poets such as George and Dora Sigerson and Douglas Hyde. Taken as a whole, the history of Irish poetry in the nineteenth century tells of the creation of what the Irish poet, critic and executed leader of the 1916 Rising, Thomas MacDonagh, could look back on and call 'the Irish Mode'. This mode was created under the constitutional conditions of the Act of Union, in which some attempted to unify and others to separate a distinctive Irish poetic culture and that of the language and traditions of its dominant neighbour.

Before Yeats (who lived the first thirty-six years of his life as a 'Victorian'), the most significant poet of Victorian Irish poetry is James Clarence Mangan (1803–49), whose achievement, like that of Macpherson in Scotland in the century before him, is based on translation. In his experiments in translation and his 'original' poems, Mangan sounds one literary language in the forms of another, creating effects of metre and voice which, when they succeed, rival those of his contemporaries in England, Tennyson, Browning and A. H. Clough. Mangan's biography overshadows his poetic reputation in accounts of his work by the Young Irelander John Mitchel, who first cast him as the unfulfilled and abject Irish artist, James Joyce, who imaginatively associated his own career with that of Mangan, and the postcolonial critic David Lloyd, for whom Mangan represents the inability of a colonial literature to be anything other than 'minor'. Mangan's life was of one doomed to hackwork and obscurity, with alcoholism and opium addiction adding to poverty and ill-health. He caught cholera and died in Dublin towards the end of the Famine.

Mangan's best poetry, though, shows how the non-English poet can create new forms, metaphors and rhythms within a non-English yet English-speaking culture. Tennyson's 'Bugle Song' is in many ways a Famine poem: both in the contexts of its composition and in the 'splendour' of its Celticism, echoes are all that sound against the seemingly final moments of personality, history and civilization. It led him later to think of the people of the west as forgotten, waiting to slide back into the ocean. Through the late 1840s, Mangan too wrote poems of Famine, like his translation of the sixteenth-century Irish poet O'Hussey's 'Ode to the Maguire', where war and weather are associated in a hostile landscape in which all difference is obliterated under rain and flood. It opens thus:

> Where is my Chief, my master, this bleak night *movrone*?
> O, cold, cold, miserably cold is this bleak night for Hugh,
> Its showery, arrowy, speary sleet pierceth one through and through,
> Pierceth one to the very bone!
>
> Rolls real thunder? Or, was that red livid light
> Only a meteor? I scarce know; but, through the midnight dim
> The pitiless ice-wind streams. Except the hate that persecutes *him*,
> Nothing hath crueller venomy might.
>
> An awful, a tremendous night is this, me-seems!
> The floodgates of the rivers of heaven, I think, have been burst wide –
> Down from the overcharged clouds, like unto headlong ocean's tide,
> Descends grey rain in roaring streams.
>
> (James Clarence Mangan, 'O'Hussey's Ode to the Maguire', 1846)

The weather that de Vere and Tennyson had pictured carrying such threat now exacerbates the poet's concern for his master, internally exiled and fleeing from a treacherous foe. In his *Penguin Book of Renaissance Verse*, David Norbrook (1992) places the Gaelic original of this poem after book V of Edmund Spenser's *The Faerie Queene*. It is a reminder not only of an indigenous bardic tradition on the run in renaissance Ireland but also of the part that Spenser played in the colonization of a country the poet felt the Irish did not deserve. In Mangan's version of the poem, it is almost as if he keeps his forebear running into the very language of the enemy, an English poem. Almost but not quite, since the language of the poem is a strange English indeed, pitted as it is with a kind of patois Hiberno-English ('*movrone*', 'me-seems') and an English full of deliberate archaisms and neologisms. The rhythm challenges the English speaker with tongue-twisters ('Its showery, arrowy, speary sleet pierceth one through and through, / Pierceth one to the very bone!') and contorted coinings ('Nothing hath crueller venomy might.')

Mangan's version of 'O'Hussey' is more than mere translation, since it is filled full both of a stubborn refusal to sound the conventional Victorian English poem and of the unavoidable assimilation of a recalcitrant literary voice into 'English'. Through what is nominally a process of 'translation', a dramatic monologue has been created which sounds the cultural defeat of one society against the forms of its triumphant enemy. Looking back from Victorian to Elizabethan Ireland, Mangan knew that bursting the floodgates of English would obliterate the distinctiveness of a culture now submerged underneath the catastrophe of Famine. In April 1846, he published this 'original' poem in *The Nation*:

Siberia

In Siberia's wastes
   The Ice-wind's breath
Woundeth like the toothèd steel.
Lost Siberia doth reveal
   Only blight and death.

Blight and death alone.
   No Summer shines.
Night is interblent with Day.
In Siberia's wastes alway
   The blood blackens, the heart pines.

Pain as in a dream,
   When years go by
Funeral-paced, yet fugitive,
When man lives, and doth not live,
   Doth not live – nor die.

In Siberia's wastes
   Are sands and rocks.
Nothing blooms of green or soft,
But the snowpeaks rise aloft
   And the gaunt ice-blocks.

> And the exile there
> > Is one with those;
> They are part, and he is part,
> For the sands are in his heart,
> > And the killing snows.
>
> Therefore in those wastes
> > None curse the Czar.
> Each man's tongue is cloven by
> The North Blast, that heweth nigh
> > With sharp scymitar.
>
> And such doom each drees,
> > Till, hunger-gnawn,
> And cold-slain, he at length sinks there,
> Yet scarce more a corpse than ere
> His last breath was drawn.

As shown in Chris Morash's *Writing the Irish Famine* (1995), many contemporary accounts of Famine were of the starving as the living dead. Here, Mangan invents a prosody of frozen numbness, a sort of zombie metre. In the regular toll of the clipped rhythm and syntax, rhythmical variation serves only the purposes of irony, as in the line where the anapaests are pulled up short in order to obliterate the exile's nostalgia: 'For the sands are in his heart, / And the killing snows'. Potato blight was the cause of Famine, and blight here brings death as the landscape is transformed into a featureless and dark place, imbued with hunger and cold. Yet the overarching conceit of the poem is to write of an *eastern* place, far away from the dying west in which the poet seemed to live. In metaphor, the poem performs a sort of translation of the Celtic into the Oriental, something with which Mangan often played in his Oriental translations, forgeries and parodies: in the same issue of *The Nation* he also published anonymously the spoof translation of a poem directed by a Persian speaker at a colonial visitor, 'To the Ingleezee Khafir, Calling himself Djaun Bool Djenkinzun'.

'Siberia' appears to enable the geographical dislocation in the metaphor to perform what many metaphors of insurrection find they have to do: secrete its message within the metaphors of a poem which appears to be located in a foreign place. Except here any rebellious message appears to hold out little consolation: the banished exile, along with all in Siberia, cannot curse the czar. The diction of the poem is filled full of English archaisms – Woundeth, toothèd, doth, heweth nigh – and even Scots, 'drees'. Mangan seems to work against the metaphor's dislocation, re-integrating English and thus effecting the obliteration of difference. 'Siberia' is tugged away from and then back into the literary language from which it might be expected to show a profound exile. Almost despite the metaphoric translation of the poem itself, the languages of Britain – English, Hiberno-English, Scots – like night and day in the poem appear to be 'interblent'. In catastrophic circumstances, Matthew Arnold's fusion or Renan's fermenting have taken place. 'Siberia' looks like an act of union.

For Thomas MacDonagh, Mangan did escape from English and was one of the key writers who established 'the Irish Mode' in Victorian Ireland. What he says of the rhythm of 'O'Hussey's Ode to the Maguire' could be said also of the rhythm of 'Siberia' in reverse: 'his escape . . . is from precipitate half-unmeasured music to a regular tolling.' (MacDonagh 1996: 54.) Mangan chains up any irregularity of measure, as if the poem sounds nothing but the short expelling of those last breaths which are so imperceptible as to be those of the exiled, imprisoned and dead. For all that it faces defeat, starvation and death, 'Siberia' is a remarkable achievement in prosody and metaphor. Yet there is another side to its apparent lesson of the final obliteration of difference. MacDonagh claims Mangan as one of the Victorian antecedents of a literary revival achieved in English, but in a speech which differs from that spoken in England. What MacDonagh has to say about the new forms of Irish poetry can be adapted to think about the ways in which other verse in English – not just Scottish or Welsh, but the postcolonial poetry of the former countries of the British Empire – could mark not just difference from the English tradition but also new poetic forms that can express new cultural identities. So, by way of example, MacDonagh shows how the work later in the century of the young W. B. Yeats achieves these aims.

Three things, according to MacDonagh, established the 'Irish mode' in English poetry: a memory of the metre of Gaelic poetry, Anglo-Irish prose speech and the rhythms of Irish music (1996: 46–57). At first this seems to be founded on a merely technical distinction, the contrast of English and Irish accentual verse. So, while 'metrical quantity proper does not exist in English' (MacDonagh's MA dissertation was on one of the few successful experimenters with quantity in English, the renaissance poet Thomas Campion), MacDonagh asserts that 'what may be called central English verse, in order to emphasize the stressed, under-emphasizes the unstressed'. By comparison:

> Irish frequently allows for the clear pronunciation of several syllables between stress and stress. Such Irish verse is not rigidly governed by the law of mono-pressures; it is generally found in songs, the tunes of which have a good deal to do with drawing the metrical feet dancing out of their bars. The less pronounced hammering of the stressed syllables is more noticeable in Irish prose speech; and on account of it English as we speak it in Ireland has a much more deliberate way of pronunciation, a much more even intonation, than the English of the English. (1996: 46–7)

The apparently unmetrical accentual verse that Yeats gives to Oisin in the passage quoted earlier comes from an attempt to imitate in English poetry effects gleaned from the Irish language, Irish music and Irish speech in English.

MacDonagh's main example is also from Yeats, 'The Lake Isle of Innisfree' (1893), where the poem shows through its metrical effects a constant effect in Irish speech. This is the opening of Yeats's poem:

> I will arise and go now, and go to Innisfree,
> And a small cabin build there, of clay and wattles made:
> Nine bean-rows will I have there, a hive for the honey-bee,
> And live alone in the bee-loud glade.

This is MacDonagh on its Irish rhythm:

> This general movement, changing from a slow beat to an easy rise and fall, happens constantly. I sometimes think it expresses, whether in accentual verse or quantitative, the mingled emotion of unrest and pleasure that comes with the break up of winter, with the south wind, with the thought of the shortness of life and the need to make haste to explore its good and simple joys – the desire to leave the unlovely, mingled with a vivid conception of the land of heart's desire. (1996: 49)

Matters of linguistics and prosody unavoidably make their way into the subject matter of the Celtic as created by Macpherson and seen in Tennyson, de Vere, Arnold, Renan and Mangan: sentimentality ('mingled emotion of unrest and pleasure'), the reaction against the despotism of fact ('not rigidly governed by the law of mono-pressures', 'the desire to leave the unlovely'), formal irregularity ('the metrical feet dancing out of their bars') and the weather ('the break up of winter, with the south wind'). But what MacDonagh is claiming is linguistic difference within the same language: in a telling phrase, he contrasts 'what may be called *central* English verse' (my emphasis) with that spoken by the Irish, and in the difference of accent he finds sounds of distinct metrical and poetic difference which may in themselves tell of unassimilable cultural division.

Reviewing Gregory Smith's *Scottish Literature: Character and Influence*, in the *Athenaeum* in 1919, T. S. Eliot asked the question 'Was there a Scottish literature?' He thought not, and concluded:

> A powerful literature, with a powerful capital, tends to attract and absorb all the drifting shreds of force about it. Up to a certain limit of dissimilarity, this fusion is of very great value. English and Scottish, probably English and Irish (if not prevented by political friction), are cognate enough for the union to be of value. The basis for one literature is one language. The danger of disintegration of English literature and language would arise if the same language were employed by peoples too remote (for geographical or other reasons) to be able to pool their differences in a common metropolis.

The 'political friction' that seemed to be impeding the attraction, absorption and fusion of Ireland and England in 1919 was the Irish War of Independence, soon to result in the first unravelling of the very cultural Union that Eliot viewed as inevitable. In Arnoldian mode here, Eliot could not have been more wrong (and he was later to encourage Hugh MacDiarmid to say as much in *Criterion* in the 1930s), but he does provide the reasons for 'disintegration', when he speaks of the remoteness of peoples which will drag cultures away from their metropolitan centre.

For every movement towards that centring, the conscious preservation of separate languages, customs, poetry and music served to perpetuate difference. The history of the consolidation of linguistic and cultural difference in the 'provincial' accents of English passes through the history of Victorian poetry. As Arnold knew, the example of Robert Burns both as poet and as collector of folk-song and lyric was instrumental in this persistence of poetry in the varieties of the English language. Following Burns as well as Wordsworth's and Coleridge's experiments in Cumbrian ballad, much antiquarian labour was expended throughout the Victorian United Kingdom in preserving the folk poetry of region, province and dialect. The great Victorian verse form, dramatic monologue, is founded on a fiction of an individual voice speaking. While Browning and later Rudyard Kipling experimented with expletive, accent and the colloquial in their monologues, Tennyson wrote monologue poems in Lincolnshire ('The Northern Farmer' poems) and even in Irish dialect ('Tomorrow'), and he was an admirer of William Barnes's West Country poems. Christina Rossetti and Gerard Manley Hopkins experimented with the unofficial metrics of ballad, nursery rhyme and hymn, and Hopkins studied Welsh and introduced Hiberno-English words into his Irish poetry. Above all, the great Victorian English writer of region, Thomas Hardy, who was a friend of Barnes and edited his poems, wrote novels and poetry deliberately accented away from the metropolitan places of 'central English'.

In Hardy, however, the separate regions of the kingdom seem to share merely in difference, communicating only their strangeness to each other. Early in *The Mayor of Casterbridge* (1886), Donald Farfrae – later to emerge as the sensible and industrious Scot, supplanter of the impetuous Wessexman Henchard – is overheard singing 'in a melody and accent of peculiar charm'. The song, 'It's hame and it's hame, hame fain would I be / O hame, hame, hame, to my ain countree!', is in Scots, and on the evidence of the stanza given in the novel, it appears to be a conventional ballad of exile and nostalgia. Hardy fabricates a text for the song from that fabricated by Allan Cunningham in Robert Cromeck's collection, *Remains of Nithsdale and Galloway Song* (1810), where Cunningham had presented it as one of his *Imitations of the Old Ballad, Jacobite Reliques, &c.* Whether Hardy is doing it deliberately or not, his version effectively conceals its political message. Although the conventional ballad homesickness of its first stanza (the basis of Farfrae's quoted version) soon gives way to the striking Jacobite image of watering the white cockade 'wi' the blude of usurping tyrannie', the lyric is one of defeat, its narrator an exile hopelessly waiting for nothing less than the widespread resurrection of the Highland dead:

> There's naught now frae ruin my country can save,
> But the keys o' kind heaven to open the grave,
> That a' the noble martyrs who died for loyaltie,
> May rise again and fight for their ain countree.

The temptation for Hardy of all authors to exploit the ironies of the defeat and irrevocable loss of a once proud culture must have been great here. But the English novelist, writing nearly one hundred and fifty years after the ruin that this song recalls, chooses to focus less on its insurrectionary history than on the contemporary cultural difference it sounds. Hardy focuses on its reception by an English audience which is moved despite its cynical local character: 'The difference of accent, the excitability of the singer, the intense local feeling, and the seriousness with which he worked himself up to a climax, surprised this sect of worthies, who were only too prone to shut up their emotions with caustic words' (*The Mayor of Casterbridge*, ch. VIII). It is the exotic charm of difference which enables Farfrae to speak to his audience of strangers, who hear that 'this stranger's sentiment was of differing quality

. . . he was to them like the poet of a new school . . . who is not really new, but is the first to articulate what all his listeners have felt, though but dimly to then'. The universal is heard once difference is noted; difference of 'accent' is a question of 'differing quality'. While he may be a 'poet of the new school', Farfrae sings of what these people feel by excavating a text which tells of violent differences in the past. His newness is the prophecy he also tells of the future of their rapidly changing United Kingdom.

See also: NATIONHOOD AND EMPIRE.

REFERENCES AND FURTHER READING

Arnold, Matthew (1973a) *On the Study of Celtic Literature*. First published 1867. In R. H. Super (ed.). *The Complete Prose Works of Matthew Arnold*, Vol. III: *Lectures and Essays in Criticism*. Ann Arbor: University of Michigan Press.

Arnold, Matthew (1973b) 'The Study of Poetry.' First published 1880. In R. H. Super (ed.). *The Complete Prose Works of Matthew Arnold*, Vol. IX: *English Literature and Irish Politics*. Ann Arbor: University of Michigan Press.

Campbell, Matthew (1999) 'Irish Poetry in the Union: Allingham's *Laurence Bloomfield*.' *European Journal of English Studies*, 3. 3, 298–313.

Campbell, Matthew (2000) 'Lyrical Unions: Mangan, O'Hussey and Ferguson.' *Irish Studies Review*, 8. 3, 325–38.

Colley, Linda (1992) *Britons: Forging the Nation, 1701–1837*. London: BCA.

Crawford, Robert (2000) *Devolving English Literature*. Second edition. Edinburgh: Edinburgh University Press.

[Cunningham, Allan] (1810) *Remains of Nithsdale and Galloway Song*. Ed. R. H. Cromek. London: T. Cadell and W. Davies.

Davies, Norman (1999) *The Isles: A History*. London: Macmillan.

De Vere, Aubrey (1894) *Selections from the Poems of Aubrey de Vere*. Ed. George Woodberry. London: Macmillan.

Eliot, T. S. (1919) 'Was there a Scottish Literature?' *Athenaeum*, 1 August 1919, 680–1.

Hardy, Thomas (1978) *The Mayor of Casterbridge*. Ed. Martin Seymour Smith. Harmondsworth: Penguin.

Hechter, Michael (1975) *Internal Colonialism: The Celtic Fringe in British National Development*. London: Routledge and Kegan Paul.

Kearney, Hugh (1989) *The British Isles: A History of Four Nations*. Cambridge: Cambridge University Press.

Lloyd, David (1987) *Nationalism and Minor Literature: James Clarence Mangan and the Emergence of Irish Cultural Nationalism*. Berkeley: University of California Press.

Lucas, John (1982) *Romantic to Modern Literature: Essays and Ideas of Culture, 1750–1900*. Brighton: Harvester.

Lucas, John (1990) *England and Englishness: Ideas of Nationhood in English Poetry, 1688–1900*. London: Hogarth.

MacDiarmid, Hugh (1934) 'The Case for Synthetic Scots.' In *At the Sign of the Thistle* (pp. 177–96). London: Stanley Nott.

MacDonagh, Thomas (1996) *Literature in Ireland*. Nenagh: Relay.

Macpherson, James (1996) *The Poems of Ossian*. Ed. Howard Gaskill. Edinburgh: Edinburgh University Press.

Mangan, James Clarence (1997) *The Collected Works of James Clarence Mangan*. Eds Jacques Chuto, Rudolf Patrick Holzapfel and Ellen Shannon Mangan. Dublin: Irish Academic Press.

Morash, Chris (1995) *Writing the Irish Famine*. Oxford: Oxford University Press.

Morgan, Edwin (1988) 'Scottish Poetry in the Nineteenth Century.' In Douglas Gifford (ed.). *The History of Scottish Literature* (III, 337–51). Aberdeen: Aberdeen University Press.

Norbrook, David (ed.) (1992) *The Penguin Book of*

Renaissance Verse 1509–1659. Harmondsworth: Penguin.

Pocock, J. G. A. (1982) 'The Limits and Divisions of British History: In Search of an Unknown Subject'. *American Historical Review*, 87, 311–36.

Renan, Ernest (1896a) 'The Poetry of the Celtic Races.' First published 1859. In *The Poetry of the Celtic Races and Other Studies* (pp. 1–60). Trans. William G. Hutchison. Reprinted (1970) Port Washington, N. Y.: Kennikat.

Renan, Ernest (1896b) 'What is a Nation?' In *The Poetry of the Celtic Races and Other Studies* (pp. 61–83). Trans. William G. Hutchison. Reprinted (1970) Port Washington, N. Y.: Kennikat.

Tennyson, Alfred (1987) *The Poems of Tennyson*. Second edition. Ed. Christopher Ricks. 3 vols. London: Longmans.

Tennyson, Hallam Lord (1897) *Tennyson: A Memoir by his Son*. One vol. edition (1899) London: Macmillan.

Yeats, William Butler (1957) *The Variorum Edition of the Poems of W. B. Yeats*. Eds Peter Allt and Russell K. Aspach. New York: Macmillan.

25

Poetry and Religion

W. David Shaw

'It is not by philosophy', said St Ambrose, 'that it has pleased God to save his people.' 'This was a piece of luck for Ambrose', one commentator has quipped, 'since Ambrose was no philosopher' (cited Sparshott 1972: 3). Though the same could be said of most Victorian poets, it is difficult to exaggerate the influence of theology and the philosophy of religion on the poets' critical theories and choice of subject matter. As a leading scholar of Tractarian poetry has observed, 'aesthetics and theology do not in the nineteenth century grow in alien soils; they are branches of the same tree' (Tennyson 1981: 61). G. B. Tennyson's judgement is confirmed by G. Kitson Clark, who concludes that 'in no other century, except the seventeenth and perhaps the twelfth, did the claims of religion occupy so large a part in the nation's life or did men speaking in the name of religion contrive to exercise so much power' (Clark 1962: 71).

Victorian religion and theology influence the poetry of the period in five major ways. During the 1830s the recovery of Biblical figures or types in the conservative hermeneutics of John Keble and his fellow Tractarians J. H. Newman and Isaac Williams begin to influence the practice of such dissimilar poets as the Tractarians themselves, Alfred Tennyson, and later Christina Rossetti and Hopkins. In the 1850s the liberal theology of the higher critics of the Bible, especially David Friedrich Strauss (and in the next decade the 'broad church' hermeneutics of Benjamin Jowett), exercises an important influence on Robert Browning. Simultaneously, the agnostic theologies of Thomas Carlyle and of such neo-Kantians as Sir William Hamilton, H. L. Mansel and T. H. Huxley give rise by mid-century to the cosmic inquisitions of Tennyson, A. H. Clough and Matthew Arnold, which soon darken into the even bleaker doubts of James Thomson and Thomas Hardy. Throughout the Victorian period the Hegelian theories of E. S. Dallas and Sydney Dobell also diffuse at large a theology of human evolution and self-making that influence Browning, Tennyson and Swinburne. Finally, as George Eliot and Matthew Arnold come to replace religion with morality and culture, respectively, Walter Pater tries to embalm religion in a new theology of art. The aestheticism that first appears in William Morris's Arthurian poems during the 1850s finds a curious counterpart in the deconstruction of both theology and metaphysics in Huxley's essays on science and religion, in Pater's *Plato and Platonism* (1893) and in Oscar Wilde's *De Profundis* (1897).

Tractarian Theology and Conservative Hermeneutics

By arguing that the Thirty-Nine Articles of the Church of England are more consistent with a Catholic than a Protestant interpretation, J. H. Newman in *Tract 90* stirs controversy by allowing an Anglican, in Thomas Macaulay's view, 'to hold the worst doctrines of the Church of Rome and the best benefice in the Church of England' (quoted in Young 1936: 71). But touched by the art and poetry of the old figural way of reading Scripture, John Keble writes *Tract 89*, 'On the Mysticism Attributed to the Early Fathers of the Church' (1840), in a less polemical spirit. Defending a conservative method of reading the Bible and writing devotional poetry, Keble insists that each analogy between the two covenants is historical. He rejects the gnostic assaults of theologians like Origen and Philo, who want to substitute for historical typology fanciful allegories that turn Adam and Eve into types of the soul and body, respectively.

In his cycle of devotional poems, *The Christian Year* (1827), Keble celebrates in the law received by Moses on Mount Sinai the Old Covenant's type of Christ's Sermon on the Mount. But, as a future Tractarian devoted to liturgical renewal, Keble also celebrates the types of such sacraments as baptism. Constituting a system of 'correspondences' between the two covenants, these types allow the poet-priest to celebrate the theological unity of Scripture. Able to mount 'in tides against the stream / Of ages gone and past', the 'ocean vast' in 'The Circumcision of Christ' (ll. 23–4), for example, recalls the mystery of Noah's deliverance from the Flood, which in the rite of baptism is also the mystery of each believer's deliverance.

One of Keble's most inventive uses of typology occurs in his poem for the 'Fourth Sunday in Lent', where the 'truest image of the Christ' is said to be Joseph, 'Old Israel's long-lost son' (ll. 51–2). This particular use of Joseph seems to be original with Keble, the advocate of reserve, who sees in Joseph's reticent affection for his brothers a typically Tractarian analogy of Christ's love for man. 'Analogy', as one critic says, is 'God's way of practising Reserve' (Tennyson 1981: 47), which is the topic discussed in two tracts (numbers 80 and 87) by Keble's fellow Tractarian Isaac Williams. As a virtue close to the heart of most Victorians, whom G. M. Young describes as 'a slow and wary race', 'reserve is at once the defence of the wise and the refuge of the stupid' (Young 1936: 13–14).

Closest in temper and inspiration to the conservative hermeneutics of Keble are the *Lyra Apostolica* (1836) of J. H. Newman and *The Cathedral* (1838) of Isaac Williams. But the only inheritors of the Tractarian devotional mode to qualify as major poets are Christina Rossetti and Gerard Manley Hopkins. In the crucible of Rossetti's simple prayers and Hopkins's daring paradoxes, Tractarianism seems 'forged anew', as one critic says, 'in a Heraclitean fire' (Tennyson 1981: 208).

Despite its figural use of Job and Noah, Hopkins's masterpiece 'The Wreck of the Deutschland' probably owes more to the Ignatian meditation than to either Keble or Newman. But lesser poems like 'New Readings' are a perfect cross between a typological lyric by Keble and a riddling prose fragment in *Guesses at Truth* by Julius and Augustus Hare. In his hermeneutical poem 'Although the Letter Said', Hopkins strikingly reverses the logic of Christ's own parable of the sower: 'I read the story rather / How soldiers plaiting thorn around CHRIST'S HEAD / Grapes grew and drops of wine were shed' (ll. 3–5). By refusing to consolidate traditional readings of the parables in Matthew 13, Mark 4 and Luke 8, Hopkins transforms the 'dull algebra' of 'schoolmen' into a lyric of riddling elegance and power. The surprise of Hopkins's hermeneutical lyrics is more akin to 'some solutions to . . . chess problems' or to 'some resolutions of suspensions so lovely in music that even the feeling of interest is keenest when they are known and over' (Hopkins 1935: 187–8).

The typological readings of Scripture that Hopkins commemorates in his 'New Readings' are replaced in his more anguished poems by a wrenching of syntax and by a sundering of words by line breaks and inserted phrases. Even a jubilant 'Te Deum Laudamus' like 'Pied Beauty' stresses unique items of ecstasy that no longer rhyme or chime predictably in Christ. Though vestiges of a Job and Noah typology survive the partial wreck of the sacramental system in 'The Wreck of the Deutschland', Hopkins's poem 'That Nature is a Heraclitean Fire' reflects the influence of a new science of flux by taking its types from geology and chemistry. Coal, an allotrope of diamond, is transmuted by intense pressure into an item of great value. In Newman's *Apologia Pro Vita Sua* (1864) some types prove too frail to survive the stress of change, but others prevail. The snapdragons at Trinity College are too fragile to endure as a figure of Newman's perpetual residence at Oxford. But Socrates and Job both confer on Newman subtle typological roles that are decisive and abiding.

Only in the devotional verse of Christina Rossetti do we encounter poems that are less a Tractarian imitation than a blend of that scriptural integrity and lyrical excellence which all typological poetry – from the Bible to Tennyson's *Maud* – exists to express. Rossetti's lyric 'Good Friday' (1862) presents in the poet's 'stony' heart a type that seems at first to be devoid of figural meaning:

> Am I a stone, and not a sheep,
>   That I can stand, O Christ, beneath Thy cross,
>   To number drop by drop Thy Blood's slow loss,
> And yet not weep?
>
> (ll. 1–4)

Recovery comes only at the end of the poem, when Rossetti finds she is a stone in the sheepfold of the Shepherd; smitten by his staff, she celebrates in Moses' power to bring water out of stone a type of Christ's much greater miracle in shedding blood for the cure of stony hearts like her own.

In her poem 'A Better Resurrection' the same metaphor of the stony heart is combined with Ecclesiastes' figure of 'the broken bowl' (12.6) to furnish Rossetti with two essential elements of a eucharistic typology: 'Melt and remould it, till I be / A royal cup for Him my King: / O Jesus, drink of me!' (ll. 22–4). No poem in *The Christian Year* is more intensely personal. And no poem better illustrates Keble's idea that God is a reticently affectionate host who has singled out each guest for special favour. Yet in a strange reversal of

Eucharistic typology that turns her into a cross between George Herbert and Bram Stoker, Rossetti also expresses her love for God by asking him to drink her blood as a kind of vampire.

J. A. Froude says that the poems by Tennyson 'which closed with *In Memoriam* became to many [broad church Anglicans] what *The Christian Year* was to orthodox Churchmen' (Froude 1884: 248). In his *Oxford Lectures on Poetry* and in his review of Lockhart's *Life of Scott*, Keble argues that, just as theologians speak through enigmas and parables to keep the uninitiated herd at bay, so the poet should throw over his deepest feelings a 'veil of reserve' (Keble 1838: 436). Familiar with Keble's theory, Tennyson uses language in *In Memoriam* (1850) 'half' to 'reveal / And half conceal the Soul within' (V, 3–4). In the universe of flux disclosed by Charles Lyell's *Principles of Geology* (1830–3) and Robert Chambers's *Vestiges of the Natural History of Creation* (1844), all types are in peril – not just the figural types that unify Scripture but also the great morphologies (the sciences of form) that allow taxonomists to identify biological and botanical species.

Struggling to preserve the concept of abiding forms in a world where change is universal, Charles Darwin finds that 'species' is just as complex a word as 'type' is for Keble and his fellow Tractarians, or as 'culture' and 'utility' are for Matthew Arnold and J. S. Mill, respectively. A species functions as a metaphor: it is a complex union of identities and differences. But if the principle of difference is carried far enough, it puts in peril the very concept of a species or a type. As the new sciences of flux and change threaten to dissolve a medieval Book of Hours into a book of moments, Tennyson wonders if even science's understanding of species can survive the shock. Whereas progressive evolution and natural theology had traced the path of an ascending escalator, Darwinian evolution replaces 'the great world's altar stairs / That slope through darkness up to God' in *In Memoriam* (55, 15–16) with a careening roller-coaster, doubtfully teleological and frightening to contemplate.

The Higher Criticism and Liberal Hermeneutics

Important to an understanding of Browning's many poems of Christian apology are the liberal hermeneutics of David Friedrich Strauss, whose *Life of Jesus* (1846) argues that parts of the Bible are unconscious fictions or myths. Of secondary interest is Benjamin Jowett's essay 'On the Interpretation of Scripture' (1860), which opposes the typological readings of Keble and the Tractarians. Jowett's five criteria of a genuine 'science of Hermeneutics' may have influenced 'Balaustion's Adventure', the most hermeneutical Greek poem in Browning's canon. Because the best 'higher' (or historical and interpretative) criticism of the Bible is based on a 'lower' (or linguistic and textual) criticism, its most authoritative practitioners are scholars like Jowett, the translator and editor of Plato's *Dialogues*, and George Eliot, who translated from German both Strauss's *Life of Jesus* and Ludwig Feuerbach's *The Essence of Christianity* (1841).

Browning's clearest reference to Strauss occurs in his poem 'Christmas-Eve', where a German professor's lecture on 'This Myth of Christ' (l. 859) distinguishes between the

Jesus of history, a matter of indifference to the true believer, and the Christ of myth, whose 'real God-function' (l. 1040) is to use Jesus' life and death as a paradigm for the placing and timing of an eternal mystery. When Strauss is mentioned again in 'Bishop Blougram's Apology', he is viewed in two different contexts. On the one hand, the worldly bishop concedes he is spiritually inferior to Strauss or Luther. Even if Strauss unwittingly damns such later Biblical critics as Ernest Renan and John William Colenso, who cannot sustain his own religious vision, he saves himself; and regardless of what happens after death, Luther finds 'A real heaven in his heart' (l. 590). On the other hand, when Bishop Blougram is trying to correct his sceptical opponent's view of faith by arguing that belief and doubt require and sustain each other, he uses Strauss as his adversary's chief example of the atheist and unbeliever, located at the opposite end of the theological spectrum from St Paul (l. 595).

Browning's monologue 'A Death in the Desert' is his closest approach before *The Ring and the Book* to a workable notion of religious myth. Like Strauss, Browning's St John puts the question bluntly: is the Christian narrative fact or fable? 'Was this once' or 'was it not once?' His evasive reply enables Browning to imitate Strauss by defending religion against literal-minded believers, who accept every detail of the narrative as historic fact. At the same time Browning can dissociate himself from less responsible higher critics, equally simple-minded, who discredit the Christian story as a mere 'fable', by which they mean a lie. The first fallacy is to reduce the logical order, in which 'might', 'will' and 'love' are eternally related, to the temporal order according to which theology has historically developed. The fallacy of some higher critics consists in the opposite error of reconstructing Christian history according to a self-repeating cycle of first principles. The historic approach of the literal-minded Christians slights the logical element quite as much as the logical approach of some higher critics slights the narrative element. Browning's own approach through his favourite Gospel-writer, St John, a constant target of textual and historical critics, leads readily into both narrative and logical vindications of Christianity without confining him to either.

In rebutting the higher critics who try to read poetry as science, Browning makes St John shift the emotive and descriptive meanings of 'fable' in the way Strauss does when opposing the concept of myth or unconscious invention to the usual dilemma: the choice between history and intentional invention. The Christian fable depends for its value on an illumination of greatness; its meanings must be self-evident once they are pointed to, for they cannot be proved by scientific means.

In his poem 'Development' Browning explores what happens when a higher critic like Friedrich August Wolf, the German classical scholar who instituted the higher criticism of Homer, tries to ground Homeric epics in ancient Near Eastern history, in the biography of Homer, or in moral allegory. Critics who try to read sacred or secular literature in these ways are doing their best to imitate science. But the attempt to ground the *Iliad* in one of Strauss's historical myths, in a chronicle of events that have been imaginatively interpreted, fails to reckon with the fact 'there was never any Troy at all, / Neither Besiegers nor Besieged' ('Development', ll. 69–70). And efforts to ground interpretation in the biography of the author fare no better. Like the Bible, the

Greek epics may be the work of many authors, and Homer himself may never have lived.

'A Death in the Desert' and the pope's monologue in *The Ring and the Book* combine the circularity of a myth with the linear design of a historical narrative. Without the stubborn facts of Biblical history, there would be no past experience to interpret. But without a retrospective understanding of the past, the speaker would be in the position of T. S. Eliot's interpreter in *Four Quartets*: he would have had the experience but missed the meaning ('The Dry Salvages', II, 45). Unless history is linear, it has none of the risk or contingency of lived experience. Unless it is circular, it is not intelligible. Since Browning's pope and St John often require history to do opposite things simultaneously, a sceptic might be tempted to infer that their art of Biblical interpretation is at once necessary and impossible.

As a close associate of Benjamin Jowett and a student of broad church theology, Browning was certainly familiar with his friend's influential essay 'On the Interpretation of Scripture', published in *Essays and Reviews* in 1860. As a classical scholar, Jowett wants to interpret the Bible with the same scholarly rigour and critical good sense that he brings to the study of Plato's *Dialogues* or that Browning's Balaustion brings to her recitation and interpretation of Euripides' play *Alkestis*. Browning assumes that interpretations can be grounded in authorial intentions, and like Jowett he seeks the comfort of consensus. But unless interpretation is redefined as a form of translation in which an obscure dialect or an obsolete iconography is deciphered, it is hard to see how it can be as strictly scientific as Jowett tries to make it. Assailing as anachronistic and dangerous the typological methods of Biblical interpretation revived by Keble in *Tract 89*, Jowett asserts that the Bible's 'greatness is of a simple kind; it is not increased by double senses . . . elaborate structure, or design' (1860: 382). His view of interpretation seems flawed, however, for it suggests that there can be only one correct reading of a work. It also implies that no critical understanding of a work could hope to prove illuminating. Jowett never fully realizes that the knowledge Balaustion brings to Euripides' *Alkestis* is not just of the kind she can look up in a glossary or handbook, but of the interpreter herself in an ideal meeting of type and antitype, of the poem and its beholder.

Kant and Agnostic Theology

In his 'Philosophy of the Unconditioned' (1829), a principal source of H. L. Mansel's and T. H. Huxley's agnostic theologies, Sir William Hamilton argues like Immanuel Kant that any attempt to understand God generates antinomies that are intrinsically unresolvable. A philosophy of religion must operate from – and demonstrate – the proposition that God exists and has certain properties: Hamilton thinks that God must be either absolute or infinite. But to say that God is both absolute and infinite is like a quantum physicist's saying that matter is at once atomic and infinitely divisible. Only a fool or an idolator would presume to say that a subject possessing such contradictory predicates is truly understood or known.

Agnostic theology reaches a crisis in H. L. Mansel's Bampton lectures for 1858, *The Limits of Religious Thought Examined in Eight Lectures*. A lecturer on Kant and the dean of St Paul's, Mansel contends that the divine nature can never be logically grasped by the mind's mutually exclusive concepts of a being that is at once absolute, infinite and a first cause. An absolute God is the negation of all relation, but the concept of a first cause is the absolute affirmation of a particular relation. If we try to peer behind these contradictory masks of God by introducing the idea of succession in time, Mansel finds we are checked by a third conception, the idea that God is infinite and therefore outside time altogether. Any attempt to know a God whose inexhaustible dynamic life cannot be enclosed within any logical scheme turns every definition of God into a profane caricature or distortion.

Like Mansel's God, the curiously contradictory God of *In Memoriam* is simultaneously personal and impersonal, singular and plural, both 'within' and 'without' the human mind:

> That which we dare invoke to bless;
>> Our dearest faith; our ghastliest doubt;
>> He, They, One, All; within, without;
> The Power in darkness whom we guess.
>
> (124, 3)

The attributes of Tennyson's God create a crisis for understanding because, being multiple and contradictory, they are not strictly conceivable.

A. H. Clough's agnosticism can be traced to his reading of David Friedrich Strauss and to his early admiration of Friedrich Schiller, whose philosophic prose and aphorisms Clough eagerly absorbed as a student at Oxford. Nor should we underestimate the influence of Clough's friend and tutor, W. G. Ward, who barely conceals his contempt for the sermons of Clough's Rugby mentor, Dr Thomas Arnold (Ward 1841: 298–364). Playing Blougram to Arnold's Gigadibs, Ward displays a deeply sceptical habit of mind designed to remove any middle ground between his own Tractarian brand of Christianity and total unbelief.

In Clough's poem 'Qui Laborat, Orat', the negatives fall with unusual force: 'O not unowned, Thou shalt unnamed forgive' (l. 17). To affirm that God is 'not unowned' is to make the most minimal affirmation possible. And perhaps God is 'unnamed' because he is not strictly knowable. Clough seems to be recalling Sir William Hamilton's philosophy of the unconditioned, the Bible of Victorian agnostics. He may also be remembering a similar idea in James Douglas's book, *Errors Regarding Religion*, which Clough consulted when doing research on Buddhist and Hindu thought for his Newdigate Prize entry, 'Salsette and Elephanta'. Douglas vigorously defends the thesis that any attempt to know God as he is, or to be at one with God, is a religious heresy. Douglas's own preference for Buddhist transcendence to any form of Hindu idolatry may have predisposed Clough to prefer a religion of silence to any religion that tries to know God as well as God knows himself.

Clough's predilection for the contradiction and uncertainty that are his intellect's greatest need culminates in his astonishing 'Hymnos Ahymnos', 'A hymn, yet not a hymn'. The opening refrain could proclaim either an orthodox belief in the ark of the covenant or a Feuerbachian faith in the divinity of the human: 'O thou whose image in the shrine / Of human spirits dwells divine' (ll. 1–2). Does 'divine' modify 'human spirits' or God's 'image'? Whether Clough is thinking of ancient Israel or Feuerbach, in either case his subject disappears behind the mind's antinomies. Having been cleansed of idols, Clough's understanding can operate only on the 'blank and void of empty mind' (l. 6), which is as devoid of sensory content as the noumenal world of Kant.

Matthew Arnold, the quintessential unbeliever, finds that the centre of society is also the place of greatest isolation. Disturbed by the slow withdrawal of the sea of faith in 'Dover Beach' and separated from the monks in 'Stanzas from the Grande Chartreuse' by his own loss of faith, Arnold like his father also seems half enamoured with the medieval Christianity about which he writes so sympathetically in his essay 'Pagan and Medieval Religious Sentiment' (April 1864). Arnold's agnosticism may have originated in the doctrine of learned ignorance advocated by his hero, Joseph Glanvill, in whose *Vanity of Dogmatizing* Arnold discovered the story of the Scholar Gipsy. A kind of seventeenth-century Hamilton or Mansel, Glanvill is an agnostic in the tradition of Nicholas of Cusa.

Victorian agnosticism originates in Sir William Hamilton's seminal review essay of Victor Cousin's course of philosophy, published in the *Edinburgh Review* in October 1829. Taking issue with Cousin's theory that God is comprehensible, Hamilton argues that 'the unconditioned is incognisable and inconceivable'. In one of the reading lists found in his early diaries, Arnold mentions Cousin's lectures on philosophy. Drawing upon the writings of the Indologian H. T. Colebrook, Cousin anticipates Hamilton's own agnosticism when expounding the Hindu understanding of God. To resemble God, Cousin explains, the yogi must 'reduce himself to pure being, by the abolition of all thought'. The 'incognisable' God of Kantian thinkers like Hamilton and Mansel was criticized by contemporaries like W. H. Smith, a reviewer of Mansel's Bampton Lectures in *Blackwood's Edinburgh Magazine* (1859), for being too Asiatic, for being 'one with the Brahm of Indian theology'. But the sublime transcendence of the Hindu God apparently appealed to Arnold, who was already familiar with the grandeur of that concept from his study of Victor Cousin, from his reading of the *Bhagavad Gita*, and, as one scholar has shown (Nagarajan 1960: 341), from an awareness of the important affinities between the Vedantic apology for art and his own ideal of disinterested objectivity.

In 'The City of Dreadful Night' James Thomson is less influenced by the agnosticism of Hamilton or Mansel than by the atheistic humanism of Feuerbach and Leopardi. His culminating vision of *Melancholia*, inspired by the engraving of the German artist Albrecht Dürer, dramatizes Feuerbach's teaching that theology is veiled anthropology, a repressed knowledge that humanity is divine, or, more precisely, that God is humanity in alienation from itself. As Feuerbach says, 'that which in religion is the predicate' the new theology must now proclaim 'the subject, and that which in religion is a subject, we must make a predicate, thus inverting the oracles of religion'. When we say God suffers, what is truly divine is the human predicate 'suffering', not the subject 'God'. The truth that theology has traditionally suppressed is the truth that 'he who suffers for others, who lays down his life for them, acts divinely, is a god to men' (Feuerbach 1957: 60).

Because he acquires the double aspect of Dürer's Melancholia, who retains like Keats's Melancholy and Moneta a double identity as muse and destroyer, Thomson's speaker can share in the goddess's sublimity and be 'himself', in Pope's words, the 'great Sublime he draws'. In her struggle towards a vision that would comprehend all intellection, all suffering and all joy, Melancholia embodies the mind's repressed knowledge of its own supremacy. Vindicating Hegel's teaching that there is nothing behind the veil which is not already in front of it, Melancholia is an image of the new Feuerbachian god. She is the divine self-consciousness Thomson has been seeking.

Though nineteenth-century atheists and unbelievers could be jailed for blasphemy, 'word crimes' are less a matter of unbelief and atheism than of lower-class vulgarity and of the coarse *manner* in which subversive teachings are diffused. Victorian society can forgive the delicately wrought scepticism of Tennyson's *In Memoriam* or the cognitive atheism of Hamilton's and Mansel's Kantian philosophies of religion. It can even condone the high church agnosticism of Matthew Arnold, whose 'Stanzas from the Grande Chartreuse' seem to admire everything about Catholicism except its Christianity. What Victorian culture finds harder to forgive is the rude candour of those freethinkers and secularists whom it prosecutes for blasphemy, including William Hone, Edward Moxon, Jacob Holyoake and the redoubtable G. W. Foote, whose appreciative review of *Jude the Obscure* was the single notice of his novel that Hardy chose to preserve. Lacking the education of an Oxford professor of poetry, Foote is imprisoned not for his heretical ideas but for his vulgar diction, inferior social status, and access to that wide working-class audience that Arnold calls the 'Populace'.

As Hardy recognized, subversive thought is less subject to censure in poetry than in prose. Though Hardy's poems of cosmic inquisition are just as blasphemous as *Jude the Obscure*, his idea in 'God's Education' that God's creatures must morally instruct their creator is surely no bolder or more heretical than the primitive evolutionary theology of Browning's 'Caliban Upon Setebos' or than Tennyson's disturbing idea in *In Memoriam* (34, 7–8) that God may be a 'wild poet' working 'without a conscience or an aim'.

Hegel and Theologies of Self-Making

All Victorian readers of Jowett's *Essays and Reviews* (1860) would be indirectly familiar with G. W. F. Hegel's idea that, in order to complete his original creation, a God of becoming requires his worshippers to actualize the freedom that is his greatest gift to the world. They would also have encountered a version of this doctrine in Jowett's influential essay 'On the Interpretation of Scripture', which just as resourcefully applies Hegel's principle of development to Christianity as Jowett's commentary on Plato's *Dialogues* weds Hegel's ideas to Greek thought. The method is carried furthest in the substitution of human self-making for divine activity in such left-wing Hegelians as Strauss and Feuerbach, whose legacy leaves its dissolving trace on Browning's 'Development' and his 'Epilogue' to *Dramatis Personae*.

I am inclined to take Browning at his word when he protests to F. J. Furnivall, the Victorian Browning scholar, that he had no first-hand knowledge of either Hegel or Kant (Irvine and Honan 1974: 502, 508). But I am also convinced that in trying to remove some of the difficulties that are posed by the merely ideal Christology of Friedrich Schleiermacher, the German theologian he read in translation, Browning arrives independently at a solution that strikingly resembles Hegel's answer to the same problem: I am referring to his doctrine of a double Trinity.

Neither Strauss nor Feuerbach, whom Browning read in translation, discusses Hegel's doctrine of a double Trinity. And Browning did not have enough command of German to read Hegel in the original. But the many similarities between Hegel's double Trinity and the interplay in Browning's poetry between historical Christianity and a timeless trinitarian logic are too striking to ignore. Like Hegel, Browning discerns behind the persons in the Trinity an interaction of idea, spirit, nature. Only the middle term, love, unites the abiding truth of the second or pre-worldly Trinity with the incursion into history of the first Trinity. As Browning's pope argues, there is evidence in nature of divine power and knowledge, but no evidence of a good or veracious God: 'Is there strength there? – enough: intelligence? / Ample: but goodness in a like degree?' (*The Ring and the Book* X, 1363–4). As soon as he adds to 'intelligence' and 'strength' the missing middle term, which Hegel calls 'Spirit' and which Browning's Pope calls 'love without a limit', then the sacrificial quality of this love requires God's entry into history. As the second person of the Trinity, love 'supplies' the 'tale' of historical religion. But as the middle term of a timeless dialectic 'beyond the tale', love or spirit also overreaches history.

Christ is the Hegelian spirit (love). God is the Hegelian idea (power). And the world is the Hegelian nature, which Browning associates with knowledge. If Christ is to unite these two Trinities, he cannot be described as a mere moral teacher. To venerate Christ as a Jewish Kant, who instructed man in the 'simple work' of moral 'nomenclature', is like praising, 'not nature, / But Harvey, for the circulation' of the blood ('Christmas-Eve', ll. 971–3). But Christ overreaches the law he expounds. Browning's assertion that the actual world is overreached by love or spirit rests on the assumption that it is overreached by God (or the Hegelian idea). And this idea can overreach the world only if the spirit or love which recognizes this truth is not a mere finite spirit, a mere good man, but an infinite God-man that forms the middle term of a double Trinity, directing Browning, as it directs Hegel, 'from the cistern to the river' ('Christmas-Eve', l. 1015).

If, however, no historical Christ existed, how could Hegel, Schleiermacher or Browning's David in the poem 'Saul' ever hope to know this fact? A sceptic like Strauss would argue that Schleiermacher's feeling of depending on a Christ who is historical and not just an idea in his mind might be delusively stimulated by a mad scientist or wizard. In 'Saul' there is only one way Browning can escape Strauss's critique of Schleiermacher's 'Eclectic Theology' in the third volume of *The Life of Jesus*, which Browning read in George Eliot's 1846 translation. It is by crossing Schleiermacher's psychological analogy, which is grounded in a feeling of dependence, with a figural analogy, which makes David's sacrificial love for Saul a figure or type of a suffering God-man who is more solidly historical than Schleiermacher's merely ideal Christ. If David's love is self-sacrificial and God's is not, then David enjoys, in G. K. Chesterton's phrase, 'a secret and blasphemous superiority' to his creator. However unorthodox Browning's ideas about the imperfection of both humanity and God may be, I think Chesterton is right to claim they are 'great thoughts, thoughts written by a great man, and they raise noble and beautiful doubts on behalf of faith which the human spirit will never answer or exhaust' (1903: 179).

A secularized version of Hegel's theology of self-making also appears in Tennyson's late and unjustly neglected poem 'The Making of Man'. According to Tennyson humanity has only a negative identity until it has earned the right to say, in a final hymn of praise to man, 'Hallelujah to the Maker "It is finished. Man is made"' (l. 8). More sustained and complex are Swinburne's two poems of self-making, 'Hymn of Man' and 'Hertha'. Though Swinburne may have known nothing of Hegel's thought directly, he seems to have encountered in William Blake, in Jacob Boehme, and perhaps even in Indian thought a form of Hegel's spiral journey out of being into non-being, then back into becoming. Such is the trajectory of Hegel's Idea, which at the end of the *Logic* returns to a higher form of its original unity. In 'Hymn of Man' Swinburne claims that 'each soul that labours and lives' by moving through distinguishable moments has the power to 'recreate' the god 'of whom [all souls] are creatures' (ll. 55, 48). Swinburne's fullest exploration of self-making is his difficult poem 'Hertha', whose deity combines the spiral journey of Hegel's absolute with the deep and appealing Hindu idea that the cosmos undergoes an infinite number of deaths and rebirths.

One Hegel scholar has noted that Hertha is Hegel's absolute spirit, 'glorified in his power to transcend everything imaginable and everything thinkable' (Loewenberg 1929: xxx). Hertha's making and doing do not merely proceed from what she *is*. Instead, her actions *constitute* what she is. Hertha is the deity 'which began' (l. 1), not merely in the sense that she originated life, but also in the sense that she herself has originated. Until she passes into nature, she is only the indifference of sheer possibility: 'Out of me man and woman, and wild-beast and bird; before God was, I am' (l. 15).

At least one scholar of Victorian religion, Alan P. Sell, has asked how far the period's Hegelian theories of knowledge and its idealist philosophies of religion are compatible with Christian belief (Sell 1995: 187–225). Whereas idealists like Edward Caird and C. C. J. Webb tend to sink the soul of the individual believer in the absolute, personal idealists like A. S. Pringle-Pattison start, not with the idea of a self-worshipping God who eliminates genuine human worship altogether, but with 'the historical development of humanity as the process in which the Absolute comes to itself' (Pringle-Pattison 1887: 185). Victorian religious apologists like the neo-Hegelian Browning scholar Sir Henry Jones are not rigorous philosophic thinkers. And the most exacting and by far the most luminous of the British idealists is F. H. Bradley, a philosopher who, in his stern warnings against religious idolatry, might be called the opposite of a Christian apologist. In a confession of his 'Ultimate Doubts' in *Appearance and Reality* (1893), Bradley, the greatest of the English Hegelians, announces that God's justice and love cannot be preserved as ultimate attributes of the absolute, which in his own austere words 'is not personal, nor . . . moral, nor . . . beautiful or true' (Bradley 1893: 472). This denial of ultimate reality to God so shocked Bradley's contemporaries that the Clarendon Press threatened to stop publication of what was to become Bradley's most influential book.

Moral Theology and the Religion of Art

T. S. Eliot believed that when religion becomes intellectually indefensible to Matthew Arnold's cultured humanist, two heresies were likely to result. Either morality may be made a substitute for religion, as in some of the poems and prose fictions of the ethically rigorous but morally unorthodox Robert Browning and George Eliot. Or alternatively, in the verse of such aesthetes as the young William Morris, Swinburne and D. G. Rossetti, the art of religion may be replaced by a pure (or decadent) religion of art. In Eliot's words, 'Arnold's books about Christianity seem only to say again and again – merely that the Christian faith is of course impossible to the man of culture . . . From this proposition two different types of man can extract two different types of conclusion: (1) that Religion is Morals, (2) that Religion is Art' (1932a: 434).

Unlike George Eliot and Matthew Arnold, for whom religion is 'morality tempered with emotion', both Browning and F. H. Bradley acknowledge that religion is an autonomous activity, qualitatively distinct from both morality and art. What remains a mere possibility for Bradley's moral philosopher, incapable of being fully realized at even the highest stage of ethics (or 'ideal morality'), becomes for Bradley's religious believer not an 'ought' but an 'is' – an achieved fact. Similarly, a knight of faith like Browning's Caponsacchi is as genuinely heroic in *The Ring and the Book* as Soren Kierkegaard's Abraham is in *Fear and Trembling*. But in Browning's complex moral monologues, important Socratic affinities still exist between Browning and the author of *Ethical Studies* (1876), even though Bradley's treatise appeared too late to influence most of Browning's own dramatic monologues.

The subversive turn in Browning's ethical thought occurs at the moment when the ethical moralist, the champion of 'my station and its duties', is catapulted into the sphere of what F. H. Bradley calls 'ideal morality'. Here he must function as a Socratic practitioner of what might paradoxically (but more accurately) be called 'ethical immorality', a Socratic effort to maximize personal value even at the cost of violating cultural *mores* or norms. The catalyst in this process is the Faustian overreacher, a revolutionary character like Browning's Paracelsus, who strains against the limits of mere custom or convention.

The hedonist who advocates 'pleasure for pleasure's sake' is a Don Juan who refuses like the lover in 'Le Byron de nos Jours' or 'Two in the Campagna' to will an endless repetition of the good moment. Instead of wanting one thing, sex, an infinite number of times, he wants to experience an infinite number of things in a single instant, like Faust. Browning's critique of Don Juan's bad faith and boredom resembles Bradley's and Kierkegaard's criticism. Equally self-defeating are the empty precepts of an unethical moralist like Browning's prior in 'Fra Lippo Lippi'. Embodying Bradley's doctrine of 'duty for duty's sake', the prior blocks the moral, artistic and even spiritual development of the monk. Even Browning's dull grammarian or his faithful but plodding poet in 'How it Strikes a Contemporary' mark the limits of Bradley's injunction to discharge the responsibilities of one's 'station and its duties'.

Two of the most eminent 'ethical immoralists' of the Victorian era are George Eliot and Browning. Eliot lived out of wedlock with G. H. Lewes while his deranged wife was still alive. And Browning eloped with Elizabeth against her tyrannical father's will. Given the extraordinary social circumstances of their acts of deliverance, however, the self-realization of Browning's Caponsacchi and of the Perseus-like saviours in 'The Glove' and 'Count Gismond' is ultimately just as ethical as Eliot's rewarding union with Lewes or Browning's heroic elopement with Elizabeth.

It is true that such deeds of self-realization are not conventionally moral. As assaults upon King Nomos or the dictates of mere convention, they may even seem immoral. Hence the paradox of a subversive Socratic hero or heroine who in defying the moral law may with some justice be called an 'ethical immoralist'. In Bradley's memorable words, 'man is not man at all unless social, but man is not much above the beasts unless more than social' (1876: 223). Or as Chesterton says, in eloping with Elizabeth Browning had 'the same difficulty as Caponsacchi, the supreme difficulty of having to trust himself the reality of virtue not only without the reward, but even without the name of virtue'. The moral Socrates must be prepared to seem immoral. When the hour comes, he must be ready to walk 'in his own devotion and certainty in a position counted indefensible and almost along the brink of murder' (Chesterton 1903: 108–9).

While Browning and George Eliot are celebrating the heroism of ethical immoralists, Victorians like Swinburne, D. G. Rossetti and William Morris are substituting for the art of religion a religion of art. A striking example of this important development can be studied in the purist art of Morris's monologues in *The Defence of Guenevere and Other Poems*. Morris's Arthurian monologues have their priest, rite, church and congregation, but no God. Their art is endotelic, an art of surface masks, which preserves the sacred space of theology as a place apart from the secular world, without any of theology's controversial doctrines or creeds. Ralph Waldo Emerson observes that the Victorian Church of England 'keeps the old structures in repair, spends a world of money in music and building; and in buying Pugin, and architectural literature'. He believes that because the church 'is marked by the grace and good sense of its forms, by the manly grace of its clergy', it helps promote the new religion of art. For as Emerson concludes, 'the gospel it preaches is, "By taste are ye saved"' (Emerson 1908: 111).

One of the most seductive and phantom-like features of 'The Defence of Guenevere' is its redefinitions, which allow moral and religious ideas to survive as beautiful aesthetic ghosts. Though the words 'gracious' and 'true' retain their favourable emotive meanings, their descriptive meanings are altered beyond recognition:

> will you dare,
> When you have looked a little on my brow,
> To say this thing is vile?
>
> (ll. 236–8)

                         am I not a gracious proof –

   . . .

                        also well I love to see
That gracious smile light up your face, and hear
Your wonderful words, that all mean verily

The thing they seem to mean.

                               (ll. 241–50)

As 'grace' declines from the favour of a gracious God or virtuous knight to mere grace of manner or bearing, virtue and vice become matters of good or bad taste. Words mean 'verily', Guenevere insists, if they are 'the thing they seem to mean'. But if appearance is the only reality and words are mere sensory marvels, like the ripples of sound that rise in Guenevere's throat, they cannot be what they seem to be. If truth has any referential meaning, Lancelot cannot be true. And if he is true, the word 'truth' has to be redefined as a pure intuition of moral values. Since a perception of good and evil is as immediate as a sensory presentation of blue or red, moral judgements are assimilated, as in the ethical theories of G. E. Moore, to the perception of a colour. For Morris, the poet behind the mask, Guenevere's understanding of truth is a self-voiding concept, made obsolete as a ghost at the very moment the mind's power to mirror the world is invoked to reaffirm the traditional distinction between what a thing is and what it refers to or means.

Though few of Morris's Arthurian characters are as holy as Galahad, they are all secular equivalents of the holy, because they inhabit a spiritual territory of chapels, palaces and tombs that Morris rigorously segregates from the workaday world. Guenevere's forensic rhetoric is purist art in disguise, because like purist art (as opposed to a craft like book-binding or an art like architecture) it is conspicuously useless and impractical. Because nothing Guenevere says is likely to convince a jury not already converted to her cause, the gratuitousness of her performance turns into a sustained travesty of the aesthetic ideal Morris formulates in his mature prose criticism. Far from throwing the halo of the sacred over art's absence of point, Morris like Ruskin defends in his criticism a theory of art for work's sake, not art for art's sake. Declaring that 'art is man's expression of his joy in labour', Morris opposes any purist separation of art or craft from the everyday world.

In Morris's purist poetry severe abstention from all practical habits of perception that would associate blue with fidelity, for example, or green with amorous passion requires a medieval scholar like Johan Huizinga heroically to suppress his understanding. Readers must see with Ruskin's 'innocent eye' what a child might see, or what the retina of the eye might register if it could be cut off painlessly from the brain. To renounce represen-tation by offering immediate presentations of tear-filled voices or rippling words rising in the throat is to emancipate the sensory medium.

Whereas T. S. Eliot's 'blue' in 'Ash Wednesday' has an assigned connotation, 'blue of larkspur, blue of Mary's colour' (IV, 10), Morris's 'blue' is an unconsummated symbol. Its meaning exhausts the freakishness of arbitrary caprice:

'And one of these strange choosing cloths was blue,
Wavy and long, and one cut short and red;
No man could tell the better of the two.
'After a shivering half-hour you said:
'God help! heaven's colour, the blue:' and he said, 'hell.'
('The Defence of Guenevere', ll. 34–8)

It is possible, of course, that the use of 'blue' as a floating signifier is historically grounded. Morris may expect us to know that blue, originally a symbol of fidelity in love, came in the Middle Ages to represent its own opposite. As Huizinga explains, 'by a very curious transition, blue, instead of being the color of faithful love, came to mean infidelity, too, and next, beside the faithless wife, marked the dupe. In Holland the blue cloak designated an adulterous woman, in France the "cote bleue" denotes a cuckold. At last blue was the color of fools in general' (1949: 292).

Though it is historically accurate to say that Morris dramatizes the phase of culture that Huizinga analyses in *The Waning of the Middle Ages*, a historian of ideas would be equally justified in arguing that Morris is not merely re-presenting medieval symbolism in its decline but is also exploring the nature and function of the presentational forms that his Victorian contemporary, H. L. Mansel, analyses in *Prolegomena Logica* (1851). Unlike a conceptual representation, Mansel says, the poet's presentational images can be immediately 'depicted to sense or imagination'. Whereas representative or discursive signs 'fix the concept in understanding, freeing its attributes from the condition of locality, and hence from all resemblance to an object of sense' (Mansel 1851: 14), the poet's presentational images are examples of representative ghosts, or what Susanne Langer (1948) calls 'unconsummated symbols'.

As in music, towards whose condition Pater says all art aspires, the presentational language of Mansel's poet possesses, in Langer's words, all 'the earmarks of a true symbolism except one: the existence of an assigned connotation' (1948: 195). Because Morris's Arthurian monologues abound in presentational language that possesses the outward form or the ghost of a representational sign without its conventionally assigned significance, the lovely cadences or 'falls' in his verse, which are vocal but not moral or theological 'falls', approximate music's 'unconsummated' form of symbolism. In short-circuiting the process of using a word to represent a concept that is then denoted by a sensory object, Mansel's presentational forms play an increasingly important role in late Victorian aesthetics. They influence the poetic theories and practice of such Victorians as Arthur Hallam, David Masson, Pater and Swinburne, who often use images to project meanings too elusive for conceptual language to express. By analysing the intuitional theory of logic and knowledge that informs such images, Mansel's *Prolegomena Logica* offers an explanation of purist poetry's anti-mimetic mimesis, including its 'religion of art'. The *Prolegomena* is a work we know Pater admired, since he praises its 'acute' philosophy in his essay on 'Style'. Mansel's treatise almost certainly influences Pater's own purist criticism, including the well-known analysis of Morris's verse in Pater's 1868 essay on 'Aesthetic Poetry'.

To turn the art of religion into a religion of art by emptying a theological poem of spiritual content is often more difficult than reductionists assume. For as Swinburne shows in his 'Hymn to Proserpine', any act of burying the gods carries the seeds of its own destruction. As long as change persists, Persephone cannot die, because she is the genius of change itself. To predict that even the newly triumphant Christ will die is to forget that no gods will die as long as there are worshippers to extol them or infidels to write their epitaph: 'Yet thy kingdom shall pass Galilean, thy dead shall go down to thee dead' (l. 74). A phrase like 'All delicate days and pleasant' (l. 48) creates a hole at its centre. Like Milton's locution 'in this dark world and wide', where the blind poet seems to lose his way in a world too spacious for him, the use of a correlative conjunction that is not required by the meaning mocks the emptiness of a soft pastoral world soon to be 'cast / Far out with the foam', like Tennyson's lotos-eaters as they sweep 'to the surf of the past' (ll. 48–9). But even as Swinburne's sceptic relishes the death of a slave morality in which the sheep conspire to persuade the wolves that it is sinful to be strong, he cannot ironically reconcile his elegiac prophecy about the death of Christianity with his other resounding axiom about the eternity of consciousness: 'Fate is a sea without shore, and the soul is a rock that abides' (l. 41).

The substitution of the religion of art for the art of religion is nowhere more evident than in D. G. Rossetti's sonnet 'The Hill Summit', where dazzling sensations of 'this feast-day of the sun' turn the blazing 'altar' spread 'for vesper-song' (ll. 1–2) into a visual marvel. The summit Rossetti climbs is clearly a Pisgah-height, a hill of contemplation where he might be expected to receive some supernatural vision. But he enjoys elevated geographical vistas without the anticipated revelation. By the end of the sestet, as he watches 'the last bird fly into the last night' (l. 14), intimations of a religious meaning have so faded that Rossetti seems in love less with the liturgy of 'this feast-day' than with visual impressions alone.

It is only a short step from D. G. Rossetti's purely aesthetic use of religious language to a decadent use of words that are in love with their own sound. In Tennyson's 'The Last Tournament', for example, the spectacular low point of *Idylls of the King*, the voiding of the rituals of courtly love caused by Tristram's and Isolt's breaking of their vows creates an instant kind of bankruptcy. In decomposing the unity of language to give a separate excitement or thrill to each individual phrase and word, Tristram's rhetoric proves at least as decadent as the hollowed-out rituals of the Tournament of the Dead Innocence. The great waves breaking upon the coast, 'Whitening for half a league', and then thinning themselves 'Far over sands marbled with moon and cloud' ('The Last Tournament', ll. 464–5), beautifully evoke an age of faith. But since Tennyson also uses the waves to describe something ugly and bathetic, the heavy-headed fall of a drunken knight, the irrelevant splendour seems merely decadent. One sign of this decadence is Tennyson's habit of decomposing his verse to give special prominence to the similes, and of decomposing the similes to give place to the sound pattern or the resonance of an individual word:

> and the wan day
> Went glooming down in wet and weariness
> (ll. 214–15)

> I have wallowed, I have washed – the world
> Is flesh and shadow – I have had my day.
> The dirty nurse, Experience, in her kind
> Hath fouled me – an I wallowed, then I washed.
>
> (ll. 315–18)

Whether at the service of Tennyson's narrator or the Fool, words in love with their own alliterating consonants and vowels assume a mercenary, venal quality. In turning the art of religion into a religion of art, they mock the faith of Arthur's knights and the rituals of his court.

Conclusion: The Poetic Legacy of Victorian Religion

We have seen how Tractarian pieties are reborn in the supple devotional verse of Christina Rossetti and in the Heraclitean fire of Hopkins. The liberal theologies of Strauss and Jowett also inspire several of Robert Browning's most daring experiments in Christian apologetics and myth-making. Hegel's philosophy of religion proclaims the dignity of self-making; and in Tennyson and Swinburne it revives the Romantic faith that every human being is by birth and by nature an artist, an architect, a fashioner of worlds. By celebrating the marvel of commonplace impressions, the enhancing nominalism of Pater and Morris also restores the sacredness of everyday life. But the most abiding legacy of religion to Victorian poetry is the quality of the poetry's religious despair and the intellectual urgency of its search for an *agnostos theos* or unknown God.

Ironically, all the contradictions which are used to keep rationalists like Browning's Guido, Karshish and Cleon away from the knowledge of an unknown God are what lead Browning himself toward it. Lending authority to such theological testaments and edge to their magnificently balanced paradoxes and dilemmas are the skill and honesty of poets as different as Browning, Tennyson, Christina Rossetti and Hopkins. Each poet tries to replace the senseless compulsion of a world 'red in tooth and claw' with that persuasive unity of power, love and knowledge foreseen by Browning's David in his most audacious and convincing vision of the Trinity. Even in 'Dover Beach' the unbelieving Arnold counters the melancholy long, withdrawing roar of the sea of faith with an appeal to Sophocles, with medieval therapies for the agony and strife of human hearts, and with a memorable allusion to Wordsworth's power both to hear and subdue 'the still sad music of humanity'.

When Tennyson steps off the moving platform of 'the great world's altar-stairs' in *In Memoriam*, he is swallowed up in an abyss of grief and dissolution. He never seems to get over the impermanence of everything he sees, the fragility of his love for Hallam, the taste of death in the new geology of Chamber and Lyell:

> The hills are shadows, and they flow
>   From form to form, and nothing stands;
>   They melt like mist, the solid lands,
> Like clouds they shape themselves and go.
>
> (123, 5–8)

As a poet of 'honest doubt' who suffers from Pascal's fear of terrifying waste spaces, Tennyson cannot bear the thought of life's being ultimately meaningless. Unique to *In Memoriam* is the quality of its religious despair. But as T. S. Eliot says in his great essay on the poem, 'to qualify' Tennyson's 'despair with the adjective "religious" is to elevate it above most of its derivatives. For *The City of Dreadful Night*, and *A Shropshire Lad*, and the poems of Thomas Hardy, are small in comparison with *In Memoriam*: It is greater than they and comprehends them' (1932b: 336).

See also: TRACTARIAN POETRY; HYMN.

REFERENCES AND FURTHER READING

Bowen, Desmond (1968) *The Idea of the Victorian Church: A Study of the Church of England 1833–1889*. Montreal: McGill University Press.

Bradley, F. H. (1876) *Ethical Studies*. London, Oxford: Oxford University Press.

Bradley, F. H. (1893) *Appearance and Reality: A Metaphysical Essay*. Oxford: Clarendon Press.

Chesterton, G. K. (1903) *Robert Browning*. London: Macmillan.

Clark, G. S. R. Kitson. (1962) *The Making of Victorian England*. London: Methuen.

Eliot, T. S. (1932a) 'Arnold and Pater.' In *Selected Essays* (pp. 431–43). London: Faber and Faber.

Eliot, T. S. (1932b) '*In Memoriam*.' In *Selected Essays* (pp. 328–38). London: Faber and Faber.

Emerson, Ralph Waldo (1908) 'Religion.' First published 1856. In *English Traits, Representative Men and Other Essays by Ralph Waldo Emerson* (pp. 106–15). London: J. M. Dent and Sons.

Feuerbach, Ludwig (1957) *The Essence of Christianity*. First published 1841. Trans. George Eliot. New York: Harper Row.

Froude, J. A. (1884) *Thomas Carlyle: A History of His Life in London 1834–1881*. London: Longmans, Green.

Hopkins, G. M. (1935) *The Letters of G. M. Hopkins to Robert Bridges*. Ed. C. C. Abbott. London: Oxford University Press.

Huizinga, Johan (1949) *The Waning of the Middle Ages*. New York: St Martin's Press.

Irvine, William, and Park Honan (1974) *The Book, the Ring, and the Poet: A Biography of Robert Browning*. New York: McGraw-Hill.

Jowett, Benjamin (ed.) (1860) *Essays and Reviews*. London: Longman, Green, Longman, Roberts.

Keble, John (1838) 'Review of Lockhart's *Life of Scott*.' *British Critic and Quarterly Theological Review*, 24, 423–42.

Langer, Susanne (1948) *Philosophy in a New Key*. New York: Mentor.

Loewenberg, J. (ed.) (1929) *Hegel Selections*. New York: Scribner.

Mansel, H. L. (1851) *Prolegomena Logica: An Inquiry into the Psychological Character of Logical Processes*. Oxford: Oxford University Press.

Moss, Joss (1998) *Word Crimes: Blasphemy, Culture and Literature in Nineteenth-Century England*. Chicago, London: University of Chicago Press.

Nagarajan, S. (1960) 'Arnold and the *Bhagavad Gita*: A Reinterpretation of *Empedocles on Etna*.' *Comparative Literature*, 12. 4, 335–47.

Pringle-Pattison, A. S. (1887) *Hegelianism and Personality*. Edinburgh: Blackwood.

Sell, Alan P. (1995) *Philosophical Idealism and Christian Belief*. New York: St Martin's Press.

Sparshott, F. E. (1972) *Looking for Philosophy*. Montreal, London: McGill-Queen's University Press.

Tennyson, G. B. (1981) *Victorian Devotional Poetry: The Tractarian Mode*. Cambridge, Mass., London: Harvard University Press.

Ward, W. G. (1841). 'Review of Arnold's *Sermons*.' *British Critic and Quarterly Theological Review*, 30, 298–364.

Wheeler, Michael (1990) *Death and the Future Life in Victorian Literature and Theology*. Cambridge: Cambridge University Press.

Young, G. M. (1936) *Victorian England: Portrait of an Age*. London, Oxford: Oxford University Press.

26

Poetry and Science

Alan Rauch

The intersections of literature and science – or literature and technology for that matter – are too varied and complex to be mapped in ways that are simply categorical or purely formulaic. It has been an unfortunate tradition to scan literary genres simply for overt references or clear thematic links to 'science', but a well-considered understanding of the impact of science and technology on literature is deeper than that. Cultural interpretations of science and technology should integrate an understanding of the impact not merely of knowledge, but of knowledge structures; in other words, establishing connections within science and culture means that one must not only inquire into the content of one discipline or another, but into the modes through which intellectual inquiry is conducted.

The very structure of poetry, which can be governed by 'rules' that guide the practice of poetic form, is itself 'scientific' and thus, like so many other genres of writing, is empathetic to the rule-governed practices of scientific inquiry. Recognizing the ways in which scientific thought shaped structures of Victorian poetry is critical to the understanding of both the period and the genre. For example, the broad appeal of the dramatic monologue is founded on its capacity to address concerns about the significance of the individual in an unforgiving universe. It is critical that any treatment of science and poetry engage structure, content and context all at once.

No single issue permeated Victorian science and culture, but the idea of materialism was certainly broad enough in scope and troubling enough in its implications to justify a claim for its centrality. The Victorians had to re-envision their world, not as a benign place ordained for man by God, but as a system that was reducible to immutable physical and natural laws. This 'new' system did not play favourites and did not show mercy, even in terms of its own existence; as the laws of entropy made clear, the sun itself would eventually dissipate into oblivion. As the poet and sometime researcher into psychic phenomena F. W. H. Myers wrote in his essay 'Modern Poets and the Meaning of Life' (1893: 95), the 'alien and impersonal character of all these laws convinces us that the universe is in no way constructed to meet the moral needs of man'.

Poets must resolve, Myers continues – drawing on Algernon Swinburne as his example – that 'even if there be no moral purpose already in the world, man shall put it there;

that even if all evolution be necessarily truncated, yet more evolution, so long as our race lasts, there shall be; that even if man's virtue be momentary, he shall act as though it were an eternal gain' (1893: 98). The escape from materialism, late in the century, was facilitated in part by the emergence of psychology (to say nothing of psychic research), which helped shift cultural focus towards the function of the mind in apprehending the external world. This shift was fundamentally driven by a preoccupation with the materiality of the world that could be traced back a century.

There is no figure more important in the emergence of scientific materialism in the nineteenth century than John Dalton (1766–1844), the son of a Quaker weaver, who advanced the atomic theory of matter in 1805. In *A New System of Chemical Philosophy* (1808–10) Dalton applied the term *atom* to indicate the 'ultimate particles' out of which materials were made. These particles, for which Dalton created pictorial symbols, were fixed and unchangeable for each material, although they could combine in certain definite proportions to form 'compound atoms', or what we now call molecules. The emergence of a relatively simple, and easily depicted, set of laws to explain the chemical basis of materiality contributed to the growing sense that the substance of the world, whether organic or inorganic, was reducible to laws and properties measurable by science.

Not only was the visible material world subjected to intense scrutiny, the discipline of physics was developed to focus on the less tangible properties of human experience, including light, heat, sound, electricity and magnetism. It was becoming clear, through the work of scientists such as Michael Faraday (1791–1867) and James Clerk Maxwell (1831–79), that these forces were not independent of one another. The poorly understood concept of the ether and the matrix of space in the world was being minutely resolved. Faraday observed that polarized light was affected by magnetic fields, leading eventually to Maxwell's demonstration that the interaction between electric and magnetic forces produced vortices of energy or fields. Maxwell not only proposed that light itself was composed of electricity and magnetism, but that it undulated in wave-like patterns. While his mathematics were far too abstruse for the common reader, his quantification of the speed of light tamed one of the most intractable elements of nature.

A significant participant in the growth of the physical sciences was William Thomson, Lord Kelvin (1824–1907), whose researches included investigations into the wave theory of light, but who is best remembered for his work in thermodynamics. Drawing on the research of James Prescott Joule (1818–89), who found a correspondence between mechanical work and the production of heat, Thomson proposed what we now know as the first and second laws of thermodynamics. While the first law indicates that energy is conserved when both heat *and* work are taken into account, the second recognizes that heat will only pass to cooler objects and therefore, inevitably, dissipate. This concept, readily observable in the mundane world of household objects, was applied equally to organisms and, even more significantly, to the sun. Entropy, as this process of heat loss came to be known in the 1860s, was deeply troubling in that it suggested that individuals, the world and the universe all faced an inexorable decline into nothingness.

As the second law of thermodynamics indicates, compelling questions about science in Victorian poetry are inextricably linked with a crisis of faith. Poems such as Tennyson's *In*

Memoriam (1850) invoke scientific learning to explore both the loss and the recovery of faith in a scientifically governed world. But expressions of doubt inflect many other works which may or may not invoke science and technology directly. Poems dedicated to the status of workers and labourers, for example, inevitably address, if only by implication, the fabric of science, technology and culture. In his *Essay on Population* (1798) Thomas Malthus, a crucial influence on Karl Marx and Friedrich Engels, offered a disconcerting lesson to readers who wanted to balance faith and science. His argument, that sustainability must necessarily limit population, put moral concerns directly in conflict with a rule-governed world where empathy, charity or frailty must succumb to scientific principles. Throughout the century, science offered a constant challenge to structures of faith and belief. Efforts to reconcile the two include the *Bridgewater Treatises*, a series of volumes commissioned by the earl of Bridgewater in the 1830s to demonstrate 'the Power, Wisdom and Goodness of God as manifested in the Creation', and *Essays and Reviews* (1870), a compilation of essays which wrestled with ideas of faith and science in Darwin's aftermath.

The remarkable growth of knowledge in the early nineteenth century exposed the Victorians to other cultures and to other values, which were often viewed in the context of science. Physiological differences between men and women, as well as ethnographic differences among cultures, were discussed and debated in popular scientific and technical publications. Thus, what we call subjectivity and identity, as well as those roles often defined by gender, ethnicity and cultural heritage, must also be considered seriously in the complex intersection of science and poetry. This is particularly true because of the fascination with other cultures, whether native peoples of North America, or people from Africa, India and the sub-tropics. In the latter part of the century this fascination produced the new disciplines of anthropology and ethnography. Sir John Lubbock's *Origins of Civilisation* (1870) and Sir Edward Tylor's *Primitive Cultures* (1871) firmly established anthropology and ethnography as sciences, rendering human culture as valid a subject of scrutiny as human physiology. In the 1890s the idea that human cultural and religious practices could be viewed systematically was realised in the massive work *The Golden Bough* (1890–1915) by Sir James Frazer.

The influence of science in this period owes a great deal to broad cultural and economic movements that changed patterns of interaction between social classes. New demographics, generated by the industrial revolution, helped dramatize the distinction between urban and pastoral. What is more, the industrial revolution was also responsible for increased literacy and a growing sense of community among labourers. This new population of readers and, on occasion, writers participated in the creation of a tradition of working-class and, later, Chartist poetry. 'Poetry', as Anne Janowitz has noted, 'was both a flattering mirror to a movement-in-formation, offering conventions for group identity, and a social matrix within which people could discover themselves as belonging to an ongoing set of traditions, goals, and expectations' (1998: 135). The value of that role, evinced in working-man poets such as Thomas Spence, Ernest Jones and Thomas Cooper, is evinced in the nineteenth century's best-known fictional poet, Alton Locke. The brainchild of Charles Kingsley, himself a poet, the figure of Alton Locke represents the successful – if not the plausible – synthesis of Christianity, Chartism, poetry and science.

Beyond the fictional *Alton Locke* (1851) many poets were deeply concerned about the fate of the labouring classes in an increasingly industrial environment. Their poems may not have captured the imagination in the way that Charles Dickens, Elizabeth Gaskell and Kingsley did in fiction, but they were none the less poignant and well known. The most widely read was Thomas Hood's 'The Song of the Shirt' (1843), a lament for the labouring classes and an appeal for an increase in wages. Caroline Norton (1808–77), expresses similar concerns in the early stanzas of her epic-length 'Voice from the Factories' (1836). 'Poor little FACTORY SLAVES', she writes in a rallying tone, ' – for YOU these lines complain.' In a much later poem, 'The Lady of La Garaye' (1866), she addresses the impact of factories not merely on workers, but on nature itself:

> Some factory work whose wheels with horrid force
> Strike the pure waters with their dripping beams,
> Send poison gushing to the crystal streams,
> And leave the innocent things to whom God gave
> A natural home in that translucent wave
> Gasping strange death, and floating down to show
> The evil working in the depths below, –
> So man can poison pleasure at its source.

Cultural and social differences were also reflected in dialect poems, such as those of William Barnes (1801–86). Poems of social protest and economic injustice remained a mainstay of politically motivated poets such as John Davidson (1857–1909), whose 'Thirty Bob a Week' (1894) became extremely popular, reflecting an awareness of intersections of class that were unprecedented.

Poetry began to address matters such as industrialization, and the genre found new readers in Mechanics' Institutes as well as circulating libraries. The development of British transportation, facilitated by the macadamizing of roads and the construction of bridges, canals and railways, not only facilitated the distribution of books, but actively shaped new social concerns that were addressed in the poetry of the time.

Other new technologies affected poetry in ways that are more difficult to trace. A notable example is the daguerreotype, invented in 1839, which had the capacity to record images more accurately than ever before. As a consequence of the scientific precision of the daguerreotype, concepts of imagery, whether in painting or in poetry, were modified. An 1844 review of R. H. Horne's collection of critical essays *A New Spirit of the Age* (to which Elizabeth Barrett contributed) indicates how quickly the term 'daguerreotype' slipped into discourse. 'The attempt to daguerreotype the living features of the most distinguished men of the age', the reviewer chides Horne, 'is no slight one: it implies boldness, at least, if it does not argue presumption' (Browning and Browning 1984: 418). Photography would have a long and controversial future, as an instrument of art and of science, but the repercussions of the new technology were almost immediate. The strategy of the Pre-Raphaelite school, for example, seemed calculated to resist the temporal fixity of photography, by bringing imagined worlds to life with the precision of language and art. The historically vivid and complex poems of Alfred Tennyson and Robert

Browning also suggest an imaginative capacity that disdains the prosaic limitations of early photography.

The Victorian transition from the Romantic sense of transcendence of nature owes a great deal to science. As more materialist explanations of organic origins were being developed, more pragmatic approaches to the 'real' emerged. French theorists, such as Jean-Baptiste Lamarck, Georges-Louis Leclerc (Comte de Buffon) and Georges Cuvier, had begun to suggest modes of transmutation, adaptation and geological change that militated against the idea of fixed species and a narrow view of creation. The biology of the period owed a debt to Linnaeus, whose collections were acquired by the Englishman Sir J. E. Smith (1759–1828), founder of the Linnaean Society in 1788. Linnaeus's rational taxonomy of nature initiated ventures, including Charles Darwin's own voyage on the *Beagle*, that would contribute new species to the growing catalogue of nature. Comparative anatomists such as Cuvier and, in England, Sir Richard Owen investigated the refined structures that fitted animals to their particular environment. Animal structures that were once merely beautiful were now understood to be shaped by a long history of environmental forces and utilitarian need. The process that shaped these structures and left traces of the past in the form of fossils and vestigial organs revealed a logic that was not inherent in the idea of special creation.

Many Victorians, including Darwin, admired William Paley's *Natural Theology* (1802) and its compelling insistence on divine order. But the book also generated interest in scientific and materialist explanations of nature that inevitably posed questions of development and transformation. *Natural Theology* and Darwin's much later *Voyage of the Beagle* (1836) are touchstones for the Victorian fascination with natural detail and the ability to grasp details through the senses.

The detailed analysis of the heavens and the earth also brought creationist notions into question. In his *Theory of the Earth*, published in the late eighteenth century, James Hutton accepts the divine creation of the earth, but also notes that there is 'no vestige of a beginning, no prospect of an end'. The most celebrated geologist of the nineteenth century, Charles Lyell, supported Hutton's claim through the concept of uniformitarianism, a principle that geological change occurs slowly, incrementally and often imperceptibly. Lyell's conception of the world dismissed catastrophism, whether divinely ordained or even naturally produced, as a plausible explanation for the geological history of the earth. For poetry and the novel, Lyell's work made two things clear: the earth required aeons to develop; and seemingly minor forces such as wind and erosion have shaped the most monumental geological formations on the planet. The notion that the smallest forces might have the largest consequences was itself attractive to many poets, including Browning. While debates about the specific age of the earth led to different conclusions, James Hutton's (1726–97) early observation, that attempts to discover the age of the Earth would produce 'no prospect of a beginning and no vestige of an end', still seemed to hold.

One of the foremost popularizers of astronomy was Mary Somerville, whose *Mechanism of the Heavens* (1830) introduced the theories of the renowned French astronomer Pierre Simon Laplace to English readers. Somerville's *On the Connexion of the Physical Sciences* (1835) was also a popular success. She was one of a number of women writers whose role in the popularization of science in the early nineteenth century cannot be overestimated. Jane Marcet wrote popular works on chemistry and natural philosophy, and Caroline Herschel, sister and aunt to two great astronomers, was well known in her own right. Children's authors such as Maria Edgeworth, Mary Howitt, Jane Loudon and Sarah Trimmer introduced many young readers to science. The proliferation of science throughout popular literature indicates one way in which the writers of the age became informed about scientific discoveries, inventions and speculations.

As literacy increased among the working and middle classes, reading materials became more accessible. The positive value of knowledge – especially for the working classes – was itself a common topic in poetry. Eliza Cook's 'Lines Written for the Sheffield Mechanics Exhibition, 1846' (1849) is typical:

> Knowledge, bright Knowledge, so *thy* sun must shine,
> And leave unchanged the Spirit-stream divine
> Knowledge, fair Knowledge, 'tis alone thy way
> Can melt the bars of mortal ice away.
>
> . . .
>
> Fair knowledge pleads the Universal Cause;
> Truth in her Language – Justice in her laws:
> Leading rude ignorance with gentle hand,
> To join Creation's highest, noblest band.
>
> (ll. 32–42)

In her 'A Song for the Workers: Written for the Early Closing Movement' (1870), Cook's commitment to workers sustained her enthusiasm for knowledge despite growing evidence of the impasse between workers and new technologies. But as important as knowledge was to the 'improvement' of the working classes, the wide availability of knowledge texts was also a boon to educated readers in the provinces. Charlotte Brontë's mundane life in Haworth parsonage was enlivened not merely by *Blackwood's*, but by the materials available in the library at the nearby Keighley Mechanics' Institute. The consolations of knowledge, especially for a life lived in relative isolation, are perfectly evident in her poem 'Reason':

> Come Reason – Science – Learning – Thought –
>   To you my poor heart I dedicate;
> I have a faithful subject brought;
>   Faithful because most desolate.

Although broad visions of knowledge seem optimistic, a detailed appreciation of the advances in science was also disconcerting, particularly as writers sensed that scientific laws might dislodge divine order. Writers balanced a diminished place for God with the excitement generated by a world infinitely more complex and engaging *because* of scientific knowledge. Epistemological issues, previously the subject of philosophical debates with little public exposure, achieved unprecedented attention in popular discourse. The language of science, although accessible, was still too remote and abstruse to be useful in negotiating, reconciling or even comprehending life in a scientific age. Nevertheless, poetry could draw on a vocabulary that allowed readers to escape the jargon of science for a more personal engagement with the natural world that might speak to concerns about faith and order.

The poet most clearly identified with this approach was Tennyson. Devastated by the early death of his friend Arthur Hallam, he strove, in *In Memoriam*, to preserve human faith when confronted by unsparing nature. The poem, which represents scientific and cultural anxieties, anticipates Darwin in its evocation of a world of prehistoric terrors and of the contemporary struggle to survive. Tennyson was anxious to stay abreast of scientific advances. 'I want you to get me a book which I see advertized in the *Examiner*', he wrote to Edward Moxon, his publisher, in 1844, 'it seems to contain many speculations with which I have been familiar for years, and on which I have written more than one poem. The book is called *Vestiges of the Natural History of Creation*.' Robert Chambers's shocking *Vestiges of Creation*, which advanced a poorly contrived but none the less provocative system for the transmutation of species, created a sensation among readers, clerics and some scientists. Tennyson had already made significant progress on *In Memoriam*, and Chambers's *Vestiges* confirmed the cruel power of nature that he had observed in all of his scientific reading. Tennyson's early poetry had already engaged scientific themes that would eventually coalesce in *In Memoriam*. In 'The Kraken' (1830) he offered an interesting vignette of an animal both within and outside of nature. A creature surrounded by 'huge sponges of millennial growth', the literal Kraken becomes mythic as it rises to the surface to roar and then, inevitably, to die. As Tennyson's 'Tithonus' (1833) makes clear, he is absorbed by the notion of an infinite world where each creature and species makes only a brief appearance. He resisted the idea that time would erase the value of human life, by locating divinity within time itself, a tactic that allows him to reconcile the impossibly short life of human experience with divine infinitude. 'Thou hast not gained a real height', the poet is told in 'The Two Voices' (1832), 'Nor art thou nearer to the light / Because the scale is infinite' (ll. 91–3). *In Memoriam* begins by recognizing that the struggle for the survival of species comes at the expense of the lives of individuals:

> Are God and Nature then at strife,
> > That Nature lends such evil dreams?
> > So careful of the type she seems,
> So careless of the single life.
> > > (55, ll. 5–8)

Later, a more extended temporal vista reveals nature's indifference even to the survival of species:

> 'So careful of the type?' but no.
> > From scarped cliff and quarried stone
> > She cries 'A thousand types are gone:
> I care for nothing, all shall go.'
> > > (56, ll. 1–4)

Tennyson at last rediscovers his faith, but unlike William Paley, who found in the insect's eye evidence of the divine handiwork, Tennyson does not find God in the details of creation:

> I found Him not in world or sun,
>   Or eagle's wing, or insect's eye;
>   Nor thro' the questions men may try,
> The petty cobwebs we have spun.
>
> (124, ll. 5–8)

One of the triumphs of *In Memoriam* for Victorian readers is that Tennyson ignores the now tired arguments of Paley and does not diminish or dismiss the achievements of science. He models his rediscovered faith on the evolutionary pattern that science had proposed. Hallam becomes a representative of a 'higher race', who has achieved through death a 'higher place'. Norman Lockyer, the astronomer and founder of the journal *Nature*, found Tennyson's integration of poetry and science exhilarating. In his brief essay, 'Tennyson as a Student and Poet of Nature', Lockyer notes that:

> Tennyson's great achievement has been to show us that in the study of science we have one of the bases of the fullest poetry, a poetry that appeals at the same time to the deepest emotions and the highest and broadest intellects of mankind. Tennyson, in short, has shown that science and poetry, so far from being antagonistic, must for ever advance side by side.

While Tennyson's engagement with science addresses questions about how to preserve human values in a world governed by scientific law, Robert Browning is deeply concerned about changes in individual responsibility in what might be called a 'clockwork' world. In Browning's dramatic monologues, the individual is pitted against a social world that is controlled by inhuman forces. Browning's narrators are survivors whose abilities to overcome social or natural obstacles provides insight into their success and ascendancy. Browning, like the character he describes in 'How it Strikes a Contemporary' (1855), finds meaning in material reality by 'Scenting the world' and 'looking it full in the face'. Bishop Blougram ('Bishop Blougram's Apology', 1855) is Browning's version of Worldly Wiseman, who realizes the intrigue and competitiveness inherent in all human actions, including those that generate the ritual practices of religion. For Blougram, religion is a 'game' of sorts that is grounded on human structures of belief, rather than empirical or pragmatic evidence:

> And now what are we? Unbelievers both,
> Calm and complete, determinately fixed
> Today, tomorrow and forever, pray?
> You'll guarantee me that? Not so, I think!
> In no wise! All we've gained is, that belief,
> As unbelief before, shakes us by fits,
> Confounds us like its predecessor.
>
> (ll. 173–9)

Blougram challenges a naivety that he finds ingenuous in the light of contemporary scientific understanding. He taunts Gigadibs for his failure to comprehend that the epistemological war between religion and science is itself timeless:

> How you'd exult if I could put you back
> Six hundred years, blot out cosmogony,
> Geology, ethnology, what not
> (Greek endings, each the little passing-bell
> That signifies some faith's about to die),
> And set you square with Genesis again.
>
> (ll. 678–844)

Browning is interested in the possibility of a common bond between science and religion that ultimately depends on the inability of the human mind to grasp either part in full. He wants to reveal the artificial constructions inherent in both modes of thought. Is the orchestrion of 'Abt Vogler' (1864) an instrument produced by a superior intelligence or is it merely a conventional organ, a variant of so many similar predecessors? An unquestioning belief in Abbé Vogler is necessary in order to accept the former. Accepting the latter is to accede to the mundane and foreclose the possibility of the exceptional. Browning's Caliban, in 'Caliban upon Setebos: or, Natural Theology on the Island' (1864), raises similar questions as Caliban tries to reconcile himself to a power that, however superior, may yet be 'decrepit', may be dozing, and may even be dead. With only a natural theology to guide him, that is to say without *revelation*, Caliban finds that he is left with a series of questions about his own existence rather than answers.

Browning's *The Ring and the Book* (1868–9), which emerged from his reading of a bound collection of manuscripts that he purchased in Florence, reflects yet another way of conceptualizing scientific practice in his poetry. *The Ring and the Book* may be based on primary materials gathered together and discovered by Browning; nevertheless, the monologues he uses to coordinate these facts contradict each other. This 'experiment' in what might be called 'interpretative empiricism' is Browning's contribution to a key Victorian debate about the nature of objectivity.

In the poetry of Arthur Hugh Clough the problem of living in a world governed by material rather than spiritual laws is addressed more directly than in the poems of Tennyson and Browning. In *Amours de Voyage* (1858), Eustace, like Clough himself, is troubled by the burden of knowledge. 'Take me from this regal knowledge', Eustace complains, 'let me contented and mute with the beast of the field . . . tranquilly lie.' The opposition between the organic self and the intellectual self also underlies the 'two minds' that form 'Dipsychus' in Clough's final major poem. Acknowledging that 'the very faithful have begun to doubt', this examines the consequences of such doubt, the reality of a world in which there is no God:

> I dreamt a dream – till morning light
> A bell rang in my head all night
> Tinkling and tinkling first, and then,

> Tolling; and tinkling; tolling again
> So brisk and gay and then so slow
> O joy! And terror: mirth and woe.
> Ting ting, there is no God, ting, ting:
> Dong, there is no God; dong
> There is no God: dong; dong.
>
> (7, ll. 7–15)

T. H. Huxley, who coined the word 'agnostic' to describe his own crisis of faith, was concerned about the ethical and moral status of humans as biological organisms that were necessarily governed by organic laws. Similarly, Clough is concerned about the animal nature of humanity: 'Could I believe that any child of Eve / Were formed and fashioned, raised and reared for nought / But to be swilled with animal delight?'

In 'Dipsychus' (scene 7), Clough documents more fully than any of his contemporaries the movement away from – or perhaps the rationalization of – the spiritual:

> 'There is no God', the wicked saith,
> 'And truly it's a blessing,
> For what He might have done with us
> It's better only guessing.'
> 'There is no God', a youngster thinks,
>   'Or really, if there may be,
> He surely did not mean a man
>   Always to be a baby.'
>
> 'There is no God, or if there is',
>   The tradesman thinks, ''twere funny
> If He should take it ill in me
>   To make a little money.'
>
> (ll. 153–65)

One of his best-known poems, 'The Struggle', shares a guarded sense of hope and possibility with Matthew Arnold's 'Dover Beach'. The battle imagery, and the invocation of both sea and struggle, to say nothing of the retreating 'Sea of Faith', seem to draw directly from Arnold:

> Say not the struggle naught availeth,
> The labour and the wounds are vain,
> The enemy faints not, nor faileth,
> And as things have been, things remain.
> If hopes were dupes, fears may be liars;
> It may be, in yon smoke concealed,
> Your comrades chase e'en now the fliers,
> And, but for you, possess the field.
>
> For while the tired waves, vainly breaking,
> Seem here no painful inch to gain,

Far back, through creeks and inlets making,
Comes silent, flooding in, the main.

And not by eastern windows only,
When daylight comes, comes in the light,
In front, the sun climbs slow, how slowly,
But westward, look, the land is bright.

The poem draws on the political struggles of 1848, which certainly absorbed Clough's attention, but it cannot be separated from his thinking about the human condition. Political struggle is predicated on the capacity of human action to resist determinacy whether it is ordained by God or by nature. Clough's westward gaze, which finds brightness only by turning away from its source, offers a more abstracted sense of hope than Arnold, who holds on to the promise of human love in a much bleaker environment:

Ah, love, let us be true
To one another! for the world, which seems
To lie before us like a land of dreams,
So various, so beautiful, so new,
Hath really neither joy, nor love, nor light,
Nor certitude, nor peace, nor help for pain;
And we are here as on a darkling plain
Swept with confused alarms of struggle and flight,
Where ignorant armies clash by night.
('Dover Beach', ll. 29–37)

Arnold may not, in 'Dover Beach', locate the brightness that Clough hopes for, but he does so in 'Thyrsis', his elegy for Clough, where he is reminded by Clough's spirit that 'the light we sought is shining still'. This passage helps distinguish Arnold's theology from Clough's. Arnold is reluctant to forego the notion of the divine and is certainly uncomfortable satirizing conventional religious beliefs. Steeped in science and fully aware of the value of scientific achievement, he is unwilling to submit the idea of existence to purely material interpretations. His own understanding of God, which he described in 'St Paul and Protestantism' as a 'stream of tendency by which all things strive to fulfil the law of their being', shares the ambiguous language that many of his contemporaries used to bridge science and religion. Darwin, for example, relied on the concept of a distinctly natural 'Power' or force in nature in the *Origin of Species* to explain natural selection, leading to an enigmatic connection to the divine. 'There is grandeur in this view of life', Darwin writes there, 'with its several powers, having been originally breathed by the Creator into a few forms or into one; and that, whilst this planet has gone cycling on according to the fixed law of gravity, from so simple a beginning endless forms most beautiful and most wonderful have been, and are being evolved.'

Arnold's real respect for scientific argument and ingenuity has not been sufficiently recognized, no doubt as a consequence of the strained debate with Huxley that ultimately led to Arnold's 1882 essay 'Literature and Science' (Arnold 1958a). Writing to Huxley in

1880, an effort to avoid conflict, Arnold claimed that the dictum about knowing 'the best that has been known and said in the world . . . was meant to include knowing what has been done in science and art as well as in letters'. The dispute was itself an important episode in a debate about what a well-educated person should know. Arnold's response to Huxley was measured, given that it acknowledged the value of a scientific education as well as the poetic qualities of science itself. Thinking of his own work, where scientifically inflected themes consistently appear, Arnold argued for the mutual interplay of literature and science. Yet he insisted that the one must be subordinated to the other. 'More and more', Arnold writes in 'The Study of Poetry' (1958b: 502), 'mankind will discover that we have to turn to poetry to interpret life for us, to console us, to sustain us. Without poetry, our science will appear incomplete; and most of what now passes with us for religion and philosophy will be replaced by poetry.' Humane letters, Arnold explains in 'Literature and Science' (1958a: 498), have:

> a fortifying, and elevating, and quickening, and suggestive power, capable of wonderfully helping us to relate the results of modern science to our need for conduct, our need for beauty. Homer's conceptions of the physical universe were, I imagine, grotesque; but really, under the shock of hearing from modern science that 'the world is not subordinated to man's use, and that man is not the cynosure of things terrestrial', I could, for my own part, desire no better comfort than Homer's line.

If much of Victorian poetry addresses the uncertainty of human significance or the role of divine providence in the face of science, there is also another facet of the poetry of the age that is informed by a tacitly scientific mode of thinking. The desire for 'particularity', as Carol Christ has noted (1975), is a distinctive feature of much of the work of the Pre-Raphaelites. The emphasis on detail in much of their poetry is evocative of the precision and technical accuracy that had emerged as a cornerstone of scientific method. Yet, as indicated earlier, the images produced by the Pre-Raphaelites also draw on the fantastic and, in doing so, resist the here and now of strict materialism. A good part of Tennyson's work (throughout his career), including 'The Lady of Shalott', 'Morte d'Arthur' and *Idylls of the King*, also reflect this sensibility. But the Pre-Raphaelites, in particular the Rossettis, have a particular eye for specificity of detail. Its vividness added sensuality to their work both in poetry and in art, but it also functioned, as in Christina Rossetti's 'Goblin Market' and D. G. Rossetti's 'The Blessed Damozel', to point the contrast between the corporeal nature of existence and the spiritual aspirations of mind.

The Pre-Raphaelites were interested in reconciling the 'material' with the 'spiritual', and often used language that bridged scientific knowledge with religious or philosophical ideas. In 'The Sea-Limits', another poem that contrasts the timeless and expansive sea with the narrow and limited span of human life, D. G. Rossetti invokes the closing lines of Shelley's 'Mont Blanc' in what seems to be an appeal to Romantic transcendence:

> Gather a shell from the strown beach
> And listen at its lips: they sigh
> The same desire and mystery,

> The echo of the whole sea's speech
> And all mankind is thus at heart
> Not anything but what thou art:
> And Earth, Sea, Man, are all in each.
> (ll. 22–8)

Nevertheless Rossetti, unwilling to locate the external universe, as Shelley does, in 'the human mind's imaginings', is content to end his poem with the Victorian assertion that the human mind and the material world coexist.

The tension between the poetic and empirical epistemologies is central to Victorian poetry. Many writers understood, drawing on their Romantic predecessors, that there is a quality of human experience that is at once ephemeral and material, and that this experience helps poetry find its proper subject matter. The work of the Catholic poet Gerard Manley Hopkins (1844–89), though outside the tradition of Anglican natural theology, very fully exemplifies this position. Hopkins's view that knowledge could only be derived from the experience of things led to his concept of 'inscape', which attributes to objects intrinsic and unique characteristics. The 'thisness' of these things, to use Hopkins's own terminology, ultimately gave them meaning. The poem 'Pied Beauty' (1877) celebrates this quality:

> Glory be to God for dappled things –
> For skies of couple-colour as a brinded cow;
> For rose-moles all in stipple upon trout that swim;
> Fresh-firecoal chestnut-falls; finches' wings;
> Landscape plotted and pieced – fold, fallow, and plough;
> And áll trádes, their gear and tackle and trim.
>
> All things counter, original, spare, strange;
> Whatever is fickle, freckled (who knows how?)
> With swift, slow; sweet, sour; adazzle, dim;
> He fathers-forth whose beauty is past change: Praise him.

For Hopkins the unique individuality of all things makes the synthesis of the natural and the supernatural possible. Hopkins wholly rejects the scientific account of the world, and yet embraces the empiricism that allows the human mind – in a divinely ordained universe – to distinguish every living thing. The revelatory quality of Hopkins's natural world distinguishes it from natural theology, which only claims 'evidence' for God's wisdom in the observable natural world. What Hopkins shares with many Victorian counterparts is a love for the richness of detail in the natural world; whether the meaning of detail can be abstracted out into laws – as in the Darwinian theory of evolution – or whether it stands on its own as an emblem of incomprehensible wonder, is a consistent intellectual stumbling block. 'To admit the primacy of the particular over the universal', argues Carol Christ:

seemed to admit an epistemological and ethical relativism Arnold wanted to avoid. Eventually the poetry of the Victorian period reversed Arnold's priorities. The characters in Browning's dramatic monologues and Hopkins's sense of inscape both spring from an insistence upon the priority of the individual over classification and a delight in the very multiplicity Arnold had condemned. (1975: 65–6)

In *The Descent of Man* (1871) Darwin explicitly rejected the notion, upheld by the renowned zoologist Alfred Russel Wallace (1823–1913), that while evolution might define all other species, humans were still the product of a 'special' creation. The notion that evolutionary laws applied to animals and humans alike immediately engaged the attention of poets. Women, in particular, found the application of natural law as opposed to social law potentially liberating, as it would allow individuals to be judged on the basis of social performance and not social conventions. Herbert Spencer's works in sociology, which applied Darwinian theory to human dynamics, were welcomed by a number of writers, most notably Mathilde Blind (1841–96) and Constance Naden (1858–89). Both poets embraced – as positive forces for women and for culture – the Darwinian recognition of constant change and development together with the idea of active agency that emerged from Spencer's social Darwinism. Blind managed to integrate unique perspectives drawing on socialism, political activism, Darwinism and religious scepticism in order to address and critique the development of social and cultural practices. Her epic poem *The Ascent of Man* (1889) deliberately invokes Darwin's *The Descent of Man* to explore the laws that have determined the growth of civilization from the very earliest origins of humanity:

> The love of life burns in their veins,
>   And from the mightiest to the least
> Each preys upon the other's life
> In inextinguishable strife.
> War rages on the teeming earth;
>   The hot and sanguinary fight
> Begins with each new creature's birth:
>   A dreadful war where might is right;
> Where still the strongest slay and win,
> Where weakness is the only sin.

The brutality inherent in the animal ancestry of humans is underscored by Blind, but humanity is ultimately redeemed by its capacity for love. Blind acknowledges her debt to the 'beautiful idealisms' of Shelley here, but, rather than accept the Romantic reliance on 'inner consciousness', Blind finds a material pathway to love that draws on evolutionary theory. 'In the continual process of selection', she writes in her essay 'Shelley's View of Nature Contrasted with Darwin's' (1886), 'there is no reason why the moral ideals of one generation should not become the stepping-stones towards their realisation in another. And in this process of evolution the final triumph of the human mind over the brute force of nature may be achieved' (1886: 22). Blind's attempts to reconcile moral improvement with the physical condition of life was consistent with the thinking of Huxley, Darwin's great advocate. Huxley acknowledged moral improvement as a component in the evolution of the humans. In a passage from his *Prolegomena to Evolution and Ethics* (1894), Huxley advances an argument for moral improvement in human culture that resonates with Blind's arguments. 'That which lies before the human race', Huxley proposes, 'is a constant struggle to maintain and improve, in opposition to the State of Nature, the State of *Art of an organized polity*; in which, and by which, man may develop a worthy civilization, capable of maintaining and constantly improving itself' (45). For Huxley, this human intervention in the evolutionary process – an historical quirk that finally cannot resist the natural order – will only endure until 'the cosmic process resumes its sway', and 'once more, the State of Nature prevails over the surface of our planet'.

Many other poets, including A. Mary F. Robinson (1857–1944), resisted this bleak prospect by insisting, in the poem 'Darwinism', that once 'the brute became the man', there would be a divine response that would both ease and end 'the new travail of the soul'. Robinson's ideas would not, however, have agreed with those of Constance Naden, whose scientific training contributed to a sceptical and empirical worldview. Her poetry, often satirical and witty, also challenges the gendered paths by which scientific knowledge made its way through contemporary culture. In 'Love Versus Learning', Naden adopts the voice of a woman torn between her love of social convention and her love of science. Having aspired to 'be a philosopher's bride', the woman accepts the proposal of an 'Oxford, M.A.' whom she discovers is 'neither a sage nor a bard':

> He's mastered the usual knowledge,
>   And says it's a terrible bore;
> He formed his opinions at college,
>   Then why should he think any more?
>
> My logic he sets at defiance,
>   Declares that my Latin's no use,
> And when I begin to talk Science
>   He calls me a dear little goose.

A similarly mismatched pairing occurs in 'The New Orthodoxy', in which an Oxford-trained suitor, Fred, is rejected by the Girton-trained Amy, who is concerned that he had 'been heard to say you can't / Pin your faith to Darwin!' and, perhaps worse, that he has been heard to 'Scoff at Herbert Spencer!' Naden concludes the poem with a neat reversal. Amy requires from Fred a strict adherence not to religious but to scientific principles:

> Write – or telegraph – or call!
> Come yourself and tell me all:
> No fond hope shall me enthrall,
>   No regret shall sway me:
> Yet – until the worst is said,
> Till I know your faith is dead,
> I remain, dear doubting Fred,
> Your believing
>   AMY.

Naden's verse, though often lighthearted, reflects a critical development in the emergence of scientific discourse as a matter of daily concern for men and for women. That women need to have a voice in science is underscored not only by Naden but by May Kendall (1861–1943), who offers a challenge to women in the poem 'Women's Future' (1894), where women are asked to abandon domestic tasks for scientific pursuits. 'Do something worth doing!', she exhorts her female readers: 'Invent a new planet, a flying machine':

> Mere charms superficial, mere feminine graces,
>   That fade or that flourish no more may you prize;
> But the knowledge of New will beam from your faces.
>   The soul of Spencer will shine in your eyes.

Kendall's belief in the liberating power of science for women is balanced by a profound respect for all living things. Her poems 'The Lay of the Trilobite' and 'The Lower Life' suggest that humans must recognize themselves as part of nature. The assumption that humans are at the upper end of a natural hierarchy is, for her, fraught with problems:

> This higher life is curious stuff,
> Too high, yet not quite high enough,
>   A mingled vial!
> This higher life is sold too dear –
> Would I could give a lower sphere
>   An equal trial!

We can hear in the poetry of Kendall and her contemporaries both an assertion of selfhood and, at the same time, an acceptance of the necessary limitations of selfhood in a universe that seems indifferent to the contributions of any single generation or individual.

Science, by the end of the century, was a highly professional pursuit that excluded amateur scientists as well as casual popularizers. The high degree of specialization and detailed knowledge that characterized the work of people like James Clerk Maxwell made it inaccessible to lay audiences. The practice of science was now confined almost exclusively to the university, where future generations of scientists were trained in laboratories and classrooms not open to the masses. But new sciences emerged, like psychology and anthropology, that were still young, still descriptive and still relatively accessible. These sciences, which emphasized the mind and the individual, opened new possibilities to poets. Still, the anxieties generated by Victorian science have not disappeared or diminished. The Victorian period was remarkable for the relatively sudden introduction of scientific thinking into aspects of general culture including poetry, the consequences of which have continued to be felt ever since.

REFERENCES AND FURTHER READING

Armstrong, Isobel (1993) *Victorian Poetry: Poetry, Poetics, Politics*. New York: Routledge.

Arnold, Matthew (1958a) 'Literature and Science.' In William E. Buckler (ed.). *Prose of the Victorian Period* (pp. 486–500). Boston: Houghton Mifflin.

Arnold, Matthew (1958b) 'The Study of Poetry.' In William E. Buckler (ed.). *Prose of the Victorian Period* (pp. 501–9). Boston: Houghton Mifflin.

Blind, Mathilde (1886) 'Shelley's View of Nature Contrasted with Darwin's.' London: n.p. [http://www.indiana.edu/~letrs/vwwp/blind/shelley.html]

Browning, Elizabeth Barrett, and Robert Browning (1984) *The Brownings' Correspondence, Vol. 8 (1833–1844)*. Eds Philip Kelley and Ronald Hudson. Winfield, Kans.: Wedgestone Press.

Butts, Richard (1985) 'Languages of Description and Analogy in Victorian Science and Poetry.' *English Studies in Canada*, 11, 2, 193–213.

Christ, Carol T. (1975) *The Finer Optic: The Aesthetic of Particularity In Victorian Poetry*. New Haven: Yale University Press.

Dale, Peter Allan (1991) 'Poetry and the Scientization of Language: "Geist" Son of "Waldmann."' *Victorian Newsletter*, 79, 4–9.

Dalton, John (1950) *A New System of Chemical Philosophy*. First published 1808. London: Dawson.

Darwin, Charles (1964) *On the Origin of Species*. First published 1859. Cambridge, Mass.: Harvard University Press.

Dean, Dennis R. (1981) '"Through Science to Despair": Geology and the Victorians.' In James Paradis and Thomas Postlewait (eds). *Victorian Science and Victorian Values: Literary Perspectives* (pp. 111–36). New York: New York Academy of Sciences.

Faas, Ekbert (1988) *Retreat into the Mind: Victorian Poetry and the Rise of Psychiatry*. Princeton, N. J.: Princeton University Press.

Fletcher, Pauline (1983) *Gardens and Grim Ravines: The Language of Landscape in Victorian Poetry*. Princeton, N. J.: Princeton University Press.

Fraser, Hilary (1989) 'Truth to Nature: Science, Religion, and the Pre-Raphaelites.' In David Jasper and T. R. Wright (eds). *The Critical Spirit and the Will to Believe: The Victorian Crisis of Faith* (pp. 53–68). New York: St Martin's Press.

Graham, Colin (1998) *Ideologies of Epic: Nation, Empire, and Victorian Epic Poetry*. Manchester: Manchester University Press.

Janowitz, Anne (1998) *Lyric and Labour in the Romantic Tradition*. Cambridge: Cambridge University Press.

Langbaum, Robert W. (1970) *The Modern Spirit: Essays on the Continuity of Nineteenth- and Twentieth-Century Literature*. New York: Oxford University Press.

Levine, George (1988) 'Matthew Arnold's Science of Religion: The Uses of Imprecision.' *Victorian Poetry*, 26. 1–2, 143–62.

Lockyer, Norman (1911) 'Tennyson as a Student and Poet of Nature.' In Hallam Tennyson (ed.). *Tennyson and his Friends* (pp. 204–91). London: Macmillan.

Lodge, Oliver (1911) 'The Attitude of Tennyson toward Science.' In Hallam Tennyson (ed.). *Tennyson and his Friends* (pp. 280–4). London: Macmillan.

McGann, Jerome J. (1995) 'Medieval versus Victorian versus Modern: Rossetti's Art of Images.' *Modernism/Modernity*, 2. 1, 97–112.

Miller, J. Hillis. (1963) *The Disappearance of God: Five Nineteenth-Century Writers*. Cambridge, Mass.: Belknap Press.

Myers, F. W. H. (1893) 'Modern Poets and the Meaning of Life.' *Nineteenth Century*, 33, 93–111.

O'Neill, Patricia (1992) 'Paracelsus and the Authority of Science in Browning's Career.' *Victorian Literature and Culture*, 20, 293–310.

O'Neill, Patricia (1997) 'Victorian Lucretius: Tennyson and the Problem of Scientific Romanticism.' In J. B. Bullen (ed.). *Writing and Victorianism* (pp. 104–19). London: Longman.

Riede, David (2000) 'Tennyson's Poetics of Melancholy and the Imperial Imagination.' *Studies in English Literature 1500–1900*, 40. 4, 659–78.

Robinson, Bonnie J. (2000) 'Individable

Incorporate: Poetic Trends in Women Writers, 1890–1918.' *Victorian Poetry*, 38, 1, 1–14.

Rowe, M. W. (1989) 'Arnold and the Metaphysics of Science: A Note on "Dover Beach." ' *Victorian Poetry*, 27. 2, 213–17.

Schneider, Mary W. (1981) 'The Lucretian Background of "Dover Beach." ' *Victorian Poetry*, 19. 2, 190–5.

Shaw, W. David (1983) 'Poetic Truth in a Scientific Age: The Victorian Perspective.' In Eleanor Cook, Chaviva Hosek, Jay MacPherson, Patricia Parker and Julian Patrick (eds). *Centre and Labyrinth: Essays in Honour of Northrop Frye* (pp. 245–63). Toronto: University of Toronto Press.

Timko, Michael (1966) *Innocent Victorian: The Satiric Poetry of Arthur Hugh Clough.* Athens: Ohio University Press.

27

Landscape and Cityscape

Pauline Fletcher

The story of the nineteenth century is in many respects the story of lost countryside and growing cities and, as displaced rural workers moved into the new industrial towns, it is hardly surprising that a nostalgia developed for green and spacious landscapes. The eighteenth century had been the great age of landscape, a term originally derived from painting. A 'landscape' was not simply to be identified as the countryside; it was countryside viewed as scenery, an artefact that the sophisticated urban visitor was able to constitute as a painting by Claude Lorrain or Salvator Rosa. The great landowners, enriched partly at the expense of a dispossessed peasantry, created such landscapes to reflect not only their power and wealth, but also their cultivated tastes. At Stowe, for example, the visitor passes through the 'Elysian Fields' to view the Temple of Ancient Virtue; but in spite of such seeming artificiality, these landscapes, especially those laid out by Capability Brown, were designed to look 'natural'. Gentle curves and serpentine lines replaced the formal, geometric gardens of earlier times; vistas stretched to the horizon, and plantings of trees and shrubs were carefully informal.

Such smooth and gentle landscapes corresponded to Edmund Burke's category of the Beautiful; the Sublime, on the other hand, was associated with awe and characterized by vastness, power and obscurity. The Sublime degenerated over time into the Picturesque, in which genuine awe of Nature's grandeur was replaced by stereotyped reactions to a catalogue of picturesque objects. Wind-blasted trees, rocky cliffs and 'ruins' became the order of the day as Brown's idealized Arcadian pastoral gave way to a glorification of wilderness that might include a derelict hovel or hermitage.

The cult of the picturesque did not last. As Carl Woodring observes: 'Not long into the nineteenth century . . . anything artificially picturesque was suspected of sham' (1989: 49). The picturesque became an easy target of satire, and, on a more serious level, of the kind of moral indignation voiced by William Cobbett in *Rural Rides* (1830).

John Ruskin shared Cobbett's moral indignation. Although he was an early admirer of alpine scenery, he refused to see squalid mountain villages as picturesque adjuncts to sublime scenery. Concluding that sublimely beautiful surroundings do not necessarily produce beautiful people, he turns away from mountains to more pastoral landscapes that are subordinate to human needs. Victorian poets, as I shall demonstrate, also tended to reject the more sublime aspects of landscape that had been celebrated by Romantic poets such as Byron and Wordsworth, often moving from the wilderness into sheltered nooks or enclosed gardens. But the landscape of retreat was not without its tensions. It might become the garden of the mind, harbouring monsters of the imagination, and for many poets a more humanized and social landscape was to be preferred. I shall discuss various versions of this humanized landscape, and also show how it might embody the political divisions of the age.

The Romantic sublime was challenged not only by the desire to accommodate human needs, but also by a radically different view of the natural world that emerged from the work of geologists and naturalists. William Wordsworth had known 'that Nature never did betray / The heart that loved her' ('Tintern Abbey', 1798, ll. 122–3), but the concept of nature that emerged from the new science was of an impersonal force, indifferent to the extinction of whole species. This bleak view gave rise to landscapes of stoic endurance and negation, although paradoxically the possibilities of a revisionary Romanticism might be inherent in the landscape of negation. And for some poets, under the influence of Tractarianism and the Oxford Movement, God and the sacramental landscape had never disappeared.

Finally, as I shall show, the poets discovered what novelists had long since known, that the city might be a fit subject for the creative imagination. The first poets to sing the city did so in terms of the horrors of the urban wasteland, but gradually an urban sensibility developed that was able to find beauty even in the crowded streets of London.

Landscapes of Retreat

Crowded streets did not appeal to the poets of the first half of the nineteenth century. Many of Alfred Tennyson's early poems express a simple desire for escape, perhaps to some remote Arcadian valley, or to magical, tropical islands inhabited by indolent Lotos-Eaters. Even more common is the enclosed garden, such as those described in 'Recollections of the Arabian Nights' (1830). These gardens of elaborate artifice are described in Tennyson's most ornate and decorative style. They celebrate art and the imagination rather than nature, and provide a retreat from the hostile world. Sometimes this retreat is specifically identified as a sacred, interior space, a garden of the poet's own mind, but such interior spaces always carry with them the dangers of isolation and solipsism. This is true of the decaying garden in 'Mariana' (1830), which is no longer an aristocratic pleasure garden or a fitting symbol of the poet's soul in a state of Romantic isolation. Mariana has come to dread her own isolation and can only yearn in impotent despair for 'him' to come. Other solitary maidens do escape. The imprisoned soul in 'The Palace of Art' (1832) goes down to a cottage in the valley, and the Lady of Shalott abandons her isolation, sacrificing both life and art.

For Matthew Arnold the landscape of retreat was less ambiguous than it was for Tennyson. Arnold was, of all the Victorian poets, closest to Wordsworth. He shared Wordsworth's deep love of the English countryside and his belief in the healing power of nature. This power was to be found mostly in secluded rural nooks or forest glades, a land-scape of refuge described by Dwight Culler as being characterized by 'the springlike and virginal quality of its vegetation' (1966: 6). The speaker in 'The Scholar-Gipsy' (1853) waits in just such a flowery, sheltered nook, which constitutes a midway point between civilization and wilderness; the speaker is hidden from the world, but he can still see Oxford, the symbol of official learning and civilization, in the valley below. In this safe spot he can dream of the gipsy, who left Oxford and civilization to become what Arnold could never be, a Romantic quester in the wilderness. In order to pursue his quest the gipsy must flee from the pastoral world in which the poet has found a refuge; he must avoid even the most seemingly innocent human contact and 'plunge deeper in the bow-ering wood' (l. 207). Arnold thus establishes the unpeopled wilderness of the deep woods in opposition to any socialized or humanized landscape.

For centuries the European imagination had found the dark forests a threatening place where innocent maidens might encounter wolves, or middle-aged poets such as Dante might lose their spiritual bearings. Arnold rescues the woods for his myth of Romantic primitivism, but in so doing he tames the wilderness and empties it of threatening qual-ities. It is illuminating to compare Arnold with Tennyson in this respect. In *Idylls of the King* (1859–85) the woods are not only savage and lawless, they are also places of dan-gerous eroticism where the evil Vivien seduces Merlin.

Arnold also has Vivien seducing Merlin in the woods, but his forest, far from being sinister, is full of bright-eyed squirrels, whistling blackbirds, anemones and primroses. In *Tristram and Iseult* (1852) the woodland bower is more ambiguously treated. It is the 'free green wood' (l. 179) where Tristram and Iseult of Ireland celebrated their forbidden love, and it is therefore a landscape hostile to Iseult of Brittany. Tristram retreats from his young wife to muse 'In the forest-depths alone' (l. 224), and we are told of such 'musing fits in the green wood' that 'They cloud the brain, they dull the blood' (ll. 248–9). For the most part, however, Arnold sees the woods as an innocent, pre-sexual paradise, and even in *Tris-tram and Iseult* the woods are not eroticized but presented as places of, mostly solitary, refuge. As Culler points out, Arnold's nooks and woodland glades may not be erotic, but they are 'intensely feminine and maternal' (1966: 7), offering a protective and sheltering haven from the duties and stressful responsibilities of adult life.

Such landscapes of retreat are common in Victorian poetry. They may be found, for example, in many of Elizabeth Barrett Browning's early poems, such as 'The Deserted Garden' (1838), which contains a 'child's nest so greenly wrought' (l. 90) beneath the shelter of a poplar tree. In Christina Rossetti's poem, 'Spring Quiet' (1866), a woodland covert offers security, whispering softly: 'We spread no snare; / Here dwell in safety, / Here dwell alone' (ll. 16–18). But Rossetti also knows that such woodland places can be sinis-ter. In 'Goblin Market' (1862) the mossy glen, far from being maternal or protective, is haunted by malicious little goblin men who offer forbidden fruit to innocent maidens. Like Tennyson, Rossetti found woodland retreats both attractive and terrifying; for both poets, wild places are often the realm of unacknowledged and dangerous desires.

The landscape of retreat also figures prominently in the poetry of Dante Gabriel Rossetti, but Rossetti's woodland bower is not pre-sexual; it is a bower of bliss, an erotic space where lovers may find a haven. Very rarely, the retreat may be a place that is open to the skies, fresh and spacious, as in 'Silent Noon' (1881), where the lovers have found a nest in a pasture ''Neath billowing skies that scatter and amass' (l. 4). However, the billowing skies suggest change; Rossetti is always aware of the forces that threaten his secret bowers, and these do not necessarily come from the human world. Even nature can threaten the lovers, and the wind in particular is seen as a destructive force of seasonal change that may strip away the protective covering. When wind, light and open space are seen as the enemies of love, the safe haven can become oppressive and stifling, as in 'The Portrait' (1847, 1870):

> In painting her I shrined her face
> 'Mid mystic trees, where light falls in
> Hardly at all; a covert place.
>   (ll. 19–21)

Here the bower becomes a shrine for the Beloved, but only for her portrait, not for the woman herself. In this dim world, where no light must penetrate, she becomes merely an artefact created by the poet. Similarly, in the fourth Willowwood sonnet the poet bends to kiss the image of Love in a well, but in so doing kisses only his own reflection. Rossetti's enclosed bowers are, in the end, solipsistic landscapes of the mind where sub-conscious fears may be encountered and where the Beloved may be transformed into the *femme fatale*. In 'The Orchard Pit' (1886) the bower screens the hidden pit of death above which the lady stands offering her apples that 'gave to these, / That lie below, her magic hour of ease' (ll. 8–9). In this 'soft dell' the lovers discover that their fine and private place is in fact a grave.

The Politics of Landscape

As we have seen, Tennyson had also discovered the perils of withdrawal, in those early poems where lonely maidens sing of their desolation and imprisonment in towers or enclosed gardens that seem most often to represent the mind of the poet. In these poems he is exploring the tension between art and life: the poetic imagination demands a land-scape of isolation that is fatal to the living creature. But as Tennyson moved away from his Romantic heritage, he discovered that the poet need not be a solitary singer, and that those symbolic gardens of the mind might be transformed into the enclosed gardens attached to the great houses of wealthy aristocrats. Such gardens should function as symbols of continuity and order, but, as Alexander Pope powerfully suggests in 'The Epistle to Burlington' (1732), the order is defined by those who create gardens as an expression of their values, status and identity. The aristocratic garden is not an innocent symbol, even for Pope. And for Tennyson in a more democratic age, the garden of a Great House is more likely to become a contested site where issues of class and privilege are explored.

In *Maud* (1855) the 'high Hall-garden' (1: XII, 412) is a symbol of power, wealth and social exclusivity, and the narrator is an outsider, excluded from the garden because he is 'nameless and poor' (l: IV, 119). Access to the garden, and to Maud herself, is granted only to the rich and titled, but Maud's officially approved suitor is a 'new-made lord' (1: X, 32), whose wealth was derived from coal mining. Tennyson is careful to destroy this garden's claim to genuinely aristocratic status. Maud herself, the desired object in the forbidden garden, is controlled not only by her brother but also by her lover, the narrator, since she has no real existence outside his narration. He sees her at first as beautiful but 'icily regular, splendidly null' (1: II, 82), the perfect icon of her social class and status. Later, he 'construes her as a product of the innocent, natural world of the garden' (Waters 1988: 253), and, finding a garden rose in the little rivulet that flows down from the Hall across his land, he assumes that it is a messenger from Maud: 'Saying in odour and colour, "Ah, be / Among the roses to-night"' (1: XXI, 849). In the lyric that follows, 'Come into the garden, Maud' (I: XXII, 850), the lover attempts to detach the garden from its social trappings and to recreate it as an innocent paradise where he can meet with Maud, but only death, despair and insanity result from the secret meeting.

A more positive image of a romantic but accessible garden emerges in 'The Gardener's Daughter' (1842), but this is largely because Tennyson chooses to ignore social facts such as the status of the lover, the presence of parents, or even whether the lover marries the gardener's daughter. No social system is imposed upon this fragile Eden. What is stressed is the fact that the garden occupies the ideal territory between solitude and society: 'News from the humming city comes to it', but 'a league of grass, washed by a slow broad stream' separates it from the city (ll. 35, 40). The love affair celebrated in this garden also occupies a middle ground; it is not fraught with the dangerous passions of *Maud*, whose protagonist descends into madness and imagines that the roses in the garden 'are not roses, but blood' (2: V, 316). The protagonist in 'The Gardener's Daughter' achieves a peaceful old age blessed by nostalgic memories of love in the garden.

The gardener's daughter has no existence outside the garden, and the frequent association of women with flowers and gardens has, as Waters points out, played a part in the construction of female stereotypes: 'Like the plants they lovingly tend, "ladies" are "naturally" delicate, ornamental, wholesome, pure and submissive, performing for their husbands and lovers the same civilizing and refining functions which flowers perform for people in general' (1988: 135). The image of a woman as the desirable rose in the garden goes back to medieval iconography, but the Victorians transformed the icon by replacing the aristocratic *hortus conclusus* (carefully considered garden), in which time and the life processes seem to be suspended, with a cosily domestic cottage garden. Even the cottage garden, however, retained some of the associations of its medieval counterpart 'through the ideological practice which sanctified women as the privileged bearers of moral and spiritual values' (Waters 1988: 255) within a male-dominated society. If the garden enshrined 'feminine' virtues, it might also be seen as a means of civilizing the working classes, who were encouraged to cultivate their flower boxes and allotments.

On rare occasions the working classes might be invited into the gardens of a great landowner bent upon making a democratic gesture. In *The Princess* (1847) Tennyson describes just such an event taking place in Sir Walter Vivian's park. This festive occasion is an attempt to provide amusement and useful knowledge for the local populace, and to promote better feelings among the various social classes. It is also a gesture that preserves and promotes the status quo, a fact that is made clear in the Conclusion to the poem, which contains a description of the panoramic view from Vivian-place of a peaceful countryside dominated by 'Gray halls alone among their massive groves' (l. 43). The landscape becomes 'our Britain', seen as a garden that is protected from dangerous, revolutionary France by the sea, still 'whole within herself, / A nation yet, the rulers and the ruled – ': Tennyson contextualizes and distances himself from the remark by attributing it to the 'Tory member's elder son' (ll. 52–3).

Tennyson's movement from the isolated garden of the mind to the richly contextualized gardens of country estate, rectory or cottage is a movement towards greater social awareness, but this does not lead the poet into the crowded city. His ideal remains a landscape of compromise, midway between the extremes of isolation and sociability, wilderness and city.

The Humanized Landscape

This midway point is a humanized landscape, an idealized realm in which human values may be celebrated in a more or less natural setting. For Tennyson, the Somersby garden of his childhood is such a place, sacred to past happiness. The carefully described garden setting of lyric 95 of *In Memoriam* (1850) creates a scene that is simultaneously pastoral, idyllic, and congenial to human activity and companionship. When, after tea and songs on the lawn, the speaker's companions depart, the darkened garden, sanctified by memories of Hallam, becomes the setting for a mystical reunion with the poet's lost friend. The Somersby garden contains no disturbing erotic overtones and is not seen as a meeting place for lovers; on the social scale it is not a cottage garden, still less an aristocratic preserve; it can safely symbolize a masculine friendship that has been idealized and spiritualized. The garden's tranquil natural beauty not only suggests that such a friendship is 'natural'; it also contains and domesticates the potentially terrifying supernatural experience that takes place within sight of the sleeping house; the occupants of the house are reassuringly close by, the garden is both 'natural' and civilized, and a pastoral landscape of cows and meadows surrounds the garden. The poem celebrates a landscape of compromise.

Elsewhere, Tennyson is conscious that the choice of a landscape of compromise might also involve sacrifice. This is perhaps most perfectly expressed in the famous lyric from *The Princess* in which the shepherd exhorts the maid to descend from the harsh and barren mountain heights to the pastoral valley, where she will hear the sweet call of hearth, home and children. Of course, this is also a call for the princess to forsake her high purpose of founding a woman's college, and to settle for love and domesticity in the valley. However, the poem does grant a measure of glory to the life of the maid on the heights; she is 'a sunbeam' and 'a star upon the sparkling spire' (VII, 181–2), and one must ask whether she will shine quite as brightly when she is weighted down with household tasks. The lyric seems to endorse the decision of the princess to abandon her revolutionary purpose, but the last two lines of the poem are both seductive and enervating: she will come down to 'The moan of doves in immemorial elms, / And murmuring of innumerable bees' (ll. 206–7). The lines echo the languid rhythms of Tennyson's 'Lotos-Eaters' (1832), and the princess, like the mariners, may be opting for a life of ease that kills the spirit.

Unlike Tennyson's princess, William Morris is able to embrace the pastoral values of the valley while preserving his revolutionary purpose. Morris had a deep love of the English countryside, but it is almost always a working countryside that he favours. Although enclosed gardens and dense forests appear in his medieval poems, they are not ultimately seen as desirable. Morris's socialist principles may have led him to reject the *hortus conclusus* as a sign of aristocratic privilege, but in any case he would have seen such gardens as too isolated and removed from the real world. The forest, on the other hand, is a hostile and dangerous wasteland. As Blue Calhoun points out, Morris 'believed in civilization – its necessity and value. The romantic quest moves away from society and into the enchanted wilderness. His Wanderers of *The Earthly Paradise* tried to be romantic and failed . . . More and more after *The Defence of Guenevere* the characteristic pattern of Morris's journeys would be not away from but toward society' (1975: 31). Morris's belief in civilization rather than in raw nature is also illustrated in his decorative arts. His designs for wallpapers, illuminated manuscripts and tapestries make use of natural motifs, but they are always highly formalized. So too, his ideal landscape is one that has been humanized and civilized; it contains fields and pastures, well-ordered villages and even small, white-walled towns. These pre-industrial towns were places of beauty containing spacious public gardens, but in Morris's imagined utopia the whole of England had become a garden: the pastoral landscape was a source of both aesthetic pleasure and practical livelihood.

Thomas Hardy also favours a humanized landscape, but he does not share Morris's utopian vision of pastoral. His rural roots give him an unsentimental view of country life, and his protagonists are not city-dwellers seeking either scenery or the healing power of nature; they are a part of the landscape. In 'A Trampwoman's Tragedy' (1909) the landscape cannot be separated from the presence of those who trudge through it: 'The sunblaze burning on our backs, / Our shoulders sticking to our packs' (ll. 5–6). The emphasis is on what the tramps endured and suffered, and the lack of visual description ensures that their painfully felt surroundings do not become 'scenery'.

In other poems where the landscape is described in more pictorial terms, it is still the human dimension that remains the focus of the poem. The acutely observed natural phenomena of 'Neutral Tones' (1867) act as an objective correlative of the speaker's emotions. Other landscapes are marked by history or haunted by the past: 'There's a ghost at Yell'ham Bottom chiding loud at the fall of night, / There's a ghost in Froomside Vale, thin-lipped and vague, in a shroud of white' ('Wessex Heights', 1896, 1914, l. 22). Indeed, many of these haunted landscapes might be described as mental constructs, but Hardy still retains a stubborn grasp of the specificity of the natural world and of its indifference to human suffering.

The Darwinian Landscape

Hardy's attitudes to nature and the natural world are strongly marked by the influence of Charles Darwin's theory of evolution, which Hardy greeted as a liberating truth; indeed, Darwin's unsentimental view of the natural world may even have had a special appeal to a man who knew the hardships of rural life. In his poem 'In a Wood' (1898) Hardy deliberately undermines the romantic view that nature can offer moral guidance or solace to the weary city-dweller. The 'City-opprest' speaker seeks a 'nest' in the wood and dreams of 'sylvan peace' (ll. 10, 12, 13), but he finds a brutally competitive world in which 'Sycamore shoulders oak' and 'Ivy-spun halters choke / Elms stout and tall' (ll. 21, 23–4). Finally, he retreats from nature to the human world where 'now and then, are found / Life-loyalties' (ll. 39–40).

Even before the publication of *Origin of Species* (1859), the romantic view of nature as transcendental had been undermined by the new science of geology, by speculations concerning the mutability of species, and by the discovery of numerous fossils. Tennyson, writing before Darwin's work was published, was so deeply troubled by the implications of the new science that in lyric 7 of *In Memoriam* he asks himself whether God and nature are locked in conflict. For centuries nature had been regarded as God's handmaiden, but now it seemed that the book of nature revealed only the workings of blind chance, and not the record of a divine plan. This is a version of nature as 'red in tooth and claw' (l. 15), and from 'scarpèd cliff and quarried stone' she proclaims her cruel indifference: 'A thousand types are gone; / I care for nothing, all shall go' (lyric 56, ll. 2–4).

A more exuberant view of the Darwinian landscape may be found in Robert Browning's work. In poems such as 'Sibrandus Schafnaburgensis' (1845) Browning depicts a landscape teeming with 'frisking and twisting and coupling' (l. 58) creatures, most of which are anthropomorphized; the struggle for survival in this populous world of 'worm, slug, eft' and 'water-beetle with great blind deaf face' (ll. 51–3) suggests a comic version of Darwin's tangled bank on which various life forms jostle for position. However, Browning does not see this struggle as evidence of nature's cruelty and indifference. He seems instead to be celebrating the wonderful fecundity and energy of a natural world in which, as critics have variously argued, God may be either present or absent. What is certain is that Browning has created another version of the humanized landscape, or rather, a microcosm of the human world populated by crickets in houses, newts that have wives with closets, and 'All that life and fun and romping' (l. 57).

On a rather more serious level, George Meredith embraced Darwinian theory as the foundation for an optimistic philosophy of the natural world and its relation to humankind. Meredith's description of a blustery spring day, when 'The wind has teeth, the wind has claws' ('Hard Weather', 1888, l. 6), has obvious echoes of Tennyson's 'red in tooth and claw'. However, in seeking the 'meaning' of nature's harshness, Meredith concludes that an easy life of pleasure would sap our strength, and that 'Contention is the vital force' (l. 75) that sharpens our faculties and develops not only muscular strength but also brain. Finally, in a progressive evolutionary process that echoes Tennyson once more, 'spirit comes to light, / Through conquest of the inner beast' (ll. 79–80).

Meredith's Darwinian vision of humankind as a part of the natural world, subjected to the same harsh laws that govern the lives of other living creatures, argues against the widely held view that for the Victorians 'humanity and nature remain unalterably separate' (Lorsch 1983: 41). It is true, however, as Lorsch has argued, that for most Victorians nature was designified, or at least, that any significance in nature had to be 'discovered' by the perceiver. However, there is a tendency to draw too easy a contrast between the 'natural supernaturalism' of Romantic transcendentalism and the Victorian sense of the natural world as emptied of meaning by scientific discovery. Long before Charles Lyell and Darwin, Romantic poets such as Wordsworth and Samuel Taylor Coleridge had already raised the question of whether nature had any inherent meaning. In his great ode 'Intimations of Immortality' (1802–4), Wordsworth had bewailed the loss of that visionary gleam that had once clothed the natural world for him, and Coleridge, in 'Dejection: An Ode' (1802), claims that it is only through human perception and imagination that nature acquires any significance. The real difference between the Romantics and the Victorians may be that whereas for Wordsworth and Coleridge the designification of nature was a tragic loss, largely attributable to their own failing powers, for the Victorians it might become a source of strength. Hardy's haunted landscapes draw his protagonist back into a confrontation with his own past that is enriching in spite of grief; and even Arnold's melancholy speaker is able to read the lesson of stoic endurance in the bleak landscape of 'Resignation', with its 'strange-scrawled rocks' and 'lonely sky' (1849, l. 268).

The Landscape of Negation

Stoicism is perhaps an apt lesson for an unromantic age that nevertheless preserves, as Arnold does, a nostalgic longing for a lost world in which visionary power was possible. Stoicism and nostalgia for the past are also characteristics of Browning's Childe Roland, a belated Romantic whose quest takes him across a nightmarish landscape of negation that is completely lacking in the wild, exuberant energy and teeming, frisking life of other Browning landscapes. It is a wasteland characterized by 'penury, inertness and grimace' (l. 61), presided over by a peevish and uncaring nature. However, even this landscape is anthropomorphized by Browning, whose hero invests the desolate scene with his own diseased imaginings. The earth itself becomes a leprous and corrupted human body with patches of moss breaking out like boils, palsied oaks, and 'a distorted mouth that spits its rim / Gaping at death' (ll. 155–6). This is, in the end, a landscape of the mind that looks back to the dreary wasteland of Tennyson's 'Mariana' and forward to T. S. Eliot.

Hardy was to use the landscape of negation in a poem written as an epitaph for the nineteenth century and, in particular, for Romanticism. The speaker in 'The Darkling Thrush' (1900) surveys a desolate winter scene in which 'The land's sharp features seemed to be / The Century's corpse outleant' (ll. 9–10). Ironically, out of this death-like landscape comes the ecstatic song of the aged and gaunt thrush, who has apparently chosen 'to fling his soul / Upon the growing gloom' (ll. 23–4). On the brink of Modernism, Hardy reveals the Romantic possibilities inherent in the landscape of nihilism and denial, but the hope for something better remains fragile and the speaker is 'unaware' of any cause for rejoicing; he remains a detached and sceptical observer, and we are reminded that for Hardy if a 'way to the Better there be, it exacts a full look at the Worst' ('In Tenebris II', 1895–6, l. 14).

Algernon Swinburne was also prepared to take that 'full look at the Worst', but he creates his own romantic exaltation out of the very landscapes of negation that would seem to deny such possibilities. In 'A Forsaken Garden' (1878) Swinburne describes 'The ghost of a garden' in which even the weeds 'that grew green from the graves of its roses / Now lie dead' (ll. 4, 7–8). This landscape of death has reached the point of perfect stasis, an eternity of non-being in which change and decay are themselves defeated, and, paradoxically, 'Death lies dead' (l. 80). Regeneration is possible, but only after a complete surrender to the forces of extinction, represented most often by the sea, although other great cosmic powers such as sun and wind come into play as well. The yearning for union with these cosmic forces is expressed partly through elements of the landscape itself. In 'The Triumph of Time' (1866) the sea-daisies, 'With lips wide open and face burnt blind', yield themselves to the sun, while the 'low downs lean to the sea' and the stream hurries to rejoin the body of the sea of which it is 'One loose thin pulseless tremulous vein' (ll. 55, 57, 58). Similarly, the speaker yearns to become 'a vein in the heart of the streams of the sea'; yielding up his separate identity, he will 'Change as the winds change, veer in the tide . . . rise with thy rising, with thee subside' (ll. 274, 276).

In 'Thalassius' (1879) Swinburne celebrates a passionate reunion with the sea as the source of his poetic power and of an 'immortality opposed to Wordsworth's' (Harrison 1990: 178). Charmed 'from his own soul's separate sense', the speaker becomes 'no more a singer, but a song' (ll. 471, 474). But such poetic power can only come from an ecstatic surrender to annihilating forces, as when the speaker in 'The Lake of Gaube' (1904) must leap into the icy water, which is 'Death-dark and delicious as death' (l. 37), before he can achieve unity with the sun. Like William Blake, whom he greatly admired, Swinburne embraces contraries. His poems explore the dangerous marginal landscapes that exist between land and sea, life and death, terror and ecstasy. He deconstructs such opposites, just as he deconstructs the opposition between the observer and the landscape. His persona becomes part of the cosmos, and through him the cosmos expresses itself in song.

The Sacramental Landscape

Swinburne's ecstatic cosmic song does not admit the presence of a benign deity in the world, but just as we are drawing the conclusion that God has indeed disappeared, Gerard Manley Hopkins provides an exception to the trend. Because his poetry was daringly idiosyncratic and was not published until 1918, he was hailed as a 'Modern'; in fact he was in many respects typical of his age, a product of the Oxford Movement and the aestheticism of Walter Pater. Hopkins writes as though Darwin had never existed. His landscapes are 'charged with the grandeur of God', and even when they are blighted by industrialism, 'bleared, smeared with toil', there is freshness beneath the corruption because 'nature is never spent' ('God's Grandeur', 1877, 1918, ll. 1, 6, 9). So Hopkins can see Christ in the power of a kestrel's flight ('The Windhover', 1877, 1918), and he can praise God for the beauty of all dappled and mutable things because 'He fathers-forth whose beauty is past change' ('Pied Beauty', 1877, 1918, l. 10).

In fact, the sacramental vision of God as inherent in the natural world had never entirely disappeared. It was given some expression by Tractarians such as John Keble and John Henry Newman, who 'use earthly phenomena as types of something outside human time' (Landow 1980: 215), and the poetry of Hopkins reflects this typological thinking. Biblical typology was also a characteristic of much Pre-Raphaelite painting, particularly that of William Holman Hunt.

Tennyson, as I have shown, had also managed to recover a version of the sacramental landscape in the Somersby garden, and towards the end of *In Memoriam* he hears Hallam's voice 'on the rolling air', and feels him as 'some diffusive power' that is 'mixed with God and Nature' (lyric 130, ll. 1, 7, 11). The agonizing question posed in lyric 55, 'Are God and Nature then at strife?' (l. 5), seems to have been answered. The presence of Hallam sanctifies the landscape for Tennyson. Hallam, as a type of the more spiritual man that will evolve, makes it possible for Tennyson to come to terms with biological evolution: 'theological type replaces biological type, or rather encompasses it, because faith reveals that God's eternal plan includes purposeful biological development' (Landow 1980: 9).

The Urban Wasteland

The urban landscape remained unsanctified, however. The rapid growth of new industrial cities had created horrendous living conditions for the urban poor, chronicled by Friedrich Engels in *The Condition of the Working Class in England in 1844*, and, with extraordinary vividness, by Henry Mayhew in *London Labour and the London Poor* (1851–2). Horror stories of families crowded into single rooms, living amongst offal and filth, dying of disease and starvation, made their way into the consciousness of the newly prosperous middle classes, often through the pages of the novels they read. Urban poetry, however, was less common, partly because the Victorians had inherited a view in which 'the country (or nature) is the source of moral good, and the city exists only remotely as an alternative and possibly destructive mode of life' (Johnston 1984: 87). Indeed, it is often assumed that 'Between William Blake's "London" and T. S Eliot's *The Waste Land* . . . the major poets turned their backs on urban life' (Thesing 1982: xv–xvi). But, as William Thesing convincingly demonstrates, this is not entirely true, and the prejudice in favour of rural retreat was not universal.

As has already been indicated, Morris valued the civilized life and yearned for a small, clean and white-walled version of fourteenth-century London. Tennyson also created idealized versions of the city, while recognizing their actual impossibility: Camelot was 'built

/ To music, therefore never built at all' ('Gareth and Lynette', 1872: 272–3). Browning's preference for humanized landscapes attracted him to city life: in 'Up at a Villa – Down in the City' (1855) the speaker draws a contrast between the boredom of life in a country villa and the excitement offered by the town, where 'You watch who crosses and gossips, who saunters, who hurries by' (l. 14). Admittedly, this is an Italian town not blighted by slums or industrial pollution, and almost certainly containing a public square where people gather to drink coffee, gossip and watch the world go by in the brilliant Mediterranean sunshine. Northern climates do not favour such activities, and Browning does not write in the same vein about English cities.

For the English, London was the great fact of urban life, alternately viewed with pride as the greatest city on earth, or with horror as the modern Babylon, an infernal labyrinth of crime, poverty and vice. Foreigners came to London to marvel and to shudder. The French historian Hippolyte Taine recalls 'stifling lanes, encrusted with human exhalations; troops of pale children nestling on the muddy stairs' (1872: 36). The major Victorian poets may have preferred country to city, but the city nevertheless had an impact on their consciousness. In 'Locksley Hall, Sixty Years After' (1889), the aged Tennyson, projecting a vision of the city that challenges the Victorian belief in progress, asks, 'Is it well that while we range with Science, glorying in the Time, / City children soak and blacken soul and sense in city slime?' (ll. 217–18).

However, the younger Tennyson's view of London had been more nuanced, and in lyric 7 of *In Memoriam* he uses the city as a metaphor for personal grief and loss. Standing in 'the long unlovely street' outside what had been Hallam's house, he must face the fact that 'He is not here', and that 'ghastly thro' the drizzling rain / On the bald street breaks the blank day' (ll. 2, 9, 11–12). But in lyric 119 he revisits the scene and this time 'the city sleeps; / I smell the meadow in the street, / I hear a chirp of birds'. Finally he experiences the desired moment of reunion: 'And in my thoughts with scarce a sigh / I take the pressure of thine hand' (ll. 3–5, 11–12). Like the garden at Somersby, and nature itself, the city is briefly sanctified by the memory of Hallam. But its state of grace is signalled by pastoral imagery of meadows and birdsong.

For Arnold the city is typically seen as 'a brazen prison' ('A Summer Night', 1851, l. 37) which is inimical to the inner life. Nevertheless, it is in 'the din of strife' of the city that 'There rises an unspeakable desire / After the knowledge of our buried life', and then 'A man becomes aware of his life's flow' and 'sees / The meadows where it glides' ('The Buried Life', 1852, ll. 46–8, 88, 89–90). Again, the use of pastoral imagery signals the good moment, but the city itself remains unredeemed.

The city threatened more than the inner life. Events such as the Hyde Park riots of 1866 and violent demonstrations in the 1880s fuelled fears of class warfare and mob rule. In the earlier part of the century Tennyson had expressed his fears of democratic change in 'Locksley Hall' (1842): 'Slowly comes a hungry people, as a lion, creeping nigher' (l. 135); these fears were intensified in 'Locksley Hall, Sixty Years After' (1886). Similar fears were expressed by other poets. In 'Tom's Garland: Upon the Unemployed' (1887) Hopkins expresses both his sympathy for Tom, the working man, and his horror at the plight of the unemployed: 'This, by Despair, bred Hangdog dull; by Rage, / Manwolf, worse; and their packs infest the age' (ll. 19–20). As Thesing comments, by the end of the poem 'the structure of feeling explodes outward into chaotic fragments' (1982: 104).

The sufferings of the urban poor are more sympathetically chronicled by a number of poets. Thomas Hood's 'The Song of the Shirt' (1846) creates a vivid picture of the toiling seamstress, and Elizabeth Barrett Browning gives a voice to the children of the Industrial Revolution in 'The Cry of the Children' (1844). Even Dante Gabriel Rossetti ventured into the territory of social commentary in his poem 'Jenny' (1870), which gives a sympathetic portrait of the life of a London prostitute.

Roden Noel, described by Thesing as possibly 'the most direct and objective of the various poetic commentators of the age' (1982: 99), pushes realistically observed detail to the point of surrealistic nightmare. London's 'million ordured courts' contain 'spectres foul yet dim / In subtle blue miasma mists that swim, / There at the dingy pane, with dull dead eyes / Faces wormfretted' ('The Red Flag', 1872, ll. 281, 285–8). In 'A Lay of Civilization, or London' (1885), the city, under 'a brown Plutonian gloom' (l. 84), is seen as a version of Dante's *Inferno*.

Poets like Noel deserve more attention, but the most significant urban poem of the age is almost certainly James Thomson's 'The City of Dreadful Night' (1870–3). Thomson anticipates Eliot in his surrealistic vision of the city as a nightmare landscape of the mind. Thomson's London breeds a 'dreadful strain / Of thought and consciousness which never ceases' (I, 116–17), and it is haunted by spectral night wanderers:

> Each adding poison to the poisoned air;
> Infections of unutterable sadness,
> Infections of incalculable madness,
> Infections of incurable despair.
>
> (XV, 793–6)

For Raymond Williams, Thomson's city 'is the physical embodiment of a decisive modern consciousness', characterized by 'struggle, indifference, loss of purpose, loss of meaning' (1973: 239).

Redeeming the City

Victorian poets such as Noel and Thomson may have forged a consciousness of the city as Inferno that would be taken up by modern poets, but Victorian energies were also harnessed to ameliorate the urban landscape. Morris's socialist and utopian vision of London in *News from Nowhere* (1890), as a city in which people had access to spacious gardens, was in fact at least partly realized by more practical and politically conservative Victorians who created public parks and garden suburbs. In London the royal parks were made available to the public, and in the new industrial cities spacious parks were created. Birkenhead Park in Liverpool, laid out by Joseph Paxton in 1834–47, became a model for others. It contained screened walks, shrubberies and enclosed spaces that allowed city-dwellers some measure of privacy, and also hid from view the hideous urban wasteland. Parks might also become showcases for botanical specimens, the spoils of empire culled from distant lands. George III had established a botanical collection at Kew, and in 1841 Kew was opened to the public. Its hybrid nature as imperial museum, public pleasure ground and botanical research facility was a tribute to Victorian enterprise.

The creation of garden suburbs was another attempt by the Victorians to bring nature into the city. J. C. Loudon's *The Suburban Gardener, and Villa Companion* (1838) and Mrs Loudon's *Gardening for Ladies* (1840) gave plans and advice to members of the new middle class intent upon creating their own little backyard Edens. Such gardens might be almost comic attempts to mimic the grand country estate, but they represented a genuinely democratic development, and they undoubtedly improved the urban landscape. The idea of the garden suburb, according to Walter Creese, 'was shaped by two very different impulses – the one, emotional and aesthetic, retained the Romantic wish to flee into wood-land alleys and places of nestling green; the other, communal in emphasis, stressed the values of social cohesion and interdependence' (1977: 52).

Arnold was able to satisfy his romantic love of 'places of nestling green' by fleeing to one of the great public parks in the heart of London. His 'Lines Written in Kensington Gardens' (1852) describes what would be a forest glade if it were not girdled by the 'city's hum':

> In this lone, open glade I lie,
> Screened by deep boughs on either hand;
> And at its end, to stay the eye,
> Those black-crowned, red-boled pine-trees stand!
>   (ll. 1–4)

The trees that 'stay the eye' in this artificial glade were no doubt cleverly positioned to block the sight of city buildings and to create the illusion of wild nature. The cries of sheep outside the enclosure moderate the 'wilderness' by suggesting pastoral surround-ings, and the glade is humanized by the intrusion of the occasional child, whose presence guarantees its primal innocence. The speaker's presence is, of course, temporary, and indeed Arnold's protagonists must always return to the busy urban world from their sheltered nooks.

All these attempts to improve the city by creating pockets of the 'natural world' within the urban landscape were based on the premise that nature was to be preferred to art. However, as the century drew to a close, a number of poets began to value the city for its own sake.

The Urban Sensibility

An urban sensibility was perhaps the natural outcome of the Aesthetic movement, with its emphasis on 'art for art's sake', and according to Woodring 'by the 1890s urban subjects surpassed the rural, certainly the pastoral, in poetry and painting' (1989: 243). The shift from country to city, from nature to art, is both promoted and parodied by Oscar Wilde in his essay/dialogue 'The Decay of Lying' (1889), where Vivian remarks in her opening speech: 'Enjoy Nature! I am glad to say that I have entirely lost that faculty . . . My own experience is that the more we study Art, the less we care for Nature. What Art really reveals to us is Nature's lack of design, her curious crudities, her extraordinary monotony, her absolutely unfinished condition.' Nature's lack of design was to be remedied by art nouveau with its emphasis on form. Its 'distinguishing curvilinear forms, smoothing the aberrations from organic plants, proclaimed simultaneously a respect for nature and the aesthetic inadequacy of nature' (Woodring 1989: 243). If form alone mattered and if all art aspired to the condition of music, then London could be transformed into nocturnes, symphonies and rhapsodies of sight and sound. So Arthur Symons, in 'Nocturne' (1889), writes of the Embankment with its 'pavement glittering' and 'The magic and mystery that is night's, / And human love without pain'. Wilde too, sees the Thames as a 'nocturne of blue and gold / Changed to a Harmony in grey' ('Impression du Matin', 1881, ll. 1–2).

However, the squalor of London was not entirely ignored. In *Les Fleurs du mal* (1857) Baudelaire had shown how the sordid life of the city could be transformed into art, and Richard Le Gallienne's debt to the French poet is clear in 'A Ballad of London' (1892), in which the city is changed from a monster of dreadful night to a 'Great flower that opens but at night, / Great City of the midnight sun'. Of course, the corruption and sin of the city might form part of its dangerous attraction. Symons explored, without moral censure, the world of London prostitutes and the fleeting pleasures they offered in *London Nights* (1895), and in 'Prologue' from *Days and Nights* (1887) he declares that art is to be found 'where cities pour / Their turbid human stream through street and mart'. These are city poems unmodified by pastoral imagery.

The new urban sensibility was not always tinged with decadence, however. Even Symons can write with simple enthusiasm about the pleasures of wandering through the crowded streets of London, and in *London Voluntaries* (1893), W. H. Henley celebrates the many moods of the city, from 'The crush, the heat, the many-spotted glare, / The odour and sense of life and lust aflare' (II, 2–3) to the splendour conferred by an autumnal sun:

> How goodly this . . . London Town can be!
>
> For earth and sky and air
> Are golden everywhere,
> And golden with a gold so suave and fine
> The looking on it lifts the heart like wine.
> (III, 42–66)

This description of the city and the natural world in harmony surely looks back to Wordsworth's 'Lines Composed Upon Westminster Bridge' (1803), although phrases like 'suave and fine' and 'lifts the heart like wine' suggest a more urban sensibility than

Wordsworth possessed. Henley is aware of the sordid aspects of London life, but the city's immense vitality fills him with excitement: 'Incomparably nerved and cheered, / The enormous heart of London joys to beat / To the measures of his rough, majestic song' (V, 70–2).

John Davidson can also write positively about London, that 'Subtle city of a thousand moods!' ('London, W.', 1905), but his own moods passed from optimism, to a brand of social protest touched by meliorism, to suicidal despair. His *Fleet Street Eclogues* (1893 and 1895) embody many of these moods in poems spoken by various characters, some of whom express longings for a pastoral retreat while others comment on the city's social problems. Davidson is perhaps best known for his dramatic monologue 'Thirty Bob a Week' (1894), which captures something of the flavour of city speech: 'Of all the rummy starts you ever sprung, / Thirty bob a week's the rummiest start!' (ll. 33–4). The speaker preserves a jaunty tone in spite of his hardships, but in later poems Davidson's pessimism becomes apparent. Ugly suburban developments devour 'The busy farm, the quiet grange', and in the city dwell workers 'in uncongenial spheres, / Who toil through dread of coming ill' ('A Northern Suburb', 1896, ll. 22–3).

All these urban poets paved the way for Eliot's powerful evocations of the city in such poems as 'Preludes' (1917), 'Rhapsody on a Windy Night' (1917) and *The Waste Land* (1922). Indeed, Eliot, with his impressionistic techniques and his use of musical motifs and structures, may be the true heir of the nineties Decadents. As for the Decadents themselves, the movement collapsed after the trials of Wilde in 1895, and most English poets fled the city, metaphorically speaking. Even during the nineties, there were many poets who did not succumb to the lure of the urban landscape. The early W. B. Yeats, for example, in spite of his connection with the Rhymers' Club, found his subject matter in Irish myth and legend rather than in contemporary London. Moreover, during this period he produced 'The Lake Isle of Innisfree' (1890), surely one of the most romantic poems of rural retreat ever written in English. The return to the country had begun and was to be continued in the work of such 'Georgian' poets as Edward Thomas. In truth, the deep English love of rural landscapes had never disappeared, but Victorian poetry was certainly enriched by the discovery of the urban landscape as a fit subject for poetry.

See also: THE POETRY OF THE 1890s; VISION AND VISUALITY.

REFERENCES AND FURTHER READING

Calhoun, Blue (1975) *The Pastoral Vision of William Morris*. Athens: University of Georgia Press.

Chadwick, G. F. (1966) *The Park and the Town: Public Landscape in the Nineteenth and Twentieth Centuries*. New York: Praeger.

Clifford, Derek (1962) *A History of Garden Design*. London: Faber and Faber.

Creese, Walter L. (1977) 'Imagination in the Suburb.' In U. C. Knoepflmacher and G. B. Tennyson (eds). *Nature and the Victorian Imagination* (pp. 49–67). Berkeley: University of California Press.

Culler, A. Dwight (1966) *Imaginative Reason: The Poetry of Matthew Arnold*. New Haven, Conn.: Yale University Press.

Fletcher, Pauline (1983) *Gardens and Grim Ravines: The Language of Landscape in Victorian Poetry.* Princeton, N. J.: Princeton University Press.

Harrison, Antony H. (1990) *Victorian Poets and Romantic Poems: Intertextuality and Ideology.* Charlottesville: University Press of Virginia.

Helsinger, Elizabeth K. (1997) *Rural Scenes and National Representation: Britain, 1815–1850.* Princeton, N. J.: Princeton University Press.

Johnston, John H. (1984) *The Poet and the City: A Study in Urban Perspectives.* Athens: University of Georgia Press.

Landow, George P. (1980) *Victorian Types, Victorian Shadows: Biblical Typology in Victorian Literature, Art and Thought.* Boston, London: Routledge and Kegan Paul.

Lorsch, Susan E. (1983) *Where Nature Ends: Literary Responses to the Designification of Landscape.* London, Toronto: Associated University Presses.

Miller, J. Hillis (1963) *The Disappearance of God: Five Nineteenth-Century Writers.* Cambridge, Mass.: Harvard University Press.

Riede, David G. (1978) *Swinburne: A Study of Romantic Mythmaking.* Charlottesville: University Press of Virginia.

Roper, Alan (1969) *Arnold's Poetic Landscapes.* Baltimore, Md.: Johns Hopkins University Press.

Schur, Owen (1989) *Victorian Pastoral: Tennyson, Hardy and the Subversion of Forms.* Columbus: Ohio State University Press.

Taine, Hippolyte (1872) *Notes on England.* London: Strahan.

Thesing, William B. (1982) *The London Muse: Victorian Poetic Responses to the City.* Athens: University of Georgia Press.

Waters, Michael (1988) *The Garden in Victorian Literature.* Aldershot: Scolar Press.

Williams, Raymond (1973) *The Country and the City.* Oxford: Oxford University Press.

Woodring, Carl (1989) *Nature into Art: Cultural Transformations in Nineteenth-Century Britain.* Cambridge, Mass.: Harvard University Press.

28

Vision and Visuality

Catherine Maxwell

The last thirty-five years of the twentieth century saw a variety of critics tackling the subject of visual representation in literature; significantly one of the founding studies, Carol T. Christ's *The Finer Optic* (1975), focused on Victorian poetry and its 'aesthetic of particularity'. Following Jerome McGann's essay 'Rossetti's Significant Details' (1969), Christ's study noted a Victorian preoccupation with small, often naturalistic, visual details, and saw a general Victorian lack of confidence in absolutes as responsible for movement away from a Romantic interest in a universal transcendental state towards the 'faithful recording of individual experience' (Christ 1975: 150). Her work inaugurated an interest in the 'naked particulars' of Victorian poetry, visual objects that unambiguously present themselves to the view of the reader.

This stress on the optical visible has remained influential. Later critics have drawn on cultural and historical factors to speculate that material practices and, specifically, the developing optical technologies of the nineteenth century have had a determinable effect in shaping the visual and perceptual worlds of Victorian literature. While Jonathan Crary's *Techniques of the Observer* (1990) rather carefully attributed the formation of a new kind of observer in the early nineteenth century less to new optical technologies than to a reshaping of subjectivity brought about by processes of modernization and rationalization, other accounts have hypothesized that innovations in optical instruments such as stereoscopes, telescopes, microscopes and the photographic camera altered the nineteenth-century viewer's visual field and consequently the visual field of various writers. Lindsay Smith's *Victorian Photography, Painting and Poetry* (1995) explicitly considers how such technologies may have shaped the kind of visual perceptions relayed by Victorian poetry. During the Victorian era, cultural spectacles in the form of theatre, music hall, public art galleries and exhibitions, promoted and propagated by new mass media, achieved a greater prominence and, along with the greater availability of illustrations and descriptive text in cheaper books, periodicals, newspapers and posters, can be thought of as helping form the visual imagination. The collection *Victorian Literature and the Victorian Visual Imagination* (1995), edited by Christ and John O. Jordan, and Kate Flint's more recent *The Victorians and the Visual Imagination* (2000) examine a variety of relationships between literary texts and different kinds of spectacle, illustration or visual technology. While Flint proposes that the invisible or the unseen might also be a key Victorian concern, she makes it clear that for her non-visibility is a more a matter of sub-visibility, infinitesimal matter or hidden ideological assumptions, which can always be rendered visible by emergent technologies or by theoretical speculation.

A more specialized version of the cultural approach to Victorian visuality can be found in studies which explore the interrelation between literature and the visual arts. Martin Meisel's study, which examines the links between narrative, pictorial and theatrical arts in nineteenth-century England, declares 'the shared structures in the representational arts helped constitute, not just a common but a popular style' (Meisel 1983: 4). The work in this field varies considerably. While some studies examine movements relevant to art and literature such as Pre-Raphaelitism, others explore the way in which writers are affected by and respond to specific art works. For example, J. B. Bullen's *The Expressive Eye* (1986), a study of visual imagery in Hardy's novels, includes discussion of how the writer's responsiveness to certain paintings influenced verbal description in his fiction. More recently critics have tended to explore the shared cultural legacy of Victorian literature and art, emphasizing the way in which both expressive forms reflect and construct certain pervasive images of gender and sexuality. This category includes Bram Dijkstra's *Idols of Perversity* (1986), Lynda Nead's *Myths of Sexuality* (1988), Lynne Pearce's *Woman/Image/Text* (1991), Elisabeth Bronfen's *Over Her Dead Body* (1992), J. B. Bullen's *The Pre-Raphaelite Body* (1997) and Kathy Alexis Psomiades's *Beauty's Body* (1997). The focus of this work falls on the depicted female body, and, to a lesser degree, the androgynous or feminized male body. Dijkstra offers an invaluable compendium of art images of women, but his interpretation is reductive. Both he and Pearce see art and literature as complicit in relaying ideas and images of women which are inherently misogynist. However, the other works offer more complex accounts of the different kinds of ideological, psychological and imaginative meanings which these representations of feminine and feminized bodies bear. That modern criticism is so preoccupied with Victorian bodily representation is hardly surprising, when a Victorian critic such as F. W. H. Myers acknowledged that 'The most direct appeals, the most penetrating reminiscences, come to the worshipper of beauty from a woman's eye', and declared 'All the arts, in fact, are returning now to the spirit of Leonardo, to the sense that of all visible objects known to us the human face and form are the most complex and mysterious' (1908: 320).

Modern work on vision, gender and sexuality intersects with an older tradition of literary analysis which focuses on images of women. In this, Mario Praz's *The Romantic Agony* (1970, first published 1933) is the key text and still a valuable resource in its wide-ranging inventory of the dominant themes and motifs of European Decadent literature. It was followed by Frank Kermode's *Romantic Image* (1986, first published 1957), a work evidently influenced by Praz, in which the girl dancer, epitome of the Modernist 'Romantic image', is seen to be the descendant of the Decadent Medusan *femme fatale*. While these older texts do not evince the kinds of political, sociological or ideological awareness associated with a modern self-conscious gender criticism, they remain vitally important in establishing the centrality of images of the female body and sexuality to any kind of analysis of vision and visuality in Victorian literature. They are important precursors to Bronfen's *Over Her*

Dead Body, in which the image of the woman's corpse is shown to carry a complex set of cultural significations, or to Psomiades's *Beauty's Body*, in which the image of the beautiful woman encodes Aestheticism's philosophy of distance and self-sufficiency. Both these authors are alert to cultural spectacle, to works of art and to material processes of reproduction, but they are also attentive to the specifically literary qualities of representation – the highly individual ways in which different writers organize and set up their visual fields and their practices of seeing. This critical ability to 'see' how a particular writer sees is also vibrantly present in Camille Paglia's survey of Western literature, *Sexual Personae* (1990), which, exploring the Victorian period through Aesthetic and Decadent painting, poetry and prose, continues the tradition of Praz and Kermode, though with conspicuous if controversial reference to gender.

Both Psomiades and Paglia provide thoughtful appreciations of the visual in Algernon Swinburne's poetry, which shows no sustained interest in visible particularity. Indeed, critics previous to Christ such as John D. Rosenberg and Robert Peters had described the Victorian love of ornate detail whilst noting that Swinburne tended to eschew such effects. Although a concentration on detail constitutes an important trend in Victorian poetry, other kinds of significant visual practice diverge substantially from a focus on 'naked particulars'. Some poetry is clearly more interested in the visionary than the ordinarily visible. Even poetry which shows an apparent interest in faithful verisimilitude may suddenly throw that reality into crisis, defamiliarize it by juxtaposing it with ideas, images and impressions that threaten its apparent matter-of-fact integrity. An interest in mythic images and motifs passed down the poetic tradition dislodges a single-minded emphasis on the concrete world, which can be replaced by a repertoire of symbolic images and figures. Moreover the reader as viewer may find himself or herself just as much absorbed by the evanescence, blurring, dissolving, fracturing, instability, indeterminacy, or double- or multi-layeredness of vision.

Many critical moments in Victorian poetry take place at the borders of vision, where optical sight becomes strained and difficult as the pressure of the imagination moves the mind from the optical visible towards the visionary, from a concentration on external reality and lived experience to internal fantasy, projection or supernatural experience, or the place where visionary experience, all too transient, fades away into the common light of day. James Richardson's *Vanishing Lives* (1988) sensitively charts the subtly nuanced fadings and dying falls of Victorian verse, although its primary concern is the sound qualities and rhythmic flow of poems rather than their visual qualities. Gerhard Joseph's *Tennyson and the Text* (1992) follows on from Richardson to show how Tennyson's aesthetic of particularity is balanced by an aesthetic of vagueness. My own study *The Female Sublime from Milton to Swinburne: Bearing Blindness* (2001) revives interest in the sublime as a means for disrupting the optical visible and reinstating the visionary, and examines the different kinds of vision experienced by male Victorian poets. My argument that this sublime is characterized as female rather than male, and that it has a feminizing effect on the male subject, rearticulates in a different way the crucial links between vision and gender in the Victorian period.

Much contemporary work on vision and visuality in Victorian poetry is still dominated by a preoccupation with particulars, with the material and phenomenal world and with material practices. This chapter tries to redress the balance by re-examining the work of the poet Thomas Hardy (1840–1928). Although Hardy only began to publish his poetry in the second half of his career when he had finished with novel-writing, he regarded poetry as his most important work and had been practising as a poet since the late 1850s. A large number of the poems which he started to publish in the early twentieth century had been written or drafted in the preceding century or took their subjects from incidents which had happened many years previously. A whole range of nineteenth-century poets from William Wordsworth and Percy Bysshe Shelley to Robert Browning, Swinburne and the Dorset poet William Barnes had a determinable impact on Hardy's poetry and on his idea of the poet. In style and form Hardy looks more in keeping with his Victorian predecessors, although his experiments in metre, tone and diction would influence later twentieth-century writers such as Philip Larkin and the Movement poets.

Periodization in literature is always an artificial affair especially when poets, as Hardy does, span two literary periods, and a recent collection contains essays on him as both a Victorian and a Modernist poet (Kramer 1999). There are good reasons for acknowledging Hardy's Modernism, not least because it disrupts the canonical version of Modernism, derived from T. S. Eliot and Ezra Pound, which until recently has shaped many critical value judgements. In defining themselves as innovative, Eliot and Pound rejected much Victorian literature for its 'out-moded' Romanticism, and Pound, who declared that the nineteenth century would be remembered as a 'rather blurry, messy sort of period' (1954: 11) and inveighed 'Against the Crepuscular Spirit' (1977: 96) he detected lingering in some of his contemporaries, would have been amazed to find Victorian poetry characterized as meticulously sharp-sighted – a quality he and his peers claimed for their own verse. Victorian particularity almost certainly influenced Eliot, Pound and various of the Imagist poets, even if they were unable to acknowledge it, while the despised crepuscular spirit was to remain a pervasive presence in the writings of those more sympathetic to Victorianism. Recent explorations of Modernism resist the conventional stand-off with Victorianism as they reveal that other early twentieth-century writers, especially women like H. D. and Charlotte Mew, far from repudiating Victorian models showed open and unembarrassed allegiance to literary Aestheticism and Decadence. Mew, a contemporary of Hardy's and a poet much admired by him, did not publish her first collection till 1916, yet is, justifiably, the subject of the last chapter of Angela Leighton's *Victorian Women Poets* (1992).

Hardy may at first sight seem to be a strange choice for such a project, for he is popularly understood as a chronicler or recorder of finely observed naturalistic detail. To read the list of titles in the contents of *The Complete Poems* is apparently to be faced by a world of material objects, concrete in its insistence even to the point of banality: 'The Levelled Churchyard', 'The Torn Letter', 'Logs on the Hearth', 'The Whitewashed Wall', 'The Pat of Butter'. This is the view of Samuel Hynes, who opines that Hardy 'is neither a symbolic nor a metaphorical writer; in his poems things remain intransigently things' (1961: 66). Yet a close look at the poems and Hardy's own thoughts on the writing of poetry gives a different picture. Hardy declared his dissatisfaction with photographic representation as a model for literary representation (Hardy 1962: 153, 351), and the form of realistic reproduction he favoured was not a concentration on externals but seeing into 'the *heart of a thing*', a technique he described as 'realism, . . . though through being pursued by means of the imagination . . . confounded with invention' (1962: 147). A substantial number of his poems work by a process of defamiliarization, in which the prosaic object presented to view is suddenly resituated or reviewed by the speaker in such a way that it ceases to be its banal everyday self and is permeated, or even subsumed and displaced, by the history, memories, impressions or associations it evokes. Such objects lose their matter-of-fact solidity and identity as they become uncanny; estranged from their everyday reality, they function as potent relics or catalysts which activate 'the intenser / Stare of the mind' ('In Front of the Landscape'; Hardy 1976: 304).

In *The Life of Thomas Hardy*, which he ghosted in the name of his second wife, Hardy recorded journal entries which show how naturalistic verisimilitude practised for its own sake left him cold. He made it clear that for him the interest of a scene depends on its human associations: 'An object or mark raised or made by man on a scene is worth ten times any such formed by Unconscious Nature. Hence clouds, mists, and mountains are unimportant besides the wear on a threshold, or the print of a hand' (Hardy 1962: 116). The marks people impose on nature when they make an artistic representation are also important. Commenting on contemporary painting and his growing interest in Turner's late style, Hardy declares that 'the "simply natural" is interesting no longer', and continues:

> The exact truth as to material fact ceases to be of importance in art – it is a student's style – the style of a period when the mind is serene and unawakened to the tragical mysteries of life; when it does not bring anything to the object that coalesces and translates the qualities that are already there, – half hidden, it may be – and the two united are depicted as the All. (Hardy 1962: 185)

This entry is prefaced by the remark:

> I don't want to see landscapes, *i.e.*, scenic paintings of them, because I don't want to see the original realities – as optical effects, that is. I want to see the deeper reality underlying the scenic, the expression of what are sometimes called abstract imaginings. (1962: 185)

Written in response to the modernity of Turner, this comment is informed by a latent Romanticism: Wordsworth's 'eye and ear' which 'half-create' and 'perceive' ('Tintern Abbey', ll. 107–8), Samuel Taylor Coleridge's cry that 'in our life alone does nature live' ('Dejection Ode', l. 48), and Shelley's declaration in the *Defence* that 'All things exist as they are perceived: at least in relation to the percipient.' It is apparent from early comments of Hardy's, such as 'the poetry of a scene varies with the minds of the perceivers. Indeed, it does not lie in the scene at all' (23 August 1865; Hardy 1962: 50), that Hardy was in line with the Romantic belief which still underpins much poetic writing in the period. In trying to distinguish with unnecessary rigour between Romantic and Victorian literatures, we have down-played similarities. The Romantic belief in the viewer's subjective power to colour and charge what is viewed remains constant throughout the period, and culminates with the late Decadent assertion of the priority of the imagination over nature. While certain Victorian commentators, alarmed by their ever-more complex sense of 'the world's multitudinousness', may have sought objective standards of truth, as in Matthew Arnold's behest 'to see the object as in itself it really is' and John Ruskin's unease with the pathetic fallacy, they were countered by those like Hardy who believed poetry's mission was 'to record impressions, not convictions' (Hardy 1962: 377).

Hardy was to call one of his most celebrated verse collections *Moments of Vision* (1917). Evoking the Wordsworthian entranced subject 'who had passed alone / Beyond the visible barriers of the world / And travelled into things to come' (Wordsworth, 'The Borderers', 4. 2. 143–5; 1797–9 version), much of Hardy's poetry celebrates 'The visioning power of souls who dare / To pierce the material screen' ('The House of Silence'; Hardy 1976: 474). For Hardy, who 'cheerfully would have given ten years of my life to see a ghost . . . I should think I am cut out by nature for a ghost-seer' (Archer 1904: 37), poetry is a domain especially sympathetic to phantoms. 'Half my time – particularly when writing verse – I believe (in the modern sense of the word) . . . in spectres, mysterious voices, omens, dreams, haunted places, etc. etc.' (Hardy 1962: 370).

It is this imaginative (if not literal) belief in the visionary and the supernatural, a world that lies beyond optical verisimilitude, which occupies me in this chapter, where the poems I wish to explore are forms of cryptic portraiture that chart relations between the phenomenal and the visionary. Noticeable in most of these poems is Hardy's use of the silhouette, which Tom Paulin has referred to as a mnemonic device (1986: 107–20); an outline that calls to mind the familiar features of a well-known personage. Silhouettes occur naturally when individuals are seen, often from a distance, outlined against the sky or a lighter background, but they also constitute an important form of eighteenth- and nineteenth-century portraiture, in which a profile view of the subject's head and shoulders is depicted either by a black paper cut-out or in black ink. Most fashionable in the period 1750–1850, these silhouette portraits were also, according to the *OED*, known as 'shades'; a word that is a particular favourite of Hardy's and that, like its Latin equivalent *umbra*, has the advantage of meaning both 'shadow' and 'ghost'. While the shade or silhouette recalls to memory the personage it represents, it is interesting for what it leaves out as much as what it includes. An evocative outline that excludes the particularity of individual features, the silhouette is like a draft or sketch, a ghost of a drawing. Its partial portraiture brings the subject to mind but, repressing the fullness of the person's presence, reminds us that she or he is not there. Thus, although as I have argued elsewhere (Maxwell 1997) all portraiture has a link with death, the silhouette has an even stronger relation in that it figures absence more graphically, so that, where the subject of the representation is in fact dead, the silhouette becomes the shade of a shade. Alternatively the empty outline of the shade can be thought to offer a greater degree of visionary or imaginative potential, in that it offers the sensitive observer the opportunity of projecting more freely his or her own memories, impressions, fantasies and associations into the charged blank space of the silhouette; that is, it sums up what is important to the observer, or, as Hardy puts it elsewhere in a discussion of impressionism, '*what appeals to your own individual eye and heart in particular*' (Hardy 1962: 184). According to this view, the shade has the potential for a plenitude lacked by a more visually exacting resemblance, as it functions as, to use Hardy's phrases, a 'visible essence' and not 'a photograph in words, that inartistic species of literary produce' (Hardy 1962: 177, 351).

The suggestive fragment or part-for-whole which prompts a fuller because *imaginative* vision is a staple of a visionary trend in nineteenth-century literature. Hardy habitually practised a synecdochic vision, declaring that 'The art of observation' lay in 'the seeing of great things in little things, the whole in the part – even the infinitesimal part' (1962: 248), and that 'the would-be storyteller' required an 'intuitive power' that allowed him 'To see in half and quarter views the whole picture, to catch from a few bars the whole tune' (1966: 137). In Hardy, as in other nineteenth-century poets, synecdoche is the figure that leads sight to vision, that tutors perception not just to register or document, but to make visible that which is normally unseen. It is well illustrated even by such as Ruskin, commonly associated with more precisionist modes of representation, in the following moving passage from *Modern Painters* 3:

> It follows evidently from the first of these characters of the imagination, its dislike of substance and presence, that a picture has in some measure even an advantage with us in not being real. The imagination rejoices in having something to do, springs up with all its willing power, flattered and happy; and ready with its fairest colours and most tender pencilling, to prove itself worthy of the trust, and exalt into sweet supremacy *the shadow that has been confided to its fondness*. And thus, so far from its being at all an object to the painter to make his work look real, he ought to dread such a consummation as the loss of one of its precious claims upon the heart. So far from striving to convince the beholder that what he sees is substance, his mind should be to what he paints as the fire to the body on the pile, burning away the ashes, leaving *the unconquerable shade* – an immortal dream. (1904: 184–5; my italics)

Ruskin describes the valuable nature of the sketch, which, in complicity with the imagination, best preserves a cherished subject matter, but the deeply charged nature of his words and figures implies that the most desirable subject matter is a memorial likeness of a dead or absent beloved. If Ruskin unconsciously links the sketch or shade-drawing with a poignant play of absence and presence, then this too is present in an apocryphal history of representation where the drawn silhouette importantly foreshadows the evolution of painting. Pliny's *Natural History* (book 35) provides two accounts, the first being of a more general nature:

> The question as to the origin of the art of painting is uncertain . . . some of [the Greeks] say that it was discovered at Sicyon, others in Corinth, but all agree that it began with tracing an outline round a man's shadow and consequently that pictures were originally done in this way. (10. 271)

In a second account, the first artist appears to be a woman, but her achievement is overshadowed by that of her father, who subsumes her work into his claim to be the first sculptor:

modelling portraits from clay was first invented by Butades, a potter of Sicyon, at Corinth. He did this owing to his daughter, who was in love with a young man; and she, when he was going abroad, drew in outline on the wall the shadow of his face thrown by a lamp. Her father pressed clay on this and made a relief, which he hardened by exposure to fire with the rest of his pottery; and it is said that this likeness was preserved in the shrine of the Nymphs until the destruction of Corinth by Mummius. (10. 371–3)

David Allen's painting *The Origin of Drawing* (1775), in the National Gallery of Scotland, chooses to regard the woman as originary artist and shows her seated on her lover's knee while tracing his profile as it is shadowed on the wall. What is particularly interesting about this story is that the young woman captures her lover's likeness as a memorial that will compensate her for his absence while he is abroad.

Shades and silhouettes evoke the forms of lost loved ones or absent individuals in a number of poems by Hardy. All the poems I shall discuss were written after the death of Hardy's first wife Emma in 1912, and the first two, 'The Figure in the Scene' and 'Why Did I Sketch' (Hardy 1976: 476, 477), have a special connection with drawing, as the speaker describes sketches he has made of a woman who has since been 'called hence'. Hardy drew a sketch (Pinion 1968: plate facing 339) of Emma at Beeny Cliffs on a rainy August day in 1870, but it would be wrong to see the poem as a transcript of the sketch, for 'The Figure in the Scene' gives the woman a prominence which the sketch does not. She is clearly centre-stage in this drama as she seems confidently to organize the scene, electing to take a role whose importance her partner does not recognize at the time:

> It pleased her to step in front and sit
>   Where the cragged slope was green,
> While I stood back that I might pencil it
>   With her amid the scene.

Yet the sketched woman, though immediately and painfully recognizable, is screened at three removes – by the cloak which protects her from the elements, by the curtaining drizzle of the rain, and by the stains raindrops have imposed on the drawing:

> And thus I drew her there alone,
>   Seated amid the gauze
> Of moisture, hooded, only her outline shown,
>   With rainfall marked across.

Joan Grundy notes Hardy's fascination with the Victorian use of theatrical gauzes to obscure outline on stage, recording how he 'recommends them at the end of his Preface to *The Dynasts* as suitable to be used to "blur outlines" and thus to "shut off the actual" in the "plays of poetry and dream" he surmises may be produced in the future', and she comments: 'Gauzes are for Hardy an intrinsic part of the human stage. Physically, in the form of mist or rain, they obscure or diminish vision' (1979: 103, 105). Yet I would suggest that the gauze – in this poem 'the gauze of moisture' – while it obscures physical sight, intensifies vision. Together with the cloak and the blots on the paper, the gauze heightens the effect and impact of the woman's 'outline'. The gauze and other screening devices, when viewed and read by the speaker, stand in for what intervenes between him and the woman: the passage of time and death. Yet these things – time and death – do not detract from or diminish the figure, but give it added emphasis. Death doubles the impact of the evocative outline, giving it a power it did not possess when the speaker limned the woman's figure. Now a 'visible essence', the silhouette sums up and summons up the woman in all her ineffable power for the speaker.

The companion poem 'Why Did I Sketch' returns compulsively to the sketch and 'a woman's silhouette'. This wryly ironic afterword is a half-hearted attempt at erasure, as the speaker urges the reader not to repeat his mistake in thoughtlessly adding into his sketch a figure which will trouble him in the years thereafter:

> If you go drawing on down or cliff
>   Let no soft curve intrude
>   Of a woman's silhouette,
> But show the escarpments stark and stiff
>   As in utter solitude
>   So shall you half forget.

But of course the speaker only adds to the power of the previous poem and the sketch it describes by retracing what he would erase or disfigure, thereby stressing its indelible impression; while the woman 'has ceased to be seen' in the phenomenal world, we know she dominates his imagination. His adjuration to the reader, evidently an adjuration to himself, shows that he can only 'half-forget'; that is, he is doomed to remember. The defences he puts in place against the past, as suggested by the 'escarpments' of the projected sketch he recommends, serve merely to reinforce the sense of his vulnerability and bereavement, his 'utter solitude'. The poem becomes, in spite of itself, another testimony to Hardy's words about the mark of humanity on a landscape, its title ghosted by the realization 'How could I not sketch?'

Hardy draws a different kind of sketch, that of a woman he has never seen, in his poem 'The Sunshade' (1976: 490). The rusty skeleton-form of an old parasol discovered in a cleft in the rocks at the seaside acts as a trigger to the speaker's imagination, and is reclothed and resurrected in his fantasy in a way that tacitly parallels Biblical narratives of divine creating power, such as Ezekiel's vision of the reunited and refleshed bones (Ezekiel 37). The deftly handled analogy of the parasol as 'skeleton' – the speaker refers to its 'ribs', its 'bones' and its 'coffin' – prepares the way for a process of embodiment as the speaker conjures up a version of the past. Such is the persuasive force of the speaker, it is hard not to see this as a genuine act of recovery rather than a flight of fancy. The recovered sunshade leads to speculations about its owner – we are asked to picture a pretty young woman with coquettish tendencies plotting her conquests at this fashionable seaside town:

> Where is the woman who carried that sunshade
> Up and down in this seaside place? –
> Little thumb bent against its stem,
> Thoughts perhaps bent on a love-stratagem,
> Softening yet more the already soft face!

Then, as a *coup de grâce*, we are asked to speculate on the woman's possible death, on her once-attractive body, now too a skeleton. The process of embodiment is inverted as the sunshade becomes abruptly a *memento mori* and the woman vividly evoked is now consigned to the grave. A touch of the morality play enters as the innocent scene of the woman's flirtation is melodramatically reviewed as Vanity Fair and matter for her regret – 'if regret dust can'. The poem moves between light and dark as Hardy forces our attention upon the separate but juxtaposed 'sun' and 'shade' constituents of his title. From the gloom of the 'coffin of stone' that hides the parasol, we move to the sunlit idyll of the woman's careless youth and then back again to the darkness of the grave. But, if we pause for reflection, we become aware that the woman herself is a 'sun-shade', a phantom and a sketch drawn by the speaker's day-dreaming fantasy. Indeed we are reminded of the creative writer's ability to manipulate his fictions and his audience by the slightly sadistic way in which the speaker animates this girl only to kill her off, and by the calculated way in which he pulls at our heart-strings. No sooner have we been led to take an interest in this attractive figure than we are rudely bereaved of her. Moreover the poem insists we accept its conjectural fantasy as a truth, an historical vignette with a moral; it allows us no space to raise objections: that the owner of the parasol might have been other than the speaker describes her, older, plainer, with no interest in 'love-stratagems', or that, even as he dilates on her possible demise, she might be sitting comfortably at home, fair, fat and forty, with a brood of children about her. Such prosaic alternatives are refused by the poem's masterful and masterly narrative, which presses ineluctably towards its desired conclusion. The poem, which works on the typical Hardy stratagem of a vision produced by a visual cue, testifies to the power of fictions and the way they are able to assume a reality of their own.

The shade as a fiction of another sort occurs in Hardy's 'The Shadow on the Stone' (1976: 530), begun in 1913, finished in 1916, and one of many writings touched by the death of Emma Hardy. The mysterious Druid stone mentioned in the first line had a biographical counterpart, which Hardy found buried in his garden at Max Gate and had raised to ground level. Around the stone the excavators discovered 'a quantity of ashes and half charred bones' (Hardy 1962: 234). Clive Holland, visiting Max Gate in 1898, recorded that Hardy showed him the stone with the remark: 'Do you believe in ghosts? . . . If you do you ought to see such manifestations here, on a moonlight night.' Ghosts and burnt offerings of a more personal nature may also have imprinted the stone on Hardy's memory, for the second Mrs Hardy reported to Irene Cooper Willis that 'Hardy found his wife burning all his love-letters to her behind that stone' (Bailey 1970: 412). However, the poem does not need these intriguing biographical details. The stone, one of the most ancient human marks on a landscape, brings with it a halo of associations concerning burial, sacrifice and regeneration. It evokes the primitive, removing us from the polite middle-class Christianity of Hardy's day to a place where other beliefs are tolerated. The stone, personified as 'brood[ing]:white and lone', gently intimates the speaker's own meditative emotion, yet simultaneously reminds us that the pathetic fallacy, extensively practised by Hardy – 'In spite of myself I cannot help noticing countenances and tempers in objects of scenery, *e.g.* trees, hills, houses' (Hardy 1962: 285) – can itself be thought of as animistic, a 'primitive' form of the imagination which is none the less a vital constituent in poetic perception. As Hardy remarked on some comments made by his friend Edward Clodd, the ' "barbaric idea which confuses persons and things" is, by the way, also common to the highest imaginative genius – that of the poet' (1962: 230). The stone serves as a monument to a certain kind of imaginative vision exercised in the poem.

The poem's preoccupation with shadows also recalls the Druidic use of large standing stones as sundials, shadow-clocks and calendars. This primitive chronology suggests that the speaker experiences the time of the imagination, which is outside of ordinary time and keeps its own calendar. Certainly the shadow that falls on the stone hearkens back to an earlier time, which mysteriously gets printed on the present moment. The poem shows us the imagination in the process of ghost-making, whereby a shadow is made into a shade. The undifferentiated shadows playing on the Druid stone are 'shaped in [the speaker's] imagining' into the shadow the lost woman was wont to cast: 'the shade that a well-known head and shoulders / Threw there when she was gardening'. 'Shade' here, evidently meaning shadow and ghost, also evokes silhouette drawing, typically of a head-and-shoulders view.

If the power of the speaker's imagination makes him see the shadow as a resemblance, the resemblance – the shade of a shade – makes him imagine that the woman he has loved and lost stands behind him. The speaker, determined to prolong this belief, protects this visionary image by refusing to look at it directly. This encounter evokes the myth of Orpheus and Eurydice; Tom Paulin remarks of the speaker, 'Like Orpheus he wants to look back' (1986: 59). But Paulin does not note how the speaker corrects Orpheus' mis-adventure. Orpheus, having charmed his way through the Underworld in order to retrieve his dead wife, is allowed to reclaim her on the condition that he does not look back at her until she has followed him back to the earth above. Orpheus should properly believe that his wife follows behind, but, doubting, has to look to make sure, and so loses her; Hardy's speaker should properly know that his lost love is not behind him, but in order to preserve her imagined presence he forgoes the desired backward glance. It is his not looking at her which keeps her 'alive', defended from rational, objectifying scrutiny. The poem testifies to the recreative power of imaginative vision over and against the empirical proofs of optical sight:

> Yet I wanted to look and see
> That nobody stood at the back of me;
> But I thought once more: 'Nay, I'll not unvision
> A shape which somehow there may be.'

> So I went on softly from the glade,
> And left her behind me throwing her shade,
> As she were indeed an apparition –
> My head unturned lest my dream should fade.

The speaker does not see a genuine apparition face to face. Arguably then this poem is not a genuine visionary poem like Milton's Orphic Sonnet 23, in which the speaker beholds the transfigured likeness of his dead wife. Seemingly Hardy's speaker cannot attain to this full vision and can only fabricate it by hints, guesses and make-believe. But Hardy is not so clear cut. The language of the final stanza is equivocal about the woman's presence, suggesting she is both provisional and real. The attribution of agency to her gives her a kind of authenticity even as it suggests that she is not a 'true' spectre: 'So I went on softly from the glade, / And left her behind me throwing her shade, / As she were indeed an apparition'. The poem might equally make us question whether there is a real distinction between imagining and the visionary, or whether they are simply points of degree on the same spectrum. Moreover, it tantalizes the reader with that space at the back of the speaker's head – the space he will not look at with his corporeal eyes – which becomes aligned with the imaginative space in which he can produce images he chooses not to share with the reader. At the heart of the poem is a mysterious and intimate privacy, a withheld vision that the speaker can see and we cannot, which allures us by being ever out of reach.

The private vision which cryptically energizes a poem and arrests the reader with its latent presence is one of Hardy's special devices. Subliminally present in the 'The Figure in the Scene' and 'Why Did I Sketch', where only the speaker can properly recreate from the 'outline' the features of his dead love, it is most powerfully employed in the last poem I shall treat in this series. All the poems I have looked at are exercises in memorial shade or shadow-drawing, but while the earlier poems draw the shades of dead women, this last one features a son mourned by his mother. The dedication of this particular woman's vision suggests that for Hardy the memorializing tendencies of the female gaze are no less potent than those of its male counterpart. Moreover this look of recovery is directed towards a shade that derives from Hardy's most literal and fascinating rendering of the technique described by Pliny.

'The Whitewashed Wall' (Hardy 1976: 685–6) is written in the form of a conversation. Two acquaintances of the woman discuss her behaviour. One wants to know why her attention seems held by the chimney-corner wall, so the other explains that a friend drew her son's shadow-portrait there, which the 'whitener' unthinkingly covered over when he came to whitewash the cottage wall. This second speaker also explains that the woman still intuits the presence of her son's portrait hidden underneath the paint and turns to it for consolation in his absence. That absence is implied to be terminal by the poem, which figures death in the reported apology of the whitener:

> 'Yes,' he said: 'My brush goes on with a rush,
>   And the draught is buried under;
> When you have to whiten old cots and brighten,
>   What else can you do, I wonder?'

The 'draught' is not simply erased but is 'buried under'; it lingers like a cadaver underneath the layering of paint, described by the second speaker as a shroud-like 'sheet of white'.

Hardy originally produced the poem for *Reveille*, the government quarterly 'Devoted to the Disabled Soldier and Sailor', after the editor John Galsworthy wrote on 30 July 1918 requesting a contribution. Hardy sent the poem in a letter dated 15 August 1918 and it was published in the November edition (Hardy 1985: 276). In the first published version, line 9 reads 'Well, her soldier-son cast his shadow there' (Hardy 1979: 686). But when Hardy came to reprint the poem in *Late Lyrics and After* (May 1922), he removed the obvious military reference as well as making some smaller alterations. This emendation significantly alters the way we read the poem, as it becomes impossible to age the son, who is defined solely by his relation to his mother. But for those who know of its existence, the first version of Hardy's poem also lingers on buried under the later one. The word 'draught' is a Hardy variant on 'draft', the usual spelling for the word meaning both a rough sketch and military conscription. The 'draught / draft is buried under' becomes a beautifully subtle way of suggesting the son's demise in battle and also of alluding to the first *Reveille* version, which lies inhearsed in the second, *Late Lyrics* poem.

The draught or shadow-drawing, the relic which conjures up the absentee, has precursors not only in Pliny but in Hardy's tender feeling for 'the mark of man' on a scene. In his commentary on 'The Whitewashed Wall', J. O. Bailey directs us to moments in Hardy's novels *Two on a Tower* (ch. 28) and *The Woodlanders* (ch. 3), where Swithun's grandmother and Grace Melbury's father preserve marks and traces left by their loved ones (Bailey 1970: 494). I find another precursor in *Tess of the d'Urbervilles* (1891), in which Retty teases Izz about Angel Clare – 'I zid you kissing his shade' – and explains to Marian how, when Angel's shadow was cast on the wall close to Izz, she surreptitiously kissed 'the shade of his mouth' (ch. 21). Hardy seems to remember this scene when the woman, like a coy lover, turns in a 'shy soft way' to 'kiss to the chimney-corner wall' on which lies her son's submerged shadow-likeness. This shade-drawing, so cherished by the woman, is more than just a banal tracing; apparently it captures a 'lifelike semblance', a 'familiar look', and, just at the moment it disappears under the whitewash, it becomes, poignantly, 'a face'. The whitening, which becomes synonymous with death, has the strange effect of making the obliterated image more like and more powerful precisely because it cannot be seen. But this is owing to the strength of the woman's determination to keep that face in view even if it is not actually visible. Although she was not the one who made the shadow-drawing – that was the act of 'a friend' whose gender is not specified – it is her devotion which continually re-marks its presence and, refusing to abandon it, makes it a reality even to others. The speaker does not deride her belief as the hysterical fantasy of a bereaved woman but tenderly endorses it in the poem's last lines, when, as in earlier poems, the identity of the shade-portrait and the absent subject are merged – 'she knows he's there' – to suggest that the woman experiences an authentic vision of her son.

That vision, even when glimpsed at a remove, suggests the all-consuming nature of the woman's feeling for her son. As mentioned before, the *Late Lyrics* version does not specify whether the son is child or adult and the poem exploits this uncertainty in its last lines, where Hardy delicately fuses eros, maternity and mourning:

> But she knows he's there. And when she yearns
>   For him, deep in the labouring night,
> She sees him as close at hand, and turns
>   To him under his sheet of white.

Birth is figured in the 'labouring' night and the form beneath the sheet could be an infant's or, even more strangely, the body of a lover or mate. Thus embodied in the mother is the woman who tends to her infant, the woman who turns to her lover in the night, and the woman who lifts the shroud of her son in a perpetual wake that is his and her reawakening.

What is haunting about 'The Whitewashed Wall' is how the power of what is hidden charges the whole poem; a humble and prosaic interior is flooded by the strangest phantasmagoria. The wall, the site of the 'draught', lacks the mystery of Druid stone, but it becomes just as uncanny under the intensity of a woman's visionary gaze. In the *Life*, a notebook entry of 1886 describes a process of revelation under conditions of extremity:

> – *January* 2 . . . Cold weather brings out upon the faces of people the written marks of their habits, vices, passions, and memories, as warmth brings out on paper a writing in sympathetic ink. The drunkard looks still more a drunkard when the splotches have their margins made distinct by frost, the hectic blush becomes a stain now, the cadaverous complexion reveals the bone under, the quality of handsomeness is reduced to its lowest terms. (Hardy 1962: 177)

This revelation of character is produced by a physical circumstance – intense cold – just as 'sympathetic' or invisible ink becomes visible when exposed to heat, but we realize that the kind of legibility Hardy describes can be read only by an observer who has a particularly discriminating and penetrating way of looking. The adjoining entry shows that the aesthetic revelation of the visionary essences of things also occurs as a result of intensity:

> *January* 3. My art is to intensify the expression of things, as is done by Crivelli, Bellini, etc., so that the heart and inner meaning is made vividly visible. (Hardy 1962: 177)

Again, writer and reader, like the woman in the poem, need to exercise 'the intenser / Stare of the mind'. This stare activates the legibility of hidden draughts or 'sympathetic ink', which, in its gradual appearance on the page, looks as though it is emerging out of the paper, coming through from a 'beyond' on the other side. Just so the 'sheet' of paint that shrouds the son is permeated by the power of his image. Because the actual picture remains, like the son's familiar look, a family secret or familial property, we cannot see the form of the dead as the woman can – 'She sees him close at hand' – but we sense the hint of a recovered outline, the image of an image, or shade of a shade, a presence shielded from direct view.

When sending his poem to Galsworthy, Hardy wrote 'The fact is that I cannot do patriotic poems very well – seeing the other side too much' (1985: 275). Evidently 'the other side' means the death and destruction caused by war, but it also carries a ghostly meaning of the visionary world on the 'other side' of the 'material screen', the world which breaks into the phenomenal and alters its appearance, turning an attempt at a patriotic poem into a moment of vision. In such a way does Hardy achieve Shelley's aim of 'always seek[ing] in what I see something beyond the present & tangible object' (Shelley 1964: II, 47), and the words Hardy used to William Archer in an interview of 1901 are fitting ones with which to end this chapter: 'But for my part I say in all sincerity, "better be inconvenienced by visitants from beyond the grave than see none at all." The material world is so uninteresting, human life is so miserably bounded, circumscribed, cabin'd, cribb'd, confined. I want another domain for the imagination to expatiate in' (Archer 1904: 45).

See also: POETRY AND ILLUSTRATION; LANDSCAPE AND CITYSCAPE.

REFERENCES AND FURTHER READING

Archer, William (1904) *Real Conversations*. London: William Heinemann.

Bailey, J. O. (1970) *The Poetry of Thomas Hardy: A Handbook and Commentary*. Chapel Hill: University of North Carolina Press.

Bronfen, Elisabeth (1992) *Over Her Dead Body: Death, Femininity and the Aesthetic*. Manchester: Manchester University Press.

Bullen, J. B. (1986) *The Expressive Eye: Fiction and Perception in the Work of Thomas Hardy*. Oxford: Clarendon Press.

Bullen, J. B. (1997) *The Pre-Raphaelite Body: Fear and Desire in Painting, Poetry and Criticism*. Oxford: Clarendon Press.

Christ, Carol (1975) *The Finer Optic: The Aesthetic of Particularity in Victorian Poetry*. New Haven, London: Yale University Press.

Christ, Carol, and John O. Jordan (eds) (1995) *Victorian Literature and the Victorian Visual Imagination*. Berkeley, Los Angeles, London: University of California Press.

Crary, Jonathan (1990) *Techniques of the Observer: On Vision and Modernity in the Nineteenth Century*. Cambridge, Mass.: MIT Press.

Djikstra, Bram (1986) *Idols of Perversity: Fantasies of Feminine Evil in Fin-de-Siècle Culture*. New York, Oxford: Oxford University Press.

Flint, Kate (2000) *The Victorians and the Visual Imagination*. Cambridge: Cambridge University Press.

Grundy, Joan (1979) *Hardy and the Sister Arts*. London, Basingstoke: Macmillan.

Hardy, Florence (1962) *The Life of Thomas Hardy 1840–1928*. London, Basingstoke: Macmillan.

Hardy, Thomas (1966) 'The Science of Fiction.' In Harold Orel (ed.). *Thomas Hardy's Personal Writings* (pp. 134–8). Lawrence, Kans.: University of Kansas Press.

Hardy, Thomas (1976) *The Complete Poems*. Ed. James Gibson. London, Basingstoke: Macmillan.

Hardy, Thomas (1979) *The Variorum Edition of the Complete Poems*. Ed. James Gibson. London, Basingstoke: Macmillan.

Hardy, Thomas (1985) *The Collected Letters of Thomas Hardy*. 7 vols. Volume V: 1914–1919. Eds Richard Little Purdy and Michael Millgate. Oxford: Clarendon Press.

Hynes, Samuel (1961) *The Pattern of Hardy's Poetry*. Chapel Hill. University of North Carolina University Press.

Joseph, Gerhard (1992) *Tennyson and the Text*. Cambridge: Cambridge University Press.

Kermode, Frank (1986) *Romantic Image*. First published 1957. London: Ark.

Kramer, Dale (1999) *The Cambridge Companion to*

Thomas Hardy. Cambridge: Cambridge University Press.

Laity, Cassandra (1997) *H. D. and the Victorian Fin de Siècle: Gender, Modernism, Decadence*. Cambridge: Cambridge University Press.

Leighton, Angela (1992) *Victorian Women Poets: Writing against the Heart*. Hemel Hempstead: Harvester Wheatsheaf.

Maxwell, Catherine (1997) 'From Dionysus to Dionea: Vernon Lee's Portraits.' *Word & Image*, 13. 3, 253–69.

Maxwell, Catherine (2001) *The Female Sublime from Milton to Swinburne: Bearing Blindness*. Manchester: Manchester University Press.

McGann, Jerome (1969) 'Rossetti's Significant Details.' *Victorian Poetry*, 7, 41–54.

Meisel, Martin (1983) *Realizations: Narrative, Pictorial, and Theatrical Arts in Nineteenth-Century England*. Princeton, N. J.: Princeton University Press.

Myers, F. W. H. (1908) 'Rossetti and the Religion of Beauty.' In *Essays Modern* [1883]. London: Macmillan.

Nead, Lynda (1988) *Myths of Sexuality: Representation of Women in Victorian Britain*. Oxford: Blackwell.

Nead, Lynda (1992) *The Female Nude: Art, Obscenity and Sexuality*. London: Routledge.

Paglia, Camille (1990) *Sexual Personae: Art and Decadence from Nefertiti to Emily Dickinson*. Harmondsworth: Penguin.

Paulin, Tom (1986) *The Poetry of Perception*. Second edition. Basingstoke: Macmillan.

Pearce, Lynne (1991) *Woman/Image/Text: Readings in Pre-Raphaelite Art and Literature*. Hemel Hempstead: Harvester Wheatsheaf.

Peters, Robert L. (1965) *The Crowns of Apollo: Swinburne's Principles of Literature and Art, A Study in Victorian Criticism and Aesthetics*. Detroit: Wayne State University Press.

Peters, Robert L. (1982) 'Swinburne: A Personal Essay and a Polemic.' In Richard A. Levine (ed.).*The Victorian Experience: The Poets* (pp. 138–57). Athens, Ohio: Ohio University Press.

Pinion, F. B. (1968) *A Hardy Companion*. London: Macmillan.

Pliny (1938–62) *Natural History*. Transl. H. Rackham. 10 vols. London: William Heinemann; Cambridge, Mass.: Harvard University Press.

Pound, Ezra (1954) *Literary Essays of Ezra Pound*. Ed. T. S. Eliot. Norfolk, Conn.: New Directions.

Pound, Ezra (1977) *Collected Early Poems of Ezra Pound*. Ed. Michael John King. London: Faber and Faber.

Praz, Mario (1970) *The Romantic Agony*. First published 1933. Trans. Angus Davidson. Second edition with foreword by Frank Kermode. Oxford, New York: Oxford University Press.

Psomiades, Kathy Alexis (1997) *Beauty's Body: Femininity and Representation in British Aestheticism*. Stanford, Calif.: Stanford University Press.

Richardson, James (1988) *Vanishing Lives: Style and Self in Tennyson, D. G. Rossetti, Swinburne and Yeats*. Charlottesville: University Press of Virginia.

Rosenberg, John D. (1967) 'Swinburne.' *Victorian Studies*, 11, 131–52.

Ruskin, John (1904) *The Works of John Ruskin*. Eds Alexander Cook and E. T. Wedderburn. 39 vols. Volume 5. London, New York: George Allen, Longmans, Green.

Shelley, Percy Bysshe (1964) *The Letters of Percy Bysshe Shelley*. Ed. F. L. Jones. 2 vols. Oxford: Clarendon Press.

Smith, Lindsay (1995) *Victorian Photography, Painting and Poetry: The Enigma of Visibility in the Nineteenth Century*. Cambridge: Cambridge University Press.

29

Marriage and Gender

Julia F. Saville

Marriage in Britain in the early decades of the nineteenth century was an institution seriously in need of reform. Still largely shaped by the requirements of a feudal, agricultural society, the legal terms of the marriage contract had yet to be revised to suit a modern, industrial democracy. Through debates in Parliament, the national press and intellectual circles, the term 'marriage' came to mean much more than the socially sanctioned union between a man and woman. It took on the function of a trope of harmony in which the settling of domestic conflicts between the sexes could represent a national capacity for liberal compromise claimed to be a special trait of Englishness. As the century progressed, this figurative function expanded and shifted. While tropes of adultery and failed marriage represented fantasies of national disorder, the harmony and productivity formerly associated with marital union were claimed for an array of heterodox alliances. This chapter aims to plot this shifting trajectory in the field of Victorian poetry, where marriage, as both theme and trope, is peculiarly diverse and prolific.

In post-revolutionary Europe, the rise of socialist and liberal discourses, combined with the rapid socio-economic changes associated with industrial development, increased the power of women to express themselves in public forums. The 'Woman Question' came to national attention in Britain, and this in turn encouraged the efforts of activists like Caroline Norton, granddaughter of playwright Richard Brinsley Sheridan, to articulate the specific legal injustices imposed on women by the marriage contract. For instance, in marrying, Victorian women were required to relinquish their existence as subjects before the law. Correlatively they forfeited their rights to own property and submitted to a sexual double standard that winked at male infidelity while condemning adulterous wives. The extreme disparity between men's and women's access to divorce exacerbated these injustices. Efforts to reform the situation resulted in the Parliamentary debates that took place during the 1850s and 1860s and culminated in the relatively ineffectual Divorce Act of 1857 and the Married Women's Property Law of 1870.

The nationwide interest in these debates, the Woman Question and relations between the sexes in general is reflected in and shaped by the treatment of marriage in poetry, and most especially by the attention given to the terms 'manliness' and 'womanliness'. More than simply synonyms for 'masculinity' and 'femininity', which refer broadly to matters of sexual conduct, 'manliness' and 'womanliness' were ideals governed by a range of attitudes towards moral, political and religious duty. They were terms that convened a cluster of contradictory moral dictates according to which the behaviour of men and women could be judged. For example, the hallmark of ideal Victorian manliness was scrupulous self-management or asceticism. The manly citizen, even as he was required to be forthright and unequivocating, was also expected to be a master of self-restraint. Manly reserve was supposedly an index of the depth of moral character; however, it could also be interpreted as sinister withholding or the cultivation of secrets. Similarly, the moral and physical courage deemed necessary to manly comportment could be perceived as brutish if not offset by a capacity for sympathy or tenderness best exemplified in the figure of the compassionate Christ. Manly conduct required constant vigilance to negotiate the fine lines between these extremes.

As the female counterpart to manliness, womanliness imposed similar imperatives on women, but where manly behaviour was directed towards the public sphere and manifest service to God, queen and country, ideal womanliness was by definition restricted to supporting male authority in the domestic sphere. The womanly woman was expected to be guileless and fully legible to her husband but, in a way that paralleled the requirements of manliness, the mistress of self-restraint and maidenly modesty. While required to be strong in moral convictions, she was not expected to voice these in public, or to indulge in any form of self-promotion, but to efface herself in the service of her husband, her children and the household's welfare.

Within these gender imperatives, the very tension between forthrightness and restraint, transparency and modesty, made 'manliness' and 'womanliness' highly unstable terms, apparently oppositional, but constantly threatening to collapse into each other. This instability is strikingly apparent in the field of poetry. As the realm of language full of feeling, private and figurative, poetry by definition conflicted with the manly imperatives of forthrightness and direct action. Repeatedly, lyric discourse had to be defended against charges of effeminacy and ivory-tower aestheticism. This gender ambivalence coincided with the drafting of resolutions to motivate the reform of marriage laws, so that poetic discourse emerged as a particularly tractable medium for exploring marriage and gender relations and the complex social negotiations they involved. No fewer than four book-length 'companionate marriage' poems were published in the late 1840s into the 1850s: Alfred Tennyson's *The Princess* (1847), Arthur Hugh Clough's *The Bothie of Toper-na-fuosich* (1848), Coventry Patmore's *The Angel in the House* (1854–62) and Elizabeth Barrett Browning's *Aurora Leigh* (1856). All include poets as main protagonists whose gender identities are made questionable by their poetic vocations.

Nation, Education, Class and Gender in the Companionate Marriage

Beside thematizing poetry as a potentially feminized discourse, the companionate marriage poems of Tennyson, Clough and Barrett Browning explore the capacity of shifting gender relations within marriage to mediate redefinitions of national identities, educational opportunities and labour practices. In their treatment of the latter, Clough and Barrett Browning also engage with the problem of class relations. None of these issues seems to concern Coventry Patmore, whose *Angel in the House* is more remarkable for its unusual conservatism – its steadfast promotion of old-world chivalric tropes and mores – than for any inventive approach to gender relations in marriage. In fact, initially, *The Angel* was poorly received and only came into its own when republished in the late 1880s, its chivalry having by then acquired a certain old-world charm (Anstruther 1992: 76–7, 97–8). From the time of the first volume's publication in 1854, the poem's title phrase has stood as a shibboleth for entrenched paternalistic views of the kind held by many Parliamentarians who, during the debates of the 1850s, were reluctant to give up the idea of marriage as a union based on hierarchy and male authority (Shanley 1989: 48).

While for Patmore marriage, with the domestic harmony it supposedly entailed, was the especial cultural accomplishment of Victorian England, for Tennyson, Clough and Barrett Browning the very initial act of betrothal was represented as the source of private anguish often fraught with national implications. For instance, by casting his tale of Princess Ida as a failed betrothal between a northern prince and a southern princess, Tennyson explores the connections between domestic and national stability. However, by focusing on royalty, he evades the specific tensions between the classes that threatened England's national stability in the 1830s and 1840s. Moreover he contains the potentially radical implications of questions raised in the betrothal narrative by means of the framing Prologue and Conclusion and the traditions of patronage and patrilineage they promote.

Clough in *The Bothie* is more radical and sceptical than Tennyson in his consideration of the ways in which marriage is inflected by, and itself contributes to, the idea of English national character. The *bildung* of his protagonist – an Oxford student-poet and self-declared Chartist, Philip Hewson, who spends the summer vacation in Scotland as one of a reading party with his tutor and five other students – is traced as a series of dalliances with Scottish lasses of varying social classes. The gender question as to which manly and womanly attributes constitute a successful marital partnership within a rapidly expanding industrial order is complicated by Scottish and English identities, each of which represents its own constellation of tensions: the pre-modern, agricultural milieu associated with the rural stability of Scotland being set against the modern, urban, professional character of aggressive English progress (see Ulin 1999). The poem's concluding view of marriage suggests more than the subsuming of assertive womanliness under a feminized manly authority (as in Tennyson's lyric invitation to 'fold thyself, my dearest, thou, and slip / Into my bosom and be lost in me'). It is also more than the effortless absorption of the Scottish into the English in a manner that erases previously existing cultural difference. Rather it is presented as a synthesis of both gender and cultural difference that becomes more than the sum of its parts. Exceeding the structures of an English symbolic order, it must be transported to the colonies (New Zealand), where a new English family will establish itself in a Scottish home as part of the growing British empire ('And the Antipodes too have a Bothie of Toper-na-fuosich').

Like Tennyson, Barrett Browning uses a failed betrothal as a narrative motivation in *Aurora Leigh*, but, perhaps as a covert challenge to the laureate's 'fairy tale', sets her poem in a contemporary Victorian setting. The marriage planned between the pragmatic English socialist reformer Romney Leigh, heir to the Leigh estates, and the part-Italian, disinherited, would-be poet Aurora is thwarted by the latter's professional ambitions. In this plot, England and Englishness are gendered male – a utilitarian, prosaic fatherland, 'this cold land of England' with 'frosty cliffs' and 'mean red houses', hostile to poetry, for '[i]n England no one lives by verse that lives'. Italy, on the contrary, is feminized as literally the mother's country and, in the tradition of Germaine de Staël's novel *Corinne* (1807), the home of female poetics. This use of gender politics to link poetics with national character underscores the marginality of poetry as a feminized discourse in Victorian England – a status which gives it contradictory properties of attractive exoticism on one hand, and triviality or inconsequence on the other. In her determination to redeem poetry and, better still, women poets as significant contributors to the discipline, Barrett Browning presents poetry writing as professional work. It requires education, followed by apprenticeship and sustained professional practice. This raises the pressing question of whether women have the intellectual capacities to meet such demands, and, if they do, whether they can fulfil professional requirements without thereby forfeiting, or at least compromising, their traditional vocations as wives and mothers.

For Tennyson in *The Princess*, the response to these questions is negative on all counts. Although the hypothesis of a segregated women's university sponsored and administrated by women is revolutionary, the elaboration of the idea reflects Tennyson's deep scepticism about it. The eventual collapse of the whole educational enterprise through a series of mean-spirited betrayals confirms the commonplace perception of women as irrational and unsuited to public-sphere activities. In the closing dialogue of the last canto, the university project – apparently a misguided, girlish scheme – is displaced by the prince's offer of marriage as genial, heterosexual complementarity. Such moments suggest that Tennyson's capacity to envision progressive, heterosexual partnerships is far less inventive and interesting than his penchant for exploring heterodox erotics between men and women. For it is when characters are under particular pressure to conform to traditional gender expectations that Tennyson envisages the most interesting forms of alternative conduct.

Often such conduct is subtly eroticized, with varying moral effect; for instance, Ida, becoming deeply immersed in the education for which she will break her betrothal and reject the conventional womanly role of self-effacing wife and mother, is simultaneously described as strangely and sensuously close to her friend, Lady Psyche. Melissa, young daughter of Lady Blanche, describes the two women as 'inosculated; / Consonant chords that shiver to one note' (III, 71–5). Here, the very Latinate unfamiliarity of 'inosculated' and its improbability in the mouth of a 16-year-old girl draws attention to the literal as well as figurative freight it carries – a joining of lips in a proto-Irigarayan physical and speculative intercourse. The intense intellectualism deemed unwomanly in Tennyson's final conception of companionate marriage is coupled here with an intimacy between women that has an energy and allure independent of men. Although threatening in terms of the poem's overtly heterosexual framework, this forms a precedent for later nineteenth-century poets, receiving some of its most vital and passionate articulations in the Sapphic poetics of Michael Field.

A different but equally interesting dynamic is apparent in male relations in *The Princess*, where moments of strict conformity rather than resistance to gender conventions are coloured with same-sex eroticism as if to heighten their symbolic weight. For instance, the prince in one of his own more manly moments prior to battle admires the martial vigour of the three southern knights: the Prince Arac (Ida's brother) and his two supporters. Here, as Eve Kosofsky Sedgwick has taught us in *Between Men*, we might notice a male same-sex eroticism legitimized by the allusion to the triangulating image of Ida (V, 244–48). In moments such as these, Tennyson opens imaginative spaces for the figuration of alternative manliness – spaces more fully explored in *In Memoriam, A. H. H.* and in the work of later poets such as Gerard Manley Hopkins.

If Tennyson is most inventive when exploring heterodox eroticism, Clough's radical contribution is his revision of marriage from a sacred union ratified by the church to a secular, materialist partnership based on a Hellenic concept of 'ergon' or social duty (IX, 86). In such a partnership, middle-class women have the opportunity to be well informed rather than intuitive, and usefully contributive rather than passively decorative. Marriage is not arranged by paternal authority or through betrothal; it is a rational choice made by both partners after protracted, independent deliberation. Unlike Tennyson, Clough does not address the issue of formal or professional education for women in *The Bothie*, which is perhaps surprising given the sympathy he showed to his sister Anne's project of improving the education available to school mistresses, and her contribution to the integration of women students at Cambridge. He does, however, address the issue of alternative vocations and professions for women with the frank question: 'Are there then so many trades for a man, for women one only, / First to look out for a husband and then to preside at his table?' (IX, 57). The tutor Adam's response to this question, 'Let us to Providence trust, and abide and work in our stations' (IX, 72), gives Philip the opportunity to question both transcendental authority and the status quo that depends on it: 'Where does Circumstance end, and Providence where begins it?' (IX, 76). Ultimately Philip accepts 'the duty of order' as an ethical imperative with the tacit assumption that the terms of that order are determined not by providence, or by circumstance, but by the individual's commitment to discover and perform her or his 'ergon'. However, by situating the newly wed Elspie and Philip in a pre-modern, pioneering agricultural context, Clough sidesteps the particular pressures that a modern industrial society exerts on traditional gender roles, for in the world of agricultural labour the separation of spheres is not as marked as it is in a bourgeois industrial world, and the distinction between men's and women's work is less clearly drawn.

Barrett Browning's own representation of the domestic negotiations necessary for a woman to function both as a professional poet and as a wife produces a version of companionate marriage that is specifically middle-class, and considerably distanced from the ideal invoked by Patmore in *The Angel*. Romney Leigh's three attempts at marriage cover the spectrum of social class, each time envisaging marital partnership as an opportunity for a woman to participate usefully in social reform. A woman with no vocation of her own might submit gratefully, as Marion Erle does, to being of service; or like Lady Waldemar, she might approach useful work as a novel diversion, visiting 'the famed phalanstery', addressing 'the lowest drab' as a sister, and plunging her 'naked perfect arms . . . elbow-deep in suds' (V, 783, 789–93). However, for a middle-class woman like Aurora, who wishes to pursue her own vocation, Romney's initial conception of marriage is not viable because it endorses the self-erasure required by the legal terms of the marriage contract in the 1850s. What the woman poet needs is a partner with figurative vision, and this Romney supposedly acquires through his literal blinding. In his final exhortation to Aurora, he urges her to 'Shine out for two, Aurora, and fulfil / My falling-short that must be! work for two / As I, though thus restrained, for two, shall love!' (IX, 910–12). There is certainly a boldness in this reversal of gender roles, as Margaret Reynolds points out (Barrett Browning 1996: 311n.2); however, such an inversion is surely only a first step towards dismantling marital hierarchy and has yet to be followed by the negotiation of more flexible power relations between the poet and her spouse.

The suggestion that Romney's blindness is a necessary part of this companionate marriage raises the question of emasculation, which haunts Victorian discourse on heterosexual gender relations within marriage. Do greater freedom and symbolic power for women require the crippling of manliness as their counterpart? This issue emerges in Robert Browning's monologue of the cuckolded 'Andrea del Sarto', believed to have been composed in 1853, when Barrett Browning was in the process of writing *Aurora Leigh*. One of the three painter monologues published in *Men and Women*, 'Andrea del Sarto' is also one of numerous male representations of female adultery that follow the companionate marriage cluster. These poems seem deeply concerned with two issues: first, the possibility that more equitable legal representation for women and the greater freedom it would allow them might compromise marriage as a bond of faith; and second, that betrayals of private marital trust represent in little an unravelling of the broader loyalties on which public order and, by implication, the British Commonwealth depended.

Uxorious Husbands and Adulterous Wives

'Andrea del Sarto' might be read as a study in unmanly and unwomanly conduct. The uxoriousness that Andrea displays constitutes a failure to manage manly energy, as he negotiates the intersection of the domestic sphere of marital relations and the public sphere of artistic production. He barters his inventive power for monetary gain and then squanders that financial power for brief, illusory intervals of domestic harmony. According to his romantic conception of the male artist as creative genius, his wife Lucrezia fails him because her physical beauty, which could be an aesthetic inspiration, is not complemented by a fine intellect. Only with the latter could she appreciate Andrea's aspirations and cooperate with his attempts to produce sublime art ('But had you – oh, with the same perfect brow, / And perfect eyes, and more than perfect mouth, / . . . Had you, with these the same, but brought a mind!' [ll. 122–6]). However, from the ironic distance allowed by the form of the dramatic monologue, the situation might be viewed as indicative of a new, dispassionate modernity. Lucrezia has mastered the entrepreneurial skills that are beyond her husband. As his business partner – his model and the agent of his commissions – she monitors his production and spends his income to procure her own pleasures. This fantasy of a wife who actively orchestrates her own dalliances, rather than passively embodying the moral ideals compatible with her husband's art, reflects the advent of a modernity in which the aura of the art work, the mystification of artistic genius, social reverence towards male authority, and the sanctity of marriage – all remnants of a Christian medievalism – give way to the art work as commodity, the artist as craftsman whose labour is marketable, and marriage not as a sacred union but as a practical contract entered into on equal terms by two consenting adults.

Considered in the light of inequities in Victorian law – both the denial of a married woman's right to own private property and the double standard that made divorce accessible to upper-class men but not to women – we might be tempted to admire Lucrezia's efficiency at arranging her own financial independence and sexual freedom. After all, Andrea's impotence and enslavement are largely the effects of his blind uxoriousness. Yet Lucrezia's silence makes it difficult to feel any strong sympathy for her. A much more sympathetic representation of female adultery as an escape from unjust legal constraints is given in William Morris's title poem in *The Defence of Guenevere, and Other Poems* (1858). Here, the adulterous woman is permitted not only to speak on her own behalf, but also to appear as a spectacle of vitality and ethical astuteness; for she is deeply aware of the moral implications of her actions.

Following the cue of the third-person framing voice, Morris's Guenevere stages herself as a vivid physical presence, a beautiful body itself profoundly responsive to beauty. Starting with the allegorical test of the two cloths – one long and blue, the other short and red – she demonstrates the injustice of a moral system in which an individual is required to make a momentous choice not on the basis of carefully accumulated information, but by trusting the arbitrary interpretative terms of symbolic convention. Without any ante-nuptial preparation – of the kind Clough envisages for Elspie Mackaye, or Barrett Browning conceives in the lengthy *bildung* preceding Aurora and Romney Leigh's final betrothal – Guenevere's acceptance of King Arthur is not an informed choice. In marrying the king, to all appearances an unimpeachable marriage partner, she in fact consigns herself to hell. Quite arbitrarily, her responses to the conventional signals of grace, moral superiority and joy that seem to inhere in the blue cloth ('[w]avy and long' and 'heaven's colour') prove mistaken. Against this allegory of failed interpretation, she poses the crucial question: is marriage no more than an irrevocable gamble requiring a woman to stake all her sexual vitality on a single, unanticipated and ill-informed choice orchestrated by male powers beyond her control? Underscoring the fact that she was 'bought / By Arthur's great name and his little love', she explains how marriage to him involves a renunciation of all pleasures of the senses (ll. 81–8).

As her argument unfolds, the question of whether or not she is guilty becomes increasingly overshadowed by the vitality of her interaction with Lancelot. In this narrative, marriage seems a cold, formal contract, and those who claim to defend its sanctity by exposing the queen's infidelity seem to work more in the interests of national chaos than in those of moral order. One of Guenevere's greatest rhetorical successes is her ability to contain scandal and protect the privacy and decorum of her relationships with both Lancelot and Arthur. Not only does she refuse to make an unambiguous confession of guilt, but she repeatedly resists her accusers' attempts to make public the details of her personal life. With her question '[I]s there any law / To make a queen say why some spots of red / Lie on her coverlet?' she draws a crucial distinction between legitimately cited evidence of a crime and scandalous invasion of privacy, whose very refutation would only compound the violation it performs. Similarly, she refuses to recount Lancelot's words of reassurance to her when their tête-à-tête in her chambers is disrupted by the brawling of her accusers: 'By God! I will not tell you more to-day, / Judge any way you will – what matters it?' (ll. 277–8).

By giving voice to the figure of the adulterous woman, Morris indicts the cruelty of a social milieu in which women are encouraged to marry on the basis of trust rather than informed choice, only to be compelled to accept the consequences even when the conventions they trusted prove radically deceptive. It may be, as Florence Boos has argued, that the chivalric ethic of the poem exaggerates womanly helplessness and thereby risks endorsing the hierarchized courtly gender relations that the reform of marriage law resisted (see Boos 1990: 101–2). Yet one might also argue that it is the very residue of medievalism inherent in Victorian marriage laws that required even the most politically active women, such as Caroline Norton and Harriet Taylor, to depend on champions like Serjeant Thomas Talfourd and John Stuart Mill to defend their cause in Parliament.

Tennyson's account of Guinevere's adultery, published a year after Morris's volume, is far less sympathetic to adulterous wives. In fact, it reflects remarkably closely the fears surrounding female sexuality that surfaced in the Parliamentary debates on divorce and marriage in the spring of 1857. Some of the fears most energetically expressed by Parliamentarians were first, that illegitimate offspring might be imposed on a husband by an adulterous wife, and second, that increased accessibility to divorce for women and the working classes would reduce marriage to 'connubial concubinage' (Shanley 1989: 41) Among the more conservative debaters was the bishop of Oxford, who proposed that adulterers should be prohibited from remarriage, a prohibition that would have applied almost solely to women (Shanley 1989: 42). This is a view Tennyson tacitly endorses in 'Guinevere': from the opening lines, which describe the queen banished and weeping in the nunnery of Almesbury, he suggests that the best she can hope for is the condescension and forgiveness of her aggrieved husband followed by a life of celibacy and penance.

As in Morris's version, so too in Tennyson's, adultery is linked to interpretative skill. Where Guenevere's choice of Arthur was based on a misinterpretation made in good faith, Guinevere's preference for Lancelot is more heavily indicted as a form of moral illiteracy. When they first meet, she only glances at Arthur (l. 402), and through her 'false voluptuous pride' (l. 636) she fails to distinguish between literal and figurative signs. Reading him literally as 'cold, / High, self-contained, and passionless, not like him, / Not like my Lancelot' (ll. 402–4), she misses the depth signalled by manly self-restraint. Only belatedly does she recognize that Arthur's reticence is a sign of his capacity for profound moral character: '[N]ow I see thee what thou art, / Thou art the highest and most human too, /

Not Lancelot, nor another' (ll. 643–5). While Tennyson cannot be accused of endorsing the sexual double standard – he does not show any greater tolerance for male philandering than for female – the emphasis he places on male continence, a man's 'maiden passion for a maid', only underscores Guinevere's failure to live up to Arthur's exacting moral standards.

The symbolic weight attached to female adultery in these two versions of the Arthurian tale is reflected with especial clarity in the physical stance of the queen in each case. On the one hand, Guenevere's spectacular physical presence is an index of her confidence in the defensibility of her position as one who has honoured the love of life above the empty forms of the law. On the other, Guinevere's abjection, her 'grovelling' (ll. 412, 578) and inability to look directly at Arthur, endorse her sense of herself as one whose beauty is 'a kingdom's curse' (l. 546). While she is literally childless, the illegitimate offspring she has metaphorically imposed on her husband are, in Arthur's words, 'the breaking up of laws, / The craft of kindred and the Godless hosts / Of heathen swarming o'er the Northern Sea' (ll. 422–5), so that she finally identifies herself to the nuns as 'that wicked one, who broke / The vast design and purpose of the King' (ll. 663–4). This equation of adultery with such wide-scale national disaster suggests the extent to which Victorian marriage represented a composite of different, but connected, social loyalties. As Herbert Tucker puts it in his discussion of the *Idylls*, 'Because Victorian monogamy represented faith of every kind, it could serve with real ideological point, as a fulcrum of empire' (1991: 707). It is this perspective on marriage as a bond of faith that women poets challenge in the last decades of the nineteenth century.

Poetry of Disillusionment: Victorian Women's Views on Marriage

With the deaths of both the Prince Consort and Elizabeth Barrett Browning in 1861, Britain lost two of its most mythologized marriage partnerships. Through the 1860s, efforts to reform marriage laws continued to be frustrated until finally the poorly composed, barely intelligible Married Women's Property Act was passed in 1870. In the wake of this Act, feminists rallied the more vigorously to the task of convincing Parliament to change the many laws reflecting the national assumption that women could be defined simply by their reproductive and domestic functions. Correlative to this political energy, a new tone of advocacy and political pragmatism emerged in women's poetry, of the kind Barrett Browning had cultivated in *Aurora Leigh*. One such political practitioner was Augusta Webster, a lively advocate of women's suffrage and formal education for girls (Leighton 1992: 167). In her writing, marriage is disengaged from the mythology of love, for to her 'a certain healthy indifference' was the essential component of a happy marriage (Leighton 1992: 173). She presents a pointedly acerbic vignette of marital relations in her dramatic monologue 'A Castaway', where she uses the form's scope for ironic distance to contemplate the moral implications of prostitution as a profession rather than a fate.

The speaker, a high-class courtesan, whose dispassionate tone resists any interpretation of her as abject or fallen, considers whether her work is any more socially demoralizing than the work of innumerable male professionals (ll. 99–101). From the prostitute's perspective, the married men with whom she deals are a homogeneous clientele; their shared consumer demand for sexual services negates any aura of moral authority to which they might lay claim. Likewise their wives are no womanly angels, but self-righteous idlers who would as soon enjoy the ethical advantage of being betrayed as exert themselves to keep their husbands' attentions. To the Castaway, the virtue of the domestic angel is no more than the effect of her lack of sexual attraction and her socio-economic privilege. While the former shields her from all opportunities for extra-marital dalliance, the latter protects her from the obligation to earn a living without the education to do so respectably. Set against this jaundiced view of marriage as an alliance characterized by boredom and hypocrisy, the courtesan's freedom, financial independence, astute analytical skills and dry wit seem infinitely more appealing.

Another, rather more distant critique of marriage as a defunct institution associated with dull routine is presented in Amy Levy's poem 'A Ballad of Religion and Marriage', one of her last compositions before her suicide in 1887. Here she presents an alternative perspective to the view of marriage as a sacrament – that 'high mysterious union, / Which nought on earth may break' so earnestly celebrated in John Keble's hymn 'Holy Matrimony' (1857). In an ironic fantasy of cosmic housecleaning, the awesome divine community of the Judaeo-Christian tradition – the angels, the Christian trinity and the wrathful Old Testament Jehovah – are '[s]wept into limbo' along with their lofty moral ideals and threats of punishment. Participants in monogamous marriage are represented as discontented troops, reluctantly performing routine duties at their assigned posts, but soon to erupt in mutiny. In the new dispensation, choice and alternatives, passion and affection, personal freedom and pleasure will abound, although in the closing quatrain, the lyric speaker wryly admits that such reform is not likely to be accomplished within her own lifetime. These brief but caustic sketches of marriage prefigure several of the views expressed by Mona Caird, whose essays 'Marriage' (published in the *Westminster Review* in 1888) and 'The Morality of Marriage' (*Fortnightly Review* in 1890) generated ferocious public debate. The former is reputed to have provoked 27,000 responses to the letters column of the *Daily Telegraph* when it first appeared (McKinney 1996: 625).

Intolerable to Caird was the economic dependence that marriage imposed on women, and the expectation of unquestioning duty that required them to produce far more children than was good for their health, or than they could adequately raise. Like Webster's Castaway, Caird deplores the hypocrisy of the ideal of womanly virtue, and like Levy's speaker, she longs for an end to the dull routine and repressive self-restraint that marriage imposes on women: 'An interval now of furious licence, if it must be, on the way to freedom, would be a kinder potion for this sick world than another century of "womanly" duty and virtue, as these have been provided hitherto' (Caird 1996: 634). In one of the most powerful passages in 'The Morality of Marriage', she stresses that even as late as 1890, English courts of law, religious teachings and social customs all define wives as the property of their husbands. To illustrate her point, she cites at some length from the dramatic monologue of Guido Franceschini, Robert Browning's villainous husband in *The Ring and the Book* (1868–9). On trial for the murder of his young wife Pompilia, Franceschini describes his relationship to her as comparable to a gentleman's relation to his hunting hawk. If she fails to meet his demands, he is entitled simply to 'twist her neck!' (V, 701–10).

Although set in late seventeenth-century Italy, Browning's representation of marital relations gone awry has much in common with the anecdotes presented by Frances Power Cobbe in her chilling essay 'Wife-Torture in England' of 1878. In such texts, the ideals of manliness and womanliness that pervade the earlier companionate marriage poems give way to the persistent recognition that a woman, once married, loses her identity and is as much her husband's chattel as are his horses, cattle, dogs or sporting birds – a representation that continues into the early decades of the twentieth century. An example is Charlotte Mew's plaintive dramatic monologue 'The Farmer's Bride' (1916), in which a bemused farmer contemplates the problem of how to cope with his young wife, who, far from conforming to his expectations of spousal companionship, shuns him as the object of profound distrust. The melancholy humour of the situation lies less in the farmer's implicit assumption that his bride is one more addition to his agricultural inventory than in the irony of the bride's animal-like, instinctive response to her would-be master. The question with which Mew's poem leaves us is whether there can ever be a truly companionate marriage as long as the contract is based on the assumption that wives are reproductive animals with no symbolic identity of their own.

Queer Unions in Tennyson, Hopkins and Michael Field

Ironically, as monogamous marriage became an increasingly popular trope for representing breaches of faith and the potential breakdown of domestic and imperial negotiation, it was at the same time used to represent same-sex unions in some of the most vital poetry of the age. As we have seen in the earlier consideration of *The Princess*, Tennyson's explorations of heterodox erotics in manly and womanly conduct are much more inventive than his ability to envisage innovative ways for men and women to relate in heterosexual marriage partnerships. His treatment of the marriage motif in his magnum opus, *In Memoriam*, is especially interesting in this regard.

One of the greatest challenges Tennyson faced in this elegy was to convey a sense of the intimacy, intensity and tenderness of the relationship he enjoyed with Arthur Hallam while framing those qualities in terms that appeared manly. For Hallam's death meant more than simply intellectual and spiritual loss for his friend; it meant intense emotional and even physical desolation too. Figures of courtship and marriage were useful for conveying these dimensions of the relationship, but they brought with them the effect of feminizing one or the other member of the male partnership in a way that unsettled standard Victorian conceptions of manly tenderness. For instance, in early lyrics such as VI and VIII, Tennyson imagines his friendship with Hallam in terms of youthful courtship. In lyric VI, he describes the pathos of a young girl eagerly anticipating the arrival of her betrothed only to discover that, ironically, he was already dead at the moment of her anticipation. This scenario of youthful joy blighted is analogous to the speaker's experience and raises questions parallel to those he faces:

> O what to her shall be the end?
>   And what to me remains of good?
> To her, perpetual maidenhood,
>   And unto me no second friend.
>
> (ll. 41–4)

The girl's life is arrested at the penultimate moment before maidenhood's promise is consummated in reproductive womanliness. Similarly, the speaker feels his own life and poetic productivity are suspended by his irreparable loss. Underlying the image of 'perpetual maidenhood' is the suggestion of Hallam as the inseminator of Tennyson's feminized poetic imagination: a suggestive reworking of the more traditional heterosexual metaphor of the male poet's feminized muse.

Sometimes, for instance in lyric IX, the cross-gendered imagery simply invites us to imagine heterosexual relationships – that between a husband and wife, or a son and mother – in order to understand the rich texture of tenderness that two men might share (ll. 17–20). At other times, the heterosexual intimacy conveys the sense of physical, eroticized companionship, as in these lines from lyric XIII:

> Tears of the widower, when he sees
>   A late-lost form that sleep reveals,
>   And moves his doubtful arms, and feels
> Her place is empty, fall like these;
> Which weep a loss for ever new,
>   A void where heart on heart reposed;
> And, where warm hands have prest and closed,
>   Silence, till I be silent too.
>
> (ll. 1–8)

The last two lines provide a fine illustration of the overdetermined function played by the recurrent image of the handshake in *In Memoriam*, an image Christopher Craft has clarified so astutely (1994: 56).

Perhaps most intriguing are those moments where Tennyson alludes to the literal betrothal of his sister Emily to Hallam in order to enrich his portrayal of a conventional intimacy between brothers-in-law, only then to displace the heterosexual marriage with the more heterodox and sublime union between men. A clear example of this occurs in lyric LXXXIV when Tennyson begins by describing the literal marriage that was to be, following this with fantasies of the pleasures he would have enjoyed with Hallam had things gone according to plan. The literal marriage would have mediated and authorized the figurative union of male friendship: as they both aged, their 'involved' spirits, 'linked . . . in love and fate', would at last be welcomed into the heavenly fraternity by a Christ who 'Would reach us out the shining hand, / And take us as a single soul'. Here, the wifely figure of Emily Tennyson, having performed the mediating duty of bringing the men together, simply fades from the picture as Christ emerges to legitimize the male union as spiritual.

While for Tennyson, Christ seems always to function as the facilitator of the lost Hallam's recuperation rather than as himself the object of Tennyson's desire, for the Jesuit poet Gerard Manley Hopkins, working in an orthodox Roman Catholic tradition, union with Christ is a fantasy that pays its own erotic dividends. Dating back to his days as an Oxford undergraduate, the motif of uniting with Christ, especially within the context of an all-male celebration of the Holy Communion, plays a powerfully eroticized role in Hopkins's poetics. Sometimes, this union is presented in the tradition of the soul's union with Christ as spiritual bridegroom in a redemptive nuptial celebration. One instance occurs in stanza 30 of Hopkins's great ode 'The Wreck of the Deutschland'; another more exuberant version in the final tercet of the Welsh sonnet 'The Starlight Night'.

Using the traditional courtly strategy of celebrating the obstacle that separates the troubadour from the object of his desire, the sonnet opens with a spirited exhortation to 'Look at the stars! look, look up at the skies!' This is followed by a series of images inviting the listener to take pleasure in the patterns of the starry sky: 'fire-folk sitting in the air!'; 'airy abeles set on a flare!'; 'a May-mess, like on orchard boughs!' Then in the closing tercet the speaker introduces his final vision of the starry patterns as celestial barnwalls beyond which Christ, the bridegroom and sublime object of desire, awaits his nuptial partner, the soul: 'These are indeed the barn; withindoors house / The shocks. This piece-bright paling shuts the spouse / Christ home, Christ and his mother and all his hallows.'

A more enigmatic allusion to hymeneal celebration is presented in the late fragment 'Epithalamion', a swimming idyll supposedly composed to honour the marriage between Hopkins's younger brother, Everard, and his fiancée, Amy Sichel. Although the fragment concludes with three equations that ask us to read 'the delightful dean' as wedlock, the water as spousal love, and the surrounding greenery as family members who witness the marriage, the main body of the verse describes a scene of young boys swimming, watched surreptitiously from the bank by a weary wayfarer. As with 'The Starlight Night', the poem opens with an exhortation, this time not to look but to listen: 'Hark, hearer, hear what I do.' Both Byrne Fone (1983: 27) and Richard Dellamora (1990: 42–3) have pointed out that we might recognize in this invocation the Greek pederastic tradition of the *eispnelas*, or inspirer, who addresses his *aitas* or hearer. I would suggest that Hopkins overlays this motif with the equally erotic Christian sacramental motif of marriage as union with Christ. If the dean is wedlock and the water spousal love, then the listless stranger, drawn by the sounds of boyish glee, experiences his own immersion in the river as a form of consummation. The allusions to heterosexual marriage and to the sacramental refreshment it brings are enough to authorize the strictly ascetic Hopkins to linger over a fantasy that approaches, but never overtly articulates, the possibility of pederastic union.

Hopkins, as I have argued elsewhere, developed his homoerotic Christian poetics as a counter-discourse to the homoerotic Hellenic discourse developing at Oxford under figures such as Walter Pater, J. A. Symonds and later Oscar Wilde (Saville 2000: 37–9). Two women poets working in quite the contrary direction turned to Greek studies developing at Cambridge to explore a same-sex alternative to the Christian institution of heterosexual marriage (see Prins 1999a). Katherine Bradley and Edith Cooper, an aunt and niece writing collaboratively under the pseudonym 'Michael Field', developed a Sapphic poetics rich in hymeneal imagery and figures of exuberant fertility.

In their joint journal, *Works and Days*, and in their letters, each of them articulates their sense of themselves as a married couple united in their collaborative poetic enterprise. For instance, in a letter of 1884 to the ageing Robert Browning, Cooper describes their writing as 'like mosaic work – the mingled, various product of our two brains'. She continues, 'I think if our contributions were disentangled and one subtracted from the other, the amount would be almost even. This happy union of two in work and aspiration is sheltered and expressed by "Michael Field"' (Sturge Moore and Sturge Moore 1933: 3). Once, in May 1886, when they visited his home at Warwick Crescent, Browning admitted to them that he and his wife never discussed their work until it was finished. To this Bradley responded later in her journal, 'these two poets, man and wife, wrote alone; each wrote, but did not bless or quicken one another at their work; *we are closer married*' (Sturge Moore and Sturge Moore 1933: 16)). In another letter, also of May 1886, this time to Havelock Ellis on the subject of which woman was responsible for which sections of their collaborative writing, Bradley insisted on their unity, alluding to the Anglican marriage service: 'As to our work, let no man think he can put asunder what God has joined' (Sturgeon 1922: 47).

Their poem 'Prologue' – published in 1893, but believed to have been written in 1878, when Bradley was 32 and Cooper nearly 17 (Sturge Moore and Sturge Moore 1933: xix) – records and celebrates their pledge to unite in poetry writing and mutual devotion ('My Love and I took hands and swore, / Against the world, to be / Poets and lovers evermore' [ll. 4–5]). Selecting the birthday of Shakespeare (master of gender ambiguity) as the date of the pledge, the lovers set themselves against the world, but defy death, allying themselves with Apollo, god of the lyre and passionate lover of the nubile Hyacinthus. And since Shakespeare's birthday (23 April) is believed to be also the date of his death, one might read here an allusion to the full circle of unbroken love represented by a wedding ring. As Chris White remarks, 'This is an implicitly political understanding of women as lovers, rather than a private and personal retreat from the world into Romantic Friendship' (1992: 42). What is more, their alliance to a community of poets counteracts the otherwise isolating and anti-social effects implicit in incestuous unions.

The generative rather than anti-social quality of their relationship is emphasized in their use of seed imagery, berries and fruit, to articulate their intellectual fecundity. In this imagery, the reproductive duties of the heterosexual wife are displaced by the vibrant intellectual intercourse denied to most married women of the late Victorian period. Two lyrics particularly effective in this regard are 'So Jealous of Your Beauty' and 'Unbosoming'. The first is a song addressed to a woman who fears the exhausting effects of 'hymeneal duty', apparently persuading her that marriage will yield fruit far surpassing the ephemeral bloom of youth. Read heterosexually, this would seem to endorse precisely the honouring of conjugal duty and women's reproductive obligations that Mona Caird denounced in her essays. Yet we might as easily read the 'marvellous pale suit' of the seed-bearing poppy head and the 'colour / Of apricot, / Ungot, / Warming in August' as images of intellectual fruit. In each case, the blossom – the 'glossy red' of the poppy or the apricot's '[f]rail flowers that spread and die / Before the sun is hot' – can be read as the poetic flower or *anthos* that develops into the fruit of collaboration gathered into the poetic anthology. In these terms, the lyric becomes a celebration of the intellectual fecundity that the Sapphic marriage promises and that conventional marriage so often prevents Victorian women from achieving. The short lyric 'Unbosoming' (1893) similarly uses the image of the summer iris to represent an affection that gains vitality as it matures. The 'zephyr-petal' of the flower gives way to 'a thousand vermilion-beads / That push, and riot, and squeeze, and clip, / Till they burst the sides of the silver scrip'.

Michael Field's specifically Sapphic lyrics do not overtly deride heterosexual love, so much as present it in the light of a poor substitute for much richer, more satisfying same-sex unions. For instance, in the lyric based on the Sapphic fragment 'To you, fair maids, my mind changes not', the love between women is presented as part of a soothing psychic equilibrium based on fine intuitive responses to mutual desires. While heterosexual love is volatile, disturbing and fraught with mutual manipulation ('Men I defy, allure, estrange, / Prostrate, make bond or free'), the homoerotic intercourse between the maids and the lyric speaker generates a surplus of energy: 'ye come to me / . . . And with your soft vitality / My weary bosom fill'. The bosom takes on the role of a repository of peculiarly feminized intellectual and emotional riches of a kind with the 'vermilion-beads' that burst forth in 'Unbosoming'.

Another Sapphic lyric, 'Come, Gorgo, Put the Rug in Place', elaborates on the Sapphic fragment 'Foolish woman, pride not thyself on a ring.' Here, the immediacy of private physical pleasure is set against the exchange of material gifts – in this case, the sardonyx ring – as a public display of the contractual agreement between lovers. Sapphic love, which calls for Gorgo's passionate reclining on the well-placed rug and delights in the spectacle of her grace and her 'fairest hands', with their 'power to thrill and cling', displays the *joie de vivre* celebrated in the 'Prologue'. It quite eclipses the affection symbolized by the ring and associated with the heterosexual convention of woman adorned and adored by men.

By the last decades of the nineteenth century, it is thus the lesbian poets Bradley and Cooper and the celibate Hopkins who produce some of the most imaginative representations of gender's potentially transformative effects on marital relations. For Hopkins, the age-old motif of Christian devotion and the soul's union with Christ authorizes a male delight in manly beauty that expands the parameters of manly tenderness without compromising principles of manly restraint. At the same time, 'the Fields' reconfigure companionate marriage as active intellectual collaboration offering a blueprint for a liberated womanliness that poetic representations of heterosexual marriage had yet to envision.

See also: SEXUALITY AND LOVE; VERSE NOVEL.

ACKNOWLEDGEMENT

My thanks to John Maynard and Jack Stillinger for suggestions, reading and encouragement.

REFERENCES AND FURTHER READING

Adams, James Eli (1992) 'Harlots and Base Interpreters: Scandal and Slander in *Idylls of the King*.' *Victorian Poetry*, 30. 3–4, 421–39.

Adams, James Eli (1995) *Dandies and Desert Saints: Styles of Victorian Manhood*. Ithaca, N. Y.: Cornell University Press.

Anstruther, Ian (1992) *Coventry Patmore's Angel: A Study of Coventry Patmore, his Wife Emily and 'The Angel in the House'*. London: Haggerston Press.

Balch, Dennis (1975) 'Guenevere's Fidelity to Arthur in "The Defence of Guenevere" and "King Arthur's Tomb."' *Victorian Poetry*, 13, 3–4, 61–70.

Barrett Browning, Elizabeth (1996) *Aurora Leigh*. Ed. Margaret Reynolds. New York: Norton.

Boos, Florence (1990) 'Justice and Vindication in William Morris's "The Defence of Guenevere."' In Valerie M. Lagorio and Mildred Leake Day (eds). *King Arthur through the Ages*. (II, 83–104). New York: Garland.

Browning, Robert (1981) *The Poems*. Vol. I. New Haven: Yale University Press.

Caird, Mona (1996) 'Morality of Marriage.' In Andrea Broomfield and Sally Mitchell (eds). *Prose by Victorian Women: An Anthology* (pp. 629–53). New York: Garland.

Craft, Christopher (1994) *Another Kind of Love: Male Homosexual Desire in English Discourse, 1850–1920*. Berkeley: University of California Press.

Dellamora, Richard (1990) *Masculine Desire: The Sexual Politics of Victorian Aestheticism*. Chapel Hill: University of North Carolina Press.

Fone, Byrne S. (1983) 'This Other Eden: Arcadia and the Homosexual Imagination.' In Stuart Kellogg (ed.). *Literary Visions of Homosexuality* (pp. 13–34). New York: Haworth.

Holcombe, Lee (1977) 'Victorian Wives and Property: Reform of the Married Women's Property Law, 1857–1882.' In Martha Vicinus (ed.). *A Widening Sphere: Changing Roles of Victorian Women* (pp. 3–28). Bloomington, London: Indiana University Press.

Kintner, Elvan (ed.) (1969) *The Letters of Robert Browning and Elizabeth Barrett Browning 1845–1846*. Cambridge, Mass.: Belknap Press.

Leighton, Angela (1992) *Victorian Women Poets: Writing Against the Heart*. Charlottesville: University Press of Virginia.

McKinney, Lauren D. (1996) 'XIV. Mona Alison Caird (1854–1932).' In Andrea Broomfield and Sally Mitchell (eds). *Prose by Victorian Women* (pp. 625–8). New York: Garland.

McWilliams-Tullberg, Rita (1977) 'Women and Degrees at Cambridge University, 1862–1897.' In Martha Vicinus (ed.). *A Widening Sphere: Changing Roles of Victorian Women* (pp. 117–45). Bloomington, London: Indiana University Press.

Prins, Yopie (1999a) 'Greek Maenads, Victorian Spinsters.' In Richard Dellamora (ed.). *Victorian Sexual Dissidence* (pp. 43–81). Chicago: University of Chicago Press.

Prins, Yopie (1999b) *Victorian Sappho*. Princeton, N. J.: Princeton University Press.

Saville, Julia F. (2000) *A Queer Chivalry: The Homoerotic Asceticism of Gerard Manley Hopkins*. Charlottesville: University Press of Virginia.

Sedgwick, Eve Kosofsky (1985) *Between Men: English Literature and Male Homosocial Desire*. New York: Columbia University Press.

Shanley, Mary Lyndon (1989) *Feminism, Marriage, and the Law in Victorian England, 1850–1895*. Princeton, N. J.: Princeton University Press.

Sinfield, Alan (1986) *Alfred Tennyson*. New York: Blackwell.

Sturge Moore, T., and D. C. Sturge Moore (eds) (1933) *Works and Days: From the Journal of Michael Field*. London: John Murray.

Sturgeon, Mary (1922) *Michael Field*. New York: Macmillan.

Sussman, Herbert (1995) *Victorian Masculinities: Manhood and Masculine Poetics in Early Victorian Literature and Art*. Cambridge: Cambridge University Press.

Taylor, Beverly (1992) '"School-Miss Alfred" and "Materfamilias": Female Sexuality and Poetic Voice in "The Princess" and *Aurora Leigh*.' In Antony H. Harrison and Beverly Taylor (eds). *Gender and Discourse in Victorian Literature and Art* (pp. 5–29). DeKalb: Northern Illinois University Press.

Tucker, Herbert F. (1991) 'The Epic Plight of Troth in *Idylls of the King.' ELH*, 58, 701–20.

Ulin, Donald (1999) 'Tourism and the Contest for Cultural Authority in Clough's *Bothie of Toper-na-Fuosich.' Victorian Poetry*, 37. 1, 71–97.

White, Chris (1992) '"Poets and Lovers Evermore": The Poetry and Journals of Michael Field.' In Joseph Bristow (ed.). *Sexual Sameness: Textual Differences in Lesbian and Gay Writing* (pp. 26–43). London: Routledge.

30

Sexuality and Love

John Maynard

We all know, or think we know, what sex is: that so varied but unmistakable pleasure that may issue in a thrill, a spasm, that experience most like a fit which is none the less gratifying. Alfred Kinsey taught us long ago to be a bit more matter of fact about this mystery of the body, to count connections and orgasms – with ourselves, with other individuals of our sex, of the other sex, both serially, of our age, older, younger, much younger; with groups of people, with puppets or machines, with preferred objects, with members of other species, with deities or Deity. Love we may think of as different, a broader business connecting us with all of the above but in ways more engaging of diverse emotions. Sex may seem to be sex – just sex; love a lot of things, romantic, familial, in friendship, in worship. Yet a pressure felt throughout the last century, perhaps most easily attributed to Sigmund Freud yet widely diffused, says the two are not so easily distinguished. The pressure is not mainly the old cynical one, wanting to say that love is just an unclear sublimation of clearer, simpler drives. It is rather the opposite, that sex, now often renamed pleonastically sexuality, is a lot more than getting it off, a momentary jerking in clitoris, penis, male or female g-spot, breasts, anus, underarm or anywhere: the body being pleasured becomes itself diverse, diffuse, a concept of 'human sexuality' more than a spot or a place. Love is something we talk of endlessly. But sex as sexuality becomes equally a textual matter: we all talk and write about *it*, without any hope for a term, perhaps rather with joy in its very interminability. So if Freud has taught us about the possible bodiliness of love, the desires vaguely conscious or not acknowledged – for neighbour's wife, for brother or sister, for Jesus or the Buddha – it has been Michel Foucault, French psychologist, historian and theorist, who showed us how we have sublimed sex into text and endless discourse of sexuality.

His view, which is where we perhaps need to start in looking at Victorian sexuality, is indeed that the discussion really gets going in the nineteenth century. If everyone was not doing it at least everyone was talking about doing it; and if they talked about not doing it, they were still talking about it. Foucault only lived to outline this view in an *Introduction* (1990) to a history of sexuality through the ages. But his approach, in which even obsessions with controlling or repressing sex are seen as contributing to a snowballing discourse on sexuality, has been exceptionally influential on those who seek to describe the nature of Victorian sexuality. Two more points should be made: that his splendid awareness of the degree to which those Victorians – said to have only been laid still to think of England, said to have covered their exposed piano legs – were all the time converting more and more of experience into sexual discourse should not encourage us to create a utopia of mere bodies merely acting pleasure before the Victorian age. His substantial, if finally tragically fragmentary history tells us each age had its ways of connecting sex with its values and major concerns – Greek pederasty with ideas of politics and education and self-making, Christian celibates with bodily freedom and weightlessness. More broadly, each culture uses sex as part of its efforts to build a discourse of humanness over the bodily tedium and emptiness of its world.

The other thing that needs to be said is that Foucault's influential overview of a proliferating discourse of sexuality does not actually cancel what he calls the repressive hypothesis, the view that the nineteenth century was a period of unnatural stifling of sexual desire and expression; it merely puts it in a broader frame. If acts of repression themselves were, as Foucault convincingly argues, contributions to that discourse that found and made sex ubiquitous, the discourse itself often remains none the less repressive. We need to be able to distinguish both the general situation of increasing sexual discourse and the binaries of repression/release opening within discourses and practices. For sexuality presents itself (to us, at the end of such a long process of discourse construction) as a virtually endless creation of binaries: madonna/whore, homosexual/heterosexual, libertine/pure, procreation/recreation, safe sex/unsafe sex: the formulation always threatening to weight some positions up in the balance and drop the others down. And most of our quarrels, really significant quarrels that cannot be washed away by imposing Foucault's big picture, have been over the morals and politics of such oppositional binaries – are heterosexuals normal, gays unnatural? Is right to life the right right or is that woman's right to choose? Is sex all right or safe enough for those over 18 but not for those under that age? – and on and on in the great number of issues most of us take very seriously, *pace* Foucault. One major way of taxonomizing such binaries is the repressive hypothesis: that since the Victorians expanded thinking massively into sexuality there has been a larger quarrel between those who would control and limit their and others' expressions of sex – whether in bed or in print – and those who would allow them. In this perspective there are still major issues of repression, or control and liberation, working themselves out in the Victorian period and after. If we see an ever broadening production of sexuality throughout both the nineteenth and twentieth centuries, from Victorian Dr Acton to Drs Masters and Johnson, from Victorian gentlemen's guides to London by night to *Hustler* magazine, we can also see some major arcs in the battle of control and release: a new concern with respectability developing with the Victorian era and perhaps cresting in the 1880s and 1890s, and a broad letting go, but with many exceptions and countercurrents, from the period around the First World War to the present.

But despite the implications of some recent historians of culture, we cannot read the individual as a motiveless cog in a machine of culture. Individual psychologies, starting with relations to parents and childhood experience of love or hate, sex or abuse, and continuing in adult experiences of love and bodily intimacy, develop the sexual proclivities of the grown individual; these not only are named and mediated by the sexual possibilities articulated in the culture but in turn shape or warp the cultural pattern; social forms and discussions are absorbed or repelled in intimate experience of sex and love; a feedback in and out of culture on the one hand, and psychic and physical life on the other, makes extremely complex any attempt to connect the individual to the social structure. If we try to imagine a model for their interaction over time we can believe they do connect, so that Freud and Foucault offer not opposing views but perspectives from different points. At any given time the individual's loving and sexual style and possibilities are determined by repressions and controls ultimately connected to the values of the outside society by the internalized superego (so Freud). Yet culture has a life of its own and can develop a fuller sexual world even as it seems to be repressing individuals (so Foucault). Oscar Wilde's trial, for instance, culminates, in society's violence against his vulnerable psyche and body, focus of his society wanting to suppress expressions of same-sex desire. Yet the trial also brings the existence of homosexuality out of Wilde's and the culture's closet decisively. A changed culture will then open possibilities to individuals of the next generation (as well as possible new limitations). Victorian society doubtless was moving to ever greater sexual discussion, but that does not overturn traditional awareness of Victorian sexual life as often a location of great anxiety, conflict, conscious suppression or unconscious repression.

Foucault (along with Peter Gay 1984, 1986) was of course right to criticize the traditional view that Victorians were merely and massively repressive about sex. In fact neither his view nor the repressive hypothesis adequately accounts for the variety of phenomena associated with Victorian sexuality. What we can see is a very complex pattern swept through by these greater bold figures of repression and proliferation. Historians before Foucault not incorrectly saw the Victorian period ushered in by moving forces wishing to limit and control sexual expression. These have been grouped together generally under the rubric of social respectability: forces of the new, greatly expanding middle class and of various evangelical religious tendencies, making a simultaneous attack on what they perceived as upper-class libertinism and lower-class profligacy. From his grand overview Foucault may rightly say this simply expands thinking about sexuality into a number of new areas. But to those experiencing this Puritan awakening it seemed a very real generation of social controls and self-policing restraints: on what could be published, on what could be said, on what could be done – especially in public. For there was a true Puritan drive towards restraining sex within the bounds of married (and usually loving) sexuality. The respectable social thinking of the middle class in the Victorian period consolidated the long tradition in English Protestantism in favour of affective married relationships as opposed to the arranged marriages and condoned adultery of the Catholic Continent. At the same time it introduced a special concern of its own with *public* conduct and appearance. The many forces of respectability easily seemed to their critics mere hypocrites combining varying disagreeable proportions of Puritanism and hypocrisy. Middle-class Victorians more often saw this movement as part of a general improvement of civic society; writers of the first two decades of the Victorian period seem voluntarily to say less than they, heirs of the much bawdier Regency period, actually know.

Later in the century the newer desire was social purity rather than just respectability. The topic of prostitution shows the difference well. Respectable forces generally focused on limiting the public appearance of prostitution, punishing seduction of girls into prostitution (1849), and attempting to bring individual women sex workers back to respectable occupations, as witnessed by the establishment of Magdalene homes and the reclaiming street walking of even such eminent Victorians as Charles Dickens and William Gladstone. Fellow travellers in these efforts included even members of the medical profession, for instance the doctor William Acton, whose book *Prostitution* (1857) has even been too central in twentieth-century accounts. Some, like Acton, campaigned aggressively for routine medical examination of prostitutes, as in France and Belgium, to prevent the spread of disease, a project compatible with respectable society's attempts at sanitary reform and indicative of a view that prostitution was a social given to be channelled and controlled. The respectable reformers were opposed by new forces of moral purity that were unleashed and concentrated by opposition to the Contagious Diseases Acts of 1864, which regulated and inspected prostitution in certain areas of military or naval activity. Under the leadership of Josephine Butler, the forces for repeal of this regulation took the form of an organized mass movement, with a major female participation and with an emphatic moral and sexual agenda on top of its social/political one. The focus was now on condemning, not regulating, prostitution, and on enforcing moral norms for sexual conduct; namely, the movement asked men to refrain from what it called fornication and limit their sex experience to married sex. In a long history, often marked by strong agitation, the forces of moral purity ultimately not only carried their demands for repeal of the Acts but even put through their own, much more controlling one, the Criminal Law Amendment Act of 1885. Through the Labouchere amendment the Act created the legal wedge for invading late Victorians' sexual privacy with a new level of moral-legal violence. That success for the forces of purity would spawn a generation of private societies working through the legal system to control both sexual activity and expression. The voluntary work of a Thomas Bowdler making Shakespeare respectable yielded to the zealous enforcement of groups with names like the National Vigilance Association, the Social Purity Alliance or the Moral Reform Union.

Foucault sees in this increasing preoccupation with regulating and controlling sexual conduct just that elaboration of a few sex acts into a large culture of sexuality that is the largest picture. Historians more interested in specificity, local diversity and uneven developments see these large tendencies pitted against or offset by a great variety of innovative sexual discussion and, to some extent, activity. We will look soon at a cross-section of these; what can be said generally is that they necessarily developed in something of a vacuum. We approach the Victorians, especially in the period before 1880, as we would people who spoke our language but had somehow lost a certain section of their brain dealing with sex. They seem *not* to speak our language about such everyday matters – to us – as homosexuality, masturbation or adultery. Partly this is a matter of changing vocabulary, masturbation being more often known as the Biblically resonant 'Onanism', adultery as the more poignant euphemism 'criminal conversation'. But we are also in a time before the spread of sexual discourse had isolated quite a few of what we think of as usual sexual experiences for especial remark, giving them a social place and a set of characteristics. Not only was homosexuality a love that dared not speak its name but it was unformed and fluid as a concept. We look at a time, as Tom Stoppard has suggested in dramatizing the agony of the person we call the 'gay' scholar/poet A. E. Housman, before the invention of love.

Two points are worth observing. First is that, though there seems to be an early development of many of our own conceptions in or about 1870, there remains, in the Foucauldian paradigm, a continual proliferation and endlessly restless redevelopment of sexual categories and discussions. More important for our purposes, the extreme lack of definition left Victorian lovers, or writers about love, a great deal of blank space in which to innovate in terms of their particular desires; and, lacking an entire vocabulary until its development late in the century, individual formations or constructions often reconfigure older ideas and vocabulary in strange ways – 'dearer than my brothers are to me' says Alfred Tennyson about his beloved Arthur Hallam – or invent new terms that, failing to have caught on, strike us as uncouth: 'Uranians' as a third sex devoted to high-level friendship, for example. In reading Victorian sexuality, we read not so much to crack an alien code that speaks of our own experience in hidden language as to open ourselves to explorations, conceptions and language that, developed out of this fluidity and inchoateness, may not fit any of ours precisely. Foucault sometimes seems to scorn the development of the great mass of sexual thinking that he chronicles. We who hear the individual out of history as we read poetry of an earlier period may, rather, revel in the diverse ways in which so central and powerful a human experience gets wonderfully elaborated and diversely articulated.

Even in exploring such language and forms we are restricted by our own modes of interpreting and thinking. How can we think beyond the ways we have already developed to read literature or understand the past? Much work on Victorian sexuality after Foucault has been concerned to seek continuities between the texts of the society and those of canonical or sub-canonical literature. The texts of society have included a heterogeneous and ever-growing class of writing or even material objects taken as readable texts: books on prostitution, newspaper reports of divorce trials, tracts on and apparatuses for birth control, memoirs of same-sex lovers finding a way to an identity, diaries of ladies and gentlemen indicating days when orgasms occurred, records of foundling hospitals, records of touristic and imperialistic sex, clitoral vibrators for medical use. In effect we attempt to name the discussions there and see how they are continued in the literature. We may look at issues confronted in both works and assess attitudes between the texts. Or we may attempt to find a politics evident in the social texts hidden in the literary format.

This is different, however, from another kind of reading in which the keys to a code open a kind of subtext to the code-cracking critic. This may be imputed to the author – Wilde's 'The Sphinx' is really about same-sex desire – or it may involve forms of psychological penetration associated with Freudian psychological traditions – underlying lesbian desire in Christina Rossetti's poems of sister relation. Here the code is clearly one from our time which – often to the suspicion of the un-Freudian – is projected back. Both can bring us productively to consider with open eyes aspects of the text. Approaches are helpful that help us think. None can assure us that we are really getting beyond our own discourses and obsessions and finding Victorian life or poetry as it truly was.

Since the mid-1980s the topic of homosexual and lesbian love has probably had the most play in sexual discussions of the Victorian period. This has been greatly enlivened by a rich theoretical discussion that parallels and often crosses it. The theory talk, while emerging from different traditions of thought, Freudian, Lacanian, deconstructive, queer or feminist, has established some premises that greatly help us in looking at issues of same-sex love and desire in the Victorian period. Perhaps most obviously, we are all social constructionists today. Which is not to say there is not controversy over any issue of ultimate causes – anyone who asks such questions will find major confusion as to genetic, psychological-developmental or environmental causes. But the consensus is rather that such unresolved questions are not historically useful. We say rather that any form in which some kind of same-sex love/desire is found will be a formation of the culture that we can meaningfully plot and attempt to define. As Judith Butler (1991) has so precisely argued, we only can speak of the presumed original (love/desire) from the presumed secondary effect, its formation. We know that Wilde engaged in sex acts with males, loved obsessively at least one male, cultivated a style of male–male intimacy and of Aesthetic transgression, thought of himself as in a tradition fostered by Greek pederastic love, expressed guilt for his same-sex acts/desires. Same-sex love/desire is revealed as a very open field in which many identities of more specific and local focus can be understood. And that in turn has encouraged a fluid sense of possible formations and recombinations, as if the number of sexual paths can be very great and may, as we see in Wilde's case, be occupied diversely by one individual. Finally, theory has suggested we be flexible about the relation of homosexual love/desire and heterosexual. It asks, as Eve Sedgwick has so effectively (1985), what the implications of Western culture's strong homophobic formations are in the face of its ever-growing homosexual constructions. And it has found great interest in formations that cross the binary homo/heterosexuality: transvestism, bisexuality, transsexuality.

Such theory has been most obviously effective in opening our eyes to same-sex love/desire in the Victorian period. Historians first saw the fact of formation itself: the love that dare not speak its name (except in Latin and Greek works most educated males knew somewhat) was given names and a nomenclature. The initial conclusion was that on or about 1870 human nature changed and homosexuality emerged (Foucault 1990: 43). It was first given ugly pathological, legal or taxonomic names but, once unleashed in human nature, it would fight its way to recognition as a valid alternate identity. The better, if usually later, conclusion was that practices and feelings, so fluid as not to be identified and labelled, became aggregated and expanded into recognized and named identities, subcultures, behavioural patterns, in the manner of a constant production of discourse that Foucault himself in fact described. This latter story has allowed us to see two aspects of the history, both social and literary, much better. First, we see a diversity of pre-1870 same-sex loves/desires. We no longer have to approach Tennyson's intense feeling for his dead friend Hallam in *In Memoriam* either by explaining it as mere friendship or by arguing that it is homosexuality after some formation invented in the later part of the century. It is what it is and our business – a very hard one – will be defining it adequately as it is: some version of relation undreamed of in our modern sexual philosophies of gayness. Similarly we can find in Gerard Manley Hopkins a very complex repositioning of same-sex desire from the beautiful bodies of tempting fellow Oxford students or brawny working men into religious desire for Christ as redeemer/lover and taskmaster (see Saville 2000). Or we can see a work like Christina Rossetti's 'Goblin Market' as creating a space of sisterly female–female affectivity and physical closeness without falling into any of our conventions of lesbianism or incest.

Second, theory allows us to see a host of patterns emerging, some of them to become more, some less predominant in twentieth-century gay, lesbian, bisexual, transsexual and transvestite formations. To suggest a few: there is the renaissance of the Greek pederastic ideal in a Platonic form, a manly pedagogic idea of love based on a somewhat teasing repression of the physical side of Greek love (see Dowling 1994); there is the born invert, otherwise unexceptional and like all other people, of sexologist and historian John Addington Symonds. There is the religiously turned sexuality of poet John Gray and sexologist Marc-André Raffalovich, moving from physical to spiritual same-sex bonding; there is the bonding, certainly with sexual desire, of Michael Field (the poets Katherine Bradley and her niece Edith Cooper), who place themselves and their fine lyrical poems, jointly written, so clearly in the tradition of a Sappho of lesbian, not opposite-sex, desire (see Prins 1999; Vanita 1996); there is the cross-class love of Wilde with his young panthers who dined with him at the Café Royal and sold their bodies to him, or the love of the Other from the empire or tourist land, as Symonds in Venice, or Wilde or French André Gide in Northern Africa (see poems in White 1999). There were the confusions of the Boulton and Park Affair (1870), in which two men were prosecuted for appearing in public London places in drag, and the Cleveland Street Scandals (1889), in which a male brothel came to public attention. These unequal historic events (one about persistent transvestism, the other about male prostitution in high places) were matched by unequal societal response, essentially movement from capital punishment for actions (sodomy, for which Henry Nicoll was the last executed, in 1833) to heavy penal servitude for sodomy and some penalty for 'indecent assault' (1861), to prosecution as a misdemeanour under that Labouchere amendment of the Criminal Law Amendment Act (1885) for 'any act of gross indecency', punishable by up to two years' term with or without hard labour. The forces for purity were now hunting down aberrant behaviour generally, as they did with Wilde, rather than specific kinds of acts. Their aim, as Foucault shows, was no longer to punish but to shape people; that failing, to categorize and offer aetiologies, marginalize and neutralize.

The writers of this later period seem to us more explicit about homosexual experience (for instance, Alfred Douglas's 'love that dare not speak its name'), but this is only because their formations begin to be, in part, recognizable through the lens of our own. Arguably, the better poetry continues to come out in work that explores feelings and desires not easily classifiable: Wilde's 'Ballad of Reading Gaol', with its deep sense of common sadistic murder as the real experience of all love, Michael Field's so sensuous poem on a dying rose, Housman's suppressed love of country lads. Less canonical poems (see White 1999) offer constructions of homosexual identity as various as the broader concerns of the society: around athleticism, cross-class connections, Orientalism, Aesthetic classicism, pederastic child loving, sense of sin or social anxiety. As a crucible of emerging identity, the culture of later nineteenth-century Oxford had encouraged a combination of manly classical values of athleticism with the new Aesthetic focus of Walter Pater. Strands that may seem to us opposed, one super-masculine, the other moving towards effeteness, often surprise us by their combination in such work. Oxford's most famous product, the Aesthetic icon Wilde, was a big man who could drink American frontiersmen under the table.

There has been a tendency in gay, lesbian and especially queer studies to set up the multiplicity of homosexual experience against a monolith called heteronormativity. It is better to see that monster as the creation of antinomic opposition, so that we can properly talk of the invention or construction of heterosexuality about the time of the invention/construction of homosexuality (see Nye 1999: 198–202). Both terms were used as early as 1883 by Symonds in his *A Problem in Greek Ethics*, but it was the development of a discourse on homosexuality that produced the need to define what Symonds calls 'normal heterosexual passion' (White 1999: 171). A kind of family heterosexuality is generated as a conservative reaction to the emergence of so many other sexualities late in the century. Before that pressure was fully felt, Victorian opposite-sex love and desire experienced, as we have already seen, many norming pressures from respectability and purity movements. But Victorian opposite-sex desire emerged from the past already divided; and despite the additional pressure to conformity late in the century, it was passed on to the twentieth century in divided form. The divisions indeed reflect major class and ideological fissures in the entire society.

There has also been a tendency to focus exclusively on middle-class desire. The failure to appreciate adequately the sexual attitudes and experience of the much greater body of working-class Victorians distorts our entire impression of the period. Indeed there has even been a tendency to read the working class by the light of middle-class preoccupations about them, especially the horror of sex as unlimited procreation that Victorians inherited from the work of Thomas Malthus. A unique study of applications for foundling hospital adoptions of their illegitimate children by working-class women provides a window on working-class sexuality (see Barret-Ducrocq 1991). Although a good number of women were prey (usually economic) to interclass misuse by employers or casual seducers, their own values must seem to us very much against the grain of stereotypes of Victorian prudes or libertines. Individual working-class women might be more or less ready to enjoy sex before or after marriage. Most women expected steady courting, fell thus into emotional connection; eventually premarital petting or bundling (a term from country courting traditions) or genital sex were indulged and accepted by their social group as preparatory to marriage. The stories on which these inside views are based are of course those where a sensible system went wrong and threatened to drive the abandoned mother into vagrancy and prostitution. That there were some such social nets to help is interesting in itself.

Barret-Ducrocq I think rightly sees middle-class literature as moralizing and distorting working-class sexuality: seeing it by the light of its occasional failures as a form of libertine excess when it was in essence based on an ideology of sexually relaxed monogamy within affective relations. Not that the middle-class representation of the seduced and abandoned working-class woman is wholly without its sympathy. The poet Mathilde Blind's 'The Russian Student's Tale' is not untypical: the seduced girl is repudiated, but not without feeling. But we need to seek out more authentic voices: working-class Scots poet Ellen Johnston's 'Lines to Ellen, the Factory Girl' on her betrothed's absence, or Eliza Cook's 'Tis Well to Wake the Theme of Love' on the death of a beloved. Or we could look at the music-hall ballads about ordinary courtship. But to survey representations of working-class sexuality in poetry is generally to fall into a nest of appropriative middle- and upper-class projections of their own anxieties.

Tales of working-class women seduced and abandoned had especial monitory force for the middle-class woman and they were legion (for instance, Adelaide Anne Procter's 'A Woman's Last Word', Dora Greenwell's 'Christina', Emily Pfeiffer's 'From out of the Night'). For middle-class girls there was no easy solution if they became pregnant by a man who abandoned them. Being known to have 'had relations' could itself exclude a girl from her status in the middle class. Elizabeth Barrett Browning's *Aurora Leigh*, for instance, ostensibly about the quest of its well-to-do heroine for mental and sexual inde-pendence, focuses in its subplot on the fate of a working-class woman, Marian Erle. Her sensational story, in which she is lured overseas for purposes of sexual defilement and pros-titution, seems a warning of the real dangers to women seeking independence. The story became a prototype of a real-life hysteria among the middle classes when, much later in the century, the journalist W. T. Stead abducted a working-class woman himself in order to expose such possible practices in his journal, the *Pall Mall Gazette*, under the lurid headline 'The Maiden Tribute of Modern Babylon'. A more focused treatment of this anxiety over sexual loss of status is offered in the fine poems of Augusta Webster, early suffragette and poet of the last third of the century. 'A Castaway', in a domestic dramatic monologue mode, and 'Circe', in a mythic one, both allow the fallen woman to speak from an educated middle-class subjectivity, to realize the unsentimental mixture of pride, wilfulness, anger and self-destructiveness, as well as shrewdness and good sense, in the woman who has gone over to a life beyond respectability.

On the near side of respectability, this system of female sexuality distorted ways of thinking about middle-class and to some extent upper-class women's sexuality. A respectable ideology wished to say that women were so free of desire that they could easily avoid sex before marriage and evade any temptation of adultery. Yet the greatest fear was that, left to herself, a woman might become only too fond of sex, as prostitutes were some-times thought to be. To have, at such a basic level, an essentially paradoxical notion forced on them must have been difficult for middle-class women. They were, unlike men, free of desire; yet could become excessively sexy, but not with their respectable spouses, whom they were none the less supposed to please while taking no pleasure. Such a series of double binds comes out in Victorian poetry not so much as a discussion of women's sexuality directly as in a perplexed, skewed vision of women in sexual situations. Tennyson's Mariana in the moated grange yearns dreadfully for her lover, yet her pendant Lady of Shalott is destroyed when she gives in to her desire. Matthew Arnold's Marguerite is an obscured object of desire, the more desired the more impossibly distant. Dante Gabriel Rossetti's more directly sensual portraits, in oil as well as poetry, gain warmth and desire as they are placed out of reach – a traditional Petrarchan move that Rossetti took more seriously and lived out most painfully.

Commentators have noted the way in which aestheticized dead women appealed to the male's need to suppress fear of his own death (see Bronfen 1992); but focusing on dead women also allowed them to be used as objects of desire without fear that their paradoxical dead/alive sexuality could be made operative. Browning's Pompilia in *The Ring and the Book*, nearly dead and laid out like a saint in church, can be given strong speech of her own (unlike the Duke's last Duchess) without ceasing to be her author's icon of Mary-like endurance and appealing passivity; similarly she need no longer face her inability to stomach her husband's lust or her growing feeling for the handsome priest Caponsacchi – with whom she need be united in heaven only. Victorians' well-observed fascination with love/sex after death allows postponement of the double bind here below in favour of heavenly passion. Especially later in the century, women became icons of Aestheticism's transformation of desire into art, a tendency already present in those Tennysonian females who were both desired objects and vehicles of artistic subjectivity. Creating them as alluring objects of desire, Aestheticized representations of women simultaneously took away all sexual agency. Such confusion over sexuality may indeed have left Victorian women speechless, unable to speak their culturally confused desire. They were then easily prey to the favourite psychological label of hysteria, which could further erode their sense of personal agency. Foucault saw the hysterical woman as a type produced, in life and literature, by the sexual discussion of the age.

The adulterous woman especially focused the paradox of female sexuality: she had presumably been cool enough in marriage but then found her other nature outside of it. If it was generally said to be a subject disallowed in English (as opposed to French) nineteenth-century novels, adultery was squarely before the society in detailed newspaper reports of criminal conversation ('Crim. Con.') cases (see Leckie 1999) after the new divorce law (Matrimonial Causes Act) of 1857, and it was a major subject of poetry, which, as a more difficult art not necessarily read aloud in the family, was not under the same regime of control as the novel. Arnold's *Tristram and Iseult* is explicitly a comparison of the sexless wife and sexual adulteress, *two* Iseults. The figure of happily adulterous Guinevere looms especially large in Victorian poetry, as the romance figure of courtly love is reprocessed by a society where the abomination, adultery, none the less hides a place of female desire. Because he must make her a woman of dignity equal to her role as wife of the near-saintly Arthur, Tennyson is elegiac over Guinevere's passion for Lancelot in *Idylls of the King*. They are both noble lovers who must yield to desire that they themselves consider unworthy and that so manifestly destroys the realm, as it was felt to destroy the domestic world in Victorian society. In his very different monologue, 'The Defence of Guenevere', William Morris recreates Guinevere in unrepentant scarlet, refusing testimony in her own (medieval) Crim. Con. trial, ready to go off with her rescuing lover and totally evade the process. Tennyson deplores; Morris celebrates; the binary remains. Even Browning's attractively pro-sexual 'The Statue and the Bust' leaves the lady-bust stranded in her conflicting double nature, wanting passionate escape, choosing stasis after all. It is easy to carry this analysis from creative literature to direct discourse of women's sex body parts. After 1800, as Thomas Laqueur (1990) has so well discussed, the body of woman was usually no longer seen as homologous sexually to man's but as Other, somehow incapable, in its reconfiguration of workable male parts, of natural desire leading to satisfying sex; desire is there but not the proper articulation to satisfy it.

It is not true, however, that Victorian middle- and upper-class women universally either lay still and thought of England (their reproductive military service) or became lustful prostitutes and adulteresses. We have had trouble getting into bed with Victorian couples and finding out what exactly was going on under the sheets. But we do know women had orgasms – on the evidence of the early sex survey by Dr Clelia Mosher at the turn of the century (the Shere Hite of her time) and diary evidence gathered assiduously by Peter Gay (1984, 1986). Victorian ideology certainly included a position celebrating married sexual love. For these writers (usually aggressively Protestant, such as Charles Kingsley or Charlotte Brontë), sex is, as for a religious Puritan such as Milton, a good in itself, though easily abused or misdirected. Elizabeth Barrett's *Sonnets from the Portuguese*, reversing the tradition of male speakers celebrating/verbally dominating their ladies, uses the poet herself as a model of oncoming marital sexuality. The images are strong ones, of awakening desire replacing family bondings, and desertion of religious anticipation for present sensual relation.

It is perhaps the idealism of this rather prominent, possibly majority, Victorian ideology of married lovers that strikes their less assured twenty-first-century successors. Possible failures of their ideal, complications or aberrant desires seem not to crowd in, as they do with us, at the prospect of emotional and sexual monogamous fidelity. But that was perhaps not so much ignorance of the way of the world as strong belief in their unworldly discovery of a kind of presence on earth. And yet Robert Browning thematizes the difficulty of achieving such presence even in generally successful relationships. His 'Two in the Campagna' almost have it but keep losing it, finding the idealist linking of two bodies and souls a harder order than they believe it should be. The traditionally romantic (in the common sense) 'By the Fireside' recounts how the couple came together into full presence in a mythic place of nature and religion, but of course it is a good moment long gone even though celebrated as the foundation of the couple's relation. The later 'James Lee's Wife' is explicitly about the pain of the dissipation and losing of connection.

George Meredith's expansive sequence of expanded sonnets, *Modern Love*, stands out, with Robert Browning, as not mythologizing relationship problems into reification of women's nature or pictures of the decline of 'Western civilization'. While Tennyson's *Idylls of the King* lays the blame on Guinevere and tries not to criticize the peerless but sexless Arthur, some kind of adultery is present on both sides in Meredith's poem. Meredith, who did in life blame his adulterous wife, here tries at least to be even-handed, though his very feminism cannot help emerging as blaming her more than him for failure to think. Both are, however, modern lovers, players of farcical roles who do not realize that actual tragedy awaits them, ironically as a direct result of their attempts to re-establish dead relations rather than accept the necessity of divorce. The sequence appeared only a few years after the Matrimonial Causes Act of 1857 made divorce a practical, if highly publicized, possibility without a special Act of Parliament.

Varieties of masculinity and masculine sexuality are often, however, the source of passions that spin Victorian plots in life and art. As recent studies have shown, masculinity in such a fast-changing age was not an essential given but fractured into many competing models, forced to exhibit themselves in a way that immediately confused genders. The male types were themselves often under threat of internal fracture from inconsistencies in the role itself, its estrangement from emerging social realities, or its excessive norming pressures on the individual: being a gentleman, a male saint, a captain of industry or a cultural icon could exact its psychological price. In sexual terms we find masculinities that surprise us: effeminate traditions from the dandy or Byronic hero offering allure to women rather than indifference; or male sexuality defined not as active or aggressive but as restraint or feminine gentleness. Breakdown and the so-dreaded failure were always possible. The Tennysonian male in distress of 'Locksley Hall' or *Maud* seems to want only happy relation; but we find a fundamental instability in his nature. Fulfilled love seems not a high point on which to build a lifetime but the pinnacle from which one immediately falls off into tragedy. That warfare and empire building are the only alternatives to brooding or insanity suggests the psychic goal all along may have been homosocial, finding re-masculinating male companionship or bisexual triangulation rather than dyadic married loving. We know this in Tennyson not only from Hallam, but in the complicated male–male relations of *Idylls of the King*, where the strongest leg of the triangle of Arthur, Lancelot and Guinevere seems to be that between king and knight, or where Tristram, that master of triangles, seems oddly to invite Mark's fatal blow as he deliberately bides his time with Mark's queen and his lover, Isolt. Also in the Pre-Raphaelites, who were first and foremost a brotherhood. In life they shared their interest in 'stunners' – beautiful and not very self-determining women, usually from lower-class positions. D. G. Rossetti and William Morris notoriously shared Morris's wife Jane at different periods of her life. While Morris has a significant string to his lyre in celebration of male friendship, Rossetti more interestingly offers himself as the poet of opposite-sex fascination. His great *House of Life* sonnet sequence of course mixes promiscuously sonnets about his life with his wife, Elizabeth Siddal, and his long affair with Morris's. Courtly love, which needs to be understood as a psychic positioning of women between men, provides much of the apparatus for a series of amorous new lives. The greater physicality of Rossetti's meditations on his affair with Jane brings us closer to the bone – male sharing with/sticking it to other males in sexual betrayal rather than the soul possession ritualized by courtly love. 'Nuptial Sleep' even records the experience of post-orgasmic mutual lost consciousness – as Morris perhaps noted. In both love relations Rossetti is clear that his consciousness is what he looks to love to build, not primarily a relation with another. Love, though it fails, makes us more aware of ourselves, more attuned to the *finesses* of our thoughts and sensations.

Here is another way in which Victorian religion could compensate as addition rather than alternative for Victorian lovers. Failure here, as Browning liked to philosophize in verse, could point to perfection in heaven. Rossetti imagined Siddal as more attractive waiting for him above; and this was not merely male desire stimulated by absence; Siddal's own poems – for instance 'He and She and Angels Three' – think of heaven as the place where she and her lover's soul will be happily united before God. In *The Unknown Eros* Coventry Patmore finds earthly love a premonition of sexual ecstasy in heaven, here at least a truly religious experience: love with God superseding even heavenly married love itself.

Many males exhibit the same division of love and sex found in some Victorian women. Indeed the social structure of repression and abandon that nurtured division in women may have been a large-scale projection of male investment in what Freud famously called the most common form of degradation in the male sexual life, a.k.a. the madonna/whore syndrome. Encouraged to seek release with actual prostitutes rather than seduce women of their class, middle-class young men had every reason to fall into a separation of love and sex that could then become the foundation of cold marriages. 'A good house makes a good home' is the cynical foundation of lives lacking female lineaments of gratified desire and offering only exploitative ones to males. Love triangles generally, as we have been seeing, are everywhere in Victorian poetry on love and sex. But few poets dared explore this dangerous psychic area, although male infidelity had been authorized by law until the Matrimonial Causes Act of 1857 and even then was not made sole grounds for granting a woman a divorce. Browning almost uniquely in his difficult *Fifine at the Fair* publishes the news of the husband's fancy talk to his wife Elvira coupled with an underlying sexual drive towards young, courtesan-like Fifine. This Victorian Everyman husband is significantly Don Juan – now the marrying type and somewhat unclearly positioned, as were the Brownings, between the middle class, where lip service was paid to affective marriages, and the upper class, where the Continental system of arranged marriages often still prevailed. Rossetti's 'Jenny', by contrast, does not probe the divided psyche of the male but rather projects his and his culture's confusion onto poor Jenny and her trade.

The division of love/sex into loving feelings centred on icons of maternity and domesticity and sexual ones centred on dangerous *femmes fatales* became widely diffused in the course of the century. Men shaped into self-division, then encouraged division between women. The unified bawdy-mother (and businesswoman) possible in the eighteenth century and even the Regency was divided in ideology, as we have seen, into sexless and respectable or sexy and fallen. Males were also told by the culture that they could not have it all, at least not in one woman. By the end of the century, the division was so great that it spawned a generation of poets seemingly obsessed with the difference between the purity of their ideals and the degradation of their desires. A *poète maudit* such as Ernest Dowson, obsessed in real life with a tavern keeper's daughter, writes of his eternal fidelity and his regular degradation. But even in mid-century, if the *femme fatale* was less evident, domesticity was casting a pall over sexual representation, for instance in the work of the young Patmore, where bold and exploratory themes of childhood self-seduction ('The Woodman's Daughter') and sexual anxiety on the eve of marriage were self-censored and replaced with the sexless domesticity of his *The Angel in the House* (see Maynard 1993).

It was usual in twentieth-century discussions of Victorian women to fall into a kind of purity discourse in which male need for sex, which any male knows is as much part of his socially constructed self as hunger for food, played the heavy. More fairly, middle-class restraints took their psychological toll on middle-class men who were urged to put off marriage during their highest testosterone period. Some few, like the notoriously grati-fied Walter, anonymous author of perhaps the most monstrous sexual private life of them all, *My Secret Life* (published *c.* 1890), went about paying and poking all the working-class girls they could corrupt or prostitutes they found interesting. Arthur Hugh Clough was perhaps more typical in his ambivalence and anxiety. A nice Balliol boy, he found himself greatly tempted by attractive prostitutes in great southern cities, namely Naples and Venice. These became sites of major poems, the two 'Easter Day' poems and *Dipsychus*, in which condemnation of sexual 'sin' is pitted against a worldly recognition of the immor-tality of desire in mortals. In the end the devil carries the day against Clough's Everyman of divided soul. Somewhere Clough recognized the deeper sins, of taking boys out of the more normal stream of courtship, of their consequent exploitation of working-class bodies: his attractive idyll *The Bothie of Toper-na-fuosich* allows an Oxford boy to join in country courtship while on vacation in the Scots highlands, and to lead his love match tri-umphantly into early affective marriage and a new life as settlers in New Zealand away from the class/sex system.

'Sex and the city (of London)' for single Victorians is relatively easy for us to imagine. We stretch our historical imagination harder when we try to imagine the sexuality of others. There is the Victorian middle-class man (or woman) of tremendous talent who seems to us almost neutered – Edmund Lear, Lewis Carroll, Christina Rossetti, Gerard Manley Hopkins – yet whose life and work suggest intense energies going into channels we do not quite understand. Carroll of course with his photography of naked girls has been a long-standing enigma, though his parodic and absurdist poems hardly reveal a sexual issue. Lear has been thought to have been not celibate avuncular but interested in males, but his 'The Owl and the Pussycat' remains perhaps the most touching of Victorian love lyrics – open to any couple whatsoever, from Venus and Mars, from one class and another, from different cultures, different genders or same genders.

For years biographers tried to connect Christina Rossetti's work to failure in opposite-sex love; others may now try to read her life as lesbian in some modern sense of the word. What we find in the work is a passionate fixation on life as a form of death, often repre-sented by speakers from the grave. Renunciation seems the sexiest activity and her bril-liant poetics of negation convinces us it is. In 'Goblin Market' sister love, as being willing to risk dying in violent sexual encounter with men to save one's sister, is the sexual centre of a poem that discards the ordinary sensuous attractions of men and only lightly praises themes of domesticity and procreation at the end. 'The Convent Threshold' obscurely refuses a relation crossed by 'blood' and accepts its own crushing denial of sexuality in this world only to reclaim it in the next. Hopkins's gloriously intense poetry, which, as noted above, many be seen in our terms as arising from a largely repressed same-sex desire, nevertheless sexualizes, in very broad, ungendered language, so much of experience. Nature he meets with intense, even masturbatory passion. God himself is a creature to touch and feel, to wrestle with as a kind of rough-trade lion. These are intensities that speak to us of sexual energies, yet also speak most unclearly their identity to our unfamiliar ears. Housman too is easily converted by us into the repressor of his single same-sex passion; but we may be inventing for him a simplified version of his ascetic passion for renunciation and his nostalgia for lost connection when we thus explain his poetry as simply about his love for the athletic but heterosexual Jackson. Tennyson himself, more than homosocial in *In Memoriam*'s adulation of dead Hallam, on the edge of psychosis in the opposite-sex urge of Maud's lover, offers us another kind of odd masculinity in the much-praised song 'Now Sleeps the Crimson Petal' from *The Princess*, where beautiful sensual desire, yearning and tremulous, calls the male to the female, male passive, female active. And he further confuses us by inhabiting so comfortably, even transvestitely we are tempted to add, passive, masochistic women such as the Lady of Shalott, Oenone or the two Marianas. The hysterical woman that Foucault considered the creation par excellence of the expanding nineteenth-century sexual discourse perhaps turns out in this poetry to be an hysterical man in drag. Even Browning created lovers beyond our usual ken: the lover of Porphyria, who finds a way to enjoy his cake having eaten her too, or the speaker of 'The Last Ride Together', who finds his experience of love more important than any reciprocity on the part of his putative mistress. Here again we find what seems to us odd repression side by side with odd freedom.

The Victorian aristocracy maintained, through its financial freedom and political hegemony, the possibility of continuing into respectable times much of the spirit of eighteenth-century libertinism. Diversity on sexual as on political issues characterized the aristocracy, from severely proper gentry and monarch to dissolute indeed. But it is the latter that contradicts our popular idea of Victorianism. We can hardly imagine how the ageing Lord Hertford could appear prominently about London with an entourage of whores. Oscar Wilde's poet mother Speranza tolerated her doctor-husband's upper-class Irishman's infidelities, letting it be known that only vulgar persons objected to such irregularities. Algernon Swinburne, scion of an old gentry family, was fascinated by the marquis de Sade and Baudelaire; and he found in his privileged world freedom to indulge his masochistic bent and in the relatively uncensored world of learned, classics-filled English poetry the opportunity to express his desires – as he had openly in life with the beautiful and intelligent courtesan Adah Isaacs Menken. *Poems and Ballads* (1866) seemed to have and still seems to have, even after D. H. Lawrence and Henry Miller, a pornographic and masturbatory quality, not so much one-handed reading as writing.

Swinburne's serious agenda, to propose a new paganism to replace tired Christianity, which would lead to important poems about liberalism and freedom, might go along with an attempt to render a sexually more vibrant world; but Swinburne tells more often than shows. It is more nearly a question of special sexualities, just developing in Western consciousness along with homosexualities, seizing on the pagan world for display. Swinburne articulates a number of these, especially the identification of sex and pain that we easily call sadomasochism but that was especially being identified in his time in the work of Leopold von Sacher-Masoch (see Deleuze and von Sacher-Masoch 1991, including Masoch's *Venus in Furs*, 1870). In an excessive involvement in an area of sexual experience common to all people in lesser forms, Swinburne exhibited the ritualistic, repetitive use of kinky activities that characterizes fetishism. Like Masoch himself, he demonstrates the rede-

ployment of fetishism from religious concerns to sexual phenomena, a movement generally prominent in the nineteenth century (as is the parallel redirection to economics in
Karl Marx) and of course culminating in Freud's oedipal theory of fetishism warding off
fears of castration.

Swinburne's own masochism was identified with what has been called the English vice,
whipping: supposedly from birching at school, for him aristocratic Eton. The studies of
Poems and Ballads connect a repetitive sexual cue to a broad range of experience, turning
a fetish back into the power structures that it mimics in hard metres that seem to emerge,
as Yopie Prins (1999) has argued, from the experience of bodily flagellation itself. We
hear of any number of actual *femmes fatales*, Faustine, Dolores, the *femme* Venus; and
Swinburne easily interweaves other coming sexualities, Sapphism, hermaphrodism,
necrophilia, with the predominant sado-masochism and its gender-bending creation of
immasculated women. As in so much literature that has a sexually performative element
– that aims at creating sexual desire – there is, however, a double experience: of true monstrosity and of monstrosity used to titillate. At the worst, we approach the repetitive and
usually tedious world of masochistic controlling ritual and Victorian pornography that
Steven Marcus (1985) long ago described, though Swinburne (master self-parodist) is
usually too playful, too self-conscious to be merely pornographic. The play between provocation in literature and sexuality as an aspect of life is clear in Swinburne's exceptional
elegiac poems, such as 'A Forsaken Garden', where melancholy dwelling in the pain of
lost love creates a world and a speaker first, and only secondarily ritualizes the frisson of
the hidden whip or stiletto heels.

Swinburne's conscious affinity with the libertinism of the marquis de Sade suggests a
more class-specific orientation. For the literature in de Sade's eighteenth-century and aristocratic tradition, all sex was the right of the seigneur; categorization, sexual identities
and fixed roles were for people without the nobility's freedom (of money, education, use
of others). The Victorian continuer of the libertine tradition felt empowered to enjoy all
forms of sexual delight and to answer to no one. His power, his money, opened all sexual
pathways equally. Hence de Sade enjoys equally male or female partners, active or passive
roles in sex. Hence the famous Walter of *My Secret Life* enjoys threesome or male–male
sexual acts without ever thinking to build an identity around them – whatever we may
conclude about him.

Victorian poetry could stand the weight of Swinburne's sexual preoccupations, despite
Robert Buchanan's famous mud-slinging article, 'The Fleshly School of Poetry' (1871),
which located Swinburne's and D. G. Rossetti's work as a site of controversy over sexuality in literature. The work of both could stand it because poetry could still be offered,
despite Tennyson and Elizabeth Barrett Browning's wide readership, as an art for the
few, not for the many who read the novel. Victorian laws against obscenity were usually
interpreted by the light of their effect on the readers whom the work was likely to find
(the so-called Hicklin Standard). Those who tried to reach a wider audience for a literature that celebrated sex had quite a different place from the poets; and that place was
Holywell Street, street of illegal pornography – or jail, where from time to time its
entrepreneurs, or more serious publishers of provocative French novels (such as Ernest

Vizetelly, publisher of Emile Zola's *Nana*), ended up. Learned poets such as Swinburne or the Browning of *Fifine at the Fair* wrote something between Latin and Greek, those store-houses of different sexualities, and plain English. They thus already pointed towards the direction the novel would take in the early modern period, as it intellectualized and aestheticized the presentation of sex.

Few female poets occupied the libertine place of a Swinburne, however. Gentry or aristocrat women poets existed – Elizabeth Barrett Browning, for instance, from the fallen but still grand plantation family of the Barretts; and her *Aurora Leigh* and 'The Runaway Slave at Pilgrim's Point', like middle-class Robert Browning's *The Ring and the Book*, discuss the sexually hard subjects of rape and seduction or rape miscegenation. Augusta Webster, daughter of a vice-admiral, is perhaps the closest to this libertine position, again with her celebration of the seducing woman as 'Circe' and her realistic, unsentimental treatment of the courtesan in 'A Castaway'. Of what I might call libertinism of the heart, the letting go of feelings of love, desire, needing, which Swinburne's poems of identity and emotion or D. G. Rossetti's sonnets show, there is a great deal in Victorian women poets. Charlotte Brontë, as in the poem 'Reason', makes a sophisticated but also agonized turn on the rather generic Sappho poem of the earlier nineteenth century in which an opposite-sex-oriented Sappho, created by Ovid, drops her lyre and jumps off a cliff for love of ferryman Phaon. (See, for instance, Felicia Hemans's 'The Last Song of Sappho', L. E. L.'s 'Sappho's Song' or Christina Rossetti's 'Sappho'.) Christina Rossetti's great poems of female masochism, such as 'The Convent Threshold' and 'Autumn', are exceptionally powerful renditions of love pathos, as are some of the abandonment and Magdalene poems mentioned above. At the top of the register are poems by Emily Brontë celebrating, as in 'No Coward Soul is Mine', the individual spirit and its love-seeking nature as the spark of divinity. Her speakers, male and female, are exiles from an imaginary aristocratic saga of power and desire.

Still, it is only in voices of same-sex desire that we hear female sexuality much celebrated by women, perhaps because public acknowledgement of opposite-sex desire, of the kind Elizabeth Barrett Browning was bold enough to make in her *Sonnets*, exposed a woman to charges of scandal or lubricity. Although we find Anne Lister, independent woman of the gentry class, as early as 1824 using Byron to mediate her seduction of Maria Barlow, and there is of course the openly acknowledged marriage of the Ladies of Llangollen (Eleanor Butler and Sarah Ponsonby) in the late eighteenth century, Victorian verse expression emerges late in the nineteenth century, especially in the constructed Sapphic celebrations of desire in the poems of Michael Field. Ruth Vanita (1996) presents evidence that Sappho's lesbianism was understood from 1800 on, but even Michael Field is hesitant to express same-sex desire too directly; similarly, the fine Anglo-Jewish poet Amy Levy shows little poetic sign of her sexual orientation. Vanita guides us to look for much more muted expression of desire, for instance in women's use of flower imagery in referring to clitoral rather than phallic *jouissance*, though most of her examples are within a male tradition of aesthetic, whole-body sexuality. Yet we must recall that the area of female same-sex relation and desire was open to Victorians in a way it can never be to us, open to many shades of love and desire not subject to a label; so poetry need not be explicit in suggesting friend–friend, mother–daughter or sister–sister relations to posit feelings of desire. Here again, the Victorians violate all our categories: unable even to mention lesbianism in reviews of French novels, they had an extraordinary freedom to put what we feel are distinctly amorous and sexual feelings into their same-sex connections. While we agonize over bisexuality, wondering if it is a sexual identity or a half-way house (Garber 1995), they comfortably love friends and sisters and husbands with apparently equal feeling, even passion. Triangles (see Garber 1995: esp. 428–31), so problematic to us, seem standard configurations to them.

Setting sexuality in relation to class has allowed me to avoid those terrible generalizations about Victorian sexuality and love that suggest there was some pattern of desire that was typical of this large and complex civilization. With more space I could insist as well on the many other varieties of background, culture and experience that shape or define sexual desire and expression. Rural or urban, north or south, English, Welsh, Scots or Irish, Church of England, Catholic or dissenter: these and so many other differences influenced the culture of love and sexuality. And of course no amount of social history and New Historical research into cultural patterns can discount the intricacies of individual difference, genes, relations to parenting, sibling relations, which all produce different patterns in intimate life. I hope I have already made clear how different successive periods of the century that effectively invented sexuality were yielding at the end to a more recognizable set of competing taxonomies.

In my remaining space I want to suggest some of the larger discourses into which sexuality was organized. It was natural for twentieth-century scholars to stress the medicalization of sexuality as an aspect of the emergence of modern secular society. Certainly we have found doctors taking a large (though, we should note, ultimately losing) part in the debate over prostitution. Their ultimate failure in their efforts to construct sexuality as a health issue was a victory of an emergent female politics but also a setback for attempts to limit venereal disease. Histories of Victorian sexuality equally stress medical debates over the healthiness of masturbation, the barbarous practice of clitoridectomy (generally not approved of – see Miller and Adams 1996), circumcision (controversial) or methods of birth control. By the end of the century Symonds and especially Havelock Ellis, like Freud in Austria, begin the work of survey and scrutiny of sexuality that was continued in the twentieth century by Kinsey, Masters and Johnson, or John Money. 'Scientific' approaches to neurosis or what was called hysteria included not only the neurologist Jean-Martin Charcot's and Freud's ideas of psychosexual aetiology, but also practical-minded English use of clitoral vibrators to relieve (female) patients' sexual tensions (see Maines 1999). We are again amazed to find this *jouissant* activity treated as a respectable physical therapy because it involved no penetration.

As the examples suggest (one thinks of those elaborate machines to prevent male erection and wet dreams – see Porter and Hall 1995), the early attempts to bring the mysteries of human sexuality under scientific scrutiny brought darkness as often as light, a point well made by Foucault in his ironic look at the pretence of creating a *scientia sexualis*. Certainly in efforts to understand variant sexuality, scientific discussion was as cruel in its pathologizing and museum-shop labelling as traditional discourses, even where, as with the physician and psychiatrist Richard von Krafft-Ebing, the political intention was liberal. Sexual psychology could help people but could also create new disabilities. Many twentieth-century commentators have concluded that Freud suppressed his patient Dora's same-sex desire and that, more broadly, approaches to hysteria overlooked underlying issues of sexual identity and female self-determination (see, among many works on the subject, Kahane 1995).

What we find in the burgeoning discourses at the end of the century in anthropology, psychology and sociology is a taxonomic knowledge that leads to our own current discourses. Yet we are bound now to understand it as at best a necessary fall from the openness and fluidity of Victorian sexuality. Fetishism, sadism, masochism, hysteria, homosexuality, transvestism, oral sex: all these garden-variety terms of our ordinary sex lives, along with exotics like coprophilia or scopophilia, begin to be named and thus in some sense made to exist as a world of discrete actions and personal identities. The concomitant development of the concept of an unconscious as the seat of sexual desire possibly unknown to the subject furthers the sense of a total system working in each sexual type and creating its own mode of sexual being. We may wish the terms away and try to see all love, desire and sex as individual, in some sense universally queer, but find them now hard to live without. At best we revise that knowledge, see homosexuality as a path (or paths) not a pathology, hysteria as a situation of a subject rather than a sickness, fetishes as pleasure opportunities rather than problems. We must struggle, as I have, to see other histories beyond the taxonomic blinders they impose on our vision. We may well puzzle over this question: would we, if we could, wish to burn all those books, Krafft-Ebing, Symonds, Ellis, Freud or the emerging studies of anthropologists, and return to the less structured, sometimes attractive, sometimes horridly ignorant and assertive world of Victorian sexuality that I have been trying to unfold?

We find, in the poetry, interestingly mainly that by women, some versions of rethinking courtship in the light of science, usually Darwinian. Constance Naden's 'Evolutionary Erotics', 'Scientific Wooing' and 'Natural Selection', as well as Mathilde Blind's more serious work *The Ascent of Man*, all reimagine sex in the light of Charles Darwin's theories. Women poets' mastery of Darwinian discourse also stands as a performative protest against the tendency in evolutionary theory to find a different genealogy for different sexes. Women were often treated as another kind of inferior race in the spawning and vile nineteenth-century discourses of racial difference to which evolutionary theory seemed to give an opening (see Russett 1989). Long before the New Woman novel of the end of the century gave a voice to women in conceptualizing their roles through up-to-date awareness of science, women poets had taken on the authority for articulating their identities. By contrast, male appeals to nature, as in Meredith's 'Love in the Valley' or Browning's sexy 'Meeting at Night', seem broadly to participate in gender differentiations in which the desired female is part of the world of nature, desired like the farm, waves or beach, but also held lower than male understanding and perception. This is the more striking as both Meredith and Browning are males who also write consciously against patriarchal control.

But of course sexuality, as Foucault very well knew, had long been the province of religion, where there had been before and continued to be in the nineteenth century a very full discussion on most of its aspects. Victorians, depending on their degree of secularism, looked varyingly to science or religion for views of sexuality. Repressive attitudes towards sodomy, same-sex relations, unmarried 'fornication,' promiscuity or birth control were authorized in some religious groups, as they still are today, from the Bible. By the same token, Victorians appealed to religious authority in arguing for more liberal positions. Charles Kingsley, Anglican priest and novelist, created religious (and nationalist) discourses to justify his very sexual vision of Christian marriage; similarly the Brownings chose love and sexual marriage within a general if vague religious context. By contrast, Hopkins's tortured redirection of same-sex desire from man to Christ, Christina Rossetti's abandonment of the love sonnet for the sonnet of renunciation ('Monna Innominata') and John Gray's priestly resolve for celibate homosexuality (only Platonic relations with his friend Raffalovich) all suggest Platonic versions of the celibate position. That celibate places in high Anglican and Catholic religions offered sites for same-sex relations may explain why emergent homosexuality seems so often located in those versions of Christianity.

Between the two positions are many tortured poets who work hard but not always successfully to bring together their religious hopes and their carnal desires – a conflict that is in itself a very traditional trope of Christian life. Clough's 'Easter Day' sees sexual desire rising as belief in Christ falls. Tennyson uneasily balances sexual disruption and spiritual desolation: Mariana is in despair over love loss, as is the hero of *Maud*; officially the world of *Idylls of the King* loses its faith in Arthur and his God and falls into sexual anarchy; but we may also read this in reverse. D. G. Rossetti's poems confuse himself as well as his readers with their mixture of religious and sexual language, uncomfortably moving between sensuality and religious epiphany in two directions at once, as if to sacralize sexuality while also sexualizing religion. The convert Patmore has celibate relations with his second wife while writing odes turned towards sexual relations with deity, then has a child by his third wife, having his sex and postponing it too. Hardy's early lovers find love loss and god-forgottenness go together: life is most often an agony of godlessness and lovelessness – as it is even in the wonderful *Poems of 1911–12* reflecting on the death of his first wife and the earlier death of their love. Religious meaning in the world and religious standards of sexual relation are unwritten together in the poems, as they also are in *Jude the Obscure*.

The intercourse between religion and sexuality that we find in such poets is especially salient in the widespread Victorian preoccupation with love and sex in heaven. Such a fascination reminds us yet again that Victorian sexuality was not less than but often very different from our own. Tennyson dreams and day-dreams of reunion with Hallam in heaven; Browning absolves Pompilia and Caponsacchi of charges of adultery here below but happily lets them plan a perfect circle above, as he would later in dreaming, as in 'Prospice', of reunion with Elizabeth. Rossetti's damozel waits warm for him in heaven. 'You can take it with you' seems a common refrain.

If the twentieth century rendered sexuality as a private place in a private world, the nineteenth as relentlessly publicized what we call private life. Sexuality was a family affair: which meant that representations of incest were manifold, whether quite recognized as such or not. Victorians with no aid from the coming late Victorian Freud instinctively connected sons and mothers, daughters and fathers. Mother–daughter connections became, as Vanita (1996) has argued, locations of female same-sex desire. The Michael Fields build a life of love and poetry together as a family romance of aunt and niece, only threatened by the penetration of an opposite-sex force in the form of a suitor to niece Edith. Even the famous cases of 'child loving', Ruskin's for Rose la Touche, Carroll's for Alice Liddell and the little girls he loved to photograph in the buff, smell of tolerance for warm feeling generated from fatherly, or avuncular, positions. If Victorians not in the upper classes had love choice in courting and marriage, they were also expected to marry feelings and love with their beloved's family; and failures to do so, as in *Maud*, where lover kills brother Hamlet-style, dooms a relationship. Fallen women, usually driven out of the family in poetic fictions, are first betrayed by mother or brother. If they actually succeeded in marrying, Victorian males felt married to the family so much that the wife's sister was an especial area of difficulty: a serious issue in the lives of Dickens or Austrian Freud, it also provided legal comedy, and not just in Gilbert and Sullivan, with society saying no to marriage with a deceased wife's sister while nature found that most attractive of objects of desire in one's own home sharing responsibility for children and housekeeping. The governess was of course the available version of this second angel-figure in the house: reader, Patmore – and many another real Victorian – married her (or bedded her).

Sexuality in the family orients sexuality in society. As we have seen, different sexual natures are attributed to women in and out of respectability; and unmarried middle-class women (of whom there were many) are often treated as neutered – though a good percentage of successful women poets who controlled a lot of the discourse on women and love never married. Men at home are in control of their lust; in society they are allowed to show their animal needs – like cats in and out of the house. Middle-class women going shopping, displaying themselves as they view displays in arcades and expanding shop windows, begin to take on their own alternative sexual natures, just as working women had in the factory or, later, in the department store. Oscar elegantly at home with wife and children is not the Oscar of the Café Royal. The family home as a workplace for the family's domestics creates sexual confusion, a place where family intensity encourages incest-like sexuality between master/young master and employee across class and role. A now famous couple, Arthur J. Munby and his wife Hannah, even played out their domestic roles of employer–employee while in fact living together as man and wife.

At the furthest extreme, national construction of the British as imperial authorities structures sexual relations with the conquered and administrated Other. Tennyson's heroes, like the young man of 'Locksley Hall', think of sexual dominance over dusky races as theirs for the taking; Rudyard Kipling offers a sentimental version of the same in 'Mandalay', where the returned Tommy recalls easy love with enticing Supiyawlat of the 'yallar' petticoat back in the East. As often the discourse is of the traditional dominant sexual position of conquering (or touring) men over their thereby feminized Others, a role of penetrator and pathic hardly invented by the British in the world history of same-sex relations between men (see Greenberg 1988). The situation of empire seems even to authorize same-sex relationship. We do not have to stress that the 'knew' in 'The finest man I knew' was regimental *bhisti* Gunga Din, in the poem of his name, to know patronizing desire of the Huck Finn/Jim sort when we find it.

Victorian poets as well as novelists see love and sexuality as society's business. The two great epics of Victorian poetry are actually about society's relation to sexuality. *The Ring and the Book* can be seen as a sensation novel in verse based on his famous source a seventeenth-century Italian equivalent of a Crim. Con. report, the Old Yellow Book. *Everyone*, right up to the pope himself, is into poor Pompilia's pants and body wounds, trying to establish innocence or guilt. The values and destiny of a society hang not on arms and conquest, not on justifying God's ways to men, but on establishing the proper view of this sex-farce of domestic love and legal war. If Browning reads a lesson to patriarchy about the demise of traffic in women, marriage rape and male ownership of female bodies, Tennyson in *Idylls of the King* warns patriarchs of the danger of adulterous love to the safety of the kingdom and empire: the worm in the bud of an ever-expanding, self-justifying Camelot. Divorce Victorian style is played out as society drama, farce again, in Meredith's *Modern Love*: adultery does not allow exit from society, as for twentieth-century Lady Chatterleys, but throws our lovers into increased social promi-nence, performers on the high wire in a societal circus. The rivalry of males, so much in evidence in the construction of aggressive middle-class Victorian masculinity, finds issue in Tennyson and Meredith in what Leckie (1999) has called an epistemology of adultery, with an aggrieved party central to a plot of discovery of injury, but thereby feminized as passive complainant rather than active revenger.

Elsewhere Victorian arguments over same-sex desire play out as sodomitical challenges to a manliness needed for civic virtue, or as revivals of soldierly ancient Greek society based on male–male pedagogic and supportive desire (see especially Dowling 1994). The 'sodomite' Wilde is demoted from the Aesthete leader of high society, whose sexuality is read as artistic personal cultivation, to its convict outcast. For Victorian women poets, loss in love walks hand in hand with loss of social position. This perhaps explains the regular negativity of their treatment of love, as for instance in poems by Edith Nesbit and May Probyn: in the balance hung not just loving happiness or sexual gratification but a life situation. Sexual issues have often been taken by feminists as obscuring women's social position in patriarchal society; but we can reverse that and say that the vulnerable and weak position of middle-class women in courtship and sex actually constituted a major social disability. Familiar plots, such as those of seduction and betrayal, connect to social definitions of appropriate roles and the ever-present danger of scandal; even the, to us, innocent plot of mutual initiation is necessarily an unfolding of great ambivalence to Victorians, bound to be interrupted as it is for the lovers of Porphyria, Maud or the woodman's daughter – or Hetty in George Eliot's novel *Adam Bede*. Tales of love out of wedlock quickly emerge as tales of social isolation, where society will expect an awakened conscience to destroy any brief idyll and return the individuals to its connec-tions; the other plot can only be the ultimate disconnection of death. As we have seen, Victorians allowed such subjects to be discussed rather freely in poetry, though far less so in the novel. But we should never misinterpret this openness as freedom from societal pressure on its forms of representation.

Science, religion, society: these are only the three largest discourses into which Victorian discussions of sexuality and love were structured. Students of the subject keep finding new, important areas of discussion in which what we think of as private events are to the Victorians a part of their construction of the world. That they had not one structure by which they organized their world, not one discourse, but a host of competing and often quarrelling ways of organizing their knowledge and feelings on these subjects (which in turn kept changing over a period of about seventy years), makes the study even more interesting. We must not look for ending solutions, ultimate integrations of our knowledge of the Victorians into great epistemes or sciences of knowledge. Rather we have the pleasure of disturbing our own unexamined views in the very hard business of trying to understand the complexity and variety of theirs.

See also: MARRIAGE AND GENDER.

REFERENCES AND FURTHER READING

Barret-Ducrocq, Françoise (1991) *Love in the Time of Victoria: Sexuality, Class and Gender in Nineteenth-Century London*. New York: Verso.

Bronfen, Elizabeth (1992) *Over Her Dead Body: Death, Femininity and the Aesthetic*. New York: Routledge.

Butler, Judith (1991) 'Imitation.' In Diana Fuss (ed.). *Inside/Out: Lesbian Theories, Gay Theories*. New York: Routledge.

Castle, Terry (1993) *The Apparitional Lesbian: Female Homosexuality and Modern Culture*. New York: Columbia.

Deleuze, Gilles, and Leopold von Sacher-Masoch (1991) *Masochism*. New York: Zone.

Dowling, Linda (1994) *Hellenism and Homosexuality in Victorian Oxford*. Ithaca, N. Y.: Cornell University Press.

Fisher, Trevor (1997) *Prostitution and the Victorians*. New York: St Martin's.

Foucault, Michel (1990) *Introduction. Vol. I of The History of Sexuality*. New York: Vintage.

Garber, Marjorie (1991) *Vested Interests: Cross Dressing and Cultural Anxiety*. New York: Routledge.

Garber, Marjorie (1995) *Vice Versa: Bisexuality and the Eroticism of Everyday Life*. New York: Simon and Schuster.

Gay, Peter (1984) *The Bourgeois Experience: Victoria to Freud, vol. I, Education of the Senses*. Oxford: Oxford University Press.

Gay, Peter (1986) *The Bourgeois Experience: Victoria to Freud, vol. II, The Tender Passion*. Oxford: Oxford University Press.

Greenberg, David F. (1988) *The Construction of Homosexuality*. Chicago: University of Chicago Press.

Kahane, Claire (1995) *Passions of the Voice: Hysteria, Narrative, and the Figure of the Speaking Woman*. Baltimore: Johns Hopkins University Press.

Laqueur, Thomas (1990) *Making Sex: Body and Gender from the Greeks to Freud*. Cambridge, Mass.: Harvard University Press.

Laqueur, Thomas, and Catherine Gallagher (eds) (1987) *Sexuality and the Social Body in the Nineteenth Century*. Berkeley: University of California Press.

Leckie, Barbara (1999) *Culture and Adultery: The Novel, the Newspaper, and the Law, 1857–1914*. Philadelphia: University of Pennsylvania Press.

Leighton, Angela, and Margaret Reynolds (eds) (1995) *Victorian Women Poets*. Oxford: Blackwell.

Maines, Rachel P. (1999) *The Technology of Orgasm: 'Hysteria,' the Vibrator and Women's Sexual Satisfaction*. Baltimore: Johns Hopkins University Press.

Marcus, Steven (1985) *The Other Victorians*. First published 1964. London: Norton.

Mason, Michael (1994a) *The Making of*

Victorian Sexuality. Oxford: Oxford University Press.

Mason, Michael (1994b) *The Making of Victorian Sexual Attitudes*. Oxford: Oxford University Press.

Maynard, John (1984) *Charlotte Brontë and Sexuality*. Cambridge: Cambridge University Press.

Maynard, John (1993) *Victorian Discourses on Sexuality and Religion*. Cambridge: Cambridge University Press.

McSweeney, Kerry (1998) *Supreme Attachments: Studies in Victorian Love Poetry*. Aldershot: Ashgate.

Miller, Andrew H., and James Eli Adams (eds) (1996) *Sexualities in Victorian Britain*. Bloomington: Indiana University Press.

Nye, Robert (1999) *Sexuality*. Oxford: Oxford University Press.

Porter, Roy, and Lesley Hall (1995) *The Facts of Life: The Creation of Sexual Knowledge in Britain, 1650–1950*. New Haven: Yale University Press.

Prins, Yopie (1999) *Victorian Sappho*. Princeton, N. J.: Princeton University Press.

Roden, Fred (2002) *Same-Sex Desire in Victorian Religious Culture*. Basingstoke: Palgrave.

Russett, Cynthia Eagle (1989) *Sexual Science and the Victorian Construction of Womanhood*. Cambridge, Mass.: Harvard University Press.

Saville, Julia F. (2000) *A Queer Chivalry: The Homoerotic Asceticism of Gerard Manley Hopkins*. Charlottesville: University of Virginia Press.

Sedgwick, Eve Kosofsky (1985) *Between Men: English Literature and Male Homosocial Desire*. New York: Columbia University Press.

Sinfield, Alan (1994) *The Wilde Century: Effeminacy, Oscar Wilde, and the Queer Moment*. New York: Columbia.

Vanita, Ruth (1996) *Sappho and the Virgin Mary: Same-Sex Love and the English Literary Imagination*. New York: Columbia University Press.

White, Chris (ed.) (1999) *Nineteenth-Century Writings on Homosexuality*. New York: Routledge.

Index